English Legal System

This book offers a modern, contemporary and innovative approach to the core curriculum, offering clear explanations to clarify the material without oversimplification. Carefully developed learning tools are used to help students to build their knowledge of the legal system of England and Wales; moreover, all the materials needed by a reader new to legal education are here in one place.

English Legal System will also help students to translate knowledge successfully to an assessment situation (whether examination, tutorial preparation or coursework) through the acquisition and development of key skills such as problem solving and application, critical reasoning and evaluation, and research and referencing. The text has been written with the changes to legal education envisaged by the Solicitors Regulation Authority and Bar Standards Board in mind.

The focus throughout will be on recent and key case law and contemporary real-life examples, bringing the subject alive and helping students to understand the foundations on which the law in England and Wales is based. The key pedagogic features seek to embed those legal skills within the context of the content on the legal system.

The associated website provides a comprehensive learning environment that will provide further illumination of the text and graphics and that caters for a number of different learning styles with additional video and audio content.

Dr Ryan Murphy is an Associate Professor in Legal Education and Director of Learning & Teaching at the Hillary Rodham Clinton School of Law in Swansea University. He is a former Dean of Law who has a national profile in legal education and in teaching excellence. Ryan is a Senior Fellow of the Higher Education Academy and has been directly involved in shaping the Solicitors Qualifying Examination reforms developed by the Solicitors Regulation Authority. He has convened modules on Legal Skills and the Legal System of England and Wales.

Dr Frances Burton is a Senior Lecturer in Law at Buckingham University, a former Chancery barrister who has for many years taught a wide range of subjects including much of the knowledge and skills which are the subject of this book, and on academic and vocational courses at a variety of British and international institutions. As a retired judge she has also had many years' experience of the operation of the rule of law in the UK from the judicial perspective as well as from those of the practitioner and academic.

SP●TLIGHTS
SHEDDING LIGHT ON THE LAW

Routledge Spotlights Series

*A new textbook series designed to help you translate
your knowledge of the law to assessment success.*

AVAILABLE NOW:

EU Law, Gerard Conway

Equity & Trusts 2nd edition, Scott Atkins

Public Law, Michael Doherty

Contract Law, Tracey Hough and Ewan Kirk

Tort Law, Timon Hughes-Davies and Nathan Tamblyn

English Legal System, Ryan Murphy and Frances Burton

WWW.ROUTLEDGE.COM/CW/SPOTLIGHTS

SP💡TLIGHTS

SHEDDING LIGHT ON THE LAW

English Legal System

RYAN MURPHY AND FRANCES BURTON

Routledge
Taylor & Francis Group

LONDON AND NEW YORK

First published 2020
by Routledge
2 Park Square, Milton Park, Abingdon, Oxon OX14 4RN

and by Routledge
52 Vanderbilt Avenue, New York, NY 10017

Routledge is an imprint of the Taylor & Francis Group, an informa business

© 2020 Ryan Murphy and Frances Burton

The right of Ryan Murphy and Frances Burton to be identified as authors of this work has been asserted by them in accordance with sections 77 and 78 of the Copyright, Designs and Patents Act 1988.

British Library Cataloguing-in-Publication Data
A catalogue record for this book is available from the British Library

Library of Congress Cataloging-in-Publication Data
Names: Murphy, Ryan (Law teacher), author. | Burton, Frances (Frances R.), 1941– author.
Title: English legal system / Ryan Murphy and Frances Burton.
Description: Abingdon, Oxon ; New York, NY : Routledge, 2020. | Series: Spotlights |
    Includes bibliographical references and index.
Identifiers: LCCN 2019057003 | ISBN 9781138783706 (hardback) | ISBN 9781138783690
    (paperback) | ISBN 9781315768526 (ebook)
Subjects: LCSH: Law—England. | LCGFT: Textbooks.
Classification: LCC KD661 .M87 2020 | DDC 349.42—dc23
LC record available at https://lccn.loc.gov/2019057003

ISBN: 978-1-138-78370-6 (hbk)
ISBN: 978-1-138-78369-0 (pbk)
ISBN: 978-1-315-76852-6 (ebk)

Typeset in Joanna
by Apex CoVantage, LLC

Visit the companion website: www.routledge.com/cw/spotlights

OUTLINE CONTENTS

DETAILED CONTENTS

GUIDE TO THE SPOTLIGHTS SERIES

The Routledge Spotlights series is an exciting new textbook series that has been carefully developed to help give you a head start in your assessments. We've listened to lecturers and examiners to identify what it takes to succeed as a law student and we've used that to develop a brand new series of textbooks that combines detailed coverage of the law together with carefully-selected features designed to help you translate that knowledge into assessment success.

AS YOU READ

sections at the start of each chapter introduce you to the key questions and concepts that will be covered within the chapter to help you to focus your reading.

AS YOU REA

The focus of th

■ Identify th

KEY LEARNING POINTS

throughout each chapter highlight important principles and definitions to aid understanding and consolidate your learning.

KEY LEARN

■ Collective
confider
respo

EXPLAINING THE LAW

brings the subject to life through the use of practical examples to provide valuable context to your learning.

EXPLAININ

Only one as
dismissal v
Parliam

ANALYSING THE LAW

invites you to consider your own response to legal dilemmas and debates. Critical thinking is key to assessment success and, with this feature, our authors invite you to critique the law or evaluate conflicting arguments in a debate.

ANALYSIN

Take a mom
distinction.
Health S

APPLYING THE LAW

Problem questions will form a large part of your assessment and **Applying the Law** allows you to develop your problem-solving skills by showing how the law can be applied to a given situation. Learn how to interpret the law and apply it to any problem question.

APPLYING
_____

Imagine that
national cha
office tha

MAKING CONNECTIONS

will help you impress examiners, showing you how a topic fits into the bigger picture, not just of the wider subject but also across the legal curriculum.

MAKING CC
+ + + + + + + +

When you lo
of law, judic
operatio

POINTS TO REVIEW

bring together all of the principles and themes for the chapter, helping to reinforce your learning.

POINTS TO

- Tribunals car
- Their merits
- The Le

TAKING IT FURTHER

Reading widely impresses examiners! **Taking it Further** provides annotated lists of journal articles, book chapters and useful websites for further reading which have been carefully selected to help you to demonstrate an enhanced understanding of the topic.

TAKING IT F

K McMillan and
not a law book
underpin mu
ook an

GUIDE TO THE WEBSITE

LEGAL EXERCISES
to test knowledge and promote critical thinking, including exam/coursework questions and thinking points for further study and reflection.

MULTIPLE-CHOICE QUESTIONS
for self-testing, helping you to diagnose where you might feel less confident about your knowledge so you can direct your revision time in the right direction.

REVISION ADVICE AND STUDY TIP PODCASTS
will help you to improve your performance and raise your grades.

KEY CASE FLASHCARDS
will help you to revise and remember the key cases and the legal principle they illustrate.

UPDATES
on cases and legislation will help you to stay on top of all the most important recent legal developments in the subject area.

PREFACE

This text began its life back in 2013 as a discussion between Ryan and the commissioning editor at Routledge. Much has changed, not least the writing team has doubled to include Frances, in the intervening period. This is true both for the author(s) and also for the legal system of England and Wales. The referendum on the UK's membership of the European Union was but a twinkle in Prime Minister David Cameron's eye when this book was first conceived. The issue of Brexit has come to dominate political and legal discourse within the United Kingdom and has provided particular challenges in the writing of this text, which was being finalised over the period during which the arrangements for the UK's exit from the EU was being agreed. It is anticipated that the unwinding of the UK's relationship with the EU will continue to have a significant impact on the legal system for many years to come.

Brexit has, however, not been the only change afoot in the years between 2013 and 2020. Aspects of our legal system have been transformed for the better and for the worse during this time. One cannot overstate the level of change to the structure, funding and substantive rules of the legal system as it wrestles with the impact of austerity, increased demand and technological development.

Despite these changes, the fundamental aim of this text remains unchanged. We hope that the English Legal System gives a modern, contemporary treatment to the core English Legal System curriculum, offering clear explanations to clarify the material without oversimplification. English Legal System aims not just to equip readers with an understanding of the law but also to help them to refine and develop those skills that will enable them to translate this knowledge to useful application in the real world.

Texts of this length do not get written without the encouragement and belief of very many people and the authors would like to acknowledge the support of these individuals. Our warmest thanks go to our respective families who tolerate, with endless patience, the trials of the writing process whether that is late nights or piles of papers covering every conceivable surface of our homes. Ryan would like to thank his eldest son Peter (age – 6) for his helpful comments and encouragement, his youngest son Simon (age – 3) for not destroying the manuscript and his wife Sarah-Jane (age – it would be imprudent to say) for her boundless enthusiasm and tolerance for the immoveable place that this book now holds in our family. Frances would like to thank her daughter Janey (janeyburton.com) for prioritising reading, all the way through, of our emerging manuscript during the hectic pre-submission weeks, when there was a lot of it to fit together after the extended years of work and development.

We would also like to thank our colleagues and students for providing inspiration and advice on the style and content of what, we hope, is a fresh and modern examination of the legal system of England and Wales. In particular, we are grateful to Michael Jarrett who provided us with an early draft of what became the chapter on Civil Justice.

Those at Taylor & Francis have maintained unwavering faith in a project that has taken much longer than intended to deliver. Patience and support have been maintained, from the original commissioning editor – Fiona Briden – through to our most recent interaction with Chloe James and others. We are enormously grateful for their part in bringing this book to the world.

Ryan Murphy (Swansea University) and Frances Burton (University of Buckingham)
January 2020

TABLE OF CASES

TABLE OF LEGISLATION

1

CHAPTER 1
INTRODUCTION TO 'LAW' AND THE 'LEGAL SYSTEM'

INTRODUCTION

There are few, if any, who will make it through to adulthood without having come across the terms 'law' and 'legal system'. The concepts not only dominate and regulate, often without our conscious recognition, our day-to-day interactions with each other and the state but they are also part of our shared cultural conscience. Aspects of law and the legal system are never far from the public eye with countless hours of popular culture and endless pages of the press devoted to portraying (sometimes highly inaccurately) law, justice and legal systems in action.

Despite the fact that the 'law' is an accepted part of our daily lives, there are few who will be asking the questions – what is 'law' and what is meant by the 'legal system'? Fewer still will peer behind the curtain to question the nature, purpose and *effectiveness* of the law and the legal system within which it operates. This chapter is not so ambitious so as to seek to provide definitive answers to questions of the purpose or nature of law or to provide a conclusive answer as to the necessary or sufficient features of the 'legal system' but rather it is to get the reader to *start* to think about these things. Indeed, the rest of this textbook is dedicated to exploring aspects of the legal system of England and Wales.

This chapter has a number of interrelated aims. First, it considers the concepts of 'law' and 'legal system' and how they relate to legal theory. Secondly, the chapter considers how these concepts translate into the legal system of England and Wales. Finally, the chapter identifies some of the key themes that will be explored throughout the whole of the rest of the textbook and outlines how to make the most of the pedagogical features of the text.

AS YOU READ

This chapter and the next will probably be amongst the most challenging to read for someone new to the study of law, but perseverance is a key legal skill. As you read, try to think about how the concepts under discussion can relate to real-life experiences of the legal system that you know best.[1] Of all of the chapters, it is to this one that you should return frequently. It seeks to give you the framework necessary for understanding the rest of the textbook.

By the end of this chapter the reader should have an **emerging understanding** of the difference between 'law' and 'legal system'. You should be able to **critically consider** the

---

[1] If you have experience of other legal systems then turn this to your advantage by considering how what you learn about the English Legal System compares with what you know about your own system.

functions and purpose of law and legal rules and how these contrast with the functions and purpose of other forms of 'rule'.

The reader will also be able to **differentiate between** different legal systems and what this may mean for the law that emerges and how the law is administered in that jurisdiction. You will be able to **describe** how the different jurisdictions within the UK interact.

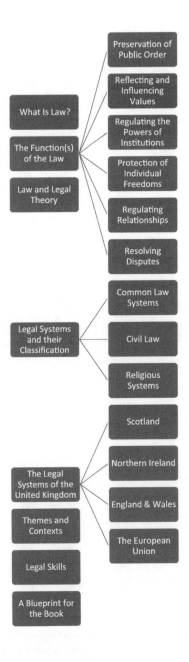

Figure 1.1

WHAT IS LAW?

Subsequent chapters of this text will explore the different *sources* of particular laws and will look at the process for creating specific categories of law. This section seeks to explore – in an accessible and straightforward way – the concept of 'law' in its broadest sense, unrelated to *particular* laws. In this way 'What is law?' is a question that has troubled the minds of lawyers, academics, politicians, judges and the public for centuries and it is not proposed that this textbook will be able to articulate a wholly satisfactory answer in one short chapter. The question of 'What is law?' provokes such interest because all concentrations of human population throughout history develop a system of laws, although the nature, form and sophistication of those laws can vary quite significantly.

At its most basic level, we could explain the law as a collection of rules that seek to govern behaviours, relationships and disputes. This definition of 'law' is attractive for its simplicity and, all else excluded, is neat and reasonably accurate. It is also an incomplete definition, ignoring as it does other 'rules' that may exist. The fact that law does not operate in a vacuum is a key theme that we return to throughout the text. Law is, of course, not the only form of rule by which we live and by which our behaviour is regulated. There are a multitude of 'rules' that vary in effect and in formality and 'laws' are just one of these sorts of rules. To take some examples:

- Families may develop 'rules' for how time is spent and on the activities that are allowed or are prohibited (for example on the time permitted to use mobile phones or social media).
- Clubs and societies may have rules that seek to regulate the governance of the club's activities (for example on how the committee members are appointed, elected or removed).
- Universities will have 'rules' as to assessment processes or on how feedback on work is produced and delivered (for example there may be rules on how essays and coursework are conducted or submitted).
- A school will have rules as to the behaviour of its pupils (for example there may be set sanctions linked to specific actions or there may be guiding principles or values to which it is expected that students will adhere).
- Games and sports will have 'rules' as to conduct that govern the way in which the game or sport is played (for example in chess there are rules as to the permissible movements of each playing piece).
- Within social groups of friends or within wider society there may be certain – albeit soft – social rules that seek to govern how we act in certain situations (for example there are so-called unspoken rules of social conduct and the concept of personal space).
- As between companies, or within particular sectors of the economy, there are soft rules which govern conduct and behaviours. They operate on a 'shared understanding' of the rules for which there may be no formal, legal consequence for breach.[2]

---

2 Although a breach of these conventions or 'soft law' may lead to 'hard law' being enacted. For example, the failure of the press to self-regulate effectively came to light during the 'phone hacking' scandal in the UK and the subsequent Leveson Inquiry led to calls (at the time of writing, still resisted) for *legislatively* backed standards of conduct.

- There are also certain moral codes by which people seek to live their lives (for example there are those who will not consume meat or animal products).
- There are also religious observances and rules that dictate the behaviour of individuals who are part of particular religious communities (for example, many faiths have rules about the preparation and consumption of certain foods and rituals and rules about prayer and worship).
- Workplaces will set rules for the conduct of their employees (for example, particular codes of dress or rules governing the use of social media during work hours).

It is also important to note that these categories of rules are not *static, exhaustive* or *mutually exclusive*. Over time – and according to particular political, social, economic and cultural considerations – rules can become more or less formal, and formerly 'informal' rules can become law.

In this way, it must be true that *legal* rules have additional or distinguishing characteristics that differentiate them from these other types of rules. The inherent fluidity to this categorisation can make identifying those characteristics very difficult. Again, at the risk of oversimplifying matters, laws could be said to be rules that the state and society agree should be deemed as such and for which there are state-endorsed consequences for breach. Laws are, as a result, a more *formal* form of rule. In this way law is elevated above other forms of rule due to its endorsement by the state – through legislation or case law – as an expression of the values and beliefs of a society. The following section turns attention towards the *function* or *purpose* of such law.

THE FUNCTION(S) OF THE LAW

Another way to consider the concept of law is to think about the *purpose of law* and the *function* that it plays in society and then the question moves from 'What is law?' to 'Why do we need law?' This helps us to understand the importance of law to society but can also help us to assess whether particular laws have met their aims and ambitions. This latter point is particularly important as having a *critical* understanding of the law will help to understand calls for reform.

ANALYSING THE LAW – APPROACHING LEGAL STUDY

An ability to **assess** the law critically is one of the crucial academic and practical legal skills that form the basis of much of the academic study of law and, indeed, its practice. When engaging with a piece of legislation for the first time, it is worth taking a step back and trying to understand not only **how** the law applies but also **what** the law was seeking to achieve.

This 'purpose' can be at a very abstract level, for example whether the law was intended to **shape** and **change** behaviour within a community[3] or whether it was aimed at **reflecting** existing expectations of behaviour within a society[4] or whether it was intended to consolidate fragmented laws into a single piece of legislation (a process termed 'consolidation').[5]

At a more focussed level the 'purpose' of the law may be understood as the very concrete outcomes that the legislation was seeking to achieve – for example, a decrease in the level of knife-related crime amongst young people may be the purpose of a piece of legislation that increased the 'stop and search' powers of the police, such as is the case under the various codes of PACE.

Understanding **purpose** (at all levels) is important for a number of reasons. In this context, by understanding the purpose of law, it is possible for the observer to comment critically on the impact (potential or actual) of law on society. As will be examined in Chapters 4 and 5 – on primary and secondary legislation respectively – the context to the passing of a particular law can have a profound impact on its effectiveness.

The website that accompanies this textbook contains more detailed examples of specific legislation with exercises for exploring their role, function and effectiveness.

What follows is a concise consideration of the main functions of law. These help to shape not only the substantive law but also how and why a particular form of law has been adopted. It is also worth noting that these are only a snapshot of the multiple purposes that law may be trying to achieve at any given point and that they should not be viewed as mutually exclusive or exhaustive (i.e. a law may be seeking to achieve more than one purpose at a time).

PRESERVATION OF PUBLIC ORDER

It is first important to attempt to define the term 'public order' before considering the function of law in 'preserving' that public order. The difficulty is that the concept of public order is rather broad and heavily contested. It can mean different things to different disciplines and the term can even have specific jurisdictional meanings within different legal systems.[6] For the purposes of this section, a broad understanding of public order is adopted and, in this sense,

------

3   For example, the Forced Marriage Acts 2007 and 2017.
4   For example, the theory of Sir Frederick Maine, set out in his seminal work *Ancient Law* (first published Murray 1861, reprinted 1906) in which he identified the socio-legal trend of earliest societies where the custom was first established, and then the regulating law followed only later.
5   For example, the consolidation of earlier commercial statutes into the Sale of Goods Act 1979 and later into the Consumer Rights Act 2015.
6   For example, within the European Union the term 'public order' is an amalgamation of the concepts of 'public policy' and 'public security'.

is understood to be the balance between competing freedoms – most notably the freedoms of association[7] and assembly[8] on the one hand and the rights of broader society to go about its business uninterrupted on the other. A thread that runs through *some* of the notions of public order is a need to protect public security and the proper functioning of the state.

The law performs an important function of 'preserving public order' by restricting or regulating certain freedoms. In England and Wales the law performs this function in a number of ways but, most notably, through the criminal law. Certain behaviour that threatens public order can, therefore, lead to criminal sanctions such as imprisonment.

EXPLAINING THE LAW – PUBLIC ORDER OFFENCES

The Public Order Act 1986 sought to codify, clarify and modernise the common law[9] offences against public order and to place them under the authority of an Act of Parliament. The main offences that seek to preserve public order are:

- Riot[10]
- Violent disorder[11]
- Affray[12]
- Fear or provocation of violence[13]
- Intentional harassment, alarm or distress[14]
- Harassment, alarm or distress[15]

It is of interest to note that public order offences under the Act are often commissioned at the same time as other offences such as assault,[16] arson[17] or criminal damage.[18]

---

7 That is, the fundamental workers' right to join workers' associations and/or other organisations, including political or-ganisations, provided they are peaceful and do not threaten public order or breach other legislation or rules protecting public order, termed in some legislation 'the Queen's peace'.

8 That is, the right in e.g. Article 9 of the European Convention on Fundamental Freedoms, and the First Amendment to the American Constitution (added 1791) to allow political, religious or other meetings of any kind for which people may lawfully wish to meet to discuss or indulge in other activities (which would cover everything from a sewing circle, through going to church to a political meeting).

9 The 'common law' is that body of law which is made by judges and is explored, in detail, in Chapter 2, Sources of Law.

10 Public Order Act 1986 s 1.

11 Public Order Act 1986 s 2.

12 Public Order Act 1986 s 3.

13 Public Order Act 1986 s 4.

14 Public Order Act 1986 s 4A.

15 Public Order Act 1986 s 5.

16 For example, common assault (the basic offence under the common law, committed by assault (threat) and battery (physical action on the person of the victim)) or the more detailed offences under the Offences Against the Person Act 1861 or more recent more specialised statutes such as Criminal Justice Acts or Police Acts etc.

17 Criminal Damage Act 1971 s 1(3).

18 See Criminal Damage Act 1971 s (1).

There is also a concern that a failure to deal with threats to public order (which are often accompanied by violence to persons or property) can allow them to spread across the country causing a complete breakdown of the functioning of the state. By way of example, in 2011 public order was threatened by mass rioting across the UK following the shooting of Mark Duggan during an attempted arrest in London. The riots quickly spread across the UK with more than 3,000 arrests for public order and other offences related to significant damage to property and looting.

In the trials that followed, and as an indication of the seriousness with which a threat to public order is treated, the courts were seen to treat those involved with the riots harshly. Adam Ahmadzai was a ringleader of a set of rioters who was initially sentenced to four years imprisonment following a Guilty plea to charges of violent disorder, robbery, criminal damage and burglary. The Crown Prosecution Service thought that this sentence was 'unduly lenient'[19] and referred the matter to the Court of Appeal who quashed the original sentence and replaced it with a sentence of seven years.

REFLECTING AND INFLUENCING VALUES OF A SOCIETY

This function of law is fairly broad and encompasses much of the function of law in a developed society. The way in which law regularly achieves this function is to capture, regulate and enforce expected standards of behaviour (often through the criminal law). In many situations there is a shared, societal understanding of what we expect of our fellow citizens. Some of these standards are deemed important enough to be enshrined in law so that they have the endorsement of the state and also the ability to be enforced or, for non-compliance, to be punished. To take an obvious example, the law reflects an accepted societal position that citizens should not be able to kill another citizen. Thus the English Legal System, with all of the usual caveats and conditions[20] about the risks of oversimplification, recognises murder as a criminal offence. With the uncertain *deterrent* effect of laws governing such important questions, the law of murder is less about encouraging citizens *not* to kill one another unlawfully but more about recognising the fact that we accept such behaviour as morally[21] wrong and wish to issue sanctions against those who violate that standard. Those laws that 'reflect' societal norms are normally relatively uncontroversial, other than in the detail or at the fringes of their application.[22] As a result it could be argued that one of the functions of law is to *reflect* and create consequence for non-compliance with already accepted standards of behaviour.[23]

---

19 This is a technical area of criminal law governed by ss 35 and 36 of the Criminal Justice Act 1988 but, for our purposes, it is possible for the Crown Prosecution Service to refer cases to the Court of Appeal where the sentence appears not to be sufficient.

20 Such as self-defence etc.

21 Whether we derive that moral judgment from some internal mechanism or by reference to religious beliefs.

22 To put this differently, most in society would agree that murder ought to be prohibited but there will be less agreement as to what should fall inside the scope of the definition of murder.

23 This is at the heart of Maine's theory that in primitive societies the law followed accepted social standards and culture.

There are also laws that seek actively to influence or change the accepted standards of behaviour within a society. These rules are often based on a changed understanding of the world and can be fuelled by technological or medical advancements. The law's purpose here is to introduce, through state action, new accepted standards of behaviour for the benefits of its citizens.

TAKING THINGS FURTHER – LAW AS AN AGENT FOR CHANGE

The website that accompanies this text charts a, seemingly small, development in the law that has played a part in changing societal attitudes and which exemplifies this function of law and relates to the increased regulation on the use of safety equipment in cars.

This function of law can be controversial and it is often that there is not a shared acceptance that regulation of activity or behaviour is necessary. Such action that is intended to lead society rather than reflect it is often for the protection of the health, safety and well-being of the population. It is for this reason that creation of such laws in the English Legal System is normally reserved to Parliament, rather than to judges through the common law, as it is Parliament that is directly answerable to the people.[24]

REGULATING THE POWERS OF INSTITUTIONS OF THE STATE

Within the English Legal System it is true to say that all are subject to the law.[25] This applies as much to the government of the day[26] (and their agents) or public authorities as it does to individual citizens. It is here that the law performs a constitutional function in delineating and controlling the powers of the state. This coin has two sides – the law grants powers to the state and controls and sets the limits of those powers.

In English law, each and every action of a public body or the government that has a legal consequence requires a legal basis that enables that action. There are various legal sources for lawful use of state powers and the function of the law in this instance is to create lawful authority for the exercise of public powers. The law adds a legitimacy to the actions of those with public powers.

The parallel function of law is to ensure that those exercising public powers do so within the limits of their lawful authority. If there is no lawful basis for the exercise of public power then the action can be challenged before the courts. Such exercise of power beyond legal authority is known as ultra vires and can render actions or decisions unlawful and void. The

---

24 This split between the powers and functions of the state is considered in greater detail in Chapter 3, Institutions of the Legal System.

25 This is a core element of the rule of law, which is one of the founding principles of the British constitution. See the influence of the theory of John Locke, that freedom is everyone being subject to the law laid down by a legislature that applies to everyone: this built on the ancient Greeks' principle that the equivalent was the similar concept of rule by 'the best men'.

26 M v Home Office [1994] 1 AC 377 (HL).

challenge before the court is called 'judicial review' and is discussed further in Chapter 13 on administrative law.

EXPLAINING THE LAW – PROROGATION OF PARLIAMENT

A recent example of the control of government power will help to demonstrate this important function of the law in controlling the powers of the institutions of the state. At the time of writing, the debate surrounding Britain's exit from the European Union was reaching its crescendo. In the Autumn of 2019 Boris Johnson, the leader of the Conservative Government and Prime Minister, prorogued Parliament[27] for five weeks, leaving the legislature with little time to scrutinise the Government in the run up to the date on which the UK was due to leave the European Union ('Brexit Day' or 'Exit Day'). A number of parties alleged that this was unlawful and so brought the issue before the courts.

Following a complicated, but expedited, journey through the courts the matter ended up before the Supreme Court in the *Miller* case,[28] which was faced with the politically charged question of whether the Prime Minister had acted unlawfully in advising the Queen to prorogue Parliament for such a long time at such a constitutionally significant moment. The Supreme Court ruled that the power to prorogue Parliament had *limitations*, chiefly that it could not be used where it 'has the effect of frustrating or preventing, without reasonable justification, the ability of Parliament to carry out its constitutional functions as a legislature and as the body responsible for the supervision of the executive'.[29] As the Prime Minister had not put forward a 'reasonable justification' for the length of the prorogation, he had acted beyond the limits of his power to request prorogation. This led the Supreme Court to the inevitable conclusion that the advice to the Queen was unlawful and void and so was the prorogation.

PROTECTION OF INDIVIDUAL FREEDOMS

The previous subsection explored the principle of legality insofar as it considered the role that law has to play in governing state exercise of power. If we turn our attention to the *individual* then law plays an equally important role in protecting individual rights and freedoms.

Unlike in the case of the exercise of power by public authorities, which requires specific lawful authority, English law has embraced the principle that individuals are entitled to conduct their business free from interference *unless* the law dictates otherwise.[30] In this way the

---

27 Ending the particular parliamentary session in readiness for a new Queen's Speech (this is a ceremonial proceeding at the State Opening of Parliament that lays out the laws that the Government will bring forward in the parliamentary session).

28 R (*on the application of Miller*) v *The Prime Minister* [2019] UKSC 41, [2019] 3 WLR 589.

29 Ibid. [50].

30 A basic principle of English constitutional law articulated by A V Dicey, *Introduction to the Study of the Law of the Constitution* (Macmillan 1885).

law, when not regulating the behaviour of individuals, performs the function of protecting individual freedoms and liberties. This can happen through the common law or through Acts of Parliament. As just one example the Human Rights Act 1998[31] protects, amongst other things, the freedom of expression.[32] This means that individuals have the right to hold opinions and to give and receive information without interference from any public authority. If a public body wishes to interfere with that right then it must comply with certain legal standards and it cannot do so in an arbitrary or disproportionate way.

REGULATING RELATIONSHIPS

In order to live life in an ordered and structured manner there needs to be some degree of certainty about the relationships we form. The law assists in this by providing a framework for governing relationships. This happens in multiple aspects of our personal and professional lives and covers a wide range of relationships.

From the perspective of an individual the law provides a framework for regulating marriages,[33] civil partnerships,[34] tenancies,[35] land ownership,[36] parenthood[37] and education.[38] It governs the goods we buy,[39] the services we receive[40] and the work that we undertake.[41]

The law also functions to regulate the relationships within[42] and between[43] businesses and how international commerce is governed.[44]

At a more abstract level the law can also govern the relationship between states.[45]

RESOLVING DISPUTES

The law also functions as a method for people to resolve disputes in a potentially dispassionate and objective way. The law provides the institutions,[46] the procedures[47] and the personnel[48] that facilitate the resolution of disputes. Chapters 8 (The Court Structure), 7 (The Judiciary),

---

31 An Act of Parliament that incorporates the European Convention on Human Rights into English law.
32 Article 9 ECHR.
33 Marriage Act 1949.
34 Civil Partnership Act 2004.
35 Landlord and Tenant Act 1985.
36 Land Registration Act 2002.
37 Children Act 1989.
38 Education Act 2011.
39 Consumer Rights Act 2015.
40 Financial Services and Markets Act 2000.
41 Employment Rights Act 1996.
42 Companies Act 2006.
43 Sale of Goods Act 1979.
44 Contracts (Applicable Law) Act 1990.
45 Vienna Convention on the Law of Treaties.
46 For example, the courts and tribunals.
47 For example, the rules of evidence and court procedures.
48 Through members of the legal profession, judges and court officials.

15 (The Legal Professionals) and 14 (Alternative Dispute Resolution) will give a more detailed examination of the framework for resolving disputes in the English Legal System.

TAKING THINGS FURTHER – WHEN FUNCTIONS COLLIDE

It is clear that the functions outlined can sometimes coincide and overlap. Equally, it is possible that some of the functions operate in tension and risk colliding. The website that accompanies this textbook explores situations where the functions of law may come into conflict and poses some questions as to how that conflict might be managed or resolved.

LAW AND LEGAL THEORY

As well as an understanding of what law may be, and why we may need it in a functional sense, there is a whole branch of legal study dedicated to the theoretical underpinnings of the *nature* of law – this branch of study is termed 'jurisprudence'.[49]

MAKING CONNECTIONS – LAW AS A 'DISCIPLINE'
+ +
The growth of the discipline and profession of law risks reducing the law to a 'subject' to be 'studied'.[50] Great care should be taken in treating law as an isolated academic discipline. Without the need of being overly philosophical, law is a construct of humankind. It does not exist without humans or society. For this reason, it should not be detached from the human experience. Law does not exist in a vacuum but is a product of economics, philosophy, politics, sociology and a whole lot more. By understanding how these disciplines interact with and exert influence on law, a much richer understanding of law can be achieved. Also, recognising how these disciplines bleed into each other will help to understand some of the peculiarities of the law and the legal system.

Not only does jurisprudence seek to explain the nature of law, it also seeks to explain the *legitimate basis* of the law and its purpose. Essentially, jurisprudence allows us to make sense of the law and to question whether, amongst other things, a particular law is *valid* as a law. In this way, jurisprudence seeks to locate and explain the authority of the law by reference to underlying philosophies or principles and to consider the limits of that authority and legitimacy. It is important to have an awareness of the major legal philosophies as they can

---

49 The word 'jurisprudence' comes from *juris prudentia*, Medieval Latin, the study of the philosophy of law.

50 Indeed, the authors both make a living from teaching the discipline of law at universities!

often help to explain the approach of legal systems to particular issues at particular points in time. Each approach to legal theory has its adherents and detractors and none perfectly describes or prescribes the operation of the legal system. In many ways, the different jurisprudential approaches could be seen as lenses through which we can examine the law and its qualities. The major schools of legal theory are outlined in Table 1.1 but the list is not intended to be exhaustive, with an almost endless supply of other constantly evolving jurisprudential theories.[51]

Table 1.1 Major Schools of Legal Theory

Theory	*Description*	*Theorists/Influence*
Natural Law Theory/Natural Rights	A belief that there is a higher form of law that transcends the law of man and that is independent of, and superior to, the law of any state. It is based on an understanding of the law of 'nature' that is common to all societies. Law, according to this theory is rational and capable of being reasoned. The proponents of this theory suggest that law is just and fair – i.e. there is a link between natural law and morality. Although now largely fallen out of favour, the principles of natural law (e.g. inalienable rights) still finds some support in the principles and law of international human rights.	Aristotle St Thomas Aquinas Hobbes Locke Fuller Dworkin (partially)
Legal Positivism	Fundamentally different to 'natural law'. A positivist would suggest that law is only 'law' when it is recognised as such by a human-made authority. Under this theory, the content of law is not questioned on the basis of	Austin Bentham Hobbes Hart Kelsen Raz

Theory	Description	Theorists/Influence
	a moral judgment. Law's validity derives from sovereignty and authority. There is a focus on the procedures by which a law is passed rather than on its moral quality.	
Legal Realism	Legal realism focusses less on high-level principles and more on how the law operates and is determined in practice – i.e. evidence of real-world impact. Law is resolved through conflict rather than consensus. According to this theory, the judiciary and the courts are the central protagonists in determining the remit of law because disagreements about the law tend to be settled by courts.	Wendell Holmes Llewellyn
Critical Legal Studies	Critical Legal Studies (CLS) shares some features of legal realism in that it does not focus on law as an abstract concept but one that is grounded in real-world experience. Critical Legal Studies notes the failings and biases of the law and legal system. A common feature of CLS is the idea that the institutions of the legal system uphold and reinforce existing political structures. According to CLS, law is often used as a way of asserting majoritarian rule over minority groups and giving a gloss of legitimacy to state action.	Marx Pyle Unger

To those new to the study of law, jurisprudence can feel detached and difficult. The theories can be conceptually challenging as the developments and 'sub-theories' clash and overlap. For the purposes of understanding a textbook on the English Legal System it is worth remembering that 'there's nothing so practical as good theory'.[52] To put this differently, legal theory can be used to explain *why* certain choices are made within a legal system and also to advocate for how they might be done differently or 'better'. Bearing in mind that individuals may *want, need* or *expect* different things from the legal system and the law may help to understand the compromises that are often reached in the formulation and execution of the law.

TAKING THINGS FURTHER – JURISPRUDENCE IN ACTION

The companion website to this text has some exercises based on fictitious legal scenarios. You can use these to test and expand your understanding of the different theories presented previously. There are explanations of how different legal theories would resolve the questions posed and there is an introduction to Fuller's hypothetical 'Speluncean Explorers' case study – a fictional scenario intended to explore how different schools of legal theorists would treat the moral and legal case of cannibalism.[53]

LEGAL SYSTEMS AND THEIR CLASSIFICATION

Attention now turns from notions of law to the concept of the 'legal system' as this is a necessary precursor to discussing the 'English' Legal System. In much the same way as a definition of 'law' is difficult to settle upon, the term 'legal system' is equally flexible and can mean different things in different contexts to different people. This textbook adopts a particularly broad understanding of the concept of 'legal system' as being the collection of sovereign processes and institutions that govern the creation, enforcement and interpretation of the law and legal rules of a particular body or state. The legal system is the way in which the *process* of law is managed, moderated and controlled. Whilst legal systems are most readily associated with countries or states – indeed this is a textbook about the legal system of England and Wales – it is also true that legal systems can be created as between groups of countries. In this way legal systems can also overlap and interact.

---

52 Kurt Lewin, 'Problems of research in social psychology' in Dorwin Cartwright (ed), *Field Theory in Social Science: Selected Theoretical Papers* (Harper & Row 1951) 169.

53 Lon Fuller, 'The case of Speluncean explorers' (1949) 62 Harvard Law Review 616.

MAKING CONNECTIONS – THE EUROPEAN UNION
+ +

The European Union is a good example of an international organisation that has a developed and sophisticated legal system that sits both outside and as part of the legal heritage of its 27[54] Member States. This legal system – which has processes for the creation and enforcement of laws by independent institutions – was created through the pooling of the sovereignty of its members.

In the seminal *Costa*[55] case, the Court of Justice of the European Union articulated its own understanding of the legal system of the EU in terms of its key features and the source of its legitimacy. The Court held that:

> The … [T]reaty has created its own legal system which, on the entry into force of the treaty, became an integral part of the legal systems of the member states and which their courts are bound to apply.

> By creating a community of *unlimited duration*, having its *own institutions*, its own *personality*, its own *legal capacity* and capacity of representation on the international plane and, more particularly, *real powers stemming from a limitation of sovereignty* or a transfer of powers from the states to the community, the member states have *limited their sovereign* rights and have thus created a body of law which binds both their nationals and themselves.[56]

Within the context of the EU at least, a legal system was characterised by certain key features – sovereignty, unlimited duration, institutions and real power. This formulation is repeated in subsequent cases emanating from the European Union and represents a core part of its identity as an emerging legal system that values its *autonomy* and *self-determination*. In this way the Court of Justice of the European Union was able to assert its own authority and reject simply accepting the rules of another law-making entity – in this instance, the UN Security Council – in the *Kadi*[57] case.

Many of the features identified by the CJEU in *Costa* are common across different legal systems, including the presence of institutions, independence and sovereignty.

Legal systems can vary significantly from jurisdiction to jurisdiction. Each is a unique product of its history, its social development, its economic and theological environment. In this way it can be difficult to categorise the different types of legal system reliably, and these sorts of labels are only partially useful. Labels can be helpful in that they seek to draw

54 Formerly 28 members before the UK departed.
55 Case 6/64 *Costa v ENEL* [1964] ECR 585.
56 Ibid. para 3.
57 C-402/05 *Kadi and Al Barakaat International Foundation v Council and Commission* [2008] ECR I-6351.

together similar treatment of law, institutions and processes. In this early chapter, which is attempting to provide an introduction to fundamental concepts, the intention is to outline some of the common legal systems and their features but not subject them to a detailed consideration.

COMMON LAW SYSTEMS

Common law systems tend to be those that place particular importance on the decisions of courts. Case law forms an important *source* of law, and judges are particularly powerful actors within the legal system. This does not mean that judge-made law is the *only* source of law in a common law legal system. It should be noted that common law systems also have legislation that usually takes priority when it conflicts with judge-made law. The legal system of England and Wales is a common law system but there are many others around the world – including the United States of America, Singapore, Israel, Canada and Australia. In this way, the former colonies of the British Empire and the British Colonies often absorbed English common law principles into their legal systems. Common law systems are common where there is not a highly codified body of statutory law and the common law then 'fills the gaps' between particular Acts of Parliament or in areas of law that lend themselves to judge-led resolution (such as contract law and the law of tort).

Another central feature of the common law is the system of precedent – discussed further in Chapter 9 – meaning that courts are, subject to considerations of hierarchy and certain rules of principle, *bound* by the decisions of other courts. It is this concept of *stare decisis* that gives the common law certainty and allows for its refinement in incremental ways.

CIVIL LAW

In contrast with the common law, a system adhering to the civilian law tradition[58] is more likely to be based on 'codes', which seek to codify and bring areas of law together into a single set of written rules. The system is the prevalent system of continental Europe and much of Africa, which is unsurprising considering that it has its basis in Roman law, also the basis of Church law in the first millennium and Middle Ages, and then incorporated in the Napoleonic Codes which spread throughout the European countries conquered by Napoleon and then through their colonies.

---

58 That is, in civil law jurisdictions, which adopt the use of a written constitution and accompanying written criminal and civil codes which set out the principles of their legislation. These codes are more flexibly drafted than the statutes of common law jurisdictions since codes are deliberately more widely framed than a common law jurisdiction statute (which tends to include within it all the required detail to achieve the purpose of the statute), whereas civil law approaches expect the more flexible codes of their jurisdictions to cover more widely expressed situations from which civil law judges will abstract a sufficiently widely framed meaning to meet the purpose of the code's law, including perhaps in situations not even envisaged when the code was originally drafted. This written constitution and codes system has, over time, since the adoption of the Napoleonic Codes in Europe and elsewhere since the early 19th century, created this 'civilian tradition' which is the opposite of the methodology of English statute and case law, which also builds on principles of the common law, recorded over time in reported cases, since we have no written constitution in which to set out such principles.

In civil law jurisdictions, the primary source of law is either that within the constitution or in the 'codes' produced by the legislature. The consequence of this is that judge-made law does not feature as strongly as it does in common law jurisdictions and there is no formal requirement for there to be rules of precedent.

RELIGIOUS SYSTEMS

A third type of system can be seen by those states that base their legal structures around a religious text or belief system. This text is the fundamental source of law and the source of the legitimacy of other forms of law, such as decided cases or legislation. The most common form of religious state in modern times is that of Islam with countries such as Saudi Arabia and Iran basing their legal system around the tenets of the Islamic faith. Sources of law tend to focus on the core religious texts as well as the writings of prominent religious scholars or prophets. There are also states which base *aspects* of their law on religious rules and other aspects are more akin to common or civilian law traditions.

This sort of legal system should not be confused with the use of dispute resolution systems based on religion. The former governs the law-making and framework of the entire legal system while the latter is just an accommodation of the legal system to allow people to use religious principles to settle their disputes. These forms of religious dispute resolution, such as Beth Din[59] or the Muslim Arbitration Council[60] are discussed in greater detail in Chapter 14 on Alternative Dispute Resolution.

ANALYSING THE LAW – THE COMPARATIVE AND PLURALISTIC APPROACH

The preceding is just a brief sketch of the main forms of legal system that are present in different states. In reality there are lots of states that 'borrow' from the different traditions and so are described as 'pluralistic' or 'hybrid' legal systems. The most obvious, for the sake of this text, is Scotland as this system borrows from both the common and civilian law tradition. As with much in law, categories are only ever the *starting* point of analysis and there is much overlapping and cross-fertilisation of legal systems. In this way legal systems should not be viewed as 'dead' or 'settled' and there will commonly be development and evolution of systems over time, such as the mutual influence of the EU and English legal systems on each other during the latter's membership of the former.

There is a whole branch of legal study dedicated to comparative law and you should bear in mind other systems as you progress through this textbook.[61] Comparative law

---

59 Used by those of the Jewish faith.
60 Used by those of the Islamic faith.
61 Peter de Cruz, *Comparative Law in a Changing World* (4th edn, Routledge 2018).

is often more than just *describing* different legal systems but involves an analysis of their similarities and differences. By comparing the approaches of law to common problems or to structures we can often learn more about our own system. Understanding similarities can be important, and English courts often look to the solutions adopted in other common law jurisdictions when considering whether to change or develop the common law.

THE LEGAL SYSTEMS OF THE UNITED KINGDOM

One of the core characteristics of a legal system is that it has a defined geographical/ jurisdictional scope. This allows us to understand the limitations of a legal system and how it interacts with other systems. This text concerns itself with the legal system of England and Wales but it would be remiss (as similar texts do) to overlook the fact that the United Kingdom has a system of systems that coexist and share certain common traditions and institutions. There are a number of jurisdictions and 'countries' that exist within the broader banner of 'UK' or 'British' or 'English' law. They also interact and collide at times and this can impact on the understanding of the individual systems.

The terminology applied to describe the law as applied within the United Kingdom is often deployed loosely with little thought for, or link to, the precise *legal or common sense meaning* of the words used. It is, therefore, important to deal with some basic terminology first before considering the detail of the system that is the subject of this book. It is here that we start to see some of the differences between the term 'law' and the term 'legal system'.

The United Kingdom is shorthand for the United Kingdom of Great Britain and Northern Ireland. Great Britain is comprised of England, Wales and Scotland and this is then 'united' with Northern Ireland to form the UK. Of itself, and for historical reasons,[62] the UK does not have a single legal system but rather is a collection of legal systems with certain shared institutions (such as the Supreme Court[63] and the Westminster Parliament). For our purposes there are **five** different forms of 'law' that are relevant – the law of the UK (that applies across all of the constituent jurisdictions), Scots law, English and Welsh law, Welsh law[64] and Irish law. There are also international laws that will be discussed where relevant throughout the remainder of the text.

---

62 The UK was formed out of a series of Acts of Union with Scotland (1707), Ireland (1800) and Wales (1536–1543).

63 Which is the highest civil court for all civil cases in the UK and the highest criminal court for England and Wales and Northern Ireland.

64 Legislation passed under the devolved authority of the Government of Wales Act 2006.

There are then **three** distinct legal systems in operation within the UK: that of *England and Wales, Scotland* and *Northern Ireland.*

TAKING THINGS FURTHER – THE COMMONWEALTH, BRITISH OVERSEAS TERRITORIES AND CROWN DEPENDENCIES

The website that accompanies this text provides an opportunity to explore how the various legal systems of the UK interact with the nations of the Commonwealth, the British Overseas Territories and the Crown dependencies. Although many of these nations and territories now have their own fully developed legal systems, it is useful to understand the broader picture and to consider the process and challenges of sharing institutions whilst seeking to develop a sense of independent identity.

SCOTLAND[65]

The legal system of Scotland is a hybrid system, calling as it does on both civil and common law traditions. Following the Acts of Union 1707, which created the UK Parliament, Scotland retained its own legal system. This means that it has its own courts and legal principles, notably in terms of property and criminal law. Historically Scotland has always been influenced by France with which it always had close relations from the Middle Ages, based on the fact that both Scotland and France constantly fought with England. Scottish monarchs regularly found French spouses more often than English ones, and inevitably this led to French influence in the upbringing of underage monarchs who succeeded fathers killed in battle.

NORTHERN IRELAND[66]

The legal system of Northern Ireland is more closely aligned to the English system than Scots law, and many of the principles that underpin the common law find their origins in English law. Nonetheless, Northern Ireland has its own legal system and capacity for law-making as well as a court system to administer the law.

ENGLAND AND WALES

When we discuss the 'English Legal System' or 'English law' we are in fact talking about the law and legal system of England and Wales. The *single* legal system that operates throughout England and Wales is often forgotten due to the shortening of the term to 'English law'. There are no 'separate' courts for Wales. Despite the fact that certain powers to make law have been devolved to the Welsh Assembly and Welsh Government, the *system* of law including the courts and professions are fused into a single system.

---

65 For more information on the Scottish legal system, see Bryan Clark and Gerard Keegan, *Scottish Legal System Essentials* (3rd edn, Edinburgh University Press 2012).

66 For a more detailed consideration of the legal system of Northern Ireland, see Brice Dickson, *Law in Northern Ireland* (Hart-Bloomsbury Professional 2018).

The remainder of this textbook is concerned with this system – how law is made, its institutions and the people who work within it.

THE EUROPEAN UNION

"The United Kingdom was, until January 2020, a member of the European Union. The EU has an independent legal system and also provided a source of law for the legal system of England and Wales. During the more than 40 years of membership, the legal systems had intertwined and cross-fertilized each other to a significant degree that will prove challenging to untangle.

In various chapters, this textbook will touch upon those challenges as they apply to particular aspects of English law and the concluding chapter considers the future impact of EU law on the legal system of England and Wales. As you read try to think about how those challenges could be reduced or eliminated. The companion website also contains updated details on the current position in relation to the UK's exit from the EU."

The case concerning the attempted prorogation of Parliament (discussed previously) gives some indication of why knowing about the different jurisdictions and how they interact is important.

ANALYSING THE LAW – THE CASE OF PROROGATION (AGAIN!)

As discussed previously, this case concerned the UK Government using its prerogative powers to prorogue the UK Parliament. This action was governed by UK constitutional law.

The prorogation led to actions challenging the legality of the Government's action being taken in two[67] of the jurisdictions of the UK: notably by Joanna Cheery in the Scottish Inner House[68] and the High Court of England and Wales by activist Gina Miller.[69] The Scottish court found that the action was unlawful. The English court found that the action was lawful. Although a rare occurrence, the cases demonstrate that there are inherent risks of operating multiple legal systems within a close political union. In this case the matter was resolved by the Supreme Court, which acts as the highest court of the UK (i.e. for England and Wales *and* Scotland) for all civil matters.[70] It ruled that the prorogation was, indeed, unlawful. By having a single Supreme Court to resolve differences in judgments, the UK is able to avoid divergence amongst its constituent legal systems on important matters such as constitutional law.

---

67 Further cases, which did not progress, were also heard in the courts of Northern Ireland.
68 Actions were taken by a cross-party group of 75 MPs and Lords. *Cherry & Others v Advocate General* [2019] CSIH 49, [2019] SLT 1097.
69 *Miller v Prime Minister* [2019] EWHC 2381 (QB), [2019] 9 WLUK 81.
70 *Miller & Cherry v Advocate General for Scotland & The Prime Minister* [2019] UKSC 41, [2019] 3 WLR 589.

The interactions of the systems can be complex and confusing. However, having an understanding not only of the systems but also of the circumstances that brought us to this situation is useful. Knowing that the UK is a political union that was achieved through particular milestones and prevailing economic, political and social conditions will help one understand some of its 'quirks' and institutional structures.

THEMES AND CONTEXTS WITHIN THIS BOOK

The legal system is just that – a *system* of interacting norms, institutions and people. It is easy to forget that, as a system, the reader should be wary of looking at any individual part of the 'system' in isolation. Not only will this give a skewed outlook, but it will also risk overlooking ways in which the 'system' as a whole can be improved. Even if studying substantive areas of law – such as contract, tort or public law – it should never be forgotten that those areas are underpinned, constrained and enabled by the *system* discussed in this textbook. In this way the legal system is both the frame of the umbrella that unites as a whole the various, disparate areas of law *and* the safety net intended to correct any undesirable effects arising from the development of the law.

Legal study is made much easier when connections are made between different parts of the system. In this way, a study of a 'legal system' is much more than just about 'how' things are done or by whom and should certainly not be seen as something to be treated as 'introductory'. The legal system is the machine that makes the law work. One way of making those connections is to identify themes that unite the different parts of the system. The following two themes will emerge as you read this text and should be considered as you read the individual chapters.

- Theory and practice – the book will introduce you to the processes and structures of the English Legal System as *intended* to apply. It will quickly become apparent that how the system operates in *practice* can be different, sometimes very different. Assessing why the 'law in the books' may be different to the 'law in action' is a very important legal skill and one which this text hopes to help you develop.
- Distribution of power – the formulation, execution and operation of law is intrinsically linked to where 'power' lies (e.g. as between Parliament and the Government or the Government and the judiciary or the Government and the people). This textbook considers the impact of 'power' (legal, political, social, economic) on the operation of the law and on the way in which the legal system operates.

LEGAL SKILLS

A study of the 'legal system' should always be accompanied with an appreciation of the legal skills necessary to understand its operation. Much has been written about the notion of 'legal skills'[71] and there are many excellent texts that are dedicated to the topic. However, there is no universal definition as to what the term means and different authors and educators sometimes use it to mean different things. This textbook adopts an open approach to the term and treats it as including:

- General transferable skills (such as communication and analysis)
- Legal study skills (such as legal research and case analysis)
- Practical legal skills (such as advocacy or drafting)

This textbook has been designed in such a way as to *embed* the acquisition, development and mastery of certain key legal skills, behaviours and competences. The authors have sought to *integrate* these skills into the design of the text and the activities and questions we encourage you to answer as you read and on the website. The text specifically does *not* have distinct sections on 'skills' as it is much more beneficial to learn those skills 'in context'.

Interspersed in the text are diagrams intended to simplify or give a visual representation of the various processes and there are comment 'boxes' throughout that provide opportunities to:

- Explore a given aspect of the legal system in greater detail
- Analyse the law by considering the implications of a given feature or development or by considering proposals for law reform
- Apply the law by considering how a particular legal rule operates in practice
- Make connections between different chapters of the textbook or to different areas of substantive law in order to gain a better understanding of the contextual detail of the law
- Take things further by directing the reader to additional resources or thinking points or by making reference to further material available on the companion website

This integrated approach works well in the written form for certain skills – such as legal research or written communication – but perhaps less well for others such as advocacy. Whereas there is much to be gained from the textbook itself, the companion website contains a significant range of further activities and examples that seek to develop your skills further. This balanced approach to providing both information and skills is one of the defining features of this textbook and its website. The accompanying website contains the following:

- Long podcasts – to form a series of 'mini-lectures' on the major chapters of the text. This will draw upon the key components and bring them to life with further examples and explanations as well as advice on how to get the most out of legal study.

---

71 With the regulator of solicitors in England and Wales proposing significant reforms to bolster the skills of new entrants to the profession – see Chapter 15 on legal professionals.

- Short podcasts – these will cover recent developments and examples that seek to keep the readers' knowledge and understanding up to date and to provide additional information on the development of the law and the legal system.
- Legal exercises – in the form of questions and activities designed to encourage the application of the law or its critical analysis.
- Multiple choice questions – in order to highlight areas of strength and weakness in understanding of specific topics and to provide feedback on performance.
- Flashcards – containing the facts and judgments of the major cases that have shaped the legal system.
- Study advice – this takes the form of general advice on the study of law and specific, worked examples of student work with strengths and weaknesses identified.

A BLUEPRINT FOR THE BOOK

The rest of this text will explore particular dimensions of the legal system of England and Wales. The book is split into four main sections, as outlined in Figure 1.2.

While the individual chapters are designed to give an isolated examination of the detail of each topic, the reader should be mindful of how that topic fits into the broader *system*. This will give a better overview of the legal system as a whole and also enrich understanding of the individual topics.

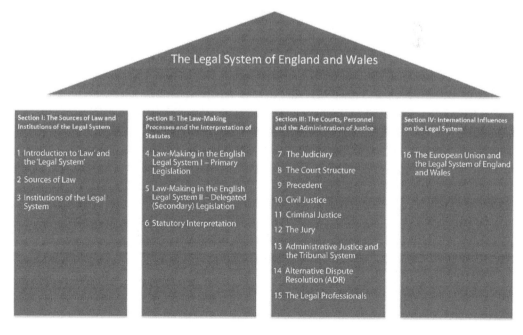

Figure 1.2 Structure of the Book

COMPANION WEBSITE

The website that accompanies this textbook contains many useful resources that you can use to consolidate and further your knowledge of the law, to hone your skills of critical analysis and to test your knowledge.

MULTIPLE CHOICE QUESTIONS

There is a bank of multiple choice questions (MCQs) that can be used to test your knowledge and understanding of the material covered by this chapter. These MCQs are a mixture of short-form, knowledge-based questions and longer ones that attempt to allow you to apply your knowledge.

PODCASTS

- The podcasts provide a summary of the area under study, bringing together the key themes and threads of analysis into a 'mini-lecture'.
- There will also be an explanation and analysis of topical and up-to-date issues related to defining law and the legal system.

2

CHAPTER 2
SOURCES OF LAW

INTRODUCTION

In determining the law of a legal system it is normal to turn to its formal, written constitution in the first instance. This will give an indication of the institutional actors capable of passing binding law under prescribed conditions. The English Legal System is different, lacking as it does a codified constitution. This, when coupled with its common law (judge-made law) heritage, means that determining and categorising the sources of English law can be more difficult than for other legal systems. Yet being able to determine and classify sources is important as it not only gives a legal system its distinct character but also enables somebody unfamiliar with a particular area of law to identify its general principles and detailed rules.

This chapter will explore the major sources of English law and attempt to put forward ways of categorising and ordering those sources. It will also introduce you to the concept of there being a hierarchy of norms,[1] with some sources of law taking priority over others within the English Legal System. Subsequent chapters will explore some of these sources in much greater detail (for example when talking about case law, primary legislation, delegated legislation and European Union law). This chapter will make cross-references to other chapters so that you can see how these sources operate independently and alongside each other. Even though greater treatment will be given in those individual chapters, it is important not to lose sight of the bigger picture of sources provided here.

AS YOU READ

This chapter focusses on **describing the major sources of law** and so you should focus your reading on those key definitions. Being able to **distinguish and categorise** sources of law is another skill to be developed during your reading of this chapter.

By the end of this chapter, you should have a broader understanding of how different sources of law **interact and be able critically to discuss** any overlaps that exist. In considering the different sources of law it is important to be able to **rank the sources in terms of priority** so as to demonstrate **critical understanding of the hierarchy of norms** in the English Legal System.

---

1   Another way of saying 'legal rules'.

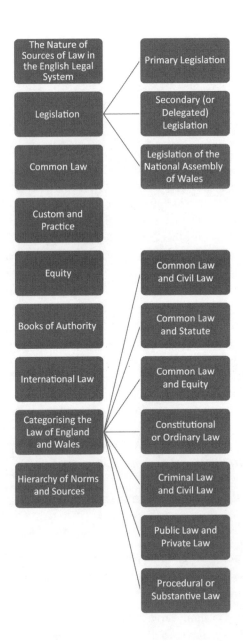

Figure 2.1

THE NATURE OF SOURCES OF LAW IN THE ENGLISH LEGAL SYSTEM

Almost all legal systems around the world are based on a formal, written constitution. The constitution will establish the legal system and explain how the relationship between its constituent parts is to be governed. The United Kingdom is one of a small number of states

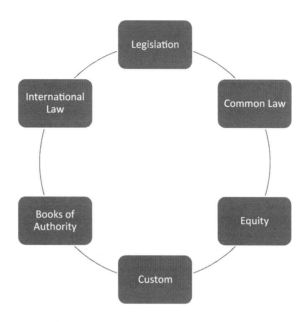

Figure 2.2 Major Sources of Law

that lack a fully codified, written constitution.[2] This is an important part of the English Legal System's culture as it allows for a more flexible system of government and a wider variety of sources to be used as law. It also adds to the evolutionary character of English law and the English Legal System. As you will undoubtedly come to learn if you formally study law in depth, just because the English Legal System lacks a formal, codified constitutional document this does not mean that it lacks constitutional rules or an order of priority amongst its sources.

The following sections will outline the major sources of law (see Figure 2.2) in the English Legal System before turning to questions of how we can classify the relationship between them or the hierarchy that may (or may not) exist between the sources.

LEGISLATION

The term 'legislation' is taken to mean the statutory law of the English Legal System, including Acts of Parliament (primary legislation) and delegated legislation (secondary legislation) – mostly statutory instruments, usually fleshing out a piece of primary legislation, i.e. providing for the detailed implementation of the statute which authorises that further detail to be legislated for by the Lord Chancellor and Secretary of State for Justice or sometimes other

---

2   Israel and New Zealand also lack a written constitution.

Ministers e.g. the Home Secretary[3] when that further detail has been worked out; though there are some other forms of routinely used secondary legislation, such as local government byelaws passed by local authorities (see the section that follows on secondary legislation). This subsection will briefly outline these two sources of law, leaving their detailed discussion to their dedicated chapters later in this work (Chapters 4 and 5).

PRIMARY LEGISLATION

Primary legislation consists of Acts of the United Kingdom Parliament which, for our purposes, have application in England and Wales. Parliament, in this sense, is taken to be the House of Commons, House of Lords and the Queen acting in combination. Prior to becoming an Act of Parliament, the draft piece of legislation is referred to as a 'Bill'. Such legislation is normally made with the involvement of each part of Parliament, but there are circumstances[4] where either additional requirements are necessary[5] or the consent of the Lords is not needed.[6] There are different ways in which Acts of Parliament can be classified and categorised (e.g. Government Bill or a private members' Bill) but the process for their passage remains broadly the same. The full law-making process is explored in great depth in the chapter dedicated to primary legislation (Chapter 4).

SECONDARY (OR DELEGATED) LEGISLATION

Secondary (or delegated) legislation consists of those measures that are passed, normally by Government Ministers, with the authority of Parliament.[7] The vast majority of pieces of secondary legislation take the form of statutory instruments but there are also other forms of secondary legislation such as orders in council and byelaws. Secondary legislation is discussed in greater detail in a subsequent chapter of this textbook (Chapter 5). For present purposes it is worth noting that the majority of secondary legislation derives its authority from an Act of Parliament, they are subject to that authority and any powers exercised under secondary legislation must be compatible with that Act of Parliament.

Secondary legislation is, therefore, largely dependent on primary legislation for its continued existence and can be challenged before the courts if it falls short of any requirement in its 'parent' Act.

---

3   Examples are found in many modern statutes as this has become a preferred way of legislating now, when the principles of the legislation are dealt with in the main statute and the detailed implementation then included in an associated statutory instrument (S.I.); e.g. the Legal Aid, Sentencing and Punishment of Offenders Act 2012, commonly referred to as 'LASPO' required a good deal of additional implementation work to be done because of its radical cuts to legal aid and much of this is in the Legal Aid, Sentencing and Punishment of Offenders Act 2012 (Consequential, Transitional and Saving Provisions) Regulations 2013, which also amended some other secondary legislation. This has been criticised because of the extensive use of the power which enables quite detailed provisions to be made outside Parliament after an Act has been duly passed (sometimes after extensive or even heated debate) following which the SI is usually then 'laid before' Parliament rather than returned for any significant approval. However, in reality the extent of parliamentary business makes this necessary or government would never get through the workload.

4   Discussed in Chapter 4.

5   For example, the referendum requirements of the European Union Act 2011 s 2(2) and Schedule 1.

6   Due to the provisions of the Parliament Acts 1911 and 1949.

7   Discussed in Chapter 5.

LEGISLATION OF THE NATIONAL ASSEMBLY FOR WALES

During the last 30 years, the United Kingdom has been through a period of structural and constitutional change known as devolution whereby powers have flowed out to certain geographical regions. These devolved regions are Scotland, Northern Ireland and Wales. For a textbook on the 'English Legal System', which is more properly known as the unified legal system of England and Wales, a brief consideration of the Welsh system post-devolution is necessary. This will allow you to differentiate it from the mainstream English Legal System that is subject to the bulk of discussion in this text.

As part of the process of devolution, there is now a Welsh Assembly and Welsh Government. In certain areas, the Welsh Assembly is able to pass 'legislation' both primary and secondary and these form part of the law as it applies to Wales. In contrast with the unlimited legislative competence of the UK Parliament, the Welsh Assembly has to act within the limits of the powers conferred upon it by the devolution settlement.[8] Since 2011 the Welsh Assembly has had the power to pass Acts of the National Assembly for Wales. These 'Acts' are to be regarded as primary legislation for Wales and should not be confused with Acts of Parliament as the former have a much more limited scope of application (both substantively and geographically) and derive their authority from an Act of the United Kingdom Parliament.[9] The Assembly can only pass primary legislation in defined policy areas. These areas of devolved power include policy areas such as: agriculture, culture, economic development, education, transport, housing etc.[10] This principle of constrained legislative competence means that a draft measure can be referred directly to the Supreme Court if there is doubt as to whether the Assembly has acted within its competence.[11] At the time of writing the Welsh Government had ordered a Commission to investigate 'Justice in Wales'.[12]

TAKING THINGS FURTHER

Chapters 4 and 5 consider the principles underpinning and processes for the creation of primary and secondary legislation. The website that accompanies this text also contains examples of each form of legislation, with annotations on how they are structured, and research exercises designed to help you to familiarise yourself with each type of source. It is always beneficial to take the abstract descriptions and analysis of particular sources given in texts such as this and to explore what those principles and sources look like in particular, concrete, measures.

If you are studying any substantive legal subjects then you could explore the legislation (primary, secondary and devolved) that has an effect on that area of law.

---

8 Started by the Government of Wales Act 1998.

9 Government of Wales Act 2006.

10 Ibid. Schedule 7 lays down the 'subjects' for which the Assembly can legislate.

11 Ibid. s 112.

12 https://gov.wales/commission-justice-wales/terms-reference.

This will help you to contextualise the substantive legal rules within the broader legal system. Equally, it is beneficial to look at legislation on areas that you have not previously studied or that you may never study. This will allow you to focus on the features and style of the legislation without becoming overly distracted by the content. Once you are familiar with the way in which primary and secondary legislation is structured and the, sometimes esoteric, language that is used, you will find legal study more straightforward.

COMMON LAW

The second major source of law in the English Legal System comes in the form of cases decided by courts. This is often referred to as the 'common law', although, as mentioned later, the term 'common law' can have many different meanings and it is important to use the term correctly in its proper context. It can refer to the case law itself and to the classification of the legal system.

The use of case law defines the English Legal System to the extent that it is referred to as a 'common law system' and is contrasted with other systems, such as those following a civil law tradition, that rely less heavily upon the use of judges in developing the law. Under the common law, there are stricter rules about the binding nature of judicial decisions and a stronger hierarchy of courts. The civil law tradition relies on extensive principles that are normally codified into single documents (or sets of documents) referred to as 'codes'.[13] The English Legal System does not adopt such a practice and so there can be significant areas of law that are not covered by legislation. It is in those areas that the common law has flourished.

If you continue with further legal study then it is inevitable that you will notice that certain areas of the law are dominated by the common law, with very little legislative activity. For example, the law of contract is primarily a common law subject with many of the major principles – such as offer and acceptance[14] – having been developed by the courts. Equally, the law of murder in criminal law is a common law offence.[15]

The common law developed organically out of local custom and practice in the different regions of England and, from the 11th century onwards, a more consistent application of principle was developed from these decided cases.[16] This led to a body of law that, by the 13th century was slowly becoming 'common' across the English territory (as it was then). It is this general applicability of common law principles across the whole of the English Legal System that differentiates the common law from continuing local customs (discussed next).

13 French and German law, for example, follow this tradition of having extensive codes.
14 *Carlill v Carbolic Smoke Ball* [1893] 1 QB 256 (CA).
15 Although sentencing on conviction is statutory.
16 For more on the history of the common law, see Harry Potter, *Law, Liberty and the Constitution: A Brief History of the Common Law* (Boydall Press 2015).

In order to develop legal certainty and consistency further, the doctrine of *stare decisis* was adopted whereby courts followed previous decisions by other courts when factual situations were suitably similar, and the facts raised the same legal issue. This adds certainty to the system as individuals can refer back to decided cases in order to predict how their dispute will be settled. This principle still survives today and makes up the basis of the rules of binding precedent. It also explains the need to record cases in the law reports for subsequent reference by lawyers, judges and students. The precise and technical rules of precedent are discussed in detail in Chapter 9 of this work.

Through case law it is clear that judges have a mechanism of developing law. In this way judges not only interpret and apply the law but are also active participants in its creation. This can be through the refinement of existing case law (allowing for an organic development of the law) or through the development of new principles. Judges can also develop understanding of the law through their interpretation of legislation. As the number of pieces of legislation, as well as their length, has grown over time the judiciary now spend a greater proportion of time interpreting statutes than was once the case.

CUSTOM AND PRACTICE

The concept of 'custom and practice' as a source of law is one that receives little attention from modern writers, but it is a source that remains important in certain (albeit limited) circumstances. It should be remembered that it was a filtering and refinement of local custom and practice that led to the development of the principles of the common law and, therefore, custom has historically contributed a great deal to the development of the legal system. In modern times, custom remains relevant where there is long-standing practice (normally the conferral of a right) that is restricted to a specific area or locality. This contrasts with the common law which is not restricted to a specific area and applies generally.

Not all customs will be recognised as a source of law and there are certain requirements for such recognition by the courts. Most importantly, the right claimed must have existed since 'time immemorial'.[17] If it is possible to demonstrate that a particular right has not been generally exercised until relatively modern times then a claim based on custom is likely to fail. This is evident in the relatively recent case of *Newhaven Port*[18] in which the Supreme Court noted that 'bathing [in the sea for pleasure] could rarely be a right obtained by custom and usage'[19] because such an activity was first recorded in the 18th century and so had not been relied upon since time immemorial. As a result of this requirement, most customs relate to

---

17 A legal concept which was defined by the first Statute of Westminster 1275 and is deemed to relate to the first year of the reign of Richard I in 1189, the date 'whereof the memory of man runneth not to the contrary' or the limit of legal memory.

18 *Newhaven Port and Properties v East Sussex County Council* [2015] UKSC 7, [2015] 2 WLR 601.

19 Ibid. [35].

rights associated to specific local professions (such as rights of fishermen[20] or agricultural rights)[21] or local traditions (such as the holding of country fairs on parcels of land[22] or rights of recreation).[23] In addition, the custom must exist as a right rather than because it has been granted with the permission of another person (such as a landowner granting permission in the form of a licence for a person to fish on their land).[24] This system of local law will remain important to maintaining the character of certain localities and has been recognised in certain statutory frameworks.

Most famously in recent times the ongoing importance of local customary law is underlined in the law (statutory and common) surrounding 'village greens'. The concept of a village green is different in popular literature and in law. The former conjures pictures of green space located in the centre of idyllic English villages, often with a pond and a May Pole. In the words of Lord Hoffman, '[n]o doubt there were, and perhaps are, village greens like that, but the law took a more prosaic view of the matter.'[25] One of the ways in which a person can demonstrate that a parcel of land is a village green is if it is a space 'on which the inhabitants of any locality have a customary right to indulge in lawful sports and pastimes.'[26] Under the Commons Registration Act 2006, such land could traditionally be registered as a village green with important consequences for development, as it is a criminal offence to prevent access to a common space such as a village green.[27] Thus, if a person could demonstrate that a customary right existed over a piece of land then that person could have it registered and therefore frustrate (or at least reduce) development of the land. Registration of a village green was recently used as an attempt to protect West Beach in Newhaven. Although the *Newhaven*[28] case was decided on another definition of 'village green', the use of a customary right to secure registration is still a possibility (one recognised by the Supreme Court)[29] and so custom as a source of law is likely to have some continuing importance that should not be too readily ignored.

The Government has attempted to curtail this type of defensive registering as a means of blocking planned developments by tightening the requirements of registration via the Growth and Infrastructure Act 2013. This will reduce the use of custom as a source of law as it will no longer be possible to register a village green in reaction to planning proposals.[30]

---

20 *Mercer v Denne* [1905] 2 Ch 538 (CA).

21 *Earl de la Warr v Miles* (1881) 17 ChD 535 (CA).

22 *Wyld v Silver* [1963] 1 QB 169 (CA).

23 *Fitch v Rawling* (1795) 2 H BL 393.

24 *Earl de la Warr v Miles* (1881) 17 ChD 535 (CA).

25 *Oxford County Council v Oxford City Council* [2006] UKHL 25, [2006] 2 AC 674 [4] (Lord Hoffmann).

26 Commons Registration Act 1965 s 22(1)(b). The other two possibilities being 'land which has been allotted by or under any Act for the exercise or recreation of the inhabitants of any locality or … on which the inhabitants of any locality
   have indulged in such sports and pastimes as of right for not less than 20 years'.

27 Inclosure Act 1857 s 12 and Commons Act 1876 s 29.

28 *Newhaven Port and Properties v East Sussex County Council* [2015] UKSC 7, [2015] 2 WLR 601.

29 Ibid. [134].

30 The Growth and Infrastructure Act 2013 s 16 amends the Commons Act 2006 by inserting a new section (s 15C) which
   reads as follows: 'The right under section 15(1) to apply to register land in England as a town or village green ceases to
   apply if an event specified in the first column of the Table set out in Schedule 1A has occurred in relation to the land ("a

EQUITY

As the common law developed, its rules became much more rigid and procedural. Equally, the range of remedies available under the common law was limited. Litigants had to bring their claim using one of a prescribed set of 'writs' which laid out the nature of the action that was being brought. As new circumstances arose, new writs were not always conceived. As a result, those bringing an action either had to make their circumstances artificially satisfy one of the writs or risk having their claim struck out. In achieving the balance between legal certainty and flexibility, the common law appeared to have favoured certainty. This led to potentially unjust decisions being held under the common law.

Where the common law failed to provide an adequate solution due to its inflexibility, individuals began to petition the King directly. The weight of these cases gradually increased, and the King passed them to his Lord Chancellor to decide as 'Keeper of the King's Conscience'. Free from the constraints of the strict rules of the common law, the Lord Chancellor was able to decide cases according to broader notions of fairness or equity. Given that the Lord Chancellor was normally a member of the clergy, the judgments given in equity were seen to have a moral, rather than a strictly legal, weighting.

This practice eventually developed into one in the 15th century that was facilitated by a parallel legal system within the court system where cases were heard by the Court of Chancery, although it was a while before this specific court was so designated: Sir Thomas More as Lord Chancellor sat in what is now called 'the Old Hall' in Lincolns Inn which dates from the late 15th century. Due to the uncertain nature of the decisions taken in equity, principles or 'equitable maxims' developed to guide the decision-making process of the Court of Chancery. These maxims were intended to be high-level guiding principles. They included, but were not limited to, the following:

- **Equity acts *in personam*** – this means that equity is concerned with persons, and jurisdiction need not be exerted over property since a decision acted on the conscience of the individual before the court who could then be required to carry out that decision which might then affect property.
- **He who comes to equity must come with clean hands** – those who seek an equitable remedy must not have acted unconscionably in the matter concerned.
- **Between equal equities the first in order of time shall prevail** – where there are two equal equitable claims then the one that arose first will prevail.

The resolution of disputes by recourse to equity also had a distinct set of remedies attached that differed from common law damages. These equitable remedies include estoppel, specific performance and injunctive relief. These remedies were always discretionary and remain so to this day, which contrasts starkly with common law remedies which are awarded as of right.

---

trigger event").' Schedule 1A triggering events include applications for planning permission, a development plan that identifies the land as a potential site for development.

This development of equity from an informal system into a quasi-distinct justice system continued and the rules became more concrete and inflexible over time as a way of dealing with the criticism that the notion of 'fairness' was subjective and an inability to predict outcomes in a given case was damaging to legal certainty. Moreover, the situation of two sets of courts exercising seemingly equal jurisdiction was bound to lead to confusion and conflict. This conflict came to a head in 1615 in the *Earl of Oxford's case*[31] where the case progressed first through the common law courts and a decision was made that a transfer of land was void under a specific statute. A further action, involving one different party, but covering essentially the same issue, was brought in the equitable Court of Chancery. The Lord Chancellor granted an injunction to prevent enforcement of the common law judgment. As a result, the common law (in the ordinary courts) and the law of equity (in the Court of Chancery) came into conflict and it was only after the intervention of the King that the conflict was resolved. James I made a declaration that equity takes priority over the common law when they are in conflict.

With the uncertainty and delay of the Court of Chancery, and the more rigid application of the equitable maxims, there were calls for a unified court system that brought together equity and the common law. This was achieved by the Supreme Court of Judicature Act 1873 which established the High Court and brought the law of equity into the same system as that of the common law. Although still housed within a separate division (the Chancery Division) to that where common law claims were heard (the Queen's Bench), the two sets of law were within one unified system with greater clarity about the division of jurisdiction. The law itself was not fused but rather the claims on equity and/or common law could be heard within a single structure, the High Court. It is in this form that equity acts as a source of law for the English Legal System. It is part of a unified legal system but retains a distinct set of rules and principles (based on the equitable maxims) that can be applied to a case, particularly where a common law solution or remedy would seem to be unfair, inappropriate or likely to lead to injustice.

MAKING CONNECTIONS – THE LAW OF EQUITY
+ +
For those studying for a degree in law, you will undoubtedly come across equitable principles and equitable remedies in other areas of study. There are entire areas of substantive law – such as the law of trusts – that are governed by equitable principles. In addition, there are many other areas of law – such as contract, intellectual property and family law – where the law of equity plays an important part, specifically in relation to remedies.

---

31 *Earl of Oxford's Case* (1615) 1 Ch Rep 1.

BOOKS OF AUTHORITY

Given the lack of consistent record-keeping in terms of judicial decisions prior to the 17th century, books of authority are treated as representing authoritative and accurate reflections of the common law as it stood at that time. These were texts written by contemporary jurists of the period and are taken to reflect the judicial decisions and practice of that era. There are numerous authors who have been held to hold such authority, including but not limited to:

- Glanvill's *Treatise on the Laws and Customs of the Realm of England* (1189)
- Bracton's *On the Laws and Customs of England* (1250)
- Coke's *Institutes of the Lawes of England* (1628–1644)
- Blackstone's *Commentaries on the Laws of England* (1765) – the work consists of four volumes relating to broad areas of law: The Rights of Persons, The Rights of Things, Of Private Wrongs, Of Public Wrongs

These books of authority can still be relied upon as authoritative sources of the law and are still used in court today, either where the common law has not significantly changed or where a reading of these texts may cast a new light on the issue at hand. As recently as 2019, the Supreme Court relied upon passages of Blackstone's *Commentaries on the Laws of England* in deciding a matter related to the security services[32] and references to the commentaries on 'public wrongs' have proved useful when discussing criminal law, particularly basic and fundamental principles of criminal justice.[33]

EXPLAINING THE LAW – THE INFLUENCE OF ACADEMIC WRITINGS

A distinction ought to be drawn between these 'books of authority' and modern academic writing. Both can be cited in court cases but only the former is regarded as being an authoritative statement of the law. Nonetheless, the writings of expert academics in law journals have certainly influenced judges in coming to conclusions on the law. For example, Lord Justice Auld in *Marks & Spencer*[34] used the analysis provided by Dr Sara Drake (an academic specialising in EU remedial law)[35] to frame his decision on a significant tax matter.[36] Judges also often point to academic criticism of the law when advocating a change in the law. This is notable in the recent judgment

---

32 R (on the application of Privacy International) v Investigatory Powers Tribunal and Others [2019] UKSC 22, [2019] 2 WLR 1219 [32] and a more substantive treatment in Pham v Secretary of State for the Home Department [2015] UKSC 19, [2015] 1 WLR 1591 [97] and [106]. This reference is by no means unusual and you will find reference to Blackstone (and other writers) peppered through the law reports at all levels.

33 R v Davis [2008] UKHL 36, [2008] 3 WLR 125 [5].

34 Marks & Spencer Plc v Commissioners of Customs & Excise [2003] EWCA Civ 1448, [2004] 1 CMLR 8.

35 Sara Drake, 'Vouchers v VAT: issues of direct effect and national time limits raised by the Marks and Spencer case' (2003) 28(3) European Law Review 418.

36 Marks & Spencer Plc v Commissioners of Customs & Excise [2003] EWCA Civ 1448, [2004] 1 CMLR 8, [29] (Auld LJ).

of the High Court in *OMV Petrom*[37] where the extensive criticism of the position of the Court of Appeal by Professor Trietel in the Law Quarterly Review was cited.[38]

This raises two important points. First, we must distinguish between *authoritative* statements of the law which form an independent source of law for the English Legal System and the writing of academics that may only influence court decisions. Second, and despite their non-binding nature, modern writers can help to *shape* the law through their writings. For example, it was often said that the judgments of Lord Goff in the House of Lords regularly showed the influence of the late Professor Peter Birks (Regius Professor of Civil Law at the University of Oxford) on the development of the Law of Restitution.

INTERNATIONAL LAW

The contribution of international law to the English Legal System is important but it acts as a less direct source than other forms of law discussed in this chapter. There are two particularly noteworthy forms of international law that are, or were, sources of law for the English Legal System.

First, and more controversially, there exists a body of law called *jus cogens* which are peremptory norms of international law from which it is impossible to derogate. This means that the rights and obligations classified as *jus cogens* cannot be displaced by agreements between different countries or by the independent actions of a particular country. There is no generally accepted list of *jus cogens* but they include things like the prohibition against state torture. These principles may influence the way in which judges decide cases under the common law but their precise status as a 'source' of law is less certain. As noted in *Mohamed v Secretary of State for Foreign and Commonwealth Affairs*,[39] '[w]hile customary international law is a source of the common law, the precise manner in which it is received into English law is a question determined by English law.'[40] In this way it is clear the *jus cogens* are at the least an influence on English law and at the most are an independent source of law. If you study public international law then 'you will be likely to explore' the academic debates that surround such examples of the *jus cogens*.[41]

37 *OVM Petrom v Glencore* [2015] EWHC 666 (Comm).
38 Guenter Trietel, 'Damages for breach of warranty of quality' (1997) 113 LQR 188.
39 *Mohamed v Secretary of State for Foreign and Commonwealth Affairs* [2008] EWHC 2048 (Admin), [2009] 1 WLR 2579.
40 Ibid. [184].
41 For a flavour of that debate, see Matthew Saul, 'Identifying *jus cogens* norms: the interaction of scholars and international judges' (2015) 5 AJIL 26 or Ulf Linderfalk, 'What is so special about *jus cogens*? – on the difference between the ordinary and the peremptory international law' (2012) 14 IntCLRev 3.

Second, there are international treaties signed by the UK with other sovereign states or with international organisations such as the United Nations or the World Trade Organisation. The nature of these treaties is to bind, at the international level, those states (known, normally, as 'contracting parties') to certain commitments. There are two primary ways in which international treaties can become part of domestic, national law. The method of incorporation will depend on whether the country/state in question is a monist state or a dualist state. Monist states are those where international law becomes part of domestic law when a particular treaty is signed by the Government. The English Legal System does not follow this model and to preserve the sovereignty of Parliament follows the dualist model.

Under the dualist model, any agreement made by the Government at the international level must be *incorporated* into domestic law by legislation. More specifically for the English Legal System, this will require an Act of Parliament to be passed in the normal way through the Houses of Parliament. Thus, although the UK was an original signatory of the European Convention on Human Rights in the early 1950s, the substantive rights contained within it did not become part of English law until Parliament passed Tony Blair's Human Rights Act in 1998. Until that point, the only rights that people had were those available as a matter of *international law* and this precluded those who had been the victim of a violation of human rights – as defined in the Convention – from launching an action in the English courts. In this way, international treaties act as a source of law for the English Legal System when they have been incorporated but potentially can be a source of *rights in international law* for British citizens when they are signed and ratified by the UK Government.

MAKING CONNECTIONS – THE EUROPEAN UNION
+++

Later chapters of this book will focus on one area where international law has had a particularly strong influence on the English Legal System, namely the consequences flowing from the UK's membership of the European Union. At the time of writing the UK was in the process of revoking that membership and the final chapter of this textbook will consider the ongoing influence of the European Union into the future. This extends beyond substantive law matters and incorporates changes to underlying structures and principles of the English Legal System.

The use of international law treaties is widespread and can cover a surprising array of subject matter from cross-border commercial matters such as intellectual property[42] or recognition of arbitration agreements[43] from other countries to public law matters such as principles relating

---

42 Berne Convention for the Protection of Literary and Artistic Works (1886).

43 Convention on the Recognition and Enforcement of Foreign Arbitral Awards (1959) also known as the New York Convention.

to the rights of children[44] and agreements against the use of torture.[45] The use of international treaties is so widespread that there are even treaties governing the use, interpretation and effect of other international treaties! The Vienna Convention on the Law of Treaties, also known as the 'Treaty of Treaties', has 85 articles governing a common way of understanding, interpreting, terminating and suspending the operation of treaties.

CATEGORISING THE LAW OF ENGLAND AND WALES

Having briefly dealt with the individual sources of law it is important to spend some time exploring the different ways in which law can be categorised. This is helpful for further understanding the varying roles that these sources play in the English Legal System. It is also worth noting that when people refer to the 'common law' they may be referring to one of many different definitions/understandings of the common law. By understanding the following subsections, you will be able to contextualise the different usages of the phrase 'common law' and avoid misunderstandings. The following is not intended to be an exhaustive consideration of the way in which law can be classified, not least because there are limitless ways in which we could try to sort and label law. The purpose is rather to give an indication of terminology and to introduce you to the idea that sources of law can be categorised differently for different purposes.

COMMON LAW AND CIVIL LAW

As was mentioned previously, one way of categorising law is to consider the legal system within which it operates (as mentioned in Chapter 1). This can give a different emphasis to the importance of particular sources and how these sources are used in the legal system. Speaking of the common law tradition, a greater emphasis is placed on the organic development of the law through decisions in individual cases. These decisions then bind future courts of equal or lower status. Common law systems, such as that found in the English Legal System, are characterised by a strict hierarchy of courts with specific rules on the times when judges are and are not bound by previous judgments. In areas with little statutory law, judicial decisions become the predominant source of law used under a common law system. In this way the legislature is not expected to act in an exhaustive way as the common law will 'fill in the gaps'. This is in stark contrast to the civil law system where more prominence is given to the statutory law. There is normally (but not always) a greater degree of codification in civil law systems with whole areas of law reduced into single sets of (albeit lengthy) codes. In France, for example, there are upwards of 60 codes, including on commercial law, family law and the procedure for dealing with criminal matters. In terms of scope, the codes can be very long with the commercial code running to more than 300 pages and the environmental code at a similar length. By attempting complete codification of certain areas, the French system is subject to updating but the codes themselves become the most important form of law after the constitution. It follows that the

---

44 United Nations Convention on the Rights of the Child (1989).
45 United Nations Convention against Torture (1984).

French system relies less on judges creating law and French judges are characterised by a more inquisitorial/interpretative role than is found in common law systems, although no national judge is ever free of external influences through dealing with other judges when international professional as well as social contact opportunities arise at the many conferences at which they inevitably speak and attend. This seems to have had a greater influence of civil law approaches on UK judges rather than the common law on the civilian culture.[46]

COMMON LAW AND STATUTE

Another way of categorising law is to make a distinction between common law and statutory law. Here, common law is normally being used to describe all case law. This is a broad conception of case law and can include the principles of equity (found within case law) and even cases that do not have precedential value. Statute is used, in this instance, to cover both primary and secondary legislation.

COMMON LAW AND EQUITY

Another typical distinction is between equity and common law. These are both forms of case law and the difference is one of historical fact (discussed previously). People making this distinction are normally interested in comparing the rigidity of the rules of the old common law system and the broader equitable principles that were applied first by the Lord Chancellor directly and later by the Court of Chancery. Understanding the distinction is still important because equitable remedies are not available as of right, as is the case under the common law, and are discretionary. This means that although the Judicature Acts sought to *fuse* the institutional organisation of equity and the common law, they remain distinct sources of law albeit, as has been said, 'now flowing along the same channel'. In this way, being cognisant of the different context within which the phrase 'common law' is used can impact on our ability to understand a given case or the analysis of a particular case.

CONSTITUTIONAL OR ORDINARY LAW

The classification of law as 'constitutional' or 'ordinary' law is important in countries that have formal, codified constitutions. This is because constitutional law is a superior form of law that has special rules and procedures that govern its creation and it normally takes priority over conflicting 'ordinary' law. For example, in the United States the Supreme Court can strike down Acts of Congress (primary legislation) that are incompatible with the US Constitution.[47]

Traditionally, such a distinction has been unnecessary in the English Legal System as, with the lack of a formal written constitution, there was no higher source of law than Acts of Parliament. While this position is still broadly true, judicial developments in the early 21st century have suggested that there is a subset of constitutional law statutes that have a certain priority when they clash with 'ordinary' statutes. What makes this all the more striking is

....

46 See further Chapter 6, Statutory Interpretation, particularly in relation to the purposive approach which has crept into English law judges' statutory interpretation toolkit.

47 *Marbury v Madison* (1803) 5 US 137.

that there is no difference in the procedure for making so-called constitutional statutes.[48] This development is taken up later in the section on the hierarchy of norms and also in the substantive chapter on primary legislation.

CRIMINAL LAW AND CIVIL LAW

A further division in the classification of law comes in the form of the differences between civil and criminal law. When we talk of civil law in this way, we mean the branch of law that governs the relationship between individuals (particularly where that relationship breaks down), as opposed to criminal law which seeks to redress wrongs done by individuals against the state. The civil law therefore encompasses private law disputes (such as breach of contract, negligence and matrimonial disagreements etc.) whereas the criminal law deals with offences of varying seriousness (such as murder, theft, speeding etc.).

Civil and criminal law are both subject to their own sets of procedures and have their own language for describing similar aspects of cases. There are more important differences such as the standard of proof required to be successful in a given case with the 'balance of probabilities' being used in civil cases and 'beyond all reasonable doubt' forming the criminal standard. Due to the significant differences in process, there are dedicated chapters on the civil (Chapter 10) and criminal justice (Chapter 11) systems later in this work.

PUBLIC LAW AND PRIVATE LAW

In some ways this categorisation is a broader version of the distinction between criminal law and civil law. Public law concerns the relationship between the individual and the state and also between the different institutions of the state. In this way, criminal law is a form of public law as it concerns the way in which the state redresses offences against it. Other branches of public law include constitutional law (which is concerned with the creation of Government and the regulation of the powers of the state and the rights of individuals against the state) and administrative law (which is concerned with the activities of Government agencies such as those administering social security or other welfare payments). The cornerstone of public law is the concept of 'judicial review' whereby individuals can challenge the actions of the Government (or its agents) before a court.

Private law, on the other hand, governs the relationship between individuals and is often used synonymously with the term 'civil law'.

PROCEDURAL OR SUBSTANTIVE LAW

This method of categorisation relies less on the type of source under discussion but rather on its purpose. Substantive law lays down the principles of a given area of law, for example the required elements of a criminal offence. Substantive law establishes the rights and obligations of an individual in a given situation. Procedural law will set out the rules and principles by

48 *Thoburn v Sunderland City Council* [2002] EWHC 195 (Admin), [2003] QB 151.

which that substantive law is *administered* (e.g. the steps needed to bring a valid claim in the High Court for a breach of contract or various rules of evidence).

SUMMARY

As we have seen previously, there are numerous ways in which we can classify law or attempt to distinguish between different types of sources of law. This is a useful skill for a person wishing to study the English Legal System and English law in greater detail as it will allow for a concept with several possible meanings to be understood in its proper context. The rest of this text will assume that the reader has mastered these distinctions. As the text progresses to more detailed, and analytical, discussion of the English Legal System it would be easy to discard the messages in this chapter. This temptation should be avoided, as a proper grounding in basic terminology and the fundamental sources of the English Legal System is crucial to understanding the more technical aspects of the system and the principles by which it operates.

TAKING THINGS FURTHER – TESTING YOUR UNDERSTANDING

The website that accompanies this textbook has exercises by which you can test your knowledge and understanding of these classifications and to enable you to be sure that you understand the correct use of key terminology in this chapter. Although it takes time to become familiar with the unique language of law and of legal sources, the greater the immersion that you have into it the faster your understanding will develop. The website also suggests specific sources that you can explore that will help you to identify some of the different classifications discussed here.

HIERARCHY OF NORMS AND SOURCES

The presentation of the sources of law for the English Legal System should not be studied in isolation. It is, of course, essential to understand and to be able to describe the basic sources of law of the English Legal System that were laid out previously. The first part of the chapter dealt with this aspect of the law. It is also important to be able to categorise, compare and distinguish between the various sources of law and legal systems. The second part of the chapter dealt with this aspect.

It is of equal importance to consider the normative framework within which these sources operate. This turns the legal sources into a series of interacting (and sometimes conflicting!) norms, some of which have priority over others. It is this aspect of the law that is dealt within this final section. Given the lack of a fixed constitutional document, it can be very difficult to ascertain and understand the order of priority amongst this multitude of sources. What makes this task even more difficult is that the position of particular sources may move over time or, at the least, our understanding of how these sources interact can change and develop as the

English Legal System continues to develop and evolve. Also, there is disagreement (amongst academics and the institutions) about the ordering of these sources and this adds to the richness of the discourse.

MAKING CONNECTIONS – CONSTITUTIONAL LAW
+ +

Further chapters of this textbook continue to explore certain constitutional principles. The rule of law, parliamentary sovereignty and separation of powers are not sources of law themselves but these principles (and their interpretation) do impact on how the sources of law are understood and can give a different gloss to a particular piece of law or even to a whole category of sources. These constitutional principles underpin the way in which the framework of the law is to be understood. These concepts are returned to in later chapters but if you are also studying constitutional law then you will delve even deeper into these concepts.

A textbook on the English Legal System written at the turn of the 20th century would have reflected a much different hierarchy of norms than is presented here. We currently stand at the start of a new era in the development of the relationship between sources with the courts seemingly keen (albeit, so far in mainly non-binding statements) to drive forward a new understanding of how the sources interact. What follows is a conceptualisation of the hierarchy between the different sources of law within the English Legal System.

Even though the English Legal System lacks a formal written constitution, it still has forms of constitutional law that take priority over other, non-constitutional sources. This constitutional law is formed through the adherence to certain principles and a core of so-called constitutional statutes that take priority over ordinary law. This was first established in the Thoburn[49] case. These statutes are partly entrenched and, unlike other statutes, can only be repealed through the express actions and words of Parliament. There is no definitive list of such constitutional statutes but the following have been held to be included in the definition:

- European Communities Act 1972
- Human Rights Act 1998
- Bill of Rights 1689
- Magna Carta 1215
- Scotland Act 1998

It is these principles and constitutional statutes that sit at the apex of the hierarchy of norms and take priority over other conflicting pieces of 'ordinary law' unless that ordinary law expressly repeals the constitutional statute.

---

49 Thoburn v Sunderland City Council [2002] EWHC 195 (Admin), [2003] QB 151, also known as the 'Metric Martyrs case'. An important case on the relationship between EU law and an Act of Parliament.

To complicate things further, the Supreme Court in its *HS2*[50] judgment has recently suggested that not all of these constitutional statutes are equal and that there may even be an order of priority between them. This is a developing area of UK constitutional law and the effect of the judgment is not quite certain, as resolution of this hierarchy between constitutional statutes was not necessary to decide the case at hand. The suggestion, but it was only a suggestion, in this case was that the principle of parliamentary privilege over its own internal affairs[51] would take priority over the primacy of European Union law.[52] The implication is that ordering these sources and determining priorities is a matter for the courts to decide in cases where a conflict arises.[53]

Following next, and subject to the constraints of the constitutional law just discussed, come 'ordinary' statutes. By 'ordinary' we mean Acts of Parliament that are not constitutional in the *Thoburn* sense.[54] This would cover the vast majority of Acts of Parliament currently in operation within the English Legal System. These, due to the principle of parliamentary sovereignty, take priority over all of the other sources. This is a principle of long-standing[55] and one that is discussed further in the chapter on law-making.

Sitting below statutory law is the common law, in the sense of the totality of case law. Acts of Parliament can displace the common law and where the two come into conflict the former takes priority over the latter. Even within the broad definition of case law the principles of equity take priority over the rules of the common law.[56]

Similarly, there is a hierarchy between the judgments of different courts. The binding rules of precedent (discussed in a later chapter) make certain judgments more authoritative than others. This is an important point not always remembered by those who are studying the law for the first time. Thus, not only does a Supreme Court judgment take priority over judgments from any other court in the English Legal System, it is also more authoritative in its statements of the law.

CONCLUSION

This chapter was intended to give an introduction to the major sources of law in the English Legal System. Reading this chapter will have provided an overview that will be invaluable for the more detailed and analytical chapters on specific sources or aspects of the English Legal System that follow. More importantly, the chapter deconstructed some of the different ways

50 R (*HS2 Alliance*) v *Secretary of State for Transport* [2014] UKSC 3, [2014] 1 WLR 3253.
51 Derived from Article 9 Bill of Rights 1689.
52 European Communities Act 1972.
53 R (*HS2 Alliance*) v *Secretary of State for Transport* [2014] UKSC 3, [2014] 1 WLR 3253, [207].
54 For debate on the meaning of this term, see Farrah Ahmed and Adam Perry, 'The quasi-entrenchment of constitutional statutes' (2014) 73 CLJ 514.
55 Michael Gordon, 'The conceptual foundations of parliamentary sovereignty: reconsidering Jennings and Wade' [2009] PL 519.
56 Alastair Hudson, *Equity and Trusts* (9th edn, Routledge 2016) 14.

in which legal terminology can be used to describe different facets of a single concept (most importantly, the 'common law'). Being aware of this rich and multifaceted use of language will improve your understanding not only of the legal system but also of any substantive legal subjects that you may study.

The chapter should also prompt you to think about how sources of law interact and how the English Legal System seeks to resolve conflict between sources when they arise. The centrality of the courts to resolving this conflict underlines the judiciary's importance in the common law system. Also, the evolutionary nature of the English Legal System should be apparent from the analysis in this chapter. The common law developed out of custom over a period of hundreds of years and was partly fused with the principles of equity after the two had existed in tandem for many years. This staged progress has also allowed for the absorption of international law principles into the English Legal System. The incorporation of the ECHR (through the Human Rights Act 1998) and the UK's membership of the European Union have caused the most significant shift of the last 100 years in how legal sources are used and understood in the English Legal System. This change to our understanding of how legal sources interact is something that is ongoing and will continue to trouble the courts in the future. This only goes to further demonstrate the fluid and dynamic nature of the English Legal System.

TAKING THINGS FURTHER

The website that accompanies this textbook contains many useful resources that you can use to consolidate and further your knowledge of the law, to hone your skills of critical analysis and to test your knowledge. This includes a set of multiple choice questions (MCQs) that can be used to test your knowledge and understanding of the material.

PODCASTS

- The podcasts provide a summary of the area under study, bringing together the key themes and threads of analysis into a 'mini-lecture'.
- There will also be an explanation and analysis of topical and up-to-date issues related to sources of law.

3

CHAPTER 3
INSTITUTIONS OF THE LEGAL SYSTEM

INTRODUCTION

There is a myriad of institutions involved in the operation of the legal system of England and Wales. The powers that these institutions exercise and how they interact with each other have a profound impact on the nature of the legal system as well as the character, form and legitimacy of the law that they create and administer.

This chapter explores the institutional landscape for the legal system in England and Wales. It is one of a series of chapters that seeks to provide an overview of the institutions and law-making processes of the legal system. It concludes with a brief account of an important constitutional principle – separation of powers – that affects the distribution of power within the legal system, a central theme of this textbook.

AS YOU READ

The chapter provides a framework for understanding the major **institutions of the legal system**, but there will be a focus on those institutions that have a role in the **law-making process** or in the **administration of justice.** By the end of this chapter you should be able to **identify the core institutions of the legal system** and critically consider their role, powers and functions.

In considering the institutions, you should **think critically about the nature of 'power' and influence** and be able to **evaluate the relationship between these institutions**. This involves understanding their function and their constitutional legitimacy. Any student of law will struggle to understand the legal system by just learning the institutions, in a standalone manner, without understanding the relationship with other chapters of this textbook. The ability to draw out themes that cross different areas of study is one that is particularly valuable to a student of law. As you read the distinct sections, attempt to **synthesise the information so as to consider the nature of power and its distribution across the different institutions of law-making**.

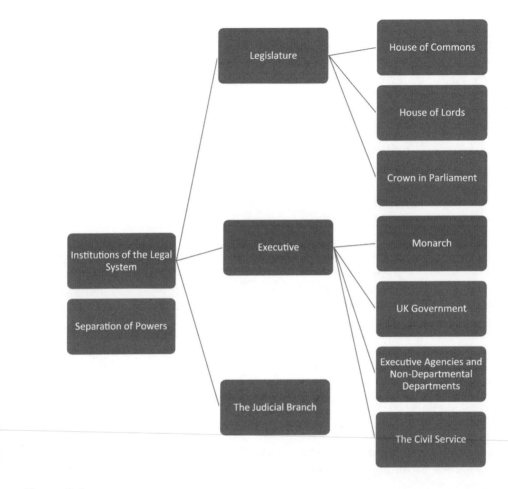

Figure 3.1

INSTITUTIONS OF LAW-MAKING

The following sections will seek to distinguish between those institutions that make the law and those that are responsible for the administration of justice. As with all aspects of the legal system, these labels are only partly effective in describing the roles, which is in part due to the fluid nature of the powers of such institutions within the legal system of England and Wales.

At its most basic we can separate the institutions of the state into three parts – the *executive* branch, the *legislative* branch and the *judicial* branch. Figure 3.2 considers the major functions of each branch and the subsections that follow consider the role in the legal system played by the major actors of each branch.

Figure 3.2 The Branches of the State

THE LEGISLATURE

Within the English and Welsh legal system, the UK Parliament is the legislature.[1] This means that the primary law-making body is Parliament. The UK's Parliament has two functions:

- To pass laws, and
- To hold the executive to account

It is the *legislative*, or law-making function, with which this textbook is concerned. The precise details of *how* law is made can be found in Chapters 4 and 5 but the remainder of this section is concerned with the structure of Parliament. The purpose of this section is to give the reader the necessary context for them to be able to understand the terminology used in later chapters. Although there are two chambers[2] within the UK Parliament, there are actually three constituent elements: the House of Commons, the House of Lords and the Queen in Parliament. In order for Bills to become Acts of Parliament, they need to pass successfully through all three[3] constituent parts.

HOUSE OF COMMONS

The lower house comprises 650 Members of Parliament (MPs) who are directly elected to represent constituencies across England, Wales, Scotland and Northern Ireland. Elections take place every five years unless certain actions under the Fixed-Term Parliaments Act 2011 prompt an early election. Elections are held according to universal suffrage and by a system known as 'First Past the Post', which means that the candidate with the most votes within an area becomes the MP for that constituency. Members of Parliament draw a salary that is set by the Independent Parliamentary Standards Authority.[4]

---

1 Although Wales also has a devolved National Assembly with 60 members, created by the Government of Wales Act 1998, which has limited powers in respect of Wales, including legislation and taxes.
2 So-called bicameral system.
3 Under certain circumstances, discussed in Chapter 4, Bills can become Acts of Parliament without the approval of the House of Lords under the provisions of the Parliament Acts 1911 and 1949.
4 A statutory body established by the Parliamentary Standards Act 2009.

Within the UK electoral system there are two main parties[5] with a number of other, smaller parties[6] who tend to gain a lesser number of seats at General Elections than the two main parties, although sometimes one of these smaller parties is needed to form a coalition with one of the two largest which would otherwise not be able to form a government without such assistance: for example in the coalition government of Conservatives and Liberal Democrats in 2010 when the previous Labour government was defeated in the General Election. There are also several MPs who sit as 'independents' (i.e. those without an affiliation to a particular party).[7] In some senses the House of Commons is regarded as the 'superior' chamber due to the fact that its members are elected by the people and this gives them, and the laws they pass, democratic legitimacy.

The House of Commons also has many Committees that help it to hold the Government to account and assure the efficient passage of legislation – some of these committees are considered in greater detail in Chapters 4 and 5.

Within the 650 elected Members of Parliament there are also several officials who perform important functions within the House of Commons. Chief amongst these is the Speaker who is elected from amongst the MPs and who chairs sessions of the House of Commons, maintains order and can suspend a particular sitting. The Speaker is supported by a number of Deputy Speakers and a Clerk who is neither a member of the House nor a civil servant and is responsible for advising the Speaker (and MPs) about parliamentary process. The Leader of the House of Commons is responsible for organising government business within the House.

TAKING THINGS FURTHER – THE OFFICERS OF PARLIAMENT

The website that accompanies this textbook has further information on the principal officers of Parliament. On the website there is a podcast that seeks to explore the impact of these officers on the legal system and, in particular, on the law-making processes within the legal system. These officers are not normally considered in a text on the legal system but the view taken here is that the personality and approach of the officers generally (and the Speaker particularly) can have a significant impact on the way in which Parliament goes about its law-making task. At the time of writing, John Bercow had just stepped down as Speaker on the 31 October 2019, and his ten-year term, in particular, demonstrates the significant impact that a Speaker can have on the legal system.

---

5 Labour and Conservative.
6 For example, the Liberal Democrats, Scottish Nationalist Party, Democratic Unionist Party, The Independent Group for Change, Plaid Cymru, Green Party and Sinn Fein.
7 Either through choice or, as recently happened to 21 former Conservative MPs in Autumn 2019, because they defied their former leader's instructions.

HOUSE OF LORDS

The upper house consists of 777, largely appointed,[8] peers. The peers are divided into Lords Spiritual and Lords Temporal. Lords Spiritual are the 26 bishops of the Church of England and the Lords Temporal are a mixture of hereditary peers[9] and so-called life peers[10] who are appointed by the Monarch on the advice of the Prime Minister.

The House of Lords is an integral part of the legislative process – a proposal for a piece of law may technically start its life in either the Commons or the Lords – but certain conventions and procedures have sought to restrict the activities of the Lords to reflect the fact that its members are not elected but rather appointed or in their position as a consequence of birth. These conventions and processes seek to allow the democratically elected House of Commons to take precedence whilst still valuing the expertise that the Lords can bring as a 'revising' chamber. For example, the Lords can no longer veto Bills but rather, as a result of the Parliament Acts 1911 and 1949, can only force a delay for the length of a parliamentary session. Equally, the Lords are unable to prevent the passage of a 'Money Bill'.[11] The impact of these restrictions for law-making is considered in greater detail in Chapter 4.

Even with the softening of the power of the House of Lords there remains a live debate about the place of the House of Lords in the modern English Legal System.

ANALYSING THE LAW – REFORM OF THE HOUSE OF LORDS

The proper composition and role of the House of Lords within the English Legal System have been the subject of fierce debate for decades.[12] There have been significant reforms to date with the Parliament Acts of 1911 and 1949 severely restricting the Lords' legislative role and the House of Lords Act 1999 reducing the size of the chamber by half and the drastic reduction to 92 hereditary peers. Since that significant reform things have somewhat stalled. There have been further reforms, including the removal of the House of Lords judicial function to the newly established Supreme Court in 2009[13] and less radical reform such as the introduction of additional ways for members of the Lords to leave the House (through resignation, retirement and exclusion).[14]

---

8 There are still 92 hereditary peers who sit as a matter of birth right and who are elected from a pool of around 750 eligible peers.
9 Those whose titles and peerage can be inherited.
10 Those whose titles and peerage cannot be passed on by inheritance.
11 A Bill that relates to government spending or taxation.
12 For a flavor, see Mark Ryan, 'A referendum on the reform of the House of Lords?' (2015) 66(3) Northern Ireland Law Quarterly 223; Lord Bingham, 'The House of Lords: Its Future' (2010) Public Law 261; Stephen Tierney, 'A new wave of constitutional reform for the UK?' (2009) European Public Law 15(3) 289.
13 By virtue of the Constitutional Reform Act 2005 s 23.
14 By virtue of the House of Lords Reform Act 2014.

There have been further efforts for more significant reform under the Coalition Government of 2010 between the Liberal Democrats and Conservatives with a proposed Bill[15] to transform the House into an elected chamber. These plans were abandoned when it became clear that back bench Conservatives would not support the Bill. The Burns Report,[16] published in 2017, recommended a further reduction in the size of the House and a restriction of terms to 15 years but this also appears to have been lost in the political and constitutional tumult of Brexit.

What is evident from the brief consideration of reform is that the issue of House of Lords reform is an ongoing debate and that some changes to the English Legal System happen in an evolutionary, rather than revolutionary way. There are occasional 'jumps' (such as the change precipitated in 1911, 1999 and 2009) towards reforms but there are often small 'steps' (such as the change in 2014).

Maintaining an up-to-date understanding of the evolution of the legal system is crucial to success in legal study and will allow for a form of 'horizon scanning' that ensures that future plans for reform (and their likelihood for success) can be identified.

Much like for the House of Commons, there are also several officers within the Lords who have the role of ensuring the efficient operation of the chamber. Some are mirrors of officers in the Commons – including the Lord Speaker and Leader of the House of Lords – but there are also others that are particular to the Lords. The most notable of these is Black Rod[17] who is the Queen's representative in Parliament and is responsible for maintaining order in the Lords and who also takes part in the ceremonial aspects of the State Opening of Parliament.

CROWN IN PARLIAMENT

As well as playing an important symbolic and substantive role in the administration of justice and the exercise of executive power, the Queen also plays an important part in the life of Parliament. She is responsible for the State Opening and, under the conditions of the Fixed Term Parliament Act 2011, dissolution of Parliament.

The Monarch's technical role in law-making is considered in greater detail in Chapter 4 but, for present purposes, it is enough to note that the Queen must give her Royal Assent to all primary legislation before it can become a valid Act of Parliament.

----

15 House of Lords Reform Bill 2012.

16 Report of the Lord Speaker's Committee on the Size of the House (published on 31 October 2017), www.parliament. uk/documents/lords-committees/size-of-house/size-of-house-report.pdf.

17 Named after the ebony staff that this officer carries on ceremonial occasions. Black Rod is not a peer, but is usually knighted if not already of that rank, and is now appointed after a search for an appropriate holder, although the post used to rotate amongst the armed forces. The present holder is for the first time a woman.

THE EXECUTIVE

Executive power within the legal system of England and Wales is exercised by a number of different individuals and public bodies. Some of the more prominent institutions of the executive are considered in the following sections as this provides useful information and context for the detailed discussion that follows.

MONARCH

The Monarch is the original source of executive power in the English Legal System. As a result Queen Elizabeth II is the symbolic Head of State. There are still some powers that the English Legal System recognises as being personal to the Queen. Examples include the appointment of the Prime Minister and, on advice, the appointment of the other Ministers that form Her Majesty's Government. The vast majority of prerogative powers of the Monarch are now exercised either on the advice of the Prime Minister or directly by Ministers on behalf of the Monarch. Even where the Monarch *appears* to have wide-ranging discretion there are certain conventions that dictate how that discretion is exercised. The selection of the Prime Minister is a good example of how the legal system tolerates an unelected Monarch that would otherwise offend against democracy.

EXPLAINING THE LAW – CHOOSING THE PRIME MINISTER

The office of Prime Minister is one of the four Great Offices of State[18] and the person occupying that position is a very visible and important part of the legal system as the head of government. Prime Ministers are chosen by the Monarch according to the Monarch's prerogative powers. Given the importance of the role it might be surprising that an unelected Monarch is able to select the head of the UK Government. However, certain *conventions* have arisen that allow for a legitimate Prime Minister to be selected.

First, the Monarch will always select a Prime Minister who sits in the House of Commons (i.e. an MP). This ensures that there is a democratic link to the people and that the democratically elected house has the best opportunity to hold the Prime Minister to account.

Second, the Monarch will always select a Prime Minister who can command the confidence of the House of Commons. Although an incumbent Prime Minister will have the first opportunity to demonstrate this, most normally the person with the best chance of securing the confidence of the Commons will be the leader of the party who secures the most seats at a General Election. This means that the Government will normally be formed by whoever 'wins' an election and so their mandate comes from the electorate and the Government has democratic legitimacy.

18 Alongside the Home Secretary, Foreign Secretary and Chancellor of the Exchequer.

THE UK GOVERNMENT

This is the most obviously recognisable part of the executive within the legal system of England and Wales. The UK Government is led by a Prime Minister and Cabinet of his most senior Ministers.[19] By convention all Government Ministers also sit in Parliament (in either the Lords or the Commons) so that they are answerable and accountable to Parliament for their actions and must subscribe to a specific code of conduct policed by the Prime Minister.[20]

As discussed previously, the Prime Minister and his Ministers will usually be drawn from the political party which won the most seats at a General Election.[21] They may govern by majority (when they have more than half of the available seats in the House of Commons), by minority (when they have more seats in the House of Commons than any other political party but still fewer than half of the seats) or in coalition with another party.

The Government organises its work within Departments that are aligned to particular policy areas.[22] It is these Government Departments that turn the aspirations of the Cabinet into policy and proposals for law. For the purposes of this textbook, the Ministry of Justice (MoJ) is amongst the most important of the Government Departments. The MoJ is responsible for the effective operation of the legal system including, but not limited to:

- The operation of the courts and tribunals[23]
- The funding of Legal Aid[24]
- Prisons
- Probation

The Government has a particularly prominent role in law-making within the legal system of England and Wales. As the Government is responsible for the way in which time is given to particular proposals in Parliament, it also has a great deal of influence over the way in which matters become law. Individual Ministers may have the power to pass delegated legislation.

EXECUTIVE AGENCIES, NON-DEPARTMENTAL PUBLIC BODIES

Supporting the work of the Governmental Departments are executive agencies and non-departmental public bodies. Executive agencies are more closely interwoven with the work of the Department with which they are affiliated. These bodies are assigned their own budgets and managed separately but retain a particularly close relationship with their associated department and Minister. Within the Ministry of Justice, for example, the Legal Aid Agency,

---

19 Including, amongst others, the Chancellor of the Exchequer, the Foreign Secretary, the Home Secretary, the Lord Chancellor & Justice Secretary and the Defence Secretary.

20 Cabinet Office *Ministerial Code* (August 2019), www.gov.uk/government/publications/ministerial-code.

21 Occasionally elections do not provide a majority Government and so parties may form Coalition Government amongst themselves; this happened between the Conservatives and Liberal Democrats following the 2010 election.

22 There are (at the time of writing) 25 Ministerial Departments, 20 Non-Ministerial Departments and more than 400 Agencies and other Public Bodies – www.gov.uk/government/organisations.

23 A task it performs through the executive agency: Her Majesty's Court and Tribunals Service (HMCTS).

24 Through the executive agency: the Legal Aid Agency.

Her Majesty's Courts & Tribunals Service and Her Majesty's Prison Service are all executive agencies.

These executive agencies are to be contrasted with non-departmental public bodies. These bodies are further detached from the Department that sponsors them and have a greater degree of autonomy. These public bodies are free from ministerial interference and the bodies are accountable to Parliament for their activity including budgets. Nonetheless they retain an important place in the legal system and can have significant influence over how the system is administered. Amongst the multitude of such public bodies, some of those most relevant to a textbook on the English Legal System include the Judicial Appointments Commission, the Law Commission, the Legal Services Board and the Sentencing Council.

As the textbook progresses the importance of the role of some of these bodies will become clearer.

THE CIVIL SERVICE

Given that governments can change every five years or so within the English Legal System, it would be inefficient if the entire machinery of the executive also had to change when a new government was elected. The Civil Service is a permanent workforce of politically neutral employees of the Crown. Civil servants are there to implement the policies of the elected government. The work of civil servants is spread amongst the government departments, each of which has a senior civil servant known as a Permanent Secretary.

THE JUDICIAL BRANCH

The judicial function is undertaken by the judiciary (judges and the magistracy) and within the courts and tribunals of England and Wales. The courts are assisted in their task by court officials and the legal professions. In this way, the judicial branch of the state contributes the following to the legal system of England and Wales:

- Application of principles of law that can be used to resolve disputes[25]
- Processes by which disputes are to be settled (including application of rules of evidence and procedural rules)[26]
- Organisation of court buildings that can be used to hear and determine disputes[27]
- Personnel including judges who, by virtue of qualification and experience, are deemed appropriate for appointment to adjudicate on disputes and jurors who hear the most serious criminal cases.[28]

Much of the remainder of this textbook is concerned with considering in some detail these judicial functions and how they contribute to the operation of the legal system of England and Wales.

25 See Chapter 6 (Statutory Interpretation) and Chapter 9 (Precedent).
26 See Chapters 10, 11 and 13 on civil, criminal and administrative justice respectively.
27 See Chapter 8 (The Court Structure) and Chapter 14 (Alternative Dispute Resolution).
28 See Chapter 7 (The Judiciary) and Chapter 12 (The Jury).

SEPARATION OF POWERS

The preceding section of this chapter has accounted for the individual role of specific institutions and bodies within the legal system, with a focus on those responsible for law-making and the administration of justice. There is a risk that these institutions are viewed as wholly independent and separate, each providing their own piece of the puzzle that is the legal system. This approach may help develop *knowledge* but will do little to aid your *understanding* of the system. The truth of the matter is that the legal system is infinitely more complex with the institutions interacting and colliding as they go about their functions and exercise their powers. In order to manage conflict and to understand properly the interactions, one must turn to fundamental constitutional principles. Of most immediate relevance is the separation of powers as it is this principle that seeks to manage and regulate the distribution of powers.

MAKING CONNECTIONS – THE INSTITUTIONS AND PUBLIC LAW
++

The doctrine of separation of powers touches upon one of the core substantive subjects covered in most studies of English law – public law, which is sometimes also characterised as 'Constitutional Law'. The discussion of separation of powers here is relatively brief and is intended to aid your understanding of the mechanics of the legal system rather than an in-depth exploration of the theoretical structures of the state.[29]

Any extended study of the English Legal System and English law will involve considering the constitutional principles that govern the distribution and control of powers between the different organs of the state. Some of those principles are discussed here and in other chapters but it may be that you return to them to consider them in greater detail at a later point in your studies or you may analyse them from a more theoretical standpoint. In addition to the separation of powers (discussed here) the **rule of law** and **parliamentary sovereignty**[30] define the character of the British constitution and, thereby, the legal system.

Under the (sometimes) flexible doctrine of separation of powers, the power of the state is dispersed over many institutions and actors. This splitting, or separation, of powers is achieved in order to ensure that power is used legitimately, that it is not concentrated in too few institutions and that there are adequate checks and balances in place to prevent abuse. In recent history,[31] the institutions of the state have been categorised using the labels described earlier in this chapter – *legislature, executive* and *judiciary*. The separation of powers goes further than merely *describing* those institutions but takes the analysis one step further by considering how those institutions interact and how they provide checks and balances to one another.

---

29 For such an examination, see Michael Doherty, *Public Law* (2nd edn, Routledge 2018).
30 Discussed in Chapter 4.
31 John Baker, *An Introduction to English Legal History* (5th edn, Oxford University Press 2019).

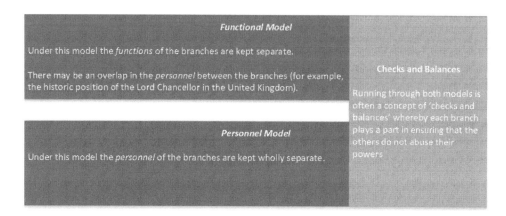

Figure 3.3 The Models of Separation of Powers

Whilst the categories or labels in Figure 3.2 are important, they only tell part of the story and are descriptive in nature. What is perhaps more important is the way in which the separation operates in practice. For this reason there are also different *models* of how separation of powers can operate within a legal or political system. Some of these models are based on the principle of non-interference in the work of the other branches whilst others focus on each branch providing a 'check' on the other branches. Figure 3.3 shows the two major models.

As one example, the Constitution of the United States of America takes a particularly strict and formal approach to separation of powers in the American legal system with the functions of the legislature (Congress – Article I), the executive (President[32] – Article II) and the judiciary (the Supreme and inferior Courts – Article III) clearly codified and defined and assigned to particular personnel. As we shall see shortly, and by contrast, the legal system of England and Wales takes a more mixed and dynamic approach.

SEPARATION OF POWERS WITHIN THE LEGAL SYSTEM OF ENGLAND AND WALES

The legal system of England and Wales exhibits the features of both of the models and adopts a mixed approach to the question of separation of powers. Rather than adopting a very fixed and rigid approach the legal system accommodates or tolerates overlaps of functions or personnel between the branches but prevents abuse of power through the utilisation of 'checks and balances'. Figure 3.4 demonstrates how some of the remaining (and historic) overlaps operate and how the 'checks and balances' seek to militate against abuse.

The checks and balances, or so the argument goes, allow the legal system to operate efficiently and flexibly but in such a way that does not lead to concentrations or abuses of power. It also means that, whilst the system is working, overlaps between functions or personnel are not deemed to be problematic.

---

32 And administration.

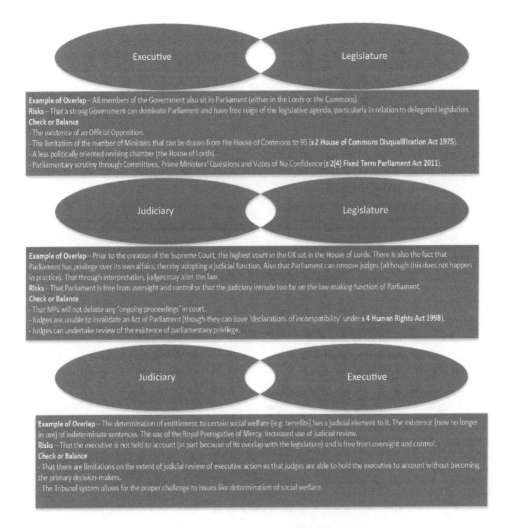

Figure 3.4 Managing the Overlaps Between the Branches of State

MAKING CONNECTIONS – ORGANIC DEVELOPMENT OF PRINCIPLE
+ +
One of the recurring themes of this text is the flexibility and evolutionary nature of
the English Legal System. As you read the other chapters and sections of the book be
sure to note this theme. It applies not only when describing the legal system but also
when considering substantive areas of law (such as tort or contract). By drawing out
this pervasive theme you will not only understand the topic at hand better but also the
wider legal system.

The more flexible and evolutionary approach to separation of powers means that the
institutional structure of the English Legal System is able to adapt and change over time. This
is not to say that there are not watershed and more substantial changes that shift the balance

of the legal system towards more or less formal forms of separation of powers. For example, the judicial committee of the House of Lords operated for many years from within Parliament despite it being the highest court of England and Wales and despite the fact that its judges were also Members of the House of Lords. The constitutional objection to the situating of judicial function within Parliament was addressed by the creation of the Supreme Court in 2009 which further separated the personnel and structures of the judiciary and legislature.[33] There is an argument that the move to a wholly separate building with a new name has emboldened the court to take a more interventionist approach to protecting separation of powers (as in the *Miller* and *Unison*[34] judgments).

Even with rules outlining the relationship between the constituent parts of the legal system and proper checks and balances, the evolutionary and sometimes informal nature of the legal system can often lead to 'gaps' in the system of accountability which is at the heart of the doctrine of separation of powers. A good example of tensions that can emerge from an informal separation of powers can be seen through the increasing use of judges as Chairs of public inquiries.

ANALYSING THE LAW – JUDGES AS LEADERS OF INQUIRY

Public inquiries can be used in a number of circumstances[35] but are often used following on from major scandals or public disasters. Such inquiries[36] can make recommendations for changes to the law.[37] The Government can propose[38] *judges* to lead such inquiries. The benefits of judges leading inquiries are apparent:

- They often have expertise in the subject matter of the inquiry.

- They have authority and credibility with the public and so the outcomes of the inquiry are more likely to be viewed as being 'acceptable'.

- They have experience of dealing with complex and emotive factual situations.

- They are used to questioning witnesses.

- They have an ability to foresee some of the practical consequences of any recommendations of changes to the law.

When acting as Chairs of such inquiries, the judges are not acting in their normal judicial capacity in the sense of overseeing a trial in a typically adversarial process.

---

33 Constitutional Reform Act 2005 s 23.

34 *R (Unison) v Lord Chancellor* [2017] UKSC 51, [2017] 3 WLR 409.

35 Inquiries Act 2005 s 1.

36 These inquiries form part of the Administrative Justice system, discussed in greater detail in Chapter 13.

37 As happened with the reform of police screening checks following the Bichard Inquiry into the Soham murders.

38 On consultation with other senior members of the judiciary as specified in s 10 Inquiries Act 2005.

However, the increasing trend of appointing judges to lead inquiries also brings particular challenges that demonstrate the problems of blurring the distinction between personnel and functions of the executive and judiciary:

- The *political* and very public nature of some inquiries can cause a blurring in the mind of the public of the judicial function (which is concerned with questions of law and not questions of politics). This can be seen in the high levels of scrutiny faced by Lord Justice Leveson during his leadership of the inquiry into press standards.

- Linked to the preceding point, there is a risk that inquiries bring to light tensions between members of the government and the judiciary. Again, the Leveson inquiry provides useful evidence of this with the then Education Secretary Michael Gove being openly critical of the direction of the inquiry with an equally robust response from Lord Justice Leveson.[39] Although judges are not acting in a judicial capacity when leading inquiries, it would be naïve to assume that those witnessing these public tensions can draw that distinction and these outbursts on both sides risk the reputation of the independence of the judiciary.

- The fact that the formal recommendations may be adopted and become law brings the judge closer to becoming a law-maker.[40]

In closing it is worth noting that the constitutional principle of separation of powers has a demonstrable impact on the shape and powers of the institutions of the legal system of England and Wales. This, in turn, affects the *operation* of the legal system and the *outputs* of law-making process. For this reason, as you continue to read this textbook reflect on how the institutional *shape* and the relationship between the different institutions impacts on the effectiveness of the legal system as a whole.

THE WEBSITE

The website that accompanies this textbook contains many useful resources that you can use to consolidate and further your knowledge of the law, to hone your skills of critical analysis and to test your knowledge. This includes a set of multiple choice questions (MCQs) that can be used to test your knowledge and understanding of the material.

39 Who made the rather pointed comment to the Education Secretary – 'I don't need to be told about the importance of free speech, I really don't.' The transcript may be found at the National Archives, discovery.nationalarchives.gov.uk/.
40 This statement is made with the full recognition that any recommendations would still need to be formally adopted into law.

PODCASTS

- The podcasts provide a summary of the area under study, bringing together the key themes and threads of analysis into a 'mini-lecture'.
- There will also be an explanation and analysis of topical and up-to-date issues related to the institutions of the English Legal System.

4

CHAPTER 4
LAW-MAKING IN THE ENGLISH LEGAL SYSTEM I – PRIMARY LEGISLATION

INTRODUCTION

Under an orthodox examination of the hierarchy of norms, primary legislation sits at the apex of a complex pyramid of legal sources (as discussed in Chapter 2). Original sovereignty lies with Parliament and Acts of Parliament have paramount importance within the English Legal System. Such Acts of Parliament are collectively referred to as 'legislation' or 'statutes'. An understanding of how such primary legislation is made (i.e. how the original sovereignty is *executed*) is, therefore, fundamental to any study of the legal system and, indeed, the study of substantive legal subjects.

This chapter explores the nature of primary legislation (i.e. Acts of Parliament or statutes) and of how such legislation is passed. The text that follows will examine the different types of Acts of Parliament, the detailed process by which a policy idea becomes a law and the roles of the various institutions in the law-making process.

The very fabric of the English Legal System is an interwoven blend of law and politics – a fact often forgotten by those lawyers who concentrate heavily on the common law (also called judge-made law or case law, since that has been built up by and through the application of principles identified in decisions of judges in the cases brought before them). This multidisciplinary understanding of law is nowhere more apparent than in the law-making process, which is currently more than usually influenced by politics as the government is absorbed in the demands of 'Brexit',[1] which has resulted in much law reform being put on hold and also in the passage of many statutes the priority for which is difficult for the ordinary person to understand while other issues, such as recommendations of the Law Commission, go surprisingly unimplemented. The answer to this type of query is that Acts of Parliament are not made in a legal vacuum and politics (and economics) influence not only the process of law-making but also the outcomes of that process. The consequence of such a relationship, and what it means for the nature and character of law, is an important theme that runs through the analysis of this chapter. Students of law often struggle with marrying law and other disciplines but noting the links between different disciplines can help you to understand the material better and to improve assessment performance.

---

1 The process by which the UK will leave the European Union.

AS YOU READ

Much of this chapter is concerned with the classification of Acts of Parliament and with giving detailed information on the process by which policy is 'concretised' into law. It is important that, as you read, **you do more than just memorise** this information. By the end of this chapter you should be able to **identify different types of Acts of Parliament** and discuss what impact the origin of a Bill may have on the application of the law.

In considering the legislative process, you should **think critically about the nature of the law-making process** and be able to **evaluate the relationship between legal and political considerations**. A much needed skill for any student of law is the ability to draw out themes that cross different areas of study. As you read the distinct sections, attempt to **synthesise the information so as to explore the theme of** *democratic input* into the legislative process.

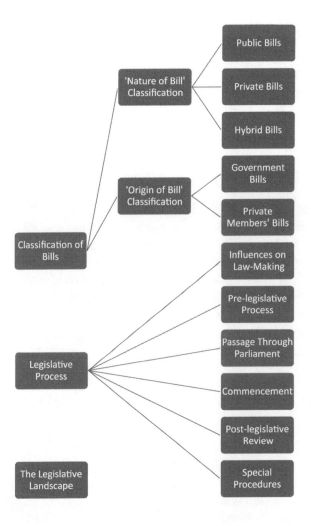

Figure 4.1

PARLIAMENTARY SOVEREIGNTY

Central to an understanding of law-making within the English Legal System is the doctrine of parliamentary sovereignty. This is a principle which holds that Parliament is the supreme legislative body of the English Legal System and that no person or body can challenge the law that Parliament passes.[2]

MAKING CONNECTIONS – PUBLIC LAW

+ +

As well as being an important feature of the English Legal System, parliamentary sovereignty is also a fundamental *constitutional* principle for the United Kingdom. If you are studying, or will study, constitutional, EU or public law then you will undoubtedly return to the principle of parliamentary sovereignty and consider it in more detail than space here allows.

There are many debates about the continued importance of the doctrine and, particularly whether it has been weakened by the UK's membership of the European Union.[3] The website that accompanies this textbook contains a short podcast that further explores the relationship between the domestic and international legal orders, with a specific focus on parliamentary sovereignty.

In practical terms, and in relation to this chapter, the importance of parliamentary sovereignty lies in the fact that primary legislation (Acts of Parliament) has a special status within the English Legal System. Acts of Parliament are a manifest expression of Parliament's sovereignty and so all other forms of law – such as secondary law or case law (both discussed in subsequent chapters) – must not violate, and cannot overturn, primary legislation. This is a marked difference to other legal systems, such as the United States of America, where the American Supreme Court has the power to 'strike down' primary legislation that violates the Constitution. No such power has (yet) been expressly[4] recognised by the English Legal System. Understanding the nature, function and process for passing primary law is therefore of paramount importance to understanding other parts of the English Legal System and is a lens through which the other chapters of the textbook could be viewed.

---

2 This principle has long been recognised in the case law – *Madzimbamuto v Lardner-Burke* [1969] 1 AC 645 (HL) 723 (Lord Reid); *R (Jackson) v Attorney General* [2005] UKHL 56, [2006] 1 AC 262 [102] (Lord Steyn).

3 For a flavour of the debate, see Nicholas Barber, 'The afterlife of parliamentary sovereignty' (2011) 9(1) IJCL 144; Mark Elliott, 'Parliamentary sovereignty under pressure' (2004) 2(3) IJCL 545.

4 Some obiter comments by the House of Lords in *Jackson* have suggested that under certain circumstances the courts may dispense with the doctrine of parliamentary sovereignty – *R (Jackson) v Attorney General* [2005] UKHL 56, [2006] 1 AC 262 [102] (Lord Steyn).

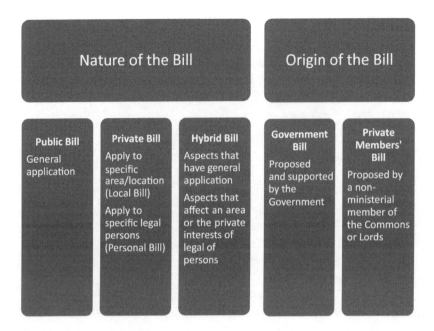

Figure 4.2 Classification of Bills

PRIMARY LEGISLATION

Flowing from the idea of parliamentary sovereignty is the principle that Parliament may legislate on any matter it wishes.[5] It achieves this legislative function through primary legislation. While going through the law-making process, pieces of intended primary legislation are initially referred to as 'Bills' and once the legislative process is complete they are then called 'Acts of Parliament'. These Acts of Parliament make up the statutory law of the English Legal System. Although primary legislation consists mainly of Acts of Parliament,[6] there are different ways in which we could categorise those Acts. The following section (and Figure 4.2) seeks to expand upon and explain those categories.

The categories 'nature of the Bill' and 'origin of the Bill' are not mutually exclusive and a Bill will be a combination of the two categories (for example, a Government Public Bill or a Hybrid Private Members' Bill).

---

5   See, for example, the case of *Cheney v Conn* [1968] 1 WLR 242 (Ch) for authority that Parliament's law is the highest form of authority in the British constitutional legal order.

6   Technically Orders in Council, made by the Queen, that have no statutory basis are also a form of primary legislation. Orders in Council (both those with and those without statutory basis) are discussed in the next chapter on secondary legislation.

'NATURE OF THE BILL' CLASSIFICATION

Under this system of classification there are Public Bills, Private Bills and Hybrid Bills and they are differentiated by either their geographical scope of application or as to the effect that they have on the whole population or a specified group of natural or legal persons.[7]

PUBLIC BILLS

Public Bills have general application in the UK or for one or more of the constituent countries.[8] Public Bills are the most common type of bill in the English Legal System. Between the 2010–2012 and 2017–2019[9] parliamentary sessions there were some 311 Public Bills that became Acts of Parliament, usually introduced into the House of Commons by the government. This has not always been the case for example in the 17th and early 18th centuries during the industrial revolution, in order to allow for the development of infrastructure, and later as Parliament had a role in granting divorces, Private Bills greatly outnumbered Public Bills.

If passed through the legislative system (as described later) Public Bills become Public General Acts.

PRIVATE BILLS

These are Bills that are not of general application but which apply to defined geographical regions or locations (Local Bills) or specific groupings of people (Private Bills). Due to their potentially oppressive nature on individual private interests these Private Bills are subject to additional requirements in order to safeguard individual rights. The full legislative procedure for Public Bills is discussed in greater detail later and this section only highlights some deviation from that normal process when passing Private Bills. The parliamentary process is much less flexible for Private Bills, partly in order to ensure legal certainty for those individuals affected.

One additional hurdle for Private Bills is the requirement that those promoting the Bill must publish in national newspapers the fact that the Bill has been brought forward.[10] Those who oppose the Bill can then, within restrictive timeframes, petition Parliament to prevent the measure from proceeding. If members of either House then register their opposition to the Bill in Second Reading it is referred to an 'Opposed Bill Committee'. An Opposed Bill Committee must determine, after listening to evidence in the manner of a court, whether the *need* for a Bill has been established. If it has, then it proceeds to the next stage of the legislative process but if the need has not been proved then the Bill will be lost.[11] No such 'necessity' test is required for Public Bills.

---

7 A 'legal person' being a company or organisation that has legal personality – *Northern Counties Securities Ltd v Jackson & Steeple Ltd* [1974] 1 WLR 1133 (Ch).

8 England, Wales, Scotland and Northern Ireland.

9 The 2017–2019 parliamentary session was the longest since the Civil War and was brought to an end in October 2019 to allow for a new legislative agenda to be put forward in a Queen's speech.

10 Richard Kelly, 'Private Bills in Parliament: House of Commons Background Paper' (2014, Standard Note) SN/PC/06508, 3.

11 Ibid. 6–7.

Private Bills are now typically supported/proposed by public authorities (such as Local Councils) in order to extend or augment their existing public law powers. For example, the Hertfordshire County Council (Filming on Highways) Act 2014 empowers the named Council to restrict the use of the public highway or permit film-makers to place objects on the highway for the purpose of making a film. Similarly, the Humber Bridge Act 2013 allows the operators of the Humber Bridge to charge tolls for use of the bridge. Private Bills can also be used to grant additional (or amended) powers to individual companies, such as the Bank of Ireland (UK) plc Act 2012 that amended the ability of the company to issue banknotes in Northern Ireland.

HYBRID BILLS

These Bills have a mixed function in that they are of general application (like Public Bills) but effect specific people or organisations (like Private Bills) in a way that is different to other people generally affected by the Bill. National infrastructure projects that have a specific impact on a local area would be likely to require a Hybrid Bill. For example the High Speed Rail project to connect London and Birmingham required such a Hybrid Bill – the High Speed Rail (London – West Midlands) Bill 2014 as did the High Speed Rail (West Midlands – Crewe) Bill 2017–2019. Other examples include the Cardiff Bay Barrage Act 1993 and the Channel Tunnel Rail Link Act 1996.

The procedure for the introduction of a Hybrid Bill is a modified version of that required for a Public Bill – the full procedure for Public Bills is discussed in a later section. For example, a Hybrid Bill does not require those supporting the Bill (normally the Government) to demonstrate that the Bill is necessary – as is required for Private Bills – but it does give those interested an opportunity to have their views heard by a Select Committee before the Bill is referred to the relevant Public Bill Committee. The Select Committee can suggest amendments aimed at compensating those affected by the Bill.

Hybrid Bills are used infrequently, with fewer than 30 being introduced since 1990.

APPLYING THE LAW – HYBRID BILLS

The passage of the (unsuccessful) House of Lords Reform Bill in 2012 further clarifies the restricted nature and narrow scope of Hybrid Bills. During the passage of the Bill, Jacob Rees-Mogg (MP) raised the question as to whether it was a Hybrid Bill as it affected a certain category of bishops within the Church of England and their ability to sit in the reformed House of Lords. In rejecting that view the Speaker of the House stated: 'a Hybrid Bill is a Public Bill that affects a particular private interest in a manner different from the private interest of other persons or bodies of the same category or class. The key phrase here is "private interest". The only interest of bishops affected by the Bill is that of being part of the legislature. That is a public interest, not a private one. Accordingly, no question of hybridity arises.'[12] Thus only Bills that affect private interests and not public offices will be considered as hybrid.

....

12 HC Deb 9 July 2012, vol 548, col 23.

'ORIGIN OF BILL' CLASSIFICATION

Alternatively, it is possible to classify Bills according to who proposes the Bill. In this regard, there are two major forms of Bill discussed next. They are Government Bills and Private Members' Bills.

GOVERNMENT BILLS

These are, as the name suggests, proposed and supported by the Government. Although not as numerous as Private Members' Bills, they have a much greater chance of success. Government Bills go through the full legislative procedure discussed later in this chapter.

Table 4.1 examines the prevalence and success rates of Government Bills over the past 20 years, split at five yearly intervals.[13]

Table 4.1 demonstrates two trends that should be borne in mind when considering Government Bills. Firstly, that the number of such Bills has declined since the 1980s. This should not be seen as the Government doing 'less', as the overall length of Acts of Parliament has grown dramatically in the last century. In 1950, for example, there were 720 pages of primary legislation spread over 50 General Acts whereas in 2007 there were 3,186 pages of primary legislation spread over only 31 Public Acts.[14] This has implications for the effectiveness of scrutiny, as the amount of parliamentary time to consider these matters has not dramatically increased. It also obviously has impact for comprehension since the complexity of modern legislation and the system of amendment of earlier Acts affected by later legislative provisions mean that an entire, lengthy, statute often needs to be read as a whole, including the consequential amendments of other Acts, before its ultimate effect can be understood.

Secondly, the vast majority of Government legislation that is proposed as a Bill will become law. It may, as is discussed later, be amended, but fundamentally the English Legal System is structured in such a way that the Government is able to pass the Bills that it wishes to pass. This raises questions about the ability of Parliament to keep an adequate check on what the Government is doing and to give full scrutiny to the laws that are put before it. This is partly a consequence of the tendency of the electoral system of the United Kingdom to return strong majority governments. The Government is then able to use its majority to force measures through Parliament.

---

13 The table to 1997–1998 is based on data from the Department of Information Services, 'Summary of Public Bills Introduced Since 1983–84' (2013, Standard Note) SN/PC/02283, 2 and the table from then until 2016–2017 is based on data from House of Commons Library, 'Number of Public Bills Introduced and Gaining Royal Assent Since 1997' (2017, Briefing Paper).

14 Based on the data from Richard Cracknell, 'Acts and Statutory Instruments: the Volume of UK Legislation 1950–2014' (2014, Standard Note) SN/SG/2911, 4–7.

Table 4.1 Success Rate for Government Bills

Parliamentary sessions	Number of Government Bills introduced	Number of Government Bills completing legislative process
1983–1984 to 1987–1988	254	247
1988–1989 to 1992–1993	216	205
1993–1994 to 1997–1998	196	194
1998–1999 to 2002–2003	172	159
2003–2004 to 2007–2008	192	166
2008–2009 to 2012–2013	131	116
2013–2014 to 2016–2017	113[15]	99

PRIVATE MEMBERS' BILLS

These are to be distinguished from Private Bills discussed earlier. Private Members' Bills are those introduced by Members of the House of Commons or Lords and are likely in reality to be Public Bills. Very many such Bills get proposed every year – more in number than Government Bills. Table 4.2 indicates the number of Private Bills introduced since the 1980s and their rate of success.[16]

If we compare Table 4.2 to Table 4.1 for Government Bills then we can note two important differences. Firstly, two to three times the number of Private Members' Bills are introduced in each time period when compared to the number of Government Bills. Secondly, the success rate for Private Members' Bills is significantly less than that of Government Bills. It could be argued that this reduces the effectiveness and diversity of legislation and further illustrates the Government's dominance of Parliament's agenda.

The very limited success of Private Members' Bills is principally owing to the fact that the Government controls the parliamentary timetable and there is very limited opportunity for

---

15 This final entry covers only four years but is consistent with the row that precedes it.
16 The table to 1997–1998 is based on the data from Department of Information Services, 'Summary of Public Bills Introduced Since 1983–84' (2013, Standard Note) SN/PC/02283, 2 and the table from then until 2016–2017 is based on data from House of Commons Library, 'Number of Public Bills Introduced and Gaining Royal Assent Since 1997' (2017, Briefing Paper).

Table 4.2 The Success of Private Members' Bills

Parliamentary sessions	Number of Private Members' Bills introduced	Number of Private Members' Bills completing legislative process
1983–1984 to 1987–1988	531	83
1988–1989 to 1992–1993	615	69
1993–1994 to 1997–1998	550	82
1998–1999 to 2002–2003	487	35
2003–2004 to 2007–2008	470	15
2008–2009 to 2012–2013	560	28
2013–2014 to 2016–2017	664[17]	29

Private Members' Bills to be allocated sufficient time to progress through the system. Under parliamentary procedure, for 13 Fridays, Private Members' Bills are timetabled in preference to Government Bills, thus allowing guaranteed time for a wider range of legislation to be discussed.

Private Members' Bills can be introduced to the House of Commons in the following ways:

1   By Ballot – in every parliamentary session 20 names are drawn from all those MPs who have an interest in bringing forward a Private Members' Bill.[18] Those members are given priority in presenting their Bill and can have them allocated to the Fridays discussed earlier that are set aside for Private Members' Bills and therefore they have much greater prospect of success.
2   By virtue of the 'Ten-Minute' rule – a Member may, on specified days, attempt to gain permission to present a Bill.[19] The Member has ten minutes (hence the name) in which to make a speech recommending the Bill to the House.
3   By Presentation – any MP can propose a Bill to be considered and choose a day for

....

17 This final entry covers only four years but is consistent with the row that precedes it.
18 Standing Order 14(9).
19 Standing Order 23.

Second Reading.[20] As the Government controls the parliamentary timetable these Bills rarely progress through the legislative process.

Most Private Members' Bills are proposed in the full knowledge that they are unlikely to become law. As such, they are often proposed as a way of raising awareness on a particular issue and allowing for debate that may spark public interest and convince the Government to take up a Bill.[21] The recent Assisted Dying Bill 2014–2015, presented by Lord Falconer, is an excellent example of a Bill that is intended to provoke debate, particularly when considering the reference that was made to that Bill in the Supreme Court's judgment in Nicklinson.[22] In Nicklinson the Supreme Court strongly suggested that Parliament consider again the issue of assisted suicide in order to ensure the UK's continued compliance with the European Convention on Human Rights.[23]

Despite how rarely they are passed, some extremely important Acts of Parliament – including those deemed by the Government to be too controversial to be promoted – began their lives as Private Members' Bills. Perhaps the clearest example of this is the Bill that became the Abortion Act 1967 which was introduced by David Steel MP and sought to allow for lawful abortions where they were carried out by registered medical practitioners.

LEGISLATIVE PROCESS

The following section will explore the law-making process (Figure 4.3) from the influences that lead to a particular piece of legislation, through the specific procedures through which primary legislation is required to pass and finally deal with scrutiny of an Act after it has been brought into force.

INFLUENCES ON LAW-MAKING

To consider only the official stages of the legislative process can give a distorted understanding of the purpose of that legislation – a theme more closely examined in Chapter 6 on statutory interpretation. Bills do not appear from the ether, fully formed and devoid of historical and political context. In order to gain a better understanding of the formal law-making process it is important to understand the institutions, events and principles that can lead to legislative proposals long before they are formalised into a draft Bill to be presented to Parliament.

The list of influences (Figure 4.4) discussed next should not be viewed as either exhaustive or as acting fully independently of the others in the list. It is often a combination of these factors working in tandem (and others) that eventually leads to a piece of legislation being brought forward.

----

20 Standing Order 57.
21 Private Members' Bills can often be effectively defeated by a simple call of 'object' when the title of the Bill is read, as happened to the Voyeurism (Offences) Bill 2017–2019 which sought to outlaw the practice of 'upskirting'.
22 R (Nicklinson) v Ministry of Justice [2014] UKSC 38, [2014] 3 WLR 200 [166].
23 Ibid. [300]–[301] (Lady Hale) who went even further and would have granted a declaration of incompatibility which would have put additional pressure on Parliament to review the issue.

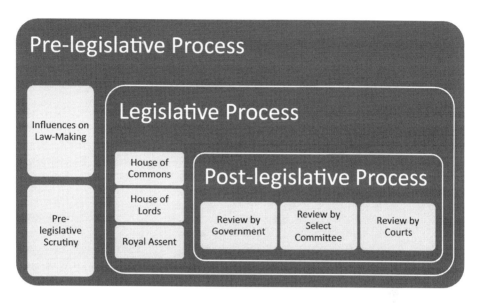

Figure 4.3 The Legislative Process

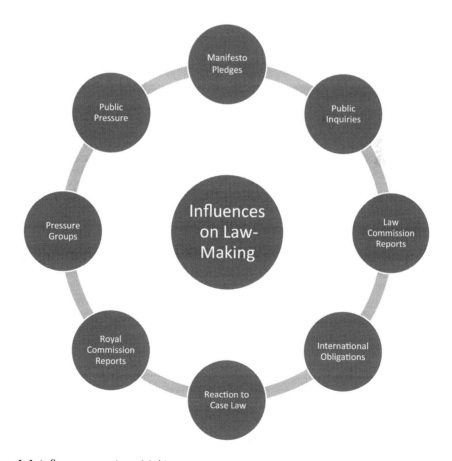

Figure 4.4 Influences on Law-Making

MANIFESTO PLEDGES

Before a General Election each political party will produce a manifesto.[24] The manifesto will detail the principles and policies that the party will seek to achieve or implement should they be returned to Government. Manifestos can be high-level political statements, such as Robert Peel's Tamworth Manifesto[25] of 1834 which sought to change the direction and philosophy of the Tory party and which is seen as the starting point of the modern Conservative party. From the principles of modern conservatism in the Tamworth Manifesto flowed support for particular pieces of legislation that would have previously been unpalatable to a Tory Leader.[26] Peel spoke in terms of principle in his manifesto but those principles could be seen to influence later law-making, such as support for the passage of the Municipal Corporations Act 1835.

Equally, manifestos can contain precise and specific promises to enact specific types of legislation. As a result and from the late 19th and throughout the 20th century the promises contained within a party manifesto began to form the core of the legislative programme that the government would adopt during their time in office. A clear example of this is the Human Rights Act 1998.

EXPLAINING THE LAW – 'BRINGING RIGHTS HOME'

When seeking election in 1997, the Labour Party placed a strong emphasis on civil liberties and human rights protection within their manifesto. The manifesto stated that:

> Citizens should have statutory rights to enforce their human rights in the UK courts. We will by statute incorporate the European Convention on Human Rights into UK law to bring these rights home and allow our people access to them in their national courts.[27]

Shortly after Tony Blair came to power his Labour Government passed the Human Rights Act 1998 in order to make good on his manifesto promise to incorporate the European Convention on Human Rights (ECHR) into the English Legal System.

A manifesto adds democratic legitimacy to the laws brought forward by the Government as the proposals are seen to have the consent or approval of the populace. Obviously, the extent to which the voting public read or understand party manifestos is debatable, as is the

---

24 An unofficial collection of all party manifestos can be found at the following link: www.politicsresources.net/area/uk/man.htm.

25 This was not a manifesto in the modern sense of the word. It was, as was the practice of the time, an address to Peel's own constituency but that was reproduced in the popular press. Nonetheless, it went further than previous examples and is one of the earliest illustrations of a party political statement of *aims* if returned to Government.

26 See, for example, the Municipal Corporations Act 1835.

27 Labour Party Manifesto 1997. Can be accessed at www.labour-party.org.uk/manifestos/1997/1997-labour-manifesto.shtml.

implication that a person voting for a particular party agrees to every item in a manifesto. Recent research on the European level suggests that policy documents, such as a manifesto, do not have a significant impact on voter behaviour.[28] Nonetheless, a manifesto does provide a link between the wishes of the electorate and the legislation that is eventually passed through Parliament.

It is important to note that a manifesto is in no way legally binding and has only political force within the English Legal System. However, that political force should not be underestimated. In 2010, the UK returned a hung Parliament – the first since the 1970s – with no political party gaining an overall majority. This situation led to the forming of a coalition government between the Conservative Party and the Liberal Democrats. As neither party was returned with a majority, their ability and willingness to abide by their original (very different) manifestos was a constant source of political tension.

ANALYSING THE LAW – THE POLITICAL FORCE OF MANIFESTOS

Perhaps the most striking recent examples of the political force of manifestos come from the legislative programme of the Coalition Government. The Liberal Democrats' 2010 manifesto contained the following promise: 'We will scrap unfair university tuition fees so everyone has the chance to get a degree, regardless of their parents' income.'[29] As they did not gain an overall majority to form a Government they entered into a Coalition with the Conservatives.

The Coalition Agreement anticipated changes arising out of Lord Browne's Review into the funding of Higher Education.[30] Eventually, the Coalition announced a policy that ran counter to the Liberal Democrats' manifesto promise in that it *increased* the cap on tuition fees. This caused a great deal of controversy both within the party[31] and the constituencies that had elected Liberal Democrat MPs. While 29 Liberal Democrat MPs either voted against the Government's policy or abstained, 27 Liberal Democrat MPs voted for the plan.[32]

Governments legislating for important matters *not* contained within their manifesto can be equally controversial. Another example from the 2010 elections serves to illustrate the point. The Coalition Government introduced the Marriage (Same Sex Couples) Bill into Parliament in January 2013. The Bill, now Act, sought to extend the institution of marriage to people of the same sex. Such a piece of legislation was not

---

28 James Adams, Lawrence Ezrow and Zeynep Somer-Topcu, 'Is anybody listening? Evidence that voters do not respond to European parties' policy statements during elections' (2011) 55(2) AJPS 370, 375.

29 Liberal Democrat Manifesto 2010, 33.

30 Lord Browne, 'Securing a Sustainable Future for Higher Education' (12 October 2010).

31 Given that all Liberal Democrat MPs had signed a pledge with National Union of Students to vote against tuition fee increases.

32 This included key members of the leadership, including Nick Clegg and Vince Cable.

anticipated by the Conservative's 2010 manifesto and provoked a great deal of debate within the Conservative Party (and within their supporters in the wider public). As the Bill progressed through the legislative procedure, more than 30 references were made, by MPs and Lords who opposed the Bill, to the fact that the Bill was not included in the manifesto and that the changes proposed to the institution of marriage were of such importance that a clear democratic mandate should be required.[33]

David Cameron's manifesto pledge to deliver an EU referendum following the 2015 General Election is another example of the political force of referendum commitments.

ROYAL COMMISSION REPORTS

Royal Commissions are set-up by the Government on an ad hoc basis and their purpose is to review an area of law and, where appropriate, make recommendations for improvements and reform.[34] Such Commissions are normally constituted of those with a specific interest or specific expertise in the area under review. Although created by the Government, they are non-political and are to be independent of Government control. The Government may then adopt the recommendations of the Commission through the passage of Acts of Parliament.

The effectiveness[35] of a Royal Commission is in part determined by the political will to adopt its recommendations. This is sometimes hampered by the delay of up to four years between the establishment of the Commission and its report being published. Such a delay will mean that often a Royal Commission that is set up by one Government could end up reporting to a different Government if there has been a General Election in the intervening period. In light of the work of the Law Commission, and the increased availability of public inquiries, the use of Royal Commissions has become less common than it once was. However, there are still occasional *calls* (even if these are not heeded) for Royal Commissions to be established. For example, Nick Clegg, during his time as Deputy Prime Minister, called for a Royal Commission to be established into the possibility of reforming Britain's drug laws.[36] The position of Royal Commissions seems, therefore, to be residual as it falls in the space created between the work of inquiries (which often deal with scandals and reviews sparked

---

33 On Second Reading in the Commons: HC Deb 5 February 2013, vol 558, cols 130, 157, 158, 165, 173, 174, 181, 182, 184, 188, 190, 200, 216, 227.
   On Third Reading in the Commons: HC Deb 21 May 2013, vol 563, cols 1162 and 1169.
   On Second Reading in the House of Lords: HL Deb 3 June 2013, vol 745, cols 945, 965, 984, 993, 1004, 1013, 1017, 1019, 1025, 1091, 1091, 1094, 1097, 1107.
   HOL (745, 10) 3 June 2013 cols 945, 965, 984, 985, 993, 1004, 1013, 1017, 1019, 1025, 1091, 1094, 1097, 1107.
34 C.f. Some Royal Commissions, including for example those on the preservation of historical manuscripts, have taken on quasi-permanent existence.
35 If effectiveness is measured by recommendations becoming law.
36 www.bbc.co.uk/news/uk-20722527.

by specific incidents) and matters related purely to law reform (even if they have a social dimension), which are within the purview of the Law Commission.

PUBLIC INQUIRIES

There is a range of different types of inquiry that may be established within the English Legal System.[37] However, it is statutory inquiries set up in response to scandals or catastrophic events that most frequently form an influence on future law-making. Such inquiries have seen an increase since the establishment of the Inquiries Act 2005, which created a statutory framework for the establishment of such inquiries by Ministers.[38] Figure 4.5 gives an indication of the structure of the Inquiries Act and some indication of the powers under it. It is unlikely that you will need to know the detail of the Inquiries Act but the diagram is intended to give some indication of the layout of an Act of Parliament that contributes to the generation of ideas for reform.

Public inquiries can be an excellent conduit for law reform and act as an increasingly important influence on law-making. However, their purpose is not solely (or even, in some cases, primarily) to propose changes to the law. Inquiries are set up primarily as fact finding exercises but can make recommendations for changes to the law.

In the years leading up to and following on from the Inquiries Act 2005 there has been an increased reliance on public inquiries, particularly those chaired by senior members of the judiciary,[39] as a method of reviewing the effectiveness of public bodies and as a response to public scandals. Judges are often appointed to lead inquiries because of their experience of dealing with evidence, their expertise in handling witnesses and their ability to foresee the consequences of their recommendations.

Recent examples of public inquiries, their reason for establishment and the impact of their recommendations are detailed in Table 4.3.

The report of an inquiry may make recommendations that find their way into law. This is not to say that *all* inquiries will make recommendations for changes to primary law. Moreover, not all recommendations will be taken up by Government, particularly given that many will report to a subsequent Government rather than the one that established it. Inquiries are often perceived to be 'a lightning conductor for the anger of the public',[40] and this can affect their effectiveness if they are set up (and report) in haste. One of the clearest examples of an emotive public inquiry leading to questionable use of law is the Bichard Inquiry into the Soham murders.

---

37 Land inquiries and other statutory schemes of inquiry.
38 Prior to this, and in accordance with the Tribunals of Inquiry (Evidence) Act 1921, major inquiries had been established via a resolution in both Houses of Parliament.
39 The power to appoint a judge can be found in Inquiries Act 2005 s 10.
40 Lord Butler, 'Despite the Doubts Over Leveson and the Mid-Staffs Report, Public Inquiries Still Play a Vital Role', *The Guardian* (London, 26 March 2013), www.theguardian.com/commentisfree/2013/mar/26/public-inquiries-vital-healing-holding-account.

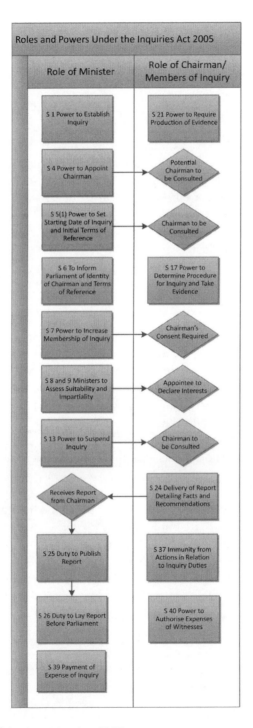

Figure 4.5 Structure of the Inquiries Act 2005

Table 4.3 Recent Public Inquiries

Chairman	Event leading to establishment of inquiry	Recommendations and influences on changes in the law
Michael Bichard	Questions over child protection following on from murder of two school girls by Ian Huntley	Criminal Records Bureau checks for those working with children
Lord Laming	Questions over the failings of social services and other agencies after the death of Victoria Climbié	Changes to child protection processes in the Children Act 2004, including the establishment of a (now defunct) national database for agencies to share information
Lord Laming Dame Janet Smith	Questions over the effectiveness of checks on doctors following the conviction of serial killer Harold Shipman	Recommended changes to the supervision of doctors and their ability to access and administer certain drugs
Sir William Macpherson	Murder of black teenager Stephen Lawrence in a racially motivated attack	Changes to police practice in light of finding that the Metropolitan Police Service was institutionally racist
Robert Francis	High mortality rates at Stafford Hospital and concerns about patient care	Some 290 recommendations; some, such as the limitation on the use of 'gagging clauses' in employment law, have been implemented by changes in the law
Lord Scarman	The Brixton Riots	Radical changes to police procedure and a new code of police behaviour introduced in the form of the Police and Criminal Evidence Act 1984
Lord Justice Leveson	The News International phone hacking scandal	Recommended additional regulation of the press; partly implemented under a new statutory framework

ANALYSING THE LAW – THE BICHARD INQUIRY

While working as a caretaker in a secondary school, Ian Huntley murdered Holly Wells and Jessica Chapman. A public inquiry was launched in 2004 to investigate the events that led to the death of the two girls and Huntley's ability to gain employment in a school despite having previous allegations of sexual conduct with underage girls.

The Bichard Inquiry that followed suggested changes to the system of criminal records checks in order to safeguard against those with certain criminal offences (or allegations of criminal offences) working with children. The recommendations of the inquiry led to the proliferation in the use of an enhanced Criminal Records Bureau check for those working with, or unsupervised around, children. It also led to police forces improving their record keeping in order to furnish bodies with criminal records disclosures.

In the aftermath of the inquiry, and its report, the use of enhanced criminal records checks increased dramatically and many offences (and warnings) of dubious relevance and those committed when the offender was very young were kept on file and disclosed to potential employers. This eventually led to the Supreme Court in *R(T)*[41] in 2014 ruling that the lack of safeguards in the system and its disproportionate[42] impact breached T's human rights and so supported the Court of Appeal's declaration of incompatibility.[43] The declaration of incompatibility prompted the Government[44] to scrap the CRB system and replace it with a less restrictive system of checks operated by the Disclosure and Barring Service.

In this instance, the inquiry raised the profile of a problem beyond that which was necessary and did little to help to achieve a balanced and appropriate solution to the problem. Indeed, the clamour for justice and 'lessons to be learned' in light of the Soham murders contributed significantly to the overburdening of the CRB system and to the breaches of individuals' right to a private life under the European Convention on Human Rights.

LAW COMMISSION REPORTS[45]

The Law Commission is an independent body established by the Law Commissions Act 1965 'for the purpose of promoting the reform of the law'.[46] Unlike Royal Commissions, the Law Commission is a permanent body dedicated to law reform which, in limited circumstances, can investigate areas of its own motion and not just at the request of Government. Regardless of the source of the initiative for a review of an area of law, all proposed works need to

---

41 R(T) v *Greater Manchester Police* [2014] UKSC 35, [2014] 3 WLR 96.

42 Ibid. [121] (Lord Reed).

43 A power under the Human Rights Act 1998 s 4.

44 Perhaps hastily in not awaiting the judgment of the Supreme Court – a point recognised by the Supreme Court: ibid. [3] (Lord Wilson).

45 https://www.lawcom.gov.uk/.

46 Law Commissions Act 1965 s 1.

be approved by the Lord Chancellor.[47] The Commissioners, of which there are four and a Chairman, are appointed by the Lord Chancellor but are independent of Government control. Nonetheless, there is a strong working relationship between the Commission and Government. In recent years some Law Commission recommendations of some obvious importance have not been implemented, particularly during the period 2010 to 2018 during which there was no legally qualified Lord Chancellor and Minister of Justice, such as when e.g. the Commission's Report of 27 February 2014 on Marital Agreements (an uncontroversial proposal which if implemented would have been likely to save both court time – and thus HMCTS' resources – and litigants' costs and certainty of outcomes in Financial Provision cases in the Family Court, and at a time when savings were being sought for all involved).

The function of the Law Commission is to:

> keep under review all the law with which they are respectively concerned with a view to its systematic development and reform, including in particular the codification of such law, the elimination of anomalies, the repeal of obsolete and unnecessary enactments, the reduction of the number of separate enactments and generally the simplification and modernisation of the law.[48]

The preceding extract demonstrates that one of the *statutory* functions of the Law Commission is to seek to be an influence for changes in the law.

The Law Commission has a rolling programme of projects and, most recently, the 13th programme of reform was launched in December 2017. The 13th programme is looking, amongst others, at the following issues:

- Arbitration
- Banks' duties to customers
- Leasehold law
- Online communications
- Children's social care
- Surrogacy

TAKING THINGS FURTHER – INVESTIGATING LAW REFORM

The programme of reform instigated by the Law Commission is constantly evolving and projects are often at very different stages. Investigating the status of ongoing projects can be very useful as it provides you with insights into the perceived problems

---

47 Government Ministers may refer matters to the Commission but the Commission is under no obligation to take forward projects on this basis.
48 Law Commissions Act 1965 s 3(1).

of the law as it currently stands and some indication of possible solutions identified by the Commission. It can also be interesting to reflect on those proposals that have not been taken forward into legislative change.

A great deal of information about the present and past work of the commission can be found on their website – www.lawcom.gov.uk.

As a result, these areas are likely to influence law-making in the near future, not least because before undertaking a review the Law Commission must seek from the Government, through the Lord Chancellor, an undertaking 'that there is a serious intention to take forward law reform in this area.'[49] In an effort to improve the implementation of Law Commission proposals, and to bring about greater transparency in Government responses, the Law Commission Act 2009 also requires the Lord Chancellor to report to Parliament the status of Commission proposals.[50]

A number of important Acts of Parliament have followed Law Commission recommendations, including the Criminal Attempts Act 1981, the Family Law Act 1986, the Landlord and Tenant Act 1988 and the Fraud Act 2006 all of which made significant changes to the law in relation to areas of concern identified by the Commission. The most recent completed programme (the 12th) provided the basis for the Digital Economy Act 2017, Intellectual Property (Unjustified Threats) Act 2017.[51]

INTERNATIONAL LAW OBLIGATIONS

As a dualist state, the United Kingdom must incorporate its international law obligations (most frequently found in international treaties) into domestic law either through primary or secondary legislation. This is to be contrasted with monist states (such as France and Germany) where international obligations become law at the moment that the international treaty is ratified. The dualist nature of the UK means that international law obligations can have a strong influence on law-making within the English Legal System. This is nowhere more apparent than in relation to the European Union which is discussed more fully in Chapter 16. There will continue to be an influence over law-making from the EU even in the case of the UK rescinding its membership.

Although a great deal of legislation that is inspired by the international legal order is of EU origin, this is not always the case. The Berne Convention of 1886 inspired changes to the intellectual property law of the UK and its provisions were incorporated partly by the International Copyright Act 1886. International influences on the process of law-making in the English Legal System are ongoing and subsequent amendments of the Berne

---

49 Law Commission, *Protocol Between the Lord Chancellor (on Behalf of the Government) and the Law Commission* (Law Comm No 321, 2010) para 6.
50 Law Commission Act 2009 s 1 inserting a new section, s 3A, into the Law Commission Act 1965.
51 Law Commission, *Annual Report 2018–19* (Law Comm No 274, 2019).

Convention have led to further changes to UK law via Acts of Parliament. For example, when the Convention was revised in 1908 some of these changes were realised by the Copyright Act 1911.

TAKING THINGS FURTHER – THE COMPANION WEBSITE

The website that accompanies this textbook further explores the influence that international courts can have on the English Legal System. There is a podcast examining the judgment of the Court of Justice of the European Union on the validity of the European Data Retention Directive. This Directive was ruled to violate fundamental rights and, as a consequence, the UK Government hastily[52] passed the Data Retention and Investigatory Powers Act 2014 to deal with the vacuum created. The podcast describes these developments and also analyses the way in which the DRIP Act 2014 was passed.

PRESSURE GROUPS

Pressure groups can be an important, if sometimes controversial, influence on the law-making process. Pressure groups seek to campaign on set issues or to protect certain groups of people or specific interests. As such, they normally focus on a single policy or set of contexts on which they campaign for law reform.

Some examples of successful campaigns led by pressure groups are included in Table 4.4.

Caution should be exercised when attempting to measure the impact of pressure groups on law-making as it is often a combination of factors that eventually lead to changes in the law. It would be unusual for a Government, when proposing a new Public Bill, to indicate that a pressure group was responsible for the introduction of the legislation. It would not normally be sensible for the Government to recognise external bodies as having influence over law-making. Moreover, pressure groups often have persistent and permanent campaigns that stretch for many years and thus tracing their direct influence on Government policy can be difficult. Nonetheless, their influence is important, can be controversial and should not be overlooked.[53]

---

52 In the words of Lord Phillips of Sudbury: 'this measure has been rushed, helter-skelter, through both Houses. It is fair to say that the vast majority of Members in both Houses are deeply worried by all that but have none the less accepted the view of the Government as to the need for that expedition.' HL Deb 17 July 2014, vol 755, col 722.

53 Riccardo de Caria, 'The constitutional right to lobby on the two sides of the Atlantic: between freedom and democracy' (2013) 2 CJICL 452, 455.

Table 4.4 Successful Pressure Group Campaigns

Organisation	Nature of campaign	Outcome
Stonewall	Lowering the age of consent for sexual intercourse between homosexual men so that it matched that for heterosexual sexual intercourse	Partial victory in 1994 with a reduction in the age of consent from 21 to 18
Disablement Income Group (and others)	Equal rights for those with disabilities in relation to access to employment and the provision of services	Enactment of the Disability Discrimination Act 1995. This prevented discrimination on the basis of disability and required employers and service providers to make reasonable adjustment to accommodate those with disabilities
Pro-Life Alliance	Sought repeal of the Abortion Act 1967	Failed to secure repeal of the Abortion Act but was an instrumental pressure in having the latest date reduced from 28 to 24 weeks

PUBLIC PRESSURE

Although closely linked to the concept of pressure groups, there can be more generalised public pressure that leads to changes in the law. This tends to come about due to events that lead to media attention.

For example, following a number of high-profile cases where young children were mauled by dogs, there was a great clamour in the popular press for greater controls over what came to be known as 'dangerous dogs'. The outcome of that media pressure was the passing of the Dangerous Dogs Act 1991. The Act categorises certain 'types' of dog and cross breeds of those types as needing special control.

ANALYSING THE LAW – THE DANGEROUS DOGS ACT 1991

Much like public inquiries considered earlier, a major problem of this type of pressure is that it can lead to hasty and ill-considered legislation. Again, the Dangerous Dogs Act 1991 is a prime example of the criticisms that can be levelled at public pressure gaining too much influence in the law-making process.

The Dangerous Dogs Act 1991 had an expedited journey through Parliament. It was not put out for public consultation. The Bill passed through all stages of the Commons within 24 hours with the debates programmed to continue until 4 a.m. in order to ensure that it could be debated in the Lords and passed before the parliamentary session ended.

In practice the Dangerous Dogs Act 1991 has been heavily criticised and much of the criticism could have been resolved had the Bill been properly scrutinised and more carefully considered. For example, choosing to ban 'types' rather than 'breeds' has led to great confusion. The intention was to allow judgments to be made by courts based on physical characteristics of the dog. In hindsight, the quality and effectiveness of the Act is to be questioned. There are now more Pit Bulls in the UK than before the passage of the Act and by concentrating so heavily on types, the Act is not sufficiently focussed on the behaviour of owners. It also required, at the time, a mandatory destruction order issued by a Magistrate, allowing the courts very little discretion in assessing the subjective danger that a particular dog creates.

One Member of the House of Lords has deemed it: 'the most outrageous law ever passed in Parliament. It is probably worse in some respects even than the suppressive tendencies of war-time legislation and the defence of the realm Act (regardless of national security).'[54] Although this comment was couched in rather strong language, the dangers of hastily passed legislation should not be ignored.

In spite of the preceding, public pressure can lead to positive changes in the law and act as an important conduit for democratic input into the law-making process. There is now a formally recognised mechanism for such public influence through the Government's e-petition website.[55] When a petition gains 10,000 signatures the Government Department responsible for the policy area will give a response. Should the petition receive 100,000 signatures then it is passed to the Backbench Business Committee who consider whether to table the issue for debate in the House of Commons.

PRE-LEGISLATIVE PROCESS
This term is most commonly used to refer to the stages that a Government Bill will go through before being presented to Parliament. Not all Bills, nor even all Government Bills, will go through all of the procedures discussed in the following sections. The order in which the stages happen (particularly in relation to drafting and the Queen's Speech) can also vary.

....

54 HL Deb 20 January 1993, vol 541, col 933.
55 https://petition.parliament.uk/.

CONSULTATION: GREEN AND WHITE PAPERS

A Government will sometimes put out ideas for legislation to public consultation. This takes place via Green and White Papers, named for the colour of paper on which they were traditionally printed. The former set out broad proposals on potential legislation and ask for comments and feedback. They are often discursive and explore the context which has led to the Government considering legislation and lay down various options for resolving the issues. The latter, on the other hand, give much firmer details of the direction that the Government would like to take on a particular policy but they are still consultation documents. As such, Green Papers are not definitive statements of policy but are rather invitations for final comment before the Government decides to bring forward (or not bring forward) primary legislation.

SPEECH FROM THE THRONE

The State Opening of Parliament is an important ceremonial event within the English Legal System. It happens in the House of Lords and signifies the beginning of a new session of Parliament. Since the passing of the Fixed Term Parliament Act 2011 and its coming into force in 2012 it was intended to become normal practice for the State Opening to happen in late Spring/early Summer as opposed to later in the Autumn or early Winter. However, as is often the case the 'law in the books' does not represent practice on the ground. The coming to power of Boris Johnson led to a Queen's Speech being held in the Autumn of 2019.

As part of the State Opening of Parliament the Monarch gives a Speech from the Throne, more commonly known as the 'Queen's Speech'. This Speech explains the Bills that the Government intend to bring forward in that parliamentary session. The legislative programme is not designed by the Queen personally but is drawn up by a Cabinet Committee called the Legislation Committee. Given Government control of the parliamentary timetable, these Bills are likely to take up a significant period of parliamentary time in the session. The Speech is then debated in both the Commons and the Lords.

DRAFTING

Bills may be, and increasingly are, published in draft form as part of public consultation. Government Bills are drafted by specialist lawyers within the Office of the Parliamentary Counsel. They must take the specific policy ideas of the various Government departments and formalise them into the Bill that will be introduced to Parliament. There has been much pressure in recent years to decrease the overly legalistic language used in Acts of Parliament and it is the task of Parliamentary Counsel to ensure that Acts are legally effective but also accessible to and understandable by the public.[56]

---

56 www.gov.uk/government/collections/good-law. See also Peter Butt, *Modern Legal Drafting: A Guide to Using Clearer Language* (3rd edn, CUP 2013) Ch 6 and 7.

MAKING CONNECTIONS – STATUTORY INTERPRETATION
+ +
The difficulties caused by poor drafting are considered in Chapter 6 on statutory interpretation but it is worth reinforcing the fact that the task facing those drafting Public Bills is formidable. They must find a form of words that is broad enough to cover every situation envisioned by the policymaker (including, where appropriate, future scenarios that may arise due to technological advances) but not so broad as to inadvertently extend the Act beyond its intended purpose.

PASSAGE THROUGH PARLIAMENT – THE LEGISLATIVE PROCESS

Most Bills may begin their lives in either the Commons or Lords but must[57] receive support from both Houses before being sent on to the Monarch for Royal Assent. Money Bills will begin their life in the Commons and, by convention, matters governing the judicial system or Bills seeking to implement Law Commission recommendations will start their life in the Lords. Otherwise, Bills may start their progress through Parliament in either House.

Figure 4.6 gives a visual representation of the major stages in the law-making process both in the Commons and the Lords for a Public Bill. These are then explored more fully later so referring back to Figure 4.6 will help the reader to track the process in a more fluid manner. The diagram assumes that a Bill has started in the House of Commons.

STATEMENT OF COMPATIBILITY

Since the Human Rights Act 1998 came into force in 2000, all Government Bills are subject to a so-called statement of compatibility. Under s 19 of the Human Rights Act 1998 the Minister responsible for a particular Bill must, before the Second Reading:

> make a statement to the effect that in his view the provisions of the Bill are compatible with the Convention rights ('a statement of compatibility'); or

> make a statement to the effect that although he is unable to make a statement of compatibility the government nevertheless wishes the House to proceed with the Bill.

It is very rare for a Bill not to receive a statement of compatibility. This is largely because a Government Minister will not wish to state openly that an Act may be incompatible with the European Convention on Human Rights. One example of a Bill that did not receive such a statement was the failed House of Lords Reform Bill introduced by the then Deputy Prime Minister Nick Clegg in 2012. The Bill proposed large scale changes to the composition of the House of Lords, including introduction of elected members. The Deputy Prime Minister explained that he was unable to give a statement of compatibility because the proposed system of electing members of the Lords would exclude prisoners[58] and this was in contravention of the *Hirst*[59] judgment of the European Court of Human Rights.[60]

----

57 Subject to the limitations of the Parliament Acts 1911 and 1949, discussed later.
58 House of Lords Reform Bill 2012–2013 clause 6 citing the Representation of the People Acts 1983 and 1985.
59 *Hirst v United Kingdom (No 2)* [2005] ECHR 681.
60 www.publications.parliament.uk/pa/bills/cbill/2012-2013/0052/en/13052en.htm paras [248]–[249].

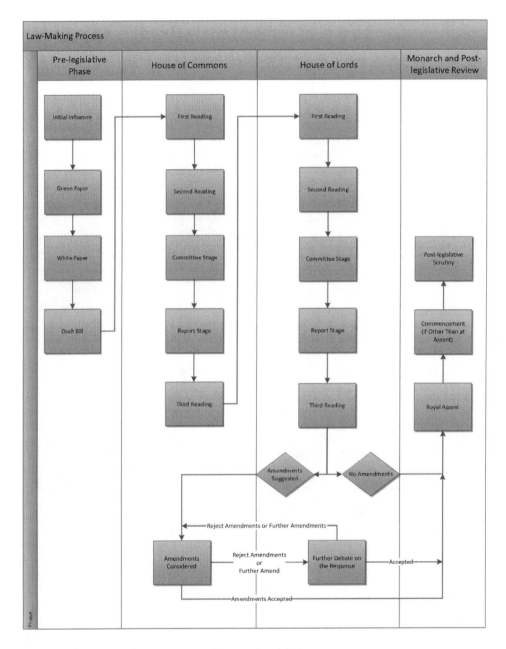

Figure 4.6 The Law-Making Process – Primary Legislation

HOUSE OF COMMONS – FIRST READING

The First Reading stage is the formal introduction of the Bill to the House. It is presented to the House by the Clerk who reads out the short title of the Bill. The Bill will then be ordered to be printed, alongside the Explanatory Notes for a Government Bill, and a date will be set for Second Reading.

HOUSE OF COMMONS – PUBLIC READING

Between the publication of a Bill and its Committee Stage it was possible that the Government or the House of Commons put the Bill out for 'Public Reading'. This involves public consultation on the Bill, the outcome of which is communicated to the relevant Committee.

Pilot public readings were given to four Bills in the 2010–2012 and 2012–2013 sessions:

- Small Charitable Donations Bill 2012–2013 (Government pilot)
- Children and Families Bill 2012–2013 (House of Commons pilot)
- Protection of Freedoms Bill 2010–2012 (Government pilot)
- Draft Care and Support Bill 2012 (Government pilot)

ANALYSING THE LAW – PUBLIC READING STAGE PILOT

The results of the Public Reading stage pilots have been mixed.

The Protection of Freedoms Bill received some 500 comments from 250 participants but the collated responses were not made available to all Committee members in advance of the Committee commencing its scrutiny, thus hampering the utility of the comments.[61] In addition, the comments were not systematically referred to but were used to inform the approach taken by individual members of the Committee. It could be argued that such an approach risks ignoring comments that do not accord with a specific member of the Committee's view.

The Draft Care and Support Bill similarly received around 1,000 responses and so public appetite for comment is strong in some areas. This is enhancing the public's engagement with the legislative process and should be encouraged.

However, the Small Charitable Donations Bill received only 85 comments, many of which were from those who had already been involved with the Bill before this stage. In none of the preceding cases did the Public Reading comments lead directly to amendments being tabled.

As the Leader of the House of Commons noted in 2012: 'the pilot results indicate that approaches to consultation should be carefully tailored to the Bill.'[62] As a result of the mixed response to Public Readings, the Government will not bring forward plans to extend the pilots to all Public Bills.

61 Richard Kelly, 'Public Reading Stage of Bills' (2014, Standard Note) SN/PC/06406, 7.
62 HC Deb 17 January 2013, vol 556, cols 44WS–45WS.

HOUSE OF COMMONS – SECOND READING

The Second Reading Bill focusses on the principles underpinning the Bill. For Government Bills, the Minister responsible for the proposal will give a statement to the House outlining the purpose of the Bill.

> ### MAKING CONNECTIONS – THE WIDER USE OF THE MINISTERIAL STATEMENT
> +
>
> The importance of the Ministerial Statement should not be understated. If the meaning of particular words in an Act of Parliament is unclear then a court may rely on Ministerial Statements in interpreting those words. This is known as the rule in *Pepper v Hart*[63] and is discussed in greater detail in Chapter 6 on statutory interpretation.

The Bill is then debated and eventually a vote on the floor of the Chamber is held. Amendments that Members (including the Minister responsible for the Bill) will be likely to table in Committee Stage can be considered and recommended for adoption at Committee Stage but the amendments themselves are not made during Second Reading.[64] Those in support of the Bill will be asked by the Speaker of the House to signify their approval for the Bill to pass Second Reading by calling 'aye', while those opposed to the Bill will call 'no'. If there is a clear and definite majority for 'aye' then the Bill is 'Read a Second Time' and if there is a clear and definite majority for 'no' then the Bill will fail to gain Second Reading. If there is any doubt then a full division is declared and Members of the Commons will go through one of two lobbies[65] to signify whether they agree to the Bill receiving its Second Reading.

It is rare for Government Bills to require a full division and rarer still for such a Bill to be defeated at Second Reading. Failure of a Government Bill to receive a Second Reading will normally be followed by the abandonment of the measure. This happened with the Shops Bill introduced by Margaret Thatcher in the 1980s which sought to change the Sunday Trading laws within the UK.

HOUSE OF COMMONS – PROGRAMME MOTION AND ORDER

Immediately after the Bill is read for a second time a Programme Order will be passed, following a Programme Motion, and this will act as a timetable for the remainder of the Bill's time in the Commons. It commits the Bill to the relevant Public Bill Committee, sets a deadline for consideration by the Committee and makes arrangements for the Third Reading which follows the Committee Stage. If a Bill passes Second Reading it is extremely unusual for a programme motion to be denied, not least because there is not normally a debate over the Order.

---

63 *Pepper v Hart* [1993] AC 593 (HL).

64 For example, the Minister responsible for the Intellectual Property Bill 2014 made comments in Second Reading about plans he had for making amendments to the Bill at Committee Stage. See HC Deb 20 January 2014, vol 574, col 40.

65 An MP can also register an abstaining vote by passing through both the Aye and No Lobby.

As a Programme Order will set the amount of time that the Bill will be debated it is an important, if often overlooked,[66] part of the law-making process. For example, it was the prospect of failure to agree a Programme Order that finally forced the Coalition Government to withdraw the radical House of Lords Reform Bill in 2012.[67] The Bill would have paved the way for an elected House of Lords. It passed Second Reading with a strong 90+ majority but the Labour Party withdrew its support due to the restricted time allowed for debate in the Programme Order.[68] With the prospect of defeat, through a combination of Conservative backbenchers and Labour party MPs, the Government withdrew the Programme Motion thus suspending the progress of the Bill. The Bill was formally abandoned later in the year.[69]

HOUSE OF COMMONS – COMMITTEE STAGE

It is at Committee Stage that the most thorough scrutiny of the Bill can take place. This happens on a clause by clause basis, enabling the detail of the Bill to be fully explored. The committees that consider the Bill can suggest amendments and these can then be debated again by the whole of the Commons at the Report Stage. The following section explores the different committees that may be involved at the Committee Stage.

PUBLIC BILL COMMITTEE

The most common form of Committee used is the Public Bill Committee.[70] These are ad hoc committees established specifically for considering a specific Bill and are named after the Bill (e.g. the Modern Slavery Bill 2014–15 was committed to the Public Bill Committee on Modern Slavery).

The constitution of the Public Bill Committee will roughly reflect the composition of the House of Commons and will normally consist of a minimum of 16 members up to a maximum of around 50 MPs. Thus, the party of Government who have the greatest number of seats in the House of Commons will also make up the majority of the Committee. The result of this is that many of the changes that are proposed in the Committee will be suggested by the Government and it is less likely that amendments that the Government disapprove of will be approved by the Committee.

Since the replacement of Standing Committees with Public Bill Committees in 2006, such Committees can also take evidence from interested parties. This means that external organisations can contribute more directly to the passage of individual Bills. For example, the Modern Slavery Bill heard evidence from the Director of Public Prosecutions; the Director of the National Crime Agency; barristers who specialise in human rights law; and the Head of the Bishops' Conference Office for Migration Policy.[71]

----

66 Few of the major textbooks on the English Legal System cover it at all.
67 HC Deb 3 September 2012, vol 549, cols 35–42.
68 Labour would have preferred unrestricted time to discuss the contents of the Bill.
69 HC Deb 3 September 2012, vol 549, col 35.
70 These, before 2006, were known as 'Standing Committees'.
71 www.parliament.uk/business/news/2014/july/modern-slavery-bill-evidence-programme-announced.

SELECT COMMITTEE

Certain Bills can be committed to a Select Committee in place of a Public Bill Committee after Second Reading. The Select Committees are permanent bodies and are aligned to Government Departments. This practice has fallen into disuse, as Select Committees can now be involved earlier in the process before a Bill is formally placed before Parliament. For example, the draft Consumer Rights Bill 2014–2015 was considered by the Business, Innovation and Skills Select Committee as part of pre-legislative scrutiny.[72] However, some Bills involving the Armed Forces[73] are examined by a Select Committee as part of the full legislative process. The most recent Armed Forces Bill to be considered in this way is the Armed Forces (Flexible Working) Bill 2017–2019 considered in Public Bill Committee on 14 November 2017, and reported without amendment. It completed its final stages (Report and Third Reading) on 29 January 2018. It came into effect in April 2019.

COMMITTEE OF THE WHOLE HOUSE

It is also possible for the Committee Stage of the House of Commons, much as it does in the Lords, to be taken on the floor of the House. This is known as a Committee of the Whole House. This tends to be reserved for matters of great constitutional importance, such as the Constitutional Reform Act 2005,[74] or those Bills that are so uncontroversial that a Public Bill Committee would not be a beneficial use of parliamentary time. Private Members' Bills often are heard in this way, as are Private Bills.

In addition, if Bills need to pass through Parliament very quickly then it may be appropriate to have a Committee of the Whole House.[75] This was the case for the Data Retention and Investigatory Powers Act 2014 which was passed over a few days in response to a case from the European Court of Justice.[76]

Other examples where a Committee of the Whole House was used include the Academies Bill and the Loans to Ireland Bill, both in the 2010–2012 session. The former sought to extend the academies school conversion programme started by the Labour Party while the latter dealt with the emergency loans made by the UK to the Republic of Ireland in the aftermath of the financial crisis. A Committee of the Whole House allows all members of the House to contribute to this clause by clause analysis of Bills.

On extremely rare occasions it is possible for a Bill to pass through a Committee of the Whole House before then being committed to a Public Bill Committee. This happened with the Human Fertilisation and Embryology Bill which contained various controversial clauses (such

72 For example, www.parliament.uk/business/committees/committees-a-z/commons-select/business-innova-
    tion-and-skills/inquiries/parliament-2010/gvt-draft-consumer-rights-bill, 20 August 2014.
73 Particularly the five yearly Bill that allows Parliament to maintain a standing army and governs certain aspects of disci-
    pline of the armed forces.
74 And, for example, the Human Rights Act 1998, the Fixed Terms Parliament Act 2011 and the European Union Act 2011.
75. For more examples, see Department of Information Services, 'Bills Whose Commons Committee Stage Has Been Taken
    in Committee of the Whole House' (2013, Standard Note) SN/PC/05435, 2–5.
76 Joined Cases C-293/12 and C-594/12 *Digital Rights Ireland* [2014] ECR I-845.

as those on admixed embryos)[77] that required a full debate as well as very technical clauses that would benefit from thorough scrutiny in a Public Bill Committee where evidence can be gathered from experts.

HOUSE OF COMMONS – REPORT STAGE

After the Committee has concluded its work, the Bill is returned to the Floor of the House where there is further debate and the Bill may be amended again. If the Committee Stage has made amendments to the Bill then it is open for MPs at Report Stage to suggest reversing these changes. The Report Stage is important as it is the last opportunity for the Commons to make amendments to the Bill.

HOUSE OF COMMONS – THIRD READING

Immediately following on from the Report Stage (often on the same day) is the Third Reading. In the Commons amendments are not permitted at Third Reading but there is a final – normally short – debate on the merits of the Bill. The debate is then followed by a vote on whether the Bill should be permitted to proceed. Failure to secure a Bill's Third Reading will normally mean that the Bill will be lost.

HOUSE OF LORDS – PROCEDURE

If a Bill begins in the Commons then it follows an almost identical procedure when it arrives in the House of Lords. The key differences in procedure are:

- The First Reading of a Bill in the House of Lords always passes without discussion.
- There is no programme motion, and corresponding Programme Order, in the House of Lords, and so debates may last longer than in the Commons.
- By default, Bills at Committee Stage in the Lords are committed to the Whole House rather than in a Public Bill Committee. In the past the House of Lords has occasionally committed to a Special Standing Committee[78] so that the House can receive specialist evidence from interested parties before the debate is re-committed to the Committee of the Whole House.[79]
- Unlike the position in the House of Commons, Bills can be amended at Third Reading Stage in the Lords.

ANALYSING THE LAW – THE HOUSE OF LORDS

The lack of a programme motion and the convention of holding the Committee Stage on the Chamber Floor is not just an historical anomaly. These practices reconfirm the

---

77 Embryos of mixed human and animal DNA.
78 Now known as Special Public Bill Committee.
79 For example, the Inheritance and Trustees Powers Bill in 2013.

important constitutional function of the House of Lords as a revising chamber and a place where detailed debate can take place in a way that is not always possible in the Commons. Indeed, the important scrutiny function of the House of Lords is often highlighted when reform is discussed. While reform of the House of Lords is a constant discussion point, it is important not to forget the role described previously and not to lose sight (in a time of increased pressure on time in the Commons) of the value of a revising chamber.

Additionally, there is a procedure known as committing to 'Grand Committee' where the Bill is taken out of the Main Chamber and discussed in a separate room. This is an option available only to Bills in the Lords. This is ostensibly a time saving measure but is technically still part of a Committee of the Whole House in that all members are able to attend should they wish and, for this reason, only a single Bill per day can be considered in this way. The major difference between a Bill in Grand Chamber and those discussed in the Main Chamber is that amendments proposed in Grand Committee must be adopted by unanimity.

AMENDMENTS

If no amendments are made by the second House that considers the Bill then it progresses to Royal Assent.

If amendments are made in the non-originating House then they must be agreed by the House in which the Bill originated. For example, a Bill starting in the House of Commons that is subsequently amended in the Lords must be returned to the Commons for those (and other) amendments to be debated and agreed. If the amendments are accepted, the Bill progresses to Royal Assent. If there continues to be disagreement between the two Houses then the Bill 'ping pongs' back and forth until one of three situations occurs:

- The parliamentary session ends.
- There is 'double insistence' by which one House insists on disagreement with an amendment and the other House insists on its support for the amendment.[80]
- The Houses come to agreement.

The first two scenarios will normally result in the Bill being lost whilst the third option results in the Bill being sent for Royal Assent.

ROYAL ASSENT

When a Bill has completed its passage through the Houses of Parliament it is sent for Royal Assent. Royal Assent is the (now largely symbolic) involvement of the sovereign within the

---

80 This is something of which the political parties are keenly aware and seek to avoid by strategically 'amending amendments'.

law-making process of the English Legal System. The process of Royal Assent emphasises the historical importance of the Monarch as the source of law within the English Legal System. It is at the point of Royal Assent that a Bill becomes an Act of Parliament.

Although it is with the giving of Royal Assent that a Bill becomes an Act, the process has been little more than a ceremonial technicality for the past three centuries. By convention the Monarch would only withhold the Royal Assent on the advice of the Government[81] and the last time that assent was refused was in 1708 when Queen Anne declined to give the Royal Assent to the Scottish Militia Bill.[82] It is to be remembered that even if it is a ceremonial technicality a Bill cannot come into force unless it has Royal Assent.

Traditionally, assent was given in person. The Monarch would take his or her place on the throne in the House of Lords and listen to the Bills being read before assent was granted. This gave way, in the time of Henry VIII, to a new procedure of assent by commission by which members of the Privy Council gave assent personally on behalf of the Monarch. This was in turn largely replaced, by virtue of the Royal Assent Act 1967, by a procedure whereby the Monarch can give their assent in writing using letters patent.[83] This written form is now the way in which the vast majority of Bills receive Royal Assent. Assent, under the written procedure, is said to have been granted when both Houses of Parliament have been informed by their respective presiding officers that assent has been received.

TAKING THINGS FURTHER – THE COMPANION WEBSITE

Acts of Parliament are structured in a fairly rigid manner. The website that accompanies this textbook contains a fully annotated statute to allow you to see the various features of an Act of Parliament on a piece of legislation that is currently in force. The website also has a short podcast on reading statutes effectively.

You can access Acts of Parliament at the following web address: www.legislation.gov. uk. You can also access Bills currently before Parliament at Parliament's website: http:// services.parliament.uk/bills/2014-15.html?group=date&order=desc.

---

81 There is even some doubt as to whether under convention the Monarch can *ever* withhold assent, regardless of the advice of her ministers. See Nick Barber, 'Can Royal Assent Be Refused on the Advice of the Prime Minister?' (UK Constitutional Law Association, 25 September 2013), http://ukconstitutionallaw.org/2013/09/25/nick-barber-can-royal-assent-be-refused-on-the-advice-of-the-prime-minster, and this issue has arisen again in the Brexit context – Robert Craig, 'Could the Government Advise the Queen to Refuse Royal Assent to a Backbench Bill?' (UK Constitutional Law Association, 22 January 2019), https://ukconstitutionallaw.org/2019/01/22/robert-craig-could-the-government-advise-the-queen-to-refuse-royal-assent-to-a-backbench-bill.

82 A Bill which sought to settle the Scottish army following on from the Acts of Union 1707.

83 Royal Assent Act 1967 s 1.

COMING INTO FORCE AND COMMENCEMENT

Before the end of the 18th century an Act of Parliament would be deemed to come into force on the first day of the parliamentary session in which it was introduced. This would mean that most legislation was introduced retrospectively and would be 'back dated' to the start of the session. This practice was increasingly seen as unfair[84] as it could mean laws having retrospective effect for nearly a year. As such, the Acts of Parliament (Commencement) Act 1793 changed the position so that the Clerk of the Parliaments[85] had to endorse an Act with the date that it received Royal Assent, and it was from this date that an Act would normally come into force.

This has the consequence that although a Bill becomes an Act upon receiving Royal Assent, this does not mean that it necessarily comes into force immediately. The current position is to be found in the Interpretation Act 1978. Section 4 of the Act reads as follows:

An Act or provision of an Act comes into force –

a) Where provision is made for it to come into force on a particular day, at the beginning of that day;
b) Where no provision is made for its coming into force, at the beginning of the day on which the Act receives Royal Assent.

There is therefore a continuum of commencement with Acts that come into force at different times. Some Acts come into force fully and immediately on receiving Royal Assent. Others come into force on a predetermined date. Others still will come into force on a date to be determined by some additional process, such as through the passage of an Order in Council or vote in the Houses of Parliament, or in the case of some statutes any enabling sections requiring preparations to be made before the bulk of the Act can come into force, only those enabling sections will come into force immediately and the rest of the Act can be brought into force sequentially at a date or dates to be determined either at the time the Act is passed or later.

EXPLAINING THE LAW – THE IMPORTANCE OF COMMENCEMENT

An example of the importance of commencement can be demonstrated by reference to the Easter Act 1928. This Act was duly passed in the last century but, despite containing only two sections, it has not yet come into force almost 90 years later. Its intention was 'to regulate the date of Easter Day' to curtail the practice of having a floating date for Easter Sunday which can currently fall on dates between late March and late April.[86]

---

84 It would now be regarded as a breach of the modern conception of the rule of law. See European Convention on Human Rights Article 7 and Tom Bingham, *Rule of Law* (Penguin 2011).
85 The Clerk is also responsible for the pronouncement of Royal Assent.
86 For example, in 2008, Easter fell on 23 March whereas it will fall on 25 April in 2038.

Section 1 set the date for Easter as the first Sunday after the second Saturday in April. However, commencement was to happen via an Order in Council that was to be laid before the Houses of Parliament for approval.[87] Due to historic disagreement within established Christian churches as to the setting of a date for Easter the necessary Order has yet to be laid before Parliament.

Although you may question the importance of setting a date for Easter, it is an important example of the dangers of simply finding statutes on the Government website and assuming that they are fully in force. You should always be aware as to whether the Act as a whole is in force.

Section 4 of the Interpretation Act 1978 also makes it clear that individual provisions of an Act can come into force at different times. The power to bring part of an Act into force is normally delegated to a Minister. This process is achieved through the passage of a commencement order, which is a form of secondary legislation (discussed further in the next chapter). This is an important, but sometimes confusing, feature of the English Legal System. The consequence is that those involved in the application of the Act in question – including the legal professions – must be aware which parts of an Act are in force at any one time, as well as if the Act as a whole is in force at all.

POST-LEGISLATIVE REVIEW

Following on from the granting of Royal Assent, Acts introduced by the Government will be the subject to formal post-legislative scrutiny.[88] This involves the Government Department responsible for that area of policy preparing a Command Paper for the relevant Select Committee on how the Act has operated in practice and whether it has achieved its objectives.[89] The Select Committee can then, if it deems it necessary, undertake a fuller review of the operation of the Act in question.[90]

SPECIAL PROCEDURES

Later 19th- and early 20th-century discussion of the legislative process would encompass only the preceding (or even only elements of the preceding) procedure. Providing that the Bill had made it through both the Commons and the Lords and had received Royal Assent then that was all that was to be considered. If a Bill failed to make it through the process then it was lost at the end of the parliamentary session.

....

87 The requirements, including the 'regard' that is to be had to the view of any Church, of commencement are found in Easter Act 1928 s 2(2).

88 www.gov.uk/government/publications/post-legislative-scrutiny-the-governments-approach.

89 This is independent of any other statutory review that may be necessary.

90 Fuller details of the process can be found in the Cabinet Office's 'Guide to Making Legislation' (July 2014) 264–273.

More recently there are numerous additional procedures that must be discussed when examining the law-making process of the English Legal System in its modern context. These special procedures and processes arise from the modern context under which Parliament legislates and are designed to deal with, amongst other things, the potential for conflict between the Houses; the transfer of powers to the European Union; and the possibility of preserving a Bill that fails to make it through both Houses in a single parliamentary session.

CONFLICT AND THE PARLIAMENT ACTS

The growth of democratic accountability and the increased importance of the lower chamber of Parliament led to questions being asked about the equality of arms between the House of Commons and the House of Lords. More particularly, the ability of the unelected House of Lords permanently to frustrate the will of the democratically elected House of Commons was controversial.

The tension over the powers of the upper chamber boiled over in the early 20th century when the House of Lords rejected the budget (in the form of a Finance Bill) of the Liberal Government in 1909. In response, the Prime Minister of the day threatened to request that the King create sufficient new Liberal Peers to force legislation through the Lords and to prevent conflicts over future Finance Bills. The outcome of the political tussle was the Parliament Act 1911. The compromise that was reached in that Act was a reduction in the power of the Lords and made the Commons the de facto superior legislating chamber.

The major innovation of the Parliament Act 1911 was the removal of the Lords' power of absolute veto for most Bills. After the Parliament Act 1911 the Lords could only delay a Bill (other than a Money Bill)[91] for two whole parliamentary sessions. Under the Act, the rejected Bill could then proceed to the Monarch for Royal Assent if it was rejected in the third session. This power of delay was reduced further by the Parliament Act 1949 so that a Bill could only be delayed for around a year (over two sessions). Thus, a Bill presented by the Commons in a second successive session can now progress straight to Royal Assent if rejected a second time by the Lords.

The 1949 Act has proved to be controversial in that it had to be passed using the powers of the 1911 Act! This was because the Lords had already rejected proposals to introduce the 1949 Bill on two previous occasions. Thus, we are left with a slightly unusual situation in that a Bill that was proposed to amend the 1911 Act had to rely on the 1911 Act in order to be passed.

Figure 4.7 illustrates the operation of the Parliament Act 1911 as amended in 1949 and how it was used to pass the Hunting Act 2004. The controversies associated with the Hunting Act are discussed later in this section.

---

91 Which can only be delayed for one month – Parliament Act 1911 s 1(1).

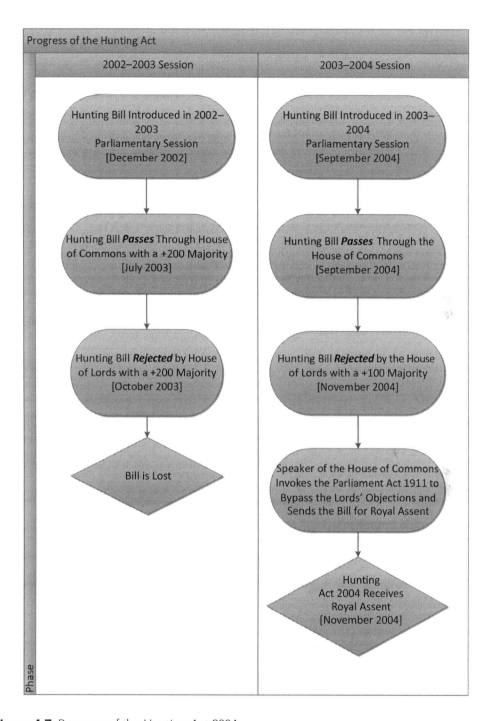

Figure 4.7 Progress of the Hunting Act 2004

The reduction of the powers of the House of Lords is obviously an important development in the democratisation of the English Legal System and in the process of reform of the upper chamber. Despite this it is important to keep a sense of perspective about use of the Acts. As well as reinforcing the supremacy of the elected Commons, the Parliament Act 1911 also acts as an important deterrent for the Lords. It encourages them to use their power of delay in a more discriminating fashion. By preserving some of the power of the Lords, essentially now a power to delay, it does not completely undermine the role of the upper chamber as a place for revising and scrutinising legislation.

The provisions of the Parliament Act itself are rarely called upon and have been used to force the passage of only seven Bills:

- Welsh Church Act 1914
- Government of Ireland Act 1914
- Parliament Act 1949
- War Crimes Act 1991
- European Parliamentary Elections Act 1999
- Sexual Offences (Amendment) Act 2000
- Hunting Act 2004

It is of interest to note that only one of the Acts just listed – the War Crimes Act 1991 – was enacted by a Conservative Government. This leads on to a further important, but indirect, function of the Parliament Acts which was to redress, in part, the inbuilt Conservative dominance of the House of Lords.

ANALYSING THE LAW – THE PARLIAMENT ACTS 1911 AND 1949

With fewer than ten Bills in more than a century requiring recourse to the powers of the Parliament Act 1911, its importance could be questioned. However, it is vital to view the Parliament Act 1911 as an early stepping-stone in the broader process of Lords reform. Moreover, the debate that surrounded the enactment of the Parliament Act 1911 has contributed to other developments that have had a more immediate impact on the legislative process. For example, the development of the Salisbury Convention in the mid-1940s was strongly influenced by recent memory of the events that led to the 1911 Act. The constitutional convention[92] named for Lord Salisbury holds that any Government Bill that seeks to achieve a manifesto commitment will not be voted down[93] by the Lords. In many cases this avoids the need to have recourse to the Parliament Act 1911.

---

92 A constitutional convention is a non-legal rule that actors within the English Legal System consider themselves (for constitutional reasons) to be bound by. See Nicholas Barber, 'Laws and constitutional conventions' (2009) 125 Law Quarterly Review 294.

93 A Bill may be *amended* provided that the amendment does not stop the Bill from progressing (i.e. it cannot be a 'wrecking amendment').

The most recent use of the Parliament Act was by Tony Blair's Labour Government to secure the passage of the Hunting Act 2004. This Act banned certain forms of hunting, including those of wild mammals by dogs. This was, and continues to be, a controversial piece of legislation.[94] In a bid to prevent the operation of the Act numerous challenges have been brought concerning its legality.[95] For the purposes of a chapter on the law-making process of the English Legal System, it is the *Jackson*[96] case that laid down important principles about the use of the Parliament Acts.

EXPLAINING THE LAW AND MAKING CONNECTIONS – THE *JACKSON* CASE
+++

The case was brought by members of the Countryside Alliance, including Jackson, who argued that the Parliament Act 1949 should not have been passed using the 1911 Act as the former amended the latter. They argued that any legislation passed under the Parliament Act 1911 was not in fact primary legislation but delegated legislation. This, so the appellants argued, meant that the 1949 Act was invalid and so the Hunting Act 2004, passed under the procedures of the 1949 Act, was also invalid.

The challenge failed with Lord Bingham stating that the Parliament Act 1911 did 'effect an important constitutional change, but the change lay not in authorising a new form of sub-primary parliamentary legislation but in creating a new way of enacting primary legislation.'[97]

For the purposes of law-making in the English Legal System the case is important because it demonstrated that Parliament can itself alter the law-making process through a regular Act of Parliament.

PRESERVATION

Traditionally, a Bill that does not attain Royal Assent by the end of the parliamentary session in which it was introduced would be lost. This adds certainty to the position and status of Bills. Also, in the days before Parliament sat frequently, it would stop Bills being maintained for a number of years. This position was changed by Tony Blair's Government in 1998 when the Financial Services and Markets Bill 1998–1999 was carried over between sessions. The procedure of carry-over is particularly important where very long and technical bills[98] are introduced which require extensive scrutiny at Committee Stage. If 'carry-over' was not possible then there is the risk that Bills would be (even more frequently) rushed through the parliamentary process with insufficient checks or scrutiny.

The beginning of the 2004–2005 session of Parliament saw the formalisation of a procedure of 'carry-over' into a House of Commons Standing Order. The Consumer Rights Bill is an example of

94 https://petition.parliament.uk/petitions/205852.
95 R (*Countryside Alliance and others*) v Attorney General [2007] UKHL 52, [2008] 1 AC 719.
96 R (*Jackson*) v Attorney General [2005] UKHL 56, [2006] 1 AC 262.
97 Ibid. [24] (Lord Bingham).
98 The Financial Services and Markets Act 2000 had some 433 sections and 22 Schedules.

an important legislative measure that was carried over from the 2013–2014 period into the 2014–2015 session before becoming the Consumer Rights Act in 2015.[99] Similarly, the controversial HS2 Bill, that paves the way for the completion of a high speed rail link between Birmingham and London, and which runs to some 413 pages, was subject to carry-over in the same session.[100] Moreover, it was already envisioned at that time that the HS2 Bill might be carried over to the 2015–2016 session[101] and in fact it did not receive the Royal Assent until 23 February 2017.

The power of carry-over can only be used for Bills introduced in the Commons that have yet to be sent up to the Lords. This last restriction does arguably limit the effectiveness of the power of carry-over but the very existence of the power indicates the willingness of the Commons to adapt its procedures better to suit the modern environment in which legislation is drafted. This is particularly important, as noted previously, in the case of Bills that contain a significant amount of technical information. It also ensures that adequate time can be allocated to long and technical Bills.

The Domestic Abuse Bill 2017–2019 was almost a casualty of the power struggle between Parliament and the Government during the unlawful prorogation of September 2019. Despite strong cross-party support the Bill was not, initially, subject to a carry-over motion and so seemed to have been lost. Following the Supreme Court's ruling that that prorogation that had caused the loss had been unlawful, the Bill was recovered and was subject to a carry-over motion before the (lawful) prorogation in October 2019.[102] This means that the Bill, now the Domestic Abuse Bill 2017–2019 to 2019–2020, resumed its passage through the law-making process.

TRANSFER OF POWERS TO THE EUROPEAN UNION

As has been mentioned elsewhere, the General Election of 2010 returned a Coalition Government between the Conservatives and Liberal Democrats. Despite the parties holding almost diametrically opposed views on aspects of European integration, the Coalition Agreement proposed amending the European Communities Act 1972 so as to require a referendum if there was to be a further transfer of powers to the European Union. This aspect of the Coalition Agreement was achieved not through amendment of the European Communities Act but rather by the passage of new primary legislation in the form of the European Union Act 2011. Indeed, the EUA 2011 went further and set up numerous restrictions on how future developments of the EU were to be be achieved through primary legislation.

The language of the EU Act 2011 is densely drafted but the core of the Act's provisions is about specific 'trigger events' that would require a referendum before the UK ratifies an EU Treaty.[103] For example, if the EU was granted new exclusive competence or existing competences are extended or if an EU institution was granted new powers to impose sanctions on the Member States then a referendum would be triggered.

---

99 HC Deb 28 January 2014, vol 574, col 834.

100 HC Deb 29 April 2014, vol 579, cols 771–774.

101 Ibid.

102 Details of the Bill, and its legislative history, can be found at https://services.parliament.uk/Bills/2017-19/domesti-cabuse.html.

103 European Union Act 2011 s 4(1)(a)–(m).

The reality of the situation, however, is more complicated than the face of the Act suggests. There has, at the time of writing, not been the need for a referendum under the EUA 2011. This is despite the fact that there have been new Treaties affecting the balance of powers within the EU.[104]

THE LEGISLATIVE LANDSCAPE: FLAT OR CONTOURED?

This chapter has very much focussed on how individual Bills become Acts of Parliament. However, it is important to remember that Acts of Parliament do not operate in a vacuum and will often interact with and contradict each other. The English Legal System has a long-established principle, that of 'implied repeal', that helps to deal with the question of inconsistencies between Acts of Parliament in a pragmatic way.

Implied repeal has traditionally been understood, from cases such as *Vauxhall Estates*,[105] to mean that where you have inconsistencies between two Acts the later Act is seen to impliedly repeal the older Act. As such the orthodox view of the English Legal System has been of a flat legislative landscape with all Acts of Parliament equally being subject to the doctrine of implied repeal.[106] The basis of implied repeal lies in the doctrine of parliamentary sovereignty, discussed previously.

The preceding means that Acts could not become 'entrenched' and Acts (no matter their importance) were all equal. However, modern developments have put increasing pressure on this concept and we can now see that discovering which Acts take priority in the case of conflict is now more complex.

> MAKING CONNECTIONS – PUBLIC LAW
> +
> The debate about the extent to which Acts of Parliament can be repealed impliedly by later Acts of Parliament will be explored in much greater depth in modules that you may study on public law, constitutional law or European Union law. However, a basic understanding of the position is necessary for an understanding of the operation of the English Legal System and of law-making.

104 For example, the Fiscal Compact Treaty.

105 *Vauxhall Estates v Liverpool Corp* [1932] 1 KB 733 (KB).

106 See this interesting blog piece by Mark Elliot, 'Reflections on the HS2 Case: a Hierarchy of Domestic Constitutional Norms and the Qualified Primacy of EU Law' (UK Constitutional Law Association, 23 January 2014), http://ukconsti-tutionallaw.org/2014/01/23/mark-elliot-reflections-on-the-hs2-case-a-hierarchy-of-domestic-constitutional-norms-and-the-qualified-primacy-of-eu-law.

Due to membership of the European Union (discussed in Chapter 16), and the case law of the Court of Justice of European Union,[107] it is recognised that EU law must take priority over conflicting national law regardless of when that national law was passed.[108] This calls into question the principle of implied repeal for the English Legal System as a later Act of Parliament must always give way to a piece of prior EU law.

The English courts were faced with the question of whether to apply the doctrine of implied repeal to matters concerning EU law in the *Thoburn*[109] case.

EXPLAINING THE LAW – *THOBURN*

The case concerned the Weights and Measures Act 1985 which gave equal legal authority to measurements of weight in both pounds and kilograms. A later amendment of the Act by secondary legislation in 1994, brought about to comply with EU law and made under the powers of the European Communities Act 1972, prohibited pounds being used as the *primary* indicator of weight in the UK. Thoburn was convicted for using scales that did not comply with the amended 1985 Act but that would have complied with the 1985 Act as originally enacted.

Thoburn argued that the Weights and Measures Act 1985 (as originally enacted) had impliedly repealed the powers under the European Communities Act 1972. As a result the later amendment to the 1985 Act using the 1972 Act was invalid.

Lord Justice Laws, in the High Court, disagreed with this argument and made some important comments *obiter* about the nature of legislation and law-making in the English Legal System. He stated that '[w]e should recognise a hierarchy of Acts of Parliament: as it were "ordinary" statutes and "constitutional" statutes. The two categories must be distinguished on a principled basis.'[110] As a result of this he stated that 'A constitutional statute can only be repealed, or amended in a way which significantly affects its provisions touching fundamental rights or otherwise the relation between citizen and State, by unambiguous words on the face of the later statute.'[111]

The outcome of *Thoburn* is that some 'constitutional' statutes, such as the European Communities Act 1972, are now immune from implied repeal and can only be repealed by express words in subsequent Acts of Parliament. Lord Justice Laws also identified other statutes, including the Human Rights Act 1998, the Scotland Act 1998, the Bill of Rights

107 Case 6/64 *Costa v ENEL* [1964] ECR 585.
108 Case 106/77 *Amministrazione delle Finanze dello Stato v Simmenthal* [1978] ECR 629.
109 *Thoburn v Sunderland City Council* [2002] EWHC 195 (Admin), [2003] QB 151.
110 Ibid. [62] (Laws LJ).
111 Ibid. [63] (Laws LJ).

1689 and Magna Carta as other Acts of similar status.[112] This means that, albeit to a limited extent, the English Legal System now has a two-tiered system of primary legislation. Although these cases were decided in the context of EU law, the principles underpinning them have been extended in subsequent cases in other contexts.[113]

The *Thoburn* case is also an excellent example of external influences – in this case the EU – transforming our understanding of the domestic legal system. In the HS2[114] case involving the planned high speed rail link between London and Birmingham, the Supreme Court indicated, *obiter*,[115] that even amongst constitutional statutes there may be an order of priority.[116] This suggests that the English Legal System has a multidimensional legislative framework with certain pieces of primary law taking priority over others.

It is important to remember this when assessing the impact of particular pieces of legislation that have a constitutional flavour. It is no longer sufficient to view each piece of legislation in isolation and it is important not only to think of whether it is of a constitutional nature itself but also whether it will conflict with earlier Acts or principles of a constitutional nature. This task of identifying 'constitutional' Acts of Parliament is complicated by the fact that they will, until labelled as such by a court, appear to be a regular Act of Parliament. So-called constitutional Acts will follow exactly the same procedure as any other Act of Parliament in their passage through the legislative process.

CONCLUSION

The law-making process, as it applies to primary legislation, is complex and highly politically charged. However, it is crucial for those wishing to understand the English Legal System to appreciate fully the importance of every step of the process that leads to primary legislation. Without understanding the *context* of how an Act of Parliament came into force it can be difficult to understand how it was intended to apply and how it will be received by both the courts and the wider public.

Moreover, and beyond the mere mechanics of the law-making process, with its many steps and procedures, it is important to note some of the broader themes that arise out of the discussion in this chapter. First, the process tells us something about the involvement (or lack thereof) of citizens in that process. At present, the role of participatory democracy in the English Legal System is somewhat limited. Citizens elect their MPs (who are only part of

112 Ibid. [62].

113 For a Scottish case on the effect of the Scotland Act 1998, see *BH (AP) v The Lord Advocate* [2012] UKSC 24, [2013] 1 AC 413 [30] (Lord Hope).

114 *R (HS2) v The Secretary of State for Transport* [2014] UKSC 3, [2014] 1 WLR 324.

115 The concept of *obiter dictum* is discussed further in Chapter 9 but for the purposes of this chapter it is to be understood as a non-legally binding part of a court judgment.

116 See *R (HS2) v The Secretary of State for Transport* [2014] UKSC 3, [2014] 1 WLR 324 at [79] and [203].

the legislature) and thereafter the role of the individual member of the public is largely over until the next General Election, some five years hence. The English Legal System has informal channels through which the individual may influence law-making, such as exerting pressure on the Government to introduce specific policies. Increasingly, there are also more formal channels for recognising the role of the citizen in the process of law-making. These are genuine steps towards greater participation of citizens, including the launch of e-petitions and the pilots of a Public Reading stage. The success of these developments will depend on whether citizens engage with the opportunities and whether the institutional actors are seen to be responding to the contributions of the public.

Secondly, and due partly to the inbuilt propensity for dominance of Parliament by the Government,[117] the effectiveness of the system of scrutiny of legislation is in question. The debates in the Houses of Commons and Lords and the work of the Public Bill Committees are intended to be the primary method of scrutiny within the English Legal System. Their work is undermined by the control of Government of the parliamentary timetable and the increase in length and complexity of statutes only exacerbates the problem. The problem of effective scrutiny has traditionally been made even worse by the tendency for General Elections to return strong majority Governments able to pass legislation through by sheer force of will. It has yet to be seen whether Coalition Governments will happen more frequently in the future and whether the promises that secured the maintenance of Scotland's membership of the UK will impact on the law-making process. These two factors may act as a force for reducing Government control, in particular in the Commons, in the future.

Thirdly, and although it may not always seem this way, the English Legal System is progressive and evolutionary. It is not a fixed system and is capable of organic changes that subtly, but importantly, and sometimes irreversibly, change the direction and nature of law-making. The most noteworthy of these in the last two centuries is probably the Parliament Acts 1911 and 1949 which allowed Parliament to legislate in a new way. More subtle changes, not normally discussed in English Legal System textbooks include the change to accommodate carry-over of Bills and the evolving system of Standing Orders that regulate Parliament but that allow for flexibility to be injected into the system. This organic development is a key feature of the whole English Legal System and will be returned to in subsequent chapters.

Fourthly, and finally, as much as this textbook encourages you to view your study of individual modules as interconnecting parts of a single system, it is equally important not to divorce law from its political, economic and social contexts. Law does not just appear fully formed and without figurative 'baggage'. An individual Act of Parliament is a product of its time, of the political climate and of the society from which it comes. It is important to remember this in any study of the English Legal System. Much law is the realisation of politics and the more you understand about the political process, the more you will understand the legal process.

---

117 For a recent reconsideration of the issue of executive dominance of Parliament, see Grégoire Webber, 'Parliament and the Management of Conflict' (2014) Public Law 100, 102–104.

THE WEBSITE

The website that accompanies this textbook contains many useful resources that you can use to consolidate and further your knowledge of the law, to hone your skills of critical analysis and to test your knowledge. This includes a set of multiple choice questions (MCQs) that can be used to test your knowledge and understanding of the material.

PODCASTS

- The podcasts provide a summary of the area under study, bringing together the key themes and threads of analysis into a 'mini-lecture'.
- There will also be an explanation and analysis of topical and up-to-date issues related to law-making.

5

CHAPTER 5
LAW-MAKING IN THE ENGLISH LEGAL SYSTEM II – DELEGATED (SECONDARY) LEGISLATION

INTRODUCTION

If, as discussed in the previous chapter, primary law sets out the framework of the legal system then secondary legislation is designed to flesh out the detailed rules and enables the decisions that operate under that framework to be taken. Alternatively called delegated or subordinate legislation, secondary legislation is the exercise of law-making powers under the *authority* and *control* of Parliament.

Such delegated legislation is an increasingly important part of a legal system that operates in the context of expansive government activity and of complex and technical regulatory environments. From tax to the control of public spaces, from the setting of constituency boundaries to the powers of professional bodies, secondary legislation affects all aspects of the legal (and political) system.

This chapter will explore the different forms of delegated legislation and how they are made. More importantly, the chapter will examine the extent of powers that can be exercised under and through secondary legislation and how that power is controlled by various actors within the legal system. A major theme of this chapter is how secondary legislation is scrutinised both within and outside of Parliament.

AS YOU READ

Think about the different forms of secondary legislation and the different purposes they may be trying to achieve. From the examples given, consider whether the different forms of secondary legislation *achieve* those purposes. Assess the **effectiveness** of the methods of scrutiny and how these methods interact with each other and how they might be improved.

Consider the different roles of Parliament, the executive and the judiciary in formulating and scrutinising secondary legislation.

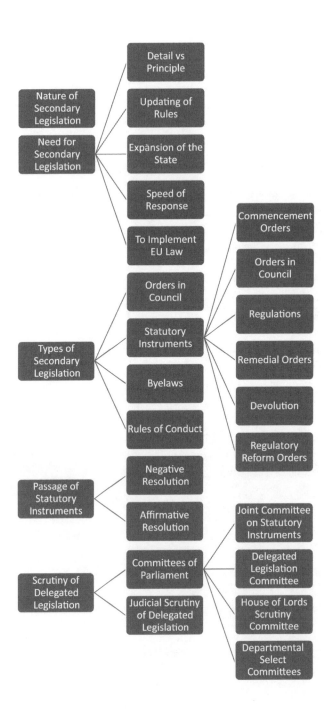

Figure 5.1

NATURE AND SCOPE OF SECONDARY LEGISLATION

This textbook presents, for reasons of efficacy, primary legislation (i.e. Acts of Parliament) in a distinct chapter from secondary legislation. However, they should not be viewed as wholly separate instruments but rather as interacting and complementary forms of legislation. Primary legislation sets down principles and secondary legislation attempts to achieve the detailed implementation of those principles. Primary legislation is like the rigid skeleton of the English Legal System[1] and secondary legislation fleshes out that skeleton.

TAKING THINGS FURTHER – SEEKING OUT SECONDARY LEGISLATION

This is a topic for which it is particularly useful for you to explore some concrete examples of secondary legislation. It is possible to browse much of the secondary legislation currently in force in the English Legal System via a Government website – www.legislation. gov.uk/browse. Visiting this website regularly can help to keep you up to date with recent legislative development.

A word of warning should be attached to the use of the aforementioned website. With more than 3,000 statutory instruments – a particular type of secondary legislation – published each year, it is easy to get lost or distracted by the volume of legislative output. You can search the database for more relevant pieces of secondary legislation, or use it to get a feel of the form, structure and style of such delegated legislation.

The companion website that accompanies this text contains a number of exercises designed to aid your familiarisation with secondary legislation and to help you to be able to *use* such legislation in your legal essays. These include a podcast where the author talks through the structure of a piece of secondary legislation; some comprehension activities to test your understanding of such legislation; and even a hypothetical problem question that will allow you to apply your comprehension skills.

Given the central position of Parliament's sovereignty in the English Legal System, most secondary legislation comes into force under Parliament's authority.[2] Such secondary legislation is authorised by a piece of primary law – an Act of Parliament – known as the Parent or Enabling Act. This will dictate to whom powers are delegated, what the powers are to be used for and how the delegated legislation is to come into force. Being familiar with the proposition that a Parent Act will contain all of the information related to the passing of a piece of a secondary legislation will help you to understand the symbiotic relationship

---

1   Which is not to say that those bones cannot be broken and recast if needed.
2   Certain prerogative powers of the Monarch can be exercised by Orders in Council, some of which are not required to be laid before Parliament.

between primary and delegated legislation. That relationship is explored in the context of the Courts and Legal Services Act 1990 in the box.

EXPLAINING THE LAW – THE COURTS AND LEGAL SERVICES ACT 1990: THE RELATIONSHIP BETWEEN PRIMARY AND SECONDARY LEGISLATION

The Courts and Legal Services Act 1990 makes provision for secondary legislation on a number of issues related to the day-to-day operation of the courts and the allocation of claims to the High Court or other courts. This is the Parent Act and Section 1 empowers the Lord Chancellor[3] to allocate categories of cases to various courts by way of secondary legislation. The Act also sets certain limits and conditions on exercise of the discretion of the Lord Chancellor. For example, any changes to the balance of shared jurisdiction between the High Court and county courts are subject to the approval of the Lord Chief Justice, who is the head of the judiciary in England and Wales.[4] For other changes, mainly to the sole jurisdiction of the High Court or county courts, the Lord Chancellor must consult with various members of the judiciary.[5] The Court and Legal Services Act 1990 also details that secondary legislation made by the Lord Chancellor in exercise of these powers is to be made but can be annulled by a resolution of either House of Parliament.[6]

In 2011, the Lord Chancellor exercised the powers under the Act and made a piece of secondary legislation called The Patents Court (Financial Limits) (No 2) Order 2011.[7] This order set a limit of £500,000 for claims brought in what were the patents county courts.[8]

Certain consequences flow from the fact that the power for secondary legislation comes from the authority of Parliament. First, the power to create the secondary legislation is vested only in the person (or persons) named in the Parent Act. In the preceding example, this is the Lord Chancellor.

Secondly, the content of secondary legislation is limited to the scope given to it by the Parent Act. This can have a positive and negative dimension. The positive dimension is that the Act may give express powers to do X, Y and Z and the person making the secondary legislation may not go beyond the powers so given. The negative dimension is that an Act may expressly

---

3   A Government position bestowed by the Queen on the advice of the Prime Minister. Since changes brought about by the Constitutional Reform Act 2005, the Lord Chancellor usually now also holds the post of Secretary of State for Justice but the positions are legally distinct.
4   Courts and Legal Services Act 1990, s 1(1A).
5   Ibid. s 1(9).
6   Ibid. s 120.
7   The Patents Court (Financial Limits) (No 2) Order 2011, SI 2011/1402.
8   These are now a specialist list of the High Court called the Intellectual Property Enterprise Court.

prevent powers from being used in a specific way. In the preceding example, the Act gives the Lord Chancellor the positive power to confer jurisdiction over certain cases to the High Court and county courts and, in the negative dimension, prohibits him from conferring jurisdiction for judicial review on the county courts.[9]

Thirdly, and linked to the previous point, secondary legislation is challengeable if it is outside the powers given by the Parent Act. For example, if the Lord Chancellor attempted to use the Act to change the jurisdiction of the Crown Court it would be possible to challenge the legality of the secondary legislation as it would be going beyond the powers (to manage the jurisdiction of the county courts and High Court).

However there have been situations where the Lord Chancellor periodically sails very close to the wind, especially in the context and relative informality of secondary legislation so authorised. A common example is his powers to make regulations under the (unpopular) Legal Aid, Sentencing and Punishment of Offenders (LASPO) Act 2012 where tight regulations on evidence to be produced for grant of exceptional funding for domestic violence applications have resulted in a very low success rate for such applications.

This is not the only example of the generous extent of such amendments which can apparently be authorised by the Parent Act, such as s 18A of the Judicial Pensions and Retirement Act 1993 which has enabled the Lord Chancellor to amend the Judicial Pensions (Fee Paid Judges) Regulations 2017, Regulation 3(1)(a) so that while using his power under s 18A to *add* extrajudicial offices into the 2017 Regulations, which were implemented on 1 April 2017, the Lord Chancellor has (in allegedly 'clarifying' the tribunal offices to be included in the new Fee-Paid Judicial Pension Scheme) also *taken away an existing right to a pension of fee paid chairmen of the old (now extinct) Rent Assessment Committees (RACs) which from 2013 became Fee Paid Chairmen of the First Tier Property Chamber (FTT)*; these were previously included because the Fee Paid Chairmen of the FTT qualified as 'an office replaced by a specified office' in accordance with the wording of the original version of the Regulations.

Curiously, it seems that when the Deputy Adjudicators to the Land Registry protested the Ministry of Justice conceded that they, since they were also now judges of the FTT Property Chamber, could be included for prior service at the Land Registry before 2013 on the grounds that they now occupied an office which had replaced a previously specified office, but declined to include the past Fee Paid Chairman of the Rent Assessment Committee (RAC) on the same basis.

Moreover the Chairman of the All Party Joint Committee on Statutory Instruments, Derek Twigg MP, could apparently not fault this when drawn to his attention; the MOJ simply said they had consulted on the draft from 15 September to 31 October 2016. An appeal by a Fee Paid Judge of the FTT who was actually affected by the change (having also been a Fee Paid Chairman of the RAC prior to 2013) was then rejected by the Employment Tribunal Judge, who was still involved

---

9   Courts and Legal Services Act 1990 s 1(a)–(b) and s 10 respectively.

in hearing the litigation between such fee paid judges and the Ministry of Justice on the basis that government policy had determined that such pensions should be provided in another manner (in fact it seems that this was what the policy was setting out to achieve by this back door since it now seems that the pre-2013 RAC Judges are to be given civil service rather than judicial pensions, and the former fall short of the latter by around 50%). This seems to be a very odd use of the Lord Chancellor's power under s 18A especially as the 2017 Regulations were so new when amended *and* while there was ongoing litigation involving some of those post 2013 office holders which was not at the time completed. It makes one wonder how many other secondary legislation changes have been similarly 'in accordance with government policy' – since this methodology seems to owe much more to the legacy of Thomas Cromwell rather than even to Henry VIII who already gives his name to the 'Henry VIII clauses' sometimes included in primary legislation (addressed in the last chapter and further on in this one).

A previous chapter of this textbook explained that Acts of Parliament, due to the sovereignty of Parliament, cannot be challenged in court. The same does not apply to secondary legislation, which can be challenged through the courts. This process is known as judicial review and its effectiveness is discussed in the section on scrutiny of secondary legislation.

MAKING CONNECTIONS – JUDICIAL REVIEW
+ +

If you study public law then you will explore, in great detail, the principles of judicial review. The vast majority of judicial review claims revolve around alleged misuse of powers conferred by Acts of Parliament, including those involving secondary legislation. This aspect of public law is increasingly important given the growth of secondary legislation and the scant scrutiny that Parliament is able to give to such delegated legislation.

The number of pieces of secondary legislation passed every year has increased in the past five decades. This is compounded by the fact that the average length of each piece of delegated legislation has also grown dramatically in the same period. Figures 5.2 and 5.3[10] depict the growth in the number of statutory instruments (the main form of delegated legislation) in recent years and the number of pages contained within those statutory instruments.[11,12,13]

Figures 5.2 and 5.3 demonstrate that while the number of UK SIs has doubled in 20 years, the number of pages has increased sixfold. This growth, when coupled with the concurrent exponential growth in the average length of Acts of Parliament,[14] has put increased pressure

---

10 See www.legislation.gov.uk/uksi.

11 This does not include other forms of SI, including those in Wales and Northern Ireland.

12 Based on data in Richard Cracknell, 'Acts and Statutory Instruments: the Volume of UK Legislation 1850–2014' (2014, Standard Note) SN/SG/2911.

13 These are the total number of pages passed in the years specified. Based on the data in the parliamentary note based on data in Richard Cracknell, 'Acts and Statutory Instruments: the Volume of UK Legislation 1850–2014' (2014, Standard Note) SN/SG/2911. The last year for which data is available is 2009.

14 See previous chapter on primary legislation for detail on this point.

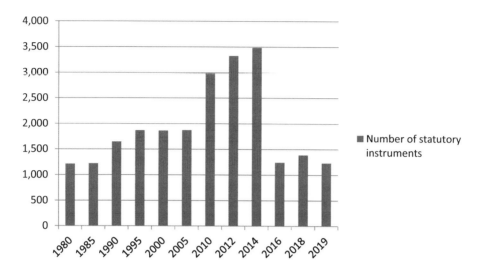

Figure 5.2 Number of Statutory Instruments 1980–2019

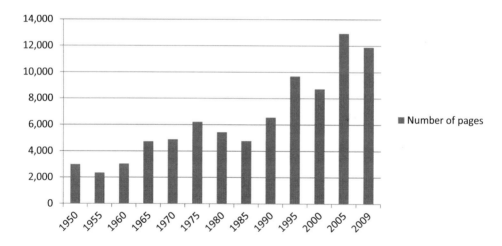

Figure 5.3 Number of Pages of Statutory Instruments 1950 – 2009

on the parliamentary process and has arguably led to a reduction in the effectiveness of scrutiny (a theme developed later in this chapter).

The charts also show a rapid contraction in the number of UK SIs laid between 2016 and 2019. This is undoubtedly a result of the Brexit negotiations which have had a stultifying effect on the legislative programme of the last two governments. It remains to be seen whether there will be a post-Brexit uplift in the volume of secondary legislation but one is expected given that the government will have significant powers to change existing legislation upon the UK leaving the EU.

Given the growth of secondary legislation, it would be easy to question whether it would be desirable to reduce the amount of such delegated legislation so that it can be properly scrutinised. However, and before making such a drastic judgment, it is important that we assess why delegated legislation is necessary. From this perspective we can see the relationship between competing interests of efficient and thorough scrutiny on the one hand and timely law-making on the other. The following section will explore the need for secondary legislation so that an informed judgment about its place in the English Legal System can be made.

NEED FOR SECONDARY LEGISLATION

Before discussing the procedure for passing delegated legislation it is important to understand why such legislation is necessary (Figure 5.4) and why it is not possible for Acts of Parliament to deal directly with the matters covered by secondary legislation. What follows is not intended to be exhaustive but to indicate why, as a matter of public policy, we may need at times to rely on delegated legislation.

DETAIL VS PRINCIPLE AND THE NEED FOR EXPERTISE

Secondary legislation complements primary legislation in that the latter deals with principles and the former with details. It is often the case that Parliament has neither the time nor the expertise to deal with some of the technical detail required for certain policy areas.

Figure 5.4 The Need for Secondary Legislation

The governance of education is a clear example of where Acts of Parliament leave much of the *detail* of regulation to secondary legislation, normally passed by the Secretary of State for Education. At the time of writing there were 30 pieces of secondary legislation concerned with education in the year 2019, compared with 63 in 2018 and 45 in 2017.[15] Although importance should not be inferred from the volume of secondary legislation alone,[16] it can be an indication of areas that lend themselves to secondary legislation. In relation to education, secondary legislation also provides for a further, linked, purpose and that is creating a regulatory framework for certain professions. Thus, there is secondary legislation on the system of performance management that is to applicable to teachers, as to include this level of detail in an Act of Parliament would be confusing and create a system that was difficult to change.[17]

UPDATING OF RULES

Sometimes it is difficult for Parliament to legislate for every situation and to foresee later developments that will change the context in which primary legislation is applied. Statutory instruments are useful, therefore, in providing flexibility in systems to allow for them to be updated. Similarly, where rules and procedures have a statutory basis but need to be altered annually then it would not make sense to pass a new Act of Parliament to achieve this. This last point is caveated with the fact that we do have a new Finance Act every year, however, owing to the changes made in the annual Budget delivered to Parliament by the Chancellor of the Exchequer when he plans the nation's annual expenditure each year. Updates to the tax codes that operate within the English Legal System are an example of the type of updating that is achieved primarily by secondary legislation.

EXPANSION OF THE STATE

Since the end of the Second World War in 1945 and partly in response to the Beveridge Report,[18] the ambit of what the Government is responsible for providing and regulating has significantly increased. This includes the establishment of the NHS, of various forms of social assistance[19] and the implementation of the National Insurance Scheme.[20] This broadening of the state required a whole series of institutions, processes and regulations to govern how the welfare system was to operate. It would not be practical for Parliament to manage and debate this level of detail. Even in more recent times, alterations and new schemes involving benefit payments have been achieved using secondary legislation. For example, the Government's controversial scheme that, on threat of sanction, forced people into unpaid periods of work

---

15 www.legislation.gov.uk/secondary?title=education.

16 There were, for example more than 1,200 pieces of secondary legislation governing trunk roads in 2013. www.legislation.gov.uk/secondary?title=trunk%20road.

17 The Education (School Teachers' Appraisal) (England) Regulations 2012, SI 2012/115.

18 William Beveridge, *Social Insurance and Allied Services* 1942.

19 Including Income Support, Council Tax Benefit, Jobseekers Allowance and the State Pension.

20 National Insurance Act 1946.

was achieved through secondary legislation[21] that was made on the basis of the Jobseeker's Act 1995.[22] Given the constantly evolving nature and the development of new schemes in areas such as social security, it would not be sensible for such matters to be subject to constant Acts of Parliament in order to change.

SPEED OF RESPONSE AND EMERGENCIES

At times, it is imperative that legislation is passed quickly. It may be that there is some emergency that requires a rapid response and to wait for Parliament to act through primary legislation would put in jeopardy some important public interest. Parliament spends a number of weeks of the year in 'recess'[23] and does not sit at these times. During these (sometimes very long) periods of recess MPs normally carry out constituency work. Moreover, even when sitting, it may be proper for decisions to be taken more quickly than the parliamentary process allows.

The Civil Contingencies Act 2004 provides for such powers to pass emergency secondary legislation. It allows *senior* members of the Government to pass secondary legislation at times of national emergency.[24] In this context a national emergency is one that threatens human welfare, will cause serious damage to the environment or in situations of war or times when terrorism threatens the security of the UK.[25]

TAKING THINGS FURTHER – POLITICISING THE CIVIL CONTINGENCIES ACT 2004

The website that accompanies this textbook demonstrates how Ministerial power can be used to weaponise delegated legislation. At the time of writing Parliament and Prime Minister Boris Johnson were locked in a fierce battle for power to control the process by which the United Kingdom left the European Union. Parliament had used *primary* law to pass the so-called Benn Act[26] which sought to force the Prime Minister to seek an extension[27] to the Brexit process in order to avoid the UK leaving the EU without a deal. One of the ways in which the Government was

21 Jobseekers Allowance (Employment, Skills and Enterprise Scheme) Regulations 2011, SI 2011/917. These regulations were successfully challenged in court in the case of R (Reilly) v Secretary of State for Work and Pensions [2013] UKSC 68, [2014] AC 453 for not providing the requisite details required by the Parent Act. This case is further discussed later.
22 Jobseekers Act 1995 s 17A.
23 Precise dates can be found at www.parliament.uk/about/faqs/house-of-commons-faqs/business-faq-page/recess-dates/recess.
24 Civil Contingencies Act 2004 s 20.
25 Civil Contingences Act 2004 s 1.
26 The European Union Withdrawal (No2) Act 2019.
27 Under Article 50 Treaty on European Union.

(allegedly)[28] looking to avoid the obligations of the Benn Act was by invoking the Civic Contingencies Act 2004.

The website contains a detailed analysis of the *primary* law and the *powers* given by the Civil Contingencies Act 2004, while also considering the merits and arguments surrounding this sort of use of powers to make delegated legislation.

TO IMPLEMENT EU LAW

As demonstrated in other chapters of this textbook, the European Union has played an integral part in the development of the English Legal System. This is equally true when it comes to a discussion of secondary legislation. European Union law, particularly those pieces passed in the form of directives, was often implemented not by primary legislation but by secondary legislation. The European Communities Act 1972 conferred upon Government Ministers powers to make secondary legislation:

> for the purpose of implementing any EU obligation of the United Kingdom, or enabling any such obligation to be implemented, or of enabling any rights enjoyed or to be enjoyed by the United Kingdom under or by virtue of the Treaties to be exercised.[29]

In light of more specific enabling Acts discussed earlier and later, the ECA 1972 gave quite broad powers to Ministers to pass secondary legislation implementing EU law obligations. Although there were limitations on what Ministers could do with the powers under the ECA,[30] the powers affected a number of very important policy areas and gave Ministers a great deal of discretion in how to implement EU law. For example, the EU passed a directive[31] in the early 1990s requiring its Member States to regulate maximum working hours and to ensure that there were adequate rest breaks and minimum periods of annual leave for workers. These rules were incorporated into the English Legal System via a piece of secondary legislation – the Working Time Regulations[32] – in 1998.

The UK left the European Union on the 31 January 2020 and entered into a transition period that will come to an end on 31 December 2020. During this time the effect of the European Communities Act 1972 is maintained and the intention is for the UK to use the transition period to negotiate a new trade deal with the EU. The time will also be used to prepare the statute book for the incorporation of EU law that is to be retained in national law. At the end of the transition period the powers of ministers to make legislation under the ECA 1972 (discussed previously) will disappear. This will not mean that the UK's (former) membership

---

28 There was heavy leaking of the plan from Downing Street.
29 European Communities Act 1972 s 2(2)(a).
30 These limitations, including those on taxation and criminal matters, can be found in Schedule 2 of the Act.
31 Directive 93/104/EC concerning certain aspects of the organization of working time [1993] OJ L307/18.
32 The Working Time Regulations 1998, SI 1998/1833.

of the EU will cease to be of relevance to secondary legislation. Indeed, untangling the EU and English legal systems will be partly achieved through secondary legislation.

As is discussed in chapter 16, the Brexit process has brought new powers to Government ministers to pass secondary legislation 'necessary' to address issues caused by Brexit during the transition period and beyond. Many of these powers are contained within the European Union (Withdrawal) Act 2018 and include so-called Henry VIII powers (discussed elsewhere in this chapter) to pass regulations that amend primary legislation. These powers can be found in s 8(1) of the EU(W)A. The section allows ministers to take measures to deal with 'deficiencies' in retained EU law and to remedy any 'failure of EU law to operate effectively'.

The concerns, about effective scrutiny and accountability, with the use of Henry VIII clauses more generally are brought into sharp focus when considering their use in a Brexit context. This has two dimensions. One is the staggering breadth of areas that may be subject to change using the powers of the EU(W)A. This is due to the fact that membership of the EU covered a broad range of policy areas. The second dimension relates to the potential volume of secondary legislation that may pass through parliamentary processes in the months of the transition period. When these two dimensions converge it becomes apparent that significant parts of English law may be subject to change by ministers with only partial scrutiny by Parliament. This raises significant concerns about accountability and legitimacy. There is something of an irony in the fact that the Leave campaign's mantra of 'taking back control' of English laws may be put in some doubt if power rests not with Parliament but with government ministers.

There are some limitations on the use of s 8 powers – s 8(7) states that the powers cannot be used, inter alia, to create a criminal offence, impose or increase taxations or establish a new public body. Even with these limitations, the powers are far-reaching and a keen eye will need to be kept on how the executive choose to use them.

TYPES OF SECONDARY LEGISLATION

So far this chapter has sought to discuss secondary legislation as a single concept. However, there are various different types of secondary legislation that serve different purposes and seek to address different needs.

ORDERS IN COUNCIL

Orders in Council are made directly on the authority of the Queen. They are formally passed by the Privy Council in the name of the monarch. There are two recognised forms of Orders in Council, those with a statutory basis (discussed later as part of the section on statutory instruments) and those with no statutory basis.

Those that are passed without statutory authority – prerogative Orders in Council – have the force of primary legislation. Although, as previously mentioned, there is a formal role for the Privy Council, the measures are normally proposed by the Government. Orders in Council made under the prerogative powers are often used in relation to those who are seen to have some sort of relationship with the Crown. In the GCHQ[33] case, for example, there were prerogative powers embodied through an Order in Council that allowed the Secretary of State for the Civil Service to alter the terms and conditions of employment of civil servants. Similarly, there are prerogative powers to pass Orders in Council in relation to appointments to certain public offices and to certain positions within the Church of England. In the modern context, the most important prerogative Orders in Council relate to international relations and the powers to enter into binding international treaties. Recent Orders in Council passed under prerogative powers have also included making changes to the Royal Charters that govern various universities.[34]

STATUTORY INSTRUMENTS

The majority of delegated legislation is achieved through the use of so-called statutory instruments (SIs). These are passed under the authority of an Act of Parliament (the Parent Act) and are numbered consecutively by the year in which they were made.

The use of such delegated legislation is governed by the Statutory Instruments Act 1946. This Act defines statutory instruments as the *expression* of the exercise of a power conferred on the Queen or a Minister by an Act of Parliament to 'make, confirm or approve orders, rules, regulations or other subordinate legislation'.[35] Thus statutory instruments are the documented exercise of powers conferred by statute on the Queen or her Ministers.[36] The Statutory Instruments Act 1946 also makes provision for the numbering, printing and publication for sale of SIs. As discussed later in this chapter, the Statutory Instruments Act 1946 also plays an important part in laying down the procedure for Parliament to scrutinise and approve/reject statutory instruments.

TAKING THINGS FURTHER – USING LEGISLATION.GOV.UK

Examples of statutory instruments can be found on the Government's legislation website.[37] This allows you to browse SIs by year or search for specific SIs on specific topics. Visiting the website frequently will give you an idea of the sorts of issues that can be governed by SIs. For example, if you search for the word 'education' then you will see

---

33 *Council of Civil Service Unions v Minister for the Civil Service* [1985] AC 374 (HL).

34 In July 2014 the Charters of the University of Bath and Surrey were altered by Orders in Council.

35 Statutory Instruments Act 1946 s 1(1).

36 Including Ministers of the devolved institutions of Scotland, Wales and Northern Ireland.

37 www.legislation.gov.uk/uksi.

that there are more than 2,500 SIs relating to education. It is unlikely that you will need to know the detailed substance of any of these SIs but (quickly) reading some of them will give a clear insight into the way in which SIs are used and the way in which they are drafted.

Each SI opens with a statement that indicates *who* is making use of the delegated powers and under the authority of which Act the use of power is being made. All SIs also come with Explanatory Memoranda. The purpose of the Explanatory Memoranda is to:

- Set out the *objective(s)* of the SI.
- Explain the *context* of the SI (including its relationship with other pieces of delegated legislation).
- Set out the *territorial scope* of the SI and confirm, where necessary, its compliance with the European Convention on Human Rights.
- Include a statement on the *policy* behind the SI. This is particularly useful as it is easy to view legal provisions in a vacuum and thus overlook the political context within which they are adopted.
- Where public *consultation* has taken place, the Explanatory Memoranda will explore the themes of the responses and also any changes made to the SI in light of those changes.
- Set out any details of *impact assessments* (on business, charities and the public sector).

Just as 'secondary legislation' is a blanket term that covers a host of different measures, the term 'statutory instrument' can also be used to describe a number of different pieces of secondary legislation. The rest of this section explores the major forms of statutory instrument that exist within the English Legal System.

COMMENCEMENT ORDERS

As was discussed in the previous chapter of the textbook, Acts of Parliament frequently do not come into force on the day that they receive Royal Assent. Indeed, individual sections of Acts may come into force at different times. The coming into force of a section, set of sections or whole Acts of Parliament is governed by a form of statutory instrument called 'commencement orders'. For example, section 56 of the Crime and Courts Act 2013 (which governs driving while having a controlled drug in your system) came into force in March 2015 as a result of a commencement order passed in 2014.[38]

The original Act will delegate powers to pass commencement orders, normally to Ministers. There are around 150 commencement orders passed in each year. Leaving the control of commencement to Ministers may mean that Acts, despite being validly passed, will never come into force. The most famous of these, as discussed in the previous chapter, is the Easter Act 1928 which is still awaiting a commencement order.

---

38 The Crime and Courts Act 2013 (Commencement No 1) (England and Wales) Order 2014, SI 2014/3268.

There are times where leaving to a Minister the decision as to the commencement of an Act can risk abuse of powers. This is well-illustrated by the *ex parte Fire Brigades Union*[39] case.

EXPLAINING AND ANALYSING THE LAW – ABUSE (AND NON-USE) OF COMMENCEMENT ORDERS

In this case the Government maintained certain non-statutory powers to compensate the victims of crime. In order to place the scheme on a more transparent foundation, Parliament passed the Criminal Justice Act 1988 which was designed, *inter alia*, to provide a new *statutory* scheme for compensation. The relevant sections[40] of the CJA were to be brought into force through a commencement order. The Secretary of State refused to bring forward a commencement order and continued to rely upon the old non-statutory powers to develop a new tariff of compensation.

The House of Lords, in *ex parte Fire Brigades Union*, was asked whether the Secretary of State's action was unlawful due to an abuse of power (i.e. the refusal to bring forward commencement). The issue was whether a Secretary of State had the ultimate and unfettered discretion to refuse ever to bring forward a commencement order or whether he just had the power to decide when commencement would happen. This is an important point and links to some of the issues discussed elsewhere in this chapter on the *scrutiny* of secondary legislation.

In deciding the case, the judiciary had to consider the *purpose* of secondary legislation and the role of Parliament and the executive in the execution of law. The House of Lords held that those with the discretion to introduce secondary legislation could not completely refuse to exercise that discretion as this would 'frustrate the will of Parliament expressed in a statute'.[41] Ministers needed to keep their minds open to the possibility of commencing an Act and should not introduce new schemes that were incompatible with the scheme foreseen by the statute.

This finding tells us two important things about the law-making process. First, the use of secondary law by Government Ministers is about a *separation of functions* between Parliament and the executive. The powers of the latter are subservient to the powers of the former. Secondly, the courts are charged with the duty of ensuring that the powers conferred by Parliament are not abused. This form of judicial scrutiny is explored in greater detail later in this chapter.

39 *R v Secretary of State for the Home Department ex parte Fire Brigades Union* [1995] 2 AC 513 (HL).
40 In particular Criminal Justice Act 1988 ss 108–117.
41 Fn39, 552 (Lord Browne-Wilkinson).

ORDERS IN COUNCIL

Orders in Council that stem from the prerogative powers of the Crown are discussed earlier. In addition, there are also Orders in Council that come in the form of statutory instruments. This means that their use is governed by the Statutory Instruments Act 1946. They have, traditionally, been used in relation to important matters of state such as those pertaining to the devolved institutions. For example, from the 1970s through to the turn of the century, a substantial amount of legislation passed for Northern Ireland was achieved via Orders in Council. These were used at times when the Parliament of Northern Ireland was suspended and overall control of the region was reverted to Westminster. An Order in Council will be made via statutory instrument (as opposed to the prerogative) where the powers granted to the Crown stem from an Act of Parliament. In relation to the situation in Northern Ireland, the power to pass Orders in Council in the form of statutory instruments came from the Northern Ireland (Temporary Provisions) Act 1972.[42]

REGULATIONS

Where an Act of Parliament leaves the detailed fleshing out of policy to statutory instruments the powers will frequently be exercised via regulations. This is important where an Act of Parliament creates a framework for a particular policy area or profession but where it does not have the capacity (or expertise) to create the detail. The governance and regulation of compulsory education and the teaching profession provide an excellent example of when regulations in the form of statutory instruments will be used.

EXPLAINING THE LAW – USING REGULATIONS TO
PROVIDE DETAIL: TEACHERS

The Education Act 2002 sets out certain requirements for schools. It is a fairly long Act with some 217 sections and 22 schedules. It establishes certain bodies related to the provision of education (such as the School Teachers' Review Body)[43] and sets the outline of the national curriculum[44] and the requirements for the governance of maintained schools[45] and independent schools.[46] Despite the length of the Act, it is only a *framework* and represents a fraction of the legislation needed to establish and maintain the environment for compulsory education.

---

42 Northern Ireland (Temporary Provisions) Act 1972 s 1(3). These powers were largely repealed by the advent of devolution in 1998. However, the Queen did retain certain powers to make Orders in Council in the form of statutory instruments in the Northern Ireland Act 1998 ss 84–86.

43 Education Act 2002 s 119.

44 Education Act 2002 ss 76–96.

45 Education Act 2002 ss 19–40.

46 Education Act 2002 ss 157–174.

As such, the Act delegates powers for some of the detail of the system to be created, maintained and amended by the Secretary of State for Education. This is achieved largely through the passage of regulations in the form of statutory instruments. For example, the arrangements by which teachers' performance in the classroom is assessed were laid down by regulations.[47] It would have been a poor use of parliamentary time to debate and consider a system of performance management for a single profession. It is much better, provided there is adequate parliamentary oversight, for the Department of Education to use their expertise to create such a system of appraisal.

As a side note, and to pick up a major theme of the textbook as a whole, although this section is about a specific type of statutory instrument, it is important not to lose sight of the fact that often different types of statutory instrument interact. Indeed, many Acts of Parliament envisage different forms of delegated powers and different ways of exercising those powers. For example, and still within the Education Act 2002, implementation of the working conditions and pay of teachers as recommended by the School Teachers' Review Body is achieved via an Order in Council.[48] The result is that, particularly where the policy area is complex, different types of SIs are used to achieve different purposes but they complement each other in the overall framework.

REMEDIAL ORDERS

Since the coming into force of the Human Rights Act 1998 in 2000, Ministers have acquired powers to make direct changes to primary legislation under limited circumstances.[49] If a court has declared a provision of UK law to be incompatible[50] with rights under the European Convention of Human Rights the powers of the Secretary of State are activated. An example of this happening was in relation to the Sexual Offences Act 2003 which was amended via a remedial order:the Sexual Offences Act 2003 (Remedial) Order 2012.[51]

EXPLAINING/ANALYSING/APPLYING THE LAW – REMEDIAL ORDERS UNDER THE HUMAN RIGHTS ACT 1998

The Sexual Offences Act 2003 contained provisions[52] for those convicted of certain sex offences to notify the police of their home address and of any plans to travel

---

47 Most recently the Education (School Teachers' Appraisal) (England) Regulations 2012, 2012/115.
48 Education Act 2002 s 120. An example of such an order is the School Teachers' Pay and Conditions Order 2014, SI 2014/2045.
49 Human Rights Act 1998 s 10.
50 Human Rights Act 1998 s 4.
51 The Sexual Offences Act 2003 (Remedial) Order 2012, SI 2012/1883.
52 Sexual Offences Act 2003 s 82.

abroad. Where the sentence was in excess of 30 months, the offender was subject to the notification requirement for an indefinite period of time. In the case of *F and Thompson (FC)*[53] it was held that the indefinite period of the requirement, with no opportunity for review, was incompatible with Article 8 of the European Convention on Human Rights. As such the Supreme Court issued a declaration of incompatibility under section 4 of the Human Rights Act 1998. This triggered the powers of the Home Secretary who passed a statutory instrument – in the form of a remedial order – to remove the inconsistency in the Act.[54] This was achieved by directly amending the Sexual Offences Act 2003 so that it allowed the opportunity for review.

From the perspective of the legal system, these remedial orders are interesting as they are a (rare) example of the different institutions of law-making working together in order to reform the law. The courts identify a problem (the inconsistency with an ECHR right), the Government proposes a solution (in the form of the order) and the legislature have the final say on whether to pass that solution into law (by affirming the remedial order). This has been described by some as a 'constitutional dialogue'[55] between the organs of state. This is a positive and welcome development but it is not without its controversies – some of which you will explore further if you undertake further study of constitutional law. The major criticisms come in two forms. First, that the power to issue such a declaration gives the judiciary a significant amount of power. Although a Government is not *legally* obliged to act upon such a declaration, there is a great deal of *political* force that will militate in favour of reform. Secondly, the constitutional 'dialogue' is not so much a dialogue as a series of events triggered with little *discussion* between the various branches of the state. Once the court has issued the declaration then the matter is essentially one for the Government, given that SIs are rarely rejected by Parliament.

The process for passing a remedial order is more involved than with passing a regular statutory instrument (as described in detail later). For this reason the use of remedial orders is relatively rare – at the time of writing there had been fewer than ten such orders issued. The most recent was the British Nationality Act 1981 (Remedial) Order 2019[56] following the Supreme Court decision in R(Johnson) v Secretary of State for the Home Department[57] on the incompatibility of the British Nationality Act 1981 with Article 14 of the ECHR.

----

53 F and Thompson (FC) v Secretary of State for the Home Department [2010] UKSC 17, [2011] 1 AC 331.

54 See the Sexual Offences Act 2003 (Remedial) Order 2012, SI 2012/1883.

55 Tom Hickman, 'Constitutional Dialogue, Constitutional Theories and the Human Rights Act 1998' (2005) Public Law 306.

56 The British Nationality Act 1981 (Remedial) Order 2019, SI 2019/1164.

57 [2016] UKSC 56, [2017] AC 365.

The Minister responsible must explain to Parliament the context that has, in that Minister's view, led to a need for a remedial order. The *proposal* for a draft remedial order must be laid before Parliament for 60 days, during which the Joint Committee on Human Rights will also report on the necessity and appropriateness of the order The Minister will also seek representations from interested parties during this time. After the 60 days has lapsed the Ministers will communicate to Parliament the nature of representations made and lay the draft order for a further 60 days after which the Minister will attempt to gain approval for a motion passing the order.

DEVOLUTION

To add a further level of complexity, in addition to UK statutory instruments, the devolved institutions are also able to make SIs. There are generally between 200 to 300 SIs issued by the Welsh National Assembly every year.[58] That compares with around double the number issued by the Scottish Parliament, reflecting, in part, the greater devolved powers that Scotland has.[59] Similarly, Northern Ireland makes between 300 and 500 SIs each year. The Welsh Assembly, the Northern Irish Assembly and Scottish Parliament are responsible for the oversight and scrutiny of statutory instruments in relation to non-reserved matters.

REGULATORY REFORM ORDERS AND CONTROL OF PUBLIC BODIES

The Legislative and Regulatory Reform Act 2006, which built on powers conferred in earlier Acts[60], allows Ministers to amend Acts of Parliament in order to promote efficiency in regulation and to reduce burdens on business and the economy. The provisions of Enabling Acts that empower Ministers to amend primary law are also known as 'Henry VIII clauses'.

EXPLAINING THE LAW – HENRY VIII CLAUSES

The Legislative and Regulatory Reform Act 2006 gives wide-ranging powers to Ministers to amend primary legislation but this does not give them *carte blanche* to amend primary law without safeguards. For example, the Act only allows Ministers to remove or reduce *burdens* on any person. Section 1 gives a relatively wide definition to the term 'burden', including 'a financial cost; an administrative inconvenience; an obstacle to efficiency, productivity or profitability; or a sanction, criminal or otherwise, which affects the carrying on of any lawful activity'.[61]

---

58 www.legislation.gov.uk/wsi.
59 www.legislation.gov.uk/ssi.
60 The Regulatory Reform Act 2001 and the Deregulation and Contracting Out Act 1994.
61 Legislative and Regulatory Reform Act 2006 s 1.

A Minister wishing to use the powers under the Act must also satisfy certain tests found within section 2. This has both positive and negative aspects. On the positive side, the use of a regulatory reform order **must**

1 Not be capable of being achieved via non-legislative means
2 Be proportionate to the aim of the policy
3 Strike a balance between the public interest and the impact on any individual

On the negative side, the use of a regulatory reform order **must not**

1 Remove necessary protection
2 Prevent the exercise of a right by another person who may have a legitimate expectation to exercise that right
3 Amend an Act that is of 'constitutional significance'

These tests, and the limitations on the *substantive* reach of such orders,[62] have the potential to act as a safeguard on the quite extraordinary powers to amend primary legislation.

The reduction of burdens on the economy may, at first hearing, sound like a perfectly reasonable proposition and removing *unnecessary* regulatory burdens on individuals or businesses is something to be welcomed. However, the Act is, and its predecessors were, controversial as they allow the Government to undo and change things done by Act of Parliament without Parliament always being able to scrutinise the change fully. It could be argued that if an Act of Parliament is defective then it is for *Parliament* and not the *Government* (in the form of a regulatory reform order) to remedy the problem. This is important as a matter of principle due to the legislative supremacy of Parliament and the constitutional rule that no other institution should be able to challenge or question the authority of Parliament.[63] As such, the *principle* behind regulatory reform orders and similar Henry VIII clauses has been criticised.[64]

The fear of regulatory reform orders is grounded on the precedent that it sets rather than the use to which the powers have been put. Regulatory reform orders have, thus far, been sparingly used (fewer than 100 since 2001) and there is little evidence that they have been abused. However, subsequent Acts of Parliament have been modelled on the LRRA. For example, the

---

62 They cannot be used, for example, to vary existing or introduce new taxes (s 5) or create or vary more serious criminal offences (s 6).

63 *British Railways Board v Pickin* [1974] AC 765 (HL) 'In earlier times many learned lawyers seem to have believed that an Act of Parliament could be disregarded in so far as it was contrary to the law of God or the law of nature or natural justice, but since the supremacy of Parliament was finally demonstrated by the Revolution of 1688 any such idea has become obsolete.' 782 (Lord Reid).

64 For the LRRA, see Tarunabh Khaitan, ''Constitution' as statutory term' (2013) 129 Law Quarterly Review 589, 597 and for Henry VIII clauses see Daniel Greenberg, 'Dangerous Trends in Modern Legislation' (2015) Public Law 96, 105.

Public Bodies Act 2011 is another, more recent example of an Enabling Act that contains significant powers given via Henry VIII clauses. The Act grants powers to Ministers to amend primary legislation to abolish, merge, amend and alter the powers of public bodies. Ostensibly about efficiency and disbanding needless 'quangos'[65] the original Bill contained insufficient safeguards. Amendments brought about during the passing of the Act significantly curtailed the potential abuse by introducing safeguards on the use of powers under the Act. For example, a Minister cannot use the powers to remove or move powers of a judicial nature; to remove enforcement mechanisms for obligations on Ministers; or to make changes to measures that act as scrutiny or oversight of actions of Ministers.[66] Similar to the LRRA 2006, the powers under the Public Bodies Act 2011 can only be used if the Minister is satisfied that changes are necessary for, *inter alia*, reasons of efficiency and economy.[67] Embodied in the Act is also a test of proportionality, meaning that use of the powers to abolish a public body must be appropriate and necessary for achieving the policy aim.[68] The inclusion of a proportionality test indicates that the use of any powers under the Act is subject to judicial review by the courts.

At the time of writing, the powers under the Public Bodies Act 2011 have been used on 22 occasions to abolish a wide variety of bodies, most recently the Advisory Committees on Pesticides and the Library Advisory Council for England.[69]

In summary, the 2006 and 2011 Acts are not dramatic in terms of their material scope and there are safeguards and restrictive tests that must be satisfied in order to use the powers within. It is always possible, should the powers be abused, to launch a judicial review in the courts to challenge the legality of a piece of secondary legislation. However, it is the creeping erosion of the role of Parliament in the law-making process that is problematic. In a system where the Government typically dominates the process, the increased use of Henry VIII clauses – that enable Ministers to change Acts of Parliament using delegated legislation – is concerning. This concern is exacerbated where Parliament's scrutiny of the use of such powers is weak. This is a point taken up later.

ANALYSING THE LAW – DISENTANGLING OUR MEMBERSHIP OF THE EUROPEAN UNION

The UK's decision to leave the European Union has brought into sharp focus the use of Henry VIII powers and the potential for abuse. The EU Withdrawal Act 2018 contains

---

65 Quangos (quasi-autonomous non-governmental organisations) were organisations to which the Government had devolved public law powers.

66 Public Bodies Act 2011 s 7.

67 Ibid. s 8. This has led to some speculation as to which bodies will be targeted by the use of the powers under the Act – see Stuart Bushell, 'In the balance' (2012) 156 Solicitors Journal 19, who argues to preserve the Legal Services Board which was the quango responsible for regulating the legal services field. The body was nonetheless replaced by the Legal Services Commission which was itself replaced by the Legal Aid Agency (LAA) on 1 April 2013.

68 Public Bodies Act 2011 s 7.

69 www.legislation.gov.uk/all?title=%22The%20Public%20Bodies%22%20abolition.

significant powers for the Government to make amendments to the statute book as a result of the UK's departure from the EU. The Government gains wide powers under s 8 to pass secondary legislation to prevent or remedy any 'failure of retained EU law to operate effectively' or 'any other deficiency in retained EU law'. These powers have been criticised for their potential to be abused. As of yet we do not know to what purpose these powers will be put (or how frequently) but it is part of a narrative that shows the limited effectiveness of parliamentary scrutiny in light of increasing powers of the Government.

The website that accompanies this textbook will contain an update on the powers of the Government post Brexit.

BYELAWS

Byelaws are primarily used as a method of achieving decentralised law-making. That is to say that they are normally passed by those with a strong connection with a particular area in order to regulate that area. As a result of this most byelaws are passed by local authorities. They are important for two reasons. They act as a form of subsidiarity[70] and bring decision-making closer to the individuals affected and are therefore more likely to engage the affected communities. Additionally, they allow for differentiation in that one rule or law may be appropriate as a solution in one area but not in another.

Like most other pieces of secondary legislation, byelaws are made under the authority of an Act of Parliament and the powers granted must be exercised in a manner consistent and compatible with a way that is in accordance with the Parent Act. A great number of byelaws made by local authorities[71] are made under the Local Government Act 1972. This Act, via section 235, enables councils to pass byelaws to ensure 'good rule and government and suppression of nuisances.' This may seem fairly wide-ranging but section 235 is a 'catch-all' provision that applies only where other Acts do not provide for powers to pass byelaws.[72] local authorities, therefore, have more specific powers to make byelaws under various Acts of Parliament. Table 5.1 gives some indication of the sorts of byelaws that can be passed, by a variety of persons, under the authority of various Acts of Parliament. Table 5.1 is not an exhaustive list of such powers but is presented in order to demonstrate the breadth of powers that can be made available via byelaws. These include the regulation of public services, the control of places of national strategic importance and the behaviour of people in specific locations.

---

70 A principle that action should be taken at the lowest level unless there are compelling reasons for it to be taken at a higher level.

71 For example, organisations like Transport for London and airport operators have powers to pass byelaws. The British Railway Board had also been given powers to pass byelaws by the Transport Act 1962 – for discussion of these byelaws see *Boddington v British Transport Police* [1999] 2 AC 143 (HL).

72 Local Government Act 1972 s 235(3).

Table 5.1 Examples of Powers Conferred through Byelaws

Enabling Act	Purpose of byelaws passed under authority of enabling Act
Town Police Clauses Act 1847, s 68	Regulating, inter alia, the conduct of hackney carriage drivers (taxi drivers) and the number of people that they can carry; fixing the rate of fares; dealing with lost property in hackney carriages.
Harbours, Docks and Piers Clauses Act 1847, s 18	Regulating, inter alia, the use of a harbour, dock or pier; the powers of the Harbour Master; admission of vessels into the harbour; warehousing etc.; regulating the use of fires or cranes or weighing machines.
Public Health Act 1875, s 164	Regulation of places of public recreation (such as public walks or pleasure grounds).
Military Lands Act 1892, s 14	The use of land held for military purposes, including securing the public against danger.
Public Health Acts Amendment Act 1907, s 82	Regulating the use of the seashore, including the erection of temporary structures (for example, booths or tents); sales taking place on the seashore; control of riding and driving.
Public Health Act 1936, s 231	Regulating public bathing, including the times during which bathing is permitted; clothing to be worn by bathers.
Public Libraries and Museums Act 1964, s 19	Regulating the use of libraries and museums, including the conduct of users.
Countryside Act 1968, s 41	Ensuring the protection of country parks, picnic sites from damage; maintaining public order.
Food Act 1984, s 60	Regulating market places, including buildings, stalls and pens; preventing obstructions; preventing spread of fires.
Airports Act 1986, s 63	Securing safety of aircraft; controlling operation of aircraft; prohibiting access to parts of the airport; restricting advertising.

(Continued)

Table 5.1 *(Continued)*

Enabling Act	Purpose of byelaws passed under authority of enabling Act
Land Drainage Act 1991, s 66	Securing efficient working of the drainage system.
Greater London Authority Act 1999, s 385	Ensuring proper management of Trafalgar Square and Parliament Square Garden by persons using those Squares.
Railways Act 2005, s 46	Regulating aspects of railway transport, including rules associated with ticketing; fare evasion; obstructions; conveyance of bicycles; prevention of nuisance; prohibition of smoking.
Broads Authority Act 2009, s 11	Registration of vessels; rules on exemptions from registration; timing of registration; setting of registration fees.

The importance of byelaws to those with delegated power lies in the fact that such people can only do things that they have expressly been given the powers to do. Thus, locating the precise nature of the power conferred, and the procedure to be followed, is crucially important to the validity of any byelaw passed. These byelaws made by local authorities must be 'confirmed' by Government,[73] after being published in local media. Given the number of local authorities and, by extension, the potential number of byelaws that apply across the geographical area covered by the English Legal System, there is a risk that law becomes inconsistent and unclear. In a bid to allow for some level consistency there has been a move to the use of model byelaws which Councils (or others) can use as a framework for making byelaws.

The growth of 'standard form' byelaws on things like the rules governing access to and use of public places raises the question as to whether the requirement of 'confirmation' by central Government is still a sensible use of ministerial time. There have been recent, limited proposals to alter the arrangements for certain byelaws and these can find their statutory basis in the Local Government Act 1972 that was amended by the Local Government and Public Involvement in Health Act 2007. The change allows for alternative processes of confirmation to be put into place for certain 'classes of byelaws'.[74] It is here that a difficult balance is to be drawn between full accountability and flexibility. The requirement of confirmation by a named Minister means that there is a chain of accountability (albeit indirect) between the Parent Act and the byelaw. The actions of the local authority would be held to account through the Ministers who themselves must answer to Parliament.

---

73 The system is different in Wales – see Local Government Byelaws (Wales) Act 2012. In Wales, byelaws can be made directly by 'legislating authorities' including councils but only after the formalities of the Act are satisfied.

74 Local Government Act 1972, s 236A.

Byelaws that create criminal offences are tried in a Magistrates' court and the punishment, determined by the specific byelaw, will be a fine typically at Level 2, 3 or 4 on the standard scale.[75] As a result, the breach of a byelaw will not lead to a custodial sentence. Where the proposed changes to the process of confirmation apply, there is also the potential for fixed term penalties to replace fines.

RULES, CODES OF CONDUCT AND CODES OF PRACTICE (TERTIARY LEGISLATION)

There is another category of legislation – normally referred to as 'tertiary' legislation – that covers extremely technical rules and procedures that govern a very narrow range of matters within a policy area. Although these powers stem from Acts of Parliament, their use receives little (or no) scrutiny from Parliament. It is typical, where tertiary legislation is appropriate, for the Parent Act to make provision for the making of regulations that can themselves further delegate powers to make rules.

The following contains some examples of the use of such tertiary legislation in the English Legal System:

- The rules that govern the operation of the powers of the Church of England are governed by rules developed (under statutory authority) by the leaders of the established church.
- There are also rules governing the minutiae of the tax and finance system. The Finance Act 2012 extended the powers of Her Majesty's Revenue and Customs to make provision for technical rules relating to VAT via tertiary legislation.[76]
- The Financial Services and Markets Act 2000, as amended by the Financial Services Act 2012, confers powers on the Financial Conduct Authority to make rules for the conduct of those covered by the Act.[77]
- The Police and Criminal Evidence Act 1984 permits the Secretary of State to develop codes of practice that the police must adhere to when exercising their powers under the Act.[78] The powers covered by such a code of conduct include those governing police search powers, detention and questioning and seizure of property.
- ACAS has powers under the Trade Union and Labour Relations (Consolidation) Act 1992 to issue Codes of Practice relating to the relationship between employers and trade union officials.[79] These codes are not legally binding but can be taken into consideration in any legal proceedings.[80]
- The exercise of powers under the Regulation of Investigatory Powers Act 2000 is also subject to Codes of Practice developed as tertiary legislation.

---

75 Currently, for England and Wales, between £500 and £2500. Criminal Justice Act 1982, s 37(2).

76 Finance Act 2012 Schedule 29.

77 Financial Services and Markets Act 2000 ss 137A–141A.

78 Police and Criminal Evidence Act 1984 s 66.

79 Trade Union and Labour Relations (Consolidation) Act 1992 s 199.

80 Ibid. s 207.

PASSAGE OF STATUTORY INSTRUMENTS

The passage of secondary legislation does not follow a single procedure, such as that which applies to primary legislation, and there are a number of ways in which it can be made. The important point to note is that the Act which authorises the passage of a particular piece of secondary legislation will also normally dictate the procedure to be followed.

Unlike Acts of Parliament, secondary legislation is not drafted by the Office of the Parliamentary Counsel but by individual Government Departments. This has the potential to cause problems in the consistency and quality of legislation. This is an aspect of secondary legislation that is discussed later. Once drafted, a statutory instrument is then completed or 'made' when it receives the signature of the person authorised by the Act to make such instruments. The majority of statutory instruments are required to be laid before Parliament either in draft form or, in some cases, after they have been 'made' by the relevant Minister. The Act of Parliament that authorises the making of a particular piece of secondary legislation will also determine the method by which Parliament shall approve the instrument.

Once statutory instruments have completed the procedure laid down in the Parent Act they are numbered consecutively in the year in which they are approved. The Proscribed Organisations (Name Changes) Order[81] was the 2,210th statutory instrument of 2014. It would therefore be labelled as SI 2014/2210.[82]

The rest of this section will explore the various procedures (Figure 5.5) that govern the passage of statutory instruments.

NEGATIVE RESOLUTION PROCEDURE

This is a passive form of approval in that it does not require specific action on the part of Parliament in order for the statutory instrument to become law. Under the negative resolution procedure, an SI will come into force unless there is a successful motion (in the form of a prayer directed to the Queen) to annul it. There are 40 days in which to secure a motion to annul the measure. Having said this, the successful passage of a motion does not of itself annul the measure and a measure that has been 'made' will remain effective until an Order in Council is passed to revoke it.[83] This further weakens the effectiveness of parliamentary scrutiny and could be said to undermine the legitimacy of secondary legislation. This is a theme discussed further on in relation to the problems caused by statutory instruments.

It is rare for statutory instruments to be prevented from coming into force via the negative resolution procedure. This is for two (interlinked) reasons. First, time to consider and debate such a motion in the Commons is extremely limited and in the hands of the Government. This

---

81 This Order added the 'Islamic State' as an alternative name for the terrorist group the 'Islamic State of Iraq and Syria' (ISIS) to the Terrorism Act 2000. This is an example of the 'updating' function of statutory instruments.

82 Full citation would be: the Proscribed Organisations (Name Changes) (No. 2) Order 2014, SI 2014/2210.

83 Statutory Instruments Act 1946 s 5(1).

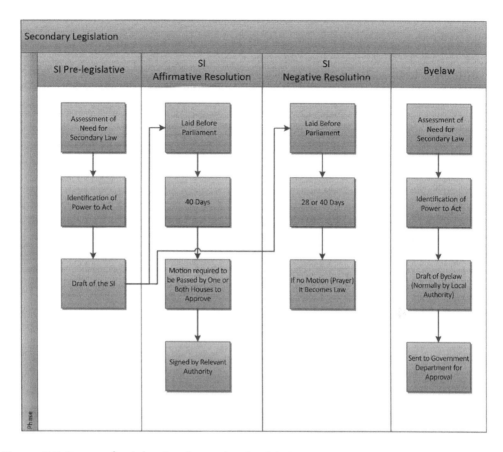

Figure 5.5 Process for Adopting Secondary Legislation

means that is not guaranteed that a negative motion, particularly if supported by only a small number of backbench MPs, would be given any parliamentary time. Secondly, the Government is likely to have a majority in the Commons and so any motion would require the Government's own backbenchers to vote against (or abstain) in any division on a negative motion. The last time a motion under the negative resolution procedure was successful was in the 1970s.[84] In this way, many of the problems caused by the dominance of Government discussed in the chapter on primary legislation are also relevant when talking about secondary legislation.

In 2017–2019 around 68% of draft SIs were required to be considered using the negative resolution procedure.

AFFIRMATIVE RESOLUTION PROCEDURE

This is a more rigorous process and requires a motion to be passed in both Houses[85] authorising the SI within a specified number of days (normally 40). Thus, unlike the negative

84 Paraffin (Maximum Retail Prices) (Revocation) Order 1979, SI 1979/797.
85 Or, in the case of SIs related to financial matters, the House of Commons only.

resolution procedure, scrutiny is active in that it requires action on the part of Parliament for the SI to become law. Given the stricter requirements, SIs which require an affirmative resolution tend to be on more important issues that should not come into force by default but that should be subject to active scrutiny by Parliament.

As with the negative resolution procedure, there is little opportunity for Parliament to amend the SI and they must approve it or reject it in its entirety. Again, much like the negative resolution procedure, it is rare for an SI not to pass the necessary procedure to become law. The last time that an SI failed to receive approval under the affirmative resolution procedure was in the late 1960s when Parliament rejected the draft version of the Parliamentary Constituencies (England) Order in the Winter of 1969.

ANALYSING THE LAW – A CLOSER LOOK AT PARLIAMENTARY SCRUTINY

What made that rejection of the draft Parliamentary Constituencies Order of 1969 even more extraordinary (and indeed a parliamentary first) was that the Home Secretary who laid the Orders before Parliament also argued that they should not be passed.[86] The failure to secure the passage of the Parliamentary Constituencies Order in 1969 is a reminder of the *political* context within which law operates. The orders in question concerned proposed changes to the development and make-up of electoral constituencies. The Labour Home Secretary in that instance – James Callaghan – laid the secondary legislation before Parliament based on the recommendations of the Boundary Commission. For a number of reasons, including the perceived bias against the Labour Party,[87] he then went on to recommend that Parliament not approve the Orders.

This saga had followed on from a failed Labour Bill to redraw the electoral map in the previous session[88] and is indicative of the politics that are involved with law-making. We should be careful not to make assumptions about the route that legislation will follow based solely on a bald reading of the Act in question. It would have been easy to assume in the preceding scenario that a piece of legislation proposed by the Government would be supported by that Government.

Figure 5.6 details the split in the proportions of draft SIs considered by the House of Lords Secondary Legislation Scrutiny Committee in the latest completed session 2017–2019.[89]

Figure 5.6 demonstrates that the vast majority of SIs are approved using the negative resolution procedure. Parliament plays only a passive role under that procedure. This is then

86 HC Deb 12 November 1969, vol 791, cols 428–432.
87 Ibid. cols 436, 451, 453.
88 That had been wrecked by the House of Lords.
89 For a more detailed report, see https://publications.parliament.uk/pa/ld201719/ldselect/ldsecleg/426/42603.htm.

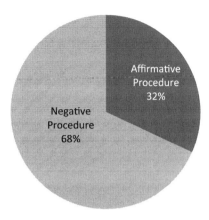

Figure 5.6 Proportion of Negative and Affirmative Procedures in the 2017–2019 Session

compounded by the sheer number of SIs passed in a session. These two factors combined lead to serious questions being asked about the effectiveness of the scrutiny of law-making in the English Legal System.

SCRUTINY OF DELEGATED LEGISLATION

A theme of both law-making chapters of this textbook is the extent to which legislation is properly scrutinised before it becomes law. Both primary and secondary legislation are subject to control and scrutiny from Parliament and others. This is particularly important for delegated legislation as, without the involvement of Parliament, there is a risk that the democratic link to the people is lost. This would undermine the *legitimacy* of legislation. The rest of this section will explore not only the way in which scrutiny happens but also the *effectiveness* of those scrutiny mechanisms.

It should be noted from the outset that statutory instruments – the major form of delegated legislation – find their basis in an Act of Parliament. Thus, Parliament has made an active choice to provide for such delegation and the creation and control of those powers are in the hands of Parliament. Those granted powers under such an Act cannot go further than the Act permits. As such, a well-drafted Parent Act can go a long way to reducing the risk of abuse.

COMMITTEES OF PARLIAMENT

As well as the formal process required for the passage of secondary legislation, there is also additional scrutiny by a system of committees in Parliament. These provide a more detailed process of scrutiny than is possible in the limited time available in the Main Chamber of the Commons or Lords. There are numerous committees that undertake different tasks in relation to scrutinising pieces of delegated legislation. The purpose of these committees is to provide a complete system of scrutiny that is based on the distinct separation of functions between the legislature and the executive. In this way, Parliament is able to act as a check on the powers of the Government.

The remainder of this section will explore the major parliamentary committees that are involved in scrutinising the use of delegated legislation. These include:

- The Joint Committee on Statutory Instruments
- Delegated Legislation Committees
- House of Lords Secondary Legislation Committee (formerly the Committee on the Merits of Statutory Instruments)
- Departmental Select Committees

JOINT COMMITTEE ON STATUTORY INSTRUMENTS (JCSI)

The JCSI is a Committee of both the Commons and the Lords and its primary function is to draw the attention of the Houses to specific aspects of statutory instruments that have been laid before Parliament. As a Joint Committee it draws its membership from both the Commons and the Lords. It meets weekly and its reports can be found on Parliament's website.[90] JCSI operates under the Standing Orders of Parliament – Orders 74 [Lords] and 151 [Commons][91] control its structure and governance.[92]

The basis for referring SIs to the special attention of both Houses includes:

- If it imposes a charge on the public revenues or contains powers to raise revenue for the Government or any public authority
- If the measure is to be excluded from review by the courts
- That the SI seems to have retrospective effect and the Parent Act does not provide for such effect
- That there has been an unjustifiable delay in publication of the SI
- That there has been an unjustifiable delay in informing Parliament of any measure that has been made without first having been laid before Parliament
- That there is doubt as to whether the measure is within the powers granted by the Parent Act or where the use of powers is unusual or unexpected in light of the purpose of the Parent Act
- That the measure requires further clarification
- Defective drafting – if JCSI notices that there are grammatical, typological or linguistically illogical aspects to the SI[93]

90 www.parliament.uk/business/committees/committees-a-z/joint-select/statutory-instruments/news/new-committee-established.
91 www.publications.parliament.uk/pa/cm201314/cmstords/900/toc.htm.
92 www.publications.parliament.uk/pa/ld/ldstords/147/14701.htm.
93 These can be found in Standing Orders 74(2) and 151(1) for the Lords and Commons respectively.

The preceding is not an exhaustive list and the Committee can consider any other issues
provided that they do not impinge upon the policy behind the measure. As such, the major
limitation on the remit of JCSI is that it is **not** intended to review the *merits* of particular SIs
but rather to highlight those that are likely to be controversial in terms of their material scope
or the use to which the powers are intended to be put. This limitation significantly impacts
upon JCSI's ability to scrutinise secondary legislation but this should be viewed in light of the
role of other committees in the scrutiny process.

MAKING CONNECTIONS – RETAINING AN 'HOLISTIC' APPROACH
+ +
When studying law we must remember that the legal system is in fact a series of
systems working alongside each other. When assessing how effectively a *particular*
committee operates in relation to its task of scrutiny, it is important not to judge that
committee in isolation but to look at the *whole system of scrutiny*. This means that
you should read this particular section of the text on the JCSI in conjunction with the
sections on the other parliamentary committees who *do* have the power to consider
the merits of a secondary legislation.

The primary purpose of JCSI is to raise red flags against specific SIs for Parliament (and the
Department responsible for drafting) to examine. This is important in relation to securing
effective protection of the rule of law, particularly where it is proposed that a measure is to
have retrospective effect or where it seeks to exclude judicial review. It leaves substantive
scrutiny of merits to other bodies and to the parliamentary processes outlined previously.
Although separating the scrutiny of the form of the legislation (as JCSI does) from the
substance/merits of that secondary legislation (functions performed by other committees)
risks fragmentation, it also leads to a degree of specialisation. By having JCSI look only at
the limited range of issues which are routinely within its somewhat superficial remit, an
opportunity is missed to flag up content which might usefully be reconsidered by the relevant
Department.

If an SI is not required to be presented to both Houses then the Commons has a Select
Committee on Statutory Instruments that performs the same function as the JCSI and that
draws its membership from the MPs who serve on JCSI.

DELEGATED LEGISLATION COMMITTEES (DLCS)

Delegated Legislation Committees are the mechanism through which the majority of the
substance of secondary law is scrutinised by the House of Commons. In this regard they have
much in common with the Public Bill Committees that scrutinise primary law.[94] Unlike the
JCSI and Select Committee on Statutory Instruments, the DLCs have the power to look at the
substance, merit and policy underlying a particular piece of secondary legislation.

---

94 Refer to Chapter 4 for more detail on the scrutiny of primary law.

Much like Public Bill Committees, the rationale for having DLCs to consider secondary legislation is for reasons of efficiency. The time on the floor of the House is limited and a committee structure allows the full detail of the legislation to be considered in a way that, for reasons of time, would not be otherwise possible. DLCs are composed of 17 members of the Commons but any member may attend and speak. The members of the DLC vote on the principle of the piece of secondary legislation, which is then returned to the Commons. If the measure is to be passed using the affirmative resolution procedure then there will be no further debate on the floor of the Commons and a vote will follow.

HOUSE OF LORDS SECONDARY LEGISLATION SCRUTINY COMMITTEE (SLSC)

The House of Lords Secondary Legislation Scrutiny Committee was previously known, from 2003 until the start of the 2010–2012 parliamentary session, as the Committee on the Merits of Statutory Instruments. It consists of 11 members and, unlike the Commons DLCs, has a fixed membership. Similarly to the DLCs of the House of Commons, the House of Lords SLSC looks at the merits and substance of measures and refers those that meet certain criteria to the Main Chamber of the Lords.[95] The Committee performs this role alongside ensuring that Public Body Orders (discussed previously) satisfy the relevant statutory tests relating to improving efficiency, effectiveness and securing appropriate accountability of Ministers.[96]

The grounds for referring a piece of secondary legislation for special attention are laid out as follows.

(a) That it is politically or legally important or gives rise to issues of public policy likely to be of interest to the House

(b) That it may be inappropriate in view of changed circumstances since the enactment of the Parent Act

(c) That it may inappropriately implement European Union legislation

(d) That it may imperfectly achieve its policy objectives

(e) That the explanatory material laid in support provides insufficient information to gain a clear understanding about the instrument's policy objective and intended implementation

(f) That there appear to be inadequacies in the consultation process which relates to the instrument[97]

---

95 www.parliament.uk/business/committees/committees-a-z/lords-select/secondary-legislation-scrutiny-committee/role/tofref.

96 The tests within Public Bodies Act 2011 s 8.

97 www.parliament.uk/business/committees/committees-a-z/lords-select/secondary-legislation-scrutiny-committee/role/tofref.

In the 2017–2019 session the Committee dealt with some 1,876 measures and brought around 7.8% of these to the attention of the House of Lords, predominantly on the basis that they were of great political importance or affected an important matter of public policy.[98]

The European Union (Withdrawal) Act 2018 conferred upon Ministers significant powers to pass delegated legislation deemed necessary to deal with the consequences of Brexit. Some provisions give a choice to Ministers as to whether they lay as part of the affirmative procedure or the negative procedure. To ensure that important changes are subject to scrutiny where Ministers seek to choose the *negative* procedure, the Committee can recommend[99] 'upgrading' to the affirmative procedure and did so on 45 (out of a possible 247) occasions. This represents almost one in five affected instruments being recommended for upgrading.[100]

The SLSC is seen as a particularly effective form of scrutiny, partly due to its fixed membership including a number of cross-bench Lords. It has given, in recent times, some fairly strongly worded reports that are very critical of certain policies and of the approach of specific government departments to secondary law. One clear example of the strength of criticism can be seen in the 28th Report of the Committee when it considered certain 'town and country' regulations that paved the way for highly controversial 'fracking'[101] operations.[102] The SLSC criticised the lack of time given to Parliament to consider such a contentious issue fully and the short period of consultation before the measure was laid.[103] The Committee also felt that the Government's consideration of cost to the public sector was 'fragmentary and apparently inconsistent'.[104] It could be argued that the scrutiny in this case was ineffective as the measures under review still became law. However, the pressure of the SLSC led to more detailed guidance and information being provided by the Government and further raised the profile of the issue amongst the public.[105]

The Committee does not restrict itself to commenting only on specific measures but has been known to comment on the general *quality* of secondary legislation. For example, in its 51st Report of the 2017–2019 Session, the Committee made comments relating to the rise in the number of correcting instruments (those measures that are passed to correct previous pieces of secondary legislation that were defectively drafted) and gave some rather scathing criticism of the *quality* of delegated legislation emanating from certain Government Departments.[106]

---

98 https://publications.parliament.uk/pa/ld201719/ldselect/ldsecleg/426/42603.htm, para 3.

99 But cannot compel the Minister to change the procedure.

100 https://publications.parliament.uk/pa/ld201719/ldselect/ldsecleg/426/42603.htm.

101 Fracking is the alternative name for hydraulic fracturing, a controversial means of extracting natural gas from rocks.

102 Secondary Legislation Scrutiny Committee, *Twenty-Eighth Report* (HL 2010–2014, 28 January 2014).

103 Ibid. para 6. The Committee noted that the measure was given less time for consultation than Government best practice would have suggested was necessary – 12 weeks as opposed to the six weeks actually given.

104 Ibid. para 13.

105 Emily Gosden, 'Pro-fracking Planning Reforms Rushed Through Despite Strong Opposition, Lords Warn' *The Telegraph* (London, 29 January 2014), www.telegraph.co.uk/news/earth/energy/fracking/10605859/Pro-fracking-planning-reforms-rushed-through-despite-strong-opposition-Lords-warn.html.

106 Secondary Legislation Scrutiny Committee, *Fifty First Report* (HL 2017–2019, 11 June 2019). The Committee noted that Government Departments were not giving adequate time for full scrutiny and lamented the generally poor nature of the Explanatory Memorandum.

The Committee, in its 2017–2019 Report criticised the:

- Continued bundling of significant and low priority amendments together
- Quality of documentation, particularly for Explanatory Memoranda
- Lack of detailed consultation or analysis of consultation[107]
- Number and type of corrections, which had risen sharply to 8%

This is important as the solution to each of these problems is in the gift of the Government (i.e. those being subject to scrutiny) and yet such issues directly impact on the effectiveness of the working of the Committee in holding the Government to account. The SLSC has not shied away from the issue and has been trying to hold the Government to account not only for the substance of individual pieces of secondary legislation but the whole efficacy of the system of delegated legislation, indicating general examples of 'poor practice'.[108]

ANALYSING THE LAW – EFFECTIVENESS OF THE 'SYSTEM' OF SCRUTINY

Previously, this chapter warned against studying the work of individual committees in isolation. The SLSC also noted this reality by commenting on the number of correcting instruments used. They recognise that drafting errors are within the remit of the JCSI (discussed previously) but also noted that such errors led to great inconvenience for other committees who may need to consider two or three versions of a statutory instrument.[109] The SLSC also commented that multiple versions (caused by corrections of poor drafting) are liable to reduce the clarity of information available for individuals who may be affected by the law.[110]

Despite the strong criticisms of the end of session report in multiple sessions these problems recurred in 2017–2019 and were exacerbated by the pressures caused on resources as a result of the planning process for the UK leaving the European Union.

DEPARTMENTAL SELECT COMMITTEES (DSCS)

The work of Government is, as was discussed in a previous chapter, split between different departments who have responsibility for various policy areas. The late 1970s saw a rise in demand for a stronger system of accountability of these departments to the House of Commons.[111] As a result of this demand the 'Departmental Select Committees' were created

107 Ibid. para 30.
108 Ibid. footnote 59 where it was noted that one SI was missing a commencement date!
109 Secondary Legislation Scrutiny Committee, *Forty Second Report* (HL 2013–2014, 13 May 2014), para 23, citing the measures emanating from the Home Office as being particularly problematic in this regard.
110 Ibid. para 22.
111 Select Committee on Procedure, *First Report* (HC 1977–1978, 588-I).

in 1979. Although their remit is not restricted to (or even focussed on) scrutiny of delegated legislation, they have a broad remit to scrutinise the work of Government. This includes the ability to examine the policies of the department, to look at the expenditure of the department, to examine the administration of the department and to produce reports for debate in the House of Commons.[112]

The Departmental Select Committees, as a result of their close work of the departments of Government, have unparalleled knowledge of the workings of central Government and of the particular department to which they are aligned. They can call witnesses and often question Ministers. This complements the work of the other Committees discussed and adds experience and expertise of particular policy areas. They are mentioned here not because they perform specific functions in relation to delegated legislation but rather because they have a more general role in relation to scrutinising the work of Government. This could take the form of post-legislative reviews of how particular SIs are operating in practice and how well they are achieving their policy aims.

JUDICIAL SCRUTINY OF DELEGATED LEGISLATION

The analysis has so far focussed on the parliamentary process of scrutiny of delegated legislation. In addition to the committee structure of Parliament, the courts also play an important role in checking on the powers of the executive (normally the Government) when they make law. Individuals are able to challenge measures on the basis that they are *ultra vires* – that is that the measure is unlawful because the person passing it acted outside of the powers conferred by the Parent/Enabling Act.

> MAKING CONNECTIONS – THE INSTITUTIONAL BALANCE AND PUBLIC LAW
> +
> There are two interrelated connections to be made here that will enhance understanding of the role of judges in this area.
>
> First, it is important to realise that judges have a constitutional responsibility to prevent abuse of power by the executive – it is a facet of both the separation of powers and the rule of law.[113] That constitutional duty finds its expression most clearly in the doctrines and principles of judicial review. For this reason, it is likely that any further study you may make of constitutional or administrative law will have a particular focus on judicial review.
>
> Secondly, through judicial review, judges are supporting another constitutional principle, namely parliamentary sovereignty. Delegated legislation, though often *proposed* by those holding ministerial posts, is *passed* under the *authority* of

---

112 Select Committee on the Modernisation of the House of Commons, *First Report* (HC 2001–2002, 224-II), para 35.
113 For more on the rule of law, see Tom Bingham, *The Rule of Law* (Penguin 2011).

Parliament. Judges are therefore aiming to uphold the will and intention of Parliament when questioning secondary legislation.

When we take the preceding two points together, we can comment on the distinction between the courts' treatment of primary and secondary legislation. You should remember, from the previous chapter, that judges cannot question the validity of an Act of Parliament (i.e. primary legislation).[114] We can contrast this with the American Legal System where judges of the Supreme Court *can* challenge Acts of Congress.[115] This is because the courts recognise the sovereignty of Parliament within the English Legal System. Indeed, this is one of the core principles of the uncodified British constitution. The same is not true of delegated legislation, which is passed under parliamentary authority but proposed and executed by 'another'. This allows courts to question whether the person who was delegated powers has *exercised* those powers in compliance with parliamentary intent.

Scrutiny by judges, through the medium of judicial review, is an integral part of the complete *system* of monitoring secondary legislation. Much of the work of the parliamentary committees, discussed previously, is what may be termed pre-legislative scrutiny – this means that scrutiny happens in advance of the piece of secondary legislation being brought into force. Judicial review complements this by adding a system of post-legislative scrutiny – this means that scrutiny happens subsequent to the coming into force of the piece of secondary legislation.

An important point to note about judicial review is that it is not necessarily intended for judges to pass comment or judgment on the *quality* or *substance* of secondary law but rather to check whether it complies with the requirements of primary law. This has been expressed by Lord Donaldson in *ex parte Hammersmith and Fullham LBC*[116] as follows:

> The referee is only involved when it is appears that some player has acted in breach of the rules. The referee may then stop the play and take some remedial action, but, tempting though it may be, it is not for him to express any view on the skill of the players or, how he would have acted in their position. Still less, following a breach of the rules does he take over one of the positions of the players.[117]

Judicial review is an excellent example of the multidimensional nature of law-making in the English Legal System as it shows the institutions interacting (Parliament, Government Ministers and the judiciary) and how the various sources of law also interact (statute, secondary law and case law).

....

114 *British Railways Board v Pickin* [1974] AC 765 (HL).
115 *Marbury v Madison* (1803) 5 US 137.
116 *R v Secretary of State for the Environment, ex parte Hammersmith and Fulham London Borough Council and Others* [1991] 1 AC 521 (HL).
117 Ibid. 561 (Lord Donaldson).

As mentioned previously, a judicial review claim can be launched on the basis of numerous grounds. Those of most relevance to a text on the English Legal System are:

1   Procedural *ultra vires*
2   Substantive *ultra vires*

Procedural *ultra vires* refers to the idea that those exercising delegated powers should follow any mandatory procedures laid down in the Enabling/Parent Act. This is illustrated in the *Aylesbury Mushroom*[118] case. In the case, the Industrial Training Act 1964 gave the Minister of Labour certain powers which were used to create, by Order, the 'Agricultural, Horticultural and Forestry Industry Training Board'. However, the Act required that 'before making an industrial training order the Minister shall consult any organisation or association of organisations appearing to him to be representative of substantial numbers of employers engaging in the activities concerned.'[119] The Minister did not undertake such consultation and so had breached a fundamental procedural requirement of the primary legislation and this led to a finding of *ultra vires* by the court.

Substantive *ultra vires*, on the other hand, relates to a situation whereby a person with delegated powers goes beyond the powers given by an Enabling or Parent Act. In the GCHQ[120] case, Lord Diplock characterised an aspect of judicial review in the following terms: 'The decision-maker must understand correctly the law that regulates his decision-making power and must give effect to it.'[121] In practical terms, this means that a successful judicial review action may be launched when a Minister (or other decision-maker) abuses their discretion,[122] attempts to use their power for an improper or alternative purpose,[123] wrongly delegates their power[124] or simply acts beyond the powers conferred by the Act.[125]

ANALYSING THE LAW – THE COURTS AND SECONDARY LEGISLATION

The recent cases of *Reilly*[126] and *Reilly (No2)*[127] demonstrate the importance of judicial review and how the grounds act as a safeguard on the risk inherent in Parliament delegating its law-making powers to members of the executive.

---

118 *Agricultural, Horticultural and Forestry Industry Training Board v Aylesbury Mushrooms Ltd* [1972] 1 WLR 190 (QBD).
119 Industrial Training Act 1964 s 1(4).
120 *Council of Civil Service Unions v Minister for the Civil Service* [1985] AC 374 (HL).
121 Ibid. 410 (Lord Diplock).
122 *R v Somerset County Council, ex parte Fewings* [1995] 1 WLR 1037 (CA).
123 *Porter v Magill* [2001] UKHL 67, [2002] 2 AC 357.
124 *Carltona v Commissioners of Works* [1943] 2 All ER 560 (CA).
125 *Prescott v Birmingham Corp* [1954] Ch 210 (CA).
126 *R (Reilly) v Secretary of State for Work and Pensions* [2013] UKSC 68, [2014] AC 453.
127 *R (Reilly No 2) v Secretary of State for Work and Pensions* [2014] EWHC 2182 (Admin).

Partly as a result of public pressure over the size of the welfare bill the Coalition Government passed the Jobseeker's Allowance (Employment, Skills and Enterprise Scheme) Regulations 2011[128] based on powers under various Enabling Acts.[129] Under the Regulations, benefit payments could be sanctioned if an individual refused to participate in unpaid work schemes.

In *Reilly* the applicant challenged the legality of the 2011 Regulations on the basis that they were *ultra vires*. Reilly had (effectively) been forced to give up unpaid work experience in her field of interest to take on a retail role with a national retail chain. She argued, in particular, that the Secretary of State for Work and Pensions had not adequately described the work scheme in the Regulation (as required by the Enabling Act) and had not published a policy describing the various schemes. As a result of the failure to comply with the requirements of the Enabling Act, the Supreme Court upheld the findings of the Court of Appeal to quash the decision, despite the fact that this would cost the Government a great deal of money in claims for repayment of the unlawfully levied penalties.

The case of *Reilly* demonstrates the importance of post-legislative scrutiny in the form of judicial review. This point is reinforced when we consider that the House of Lords Committee on the Merits of Statutory Instruments[130] had already raised concerns during the legislative process about the lack of detail in the Regulations and how much power they transferred, without recourse to Parliament, to the executive.[131] Through this lens, it could be argued that judicial review acts as an additional safeguard where the parliamentary process of scrutiny is deficient. There is even a form of weak link between pre- and post-legislative scrutiny as Mr Justice Foskett made passing reference to the work of the Merits Committee when handing down his decision in *Reilly (No1)* in the High Court.[132]

However, the effectiveness of the whole system of scrutiny can be called into question by the events that unfolded whilst the initial case in *Reilly* was still going through the judicial process. Before the decision by the Supreme Court was reached, the Government passed (and in the face of strong opposition)[133] a new Act[134] that

---

128 Jobseeker's Allowance (Employment, Skills and Enterprise Scheme) Regulations 2011, SI 2011/917.

129 Most importantly under s 17 of the Jobseekers Act 1995.

130 Now known as the House of Lords Secondary Legislation Scrutiny Committee.

131 Merits of Statutory Instruments Committee, *Twenty-Ninth Report* (HL 2010–2012, 3 May 2011), [10]–[11].

132 R *(Reilly) v Secretary of State for Work and Pensions* [2012] EWHC 2292 (Admin), (2012) 156(32) SJLB 31 [44]–[48] (Foskett J).

133 For a flavour of the debate in the House of Commons, see the Third Reading debate – HC Deb 19 March 2013, vol 560 cols 855–896. In the Lords the language was less emotive but nonetheless critical. See HL Deb 25 March 2013, vol 744 col 945.

134 Jobseekers (Back to Work Schemes) Act 2013.

retrospectively validated decisions taken under the old Regulations. This had the effect of pre-empting and nullifying the effect of any Supreme Court decision and thus rendered the judicial review somewhat toothless. In the case it appeared that the Government was able to free itself of the safeguards provided by judicial review. However, such retrospective legislation is both rare and controversial.[135]

Indeed, what followed was a further case, *Reilly (No2)*, whereby the manner in which the Government had acted was deemed to be incompatible with the right to a fair trial guaranteed by the European Convention on Human Rights. The courts also sounded a warning to Parliament about respect for the mechanisms of scrutiny provided by judicial review:

> Parliament's undoubted power to legislate to overrule the effect of court judgments generally ought not to take the form of retrospective legislation designed to favour the Executive in ongoing litigation in the courts brought against it by one of its citizens.[136]

As was discussed earlier in this chapter, the second half of the 20th century has been characterised by an increase in the volume and scope of delegated legislation. This has put significant pressure on the existing system of parliamentary scrutiny and has led to a commensurate increase in the importance of judicial review as a post-legislative form of scrutiny. Despite the logical link between increased executive powers and the need for enhanced scrutiny, the Government appears to be unhappy with such judicial 'interference'. When we consider the financial impact of cases like *Reilly* with estimates of costs of £130 million[137] this is perhaps unsurprising.

ANALYSING THE LAW – THE RISE OF JUDICIAL REVIEW

There has been a steady increase in the number of judicial review applications and this has led to some questioning whether the system is being used appropriately. In 2012[138] the Government launched a consultation paper with the intention of bringing forward reforms to the system of judicial review in an attempt to curb the 'significant growth'[139] in the number of judicial review applications. That report noted that the

---

135 One such instance was the War Damages Act 1965 which retrospectively overruled claims founded on the basis of *Burmah Oil Ltd v Lord Advocate* [1965] AC 75 (HL). For the controversies of retrospective legislation, see Geoffrey Loomer, 'Taxing Out of Time: Parliamentary Supremacy and Retroactive Tax Legislation' [2006] British Tax Review 64.

136 *R (Reilly No 2) v Secretary of State for Work and Pensions* [2014] EWHC 2182 (Admin). [82].

137 Although this figure was questioned by the High Court in *Reilly* (ibid.) [105]–[108].

138 Ministry of Justice, *Judicial Review: Proposals for Reform* (White Paper, Cm 25, 2012).

139 Ibid. para 25.

number of applications had risen from 160 in 1974 to over 11,000 by 2011. The Government went on, in 2013, to make certain procedural changes that sought to limit the rights of those seeking judicial review.[140] However, and as noted in a response to the consultation paper, the Government is not clear as to why this rise is particularly problematic and fails to take into account the significant developments in EU, human rights and immigration law that have partly prompted this rise.[141]

Governmental attempts to 'curb' judicial review should be treated with healthy suspicion. It should not be forgotten that it is often Government Ministers who are *subject* to the judgments of the courts under judicial review. Thus, there is an inherent bias whereby Government Ministers are keen to promote a narrative that increased litigation is 'judicial interference' rather than an important tool of accountability.

In summary, there is a tension between, on the one hand, the need for those upon whom public power is conferred to be able to act freely and, on the other, for those who have significant public powers to be held to account when passing and executing secondary legislation. Judicial review is intended to be a safety net, allowing for challenge not only to those SIs that unintentionally overstep parliamentary authority but also to act as an important check on the power and authority of those exercising delegated law-making powers.

CONCLUSION

Secondary legislation, despite all of its problems and difficulties, is a necessary tool of efficient governance. Secondary legislation is now a fact of life for the English Legal System. Without it, Parliament would be (even more) bogged down with debating and discussing primary legislation. For that reason, and although presented in distinct chapters within this work, it is important to read this chapter alongside the chapter on primary legislation (Acts of Parliament). Although Parliament is sovereign and, as a result, Acts of Parliament are at the apex of any hierarchy of norms within the UK, there is a danger that this underplays the importance of secondary legislation. It is below primary legislation in a hierarchy but its impact can be significant. Understanding the symbiotic relationship between primary and secondary legislation is crucial to full and proper understanding of the English Legal System as a distinct subject. It is also important to understand the nature of secondary legislation and how it impacts on many other dimensions of legal study (e.g. contract law, public law and European Union law).

The advantages that secondary legislation brings in terms of efficiency, increased local decision-making and expertise are obvious. The public good behind the principle of secondary legislation in the English Legal System is, therefore, almost beyond question.

140 Alexander Horne and Joanna Dawson, 'Judicial Review: Government Reforms' (House of Commons Library, 2013), www.parliament.uk/briefing-papers/sn06616.pdf.

141 Ibid. 5.

The problems come then not necessarily from the *principle* of secondary legislation but how that principle is *executed* in practice. There are very real concerns over the volume of secondary legislation that is passed and, more crucially, how that legislation is scrutinised and controlled. The current patchwork system of scrutiny, with its many and disparate committees, can lead to a fragmented and ineffective system of scrutiny. Given the breadth of powers given to pass secondary legislation, an effective system of scrutiny is important to prevent the abuse of powers and to maintain the quality of such legislation.

TAKING THINGS FURTHER – PERSUASIVE AND IMPACTFUL LEGAL WRITING

In order to promote your critical awareness it is important that you can do more than just state the relevant advantages and disadvantages of statutory instruments and the methods by which they are controlled and scrutinised. Students often present answers to questions about the nature of secondary law as a list of advantages and disadvantages of delegated legislation with a brief effort to evaluate the strength and this often leads to bland, generic answers.[142] Better answers attempt to weigh the relevant arguments and link them together through a common theme.

The website that accompanies this textbook contains a question on secondary legislation and an exemplar answer along with comments from Ryan. The purpose of this is to demonstrate the type of material that might appear in such an answer. Avoid the temptation to go away and 'learn' this answer but rather use it to help you identify the features of good legal writing.

THE WEBSITE

The website that accompanies this textbook contains many useful resources that you can use to consolidate and further your knowledge of the law, to hone your skills of critical analysis and to test your knowledge.

PODCASTS

- The podcasts provide a summary of the area under study, bringing together the key themes and threads of analysis into a 'mini-lecture'.
- There will also be an explanation and analysis of topical and up-to-date issues related to law-making.

---

142 This applies to all forms of legal essays and not just those relating to secondary law or even just a module on the English Legal System.

6

CHAPTER 6
STATUTORY INTERPRETATION

INTRODUCTION

In an ideal world Acts of Parliament would enter the legal system perfectly formed and drafted with such clarity and precision of language so as to raise no question over application. The world is far from ideal and the English language is full of such nuance and flexibility that even the most straightforward of statutes can raise serious questions over interpretation. This is before we consider that some statutes may be drafted imperfectly or with intentional ambiguity. The flexibility and ambiguity of words is not something unique to the field of law. Indeed, most disciplines struggle with the subtlety of the English language. However, in the legal field words contained within legislation (particularly those in Acts of Parliament) take on an increased level of importance. The words themselves *are* the law; Acts of Parliament are viewed as the worldly manifestation of Parliament's sovereignty. The words of statutes take on an almost scripture-like quality in the English Legal System. With the risk of stretching this analogy too far, and with full acknowledgement of its limitation, the English Legal System needs the equivalent of holy men, those capable of interpreting the meaning of the words and applying them to the everyday situations of the subjects. That role falls primarily to the judiciary, and this chapter will explore how judges go about this task of interpreting the law found within statutes. In order to understand the approach(es) adopted by judges fully, the chapter will begin by exploring the importance of statutory interpretation including some of the reasons that may lead to a need for such interpretations, as well as the inherent dangers of the principles of statutory interpretation itself.

AS YOU READ

This chapter broadly consists of two sections – the first of which deals with the need for statutory interpretation and the second of which deals with the 'rules and approaches'. As you read, think about practical examples of how these principles may be applied.

By the end of the chapter you should be able to **explain** the need for statutory interpretation and **discuss critically** the extent to which the rules affect the balance of power between the legislature and the judiciary.

In addition you should be able to **evaluate** the strengths and weaknesses of, and relationships between, the legislature and the judiciary.

Also you should be in a position to be able to **understand** the application of the approaches to statutory interpretation in a given hypothetical example.

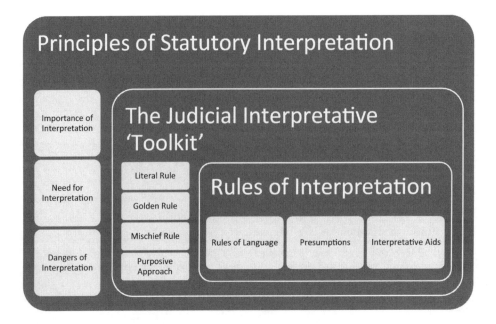

Figure 6.1

THE IMPORTANCE OF STATUTORY INTERPRETATION

FOR THE ENGLISH LEGAL SYSTEM GENERALLY

The importance of statutory interpretation should not be understated. A great number of appeals that reach the Supreme Court are concerned with interpretation of statutes. Within the context of this textbook, statutory interpretation is one of the twin pillars (along with precedent, discussed in Chapter 9) of the judicial legal order (see Figure 6.2). It is also closely related to the issues discussed within Chapters 2, 4 and 5 on sources of law and the primary and secondary law-making process respectively. As such you should avoid reading these chapters (and indeed any of the chapters of this text) in isolation. Having this more holistic view of how topics fit together will lead you to a stronger critical understanding of the material. You should also try to see how different legal subjects fit together. Should you be an undergraduate law student, it is also one of the key elements of the quality of 'graduateness' that you should acquire during your studies in law. This ability not only to make connections between the individual topics that you study but to be able to synthesise the ideas that you glean from each is central to success. During the course of this development from term to term and year to year you should then at some stage discover how much the holistic awareness of the different facets of the law with which you are becoming acquainted is bigger than the sum of its individual parts. This is what becoming an increasingly experienced

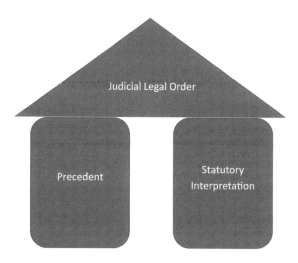

Figure 6.2 The Twin Pillars of the Judicial Legal Order

lawyer means and it can make the study of law both more interesting and more rewarding. This advice should also be heeded even when studying the more technical modules outside the English Legal System (such as contract or tort).

At its most basic level statutory interpretation is important as it allows the English Legal System to function efficiently. Rather than have Parliament attempt to cover matters comprehensively in statutes, as may be the case in a civil law system, or force Parliament to a constant cycle of redrafting, judges are given jurisdiction to interpret the law in order to answer any interpretative questions that arise in the application of the law. The majority of this chapter will be dedicated to this aspect of statutory interpretation.

APPLYING THE LAW – A FICTITIOUS EXAMPLE

Within legal education much emphasis is placed on answering problem questions and many assessments are based on an ability to apply legal principles to hypothetical situations. Obviously it is much too early in the chapter for the reader to be able to do this effectively but seeing a problem question before being given *any* legal principles to apply can be useful. It provides the opportunity to think, without the inhibition of detailed knowledge, about the problems that an area of law may present.

Imagine that the United Kingdom has a problem with a growing population of wild cats that are causing significant health problems for particular breeds of domesticated cats. After much public pressure on the issue, Parliament decides to legislate to address the problem and passes the **Feral Cat** (Destruction) **Act 2013**.

Amongst other things, this fictional Act of Parliament contains the following sections:

s 1 – It shall be an offence for any person to feed, water and give shelter to any feral cat.

s 4 – In the absence of a claim of ownership within 72 hours, an authorised Destruction Officer may destroy any cat in his possession.

s 20 – For the purposes of this act a cat shall be considered to be feral if it is of a type contained within Schedule 1 or if it is discovered to be in a public place after nightfall on no fewer than three occasions without having been appropriately microchipped by a registered veterinary surgeon, cat refuge or animal shelter.

Schedule 1 – A cat is included within this Act if it is of one of the following breeds: Persian, Siamese, American Bobtail or Peterbald.

Having read this fictitious Act, take some time to consider some of the potential problems that would arise in its interpretation. Are there any **particular words** that would need interpretation? How should the law go about resolving the meaning of these words? Does the Act, **as a whole**, have **coherence**? It is not expected that answers to these questions will be immediately apparent but it is important to think carefully about this type of exercise as it can promote deep learning and hone problem solving skills.

We will return to this example later in this part of the book and the companion website gives some further problem questions for you to consider either before reading on or as a way of testing your knowledge after reading the chapter.

The ability to attribute meaning to words is a very powerful tool. Much of the judiciary's time is taken with attempting to unravel the meaning of words as intended by Parliament. While many cases raise new points of law, many more are concerned with the correct interpretation of statutory material. By allowing this power to be exercised by judges the English Legal System has an added flexibility in that it is possible for poorly drafted measures to be 'saved' by the judiciary and for matters to develop more easily to match changes in society.

FOR STUDENTS (OF LAW AND OTHERWISE)

It is easy, amongst the technical rules discussed later, to lose sight of the practical, *educational* value of statutory interpretation to those undertaking legal study. The ability to read for meaning is one of the key skills of being a good law student. The obvious benefit is that it helps with understanding better the role of the judiciary and to analyse case law that may be required to be read during legal studies. Beyond this it is important to understand how judges approach statutes so that accurate predictions can be made about the approach likely to be adopted in relation to new legislation. The law in a given area will almost certainly change over time and sometimes the pace of change is staggeringly fast. Even where the pace of change is steadier, the amount of change can still be immensely significant. For example, the various Acts governing company law have had incremental change over the last 150 years, but the number of sections has still grown by more than 510% in that time (from around 200 to the current 1,300 sections). Individual clients, or large organisations, may be interested in the likely impact of new statutes and the ability to read beyond simple decoding of the meaning of words is a valued skill. Even when we are talking about legal documents other than statutes, such as contracts or collective agreements, the skills of interpretation are valuable. Indeed, documents – such as collective agreements or contracts – may need an interpretative approach similar to that which is applied to statutes.

MAKING CONNECTIONS – INTERPRETATION OF COMMERCIAL OR NON-COMMERCIAL CONTRACTS

+ +

By considering the relative approaches that judges take when interpreting statutes and other legal documents we can see clear links to the law of contract. Much of a commercial lawyer's time is taken up with trying to understand the meaning of contracts, often by trying to distil the objective intention of the parties from the words used. By understanding how judges undertake this role, lawyers are able to look at documents in a way that goes beyond decoding the simple, literal meaning of each word. The *East Midlands Trains* case[1] gives a clear example of how interpretation of non-statutory agreements is undertaken. The case involved the interpretation of a collective agreement and the lessons, even from this non-statute based case, can be applied in other contexts.

Even outside formal legal education, in the form of a law degree or otherwise, the ability to read for purpose is a valuable skill both in terms of professional development and for academic reasons. Being able to understand the literal meaning of words is important but it is also important to be able to determine the meaning of any piece of writing (a formal report, a company circular or even an email) not only from the literal meaning of the words but also the other contextual factors (organisational or documentary) that surround them. Studying how judges approach the task of interpretation is helpful in this regard as it demonstrates the range of approaches that can be taken and can help to construct alternative meanings that can be useful in an organisational environment.

By bringing together the strands discussed earlier, the importance of statutory interpretation becomes clear. It is vital to both the operation and understanding of the English Legal System. Different approaches to interpretation can make the world of difference to the outcome in a particular case and so formulating a set of principles that can be used to predict the various outcomes, and their likelihood of being adopted, is an important legal skill.

---

1 *Turner v East Midlands Trains Ltd* [2012] EWCA Civ 1470.

ANALYSING THE LAW – DIFFERENT APPROACHES TO INTERPRETATION

The case of *Mandla v Lee*[2] aptly demonstrates the problems that can be caused by different approaches to statutory interpretation. The case concerned the interpretation of the Race Relations Act 1976.

The facts of the case are relatively straightforward. A father wished to place his son in a private school in Birmingham. As active members of the Sikh faith and community the father and son wished for the boy to wear a turban in school. The Headmaster of the school would not allow this as it violated the school's uniform policy. The legal issue was whether Sikh was within a 'racial or ethnic group' under the Race Relations Act 1976. If it was demonstrated that Sikhs were a racial or ethnic group then the boy would be protected from discrimination; whereas, if not, the school would not have unlawfully discriminated against him.

The Court of Appeal and the House of Lords came to radically different views over how to interpret the term 'racial or ethnic group'. Lord Denning in the Court of Appeal held that the word 'ethnic' was closely linked to the concept of race. In doing so, he relied upon the Oxford English Dictionary definition of the word. This had the result that Sikhs were not to be regarded as an ethnic group (and were not, therefore, covered by the prohibition from discrimination) as they did not share racial or ethnic characteristics such as a distinct language or 'blood'. According to Denning, the only characteristic that separated Sikhs from other people was the religion of Sikhism and religion was not a protected characteristic under the 1976 Act. Lord Denning also had some words of criticism for the Commission of Racial Equality: 'I cannot pass from this case without expressing some regret that the Commission for Racial Equality thought it right to take up this case against the headmaster…. The statutes relating to race discrimination and sex discrimination are difficult enough to understand and apply anyway. They should not be used so as to interfere with the discretion of schools and colleges in the proper management of their affairs.'

The House of Lords, and in particular Lord Fraser, did not find this an acceptable method of interpretation for this case and preferred a broader interpretation, indicating that to adopt a literal approach and to apply a dictionary definition to the term 'ethnic' (as Denning did) relying on scientific or biological evidence of racial characteristics would 'be absurd'. He also strongly disagreed with the view put forward about the Commission for Racial Equality stating: 'The commission has a difficult task, and no doubts its inquiries will be resented by some and are liable to be regarded as objectionable and inquisitive. But the respondent in this case, who conducted his appeal with restraint and skill, made no complaint of his treatment at the hands of the commission.'

---

2   *Mandla v Lee* [1983] 1 All ER 1062. See Ian McKenna 'Racial discrimination' (1983) 46 Modern Law Review 759.

Which of these lines of reasoning is more convincing? Try to think *why* that line of reasoning is more appropriate in the circumstances. Which of the cases is most likely to represent the intention that Parliament had when drafting the Race Relations Act (and how might we know)? Are both *potentially* valid ways of interpreting the Race Relations Act? Also think of any factors that may influence the way in which judges undertook the interpretative task. For example, what should be made of Lord Denning's criticisms of the Commission for Racial Equality and his comments on the difficulties faced by the Headmaster of the school?

As an aside, it should be noted that, should this case have arisen in more contemporary times, it would have been covered by non-discrimination on the grounds of religious belief.

THE NEED FOR STATUTORY INTERPRETATION

It is important not only to understand the mechanical processes or rules of statutory interpretation (which are discussed later) but also to understand why statutory interpretation is needed at all. Statutory interpretation is about attempting to discern Parliament's intent from, amongst other things, the words it uses in Acts. This can be problematic because words can bear different meanings. Figure 6.3 demonstrates some (but not all) of the problems, caused in part by the problems of the English language, that lead to a need for judicial interpretation of statutes.

THE MULTIPLE OR UNCERTAIN MEANINGS OF WORDS

One of the most common problems that courts face when having to interpret statutory provisions relates to the fact that words can have wide, narrow and even alternative meanings. The case of R v *Allen*[3] demonstrates this problem. Under s 57 of the Offences Against the Person Act 1861 it was an offence to commit bigamy, that is while married if a person should 'marry any other person during the lifetime of the former husband or wife.' There was ambiguity in the word 'marry' within the Act as a person committing bigamy did not marry the second person (i.e. the second marriage was void as it was not lawful). As such, if you were to adopt the *narrow* meaning of the word the offence of bigamy was legally impossible to commit. However, if you were to adopt a *wider* meaning of the word, as the court did, so that it meant to go through a marriage ceremony regardless of its legality then the offence had been committed.

---

3   *Allen* (1872) LR1 CCR 367.

Figure 6.3 The Need for Interpretation

A more technical example of this principle can be found in *Re Paramount Airways (No2)*[4] where the Court of Appeal had to consider whether the phrase 'any person' in s 238 of the Insolvency Act 1986 was to be interpreted to mean any person within the UK or whether it could be read more extensively to include people outside the jurisdiction. Despite the uncertainty and ambiguity of the phrase the Court of Appeal held that 'the solution to the question of statutory interpretation raised by this appeal does not lie in retreating to a rigid and indefensible line. Trade takes place increasingly on an international basis. So does fraud.' This gave the Act extraterritorial application and demonstrates that even international forces can influence how a court will undertake its interpretative task.

POOR DRAFTING

In an ideal world, provisions of law would be perfectly drafted in such a way as to lead to only one possible, rational and just interpretation. However, and in addition to the other reasons identified earlier and later, it is sometimes necessary to interpret statutes because they are badly written. This is regrettable but perhaps unavoidable given the increase in legislative output over the past 70 years, both in terms of the number of distinct Acts passed and in the length of these Acts. The challenges posed by the proliferation of primary and secondary law in terms of distinct legislative instruments and page numbers

---

4   *Re Paramount Airways Limited* [1993] Ch 223, CA. Not to be confused with the American case of *US v Paramount Pictures No 2* (1948) 334 US 131.

were discussed in Chapters 4 (primary legislation) and 5 (secondary legislation) but this chapter considers the practical implications of poor drafting that makes it onto the statute book.

If we turn attention back to the 'feral cat' scenario identified earlier in the chapter, there are certain elements that demonstrate poor drafting. For example, if we were to read the Act literally, an Authorised Destruction Officer who is in possession of a feral cat pending destruction may be committing an offence under s 1. This is because they will surely be feeding and sheltering the cat during that 72-hour period! This is plainly absurd and cannot possibly be the intention behind the Act but it is one possibility that a judge must consider due to the sloppy way in which the section is drafted. However, what if the draftsperson had added, before the full stop at the end of s 1, the words 'other than for temporary purposes not exceeding seven days and pending making a determination in respect of the applicability of this Act to any cat to whom it might potentially apply'? Would that give the Authorised Officer time to ascertain, for example, whether any microchip found on a cat revealed information about an owner?

Badly written statutes put the courts in a difficult position as it is not clear what a judge should do when interpreting a defective statute and this is a point returned to later in the chapter when discussing interpretative approaches. In light of this difficulty, the judiciary tend to get impatient and vocalise their displeasure with poorly worded statutes. For example, the Landlord and Tenant Act 1987 has provided the judiciary with many opportunities for criticism of the drafting process and illustrates the difficulties that courts are faced with when ruling on unclear statutes.

MAKING CONNECTIONS – LAND LAW
+ +

Land law is another subject that you are likely to come across frequently in any study of law. When thinking about different areas of law attempt to determine what the underlining principles are that govern that area and it will help to gain a deeper understanding of the legal system as a whole.

Much of the purpose behind the Landlord and Tenant Act was to enable tenants in a mansion block to acquire certain powers to manage the disposal of their leases/property when the landlord wished to dispose of his interest in the building to a new potential landlord. The proposed mechanism was to give a right of first refusal to any tenant wishing to take up that opportunity. This was a noble and laudable proposal. However, there were a number of specific provisions within the Act that did not achieve this purpose and which, in light of the purpose, made little sense. For example, the prevention of the disposal of the protected interest in s 6 applied to the original landlord. However, the duty not to dispose of the protected interest did not apply to the new landlord (whose conduct was governed by s 12). If the purpose of the Act was to protect the interests of the tenants then the absence of a s 6 duty on the new landlord made little sense.

The provisions of the Landlord and Tenant Act 1987 were considered in numerous cases and two judgments will be briefly mentioned to give a flavour of the problems caused by the Act and the reaction of the judiciary. In *Belvedere Court Management v Frogmore Development*[5] Lord Bingham held that 'one could wish that the Act provided as many answers as it raised problems.' He was sympathetic to the difficulties involved in drafting: 'I can readily appreciate the complexity of the task which confronted the draftsman in seeking to give legislative effect to this ambitious scheme.' However, his criticism became more scathing as the case progressed: 'the history of these proceedings is a dismal commentary on a measure intended to help tenants of mansion blocks, many of them of limited means. As it is, the legal profession would appear to be the main beneficiaries of this obscure statute.' This criticism was an echo of earlier criticisms made by Browne-Wilkinson in *Denetower Ltd v Toop*[6] where the Act was described as 'ill-drafted, complicated and confused'.

THE DIFFICULTIES OF TURNING POLICY INTO 'LAW'

The problem of turning a policy into a law can be split into three distinct but interrelated issues. Firstly, what is a good idea in theory may simply be very difficult to implement into practice. This may be because social problems, although readily recognised as such, do not present easy solutions. The development of the statutory law of harassment is a good example of this problem in action. The Protection from Harassment Act 1997 (PFHA) was passed in response to growing pressure to deal with the problem of stalking that was brought to public attention by high profile instances of the damage stalking causes.

The Act sought to deal with problems by formulating a response in both civil and criminal law so that a victim of harassment could not only find satisfaction through the criminal justice system but also had a range of civil law remedies available. This, on the face of it, seems a sensible policy. Unfortunately, due to the mix of criminal and civil liability and the context of the Act itself the courts have been faced with some interpretative problems

For example, in *Thomas v News Group Newspapers*[7] the court was asked to consider whether the meaning of 'harassment' should be interpreted so as to exclude a newspaper campaign directed at a particular person. It was clear that the meaning given in the Act was capable of including newspaper articles but the question was whether it *should* include such articles given that Parliament had specifically been attempting to address the issue of stalking i.e. normally physically following, pestering and harassing a person. Given that it could not reasonably be denied that news articles could be within the meaning of 'harassment', the courts did not accept a narrow definition of the term. This case demonstrates that it is sometimes difficult to circumscribe the scope of the words in an Act so that they cover only the circumstances intended and no more.

....

5   [1997] QB 858 (CA).
6   [1991] 1 WLR 945.
7   [2001] EWCA Civ 1233, CA.

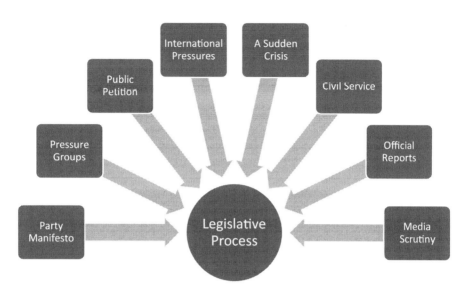

Figure 6.4 Summary of Influences on Law-Making

Secondly, the precise basis of the need for the new law may not be very clear and this level of uncertainty can feed through into the legislative proposal. This is also, in part, a consequence of the different interests that feed into the formulation of policy and legislative proposals. These interests can vary (from manifesto promises to international pressures to public or media pressure) and have already been discussed in Chapter 4 on law-making (Figure 6.4). It is not always the case that these interests pull in the same direction and, in an attempt not to wholly alienate different interest groups proposals can often be watered down and/or compromised in order to satisfy different actors. As George Orwell noted, the use of language can sometimes disclose a tension between communicated and perceived intentions: 'The great enemy of clear language is insincerity. When there is a gap between one's real and one's declared aims, one turns, as it were, instinctively to long words and exhausted idioms, like a cuttlefish squirting out ink.'[8]

Finally, and more narrowly, the parliamentary process itself can create difficulties in concretising a policy into a clear, intelligible law. In some ways, the parliamentary process can be like the childhood game of Chinese whispers, with the initial germ of a legislative 'idea' ending up very different to the final outcome that will be embodied within the Act of Parliament. While it is normally the Government that forms the policy and is responsible for presenting a Bill it is Parliament that has the final 'say' over whether the policy becomes law and the precise form of words used.

It is also important to note that at each stage of the *legislative* process the pressures identified earlier can force (or in some cases persuade) the political actors to change their view and make further amendments to the proposal. The three strands identified previously are, as

---

8   George Orwell, *Politics and the English Language* (first published 1946, Penguin 2013).

already mentioned, interconnected and interrelated. They should not be viewed in isolation but as a system of pressures and influences that can influence the passage of law at all stages and in ways that can cause problems of interpretation.

NEW SITUATIONS

At times technological or societal developments overtake a statute and these result in pressure mounting on judges to reinterpret the law to include previously unconsidered situations. There are examples of this type of problem scattered throughout legislative history. This problem tends to affect, in particular, those areas which have seen drastic technological changes. One such area is that of protection of intellectual property by the law of copyright. The Copyright Designs and Patents Act 1988 sought to protect the rights of creators of, *inter alia*, artistic works (including literary, dramatic or musical works). Since that time the age of the computer has developed and computer software has become an important, and valuable, source of innovation and creativity. As such, the question arises whether software architecture and the code that generates the program can be protected by copyright. In the first instance, and in the absence of updating by Parliament, it was for the court to decide whether to extend the Act to cover this new situation.

Another, more emotive, example of technological advances requiring changes to interpretation comes from the *Royal College of Nursing v DHSS*[9] case. The Abortion Act 1967 (s 1) created a defence to the offence of child destruction where procedures were carried out by 'a registered medical practitioner'. Under the old law there was only a common law defence for doctors. At the time of the passage of the Act abortions were carried out through surgical means. The question raised by the Royal College of Nursing was whether the developments of non-surgical abortions (possible after significant scientific developments) called for an interpretation of the Act that allowed for nurses to also be involved in the process. In interpreting the Act Lord Wilberforce considered it 'proper, and indeed necessary, to have regard to the state of affairs existing, and known by Parliament to be existing, at the time.' He felt that a change to the meaning of the Act, due to its controversial nature, should be undertaken by Parliament even if such a change was seen as necessary and sensible. This was the minority view, with the majority of the House of Lords preferring a more pragmatic approach, focussing on the purpose of the Act (to allow women to have safe abortions). The court held, in a split court, that nurses working *under the direction of a doctor* were not acting unlawfully by virtue of their involvement with the abortion procedure since the doctor was in control of the non-surgical treatment when s/he directed that it should be administered.

ANALYSING THE LAW – RESPONDING TO TECHNOLOGICAL CHANGE

The two situations discussed previously boil down to fundamentally the same issue: should the Act be interpreted in such a way as to include later technological

9   [1981] 2 WLR 179.

developments? Having said this, the interpretation applied to the Abortion Act 1967 was very much more controversial than that applied to the Copyright Designs and Patents Act. This is demonstrated by the sharp division in the House of Lords with one dissenting judge suggesting that the approach adopted by the majority was 'redrafting with a vengeance'.

Read the judgments (both dissenting and majority) in *Royal College of Nursing v DHSS* and consider the factors that make this different to the situation under the Copyright, Designs and Patents Act. Did the House of Lords come to the correct decision in this case? What would have been the consequence of ruling differently? Should the nature of the Act itself alter the way in which courts approach the question of statutory interpretation? Are there any dangers in the approach of the majority (or indeed of the minority)?

APPROACHES TO PARLIAMENTARY DRAFTING

MAKING CONNECTIONS – LAW-MAKING
+ +
You will remember from Chapter 4 that we have already discussed the nature of parliamentary drafting and the problems that can be involved in making abstract policy into concrete law. These problems are of particular importance for statutory interpretation. It would be sensible to refer back to the problems and challenges identified in that chapter as they are equally relevant when considering the need for statutory interpretation.

In formulating legal provisions there are two extreme positions that could be taken in relation to drafting. On the one hand, provisions can be very loosely drafted in a way that invites judicial intervention and that allows judges to be involved in the process of developing the law; on the other hand, Acts of Parliament could attempt to be exhaustive and try to cover every possible situation through long and detailed provisions. Neither of those positions is necessarily preferable and much will depend upon the specific context within which the Act of Parliament is drafted. However, both approaches to interpretation have inherent benefits and drawbacks. The flexible option is influenced to some extent by the approach in civil law countries which have a written constitution and a series of codes setting out the law, which is then drafted in such a way that it should rarely require amendment – unlike our statutes in England and Wales, which often have to have regular amendment.

At times it may be appropriate to draft provisions in such a way that they are flexible and adaptable. Although originally formulated outside the scope of the English Legal System, the European Convention on Human Rights, as incorporated by the Human Rights Act 1998, is an example of flexible drafting. The rights contained within the European Convention on Human

Rights are not defined by the Convention and have been developed and interpreted by the European and domestic courts over more than 50 years. The more loosely drafted a legislative provision, the more heavily weighted judicial power is.

THE 'NATURAL' AS OPPOSED TO THE 'LEGAL' MEANING OF WORDS

As well as the rich diversity of everyday meanings that can attach to words, there is the added complication that words can sometimes carry a technical meaning, be it legal or otherwise. It is part of the job of the courts to distinguish between when Parliament is using a word in a technical sense, and when the word is being used in its everyday form.

> **EXPLAINING** THE LAW – DETERMINING TECHNICAL, LEGAL OR ORDINARY MEANING
>
> _____
>
> This issue is demonstrated by the **Restriction of Offensive Weapons Act 1959.** Section 1 of the Act, as originally enacted, read as follows:
>
> s 1 Penalties for offences
>
>   (1) Any person who manufactures, sells or hires or offers for sale or hire, or lends to gives to any other person –
>
>   (a) any knife which has a blade which opens automatically by hand pressure applied to a button …, sometimes known as a *flick knife* or *flick gun*;
>
> …
>
> shall be guilty of an offence and shall be liable on summary conviction to imprisonment for a term not exceeding six months.

A question arises as to how to interpret the phrase 'offers for sale'. There are (at least) two potential meanings that could attach to this phrase – an everyday/layman meaning or a technical legal meaning. It was precisely this issue that arose in the leading contract law case *Fisher v Bell*.[10]

> **EXPLAINING** THE LAW – *FISHER V BELL*
>
> _____
>
> In the case, Bell was prosecuted under the Act outlined previously for offering for sale a flick knife. The facts were uncontroversial. Bell had placed a flick knife in the window of his shop, complete with a price ticket. He had been charged under the Act and subsequently argued that he was not, in the technical sense, offering for sale but that he was receptive to offers to buy.

....

10 [1961] 1 QB 394 (QB).

Under the general law of contract an offer, once accepted, becomes binding on the person making the offer. That is not how items displayed in shops are generally sold. It is normal that the *customer* makes the offer to buy the item and the shopkeeper then chooses whether to accept the offer or not. Therefore, the display of an item in a shop is not an offer to sell but an indication that the shopkeeper may be receptive to offers. This type of situation has been deemed an 'invitation to treat' under the common law.

The difference, to a non-lawyer, may seem very small but it is important to distinguish between the two situations for practical reasons not relevant to the discussion here. The result was that Bell was not guilty of the offence as he had not made an offer for sale but rather an invitation to treat. The court had to make the assumption (even though it was clearly an oversight) that Parliament knew the technical meaning of 'offer for sale' and had chosen that phrase despite the loophole that it created.

Some would argue that the outcome of *Fisher v Bell* is unsatisfactory. If you think for a moment about the *purpose* of the Act, then it was clearly to prevent the sale of offensive weapons and to reduce the ability for people to acquire and subsequently use such offensive weapons. The outcome in *Fisher v Bell* did not achieve that aim and seemed to allow somebody to escape justice on the basis of a very narrow and technical distinction.

MAKING CONNECTIONS – CONTRACT LAW AND BEYOND
+ +
Having said this, it is important not to view the case in isolation. This is a danger when new to the study of law: judging the outcome of each case solely on its facts and losing sight of the 'bigger' picture. This is exacerbated when we are talking about the English Legal System as a subject as it will invariably draw upon many areas of law.

This is a case that the reader will no doubt return to if undertaking the study of contract law. Think carefully about why the court was unwilling to apply a more 'common sense' approach to the term 'offer for sale' – although it might have led to a lack of justice in this particular case. Think, in particular, about the consistency that is needed within areas of law and how important the principle of legal certainty is to the legal system and how this may need to trump outcomes in particular circumstances. This is particularly so when discussing complex, but settled, legal principles such as those found within the basic rules of contract.

The argument that the court in *Fisher v Bell* had been unable to achieve Parliament's intent is somewhat confirmed by later events. Following on from the case, Parliament passed the Restriction of Offensive Weapons Act 1961 which sought to cover the situation that arose in *Fisher v Bell* by inserting into the original Act the following phrase: 'or exposes or has in his possession for the purpose of sale or hire'. It could be argued that at a broader level *Fisher v Bell* is an example of separation of powers in action (as discussed in Chapter 3 – Institutions of the Legal System) and of how statutory interpretation can promote better law-making. The court was not willing to go beyond their interpretative role and instead preferred to leave law-making to Parliament. The case highlighted a problem with the statute which was then 'solved' by the legislature. In this way, interpretation of statutes can be an efficient way of promoting and ensuring clearer drafting.

All of the aforementioned reasons feed into the need for statutory interpretation within the English Legal System. The problems are not to be viewed as being mutually exclusive but rather they should be viewed as interacting and interrelated. For example, poor drafting can mean that the law is too vague or that it is not 'future-proofed' for subsequent developments. If we return, for a moment, to the Abortion Act 1967 and the case of *Royal College of Nursing v DHSS* we can see that some of the uncertainty created by the Act could have been resolved through clearer drafting, coming as it did from a professional draftsman: 'it lacks that style and consistency of draftsmanship both internal to the Act itself and in relation to other statutes which one would expect to find in legislation that had its origin in the office of parliamentary counsel.'[11]

The preceding gives a flavour of the wide-ranging issues that lead to a need for statutory interpretation. The list is not intended to be exhaustive and should be viewed as a starting point for future exploration. Although unlikely of themselves to form the core part of an essay-based assessment question on statutory interpretation, the problems just identified can help to evaluate critically the 'tools' of and approaches to statutory interpretation. To put this differently, the aforementioned problems can require different approaches and solutions from the judiciary. Indeed, they are essential context without which it will not be able to assess the merits of the different approaches to statutory interpretation. The next section will explore how the court goes about resolving, or at least reducing, some of these problems through adopting specific approaches to statutory interpretation.

TAKING IT FURTHER – THE COMPANION WEBSITE

The companion website gives further details of statutory provisions, and case law, which form examples of the problems identified earlier. The companion website also contains further example assessment material along with worked solutions and points for further critical analysis.

Beyond this, Acts of Parliament are readily accessible on the internet (www.legislation. gov.uk). It is well worth looking at recent statutory material to help further contextualise the content studied in this chapter. Be sure to remember that studying law and the legal system is about more than simply learning the contents of various Acts of Parliament, which may in any case change significantly during the course of a scheme of study and

---

11 *Royal College of Nursing* [1981] AC 800 (HL) 824 (Lord Diplock).

later career. When accessing primary materials, do so with a purpose. For example, it could be helpful to look to see if a recent Act of Parliament will require interpretation based on one (or more) of the factors discussed.

In addition it is useful to become familiar with the key statutes in each area of law that is studied. By accessing Acts of Parliament and trying to highlight key phrases or sections that may require interpretation, it is possible to learn a lot about the principles underlying different types of law and legal practice even before formally starting to study them. This is important as it not only gives some idea of the content that will be studied but also allows a reader to think about how the various subjects fit together and whether the style of drafting is consistent within a subject area (such as land law) and as between subjects (such as between constitutional law and contract law). This will really help connections to be made between the discrete modules which may be studied concurrently.

Finally, in May 2013, the House of Commons Political and Constitutional Reform Committee published a document relating to the drafting and interpretation of legislation. See www.parliament.uk/business/committees/committees-a-z/commons-select/political-and-constitutional-reform-committee/inquiries/parliament-2010/better-legislation.

THE DANGERS OF STATUTORY INTERPRETATION

In spite of the fact that statutory interpretation is of fundamental importance to the functioning of the English Legal System, it does come with inherent dangers. Foremost amongst those dangers is the power that it gives to the judiciary. Interpretation can, and does, change or at least determine the law and in some circumstances gives the courts a greater opportunity to *make* law.

As a result of this the principles of statutory interpretation also play a constitutional role, in that they determine an allocation of power between those who make the law (the legislature – Parliament) and those who apply the law (the judiciary – the courts). As was mentioned in Chapter 3, it is important that functions and powers of the different organs of the state are kept distinct or at least that there are sufficient checks and balances on the powers of the judiciary (and, although less relevant for this chapter, Parliament). The 'rules' of statutory interpretation seek, to an extent, to demonstrate self-restraint and deference being exercised by judges. In this way statutory interpretation marks one of the key interactions between the legislature and the judiciary.

The judiciary readily accepts that there needs to be a separation of function between those who *interpret* the law and those who *apply* the law. This has been recognised by all levels of the judiciary over many years and in many different contexts where the interpretation of law is in question. A flavour of this discourse is explored later. The clearest expression of this principle comes from Lord Diplock in *Duport Steels Ltd v Sirs*:[12]

> Parliament makes the laws, the judiciary interpret them....[T]he role of the judiciary is confined to ascertaining from the words that Parliament has approved as expressing its intention what that intention was, and to giving effect to it. Where the meaning of the statutory words is plain and unambiguous it is not for the judges to invent fancied ambiguities as an excuse for failing to give effect to its plain meaning because they themselves consider that the consequences of doing so would be inexpedient, or even unjust or immoral.

The preceding quotation tells us much about the attitude of some of the judiciary to the process of and rationale for statutory interpretation. Similar expressions can be found elsewhere within the case law. For example, in *Belvedere Court Management Limited*[13] the court put the matter even more plainly when criticising the Landlord and Tenant Act 1987:

> Whilst the drafting of fully effective provisions would not be unduly difficult (and has been achieved in other legislation covering similar matters), it is not the role of the court to construct such provisions if they are not to be found expressly or implicitly in the Act as drafted. **The ease of the legislative task does not mean that the distinction between the roles of the courts and the legislature can be disregarded.** The solutions to the problems posed have to be found, if at all, within the scope of the interpretative tools open to the courts to uncover and give effect to the statutory intention.

The statement in this case is stronger than in *Duport Steels* as it is a more direct warning against judicial law-making. Thus, even where judges could be fairly certain of getting the 'right' answer in creating new law, they should be mindful of the difference between the roles of the legislature and the judiciary. As a principle it is, therefore, relatively uncontroversial to say that a large part of statutory interpretation is concerned with trying to determine the *intention of Parliament*. This focus on intention is a method by which judges legitimise what they are doing. It can be argued that judges are strengthening the separation of powers by focussing on the intention of the legislature.

Although judges happily agree that separation of powers is an important safeguard in preventing judicial law-making, there is disagreement as to the extent to which different approaches achieve or threaten separation of powers. In this way statutory interpretation also reveals some of the internal tensions that can exist as to the way in which judges go about their interpretative task. This tension is exemplified by the *Magor and St Mellons Rural District Council v Newport Corporation*[14] case. Within this case a very liberal approach to interpretation was put forward by Lord Denning. He was unhappy simply to apply the intention of Parliament and wished to go further. In departing from the orthodox approach he earned the reproof of Lord Simonds on appeal to the House of Lords who held that Denning had been part of 'a naked

---

12 [1980] 1 WLR 142 (HL) 157B–158C.
13 [1996] 1 All ER 312, [1997] QB 858 (CA).
14 [1952] AC 189 (HL).

usurpation of the legislative function under the thin guise of interpretation'.[15] The exchange between Denning and Simonds demonstrates the significance of statutory interpretation in achieving the correct balance between the role and powers of the judiciary and the legislature. On the other hand Lord Denning in the Court of Appeal had put a strong case for a more purposive interpretation when he said: 'We do not sit here to pull the language of Parliament to pieces and make nonsense of it. We sit here to find out the intention of Parliament and carry it out and we do this better by filling in the gaps and making sense of the enactment than by opening it up to destructive analysis.'[16] This was but the beginning of a long running collision of ideas and approaches between the House of Lords and the Court of Appeal, which lasted as long as Denning remained in the Court.[17] Statutory Interpretation was not the only battleground between these two highest courts in English law. While Lord Diplock and others in the House of Lords generally spoke for the classic approach to established principle in the House of Lords, Lord Denning was ahead of his time in many respects, such as in respect of the purposive approach to statutory interpretation which did not become mainstream in domestic law until well after the UK joined the EU in 1973, although from that date it was used in interpreting the EU law which then inevitably impacted on our domestic law.

ANALYSING THE LAW – ASSESSING JUDICIAL REASONING

Assessment questions for statutory interpretation typically focus on the approaches to and rules of statutory interpretation (discussed later) and not the preliminary issues that emerge from the foregoing analysis. Having said this, it is extremely useful to be able to consider the broader points of principle within any essay on statutory interpretation. These will inform, strengthen and contextualise the answer and help to evidence a critical understanding of the area of law.

Which line of reasoning – that of Lord Denning or of Lord Simonds – do you find more convincing?

In formulating an answer to the preceding question an attempt should be made to consider all of the issues discussed so far in this chapter. In particular, think about what it is that statutory interpretation is trying to achieve and how the factors leading to the need for interpretation interplay and conflict. In doing so the conclusion may well be that both Lord Denning's and Lord Simonds's views hold validity and that the multitude of problems may require more than one solution.

More recently, the dangers of judicial activism in interpretation have been brought to the fore by the European Court of Human Rights in the case of Hirst[18] where the European Court held

---

15 Ibid 190 (Lord Simonds).

16 *Magor and St Mellons Rural District Council v Newport Corporation* [1950] 2 All ER 1226 (CA) 1236 (Denning LJ).

17 Denning had previously sat in the House of Lords but returned to the Court of Appeal to assume the post of Master of the Rolls in the Court of Appeal.

18 *Hirst v UK (No 2)* [2005] ECHR 681.

that the UK's blanket ban on allowing prisoners to vote violated the European Convention on Human Rights. In doing so, they challenged a long-standing UK Act of Parliament and were accused of taking interpretation too far and were at risk of becoming quasi-legislators. We will return to the European Convention on Human Rights later in this chapter and in subsequent chapters of the textbook.

Having considered both the reasons leading to the need for interpretation and the dangers that need to be avoided in construing legislation it is now important to turn to the specific 'rules' or approaches of statutory interpretation.

THE TRADITIONAL 'TOOLS' OF STATUTORY INTERPRETATION

In order to resolve specific cases which raise questions of interpretation the judiciary has a varied toolbox comprising principles and methods that can be applied to different situations. What this text terms 'tools', others have labelled as 'approaches', 'canons' or even 'rules' of statutory interpretation. The fact that academics and judges use different terminology to describe what is, essentially, the same process further demonstrates the difficulties of the English language! Even judges vary the language used, preferring in more recent times the phrase 'statutory construction'. This text prefers 'tools', as opposed to 'rules' or 'canons', as it more accurately describes how judges use the various principles to decide cases. This is because, to a large extent, the precise issue that gives rise to a need for interpretation (as discussed in the previous section) will be determinative of which 'approach' or 'tool' a judge uses to solve the case at hand. The Australian case of *Cooper Brookes* sums up the position succinctly by stating that 'the rules [of statutory interpretation] … are no more than rules of common sense, designed to achieve this object. They are not rules of law.'[19]

Principal amongst the tools available to judges are the so-called literal, golden and mischief rules of statutory interpretation. These are often then contrasted with the purposive approach to statutory interpretation that is the hallmark of the approach taken within the European Union and to the European Convention on Human Rights. This section of the chapter will explore the preceding tools as discrete principles but it should be remembered that they interact and can sometimes be complementary in application.

TAKING THINGS FURTHER – PRACTICAL APPLICATION OF THE 'RULES'

The best way to gain a full understanding of the rules of statutory interpretation that follow is through repeated application to scenarios. The companion website that

19 *Cooper Brookes (Wollongong) Property Ltd v Federal Commissioner for Taxation* [1981] HCA 26 at 35.

accompanies this textbook contains numerous exercise that will facilitate applications of the rules to fact patterns.

Figure 6.5 gives an indication of the major rules and approaches of statutory interpretation. A diagrammatic form can be useful in terms of explaining basic structures but it should not be forgotten that a diagram may struggle to explain the *interplay* between the different rules.

THE RULES OF INTERPRETATION

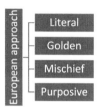

Figure 6.5 The Major Rules and Approaches of Statutory Interpretation

LITERAL RULE

The literal approach is normally the starting point for any court faced with a question of interpretation. This is because, often, it is the easiest way to resolve the case at hand and holds the least possibility of judges being accused of intruding on the legislative function. The most commonly cited example of the principle underlying the literal approach comes from Lord Esher in the 19th century:

> If the words of an Act are clear, you must follow them, even though they lead to a manifest absurdity.[20]

Similar statements can be found in another 19th-century case, *The Sussex Peerage Case*[21] where the court held:

> If the words of the statute are in themselves precise and unambiguous, then no more can be necessary than to expound those words in their natural and ordinary sense. The words themselves alone do, in such case, best declare the intention of the lawgiver.

....

20 Per Lord Esher in *R v Judge of the City of London Court* [1892] 1 QB 273 (CA).
21 (1844) 11 C; & Fin 85.

The core principle of the literal approach is that judges look to the common and plain meaning of words in trying to determine what Parliament intended when passing the Act in question. Judges do not seek to go beyond the wording used by Parliament so as to consider extraneous material that would evidence an alternative or revised understanding beyond that which the clear meaning of the words suggests. Those who favour the literal approach suggest that it should always be applied where the words are clear and unambiguous. This was confirmed recently by the First-Tier Tribunal (Tax Chamber) in *AN Checker Heating & Service Engineers v HMRC*[22] which concerned interpretation of s 29 of the VAT Act 1994. The section allowed for a reduced rate of VAT for a supply of certain energy saving materials and the very technical legal issue was whether the reduced rate could be applied to individual elements within an overall supply – in this case the components contained within a boiler that was to be installed as a single service. In the case Judge Paines had sympathy for the argument of the company but refused to depart from the literal meaning of the words contained within the Act as he was 'far from being abundantly sure that Parliament' had misunderstood the meaning of the word 'supply' in this context and that the meaning was 'unambiguous'.

There are additional standard examples of the literal approach in action that further demonstrate how it operates. The following are just two examples and should not be taken as exhaustive.

1   *Whiteley v Chappell*[23] – under the Act in question, it was an offence (punishable by up to three months in prison) to 'personate any person entitled to vote' at the election of guardians of the poor. The appellant had been accused of impersonating another person who had died before the election. The legal issue was whether he had committed the offence as a dead person is not entitled to vote. His counsel argued that his client was 'within the spirit, but he was not within the letter, of the enactment.' The court, with some reluctance, agreed deciding that the judges could not, 'without straining them, bring the case within the words of the enactment. The legislature has not used words wide enough to make the personation of a dead person an offence.' This may seem an odd result given that it allowed the appellant to escape justice for a clear wrong but the judges in the case were worried that, should they do such violence to the words in order to convict, it would set an unwelcome precedent for judicial activism.

2   *IRC v Hinchy*[24] – When making an income tax return Hinchy did not declare the full amount of interest that he had received and as a result underpaid income tax to the amount of around £15. He was charged a penalty payment under section 25 of the Income Tax Act 1952 which required that where a person did not fully declare income they would 'forfeit the sum of … treble the tax which he ought to be charged under this Act'. The IRC submitted that the penalty should be treble his whole tax liability under the Act (totalling almost £440) and not just three times the amount he had underpaid (£15). Despite the extreme nature of imposing the higher penalty, the court felt unable to alter the natural and unambiguous meaning of the words of the Act: 'The argument

---

22 [2013] UKUT 247.
23 [1868] LR QB 147.
24 (1960) AC 748 (HL).

for the more limited meaning adopted … is based almost entirely on the extravagant consequences which flow from giving the words in the present Act their natural meaning.'

TAKING THINGS FURTHER – ASSESSMENT ADVICE

It is always a good idea, in preparation for an exam or piece of coursework, to go beyond the examples given by lecturers or those found in the main textbook. By going beyond the core texts, it demonstrates to the examiner/marker that candidates have read widely and have independent research skills. Finding different case examples can help to differentiate an answer from the (potentially) hundreds of other answers that the examiner will be reading. Explore the legal databases (such as Westlaw or LexisNexis) and the open access database BAILLI to find additional and current examples. The website of the Supreme Court can also provide fruitful ground for further research of recent case law.[25]

It is also possible to differentiate answers by noting similarities (or differences) between the principles in operation in other legal systems and comparing them to the position in the English and Welsh legal system. Other common law jurisdictions also tend to favour the literal approach to statutory interpretation as the starting point for finding legislative intent and this has been the subject of some discussion in the Commonwealth. For example, the Australian High Court in *Alcan*[26] held that 'the task of statutory construction must begin with a consideration of the text itself. Historical considerations and extrinsic materials cannot be relied on to displace the clear meaning of the text. The language which has actually been employed in the text of legislation is the surest guide to legislative intention.' As previously mentioned this comes from an Australian case but is a clear and convincing line of reasoning.

Although the two cases discussed previously are dated, there are more recent cases that demonstrate that the literal rule is still applied. The case of R v Goodwin[27] also demonstrates application of the literal rule in a more contemporary context.

EXPLAINING THE LAW – THE LITERAL RULE IN THE CONTEMPORARY LEGAL SYSTEM

The case of *Goodwin* concerned the application and interpretation of s 58 of the Merchant Shipping Act 1995 which made it an offence for the 'master of … a United Kingdom ship' to do 'any act which causes or is likely to cause … the death or serious injury to any person'.

....

25 www.supremecourt.uk.

26 *Alcan Alumina Property Ltd v Commissioner of Territory Revenue* [2009] HCA 41.

27 [2005] EWCA Crim 3184, [2006] 1 WLR 546.

Goodwin was charged with this offence after colliding with another person whilst riding his jet ski. The question before the Court of Appeal was whether a jet ski was a 'sea-going ship'. If it was then Goodwin could be prosecuted under the Act. The Court of Appeal held that '[b]y no stretch of the imagination could that craft be so described.' In doing so, they applied a commonly held/layperson's understanding of the term 'ship' and were not convinced by a more strained but broader reading that, because it had some of the characteristics of a ship, then it should be considered a ship.

Despite the fact that the literal approach continues to be widely used, it can lead to unfairness and potential absurdity. This is demonstrated in cases such as *Hinchy*[28] (discussed previously) where the penalty applied was extremely severe. Other cases also reinforce the unfairness that can follow from an overly zealous commitment to the literal meanings of the words in an Act of Parliament.

A rather extreme example of the unfairness that may be caused by the literal approach can be seen in *London and North Eastern Railway Company v Berriman*.[29] The case concerned the Railway Employment (Prevention of Accidents) Act 1900 and interpretation of the phrase 'relaying or repairing the permanent way'. Mr Berriman was killed whilst oiling the apparatus connecting signal boxes and points. The question before the court was whether his widow could claim damages for breach of rules that governed staff who were 'relaying or repairing the permanent way' in accordance with the Schedule of the Act. The court felt bound to adopt a literal approach and deny Mr Berriman's widow any compensation under the Act. It did this on the basis that oiling the points was maintenance work that fell outside the ordinary, plain and unambiguous meaning of the word 'repair'. This is an extremely restrictive interpretation and one that Lord Wright (dissenting) disagreed with, preferring to hold, in part because the measure was aimed at preserving human life, that maintenance is a form of repair in that it ensures the proper working of a railway line. The view of the majority denied Berriman's widow compensation where he was exposed to significant risk. This type of unfairness militates against an overly strict observance of the literal approach.

TAKING THINGS FURTHER

The companion website contains discussion and analysis of additional case law that further demonstrates the problems that can be caused by the literal rule.

The case discussed earlier clearly demonstrates the problems caused by the literal approach. It would seem sensible to also note that some of the issues that lead to a need for statutory interpretation, which were discussed earlier in this chapter, cannot always be easily resolved

---

28 *IRC v Hinchy* (1960) AC 748 (HL).
29 [1946] AC 278 (HL).

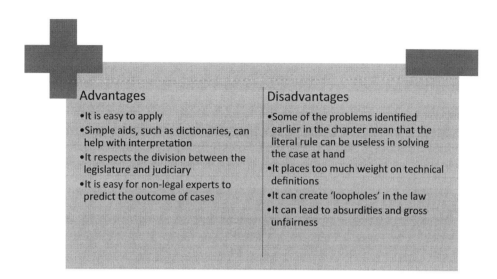

Advantages	Disadvantages
•It is easy to apply •Simple aids, such as dictionaries, can help with interpretation •It respects the division between the legislature and judiciary •It is easy for non-legal experts to predict the outcome of cases	•Some of the problems identified earlier in the chapter mean that the literal rule can be useless in solving the case at hand •It places too much weight on technical definitions •It can create 'loopholes' in the law •It can lead to absurdities and gross unfairness

Figure 6.6 The Advantages and Disadvantages of the Literal Approach

by reference to the principles of the literal approach. The most striking example of this is where technology advances beyond that envisaged by an Act of Parliament. In *Attorney General v The Edison Telephone Company of London*[30] the court was asked to consider whether the wide powers granted to the Postmaster General under the Telegraph Act 1869, for control of telegraphic communications, should extend to telephone calls despite the fact that the telephone had not been invented in 1869.

The advantages and disadvantages of the literal approach are summarised in Figure 6.6.

Due to both the unfairness and more general disadvantages of the literal rule, it is important to consider whether the other rules fill the gaps left by the consequences of the literal approach. Courts have shown willing to depart from the regular and ordinary meaning of words to avoid that unfairness but only under certain conditions. These conditions are not expressed in a uniform manner and can vary from case to case but general principles can be discerned from the judgment of Lord Simon in *Stock v Frank Jones (Tipton)*:[31]

A court would only be justified in departing from the plain words of the statute were it satisfied that: (1) there is clear and gross balance of anomaly; (2) Parliament, the legislative promoters and the draftsman could not have envisaged such an anomaly, could not have been prepared to accept it in the interests of a supervening legislative objective; (3) the anomaly can be obviated without detriment to the legislative objective; (4) the language of the statute is susceptible of the modification required to obviate the anomaly.... But it is essential to bear in mind what the court is doing. It is not declaring Parliament has

---

30 [1880–81] LR 6 QBD 244.

31 [1978] 1 WLR 231 (HL) 235.

said X, but it obviously meant Y, so we will take Y as the effect of the statute. Nor is it declaring Parliament has said X having situation A in mind, but if Parliament had had our own forensic situation B in mind, the legislative objective indicates that it would have said Y. What the court is declaring is Parliament has used words which are capable of meaning either X or Y, although X may be the primary natural and ordinary meaning of the words, the purpose of the provision shows that the secondary sense, Y, should be given to the words. So, too, when X produces injustice, absurdity, anomaly or contradiction.

This statement demonstrates that the courts will exercise great self-restraint before departing from the clear meaning of the words used in an Act.

ANALYSING THE LAW – DEVELOPING ESSAY WRITING SKILLS

Example essay question: 'Over reliance on the literal rule of statutory interpretation is completely unacceptable, prone as it is to producing injustice and absurdity'. Discuss critically

This is a typical exam or coursework-type question in this area. Make some brief notes on how you would start to answer this question and form a basic outline plan. Think about the 'anchor' words within the quotation and how you would use your knowledge gained so far in order to demonstrate critical understanding of the topic. Do any of the issues discussed in the section of the chapter dealing with the factors leading to the need for statutory interpretation alter your argument? To put things another way, could this question be answered differently depending on why an interpretation is needed?

When this topic is taught within law schools it is not uncommon for the lecturer or tutor to present and concentrate on the 'advantages' and 'disadvantages' of each approach. This gives you a very clear and contrasting view of the benefits and drawbacks of the particular approach under examination but it is not always suitable to transpose this advantages/disadvantages framework into an assessed essay. This is because your essay can come across as bland and uncritical. Taking the essay question given previously as an example, it is not enough simply to state all of the advantages and all of the disadvantages. In order to demonstrate critical thinking skills you need to be able to weight the various arguments which you are advancing and to compare them with each other: using words such as 'strong', 'very strong', 'weaker than', 'less – or more – convincing' can help to convey weighted argument.

As such, you should treat lists of 'advantages' and 'disadvantages' with a degree of trepidation and you should use them only as an *aide memoire* to help you start to form an argument.

Refer to the companion website where there are real examples of student answers, both good and bad, to this (and other) question(s) complete with comments from the examiner.

GOLDEN RULE

The golden rule is said to owe its origin to the literal rule, slightly modified in order to allow taking into account some other interpretation if an absurd result is produced by initially following the literal rule. Two 19th-century judges have contributed to this development: first, per Jervis CJ in *Mattison v Hart*[32] who suggested sticking to 'the plain meaning' unless 'injustice or absurdity would result', adding that this was the 'golden rule for construction of statutes; secondly, per Baron Parke in *Grey v Pearson*,[33] who seemed to try to put a brake on the wide deviation that seemed to be allowed if absurdity of injustice resulted, when he said that the literal rule was the starting point but wanted to replace the word 'injustice' in Jervis CJ's definition with the words 'unless that would lead to some absurdity … repugnance or inconsistency with the rest of the instrument'.

This was obviously not much of a clarification as nothing further was suggested until the 20th century when Lord Reid began to contribute to the debate in *Jones v DPP*[34] in which he said that a judge could not generally depart from the ordinary meaning of a statute but if there was more than one meaning of the words in question the judge could choose which one to follow. At first sight, this looks like narrowing the original literal rule even further than Jervis CJ and Parke B had already done but commentators seem to be claiming that in fact this *widens* a judge's choice as it means that under the golden rule s/he may be able to choose between two possibilities (1) where a word has more than one meaning, the judge should choose the most sensible one, but (2) where the words would lead to the absurdity, repugnance or inconsistency feared by Parke B then the words could be altered to avoid this: the example usually given of this obviously undesirable result is the case of *Re Sigsworth*.[35] In this case a son had murdered his mother and then committed suicide, so as there was no Will applicable the statute to be interpreted was the Administration of Estates Act 1925 as the mother was intestate. As this meant the deceased son's family would inherit her property through him, and there was a principle of public policy that a murderer should not profit from his crime, the Act was interpreted to avoid such a 'repugnant' result. Lord Denning was one of the two judges hearing this case.

There is also another case concerning a murderer son where public policy enabled an interpretation in accordance with public policy which reinforces the idea that in these cases there is a sign of the development of the later purposive approach. This second case is *R v Registrar General ex parte Smith*.[36] In this case the son (Smith) was in custody in Broadmoor as he periodically had recurring psychotic episodes, having already committed two murders. The statute to construe in this case was the Adoption Act 1976 s 51(1) as he had been adopted and he wanted to obtain his original birth certificate so he could find his natural mother which was permitted to adults under that section and with certain conditions: he had made an entirely correct application to obtain the original certificate so as to ascertain her identity,

32 [1854] 14 CB 357.
33 [1857] 6 HL Cas 61.
34 [1962] AC 635 (HL).
35 [1935] Ch 89 (Ch).
36 [1991] 2 QB 393 (CA), [1991] 2 WLR 782.

and had consented to the compulsory counselling which any applicant who had become
entitled to apply for the details in question at the age of 18 was obliged to undergo before
receiving that information and nothing stood in the way of the Registrar's obligation to
supply it since the statute stated that upon satisfaction of these conditions he 'shall' supply
it despite the natural concern that he might feel in a case such as Smith's where a natural
mother so discovered in adulthood might be blamed for the son's adoption and thus be
harmed by someone of Smith's mental state. Indeed, a psychiatrist consulted on the matter
considered that he might harm the mother if the information he sought was supplied. It
was therefore decided that, despite the plain language of the Act, Parliament could not have
intended to promote serious crime so again the Act was interpreted so that the Registrar did
not have to release the information which might have risked the natural mother's life.

A wider departure from the literal rule to avoid absurd consequences occurred in *Adler v George*.[37]
In this case the statute was the Official Secrets Act 1920, which protected certain of HM Forces
bases by prosecuting anyone found 'in the vicinity of' such a place. The accused was found
actually 'in' the base when he was apprehended and the court considered that it would be absurd
to be able to convict someone apprehended outside and not someone who had already gained
entry, so interpreted 'in the vicinity of' to include actually within the prohibited place.

MISCHIEF RULE

The 'mischief rule' is much older than either the 19th-century literal rule as originally
articulated or the golden rule as expanded that earlier rule shortly afterwards, as the 'mischief
rule' dates from the 16th-century Heydon's Case.[38] The facts of the case do not matter, as what
is important is the formulation of the proper interpretation of a statute which replaced a
rule of common law at a time when there were not many statutes and the principles of the
common law formed the bulk of the law of England. What the Barons of the Exchequer court
suggested after some debate was to ask the following four questions:

1 What was the common law before the passing of the Act?
2 What was the 'mischief' and 'defect' for which the common law did not provide? – (thus
   requiring the Act to be passed)
3 What remedy had the Parliament 'resolved and appointed' to cure the defect?
4 What was the true reason of the remedy?

A modern example of the application of the mischief rule is the case of *Smith v Hughes*;[39] the
mischief in that case was prostitutes soliciting 'on the street' to the annoyance of the public
and the Act to be interpreted the Street Offences Act 1959, s 1(1) which prohibited common
prostitutes from causing such annoyance, since it made it an offence to 'loiter or solicit in a
street or public place for the purpose of prostitution'. The women were not in fact in the street

37 [1964] 2 QB 7 (QB).
38 [1584] Co Rep 7a, i.e. reported in Coke's Reports, those of Sir Edward Coke, a barrister later Chief Justice of England
    under Queen Elizabeth I and considered to be the greatest jurist of the Elizabethan and Jacobean ages.
39 [1960] 1 WLR 830 (QB).

itself but were on balconies or at open or closed windows at street level and were attracting the attention of men by calling out to them or even by tapping on the windows. Lord Parker LCJ pointed out the mischief was people being unable to walk along the street without being accosted by prostitutes, so applying the mischief rule the prostitutes were preventing that peaceful passing and repassing despite not actually being in or on the street as they were as much in or on it on the balconies and at the windows.

The same rule was applied to taxis parked on private land adjacent to the street without a licence required for 'plying for hire in the street' in *Eastbourne Borough Council v Stirling*[40] even though the private land was the railway station and the designated space a taxi rank since it was within sight of the street from which it could be hailed.

PURPOSIVE RULE

The 'purposive rule' is the most modern in the statutory interpretation toolkit. It goes much further than any of the other rules as it looks to see what the statute was intending to achieve and thus what Parliament must have meant. We have already had Lord Denning's early attempt at a purposive approach in *Magor and St Mellons Newport Corporation*[41] at that time unsuccessful in the face of opposition from Lord Simmonds in the House of Lords. However in modern times this rule seems to trace its origins to 1973 when the UK joined the EU's predecessor, the then European Economic Community, the 'EEC' ('Common Market') and the UK and its national judges began to have contact with the Court of Justice of the European Union and they first became acquainted with the Treaty of Rome 1957 which had set up the Common Market and set out the general principles of the members' participation and interpretation of that membership. At this stage UK judges would have become familiar with the purposive approach in connection with those parts of the law which were passed to conform to European law, which required national law passed in accordance with a relevant Directive of European law to be interpreted purposively i.e. 'in the light of the wording and purpose of the Directive': *von Colson v Land Nordrhein-Westfalen*.[42]

An example of the use of this purposive approach in a national statute was in *Pickstone v Freemans plc*[43] where the statute involved was the Equal Pay Act 1970 into which a new provision, s 1(2)(c), had been added to implement the Equal Pay Directive (75/117/EEC) and was about giving the same rate of pay to workers who did 'like work' to workers of the opposite sex where there was otherwise a differently gendered rate, so that they could make a claim to be paid for 'work of equal value' if they ought to be paid the same rate for that as another worker of the opposite sex even if not doing the same job. There were subsequently many of these as the EEC and EU set about virtually completely remodelling our domestic employment law, which owes much of its modernisation to the principles of European law. In the 1970s English law also overhauled its anti-discrimination statutes, e.g. in its Sex Discrimination

---

40 [2001] RTR 7 (QB).
41 [1952] AC 189 (HL).
42 Case 14/3 [1984] ECR 1891.
43 [1989] AC 66 (HL).

Act 1975 and Race Relations Act 1976 (see for example *Jones v Tower Boot Co Ltd*[44]) and the literal interpretation would seriously undermine the developing domestic anti-discrimination law.

Even more recently Human Assisted Reproduction law has developed beyond all previous recognition. This began in 1985 with the Surrogacy Arrangements Act and in 1990 with the first Human Fertilisation and Embryology Act which quickly led to cases such as R (*Quintavalle*) v *Secretary of State*[45] in which the House of Lords needed the purposive approach to address the meaning of cell nuclear replacement (CNR) and whether it could be placed within the meaning of s 1(1)(a) of the HFEA 1990, since CNR (a type of cloning) did not exist when the Act was passed. But the more recent HFEA 2008 has catered for remarkable advances in both law and medical science applicable to this field of law and practice which occasionally throw up recondite interpretation demands such as recently in the interpretation of the HFEA in relation to whether a female to male trans person with a retained womb not removed during his gender transition surgery and who gives birth as a result of hormone treatment and IVF is a mother or a father. So far the Registrar of Births, Deaths and Marriages has decided that such a person is a 'male mother' and government lawyers addressing the High Court in proceedings taken by a man identified only as TT[46] following the Registrar's refusal to register the man as the child's 'father' claimed at the hearing in 2019 that the term 'mother' is no longer gender specific[47], despite the fact that HFEA 2008 s 27 currently defines 'a mother' as a 'woman' who has given birth and the 'male mother' in question has stated that he wishes to continue to live as *a man* (in which gender he has been recognised for some years) on the grounds that he does not want his former life as a woman to become known to his daughter since he considers this not to be for her welfare: clearly there is now some collision between the Gender Recognition Act 2004 and the HFEA 2008 which needs legislative clarification by amendment of s 27.[48] The child was conceived by IVF with the man's former male partner although the relationship has now broken up and the man is raising the child as a single parent. The child refers to the former partner as her 'other Daddy'. The Court held that, despite hitherto acceptance that 'mother' was female, the purpose of the Act being interpreted to identify the *parental* status[49] from the biological role played in the birth and not the recognised *gender* of those involved. The conclusion was, therefore, that the trans man had given birth to his daughter and so the term 'mother' was the correct term in law.

Secondly, as noted previously, judges have increasingly become familiar with the purposive practices of interpretation in European law, in domestic law made under Directives and also from association with other jurisdictions' judges in the context of a variety of opportunities in judicial comity. The approach has also received support from the decision in *Pepper* (*Inspector*

---

44 [1997] All ER 406 (CA).

45 [2003] UKHL 13, [2003] 2 AC 687.

46 R (TT) v *The Registrar General for England and Wales* [2019] EWHC 2384 (Fam).

47 www.telegraph.co.uk, 14 February 2019 and 19 February 2019.

48 A point recognised by the court 'to be a pressing need for Government and Parliament to address square-on the question of the status of a trans-male who has become pregnant and given birth to a child' [125].

49 To ensure a certain and coherent system of recording births.

of Taxes) v Hart[50] (a case on the amount to be taxed under the contemporary Finance Act s
63 was to be calculated in relation to the provision of a school fee benefit for school staff
at Malvern College boys' public school) in which it was accepted that Hansard accounts
of proceedings in Parliament could be used in a limited way in order to discover what
Parliament had intended, but only where there is ambiguity or absurdity without its use,
unless, of course, the statute in question falls into the category of those for which a purposive
approach is required because the Act in question has introduced an international Convention
or Directive into English law, see *Three Rivers District Council v Bank of England (No 2)*.[51]

CONCLUDING REMARKS ON THE RULES

In reality judges are not always faced with stark choices about the interpretation of an Act. It
is often the case that there are several alternative approaches that could be used to dispose of a
case and courts are faced with a number of competing interests. Even within a case alternative
approaches may be used to decide different issues. What the preceding is intended to
demonstrate is that one should not necessarily start the search for parliamentary intent with
a particular method of interpretation in mind. The distinct problems identified early in this
chapter, which give rise to the need for interpretation, may require different interpretative
responses. Even the context, area or extent of development of the law may prove influential
on how judges approach statutory interpretation and this is without consideration of personal
preferences of the members of the judiciary. In the case of *Twinsectra v Jones*[52] the Lands Tribunal
(now the Lands Chamber of the Upper Tribunal) was again faced with the interpretation of
the Landlord and Tenant Act. In constructing a response the tribunal formulated a four stage
process of construction:

1   That the tribunal assess the results of applying alternatives
2   Which 'leads to the least inconvenience'
3   To avoid an approach that leads to injustice
4   To 'reject' any construction that 'enables a person to defeat a statute ... or otherwise
    profit by his own wrong'

Figure 6.7 demonstrates a way of conceptualising the effect of selecting one approach or
'rule' over another. The literal approach generally results in the narrowest scope of application
whereas the teleological approach grants the widest discretion and powers to judges. Given
that the scope of discretion of judges increases as you move down the pyramid so does the
risk of accusations of judicial law-making. The court must balance these competing interests
of achieving fairness and of avoiding intruding on the legislative.

In addition to the rules and approaches to statutory interpretation identified in the current
section of the chapter, the courts are also guided by other tools, principles and presumptions
that can affect the outcome of any given interpretation.

---

50 [1993] AC 593 (HL).
51 [1996] 2 All ER 363 (QB).
52 [1998] 23 EGLR 129.

Figure 6.7 The Scope of Different Approaches to Statutory Interpretation

ANALYSING THE LAW – RETURNING TO THE HYPOTHETICAL SITUATION

As we have now explored the substantive rules and principles underpinning statutory interpretation it would seem wise to return to the problem of feral cats.

Imagine that the United Kingdom has a problem with a growing population of wild cats that are causing significant health problems for particular breeds of domesticated cats. After much public pressure on the issue Parliament decides to legislate on the issue and passes the **Feral Cat (Destruction) Act 2013**. Amongst other things this fictional Act of Parliament contains the following sections:

s 1 – It shall be an offence for any person to feed, water and give shelter to any feral cat.
s 4 – In the absence of a claim of ownership within 72 hours, an authorised Destruction Officer who is in possession of a feral cat may destroy it.
s 20 – For the purposes of this Act a cat shall be considered to be feral if it is of a type contained within Schedule 1 or if it is discovered to be in a public place after nightfall on no fewer than three occasions.
Schedule 1 – A cat is included within this Act if it is of one of the following breeds: Persian, Siamese, American Bobtail or Peterbald.

In light of the principles of law explored and discussed in this chapter, can you now identify any additional aspects of the Act that may raise issues of interpretation? How could/would you apply the 'rules' of statutory interpretation to this Act? To what extent should the courts take into account the public health concerns that led to the passage of the Act? The companion website gives additional guidance and tips on how to approach problem questions in this area and gives some 'answers' to this scenario.

PRESUMPTIONS AND PRINCIPLES

Obviously, the different methods of statutory interpretation have now themselves created a new problem, in deciding which method is most appropriate, since it is clear from the increasing adoption of the purposive approach that judges are still using a variety of the available methodologies.[53] This might be explicable in the early years after the UK joined the pre-1992 EEC but as time went on it might have been assumed that some general agreement would be reached about which method is to be used. That has still not happened, although Lord Denning in *Northam v London Borough of Barnet*,[54] quoting from the Law Commission's 1969 report recommending harmonisation, said 'the literal method is now completely out of date'. He went on, 'in all cases now in the interpretation of statutes we adopt such a construction as will promote the general legislative purpose underlying the provision and that whenever the strict interpretation of a statute gives rise to an absurd or unjust situation, the judges can and should use their good sense to remedy it – by reading words in if necessary – so as to do what Parliament would have done had they had the situation in mind.'

This echoes the Law Commission's recommendation that 'the principles of interpretation would include:

(i) the preference of a construction which would promote the general legislative purpose over one which would not;
(ii) the preference of a construction which is consistent with the international obligations of the United Kingdom over one which is not.'

However, it is unlikely that, simply because we have now left the EU shortly, the purposive construction will be abandoned in view of its proved utility in cases where the advance of science has clearly required it, such as those involving the HFEA 2008 mentioned previously.

Another principle which, however, conflicts with preference being given to a purposive approach is in relation to criminal statutes where it has always been a practice that such a statute must be clear because it imposes liability on the citizen, thus arguing for the literal rule to be used in such contexts, although this did produce an absurd result in *DPP v Cheeseman*[55] (a case of indecent exposure contrary to s 28 of the Town Police Clauses Act 1847, in which technically the offence needed to be committed in the street, but was in fact committed in a public lavatory) so the conviction was quashed, which does not sit well with the decision in *Smith v Hughes*[56] where the purposive approach secured convictions.

....

53 For example, *Smith v Hughes* (1960, Parker LCJ, mischief rule); *Fisher v Bell* (1960, Parker LCJ, literal rule); *Royal College of Nursing v DHSS* (1981, mischief rule, but disagreement between the House of Lords judges as to which was the appropriate rule to use). Law Commission, *The Interpretation of Statutes* (Law Comm No 21, 1969) recommended harmonisation of the methods of interpretation used by judges, but this has not been not adopted.
54 [1978] 1 All ER 1243 (CA).
55 [1992] QB 83 (QB).
56 (1990) *The Times*, 2 November.

Standards required of criminal statutes also generate certain presumptions:

1   Against a change in the common law unless a clear statute rebuts this, see e.g. *Leach v R*[57] (Criminal Evidence Act 1898 did not displace the rule that a wife cannot be compelled to give evidence against her husband as the Act did not mention this at all).
2   That *mens rea* is required in criminal cases, see e.g. *Sweet v Parsley*[58] (landlord of premises not liable under the Misuse of Drugs Act 1971 if she did not know of tenants smoking cannabis, as no *mens rea*, and the Act did not address the issue of *mens rea*).
3   The Crown is not bound by any statute unless the statute expressly states so (see e.g. Occupiers Liability Act, Equal Pay Act 1970, Health and Safety at Work Act 1974 all expressly state so, where others do not, there is no liability).
4   Legislation does not apply retrospectively unless expressly stated to do so (see e.g. War Crimes Act 1991 and War Damage Act 1965 do so apply as this is expressly stated, but very few other statutes contain such express statement). However s 28 of the Criminal Justice and Court Services Act 2000 does apply retrospectively despite no such statement as it is a provision to protect children, disqualifying a person convicted of an offence against a child committed before the Act was passed from working with children, which is right to apply to such offences or the purpose of the provision would be seriously undermined.

RULES OF LANGUAGE

However even where the literal rule is used there are minor rules intended to assist interpretation. These are

1   The *eiusdem generis* ('same type') rule (where general words follow specific words the general words must be interpreted as of the same class as the specific words (see e.g. *Hobbs v C G Robertson*,[59] brick not similar material to stone, concrete or slag for the Construction (General Provision) Regulations 1961 and the wearing of goggles – brick a soft material unlikely to chip off unlike the others).
2   The *expressio unius est exclusion alteris* rule (express mention of one thing excludes others) – where a list of words is not followed by others of a general nature then only the specific words are included in a statute (see e.g. *Tempest v Kilner*,[60] which had the effect of excluding shares from the Statute of Frauds 1671, as that referred only to sale of 'goods, wares and merchandise' of more than £10 to be evidenced in writing).
3   The *noscitur a sociis* rule (meaning a word is known by the company it keeps) which requires the context in which a word appears to be considered (see e.g. *Inland Revenue*

57 [1912] AC 305 (HL).
58 [1970] AC 132 (HL).
59 [1970] 2 All ER 347 (CA).
60 (1846) 3 CB 249.

Commissioners v Frere,[61] where construing an Act for help with the meaning of 'interest, annuities or other annual interest' it was concluded that only annual interest payments should count, excluding daily, weekly or monthly interest.

INTERPRETATIVE AIDS

Apart from Hansard[62] there are other 'aids' to interpretation:

1 'Intrinsic' aids – anything else in the statute that provides a clue to interpretation, e.g. long title, short title, preamble – such as the Theft Act 1968 states that it is to modernise the law of theft and includes a number of associated offences – although there are also headings and schedules that may also assist.
2 'Extrinsic' aids – anything outside the Act: this is where Hansard and Law Commission Reports come in, together with Directives and Regulations emanating from the EU which result in national legislation, but also previous Acts on the same subject, the historical setting, case law and even dictionaries of the time an Act was passed. Law Commission Reports were allowed to look for the 'mischief' after Lord Reid's strong statement in support of the purposive approach in *Black Clawson International v Papierwerke AG*[63] (but the judges in the House of Lords were still divided at that time about whether they could use it to find the intention of Parliament) and a case in which the court looked at a Law Commission Report was *DPP v Bull*[64] where the Court looked at the Wolfenden Report (*Report of the Committee on Homosexual Offences and Prostitution*).

Lord Denning tried to use Hansard long before *Pepper v Hart* in a domestic violence case[65] but was once again slapped down by the House of Lords, where Lord Scarman said any such use was 'unreliable' promoting 'confusion not clarity'. Lord Denning said not using Hansard was like 'a grope about in the dark for the meaning of an Act without switching on the light'!

CONCLUSION

Amongst all of the technical rules on the admissibility, or desirability, of using various aids to interpretation and the difficult choices over which 'approach' should gain priority, it is easy to lose sight of the core issues that underlie this whole area of law.

61 [1965] AC 402 (HL).
62 Governed specifically by the rule in *Pepper (Inspector of Taxes) v Hart* [1993] AC 593 (HL).
63 [1975] 1 All ER 810 (HL).
64 [1995] QB 88 (QB).
65 *Davis v Johnson* [1979] AC 264.

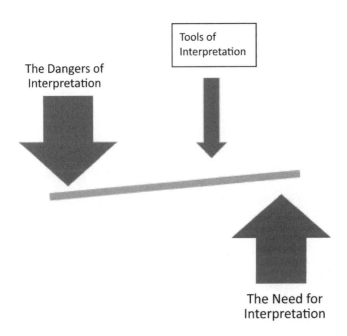

Figure 6.8 Tools of Interpretation as a Balancing Force

First, and foremost, the English language will continue to cause problems of interpretation, no matter how well-drafted or exhaustive is the discussion surrounding the passage of an Act of Parliament. In fact, much of the beauty of the English language lies in its ambiguity, nuance and subtlety. If we accept this truth, and wish to see an English Legal System capable of dealing with the increasing complexity of the world, then we must also accept judges must play a central role in the interpretative process. This will, of necessity, involve judges making determinations about the meaning of words in statutes. Rather than expressing concerns over individual cases of statutory interpretation it is more important to deal with the interaction between the myriad of reasons requiring statutory interpretation and the specific approaches to such interpretation. The art of proper construction is predicated on achieving the perfect balance between the need for statutory interpretation and the proper role of the court in the English Legal System. The tools of statutory interpretation act as a counterbalance (Figure 6.8) to prevent the courts from stepping into the shoes of the legislature while still allowing the judiciary to solve the problems provided by the written word.

THE WEBSITE

The website that accompanies this textbook contains many useful resources that you can use to consolidate and further your knowledge of the law, to hone your skills of critical analysis and to test your knowledge. The companion website contains genuine assessment opportunities for you to monitor your progress through the text. This consists of short multiple choice questions, extended essays and problem questions. There is also exemplar material available, complete with comments from an examiner.

PODCASTS

- The podcasts provide a summary of the area under study, bringing together the key areas under discussion.
- There will also be an explanation and analysis of an up-to-date case study of a recent Act of Parliament that may require interpretation from the courts.
- The author talks through a worked example of an essay on statutory interpretation, commenting on the strengths and weaknesses of the substance and approach.

7

CHAPTER 7
THE JUDICIARY

INTRODUCTION

The judiciary is at the heart of the English Legal System, interpreting and applying the law that Parliament makes to individual cases. Additionally, judges make law in certain areas. As judges are responsible for recognising and giving life to 'the law', particularly through the common law, it is vitally important that they retain their authority and the trust of citizens. Maintaining independence and public trust is not always easy but knowing the *nature* of the judicial task and the challenges that the structure of the judiciary poses will give a richer understanding of how law operates in the English Legal System on a day to day basis.

This chapter has two main aims. First to introduce the reader to the role of the judiciary and to explain (briefly) the different types of judicial office. Second, the chapter will explore some of the thornier issues (such as diversity in appointment and misconduct in judicial office) which jeopardise or threaten the attainment of one or more of the objectives of the legal system.

AS YOU READ

This chapter consists of a fairly dense set of (sometimes descriptive) information about various aspects of the judiciary. As you read, be sure to try to contextualise this information in light of the other chapters of the textbook and avoid reading it in isolation.

By the end of this chapter you should be able to **identify the different levels of the judiciary** and **distinguish between senior and inferior** judicial office holders.

In considering appointments to the judiciary you should **think critically about diversity appointment** and **evaluate the effectiveness of changes to the process of judicial appointment.** Throughout the chapter **consider the extent to which the independence of the judiciary is secured or undermined** by the points being discussed.

NATURE OF JUDGING AND ROLE OF THE JUDICIARY

Before exploring the different types of judicial office it is important to give a brief account of the role of the judiciary in the English Legal System. This will add much needed context and give an insight into the type of person who may be attracted to, and have aptitude for, judicial office.

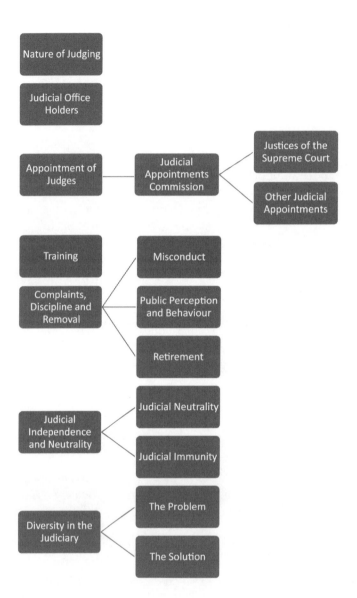

Figure 7.1

MAKING CONNECTIONS – THE JUDICIARY AND THE LEGAL SYSTEM
++
There are important links to be made with other chapters in the textbook. The judiciary
do not operate in isolation but form an integral part of the overall system. For more
on the core role of the judiciary, look at the chapters on **statutory interpretation
(Chapter 6)** and judicial **precedent (Chapter 9)**. To explore the way in which the
judiciary interacts with other parts of the legal system, look at the chapter on **sources
of law (Chapter 2)** and the **institutions of law-making (Chapter 3).** For a richer
understanding of how judges contribute to particular areas of the justice system,

refer to the **criminal justice (Chapter 11)** and **civil justice (Chapter 10)** parts of the textbook.

This section of the textbook focusses primarily on judicial office holders and does not deal with the system of lay magistrates in any level of detail, despite the fact that since early medieval times magistrates courts have been the location of the start of both civil and criminal cases and every criminal case to this day begins in a magistrates court (for which see Chapter 11).

The website that accompanies this text has a separate section dedicated to the magistracy and the role that they play in the legal system.

To talk of the 'judicial function' or the 'role of the judiciary' is to treat the 'judiciary' as if it is a single role or function but this fundamentally misunderstands the nature of the judicial task. Any text seeking to differentiate the institutions of the legal system will claim that the judiciary 'apply' and 'interpret' the law and that they act as the 'resolvers of disputes'.[1] These three pillars of the judicial system risk oversimplifying what it is that judges do and how they do it. There are multiple roles within the judiciary and different types of judges have responsibility not only for different areas of law and different types of dispute but also for different aspects of the justice system and for performing aspects of these overarching tasks of application and interpretation to varying degree. The life of a judge in the County Court can be very different to that of a Court of Appeal judge which is, again, very different to that of a judge sitting in the Crown Court. As such, the mix of functions that a particular member of the judiciary plays will also vary enormously.

Of all the branches of the state, it is the judiciary that arguably has the most varied and multifaceted role. Laid out (briefly) in Table 7.1 is a list of just some of the tasks faced by those who hold judicial office.

It is also worth making the point that the role(s) of the judiciary incorporates a temporal dimension that has changed over time and that will continue to change in the future. Aspects of the role take on different degrees of importance at different times in the development of the legal system. As discussed in the chapters on law-making (Chapters 4 and 5) and sources of law (Chapter 2), the traditional role of the judiciary has focussed on the development of the common law. This was due to the fact that statutes were not as numerous prior to the mid-20th century. The growth of statutory law, without necessary improvements to the quality of such law, has led to a greater need for judges to interpret Acts of Parliament. The interpretative role played by judges has therefore become a greater part of the judiciary's work than was once the case. The differing emphasis placed on alternative aspects of the judicial role over time is something that is even recognised by senior members of the judiciary. Lord Woolf once stated that it was 'one of the strengths of the common law that it enables the courts to

---

1   For a provocative account of the judicial role, see John Griffith, *The Politics of the Judiciary* (5th edn, Fontana Press 2010).

Table 7.1 The Tasks of Judiciary

Role	Description
Fact finders	In the vast majority of civil and criminal cases, judges find the facts.[2] This means that they establish, where issues are contested, what the true facts of the case are. This is an important role as it is the material facts that give rise to the legal issue that needs to be resolved.
Give interpretation of the law	Where Acts of Parliament (or secondary law) are unclear or could bear multiple meanings, judges are called upon to determine the meaning of the law. In this sense, the judiciary gives an abstract interpretation of what the statutory provisions mean. Judges are also responsible, where juries are involved, for explaining the applicable law to the jury.
Apply the law	Once the facts have been established and an interpretation of the law given, it is normally the judge's role to *apply* that interpretation to the specific facts in order to resolve the legal issue in question. They must also apply sentencing guidelines in the case of criminal trials.
Resolve disputes	It should not be forgotten that judges interpret or apply the law in cases where parties are in dispute. In this narrow sense, judges presiding over the courts to which applications are made provide a means of independently settling disputes. In a broader sense, and following the Woolf reforms to the civil justice system, judges are also there to encourage parties to engage with dispute resolution mechanisms short of litigation (such as mediation or arbitration), which are now at the core of dispensation of justice in all westernised jurisdictions grappling with resolution of legal disputes.
Create law	Through the common law in particular, judges make law. Their interpretation of statutes can also be considered as a form of law-making. There are distinct chapters in this textbook on judges' interpretation of the law and on the case decision method by which judges make law. As Lord Denning put it '[judges] every day make law, though it is almost heresy to say so.'[3]
Adjudicate on procedure	The English Legal System has a sophisticated and complex body of rules relating to court procedure and a whole branch of law related to rules surrounding evidence. Judges must also adjudicate on these satellite issues as and when they arise in given cases.

....

2   Where juries are used, it is the jurors' role to determine facts though the judge will give them helpful directions to
    assist them to focus on the issues to be determined. The role of juries is considered in greater detail in Chapter 12.
3   Cited in Michael Zander, *The Law-Making Process* (7th edn, Bloomsbury Publishing 2015) 344.

Role	Description
Check on executive powers	Judges can also be called upon to adjudicate on Government action and act as a check that other branches of the state have not exceeded their powers. This is primarily achieved through the system of judicial review. This control of state power is a constitutional check that maintains the proper separation of powers and preserves the rule of law.
Safeguard the rule of law	In more recent years, partly prompted by the powers under the Human Rights Act 1998 judges have taken a more active role in safe-guarding important constitutional principles such as the rule of law. For example, in the case of *Reilly (No2)*,[4] the High Court was extremely critical of the way in which the Government (and Parliament) had passed retrospective legislation to invalidate an ongoing legal dispute as this violated the principle of the rule of law.[5]
Manage cases	The judiciary now has an important part to play in an administrative and management sense. They control the court lists and the way in which the building housing the court itself operates. They must also actively manage cases and assign dates to hearings. This is important in reducing delays and preventing (or minimising) tactical applications designed to give one party an unfair advantage. Although some of these management tasks can be delegated to administrative staff, the responsibility tends to lie with more senior members at each level of the justice system.
Provoke changes	Judges are also in a position to influence the development of the law in a less direct way than mentioned previously under the title 'create law'. Where judges are unable to change the law (for example where there is a binding precedent or there is a clear parliamentary intent contrary to the position that the judge wishes to take) they can still provoke changes. A well-reasoned judgment can influence higher courts to take a different view and a convincing and powerful criticism of the current law may lead Parliament to rethink its position. This ability for judges to provoke reform has been strengthened by the passage of the Human Rights Act 1998 and the ability of judges to highlight where legislation is incompatible with fundamental rights.[6]

4   R (on the application of Reilly (No 2) and Hewstone v Secretary of State for Work and Pensions [2014] EWHC 2182 (Admin), [2015] 2 WLR 309.

5   The prospect of retroactive legislation is an anathema to the English Legal System as it offends against the rule of law – see David Stott, 'Reilly and Hewstone v Secretary of State for Work and Pensions' (2016) SLR 3.

6   Section 4 of the Human Rights Act 1998 gives judges the power to declare legislation to be incompatible with the European Convention on Human Rights and this triggers powers for the Government speedily to amend Acts of Parliament.

vary the extent of their intervention to reflect current needs, and by this means it helps to maintain the delicate balance of a democratic society.'[7] The development of international (and domestic) fundamental rights protection has also affected the way in which the judiciary approaches its task.

ANALYSING THE LAW – JUDGES BEYOND THE COURTS

In addition to the tasks (mentioned earlier) associated with their office, judges also fulfil a number of roles 'extrajudicially' and these can complement (or even jeopardise) their work. For example, judges can act as Chancellors for Universities, give lectures to various institutions[8] and also write commentaries on the law. This enhances the profile of the judiciary and the authority of their office can add significant weight to these extrajudicial roles. Despite the qualities that judges undoubtedly bring to such tasks, it can be difficult (for the public) to disassociate the judicial from the non-judicial in some cases, and for judges to ensure that they maintain an impartiality compatible with their judicial role: for example in the case of the former Mr Justice Coleridge, a leading judge of the Family Division of the High Court, whose work with broken families in Family Justice led him to set up the Marriage Foundation which promotes marriage as the optimum family format in which to bring up children (a point of view not without significant statistical support). However, in the light of contemporary equality and diversity thought he eventually had to choose between his judicial role and the Foundation, his connection with which the government considered too partisan to be compatible with essential judicial neutrality so as to respect the equal and diverse requirements of a liberal democracy which now also acknowledges the validity of less historically traditional family formats.

In particular, senior members of the judiciary are often selected to lead public inquiries into matters of public interest.[9] By doing so they are acting on the appointment of the Government in a non-judicial capacity and do not sit as a judge during the course of the inquiry. These inquiries can have an extremely high profile in the public consciousness, such as the Leveson Inquiry, and can lead to confrontations or close interactions with the Government that blur the lines between when the judge is acting judicially and when he is not.[10]

The focus here has so far been on the role of the judiciary of England and Wales. It is important to remember that English judges are now part of a broader community of judges and that has influenced both their role and their *approach* to their judicial function. For

---

7 Lord Woolf, 'Droit Public – English Style' (1995) Public Law 57.

8 For a list of speeches given by the Justices of the Supreme Court, see www.supremecourt.uk/news/speeches.html.

9 Inquiries Act 2005 s 10.

10 See the public disagreements between a Government Minister (Michael Gove) and Lord Leveson during the inquiry chaired by the latter – www.bbc.co.uk/news/uk-18256724.

example, all English judges were also European judges in the sense that they were, until 2020, part of the legal order of the European Union. Similarly, but to a lesser extent, the European Court of Human Rights has had an influence (positive or negative depending on your political hue) on judicial office holders. The impact of the UK's former membership of the European Union is discussed in a distinct chapter of this work (Chapter 16).

More importantly, English judges, educated and trained in the traditions of the common law, have in recent years been influenced by their growing acquaintance with the methodology of the judiciary of civil justice jurisdictions in Europe and this has inevitably now impacted on previously long established methods of statutory interpretation in English common law (see Chapter 6). First foreseen by Lord Denning MR in the case of *Bulmer v Bollinger*[11] (in which he had an instant vision of this influence and of the continental judiciary's purposive approach sweeping into English law like 'an incoming tide. It flows into the estuaries and up the rivers. It cannot be held back') within only a year the House of Lords was giving the green light to accepting such continental influences in interpreting English statutes.

JUDICIAL OFFICE HOLDERS

There is a variety of different levels and roles within the judiciary and this section will attempt to summarise the different positions and, for the senior/superior[12] positions, give account of their place in the legal system. There are in excess of 4,000 judicial office holders[13] and a further 20,000 lay magistrates. This chapter will focus on the judicial office holders in the higher courts in the English Legal System, but the lay magistrates will be dealt with separately, as will the judiciary involved in the system of tribunals. The tribunals are historically – and to some extent still functionally – distinct and their judiciary has its own hierarchy, with rarely a crossover with the courts unless on appeal. The rationale for this separation of treatment will be obvious in the distinct sections on the lay magistrates and tribunals (Chapters 11 and 13).

The structure of the senior judiciary has gone through significant changes in the last ten years. Most importantly, responsibility for the *leadership* of the judiciary has transferred from the Lord Chancellor to the Lord Chief Justice. This occurred through the Constitutional Reform Act 2005 which separated the office's former connections with the judiciary and profession from the core responsibility of the office as a member of the Government, not least because (as head of the judiciary) this dual responsibility clearly fell foul of the doctrine of separation of powers as discussed in Chapter 3. The Lord Chancellor is thus now merely a position in Government, held concurrently but not necessarily by the Secretary of State for Justice. This

---

11 [1974] Ch 401 (Ch).

12 Superior judges have unlimited jurisdiction (provided that jurisdiction has not been limited by statute) and so can theoretically sit anywhere and decide fully on aspects of procedure – see *Al Rawi v The Security Service* [2011] UKSC 34, [2012] 1 AC 531 [72].

13 www.judiciary.uk/publications/judicial-diversity-statistics-2019-2.

move is a significant shift made to ensure the ongoing independence of the judiciary and it coincided with changes to the House of Lords.[14] The Lord Chancellor no longer needs to be legally qualified – s/he must instead be qualified 'by experience'[15] – as contemporary Lord Chancellors are no longer eligible to sit in any judicial capacity. Before David Gauke, the last legally qualified Lord Chancellor was Lord Falconer of Thoroton, in the Labour government which left office in 2010, who has since held the equivalent Labour Shadow post. Recent Conservative and Coalition ministers who could have done likewise have resigned.

Justices of the Supreme Court – The Supreme Court came into existence in 2009 and replaced the Appellate Committee of the House of Lords. The first Justices were drawn from the existing Lords of Appeal in Ordinary and have subsequently been appointed through ad hoc selection commissions (discussed later). There are 12 Justices, one of whom will serve as the President (at the time of writing Lord Reed) and another who will serve as the Deputy President (at the time of writing Lord Hodge). Sitting in the highest civil court in the United Kingdom and the highest criminal court in England, Wales and Northern Ireland[16] means that the Justices are the most high profile judges in the English Legal System. By convention, two of the Justices will be senior Scottish judges with a further Justice being selected from Northern Ireland. This is not a statutory requirement but the Constitutional Reform Act 2005 does require that, when making appointments, consideration is given to the expertise of the judges (as a whole) and that there is adequate knowledge of the law of the constituent parts of the United Kingdom.[17]

Lord Chief Justice – The Lord Chief Justice is the most senior office holder within the judiciary of England and Wales. As well as leading the judiciary as the President of the courts of England and Wales, the Lord Chief Justice is also a Head of Division,[18] leading the Criminal Division of the Court of Appeal. The Lord Chief Justice also has the role of making representations to Parliament on matters that he deems to be of importance to the judiciary.[19]

Heads of Division – The next most senior judges are the Heads of Division. The Master of the Rolls leads the Civil Division of the Court of Appeal while the President of the Queen's Bench Division,[20] the Chancellor of the High Court[21] and the President of the Family Division lead the respective Divisions of the High Court.

Lord and Lady Justices of Appeal – These are superior judges who sit ordinarily in the Court of Appeal. There are 38 such Justices.[22] When appointed to the Court of Appeal, Lord and Lady Justices become members of the Privy Council.

---

14 Whereby the judicial function of the Lords was transferred to the newly established Supreme Court.

15 Constitutional Reform Act 2005 s 2(1).

16 There is a separate criminal court system in Scotland.

17 Constitutional Reform Act 2005 s 27(8).

18 Constitutional Reform Act 2005 s 7(1).

19 Constitutional Reform Act 2005 ss 5(1) and (5)(a).

20 This post had previously also been held by the Lord Chief Justice but the responsibility was passed to a new post, created in 2005, when the latter became head of the judiciary.

21 This was a post that had previously been undertaken by the Lord Chancellor.

22 Senior Courts Act 1981 s 2.

Puisne[23] judges – These are the least senior of the superior judges. They sit in the High Court and are given knighthoods when they take up their office.

Inferior judges – There are also a collection of inferior judges who usually sit at lower levels within the legal system. These can be summarised as following – Circuit judges who sit in the County Courts, Family Court and Crown Court; District Judges who sit in the County Court; and Recorders who sit in the County Court and Crown Court. However Recorders must be distinguished from most of the other inferior judges since they – although at that level only part time and fee paid – comprise the first rung of the judicial ladder towards permanent appointment in the High Court and above. There are also 'Masters' (who are the equivalent of District Judges in the County Courts) who sit, largely on interlocutory – interim administrative – matters, in the Queen's Bench and Chancery Divisions of the High Court. The District Judges and Masters – although they form the hard working backbone of the superior courts – do not usually expect to be promoted to permanent appointments in the superior courts although there are exceptions, e.g. Dame Elizabeth Butler-Sloss, now Baroness Butler-Sloss who began in the Tribunal Judiciary and was then a Registrar of the Family Division (equivalent of a Master of the Queen's Bench and Chancery Divisions, later becoming today's District Judges of the Family Division) before being appointed to the High Court (as only the fourth woman to reach that Court, after Elizabeth Lane, Rose Heilbron and Margaret Booth).

The superior judges have unlimited jurisdiction in the sense that their powers come from (and are limited by) statute rather than the common law. This means that the authority for their action comes from their judicial office rather than from the court in which they sit.[24] By contrast, the inferior judges have a statutory basis for their jurisdiction and must sit in a place that is designated as a court.

ANALYSING THE LAW – THE POWER OF JUDICIAL PERSONALITY

A reading of the two opening sections of this chapter could paint something of a bland picture of the judiciary of the English Legal System. However, judges are not raised in captivity away from all human influence. Indeed, judges will have had a distinct career (albeit one likely to have been linked to the law) before taking up judicial office.

Judges have personalities and world views that are informed by, amongst other things, their education, employment and social backgrounds. This fact is important as it may affect (even subconsciously) the way in which they go about discharging the duties of their judicial offices. One of the great joys of studying the English Legal System is to embrace this fact and to understand that judges have character strengths and flaws that help to shape the life of the judiciary and the development of the law. That is not

---

23 Pronounced 'puny'.
24 See *Ipswich Board of Finance v Clark* [1973] Ch 323 (Ch) for a powerful example of this principle in action.

to say that judges are partisan or that they come to judgments not based on their understanding of the *law*; it is simply to note that their understanding of the law *and of the judicial function* may be coloured by their human experiences as much as by their legal experiences.[25]

If we look even at just the 20th century it is possible to study some of the notable characters of the English Legal System and to make some comment on their contribution to the judicial task. To take Lord Denning as just one, very famous, example, he has been described as being the most 'best-known and best-loved judge in the whole of our history'.[26] He had a determination to drive forward development of the common law and was noted for his creativity, for example resurrecting the long dead concept of promissory estoppel in contract law.[27] This was a much more proactive approach to the judicial function of law creation than prevalent in many of his contemporaries. As Master of the Rolls, and through sheer force of character, Denning also convinced other members of the Court of Appeal to attempt to alter the very rules of binding precedent in *Davis v Johnson*.[28] The House of Lords, with rather sharp words for Denning, rejected this attempt by reaffirming 'expressly, unequivocally and unanimously'[29] the existing rules of precedent. Nonetheless Lord Denning's attempts to free the Court of Appeal from the strict rules of precedent demonstrate the different way in which judges can view the judicial role.

As an example of background impacting on approach to the judicial function we can look to Lord Atkin's Christian faith which was a 'strong constant in his life'.[30] Lord Atkin was part of the majority that decided *Donoghue v Stevenson*[31] and he based his judgment on the 'neighbour' principle, even alluding to the parable of the Good Samaritan.[32] It is almost beyond question that the correct decision was reached in *Donoghue* – that the manufacturer owed a duty to end users of its products – but the path to it for Lord Atkin was eased by his ability to relate the issue to his faith. Although the concept of a 'legal neighbour' is different to that of the Christian concept of 'neighbour', it is clear that Lord Atkin's Christian morality could have influenced his decision.

Lady Hale's dissent as the only female member of the court in *Radmarcher*[33] is also a notable example of the justices' backgrounds potentially influencing their approach to decision-making.

---

25 For a detailed discussion of this concept see John Griffith, *The Politics of the Judiciary* (5th edn, Fontana Press 2010).

26 Tom Bingham, *The Business of Judging: Selected Essays and Speeches 1985–1999* (OUP 2000) 409.

27 *Central London Property Trust v High Trees House* [1947] KB 130 (KB).

28 *Davis v Johnson* [1978] 1 All ER 841 (CA).

29 *Davis v Johnson* [1979] AC 264 (HL).

30 Geoffrey Lewis, *Lord Atkin* (Bloomsbury 1999) 20.

31 *Donoghue v Stevenson* [1932] AC 562 (HL).

32 Ibid. 580 (Lord Atkin).

33 *Radmarcher v Granatino* [2010] UKSC 42, [2011] 1 AC 534.

APPOINTMENT OF JUDGES

CONTEXT

The appointment of judges, and particularly the most senior members of the judiciary, has long attracted criticism.[34] The history of judicial appointments is fascinating and rich but is largely beyond the scope of this text on the entire English Legal System.[35] Nonetheless, a flavour of that history is important to understanding the significance of the reform that has taken place in recent years.

In the dim and distant past, judicial appointments were solely in the gift of the Monarch and judges served at the 'King's Pleasure' as part of the King's Court. This meant that not only did potential judges need to find favour with the ruling monarch but that they had to maintain that favour in order to make a career in the judiciary and not be removed at the whim of the reigning monarch. This position was changed in the 18th century by the Act of Settlement 1701[36] which transformed judicial appointments to ones held indefinitely *'quamdiu se bene gesserint'* (during periods of good behaviour). This removed the stranglehold of ongoing patronage from the Monarch. The current wording for this principle can be found in the Senior Courts Act 1981 which states that senior judges will 'hold that office during good behaviour, subject to a power of removal by Her Majesty on an address presented to Her by both Houses of Parliament'.[37] This adds security of tenure for judicial office holders, which is a fundamental part of securing the independence of the judiciary. Securing such a vote in both Houses of Parliament would be unprecedented for the modern judiciary.

In fact no senior judge has ever been removed for misbehaviour, and rare too is even removal of a Circuit Judge (Judge Bruce Campbell was eventually removed from sitting by the then Lord Chancellor, Lord Hailsham, but was allowed to keep his judicial pension). There was also more recently a Court of Appeal Judge who was criticised for a serious procedural error (which nevertheless gained only sharp criticism from the Court of Appeal which dealt with his procedural error and three months of 'gardening leave' before his imminent retirement).

Recorders enjoy the protection of the significant parliamentary formality required for dismissal, no doubt largely because neither part time Recorders, nor either the original 19th-century tribunals or the 21st-century Tribunals Service existed in the 17th century when what is now the higher judiciary needed to be protected from the spite or even simple displeasure of the monarch. For more on this important topic of judicial behaviour and discipline, see the section on complaints, discipline and removal from judicial office.

....

34 For a flavour of the debate, see Brenda Hale, 'Equality and the Judiciary: Why Should We Want More Women Judges?'
    (2001) Public Law 489 and Kate Malleson, 'Creating a Judicial Appointments Commission: Which Model Works Best?'
    (2004) Public Law 102 particularly at 103–109.
35 If you are interested in the history, then see John Griffith, *The Politics of the Judiciary* (5th edn, Fontana Press 2010).
36 Article 7.
37 Senior Courts Act 1981 s 11(3).

Even with the passage of 300 years since the Act of Settlement there has still been controversy as late as the 20th century over the secretive and overtly partisan way in which certain members of the judiciary have in the past been appointed. As recently as the 19th century, certain appointments were still seen to be politically motivated and not based wholly on merit.[38] This was because the Lord Chancellor was responsible for the appointments and his office, as discussed elsewhere in this text, was overtly political. Even a Prime Minister of the time, Lord Salisbury, commented that 'party claims should always weigh very heavily in the disposal of the highest legal appointments. In dealing with them you cannot ignore the party system as you do in the choice of a general or an archbishop.'[39] These comments are revealing of the prevailing Conservative attitude of the time about the separation of powers and the independence of the judiciary. This links to the point made at the start of the chapter that the nature of the judicial role is not static and changes and evolves over time as political as well as legal thought changes.

The bench was equally seen to be reserved to barristers of long standing. Thus, solicitors were practically excluded from sitting in the senior courts of England and Wales. This was traditionally linked to the greater experience of the court process and of advocacy that went with being a member of the Bar. As rights of audience have expanded and a greater diversity of experience is seen as valuable for life on the bench, this qualification has slowly diminished.

The Courts and Legal Services Act 1990 significantly broadened the qualification requirements and allowed solicitors to be appointed to more senior judicial offices, although it is still perceived as easier to become a senior judge after a career at the Bar (due partly to the Inn structure for barristers).[40] In contrast to other judicial systems, a life on the bench is seen as a secondary career that follows on from a life in practice. This can exclude those who would have been suited to hold judicial office but who had not spent time as a solicitor or barrister. Lord Mackay as Lord Chancellor in the late 1980s was first to experiment in appointing academics as Recorders and at that time included Baroness Hale, later a full time High Court and Court of Appeal Judge, and the President of the Supreme Court. Lord Irvine, as Lord Chancellor in the New Labour government of 1997 relaxed the family unfriendly conditions for women and other minorities in his encouragement of a wider pool of applicants, famously remembered for his mantra when announcing these changes: 'Don't be shy: apply.' The Tribunals, Courts and Enforcement Act 2007 sought to alter previously restricting frameworks to a degree, by lifting some of the restrictions on the holding of judicial office and to reduce the qualifying time period before a person can apply for certain forms of judicial office. For example, the Lord Chancellor has used the powers under s 51 to extend the eligibility criteria for certain posts to include trade mark attorneys and Fellows of the Chartered Institute of Legal Executives.[41]

---

38 For an extensive examination of the issue, see Adam Geary, Wayne Morrison and Robert Jago, *The Politics of the Common Law: Perspectives, Rights, Processes and Institutions* (2nd edn, Routledge 2013) 190.

39 Lord Salisbury cited by Robert Stevens, *The English Judges: Their Role in the Changing Constitution* (Hart Publishing 2005) 14.

40 This led, indirectly, to Lord Collins becoming the first Lord of Appeal in Ordinary who had started a legal career as a solicitor.

41 Judicial Appointments Order 2008, SI 2008/2995 Schedule 1.

While the preceding paints a somewhat closed picture for attaining judicial office, there are examples of the most senior appointments being made to those who had never previously held full-time judicial office. In modern times, the most notable of these is Lord Sumption, who had spent the majority of his legal career as a barrister and had not previously held a full-time judicial post. Lord Sumption was the first person to be appointed to the Supreme Court in this manner but the situation was not unknown in the time of the House of Lords with Lords Reid, Carson and Radcliffe being other examples. Most recently it was announced that Professor Andrew Burrows[42] will take up a position on the Supreme Court in June 2020.

With the changes to the Lord Chancellor's office, brought about by the Constitutional Reform Act 2005, there were also significant changes made to the way in which certain judges were appointed. This was further to bolster the independence of the judiciary and to ensure greater transparency and diversity in the selection of judicial office holders. The Constitutional Reform Act 2005 achieved this by establishing a new Judicial Appointments Commission (JAC) that has become an integral part of the appointments process. As we shall see, the final recommendation will still come in most cases from the Lord Chancellor but his (or her) discretion has been severely limited to the extent that involvement in the process is more symbolic than substantive.

JUDICIAL APPOINTMENTS COMMISSION

The governing provisions[43] of the JAC, found within the Constitutional Reform Act 2005, deal briefly with membership of the Commission, leaving the detail to a Schedule at the end of the Act.[44] Figure 7.2 summarises the governance structure of the JAC.

The vast majority of appointments to the superior levels of the judiciary within the English Legal System are made on the recommendation of JAC. The notable exception is the Supreme Court, which has a specific process by which new Justices are selected. The following section will seek to summarise the appointments process as it applies to both the Supreme Court and to those covered by the JAC scheme, dealing first with the Supreme Court process.

JUSTICES OF THE SUPREME COURT

If a vacancy arises for a Justice of the Supreme Court, be it an ordinary judge or the President/Deputy President, then an ad hoc Selection Commission must be convened by the Lord Chancellor.[45] The commission is required to select on the basis of merit[46] and will consult with senior members of the judiciary who are not part of the commission, the Lord Chancellor and the First Ministers of the devolved regions.[47] The workings and composition of

----

42 An honorary QC and Professor of English Law at the University of Oxford, who has also been a part-time Recorder, Deputy High Court Judge and Law Commissioner – www.supremecourt.uk/news/lord-reed-appointed-next-president-of-supreme-court-alongside-three-new-justices.html.

43 Constitutional Reform Act 2005 s 61.

44 Constitutional Reform Act 2005 Schedule 12.

45 Ibid. s 26(5).

46 Ibid. s 27(5).

47 Ibid. s 27(2).

Figure 7.2 Membership of the Judicial Appointments Commission

a selection commission for the Supreme Court is laid out in Schedule 8 of the Constitutional Reform Act 2005.

A selection committee for a Justice shall comprise of the President of the Supreme Court, the Deputy President, and one member from each of the appointment bodies in England and Wales,[48] Scotland[49] and Northern Ireland[50] who will be nominated by the Lord Chancellor. One of these members is required to be non-legally qualified. The special commissions are free to decide upon the most appropriate selection process[51] but the final recommendation of this Selection Commission is notified to the Prime Minister by the Lord Chancellor for recommendation to the Queen. This stage is of symbolic importance only as the Constitutional Reform Act 2005 compels the Prime Minister to recommend this person to the Queen[52] and he is expressly prohibited from recommending another person.[53]

48 Judicial Appointments Commission.
49 Judicial Appointments Board for Scotland.
50 Northern Ireland Judicial Appointments Commission.
51 Constitutional Reform Act s 27(1).
52 Ibid. s 26(3)(a).
53 Ibid. s 26(3)(b).

OTHER JUDICIAL APPOINTMENTS

The establishment of the Judicial Appointments Commission has added significantly to the transparency and openness of appointments within England and Wales and is an important factor in maintaining trust in and respect for an independent judiciary. It may be convenient to talk of the 'system of judicial appointments' but there is not a single system for selecting judges. The system will vary (or at least the underlying provisions governing the appointment will be different) depending on the role and seniority of the judicial appointment in question. Distinct sections of the Constitutional Reform Act 2005 apply to different judicial office holders and dictate the process by which the JAC should make its recommendations. The JAC system covers the appointment of the Lord Chief Justice and other Heads of Division,[54] Lords Justices of Appeal[55] and puisne judges of the High Court.[56]

Despite the fact that there are different structures in place for different groups of judges, all selections for appointments are subject to certain overriding requirements. A panel of the JAC cannot make a selection for appointment to a judicial office unless it is satisfied that the person is 'of good character'.[57] More importantly, the JAC must make all selections based solely on merit.[58] This last overriding requirement sends a powerful message about the future of judicial appointments and is an indication that although the Lord Chancellor is still involved in the process, his political influence can no longer affect the outcome in any meaningful way. In taking its decisions the JAC has developed certain competencies that guide its selection process. These are: *intellectual capacity; personal qualities; an ability to understand and deal fairly; authority and communication skills; and efficiency.*[59] The 'efficiency' criterion is of significant importance owing to the demands now made on judges of every level in disposing of business in a timely manner due to the stringency of the austerity cuts that have had to be made in Her Majesty's Courts and Tribunal Service.

Figure 7.3 indicates the procedure that the JAC follows for making its selection and proposing its recommended candidates.

ANALYSING THE LAW – THE LORD CHANCELLOR AND JUDICIAL APPOINTMENTS

As has been seen throughout this section, there have been substantial changes to the way in which judicial appointments are made. From a secretive, insular and potentially politically driven process, we now have a system that is (more) open, transparent and

54 Ibid. ss 66–75.
55 Ibid. ss 76–84.
56 Ibid. ss 85–94B.
57 Ibid. s 63.
58 Constitutional Reform Act 2005 s 63.
59 https://jac.judiciary.gov.uk/925-qualities-and-abilities.

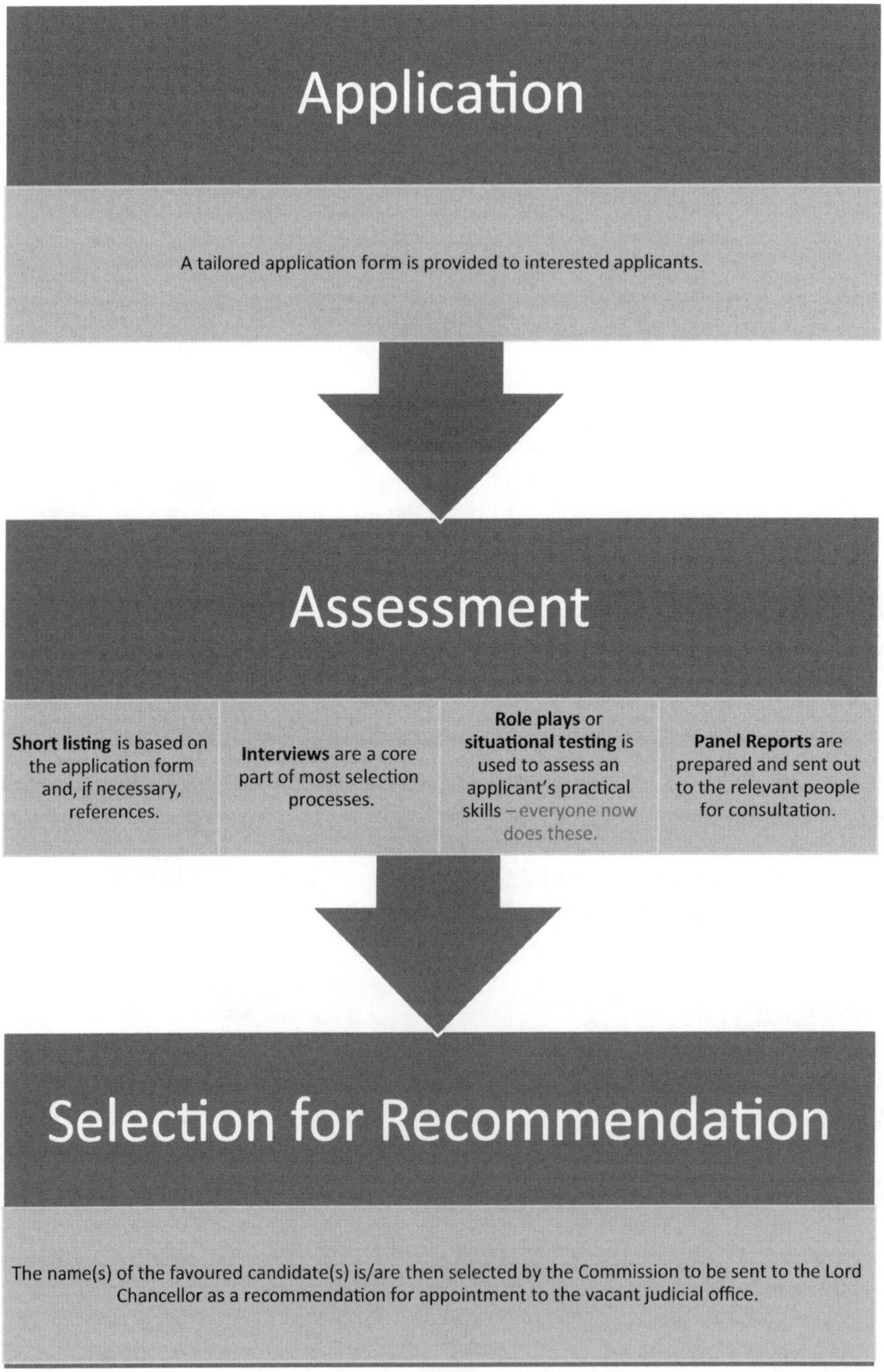

Application

A tailored application form is provided to interested applicants.

Assessment

Short listing is based on the application form and, if necessary, references.	**Interviews** are a core part of most selection processes.	**Role plays** or **situational testing** is used to assess an applicant's practical skills – everyone now does these.	**Panel Reports** are prepared and sent out to the relevant people for consultation.

Selection for Recommendation

The name(s) of the favoured candidate(s) is/are then selected by the Commission to be sent to the Lord Chancellor as a recommendation for appointment to the vacant judicial office.

Figure 7.3 The Process for Selection and Recommendation of Judicial Appointments

subject to an overriding requirement for a meritocratic approach. Nonetheless, the final appointment is still made by the Queen on the advice of the Lord Chancellor or Prime Minister. It may seem, at first glance, unusual for the opportunity, provided by the Constitutional Reform Act 2005, to remove the influence of the Lord Chancellor so completely from the appointments system to have been overlooked, but on reflection this is not unusual as long as the UK has a monarchy which still nods to the long history of the development of the common law through the customs and culture of a thousand years.

To take a more radically modernising approach, as some had advocated, would be to do what is vernacularly called 'throwing the baby out with the bath water', i.e. ignoring the continuing, but albeit more limited, role that the Lord Chancellor plays in the judicial system. The Lord Chancellor, despite in modern times neither a cleric (as in the Middle Ages) nor a lawyer, as in the last few centuries, is under a statutory duty to ensure the independence of the judiciary.[60] It would be difficult for the Lord Chancellor to fulfil this role properly if he was not involved, even symbolically, in the judicial appointment process. In many ways, it is important that this duty lies with a political appointment rather than a judicial one. For example, this situation means that the Lord Chancellor can be held to account for this duty in Parliament. Equally, during discussions of Government policy in Cabinet, the Lord Chancellor can ensure at an early stage that planned policy does not jeopardise the independence of the judiciary, thus also bolstering the authority of the judiciary. It also means that any conflict between the judiciary and the Government can potentially be neutralised from within Government, without the judiciary having to defend themselves publically. In this respect we can contrast the heavily criticised (non-)approach to this task taken by Liz Truss in the aftermath of the Daily Mail's infamous and scandalous 'Enemies of the People' headline[61] who failed to provide protection to the independence of the judiciary with that adopted by the present Lord Chancellor Robert Buckland following the prorogation case who made prompt and public statements in support of the independence of the judiciary.[62] An overly formal approach to separation of powers would not allow this overlap to exist but it is beneficial, in the whole, to the judiciary.

Some of the preceding analysis is reflected in the recent discussion within the House of Lords Constitution Committee which published a report in 2014 on the continuing role of the Lord Chancellor in the English Legal System.[63] Reading the report will give you an additional insight into the reforms of the office of Lord Chancellor and the valuable contribution that the office will continue to make to judicial appointments and the broader justice system in the future.

....

60 Constitutional Reform Act 2005 ss 3(1) and 3(6).

61 Which followed the High Court's initial decision in R (Miller) v Secretary of State for Exiting the European Union [2016] EWHC 2768 (Admin), [2017] 1 All ER 158. For comments of the Lord Chancellor, see Answers to Oral Questions on 8 October 2019 (Volume 664, 912599).

62 R (Miller) v The Prime Minister and Cherry v Advocate General for Scotland [2019] UKSC 41, [2019] 3 WLR 589.

63 Select Committee on the Constitution, The Office of the Lord Chancellor (HL 2014–15, I-75).

TRAINING

From 1979 to 2011, training for judges was provided by the Judicial Studies Board. This was replaced in 2011 by the Judicial College which now covers an expanded number of judicial office holders, including those working in tribunals or coroners.[64] The Lord Chief Justice is the person responsible, via section 7(2)(b) of the Constitutional Reform Act 2005, for the ongoing training of the judiciary and so plays an important role in the life of the Judicial College. The Lord Chief Justice is supported in this aspect of his role by the Board of the Judicial College, which is its governing body. The current Chairman of the Board is Lady Justice Rafferty.

As a permanent body, covering a significant number of judicial office holders, the Judicial College now has a strategy[65] setting out its goals and immediate objectives. The overriding objective of the College is to provide training of the highest professional standard which:

1 Strengthens the capacity of judicial office holders to discharge their judicial functions effectively including any leadership and management functions;
2 Enhances public confidence in the justice system;
3 Treats the training of fee-paid and salaried judicial office holders in the same roles with parity;
4 Promotes the professional development of judicial office holders and support career progression; and
5 Satisfies the business requirements of judicial leaders.[66]

From the preceding it can be seen that the Judicial College has a function that extends beyond keeping judges updated with legal developments in their field of expertise. Rather, it is seen as a fundamental part of achieving the wider mission of the English Legal System and recognises the practical, administrative, public service and management aspects to the role of a judicial office holder. This is reflected in the governing principles of the College which signify that judicial training should focus on:

1 Substantive law, evidence and procedure and, where appropriate, expertise in other subjects
2 The acquisition and improvement of judicial skills including, where appropriate, leadership and management skills
3 The social context within which judging occurs[67]

The training includes induction to the role played by the judiciary, seminars on substantive and procedural law as well as sessions aimed at building softer skills. This

64 From April 2013 coroners are also covered by the Judicial College, by virtue of regulations made under the Coroners and Justice Act 2009 s 37.
65 Currently covering 2018–2020: www.judiciary.uk/wp-content/uploads/2017/12/judicial-college-strate-gy-2018-2020.pdf.
66 Ibid. para 12.
67 Ibid. para 13.

reaffirms a commitment to life on the bench being an ongoing career choice, rather than simply a reward and path to retirement for illustrious barristers. The training provided by the Judicial College also acts as a mechanism by which a judicial office holder can expand upon the range of cases that can be heard under any judge's initial or existing 'ticket'. Some of the courses offered are mandatory for those wishing to hear cases in new areas.

For the sake of giving some sense of the scope of activity undertaken by the Judicial College, in 2017–2018, it delivered more than 300 courses to almost 12,000 participants.[68]

COMPLAINTS, DISCIPLINE AND REMOVAL FROM JUDICIAL OFFICE

In order to ensure the independence of the judiciary, judicial office holders have a certain security of tenure and the mechanisms for removing them from office are complex and rarely invoked. Outside of retirement and resignation,[69] senior judges can only be removed for serious failings in character and with the backing of both Houses of Parliament. Thus an English judge has never been removed by this method. Judges of the inferior courts can be removed more easily than judges of the senior courts. Nonetheless, it is still relatively rare for judges to be removed from office. This section will deal firstly with issues of conduct before moving on to discuss the retirement of judges.

MISCONDUCT

The Lord Chancellor and Lord Chief Justice are jointly responsible for discipline of the judiciary[70] and much of that work is undertaken by the Judicial Conduct Investigations Office (JCIO), which from 2013 replaced the Office for Judicial Complaints.[71] The volume of complaints dealt with by the JCIO remains relatively low, with around 2,200 complaints in 2017–2018.[72] A large number of those complaints were regarded as inadmissible because they related to judicial decisions or case management issues.[73] Table 7.2 shows the categorisation of complaints in 2017–2018.

Of the 2,200 cases there were 58 that required disciplinary sanction. Table 7.3 describes the various sanctions and indicates the number of each in the reporting period (2017–2018).

---

68 Judicial College, *Review of Activities* 2017–2018.

69 Judges rarely return to active practice after serving on the bench and some judiciary are prevented from doing so.

70 Constitutional Reform Act s 108.

71 The Judicial Discipline (Prescribed Procedures) Regulations (2014) SI 2014/1919 gives more details.

72 Judicial Conduct Investigations Office, *Annual Report* 2017–2018 – electronic version available here: https://judicialconduct.judiciary.gov.uk/reports-publications.

73 Ibid. 7.

Table 7.2 Categorisation of Judicial Complaints

Complaint type	Number
Not specified	42
Inappropriate behaviour	498
Delay	55
Conflict of behaviour	15
Failure to meet sitting requirements	10
Motoring offences	5
Misuse of judicial status	4
Civil proceedings	3
TOTAL	687

Table 7.3 Sanctions for Judicial Conduct

Sanction	Number
Formal advice	11
Warning	7
Reprimand	4
Removed	17
Total	**39**

PUBLIC PERCEPTION AND BEHAVIOUR OF THE JUDICIARY

It is easy to find examples of poor judgment, some amounting to serious misconduct, amongst members of the judiciary. These examples almost invariably end up in the popular press, regardless of whether they pass through the official complaints process. It should be borne in mind, however, that these represent little more than anecdotes, albeit ones which are salacious or scandalous enough to reach the public press. In a world of 24/7 news and press coverage and the increased accessibility of the courts, it is perhaps not surprising to witness members of the judiciary finding themselves unexpectedly (and unwittingly) the subject of newspaper articles or news reports. Although the scrutiny of judges has traditionally focussed on the substance of their judgments, increasing the lens of public perception is turning to individual comments made by judges during the course of proceedings.

EXPLAINING THE LAW – JUDGES DEMONSTRATING POOR JUDGMENT

What follows is a selection of recent examples of what can, at best, be described as poor judgment on the part of members of the judiciary. They are not intended to be extensive or exhaustive but merely show the way in which the press is able to bring judicial behaviour to the attention of the public. The cases range from misguided statements linked to judicial office to more serious cases of misconduct (either in the judge's private capacity or in their judicial office) to evidence of criminality.

- In October 2012 a Recorder (a part time fee paid member of the lower judiciary) was arrested for perverting the course of justice and was subsequently jailed for 16 months in May 2014.[74] She was removed from the judiciary in August 2014 and also disbarred. She had lied to the police in witness statements and had even altered an earlier witness statement. What makes this case all the more extraordinary was that it involved the case of a Cabinet Minister (Chris Huhne) and his wife who had been prosecuted for perverting the course of justice in relation to speeding tickets. This case demonstrates the sometimes uncomfortably close relationship between the judiciary and the executive.
- In March 2015 three judges (a part time recorder, a part time deputy district judge and a district judge) were removed and a further judge resigned after it came to light that they viewed pornography on computers provided for the purpose of their executing their judicial duties.[75] While the viewing of the material was not unlawful, the misuse of office equipment was deemed serious enough to warrant an investigation and removal from office.
- In January 2015 a Circuit judge came under intense criticism for suggesting that a 16-year-old student had 'groomed' her 44-year-old teacher in a case against him. The judge's comments were used to justify a suspended jail sentence and were said to undermine the seriousness of the conviction for the offence.[76]
- In 2014 a judge resigned after making a racist comment about a victim of harassment. He is alleged to have said that 'With a name like Patel, and her ethnic background, she won't be working anywhere important where she can't get time off.'[77]
- In 2015 a High Court judge was subject to intense press scrutiny and criticism for saying that 'proper allowance must be made for what is, almost certainly, a different cultural context'[78] when considering an alleged situation of violence against a child. Sections of the press took this to mean that the judge was endorsing a different

---

74 www.bbc.co.uk/news/uk-28675376.
75 www.theguardian.com/law/2015/mar/17/three-judges-removed-and-a-fourth-resigns-for-viewing-pornography-at-work.
76 www.theguardian.com/uk-news/2015/jan/14/former-london-teacher-convicted-over-affair-with-teenager.
77 www.theguardian.com/law/2014/dec/07/judge-resigns-racist-remark-about-victim-richard-hollingworth.
78 *A (Wardship: Fact Finding: Domestic Violence)* [2015] EWHC 1598 (Fam) [67].

application of the law to newly arrived immigrants.[79] Focus was placed on this one comment in a 75-paragraph judgment which, if read in the whole, does not support some of the accusations made in the press that the judge was 'out of touch' with the modern world.

The preceding examples should not be treated as representing the conduct of the vast majority of judicial office holders and, as with many of the other examples, poor judgment should be placed into the full context before an assessment of poor conduct is made.[80] **It could even be argued that these examples are notable because they are so few in number in a justice system that deals with such a volume of cases in a given year.** Nonetheless, these are cases that have caught (or, more cynically, been brought to) the public's attention.

The public's interest, or at least the interest of the popular press, in the unfortunate comments or actions of judges is explicable precisely because it goes to the heart of what society expects of its judges – good judgment. The comments may cause a moment of incredulity or outrage (or even amusement in some cases) but they do place at risk something of much greater value and that is public confidence in the authority of the judiciary. These remarks are doubly damaging when they confirm stereotypes of judges as 'out of touch' due to their social class or gender, a point discussed elsewhere in this chapter when considering the diversity of the judiciary. Moreover, these comments can sometimes be taken out of context and do not represent, in isolation, the full reasoning of the judge in a given case. Nonetheless, they are more high profile, particularly for the public, than the official complaints process and so should be given due consideration.

There are, of course, even more subtle ways for judges to be called to account for their conduct and behaviour, particularly as the official complaints process cannot be used to remedy incompetence or poor judgment in coming to their judicial decision in a particular case. Here, the appeals process itself can act as a form of rebuke where a judge does not live up to the high standards expected of the judiciary. This is evident in *Crinion v IG Markets*.[81]

ANALYSING THE LAW – PLAGIARISM AND JUDGES

In *Crinion*, the first instance judge had largely copied the submission(s) of one side of the dispute and passed it off as his judgment. The appeal was unrelated to the

---

79 www.independent.co.uk/news/uk/home-news/judge-says-cultural-context-should-be-considered-when-investigat-ing-allegations-of-parental-child-abuse-10308692.html.

80 For an interesting and lively analysis of judicial behaviour, see Gary Slapper, 'The judiciary – a performance review' (2015) 75 SLR 16.

81 *Crinion v IG Markets Ltd* [2013] EWCA Civ 587, [2014] 2 All ER (Comm) 55.

substance of the case and focussed almost entirely on the issue of whether the first instance judge should have simply copied the claimant's arguments in the way that he did. The extent of the copying was such that it appeared that the *original* document that described itself as the judgment was an amended electronic version of the submission from counsel.[82] The appeal was dismissed by the Court of Appeal but contained within the judgment were some strong words of rebuke for the first instance judge. Sir Stephen Sedley gave the strongest criticism indicating that the approach taken by the judge was 'unacceptable'[83] and that he hoped that 'a judgment like the one now before us will not be encountered again.'[84] Lord Justice Longmore agreed, stating that he trusted that 'no judge in any future case will lift so much of a claimant's submissions into his own judgment as this judge has done and that, if substantial portions are to be lifted, it will be with proper acknowledgment and with a recitation of the defendant's case together with a reasoned rejection of it.'[85]

In light of the fact that the appeal was *dismissed* this seems like strong criticism for what the judge had done. This was not dealt with as a complaint and so would not have been recorded in the official statistics but is a clear sign that judgments of appeal courts can be used to rebuke members of the judiciary who have acted in questionable ways.

A different, but related, point can be seen in *ex parte BskyB v Essex Police*[86] where a judge's formulaic approach to applying the law without justification was in issue. The judge had granted certain production orders for the police to gain footage held by broadcasters covering the Dale Farm evictions in 2011. In dealing with the appeal, Lord Justice Moses noted that the judge involved had not adequately justified the need for such orders and the case 'affords a good example of the need for a judge to be scrupulous in specifying the evidence on the basis of which' he reaches his conclusions.[87]

This further demonstrates that the appeals system not only allows faulty judgments to be remedied but that it also can act as a way of reminding judges of important aspects of their role that may have been overlooked.

RETIREMENT

Judges have a compulsory retirement age of 70.[88] This is a reduction of previous compulsory retirement ages and has helped to drive down the average age of judicial office holders. This is part of a coordinated effort to promote greater diversity in the judiciary and is discussed

---

82 Ibid. [11].
83 Ibid. [39].
84 Ibid. [40].
85 Ibid. [44].
86 *R (BskyB) v Chelmsford Crown Court* [2012] EWHC 1295 (Admin).
87 Ibid. [33] (Moses LJ).
88 Judicial Pensions and Retirement Act 1993 s 26(1) and Schedule 5, Senior Court Act 1981 s 11.

elsewhere in this chapter. The reduction has also had the unfortunate consequence of denying the more senior members of the judiciary the opportunity to continue to sit. Most notable in this regard was the retirement of Lord Bingham, who was unable to serve in the Supreme Court in 2009, despite the fact that he had been instrumental in the design of the new court replacing the appellate committee of the House of Lords.

During their time in office, judges are also able to contribute to a generous[89] pension scheme that, after 20 years of eligible service, will pay an annual pension equivalent to half of the officer holder's pensionable pay.[90] This rate is reduced by 1/40 of the pensionable pay for each year of missing service.[91] This is in addition to a lump sum of two and a quarter times the pension[92] on retirement and death benefits payable to close dependents.[93] Those members of the Supreme Court who are also members of the House of Lords will, when they retire, be able to return to the Lords and continue to vote, sit and serve on committees.[94]

JUDICIAL INDEPENDENCE AND NEUTRALITY

Judicial independence is one of the cornerstones of the English Legal System and is essential to ensure the authority and neutrality of the justice system. Public confidence in the justice system is predicated on the notion that judges make their decisions on the basis of the law and not on external pressures applied either by politicians or even other judges.

MAKING CONNECTIONS – PUBLIC LAW
+++++++++++++++++++++++++++++++++

The issue of judicial independence is a topic to which you will undoubtedly return if you are also studying constitutional law. It is the cornerstone of the separation of powers and certain conceptions of the rule of law.[95] These topics were briefly explored in earlier chapters and the analysis there should be reconsidered here.

Not only is judicial independence paramount to these constitutional principles but it is also vital to the way in which the judiciary is *perceived* by the public. Public confidence in the judiciary is reinforced if they are seen to be a separate entity to the executive who enforce the law and the legislature who pass the law.

---

89 Although, like many public sector pension schemes, the benefits have been decreased while the requirements for gaining a full pension have increased.

90 Judicial Pensions and Retirement Act 1993 s 3(1).

91 Ibid. s 3(2).

92 Ibid. s 4(1).

93 Ibid. s 5.

94 Constitutional Reform Act 2005 s 137.

95 Robert Stevens, 'A loss of innocence? Judicial independence and the separation of powers.' (1999) 19 OJLS 365 or Roger Masterman, *The Separation of Powers in the Contemporary Constitution: Judicial Competence and Independence in the United Kingdom* (CUP 2010).

The Lord Chancellor is formally responsible for defending the independence of the judiciary. The contrasting effectiveness of different Lord Chancellors as they execute this function is discussed earlier. The duty was placed on a statutory footing in 2005 and the duty also extends to other Ministers of the Crown.[96] The Constitutional Reform Act 2005 requires an incoming Lord Chancellor to take an oath which reads as follows:

> I, [name], do swear that in the office of Lord High Chancellor of Great Britain I will respect the rule of law, defend the independence of the judiciary and discharge my duty to ensure the provision of resources for the efficient and effective support of the courts for which I am responsible. So help me God.[97]

The oath and the statutory duty may seem like little more than empty rhetoric but there is evidence that various Lord Chancellors have taken this duty extremely seriously and have tried to enforce it by heading off criticism of judges by other members of Government. One example cited by Gee is where a written apology was issued after a junior Government minister criticised the sentence handed down by a judge to a sex offender and was rebuked by the Lord Chancellor.[98]

It is in this area of the judiciary's interaction with the other institutions of the state that the independence of the judiciary takes on particular importance. By being independent from the legislature and executive, the senior judiciary has also been able to drive forward the development of the rule of law as a way of balancing the powers between the different parts of the state. Overt recognition of the different functions that can be brought about because of this independence was given in the Prolife[99] case. In that case, Lord Hoffmann held that:

> Independence makes the courts more suited to deciding some kinds of questions and being elected makes the legislature or executive more suited to deciding others. The allocation of these decision-making responsibilities is based upon recognised principles. The principle that the independence of the courts is necessary for a proper decision of disputed legal rights or claims of violation of human rights is a legal principle.[100]

Lord Hoffmann's contribution suggests that judicial independence offers the judiciary not only protection from interference by Parliament and the Government but also confers upon them additional duties within the constitution. The Jackson[101] case is an example of the courts taking this further and using rule of law to rebalance the constitution. In that case, albeit in non-binding obiter statements, several of the Law Lords took the radical view that the powers of Parliament were limited by the principle of rule of law and that there could be a place for judges finding that an Act of Parliament was invalid if it interfered with constitutional principles in a significantly serious manner.[102]

---

96 Constitutional Reform Act 2005 s 3.

97 Promissory Oaths Act 1868 s 6A as amended by the Constitutional Reform Act 2005 s 17.

98 http://ukconstitutionallaw.org/2014/08/18/graham-gee-do-lord-chancellors-defend-judicial-independence.

99 R (Prolife) v British Broadcasting Corporation [2003] UKHL 23, [2004] 1 AC 185.

100 Ibid. [76].

101 R (Jackson) v Attorney General [2005] UKHL 56, [2006] 1 AC 262.

102 For comment on the case, see James Allan, 'The paradox of sovereignty: Jackson and the hunt for a new rule of recognition?' (2007) 18 KLJ 1.

As well as the need for Government ministers to exercise caution in criticising judicial decisions, there are broader restrictions on the reporting and critical discussion of ongoing proceedings in court. These restrictions cover more than just the principle of judicial independence but they do have an element of preventing judges from being influenced by outside forces. This principle, known as the *sub judice* rule, is intended to insulate ongoing proceedings from outside influences. This principle is most commonly discussed in relation to Members of Parliament being precluded from debating ongoing cases but there is also the possibility of journalists committing the offence of contempt of court if their reports are seen to be interfering with the proper administration of justice.[103]

The view on the measures necessary to preserve judicial independence and neutrality has evolved over time and is by no means static. For example, it was once viewed as unacceptable for members of the judiciary to give interviews to the press or participate in documentaries. This view came most strongly from Lord Kilmuir (Lord Chancellor in the 1950s) who formulated what came to be known as the Kilmuir Rules which reiterated the 'importance of keeping the judiciary in this country insulated from the controversies of the day'.[104] Long since abandoned, the Kilmuir Rules add further evidence to the argument that the duty placed upon the Lord Chancellor to protect judicial independence is more than just symbolic and it is intended to enshrine pre-existing principles and practice.

JUDICIAL NEUTRALITY

As well as duties being placed on members of the Government, the judiciary also has responsibility for safeguarding and self-regulating their conduct to avoid harming judicial independence. This is primarily achieved through the idea that no member of the judiciary should be a judge in his (or her) own cause. This means that judges who have an interest in a case to be decided should declare that interest and, if it would give rise to a danger of bias, recuse themselves from the case. The case law on this issue is voluminous and requires judges to consider both financial and non-financial interests before sitting on a case or they risk accusations of actual or perceived bias. Perhaps the most notable example of the principle in operation is of Lord Hoffman in a case involving General Pinochet.

EXPLAINING THE LAW – LORD HOFFMANN AND THE CHILEAN GENERAL

In the *Pinochet* case the issue of judicial independence and the rule against bias came to the public's attention with accusations of bias levelled against Lord Hoffmann when sitting as a judge in an appeal in the House of Lords. The history of the case is complex but involved the extradition of General Pinochet who had led a bloody military coupe in Chile. He subsequently came to the UK for medical treatment and an

103 Contempt of Court 1981 s 1.
104 Cited in John Griffith, *The Politics of the Judiciary* (5th edn, Fontana Press 2010) 42.

extradition order to Spain was sought for him to answer alleged charges of murder and torture. The House of Lords ruled in favour of extradition by a narrow majority.

It was subsequently revealed that Lord Hoffmann (who had been in the majority) was a Director of a public interest group (Amnesty International) which had been permitted to intervene in the proceedings. Additionally, his wife also worked for Amnesty. Although there was no suggestion that Lord Hoffmann had acted in an improper manner in determining the case, there was a risk of the appearance of bias. The House of Lords was asked (in an unprecedented application) to review its decision with a different panel of judges. It took this opportunity to set aside the decision and to re-hear the case. The decision (but not the reasoning) was the same in the subsequent case but it was one that excited public interest in the issue of judicial independence and neutrality and did a great deal to harm the reputation of the legal system.

The case demonstrates the importance of the principle in a very high profile way. If we strip away the dreadful historical context of *Pinochet* we are left with a very simple principle. The underlying principle is that a person with an interest in a claim should *declare* that interest and recuse themselves from sitting in the case. This has been expressed in the Latin maxim: *nemo iudex in sua causa* (no person should be a judge in their own cause). Indeed, the cause supported by Lord Hoffmann was both charitable and largely beyond reproach and the criticism was not of his supporting such an organisation as Amnesty. Lord Hoffmann's failing, and it was a serious one, was in not *declaring* his interest and choosing not to step down from the case or to hear argument from the parties about his suitability to sit.

A more recent example of *personal* connections rendering a judge unsuitable to hear a case can be found in the Court of Appeal decision in *AWG v Morrison*.[105] The case concerned a potential witness in a fraud trial who was known, in a personal capacity, to the judge. The judge lived in a nearby village to the witness and their children knew each other and they had dined together. In the words of the judge: 'I would have the greatest difficulty in dealing with a case in which Mr Jewson was a witness where a challenge was to be made as to the truthfulness of his evidence.'[106] The independence of the judge was therefore not only apparently in question but, through his own admission, *actually* in question. As the witness was not seen to be essential to the case, he was substituted and the judge did not recuse himself, against the wishes of the claimant (the appellant in the present case). The Court of Appeal reiterated the importance of judicial neutrality by emphasising that judicial impartiality 'is the fundamental principle of justice'.[107] The conclusion was that even though the witness was not called, there was a risk that the judge would be 'subconsciously biased by his long acquaintance with

105 *AWG v Morrison* [2006] EWCA Civ 6, [2006] 1 WLR 1163.
106 Ibid. [4].
107 Ibid. [6].

Mr Jewson'.[108] This case highlights that judges must handle the question of apparent bias particularly carefully and consider recusing themselves if they have any connection with a case. This is in spite of any attempt by the judge to mitigate the risk. The strong message from the Court of Appeal was that inconvenience and cost to parties cannot be used to counteract claims of judicial neutrality.[109]

As well as *personal* interests, judges must ensure that their financial interests do not bring their independence or neutrality into question. The classic example of this was found in the circumstances regarding the Dimes[110] case which is less high profile (in non-legal circles) but no less important than the *Pinochet* case. In that case it was held that Lord Cottenham had been wrong to sit on a case involving a company in which he held shares as his financial interests would raise the potential for the appearance of bias.

A recent example of the importance attached to judicial independence can be seen in *Sky UK v Office of Communications*[111] which involved matters of competition law before the Competition Appeal Tribunal. The facts are complicated and follow an unhappy train of litigation which resulted in the matter being remitted from the Court of Appeal to the Competition Appeal Tribunal to be reconsidered. Ofcom had objected to the *same panel* re-hearing the issue on numerous grounds but most importantly on the basis that there was a real risk of bias on the part of the panel. This took several forms but, crucially, the argument turned on a speech given by the Chairman of the panel (President of the Tribunal at the time) in June 2013. During the course of a long speech, the President made some comments that, Ofcom alleged, could have been taken to refer (in negative terms) to them and the matter that was at that time before the Court of Appeal. Ofcom were not named in that report but a Guardian article coincidentally published on the same day as the speech was given named Ofcom and discussed their ongoing consultations with Government and the appeal case in question. Ofcom suggested that the President's speech could be perceived to be a *response* to the Guardian article and so there could be an inference that the comments made in the speech were also about Ofcom. The argument put forward by Ofcom was that this raised the real possibility of an appearance of bias and that this was enough to require recusal.[112] The Chairman rejected many of the arguments put forward but accepted this last argument and stood down from the panel hearing the remitted case. The *Sky UK* case demonstrates the ongoing importance of judicial independence and the toxicity of a charge of bias. Even a throwaway comment in a lengthy speech, combined with external factors such as newspaper articles written by third parties, can be enough to taint a member of the judiciary and require their recusal from a given case. This underlines how seriously judges need to consider their comments, even (perhaps especially) when they are speaking extrajudicially.

....

108 Ibid. [10].
109 Ibid. [30].
110 *Dimes v Grand Junction Canal Proprietors* (1852) 10 ER 301.
111 *Sky UK Limited v Office of Communications* [2015] CAT 9.
112 Ibid. [79]–[101].

JUDICIAL IMMUNITY

To ensure that judges are free to exercise their jurisdiction without fear of repercussions there is a form of judicial immunity for tasks carried out in furtherance of a judicial function. This immunity was reaffirmed by Lord Denning in *Sirros v Moore*.[113]

EXPLAINING THE LAW – JUDICIAL IMMUNITY

The case of *Sirros* involved an individual attempting to sue a judge (and police officers) for assault and false imprisonment after the judge ordered Sirros to be held in custody following on from a deportation appeal. Lord Denning had to rule on whether a judge could be held liable for things done in the course of discharging his judicial duties. Denning noted that since the 17th century 'it has been accepted in our law that no action is maintainable against a judge for anything said or done by him in the exercise of a jurisdiction which belongs to him.'[114] He went on to hold, in the strongest possible terms, that the judicial immunity was absolute: 'No matter that the judge was under some gross error or ignorance, or was actuated by envy, hatred and malice, and all uncharitableness, he is not liable to an action.'[115] The remedy, according to Denning and the other Lords Justices was to appeal against the decision of the judge. The position in *Sirros* was confirmed more recently in *Pius v Fearnley*.[116]

It may seem unjust to give judges too free a hand in how they deal with cases. However, it is a necessary requirement to ensure that judges are free to give judgment and to make the orders that they feel necessary. As well as the appeal system, as noted by Denning, there are other mechanisms by which judges can be held to account, not least the complaints system outlined previously.

Although judges cannot be held *personally* liable for actions taken while acting judicially, it should be noted that the immunity in *Sirros v Moore* does not preclude the potential of a civil suit against the Government for errors of law committed by the judiciary in certain areas of law. For example, a member of the judiciary who committed a sufficiently serious breach of European Union law may have rendered the UK Government liable in damages – the so-called state liability principle.[117] One of the key arguments put forward against such liability in *Kobler v Austria* related to the independence of the judiciary. The response of the Court of Justice of the European Union was that the liability was not personally attached to the judge and so there is no prospect of independence being called into question.[118]

---

113 *Sirros v Moore* [1975] QB 118 (CA).
114 Ibid. 132 (Lord Denning MR).
115 Ibid.
116 *Pius v Fearnley* [2013] EWHC 2216 (Ch).
117 For the seminal case on judicial error, see Case C-224/01 *Kobler v Austria* [2003] ECR I-10239, and for the issue being discussed in the UK context see *AG v Cooper* [2010] EWCA Civ 464, [2011] QB 976.
118 Ibid. para 42.

DIVERSITY IN THE JUDICIARY

THE PROBLEM

There has been long-standing recognition from both within and outside of the judiciary that more could be done to ensure that there is a greater diversity in the range of people appointed to judicial office. This recognition has come in the form of multiple (critical) reviews of diversity in the judiciary and has even found expression within decided cases.

> **EXPLAINING** THE LAW – LADY HALE AND THE CASE OF FINANCIAL PROVISION
>
> ---
>
> The case of *Radmacher*[119] was a high profile family law case concerning financial provision on the breakdown of a marriage. The couple concerned had made an 'ante-nuptial agreement,'[120] and the Supreme Court had to consider the weight to attach to such an agreement when granting financial revision. It was an important case in terms of substantive family law and was made all the more interesting by the fact that the Supreme Court was split down gender lines with the all-male majority against very strong dissent from the sole female voice in the court. During the course of her judgment Lady Hale noted that '[i]n short, there is a gender dimension to the issue which some may think ill-suited to decision by a court consisting of eight men and one woman.'[121]

While the issue of diversity has been recognised, and great strides have been made to redress the balance, the problem has proved extremely difficult to address. In 2009 Jack Straw (the then Lord Chancellor) established an Advisory Panel on Judicial Diversity that found, in 2010, that previous attempts had not led to significant progress with judicial diversity.[122] This may well be just a matter of waiting for changes to filter through the system. The career trajectory of judicial office holders is relatively lengthy, with senior appointments often being made late in a legal career and from well-rehearsed routes. This would suggest that, as time progresses, greater diversity will occur in a 'bottom-up' manner with tiers of the judiciary evidencing different levels of diversity. With this is mind the Advisory Panel established a 2020 strategy for improving judicial diversity.[123]

Moreover, becoming a member of the judiciary has not traditionally been seen as a primary career path but rather one that follows on from a career in legal practice and, in particular, from being a barrister and – mostly in the lower judicial ranks – a solicitor or chartered legal executive. This means that well-established problems with diversity in legal practice will have significantly narrowed the pool of applicants eligible to be considered for judicial office.

---

119 *Radmacher v Granatino* [2010] UKSC 42, [2011] 1 AC 534.

120 That is an agreement on the division of assets on separation that is entered into *before* the marriage takes place.

121 *Radmacher v Granatino* [2010] UKSC 42, [2011] 1 AC 534, [137] (Lady Hale).

122 https://www.judiciary.uk/publications/advisory-panel-recommendations/.

123 www.gov.uk/government/news/progress-on-judicial-diversity-but-more-to-do.

The lack of diversity in the judiciary is multifaceted in that there are a number of groups that are currently (or have historically been) underrepresented. Particular focus has, in the past, been on the lack of women in the judiciary, whereas more recent criticism has been about lack of diversity in terms of ethnicity and socio-economic groupings.

The lack of presence of women judges was not simply a matter of circumstance but was, to an extent, embedded within the framework of the English Legal System. For example, reference was made only to the title of 'Lord Justice of Appeal' in the Senior Courts Act 1981.[124] This caused considerable practical problems when Elizabeth Butler-Sloss was elevated from the High Court[125] to the Court of Appeal in 1988. As an interesting aside, she was only the fourth woman judge of the High Court and was, as were the other women judges, assigned to the Family Division. This automatic assignment to the Family Division is further evidence of the institutional assumptions made about women in the judiciary, even as recently as the 1980s. An even more striking example of this was Dame Rose Heilbron, who had made a particular name in high-profile murder trials,[126] who was also assigned to the Family Division of the High Court.

The defect with Dame Elizabeth Butler-Sloss's title was not formally remedied until the early years of the new millennium when the 1981 Act was amended to include the title 'Lady Justice of Appeal' alongside the masculine version of the title.[127] In her early years, she was accordingly officially referred to as a Lord Justice of Appeal, although counsel had come to refer to her in the rather tortuous manner of 'My Lady, Lord Justice Butler-Sloss' in court. As Master of the Rolls, and to end this 'plainly absurd' usage, Lord Bingham issued a Practice Direction which encouraged counsel to use either 'My Lady' or 'Lady Justice Butler-Sloss' in court, even if her formal title would need to be changed by statute.[128]

Similarly, the route for progression to senior posts used to come either through direct appointment of leading QCs or occasionally through promotion from the Circuit Bench and the long periods away from home while sitting full-time 'on-circuit' trying crime at Assizes and later in the Crown Court disproportionately impacted on women judges. Lord Irvine, Lord Chancellor in the New Labour government of Tony Blair in 1997, attempted to address the circuit sitting problem by offering potentially more flexible arrangements to suitable candidates and by encouraging more women to apply from both the Association of Women Barristers and from women solicitors.

Table 7.4 summarises the position in relation to different groups of people within the more senior ranks of the judiciary as at June 2019.[129]

---

124 Senior Courts Act 1981 s 2(3).
125 She had been only the fourth woman judge of the High Court.
126 Having been the first woman to be leading counsel in a murder trial.
127 Courts Act 2003 s 63(1).
128 Practice Note (Mode of Address: Lord Justice Butler-Sloss) [1994] 1 FLR 866.
129 For appointments below the Supreme Court, data was found from – HMCTS, *Judicial Diversity Statistics 2019* (11 July 2019).

Table 7.4 Gender Split Amongst the Judiciary

Judicial office	Female – NB (%)	BAME – NB (%)
Justice of the Supreme Court	3 (25%)	0 (0%)
Heads of Division	0 (0%)	0 (0%)
Court of Appeal Judges	9 (23%)	2 (6%)
High Court Judges	26 (27%)	3 (3%)
Deputy High Court Judges	22 (25%)	8 (13%)
TOTAL	62	13

The picture painted by this data is (depressingly) consistent with a paucity of representation for women in the highest levels of the judiciary. The situation is particularly stark in terms of representation of minority ethnic groups. The next section will discuss the ways in which the judiciary has sought to remedy the imbalance and to promote greater diversity.

THE SOLUTION

The JAC is under a statutory duty, when executing all aspects of its work, to consider how to 'encourage diversity in the range of persons available for selection for appointments'.[130] It is important to note that this push for diversity is subject to the overriding requirement for selection to be on the basis of merit.[131] Thus, although there is statutory recognition of the problems with the lack of diversity in the judiciary, this will not mean that those from underrepresented groups will be selected for appointment without also demonstrating that they have the aptitude and ability to be a successful member of the judiciary. In this way equality is achieved alongside, and not instead of, merit.

By loosening the eligibility criteria for holding judicial office, the system has broadened the category of persons who can be selected and this will, in turn, lead to greater diversity in the judiciary. Lord Collins (as the first solicitor) and Lady Hale (as the first woman, and who had served a long spell in academia, including initially a short period in part time practice at the Bar, followed by a key period with the Law Commission in which she worked on the seminal child and family Law statute, the Children Act 1989) are contemporary examples at the very highest level of the Supreme Court of how diversity has improved in more recent years, culminating in her since having been the first woman Deputy President and also the first woman President of the Supreme Court. Meanwhile there have been two BAME appointments to the High Court, Dame Linda Dobbs (who was also the first such appointment) and Sir Rabinder Singh, who has recently been promoted to the Court of Appeal as its first Lord Justice from a BAME background.

....

130 Constitutional Reform Act 2005 s 64(1).
131 Ibid. s 64(2).

A consequence of the changes to eligibility is a greater freedom to recruit potential judges from a wider field than was previously possible. For example, the High Court has been subject to a recent pilot under the banner of the 'Diversity Support Initiative'.[132] The pilot offered a structured support programme of work shadowing and mentoring for those who had never held judicial office. The pilot was designed to prepare those from non-traditional backgrounds (i.e. non-judicial office holders) for the JAC selection exercise to be appointed to the High Court. The pilot was restricted to certain categories of person currently underrepresented in the High Court.[133] Those taking part in the programme were not guaranteed to be selected, due to all selections being made on merit, but the programme was designed to encourage diversity and to allow those from a non-judicial background to compete more effectively with those applicants who were more familiar with the court process.

THE WEBSITE

The website that accompanies this textbook contains many useful resources that you can use to consolidate and further your knowledge of the law, to hone your skills of critical analysis and to test your knowledge. This includes a set of multiple choice questions (MCQs) that can be used to test your knowledge and understanding of the material.

PODCASTS

- The podcasts provide a summary of the area under study, bringing together the key themes and threads of analysis into a 'mini-lecture'.
- There will also be an explanation and analysis of topical and up-to-date issues related to the judiciary.

---

132 Launched jointly by the Lord Chief Justice and Lord Chancellor who are also under a statutory duty to encourage diversity – Constitutional Reform Act 2005 s 137A.
133 Women, BME and those from a less-privileged background.

8

CHAPTER 8
THE COURT STRUCTURE

INTRODUCTION

Courts dealing with English law in the jurisdiction of England and Wales are largely divided into senior and inferior courts, but must also be distinguished as courts of first instance and appellate courts, which do not necessarily follow the same division, since even some inferior courts have appellate functions, as will be explained as we go along.

At the top of the tree the Supreme Court of the United Kingdom[1] is also the final appellate court for Scotland[2] and Northern Ireland, while both separate geographical territories have their own systems of law, of which Northern Ireland's is more like the common law of England and Wales. Scotland's system, however, is completely different from English law, being a hybrid rather than purely common law system, owing to the influence of the civil law of France, generated by Scotland's 'Auld Alliance' with that country, prior to the Union with England and Wales in 1603.[3] This means that the present day Supreme Court applies two separate systems of law in relation to appeals from Scotland and from England and Wales, which is sometimes very noticeable within the same subject area. An example of this is the completely different approaches to the breakdown of cohabitation relationships in the two jurisdictions, where Scotland has a statutory system to be found in the Family Law (Scotland) Act 2007, exemplified in the Scottish appeal of *Gow v Grant*,[4] while England and Wales have no such statutory provision, so that the applicable law is that of constructive trusts, as in the English appeal of *Jones v Kernott*.[5]

Northern Ireland law is not much different from that of England and Wales, being a common law system, which nowadays includes some English statutes in which some sections are expressed as either applying or not applying to Northern Ireland, again with the final appeal court at the Supreme Court.

AS YOU READ

Much of this chapter is concerned with the way in which cases heard by our judges are distributed amongst our various courts, and with giving detailed information on the process by which this is done and how the system works in general.

It is important that, as you read, **you do more than just memorise** this information. Attempt to **synthesise** what was said about the judiciary in Chapter 7 as this will breathe life into

-----

1 Which is neither a senior nor inferior court!
2 In civil matters only. The highest criminal court in Scotland is the High Court of Justiciary.
3 The practical union the accession of James I following the death of Elizabeth I; the parliamentary union did not come until 1706 (the English statute Act of Union, and 1707, the equivalent Scottish Act).
4 [2012] UKSC 29, (2013) SC (UKSC) 1.
5 [2011] UKSC 53, [2012] 1 AC 776.

the court structure. Think **critically** about the implications of the structure of the court system that has been arrived at in the English Legal System and **reflect** and **compare** with the structures adopted in different jurisdictions. A particular area of focus ought to be on the reforms to the highest court in England and Wales with some **critical thought** given to what the change has meant for the wider legal system.

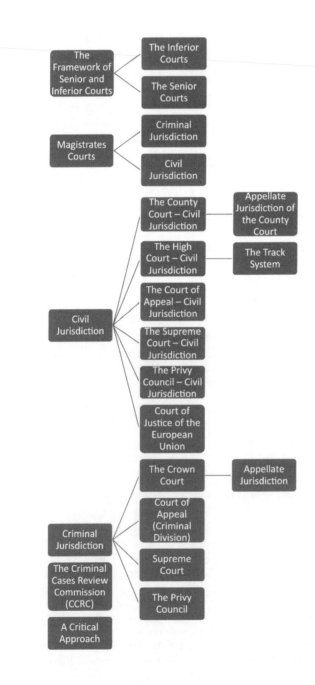

Figure 8.1

THE FRAMEWORK OF SENIOR AND INFERIOR COURTS

This chapter explores the framework of the courts in England and Wales, from the Magistrates at the bottom to the Supreme Court at the top, this being the best direction in which to progress, since nothing starts at the top in the Supreme Court, whereas most cases will start in one of the two inferior courts, the Magistrates' which have both civil and criminal jurisdiction, or the County Court, which is exclusively civil. Since 2014, the contemporary County Court has become a national court, sitting both in the capital and locally in regional centres, as opposed to the former county courts' identity as a network of individual courts in appropriately spread geographical locations. The new identity as a national court has not changed the modern County Court's location in the frame work as an inferior court.

Above this lowest level are the senior courts, the High Court and Court of Appeal, after which we arrive back at the top, at the Supreme Court again.

Also in the class of senior courts is located one in the group of national courts which sit both in the capital and locally: this is the Crown Court which is exclusively criminal in jurisdiction and is a senior court. The other specialist national court, set up in 2014 under the Crime and Courts Act 2013, is the Family Court which also sits both in the capital and locally in the regions, but which is not a senior court on the same level as the High Court, Court of Appeal and Crown Court.

These senior courts include courts of both civil and criminal jurisdiction, which have their origins (in the distant early Middle Ages) in the King's Council, the 'Curia Regis' out of which all subsequent courts evolved, either organically out of the Council itself when convenience dictated, or by statutory creation: thus all courts are still HM the Queen's Courts, and judges of every level sit under the Royal Arms, which are prominently displayed on the wall behind them as they sit on the bench.

These judges now include those of the relatively newly unified Tribunal Service,[6] and the entire courts and tribunal system is now known as HM Courts and Tribunal Service, or 'HMCTS', thus still distinguishing between courts and tribunals. This chapter will therefore not address the tribunals, although the courts and tribunals have now been joined up in HMCTS, as the tribunals have a separate identity and function, and thus a separate chapter (Chapter 13).

TAKING THINGS FURTHER – VISITING COURTS

While reading about the court system is very important, nothing brings home the workings of the system quite so clearly as a visit to an actual court. Making some actual

---

6   The Tribunal Service was created by the Tribunals Court and Enforcement Act 2007, but not all tribunals were in practice transferred in immediately (most in the following three to four years, though some e.g. the Residential Property Tribunal not until after 2011). The amalgamation within the Ministry of Justice as HMCTS was in 2011, following a consultation in 2010.

court visits will allow you to think more critically about how the courts work in dealing with the cases before them and thus facilitate evaluation of the systems that you observe there.

A much needed skill for any student of law is the ability to draw out themes that cross different areas of study. As you read the distinct sections, you should attempt to synthesise the information so as to make connections: for example you may be studying both criminal law and contract law, the first of which you will encounter in your local Magistrates Court and the second in your local County Court. Of course if you live and/ or study in London you can go to the High Court as well and in most parts of the country there will be an accessible Crown Court for attending more significant criminal trials than the initial appearances and trials of petty crime that characterise the Magistrates. Finally, in Parliament Square at Westminster, the Supreme Court welcomes the public, providing helpful summary sheets at reception for each of the cases heard in the building – usually one in the Supreme Court room which has a number of rows for public seating at the rear of the room to which there is free access – and one in the Privy Council jurisdiction which sits in their secondary court. Thus although these cases are by definition complex and probably involve both unfamiliar topics and more recondite points than those early in their studies may normally be used to, which is why they are on appeal in the Supreme Court or Privy Council, a visit affords a unique opportunity to see leading advocates in action and to hear the Lords Justices questioning them as they argue their cases. Moreover a video of every day's full hearing is always loaded onto the Court website the next day, for further perusal at leisure.

So when you visit these courts always look for cases in their lists which you will best understand, perhaps because you will have been studying the substantive content of the law to which they relate.

However to begin with your court visits are bound to be informative whether or not you understand much of the content of the cases you are observing, as to start with you will be noticing routine features of the court itself and of the personnel involved which you will then recognise as either much the same or similar but with some variations in the next court that you go to, although as time goes on and your visits progress you will get more out of the visit in actually understanding the content of the case for each side.

Meanwhile Figure 8.2 shows the complete court structure (excluding the tribunals which we will follow in Chapter 13).

THE INFERIOR COURTS

Before the arrival of the essentially Norman 'Curia Regis' through which the early Norman Kings dispensed justice after the Conquest of 1066, there was a well-developed Saxon system of low level local justice administered through regional law enforcement by royal officials similar to the later county sheriffs and by local lords on their manors – which the conquering Norman King took over and promptly restocked with Norman lords who

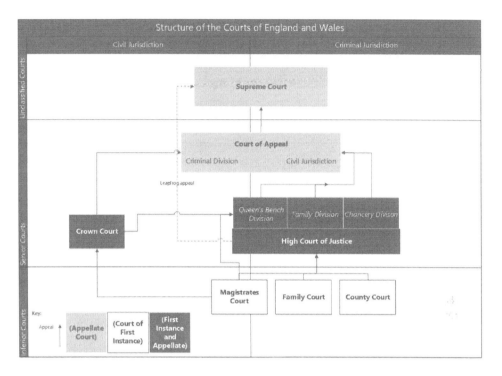

Figure 8.2 The Court Structure of England and Wales

could be safely left to keep order for him in England whenever their master, who remained also Duke of Normandy, was obliged periodically to return to France to attend to the affairs of his Duchy.

From this pervasive rural network of local courts around England and Wales eventually grew the formally organised regional magistracy, dealing with minor cases in both civil and criminal law, a system which has come down to us today. Thus, for example, 200 years after Henry II, the magistrates were so well established that they were given the job of enforcing agricultural wages under the Statute of Labourers 1351, passed to control the wages of the depleted agricultural workforce, which had been halved in the Black Death of 1349, but on which the medieval kingdom depended for sufficient labour, both to farm the land for food and to work in the lucrative wool trade, the country's most crucial financial resource.

THE SENIOR COURTS

Similarly, from the itinerant Curia Regis of the medieval kings were eventually developed the senior courts, when it was ultimately realised that dispensing the king's justice could more conveniently be split off from his council, which could then become his privy council or main organ of government. This was partially a practical concern as the old structures could not then have indefinitely accommodated all the judicial functions into which they had been expanded by Henry II, known as 'the Lion of Justice', and his successors. There was something

to be said for the administrative convenience of having a stationary principal fount of justice
in which the King could delegate to a principal judicial officer and his staff.

This was, moreover, more practical for all concerned since when not travelling around
his realm, as medieval monarchs did, Norman kings were based in London, to which the
Conqueror had shrewdly re-located the capital from the centre of the Saxon 'Witan' at
Winchester. The Senior Courts Act 1981 names the Crown Court, the High Court of Justice
and the Court of Appeal as the 'senior' courts of England and Wales.

The chapter will proceed by examining the courts with jurisdiction to hear civil cases before
progressing to those with jurisdiction to hear criminal cases. Let us start with the Magistrates
since the first distinction that we need to make is between civil and criminal law, and the
Magistrates do both, so this is as good a place as any to jump in at the deep end. Following
initial coverage of the Magistrates, in this part of the chapter we shall concentrate on the flow
of the Civil Court structure, mentioning where there is a criminal jurisdiction alongside, but
leaving a similar, more detailed account of the Criminal Court structure until after completing
that for the Civil Courts.

_____

MAGISTRATES COURTS – CIVIL AND CRIMINAL JURISDICTION

Every town of sufficient size not to be called a village will probably have a Magistrates Court.[7]
In larger towns it will probably share buildings in a Court Centre with the local County Court,
although the Magistrates section will also sometimes be called the 'Youth Court', a division of
the Magistrates which deals with youth justice and is not supposed to sit at the same time as
the (adult) Magistrates Court is in session, the idea being to keep youth justice separate from
adult crime, and thus the young and impressionable offenders away from hardened criminals;
so if premises must be shared the courts routinely sit at different times or on different days.

The Family Court will probably also be located in the Court Centre, especially if it is a Civil
Court Centre, or Combined Court Centre, with the Crown Court often in the same building as
well, although this is not always the case.

CRIMINAL JURISDICTION

All criminal cases commence in the Magistrates Court, where a person charged with a crime
must be brought before the magistrates and either tried or committed for trial elsewhere –
usually this will mean transfer to the Crown Court in the case of more serious crimes that
must be tried in the Crown Court but there are some others which can be tried in either
court, either where the magistrates consider a serious crime would be better tried, or
the Crown Court penalty would be more suitable than their own more limited powers of

<hr>

7   A complete list of courts can be found here – https://courttribunalfinder.service.gov.uk/courts.

punishment, or where the accused elects trial by jury in a case that could be tried in either the Magistrates Court or Crown Court. Alternatively an accused could be committed for trial on another day.

Magistrates courts are mostly presided over by unqualified and unsalaried Justices of the Peace appointed from the local area for which that court dispenses justice and who usually sit in benches of 2 or 3, though a single magistrate may try a summary offence not punishable by imprisonment, e.g. driving without insurance, non-payment of TV licences. The relevant statutes are the Magistrates Courts Act 1980 as amended by the Criminal Justice and Courts Act 2015. As they are mostly not legally qualified and voluntary, though trained and able to claim expenses, lay magistrates are basically finders of fact but advised on the law by a Legal Advisor, formerly known as a Magistrates Courts Clerk. However there is also a class of salaried and qualified magistrates,[8] formerly called Stipendiaries, and now styled 'District Judges (Magistrates Courts)' who, while having the same jurisdiction, can sit alone and are often found in busy urban courts.

CIVIL CASES

The Magistrates used to have substantial Family Law jurisdiction, but since the inauguration of the Family Court in 2014 the magistrates who used to sit in the Magistrates Court as a domestic court – dealing with small financial claims between spouses and in respect of maintenance of children – have gone to sit at the lowest level of the Family Court where they are called 'Judges of the Family Court', as are all other judges of the different levels of that court, and the Magistrates' Legal Adviser (clerk) has been given other Family Law duties there where, *inter alia*, they now perform the initial sift of divorce, nullity and civil partnership dissolution petitions.

There still remains, however, some small first instance civil jurisdiction, predominantly licensing, and recovery of some civil debts, for example in relation to income tax.

The Magistrates are amongst the oldest of courts, having had their origins in small local jurisdiction in the early Middle Ages. By the mid-14th century they were sufficiently established to be entrusted with the enforcement of the Statute of Labourers, leading to their being progressively used to keep local order in various ways, so it is easy to see where their formal title as 'Justices of the Peace' came from. The fact that they mostly now do appeals from licensing authorities, and used until recently to deal with small domestic issues in family law, indicates their parochial nature.

However, today their most important function is criminal, in trying small crime and committing for trial to the Crown Court. Given the lack of expensive juries or salaries, the Magistrates Court provides deals with a significant volume of cases in a cost-effective way.

....

8   These salaried magistrates must have been barristers or solicitors for at least seven years: Courts and Legal Services Act 1990, Access to Justice Act 1999. There are about 30,000 lay magistrates and about 100 District Judges (Magistrates Courts).

THE COUNTY COURT – CIVIL JURISDICTION ONLY

As explained earlier, this is (since 2014) a single national court (similar in status to the Family Court which determines all family cases that do not need specifically to go to the High Court). However, despite now being classified as a single national court with its own seal which sits in many different locations around the country as the national Crown Court does, the contemporary County Court is still technically the inferior court it has always been since the first network of County Courts was set up in 1846; that is to say it is a creature of statute in which its governing legislation sets out its jurisdiction, which is first instance civil only, but concurrent with the High Court (save as to some subject matter, financial and territorial limitations, in that e.g. proceedings generally have a local link and if one or both of the parties are resident elsewhere a case is usually transferred to a court near to the residence of the defendant if started in another area).

The County Court is thus subject to the supervisory prerogative jurisdiction of the High Court and the orders of *mandamus, certiorari* and prohibition, and pursuant to the Senior Courts Act 1981 s 29(3), the High Court can quash any decision of the County Court if it has exceeded its jurisdiction. The contemporary County Court therefore has no inherent jurisdiction, unlike the High Court, nor do High Court judges routinely sit in it, as in the Family Court and Crown Court, and it has the character of providing local access to a civil jurisdiction similar to the High Court but more cost effectively. A County Court is thus likely to be found in a larger town with a Civil or Combined Court Centre, and there are currently many locations, usually to be found in precisely the same buildings as the former County Courts sat in. It is a court of record although classified as an inferior rather than senior court.

The original 19th-century County Court concept was based on the old county sheriff's courts, namely summary justice in a local court, although there is no historic connection between them, and the contemporary statutory creation was aimed at saving money following Sir Henry Brooke's 2008 Report *Should the Civil Courts Be Unified?*[9] This resulted in a recommendation *not* to make this change (as had however already happened in other common law jurisdictions, e.g. Ontario in Canada) but also for the closure of a number of court buildings, the introduction of more online and electronic handling of cases, together with the implementation of two new specialist centres – the County Court Money Claims Centre at Salford[10] and the County Court Business Centre in Nottingham.[11] These are designed to save money by improving case management.

The County Court now automatically tries most lower value civil claims unless there is some reason for starting or trying a case in the High Court, which can be done in the alternative, but which will usually be more expensive in every way (not least in court fees and the cost of representation) although, following the Woolf Reforms 1994–1998, both courts use the

---

9 Brooke, LJ, Judicial Office, August 2008.

10 Issuing claims and offering an online determination for claims for fixed amounts under £100,000, see https://www.gov.uk/make-money-claim.

11 This facilitates removing repetitive staff intensive cases from County Courts to a computer-supported environment.

same Civil Procedure Rules (CPR) 1998 and the same fast track and multi-track approach, also introduced by Woolf (see later in this chapter).

There are some exceptions to the general principle of starting low value claims in the County Court as some cases must be started in the High Court e.g. in Defamation but there will usually be no significant advantage in incurring higher costs in the High Court, except perhaps the chance of obtaining a higher quality of judge. However, even that cannot be guaranteed since the High Court now uses many Deputies who well may not be more erudite, especially as some locations of the County Court have specialist judiciary assigned there to try the more complex Chancery and commercial lists, and who may therefore be perfectly capable of addressing complex points that would thus have no need of going to the High Court in the hope of encountering a superior quality of judge.

The relevant statutes are the County Court Act 1984 as amended by the Crime and Courts Act 2013, s 17 and Schedule 9, which created the single national County Court in place of the former system of individual County Courts to hear small cases originally set up in 1846. The judiciary are principally Circuit Judges, assisted by District Judges and Deputy District Judges, but any High Court or Court of Appeal judge, and also any Recorder, may also sit there. The Court's great relevance to students of law is that it tries contract and tort cases[12] thus affording a suitable diet of subject matter of relatively simple cases for court hearings to be observed by those studying the legal system.

The other significant feature of the County Court is its small claims jurisdiction. This usually involves contract, tort (especially personal injury), landlord and tenant and perhaps probate claims. The small claims procedure is simple, conducted by a District Judge, and should allow parties to appear without legal representation, with the consequence that costs are not normally awarded. This should lead to quicker, cheaper and less stressful outcomes. Dispute resolution other than by means of litigation is encouraged and most courts will have some dispute resolution service available.

APPELLATE JURISDICTION OF THE COUNTY COURT

There is a limited appeal system whereby District Judges' decisions may be appealed to a Circuit Judge of the same court. Such appeals have their origins in the analysis of civil appeals by Brooke LJ in the case of *Tanfern Ltd v Gregor Cameron-Macdonald*,[13] in which it was established that in civil cases an appeal lies to the next judge in the hierarchy.

THE HIGH COURT – CIVIL JURISDICTION

This, in its modern dress, is the direct descendant of the medieval King's Court, which morphed into the Court of King's Bench now represented by the Queen's Bench Division

12 Subjects normally encountered early on in the study of law.
13 [2000] 2 All ER 801 (CA).

of the High Court of Justice. In the intervening hundreds of years there have been various other Divisions of the High Court, but today the principal ones are the Queen's Bench Division, Chancery Division and Family Division. There was a suggestion by the Heilbron-Hodge Committee (which in 1993 produced one of the reform reports prior to the Woolf Reforms 1994–1998) that the Queen's Bench and Chancery Divisions should be merged, but thankfully this was never seriously considered, as to do so would have created unnecessary complexity and lost the best features of both Divisions.

The Queen's Bench Division (QBD) deals predominantly with contract and tort claims, i.e. the original common law diet of common law courts, as opposed to the traditional Chancery topics (see text under Chancery Division) although the Division can take a variety of other cases if it wishes. However the QBD also has three sub-divisions:

- The Commercial Court with specialist judges to deal with insurance, banking and similar topics connected with City financial business, such as Lloyds[14] 'names' losses caused by high insurance claims; they also use expedited procedures, make determinations on documents in some cases without a hearing and promote out of court dispute resolution e.g. through the City Disputes Panel.
- The Admiralty Court (a specialist maritime law court dealing with losses to cargo and ship collisions, with a specialist judge sitting with two assessors from the Masters of Trinity House[15] to advise on seamanship and navigation).
- The Technology and Construction Court (which deals with any cases involving technical complexity such as building and construction generally, engineering and computer technology, including cases of any such complexity referred to it by the Chancery or Queen's Bench Division).

There is also the Divisional Court of the Queen's Bench Division, distinct from the three QBD Divisions mentioned previously, which is an important court for the purpose of hearing applications for judicial review, statutory appeals and *habeas corpus*, and when it exercises these functions it is known as the 'Administrative Court'.

The Chancery Division traditionally deals with corporate and personal insolvency, mortgages, leases, property generally, partnership, intellectual property, patents, trade marks, copyright, disputes relating to trusts and settlements, inheritance and administration of estates, wills and specialist company law matters for which there is a specialist Companies Court within the Division. Another specialist court within the Division is the Patents Court. However in recent decades the Division has also undertaken much heavy commercial litigation and less of the traditional old Chancery documentation work in connection with trusts and settlements owing to the diminution of volume of such work. Cases are determined by a single judge and juries are never used.

---

14 Lloyds of London being the underwriters for many policies and a historic core city business.
15 Founded in 1514 Trinity House is an ancient maritime authority responsible for all lighthouses and navigational aids in England, Wales, the Channel Islands and Gibraltar, and also a deep sea pilotage authority in relation to ships sailing in Northern European waters, clearly providing specialist expertise in maritime matters.

The Family Division deals with cases in relation to adult relationships such as marriage, civil partnership and their dissolution; child law generally including child protection for which the state[16] is responsible; wardship and cases involving children's rights to determine their own medical treatment, in respect of which the High Court has an inherent jurisdiction. However there are many provisions in the governing statutes and in the Family Procedure Rules 2010 as amended that deal with transfers to and from the High Court to the Family Court which now has High Court judges sitting in it along with Circuit Judges and Magistrates owing to the various levels at which the Family Court is designed to operate. This last point is important as it avoids the former necessity to apply to different courts, thus introducing more flexibility and saving the Family Division of the High Court for cases which really require the expertise of the judges normally sitting there.

The Division also deals with international child abduction under the Hague Convention to which the UK is a signatory, and this is an example of the specialist expertise for which the Family Division of the High Court is most conveniently reserved.

The more routine work, such as under the Marriage Acts, Matrimonial Causes Act 1973 and associated legislation, Civil Partnership Act 2004, Gender Recognition Act 2004, Children Act 1989, and similar statutes, is now allocated to the Family Court, in which High Court judges also sit as Judges of the Family Court, the purpose of which being to bring all levels of Family Justice into one court where possible in order to reduce the necessity for transfers between levels or locations of court, although sometimes geographic or other reasons still require a transfer to another location of the Family Court, or indeed to the High Court at the Royal Courts of Justice, owing for example to sensitivity of a case requiring superior security which a local Family Court might not be able to provide due to local resourcing limitations.

TAKING THINGS FURTHER – THE RELATIONSHIP BETWEEN THE HIGH COURT AND COUNTY COURT

Despite the 2008 Brooke Report's recommendation that the High Court and County Court should not be unified, and although the High Court is a senior court and the County Court an inferior court, that is not to say that the two courts do not work together in some ways to provide a holistic system of first instance civil justice. Besides the possibilities of transfer between the two courts, they both share the same Civil Procedure Rules (CPR) 1998 which were a key product of the Woolf Reforms 1994–1998, and have done so since the CPR replaced the two distinct sets of Rules for each level[17] when the two former practitioner's texts were replaced with a convenient single publication – although the

---

16 Through the local authority.

17 In previous use were the Rules of the Supreme Court (RSC) for the High Court, called 'The White Book' for the colour of its cover, and the County Court Rules (CCR) for the County Court, known as the Green Book, since that was the colour of its cover. The CPR 1998 as amended were thus in themselves, and remain, a unifying factor at the two levels of first instance civil justice, as they set out a uniform code in one book (and the current practitioner's book of the 1998 joint rules, the CPR, is still known as 'The White Book' since the white binding has been retained for the single contemporary practitioner's text).

contemporary content is so extensive that two heavy volumes are now required so as to include all the associated material that a civil practitioner using both courts might need while before either of them, including the relevant onward civil appellate routes along which civil cases might progress.

In addition to using the same CPR for procedure, both County Court and High Court use the same tracking and proactive judicial case management systems that were a key Woolf innovation (and which are discussed in more detail in Chapter 10). This is not the place to introduce detailed civil procedure, especially since the courts are currently undergoing extensive modernisation, including progressive digitisation, but some outline will be useful in understanding how litigation works in both County Court and High Court.

THE TRACKS SYSTEM AND CASE MANAGEMENT

This was inspired by the long established small claims court originally in use in the old style county courts, where low value cases were heard in consumer disputes, housing and even personal injury, and procedure was flexible so that the judge could run hearings in whatever way appeared most suitable, including when parties might not be professionally represented. However in addition to small claims two other tracks were added by the CPR – a fast track and a multi-track – so that cases over a small claims limit but still of relatively low value could be fast tracked, whereas those over such low value or of greater complexity or both could be allocated to a multi-track. This enabled fast track cases to be heard relatively quickly, and in no more than a day, with fixed costs and a limitation on experts, whereas those apparently more suitable to the multi-track could be consigned to the proactive hands of judicial case management which enabled a creative case management judge to set up pre-trial reviews, preliminary hearings, time limits and other directions, thus controlling both costs and delay.

Allocation to the appropriate track is achieved by issue to both parties of an allocation questionnaire which the parties complete with sufficient information for the case management judge to form a view as to the appropriate track, i.e. value, complexity, likely length of the hearing and also adding their own wishes and preferences, to which the court may or may not accede as the case may dictate. This is because the object of these systems is to use only a proportionate amount of the resources of the court rather than to allow cases to run for a disproportionately long time for the value of the case. This aim is dictated by the overriding objective in the CPR r1.1 which requires that cases are dealt with justly and that the parties are on an equal footing. Since the introduction of the CPR the aim has also always been to encourage dispute resolution (DR) at all stages, including adjournment wherever possible to enable the parties to try one other form of DR – these alternative forms of DR are discussed in Chapter 14.

The CPR also introduced the concept of 'pre-action protocols' to ensure that the defendant fully understands the claim and has a chance to consider settlement and that neither party is embarking on litigation unnecessarily. As the pre-action protocols are required by the Rules, failure to observe them is likely to be penalised in costs.

THE COURT OF APPEAL – CIVIL JURISDICTION

The next court in the hierarchy above the High Court is the Court of Appeal, which has two Divisions, the Civil Division and the Criminal Division: this section of the chapter however deals largely with its civil business; for the criminal aspects see later.

The Court of Appeal (Civil Division) is presided over by the Master of the Rolls (MR) who is also Head of Civil Justice. The title of this office had its origin in the Middle Ages when this judge did indeed keep the 'rolls' on which were recorded decisions of the King's Courts, and in modern times he (there has not yet been a woman judge as Master of the Rolls) is also responsible for some aspects of the regulation of solicitors, e.g. he determines the cost of solicitors' practising certificates.[18]

Permission to appeal is almost always required for an appeal to this court[19] and the contemporary rationalisation of appeals requires that there should generally only be one appeal, rather than a case going from court to court up to the Supreme Court, so many appeals will not progress further than the Court of Appeal. Some may never go to the Court of Appeal but directly to the Supreme Court, the final UK appellate court, by the 'leap-frog' process provided by the Administration of Justice Act 1969 ss 12–15 (this means it must be on a point of law of general public importance and on the construction of a statutory provision or be in relation to a decision by which the trial judge is bound, all parties agree to the appeal and the Supreme Court gives leave to make it).

Where a second appeal is required beyond one already made from the judge of first instance (what is known as 'a second tier appeal') there must be an important point of principle or practice or some other compelling reason for the appeal sought, and the Court of Appeal must consider this to be the case.

The Court of Appeal was first set up under the Judicature Acts 1873–5 and at the time was part of what was then known as 'the Supreme Court of Judicature' which also included the High Court. However the then 'Supreme' Court could no longer co-exist with the Supreme Court that we know today, set up in 2009 to replace the House of Lords as the final appeal court of the UK, so the Court of Appeal is now part of the group which has been renamed the 'Senior Courts' (the High Court and Court of Appeal) and the name of the Supreme Court Act 1981, which dealt with a number of matters of jurisdiction of the former 'Supreme Court of Judicature' was changed to 'the Senior Courts Act 1981' in order to address the creation of a new Supreme Court to comply with the separation of powers required by the Constitutional Reform Act 2005.

All the senior judges who hold offices identified in the Constitutional Reform Act 2005 sit in the Court of Appeal, i.e. the Lord Chief Justice (LCJ), Chancellor (formerly called the 'Vice-Chancellor') of the Chancery Division, the Master of the Rolls and the President of the

18 Solicitors Act 1974 s 11(1).
19 Access to Justice Act 1999 s 54 and CPR Part 52.

Family Division. There are also 38 Lords Justices of Appeal and some High Court judges (and sometimes retired High Court judges) are often invited to sit, since there are usually several courts of either three or five judges required daily, which places some pressures on the court, since there will also be other courts sitting as benches of one or two judges in order to hear oral applications for leave to appeal, and others considering applications on paper. In recent times the court has much increased its capacity, now hearing as many as nearly 4,000 cases in a year.

THE SUPREME COURT

Appeals from the Court of Appeal go to this final UK appellate court, which replaced the Appellate Committee of the House of Lords in October 2009, alongside others from the Court of Session in Edinburgh,[20] and the courts of Northern Ireland. There are 12 Justices of the Supreme Court, who are no longer given a peerage as when they were elevated to the House of Lords Appellate Committee, though they may already have one, e.g. Baroness Hale was appointed to the House of Lords Appellate Committee before 2009, as were her two predecessors as President, Lord Phillips of Worth Matravers, and Lord Neuberger of Abbotsbury. Either the Court of Appeal or the Supreme Court must give leave for an appeal to the Supreme Court; it is usual to ask the Court of Appeal first and then if the application is refused the appellant may apply to the Supreme Court.

Appeals are usually on questions of law, and of a complex nature, although an appeal on a question of fact is possible in civil cases (unlike in the case of criminal appeals). Now that the Court has been operational for ten years, there has been an interesting article on its judicial leadership in a recent issue of the academic journal Legal Studies[21] which analyses the way in which its Justices have worked together in all cases heard so far.

THE PRIVY COUNCIL

Appeals go to the Privy Council if from outside the UK, e.g. the British Overseas Territory of Bermuda and certain Caribbean jurisdictions which have not abolished this appellate channel. In this way the Privy Council is not part of the court system for the English Legal System but is mentioned here for completeness. The Justices are the same as those who sit in the Supreme Court with the addition of some Commonwealth judiciary members who sit on cases from their own jurisdictions. It is also the final appellate court for the Channel Islands and the Isle of Man, where some English judiciary sit on those islands' appeals (in the Channel Islands as Deputy Bailiffs and in the Isle of Man as a Judge of Appeal).

---

20 On civil matters only.
21 Rosemary Hunter and Erika Rackley, 'Judicial leadership on the UK Supreme Court' (2018) 38 Legal Studies, 191–220.

COURT OF JUSTICE OF THE EUROPEAN UNION

Until the end of January 2020, the UK was a member of the institutions of the European Union, including the Court of Justice. The UK provided a judge to sit in the main court and a further two in the so-called General Court. Although those judges have now left the CJEU, the English legal system will remain subject to the jurisdiction of the European courts during the transition period to the end of December 2020. Even after the end of the transition period, the case law of the Court of Justice of the European Union will remain relevant in understanding the interpretation of retained EU law. This ongoing role is discussed in detail in chapter 16 and when discussing precedent in chapter 9.

The CJEU has jurisdiction to hear questions on the interpretation of EU law referred to it by the domestic courts, including for the moment, those courts of the English legal system. During the UK's membership, this was achieved by means of the 'preliminary reference procedure' detailed in Article 267 TFEU. The power to refer remains active during the transition period but is based within the Withdrawal Agreement rather than Article 267 TFEU.

The CJEU can also, for now, hear cases brought by the Commission against the UK for alleged breaches of European Union law under Articles 258-260 TFEU. This includes the ability for the CJEU to complete cases that are pending at the time that the transition period ends. The CJEU will also retain the jurisdiction to decide cases brought for up to four years after the end of the transition period (i.e. until the end of 2024), for breaches of EU law that occur *during* the transition period.

It should be made clear that the CJEU has never been an *appellate* court within the English legal system, even during the time that the UK was a member state of the EU. In this way the CJEU sits slightly outside the formal court structure but its binding judgments of interpretation have a significant impact within that structure.

THE CRIMINAL COURT SYSTEM

Beginning at the bottom, as with the civil process, the first level in the criminal courts is the Magistrates. This court system has a much more extensive role than as at the bottom rung of the civil ladder, since all criminal cases begin in the Magistrates Court.[22] This court, together with the Crown Court, comprise the launch pad for first instance criminal hearings.

The Magistrates have both a relatively limited first instance trial role, for less serious crimes ('summary offences'[23] and some offences which can be tried 'either way' i.e. in the

---

22 Magistrates Courts Act 1980 s 18A as amended by the Criminal Justice Act 2003.

23 For example driving offences under the Road Traffic Acts, and many other statutory offences.

Magistrates' or the Crown Court)[24] and also a committal role, to decide preliminary matters (such as 'bail' and 'remand') and to send more serious crimes ('indictable offences')[25] for trial at the Crown Court, which also has an appellate role in determining appeals from the Magistrates. No criminal cases actually start in the Crown Court without going before the Magistrates first for committal if not being tried there.

From first instance, criminal courts have their own appellate ladder similar to civil cases, to the Court of Appeal (Criminal Division) and then to the Supreme Court, save for the fact that the High Court's Administrative Court (in the Queen's Bench Division) also has a special role in hearing a particular class of appeals on point of law from the Magistrates, by way of 'case stated'. It will be remembered that the bench of magistrates unless a stipendiary magistrate sitting alone – now called a 'District Judge (Magistrates Courts) – would not be legally qualified so this 'case stated' appeal route was originally created to enable a more complex point of law to be considered by the qualified and infinitely more experienced High Court judiciary in the QBD, and in documentary form. Hence the origin of the term 'case stated', since the Magistrates Court could be asked to 'state a case' for the High Court judiciary to consider on this special form of appeal.

THE MAGISTRATES' CRIMINAL JURISDICTION

Crimes are investigated and, where appropriate, charged by the police and then prosecuted by the Crown Prosecution Service, a statutory body set up for the purpose in 1986.[26] The CPS then takes over the offence charged and prosecutes it, since as in most common law systems the criminal court process is adversarial. In adversarial systems the two parties, prosecution and defence, present their opposing cases, the prosecution in order to put the case for the state which has charged the accused with the relevant crime and the defence for the accused, who will have access to both solicitors to prepare the case for his defence and barristers to present it and to challenge the prosecution's case as presented by the prosecution witnesses called to give evidence in support of the charge. In the Magistrates Court, where there is never any jury, the magistrates then decide on guilt on the basis of the evidence called, which must prove guilt beyond all reasonable doubt (unlike the civil standard of proof which is on a balance of probabilities) and they then also decide on the sentence, for which there is structured guidance according to the type of case and a number of other variables.[27]

---

24 For example less serious assaults, criminal damage, less serious offences under the Theft Act 1968.

25 For example treason, murder, attempted murder, manslaughter, rape, serious assaults, aggravated burglary, i.e. cases too serious for trial by the magistrates but needing a professional judge and a jury. Judges are 'ticketed' for these cases within four classes of seriousness of indictable offences, the most serious being allocated to a High Court Judge, and the less serious to a Circuit Judge or Recorder.

26 Prosecution of Offences Act 1985 s 3(2). A case may sometimes come to them from other sources as well, e.g. from the local authority in relation to prosecutions for trading standards breaches.

27 www.sentencingcouncil.org.uk.

MAKING CONNECTIONS – ADVERSARIAL AND INQUISITORIAL DIFFERENCES
+ +
This adversarial system is completely different from the civil law systems' approach which is inquisitorial. Another feature of the adversarial system is that the prosecution has a duty to disclose all material evidence to the defence, whereas the defence is under no duty to disprove the prosecution's allegations, since on the contrary (except in very limited circumstances) the prosecution must prove its case or the accused cannot be convicted.

If the offence is serious ('indictable', i.e. must be tried on indictment in the Crown Court) the accused will only make his/her first brief appearance before the magistrates, who will formally commit for trial by the Crown Court, grant legal aid and bail if appropriate or remand in custody if not. There is otherwise no hearing at this level, and the accused will not enter a plea until the Crown Court where a judge will hold a Plea and Case Management Hearing (PCMH). Preliminary hearings in the Magistrates' Court were discontinued by the Crime and Disorder Act 1998.

If the offence is an 'either way' offence (also called a 'hybrid offence') the accused will have to enter a plea at the Magistrates' Court, whereupon if the plea is Guilty the magistrates may sentence straight away, or they may elect to commit to the Crown Court for sentence, if e.g. they consider their powers of sentencing are inadequate. If the plea is Not Guilty the magistrates will hold an allocation hearing[28] to decide where the case will be heard[29] although some cases involving children and serious or complex fraud cases are usually sent straight to the Crown Court.[30] The magistrates have published guidelines to help them to decide whether a case is suitable for summary or Crown Court trial.[31]

If the offence is 'summary' only the accused is not entitled to trial in the Crown Court and trial will take place before the magistrates without a jury. This is the main diet of the Magistrates' Court. Appeals against conviction and/or sentence go to the Crown Court or to the Administrative Court of the Queen's Bench Division, by way of case stated.

Despite the overall impression sometimes portrayed by the media that the UK is completely crime ridden, in fact only a very small number (less than 5%) are indictable offences going to the Crown Court, including the separate category of 'either way' offences where the trial could take place before the Magistrates or the Crown Court. The remaining 95% or more are less serious and are disposed of by the Magistrates.

---

28 Criminal Justice Act 2003.
29 This is determined under the Magistrates Courts Act 1980 s 19. It is only a mode of trial hearing, not to determine guilt or innocence. If the magistrates decide the case is suitable for summary trial the accused will be told he can choose whether to be tried by the magistrates or by the Crown Court with a jury: s 20.
30 Crime and Disorder Act 1998 ss 51B and 51C.
31 Criminal Justice Act 2003 s 170.

THE CROWN COURT

Crown Court procedure is completely different from the Magistrates Court, since the findings of fact (by the jury) and the direction on the law to the jury (which is in the hands of the judge) are separated, since the judge has no say in the jury's decision (though s/he will direct the jury on the law) and the jury has no say in the sentence (which is up to the judge, albeit in accordance with structured guidance). The role of the jury is considered further in Chapter 12.

Since the Crown Court is a national court which also sits regionally around the country it will be the centre for criminal trials in its regional location. This is the same in London, where the Central Criminal Court (the Old Bailey near St Paul's Cathedral) is the main London Crown Court though there are others e.g. Southwark Crown Court, on the South Bank of the Thames near London Bridge; Snaresbrook Crown Court in NE London; and Croydon Crown Court in the SE London suburbs. As the Court is a national court it has jurisdiction to hear all criminal trials wherever committed although mostly cases will be tried regionally unless of such notoriety that a fair trial might not be easily available locally in which case it is usual to hear such a case at the Old Bailey.

In this sense, judges of the High Court still go out 'on circuit' to hear cases in regional locations of the Crown Court, since owing to the ticketing system for Crown Court cases High Court judiciary will be needed who will otherwise normally be sitting in London at the Royal Courts of Justice in the Strand. Although some lesser indictable offences can be heard by Circuit Judges and Recorders who may be available locally, the top two classes of seriousness amongst the indictable offences will require High Court judges.

APPELLATE JURISDICTION OF THE CROWN COURT

The Crown Court also hears appeals from the Magistrates, against conviction and sentence. No permission is required and only the convicted accused can appeal. The prosecution has no right to appeal to the Crown Court against a decision of the Magistrates. An appeal to the Crown Court will be a complete rehearing 'de novo', with witnesses but without a jury, and the Crown Court can vary the decision or confirm it but it cannot increase the sentence beyond the magistrates' limits.

Alternatively the prosecution and defence can each appeal to the Administrative Court of the QBD on the grounds that the magistrates' decision was wrong in law, which is not a rehearing, but an appeal by way of case stated on the basis of legal argument, and if that is not successful a further appeal can be made to the Supreme Court, provided it is on the basis of a point of law of general public importance and leave must be obtained from either the Administrative Court or the Supreme Court.

COURT OF APPEAL – CRIMINAL JURISDICTION

This Court was created in 1966 to replace the old Court of Criminal Appeal, created in 1907, to hear criminal appeals only. It is presided over by the Lord Chief Justice, the most senior criminal judge. The Master of the Rolls presides only over the Court of Appeal (Civil Division) which we have already dealt with in the Civil Courts section of this chapter. Possibly a positive aspect of Brexit, which otherwise is not currently receiving much positive media attention, is that English judges may spend less time liaising with their European civil law system counterparts, thus reducing opportunities for foreign judicial jokes about England's 'Master of the Rolls' which unfortunately routinely translates into French in newspapers as 'Maitre des Petits Pains' (*bread rolls!* – rather than the vellum variety on which medieval law reports were printed for which the French language does not seem to have provided journalists with an appropriate term).

THE COURT'S JURISDICTION AND ITS JUDGES

The Court hears appeals against conviction or sentence in the Crown Court, but does not entertain further appeals from the Divisional Court of the Queen's Bench Division which go directly to the Supreme Court.

There are also special requirements provided by the Criminal Appeal Act 1968 as amended by the Criminal Appeal Act 1995, s 2 about the way in which the Court of Appeal (Criminal Division) is to approach the appeal. The Act provides that the Court *shall* allow an appeal if the judges hearing the appeal feel that the conviction is '*unsafe*', and in all other cases they shall dismiss the appeal.

The judges of the Court of Appeal (Criminal Division) are the Lords Justices of Appeal of the Court of Appeal and are not restricted to former purely criminal specialists. Some High Court judges also sit periodically and it has become a custom to invite retired High Court judges to sit especially when there are not enough judiciary to go round when listing is particularly busy. It is easy to identify such sittings since the Court of Appeal judges still in office are always referred to in Law Reports by their Lord Justice's designation, e.g. as Smith LJ, whereas a retired High Court judge would be referred to by his out of office title, namely his knighthood, as e.g. Sir Jeremiah Smith. Lords Justices of Appeal promoted from the High Court will already have a knighthood, traditionally given on their elevation to the Bench, so it was agreed at the time of the Judicature Acts 1873–5 that to distinguish Court of Appeal judges from those of the High Court, the Lords Justices would also be created Privy Councillors, thus obtaining the suffix 'PC'.

SUPREME COURT

Like the Court of Appeal, the Supreme Court requires permission to be granted before an appeal can be accepted, either by the Court itself or by the Court of Appeal. It is usual to seek permission first from the Court of Appeal and if that is refused application is made to the Supreme Court. However there is also a statutory requirement[32] that the Court of Appeal must certify that the case involves a point of law of general public importance and that it appears that it is one which should be considered by the Supreme Court. Either the Court of Appeal or the Supreme Court must also give leave to appeal.

---

32 Criminal Appeal Act 1968 s 33.

THE PRIVY COUNCIL

This 'alter ego' of the Supreme Court hears criminal appeals from some Commonwealth and British Overseas Territories that have retained this appeal channel as in the case of civil appeals. In the case of appeals to the Privy Council, special leave must be given for a criminal appeal which will not be given unless there are exceptional circumstances, for example a substantial injustice has occurred and the accused has not had a fair trial.

THE CRIMINAL CASES REVIEW COMMISSION (CCRC)

This is not actually a court but an alternative channel for final appeals where appeal time limits have been missed, leave to appeal out of time has not been given and yet there is a sense that there has been a miscarriage of justice. Sometimes such miscarriages of justice are only actioned long after the actual conviction, e.g. in the case of Derek Bentley, convicted and executed for the murder of a policeman in 1953, pardoned in 1995 and his conviction for murder finally quashed in 1999.[33]

TAKING THINGS FURTHER – VISITS TO THE CRIMINAL COURTS

Criminal Courts are particularly worth visiting since it is usual to be simultaneously studying the English Legal System, legal method and criminal law, thus affording an ideal opportunity to attend court hearings in a subject area in which you will have already acquired some subject knowledge. After the Magistrates Court the next most accessible is likely to be a local Crown Court sitting, where attendance in the public gallery is usually not a problem (as it may be in London where e.g. the Old Bailey often has queues for admission).

Another opportunity for obtaining some hands on experience of criminal court hearings is to seek a 'marshalling' placement with a criminal judge (i.e. 'shadowing' a judge in a local Crown Court) or a 'mini-pupillage' with a barrister or set of Chambers, or vacation placement with a firm of solicitors, in both cases with a practitioner who has a predominantly criminal practice. More information about this can be found on the accompanying website where it is more convenient to address ways of obtaining such useful experience.

---

33 R v Derek William Bentley (deceased) [2001] 1 Cr App R 21 (CA). Per Lord Bingham, LCJ, in introducing the referral from the CCRC, treated as an appeal to the Court of Appeal, 'rarely has a court been called upon to review the safety of a conviction recorded over 45 years ago' but finding the summing up of the trial judge so prejudicial as to make the conviction unsafe, so that 'the summing up in the present case had been such as to deny the appellant that fair trial which was the birth right of every British Citizen'.

A CRITICAL APPROACH TO THE COURT STRUCTURE

Both the civil and criminal courts have been the subject of extensive reports and suggestions for reform but, except in the case of the civil courts (where a suggestion to amalgamate the County and High Courts was rejected by the Brooke Report in 2008) there has been no suggested reform to alter the structure of the criminal courts since the last major recast of their systems by the Courts Act 1971 which abolished much historic framework[34] not really suitable to modern times. Such research and reform as there has been in the criminal system has been targeted towards criminal process rather than the courts as such and is addressed in Chapter 11 on Criminal Justice where it sits more appropriately.

Contemporary reform in respect of both the civil and criminal courts has therefore more recently focussed on court buildings and on the practicalities of adapting procedure to the increased use of IT than on any changes in what appears to be the now firmly established court framework, despite the fact that projected reform repeatedly refers to 'the digital court'.

ANALYSING THE LAW – MAKING SENSE OF THE CIVIL AND CRIMINAL COURT STRUCTURE

A basic understanding of the framework of the courts, and of how civil and criminal jurisdictions are interwoven at various points in the overall picture, is essential for an understanding of the operation of the English Legal System and of the administration of justice. In order to do this effectively, and to avoid unnecessary repetition, some cross referencing will be required to other chapters, such as that on legal professionals,[35] the judiciary,[36] juries,[37] and civil,[38] criminal[39] and administrative justice.[40]

However the very best way to become familiar with the courts is to visit them and to participate actively in hearings by understanding not only the stage that a case has reached in any court visited, but also the content of the dispute. In this respect paradoxically the Supreme Court, the highest of all, is the most student friendly of any court in the framework, since that Court's principle of open access to the public welcomes students who do not need to be on an organised tour and the Court also thoughtfully provides a briefing sheet for each case heard on any day, videos posted the following day of hearings and simultaneous televised sessions on their website.

34 Such as the historic assizes where, from 1559 to 1971, High Court judiciary toured the country to try major crime (replaced by the national, regionally sitting Crown Court with four different levels of judicial 'ticketing') and the Quarter Sessions (replaced by the constantly sitting modern Magistrates Court).
35 Chapter 15.
36 Chapter 7.
37 Chapter 12.
38 Chapter 10.
39 Chapter 11.
40 Chapter 13.

These are all obviously resource intensive and not possible to be replicated at every court managed by HM Courts and Tribunals Service. Nevertheless every court displays a list of cases to be heard every day and at other courts ushers can be helpful in indicating to visitors which cases in which courts in their building might be worth attending in the public gallery.

CONCLUSION

Beyond the text and diagrams of this chapter, it is important to note some of the broader themes that arise out of the essential information set out. First, the framework of courts is not exclusively either civil or criminal in either set of courts involved in their apparent specialisms. Despite the framework of the specialist Divisions of the High Court, at Court of Appeal level and above in the Supreme Court, our top judiciary are generalists rather than narrow specialists, steeped in the general principles of English law and of the application of it in our unique ways of statutory interpretation and application of judicial precedent, as they were in their rudimentary first inception as members of the medieval King's Council. This is regularly made clear when it is evident from reports of decided cases that whatever their previous background in practice and on the Bench, the Lords Justices of the Court of Appeal and the judiciary of the Supreme Court are expected to sit on both civil and criminal appeals in accordance with the demands of the service.

Secondly, partly due to the pressures of contemporary life, much more is expected of the modern judiciary of England and Wales and of the United Kingdom because Parliament is so overwhelmed with detail generated by the ever widening reach of government policies that Law Reform is not being undertaken by Parliament even when it is urgent.[41] Thus it is sometimes being left to the senior judiciary to develop the common law where that is possible without usurping the role of Parliament.[42] Despite the duty of the Law Commission under the Law Commission Act of 1965 (for England and Wales) to advise the government of the need for essential law reform, and the separate Act (also in 1965) for Scotland, the Scottish jurisdiction has had recent family law reform when required[43] even though England and Wales have not, and as in the case of other unaddressed family law reform already mentioned similar legislation to Scotland's in 2007 is urgently required. In these circumstances a clear court framework, in both civil and criminal contexts, is a positive

41 Such as in the case of No Fault Divorce, which most other jurisdictions of modernised countries now have, but which it has recently been highlighted in the case of *Owens v Owens* [2018] UKSC 41, [2018] AC 899 England and Wales does not; and this is only one of several urgent family law reforms which could be saving time and resources in the Family Court, costs savings that the government has already indicated are urgently needed in the administration of justice.

42 As noted by the Supreme Court in *Jones v Kernott* [2011] UKSC 53, [2012] 1 AC 776 in connection with the failure of the English government at Westminster to legislate for cohabitation breakdown as was achieved in Scotland in 2007.

43 For example the Family Law (Scotland) Act 2007, which gave rights to cohabitants in Scotland while England and Wales still lag behind over a decade later.

advantage which should be encouraging time to be made by the Westminster government (which is always claiming shortage of resources) for the necessary legislation which would take full advantage of the fact that the court infrastructure is already satisfactorily in place to create some significant economies in the administration of Family Justice which would be likely to impact further on the overall administration of justice bill.

THE WEBSITE

The website that accompanies this textbook contains many useful resources that you can use to consolidate and further your knowledge of the law, to hone your skills of critical analysis and to test your knowledge. This includes a set of multiple choice questions (MCQs) that can be used to test your knowledge and understanding of the material.

PODCASTS

- The podcasts provide a summary of the area under study, bringing together the key themes and threads of analysis into a 'mini-lecture'.
- There will also be an explanation and analysis of topical and up-to-date issues related to the court structure.

9

CHAPTER 9
PRECEDENT

INTRODUCTION

Courts dealing with English law in the jurisdiction of England and Wales employ systems of statutory interpretation[1] and the use of precedent which are radically different from those of the civil justice systems. In England and Wales we have no codified constitution, the law is partly statutory and partly 'case law',[2] i.e. previous determinations of the judges, which have been collected together in the various series of 'law reports' since the Middle Ages; these previous determinations are what has developed the original common law of the land, the principles of which have given English law its unique flavour.[3] In this way, statutory interpretation and principles of binding precedent give the law of the courts legitimacy and authority and thus form the two pillars of the judicial legal order in England and Wales.

This is in contrast to civil law jurisdictions, which have a codified constitution that already guides their judiciary, before their judges even consult the various codes, civil and criminal respectively, which are made under the Constitution of their particular jurisdiction; and these two sources together are sufficiently widely framed to permit a judge to apply the principles of both without the relatively frequent amendments which are sometimes necessary in English statutes. That is not to say that there are not reported cases in civil law jurisdictions, although judges in those jurisdictions do rely more on the principles of their constitutions and of the codes made under them in those civilian jurisdictions; but the use of previous judicial decisions is not as mainstream and widespread as in English law which also depends on a system of hierarchy of courts, so that in English law a previous decision of a court is binding on all courts below the court of the previous decision and may be overruled by a higher court in the hierarchy.

These two unique features of statutory interpretation and the doctrine of precedent in English law are the most 'different' aspects of the English Legal System, which distinguish England and Wales from the civil law systems of the rest of Europe, although there are some jurisdictions in Europe and the EU which are regarded as 'hybrid', i.e. neither civil nor common law, e.g. Scotland, which was since medieval times much influenced by France, and continued to be so influenced in later years and indeed modern times when in the late 18th and early 19th centuries France became a leading civil law jurisdiction as its law was modernised and based on a constitution and the Napoleonic Code, and also Germany where

---

1   See Chapter 6, Statutory Interpretation.
2   And NB case law, as in reported cases, in the various series of law reports, is always written 'case law' (never 'case laws') as case law is a generic term, like the 'common law', which is another name for the law that comes from reported cases.
3   See Chapter 2, Sources of Law.

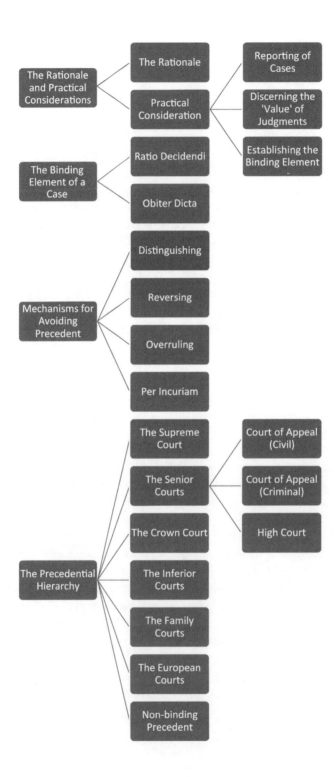

Figure 9.1

its modern unified law following the unification of the late 19th century has exhibited some aspect of both common law and civil law systems.

AS YOU READ

Much of this chapter is concerned with the mechanics of the use of precedent in English law and in particular how precedent is used in the hierarchy of courts and how the system works in general. It is important that, as you read, **you do more than just memorise** this information. It is particularly important when studying precedent that you **understand the terminology** deployed in discussions about cases. As with learning about the courts themselves you need also to **practise reading case reports** in the various series of law reports and to find *ratios* and *obiter dicta* yourself. This will help you to develop your skills of **critical analysis** and will help you in **applying the law** to new situations. Much of the time of all those involved in the legal system is devoted to decoding and discerning the principles applied in a given case.

While reading such cases, you should be beginning to **think critically about how the courts work in dealing with the doctrine of precedent in cases before them** and thus to be able to **evaluate the system**.

THE RATIONALE AND PRACTICAL CONSIDERATIONS FOR PRECEDENT

THE RATIONALE

The underlying rationale and principle of precedent is straightforward – that cases which raise similar or identical legal issues should be decided in a similar way. Unfortunately, the practical realities of precedent are much more complex. As we shall see, the doctrine of precedent is steeped in difficult language and operates within a hierarchy of courts and is subject to underlying rules and principles. It would be sensible to discuss first the rationale for precedent before explaining how it finds expression in the common law and then considering the rules and principles that govern its exercise.

Given that the legal system of England and Wales is a *common law* jurisdiction[4] we already know that case law has a particular importance for the development of the law. In the absence of a fully codified constitution or comprehensive civil code, judges are left to 'fill the gaps' in the law through the cases that come before them. Although Parliament is now a keen legislator, it has not always been so and prior to the 19th century the volume of legislation was low meaning that the courts had bigger gaps to fill. For example, in the areas of contract

---

4   As discussed in Chapter 1.

and crime in particular the legislative landscape was fairly barren. Even at a time of greatly increased activity from Parliament, courts are required to continue to operate within the 'gaps' and to consider how abstract legislation is to be applied in particular cases. This puts case law front and centre in not only *interpreting* statutory law but also in creating, developing and refining legal principle. In order for this law to have the confidence of its citizens there must be a degree of certainty.

ANALYSING THE LAW – LEGAL CERTAINTY

It is to be remembered from Chapter 1 that one of the functions of law is to regulate relationships between individuals. Thus, there needs to be a degree of certainty not only about the principle but also as to how it will be applied in particular cases. This is part of the doctrine of 'legal certainty' which is a core requirement of the rule of law.[5] The natural consequence of legal certainty in the context of case law is that it provides a compelling argument for the *binding nature* of legal judgments. By this we mean that decisions taken should be binding on future courts.

In this way the doctrine of precedent should be treated with particular care. It is much more than just a set of technical rules that govern how judges arrive at outcomes. Precedent is achieving one of law's most fundamental purposes – giving people certainty as to their rights and obligations.

The corollary, and sometimes contrasting, principle that arises from legal certainty is that of *res judicata*.[6] This principle requires there to be a degree of *finality* to judicial decision-making and prevents parties, other than by appeal, from continuing to seek redress for the same issue within the courts. When all appeals have been exhausted the decision, whatever its merits, is final as between the parties. This gives certainty on an individual level to the parties to a case.

In this way, precedent provides certainty in the law for *all* and *res judicata* provides certainty to the parties in a given case.[7] The court in *Cassell*[8] put the matter rather well when holding – 'some degree of certainty is at least as valuable a part of justice as perfection'.

Precedent, and its attendant rules, allows the legal system to achieve a mix of certainty and flexibility. The certainty has been discussed previously but the flexibility is also important.

---

5   For a nuanced consideration of the principle of 'legal certainty' in English law, see Lord Mance, 'Should the Law Be Certain?' (The Oxford Shrieval Lecture), 11 October 2011, www.supremecourt.uk/docs/speech_111011.pdf.

6   Meaning that a decision, when taken, will be final.

7   Even if the principles of *res judicata* themselves are still the subject of litigation! Most recently in *Peter Farrar v Leongreen Limited* [2017] EWCA Civ 2211, [2018] 1 P&CR 17.

8   *Cassell v Broome* [1972] AC 1027 (HL) at 1054.

There are conditions, that we will come to, that allow for the common law to evolve through the doctrine of precedent. Principles are set and followed but may also be *refined* over time by subtle judgments that distinguish themselves from one another or more senior courts can overturn earlier precedents that are deemed inappropriate. In this way, precedent achieves a balance between *certainty, justice* and *progress*.

The language of this doctrine of precedent which exists in English law is quaint in itself, since the doctrine is also known as *stare decisis*, which is Latin[9] for 'let it stand' (Latin having first been the language of English law in the early Middle Ages, when it was also the language of the Church, and the only people who were literate were clerks in the Church at a time when the rest of the population, often including the King, was illiterate). Thus Latin survived as a live spoken and written language until well into the Middle Ages and beyond in the law, although it was after a time not the Latin of imperial Rome but a softer, more simplified version which endured until the period of the Woolf Reforms (1995–1998) by which time English was officially promoted for use in court as part of an overall policy of simplification of court practice. One of the areas in which Latin has doggedly survived is in describing the doctrine of precedent.

In this way the principle of *stare decisis* is deceptively straightforward – decisions that resolve legal issues in particular cases will be binding on future courts when the same legal issue arises.

PRACTICAL CONSIDERATIONS

With ready acceptance of the *concept* or *principle* of precedent, we turn now to some of the thornier practical and theoretical issues that flow from that principle. It is here that we start to come across some difficulties and challenges that need to be overcome in order to establish an effective and workable system of precedent.

THE REPORTING OF CASES

The first practical consideration is that if judgments are to be binding statements of principle then those judgments that create or develop principles need to be available for reference by lawyers and citizens. This is not only a practical concern but a core aspect of the accessibility of the law under the principle of the rule of law. What follows is a brief history of case reporting that is intended to explain why there are often numerous citations of cases and to explain why it is important to consider the 'most authoritative' case report in legal writing and research.

In the medieval times collections of cases were gathered into 'year books' that were published at infrequent intervals. With the advent of the printing press, the 16th and 17th centuries saw a rise of commercially available 'law reports'. These were not governed by the court system or state and were a creation of (normally) high profile lawyers whose account of the case could

---

9   Books of Latin legal phrases were still being published at the turn of the 20th century – E Hilton Jackson, *Latin for Lawyers* (Sweet and Maxwell 1915).

be relied upon. The reliability and weight placed upon those reports by lawyers and the courts was largely dependent on the reputation of the lawyer involved and so these reports – known as nominate reports – would often carry the name of the Barrister (e.g. Burrow or Plowden Reports). These reports were not consistently formatted nor were all cases of importance necessarily reported and some were of questionable quality.[10] Newspapers took up the mantle in the mid-1800s with the advent of, amongst others, the *Law Times* reports. Again, the quality of these was variable in part because judges still gave judgment only orally and so the accuracy could be difficult to monitor.

By 1865 there were a number of commercial law reports and commoditising the judgments of courts was seen to be problematic, particularly because of the risks of inaccuracy and the infrequency of the publications. The solution was the creation of the not-for-profit[11] Incorporated Council of Law Reporting that would produce 'authorised' law reports – known as the Law Reports. These are considered the most authoritative reports of cases and must be cited in court if available[12] and will contain all cases that introduce or modify principles or which settle questions over uncertain areas of law. This may all seem rather technical and distant and may have a whiff of pedantry and awkwardness about it. However, the Court of Appeal issued a stern (and potentially costly) reminder to lawyers about the importance of adhering to the practice of citing the most authoritative case reports and expressed its 'deep regret' with non-compliance with the procedures on the presentation of authorities:[13]

> judges of this court have limited time for pre-reading in advance of an appeal. Adherence to the practice directions means that that limited time can be more productively spent. Parties can expect that the cost of preparing a non-compliant bundle of authorities is at risk of being disallowed.

This makes clear that the judiciary may even penalise those who ignore the Practice Direction on the citation of authorities in the costs that they are able to recover!

Any selection of cases for publication involves a risk in that an important case may be overlooked but the alternative of publishing *every* judgment of the courts would be unsustainable. This means that any number of cases are not 'captured' within the official, authoritative Law Reports. Such cases, when cited, are denoted by 'unreported' after the party names. This sort of case may have come to notice through having been reported briefly in a monthly journal noting developments in the main fields of law (such as Current Law, which is bound and kept in that form in most practitioner and some academic libraries) or a

---

10 For example, the reporter Espinasse, of whom a judge said that he was not going to rely on the reports of Espinasse 'or any other ass'.

11 On establishing the ICLR, the bar committee rejected the notion that the government should fund the publication of reports and this remains true to this day. Unofficial but perfectly acceptable reports still exist today, with the All England Reports probably being the most significant, recording as they do cases from the Supreme Court, Court of Appeal and High Court.

12 Practice Direction (Citation of Authorities) [2012] 1 WLR 780.

13 *Parry v Keystone Healthcare* [2019] EWCA Civ 1246, [2019] 4 WLR 99 [26]–[27].

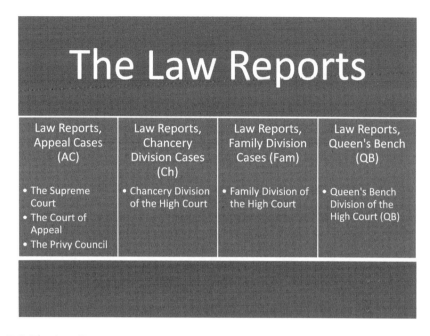

Law Reports, Appeal Cases (AC)	Law Reports, Chancery Division Cases (Ch)	Law Reports, Family Division Cases (Fam)	Law Reports, Queen's Bench (QB)
• The Supreme Court • The Court of Appeal • The Privy Council	• Chancery Division of the High Court	• Family Division of the High Court	• Queen's Bench Division of the High Court (QB)

Figure 9.2 The Law Reports

specialist or general professional journal (such as *Solicitors' Journal, New Law Journal, Family Law*) or even an academic journal (such as *Law Quarterly Review, The Conveyancer*).

A diagram of the major series of the official Law Reports can be found in Figure 9.2.

In addition to the main series, the ICLR also publish several other (mostly specialist) series of reports that seek to gather together important judgments and may be cited where a Law Report version is unavailable – for example, the Weekly Law Reports (WLR),[14] the Business Law Reports and the Industrial Cases Reports (ICR).

In 2001 the courts took a further step forward in terms of the accessibility of their judgments through the issuing of a Practice Direction on the use of 'neutral citation'.[15] This was a recognition of the increasing digitisation of both reports and judgments. Neutral citation involves identifying the judgment rather than a law report. Each judgment is coded according to the court and is then given a sequential number when it is handed down and each paragraph of the judgment is also numbered. The format of such neutral citations is as follows:

[YEAR] | COURT CODE | JUDGMENT NUMBER and, if relevant, [PARA NUMBER]

---

14 'The Weeklies' are an ICLR series of all but 1 WLR that go into the annual bound volumes cited in the normal way as [2019] AC etc.

15 Practice Direction *Judgments: Form and Citation* [2001] 1 WLR 194.

And so the fourth paragraph of the 1,246th case of the Civil Division of the Court of Appeal in 2019 would be as follows:

[2019] EWCA Civ 1246 at [4]

TAKING THINGS FURTHER – DEVELOPING LEGAL WRITING SKILLS

If you progress onto further legal study then case citations will become second nature. At the earlier states they can be confusing and difficult to navigate. The companion website gives some examples of how to construct references to cases and some exercises to test your understanding of this important area of legal writing. As you read other texts, pay particular attention to the footnotes and consider how the author has constructed their reference and what it tells you about the authorities cited.

The major developments in case reporting have been precipitated and encouraged by technological advances – the advent of the printing press and electronic case reports are just two examples. This process of technology influencing and driving forward the law and the processes of the legal system is apparent not only in this chapter but forms an important theme of the textbook as a whole.

DISCERNING THE 'VALUE' OF JUDGMENTS

It should be clear from the study of the court structure in Chapter 8 that there are different levels of court – for example the inferior and Senior Courts – and it would not make sense for inferior courts to bind all courts in the system. This means that there need to be rules by which we establish the 'precedential value' of the different tiers of the court system and consider the extent to which those tiers are bound by their own judgments. Another practical consideration is the extent to which judgments from outside of the jurisdiction influence the judgment of an English court. Both of these considerations are discussed in more detail in the following sections.

ESTABLISHING THE BINDING ELEMENT

As we shall shortly discover, not all aspects of a judgment are binding. The binding element is, in short, that principle which was necessary to resolve the legal issue. Unfortunately, judgments do not always make clear which parts are intended to be binding and, when multiple judges sit, the task of unearthing the binding element of the case can be devilishly tricky.

THE BINDING ELEMENT OF A CASE

A judgment will contain a great number of 'statements'. Some of those statements will be points of new principle, some will be speculation about issues outside of the present dispute, some will be relevant only to the parties (such as cost orders) and some will be purely 'ornamentation'.

A judgment will include a summary of the facts – material or otherwise. The material facts are those that give rise to the question of principle that the court must resolve in order to settle a case. Whether a fact is 'material' will depend upon the principle in issue. Some facts are clearly just part of the parties' 'stories' and judges sometimes have the air of a frustrated author in how they articulate those facts. Most prominent amongst these was Lord Denning who was known for his ability to bring to life the facts of cases, introducing one case about a traffic accident with the now famous line: 'It was bluebell time in Kent'[16] and, in another case painted the scene of a village cricket pitch as the backdrop to a case about the law of nuisance:

> In summertime village cricket is the delight of everyone. Nearly every village has its own cricket field where the young men play and the old men watch. In the village of Lintz in County Durham they have their own ground, where they have played these last seventy years. They tend it well. The wicket area is well rolled and mown. The outfield is kept short. It has a good club-house for the players and seats for the onlookers.[17]

RATIO DECIDENDI

A very large part of the study and practice of law is in the scouring of the case reports to separate the binding point of principle from 'the rest'. Or in convincing the court that a particular case raises different issues to that in the authority cited by the opposing side. Or in persuading the senior courts that they should reconsider and potentially overrule decided cases. In order to achieve any of these purposes it is important to first be able to discover the binding principle.

This binding principle is called the ratio decidendi, which is Latin for the reason for deciding the case in the way the judge did, on the basis of the material facts. Lawyers often simply call this the 'ratio'; so if you are asked 'What is the ratio of the decision?' in relation to any case report, it is that central binding principle, otherwise known as the ratio decidendi, which is the principle which the judge relied on to find for one party or the other.

An example, although a difficult one, of this might be the famous case of Donoghue v Stevenson[18] that of the decomposing snail found in a ginger beer bottle which laid the foundations of the law of negligence and of the duty of care. The main issue in this case, which was decided on 26 May 1932, was whether the manufacturer of the drink within the bottle (along with the snail's remains) owed a duty of care in tort to the eventual consumer of the beverage, since the central issue was that a duty of care was owed to one's neighbour but who then was that neighbour? There was a distinguished bench including Lords Buckmaster and Atkin; the result of the judges' deliberations on the factual matrix and the evidence in

16 *Hinz v Berry* [1970] 2 QB 40 (CA).
17 *Miller v Jackson* [1977] QB 966 (CA) at 976.
18 [1932] AC 562 (HL).

support was that the manufacturer did owe a duty of care to anyone who came in contact with the contaminated drink as it was reasonably foreseeable that anyone might drink it and 'everyone' was that manufacturer's neighbour for this purpose, so such a duty is therefore owed in those circumstances. Therefore, such a product should be fit for its anticipated use. To demonstrate the other point made earlier in this chapter, *Donoghue* was a landmark case in itself but it also led to further developments of the law of tort as it was refined and applied to new circumstances (where the material facts led to a dispute based on the same legal principles).[19]

TAKING THINGS FURTHER – IDENTIFYING THE *RATIO*

The case of *Youngsam*[20] (discussed later in relation to the power of the Supreme Court to depart from its own decisions) gives a sensible account of the nature of both ratio and obiter. It is worth reading this case in full given that it is rare for the judiciary *overtly* to enter into an analysis of these terms that are so important to the doctrine of precedent.

OBITER DICTA

By way of contrast, the judge in any reported case may have said other things about other principles which were not central to the case or the decision, and these are not part of the *ratio decidendi*. Such statements are known instead as *obiter dicta*, which is Latin for 'things said by the way' or 'outside' the central issue. It may be tempting to dismiss the value of such *obiter* but this would overlook the value that it can bring to the legal system. The most useful *obiter* can be split into two categories.

First, statements of law made during the course of a judgment that are not based on the material facts or are based on hypothetical situations. Denning's (J) judgment in *High Trees House*[21] is a famous example of the power of *obiter*. In this case, and speaking *obiter*, Denning postulated that on alternative facts the law would have *estopped* the behaviour of the respondents and this would have had the effect of re-animating the long neglected doctrine of promissory estoppel. In later cases, relying on Denning's persuasive reasoning (which was not in any way legally binding) the courts did in fact resurrect the principles of promissory estoppel.

Second, statements of law that *are* based on the material facts of the case but which do not form the basis of the decision (for example a dissenting judgment).[22] These are equally useful

---

19 See *Hedley Byrne v Heller* [1964] AC 465 (HL) for an express acceptance that *Donoghue* was to be the first in a number cases that would develop and extend the 'neighbour' principle.

20 R (*Youngsam*) v *The Parole Board* [2017] EWHC 729 (Admin), [2017] 1 WLR 2848.

21 *Central London Property Trust Ltd v High Trees House* [1947] KB 130 (KB).

22 Judges in the English Legal System do not always agree within a case, which is why the most senior courts always have an odd number sitting on a case to ensure that an outcome can be reached. Those judgments in the majority form the binding legal precedent whilst the comments of the minority (in dissent) do not form part of the binding aspects of the case.

because, as said elsewhere, the law is not static. Thus dissenting judgments can be useful in the future, should a court with the ability to overturn existing precedent wish to call upon the logic of those judges who earlier formed a minority.

TAKING THINGS FURTHER – THE WEBSITE

The website that accompanies this textbook contains a number of exercises that allow you to test your understanding of the terms *obiter* and *ratio* and give some more practical advice on how you may uncover them in decided cases.

MECHANISMS FOR AVOIDING PRECEDENT

Wherever the doctrine of precedent applies, there may be good reason for not wishing to follow a specific decision which is otherwise binding in the court in question. In these circumstances there are four possible ways of achieving this: distinguishing the precedent on the facts, so it does not apply; reversing of the decision by a higher court in the same case; declaring that the decision was made *per incuriam*; or overruling by a higher court in a later case involving a different legal dispute.

DISTINGUISHING

In the adversarial system that is in operation in England and Wales, opposing legal representatives will provide to the court their 'skeleton argument', including a list of authorities upon which they will seek to rely. It could be that it would be fatal to one side's case if the court accepted the reading of the law put forward by the opposing side. For this reason an advocate may wish to argue that the precedent does not apply. One way of achieving this is by arguing that the present case should be 'distinguished' from the authority in question. This involves persuading the judge that *the material facts* of the instant case are different from those of the precedent to the extent that the same legal issue does not apply or that the legal issue ought to be resolved differently.

This must of course be done with care as there is a duty on an advocate not to mislead the court and even if the judge accepts the advocate's argument the ultimate decision might still be reversed on appeal. If the judge successfully accepts the distinguishing arguments, then the judge will be developing the law in deciding that that precedent does not apply in the circumstances of the case before the court on that occasion but the decision is nevertheless made on the basis that the facts necessary to apply the precedent did not match those of the precedent in that particular case.

REVERSING

This will only occur if there is a successful appeal against the applicability of the precedent at the first instance hearing on the basis of *the law*, e.g. the Court of Appeal's decision is reversed by the Supreme Court because the precedent should not have been applied. Reversing therefore happens within the history of a single case and prevents the lower court's error from becoming part of binding precedent in the future.

OVERRULING

This occurs when the Court of Appeal or Supreme Court finds that an earlier case was wrongly decided. The most famous case of this type is probably the 1992 attempted marital rape and assault prosecution of R v R (Marital Exemption),[23] so famous that it was not necessary to be studying law in order to have noticed this case at the time. The appeal arose because there was a long-standing principle of English law that a husband could not be guilty of raping his wife since on marriage she had irrevocably consented to sexual intercourse with the husband. In this case the parties had separated, and the wife was living with her parents. The husband nevertheless took an opportunity to attempt to have intercourse with her against her will and was charged with attempted rape. His defence relied on Sir Matthew Hale's *Pleas of the Crown* (1736) which stated 'the husband cannot be guilty of rape committed by himself upon his lawful wife, for by their mutual matrimonial consent and contract the wife has given herself up to him in this kind unto her husband which she cannot retract'. The husband was convicted and appealed on the basis that, as he could not be convicted of rape, he could not be convicted of the attempt either.

The House of Lords unanimously rejected his defence, overruling the previous common law, in a decision of Lord Keith of the Kinkel to the effect that Hale might have been right about the state of the common law in 1736 but that in 1992 this could no longer be claimed owing to the change in the nature of marriage (in 1992 a partnership of equals with remedies available for ill treatment of the wife being no longer a subservient partner, or as Lord Keith stated, 'a chattel'). This was really inevitable in view of the changes that had taken place in Divorce Law[24] and in Equality and Diversity and Race Relations Law[25] and despite the long standing nature of the common law principle Hale referred to, which was itself based in a long past concept of matrimony which by 1992 was no longer rooted in religion or the practices of the Church in relation to matrimony and its dissolution.

It is more common for the Supreme Court to overrule the decision of a lower court than to reconsider its own earlier cases,[26] but there are recent examples of the Supreme Court overruling its own precedents.[27]

----

23 [1992] 1 AC 599 (HL).

24 Divorce Reform Act 1969, Matrimonial Causes Act 1973.

25 Equal Pay Act 1970, Race Relations Act 1976.

26 The circumstances in which the Supreme Court is able to depart from its own judgments are dictated by the Practice Statement, *House of Lords: Judicial Precedent* [1966] 1 WLR 1234 and is discussed later in greater detail.

27 See, for example, *Knauer v Ministry of Justice* [2016] UKSC 9, [2016] AC 908 where the court overruled its previous decisions in *Cookson v Knowles* [1979] AC 556 (HL) and *Graham v Dodds* [1983] 1 WLR 808 (HL).

PER INCURIAM

This is a somewhat limited form for avoiding what would otherwise be a binding precedent. It can only be used where it can be demonstrated that the previous case was decided without reference to a statutory provision or other case that would have changed the outcome. To put it differently, and to use the meaning of *per incuriam*, that the case was decided carelessly or in ignorance of relevant authority. The Court of Appeal described *per incuriam* as those:

> decisions given in ignorance or forgetfulness of some inconsistent statutory provision or of some authority binding on the court concerned: so that in such cases some part of the decision or some step in the reasoning on which it is based is found, on that account, to be demonstrably wrong.[28]

Given the quality of advocates and the judiciary in the senior courts, such occurrences ought to be rare and exceptional. Indeed, although this method of avoiding precedent is frequently pleaded, it is rarely successful. A recent example of an unsuccessful attempt at *per incuriam* can be found from the Lands Chamber of the Upper Tribunal.[29]

THE PRECEDENTIAL HIERARCHY

This, however, is not the end of the story as far as the use of such binding precedents are concerned. A decision which qualifies for the doctrine of *stare decisis*, and which cannot be 'avoided', must also fit within the hierarchy of courts which must (or need not) accept the decision as binding on them. The basic principle in relation to this issue is that all courts below that in which the decision was made are bound and must follow the decision made in the relevant case, whereas those above do not have to, and in any case may overrule it in a later case. But not all courts make binding decisions at all, as only those of the Senior Courts and the Supreme Court must be followed.

Thus, a decision made in the Court of Appeal is binding on all lower courts except the Supreme Court; however, it is also binding on the Court of Appeal itself, subject to some exceptions (see later in this chapter). Depending on the nature of the case and composition of the Court of Appeal the Supreme Court might also find such a Court of Appeal 'persuasive' (which means that while of course not bound by the decision – since the Court of Appeal is inferior to the Supreme Court – the Supreme Court might still find that a decision from a bench in the Court of Appeal, especially one which included one or more specialist judges of high repute, should not be entirely ignored and might adopt and improve on it.

Table 9.1 gives some indication of the various courts and their relationships.

28 *Morelle v Wakeling* [1955] 2 QB 379 (CA).
29 See *Firstport Property Services Ltd v Settlers Court RTM Company Ltd* [2019] UKUT 243 (LC) at [4] for the argument and [59]–[63] for the rejection.

Table 9.1 The Precedential Hierarchy

Court	Bound by others	Self-binding	Binds others
Supreme Court [SC]	[CJEU][1]	Yes – subject to Practice Direction of 1966	All other courts
Court of Appeal (Civil) [CA]	[SC]; [CJEU]	Yes – subject to the *Young* criteria	[HC]; [CC]; Inferior Courts
Court of Appeal (Crim) [CA]	[SC]; [CJEU]	Yes – subject to the *Young* criteria and an exception where individual liberty is at stake	[HC]; [CC]; Inferior Courts
High Court [HC] – Appellate Jurisdiction	[SC]; [CA]	Yes – subject to the *Young* criteria and an exception when considering criminal cases where individual liberty is at stake	[CC]; Inferior Courts
High Court [HC] – Supervisory Jurisdiction	[SC]; [CA]	No	Inferior Courts
High Court [HC] – First Instance Jurisdiction	[SC]; [CA]; [HC] – Divisional Courts	No	Inferior Courts
The Crown Court	[SC]; [CA]; [HC]; [CJEU]	No	No
The Inferior Courts	All other courts	No	No

THE SUPREME COURT

It will be remembered that the Supreme Court (formerly the House of Lords) is the highest appellate court in the English Legal System and so it ought to be no surprise that its decisions are binding on all courts that are, necessarily, lower than it in the hierarchy. Traditionally the House of Lords decisions were even binding on itself, with an inability to be able to overturn its own earlier judgments. This was made clear in the *London Tramways*[30] case where the House of

---

1   The position of European Courts is considered later but is much altered by the UK's exit from the EU.

30   The *London Tramways Company v The London County Council* [1898] AC 375 (HL).

Lords unanimously declined to overturn its own previous decision on the basis that to do so would lead to:

> the disastrous inconvenience – of having each question subject to being reargued and the dealings of mankind rendered doubtful by reason of different decisions, so that in truth and in fact there would be no real final Court of Appeal.[31]

Essentially this was an argument based on legal certainty and res judicata.

The present situation, since 1966, has been a complete change of heart in that the House of Lords (and now the Supreme Court) can overrule its own decisions. This principle is now articulated in a Practice Direction.[32] The Supreme Court having taken over seamlessly from the House of Lords as the final appellate court of the United Kingdom has not thought it necessary to re-issue or adapt for re-issue the 1966 Practice Statement,[33] so while in theory bound by its own decisions can depart from them when necessary on the same basis as the 1966 Direction.

The 1966 statement made reference to the fundamental value of precedent to developing legal certainty and providing 'at least some degree of certainty' for individuals.[34] Against this the Law Lords had weighed the injustice that can be caused by an overly rigid adherence to the rules of precedent.

The power to overrule is used sparingly and, normally, with express reference to the balancing exercise within the Direction. Perhaps its most famous use was in its Shivpuri[35] case on the potential criminal liability for attempting to commit a crime that was, in fact, impossible to commit where it overruled its judgment in Anderton[36] from the previous year.

Nonetheless, there are more recent examples that demonstrate the genuine balancing that needs to happen before the Supreme Court should depart from one of its previous rulings. In Knauer[37] the Supreme Court – without criticising – found the reasoning in two House of Lords cases to be flawed but this, of itself, did not persuade the judges to invoke the 1966 Practice Statement, something that the justices should be very 'circumspect'[38] in doing. The Court relied on three factors in coming to its decision to depart from its own prior judgments in this case:

---

31 Ibid. 379.

32 Practice Direction Judicial Precedent [1966] 1 WLR 1234.

33 And has judicially made reference to the fact that the Court will continue to rely upon the Direction which is 'part of the established jurisprudence relating to the conduct of appeals' Austin v Mayor and Burgesses of the London Borough of Southwark [2010] UKSC 28, [2011] 1 AC 355 at [24].

34 Practice Direction Judicial Precedent [1966] 1 WLR 1234.

35 R v Shivpuri [1987] AC 1 (HL).

36 Anderton v Ryan [1985] AC 560 (HL).

37 Knauer v Ministry of Justice [2016] UKSC 9, [2016] AC 908.

38 Ibid. [23].

1 The prior judgments were illogical and causing unfairness.
2 The lower courts were avoiding the effects of then judgments through artificial use of
   'distinguishing' which meant that legal certainty was already being undermined; thus the
   advantages of precedent in this case were already being eroded.
3 There had 'been a material change in the relevant legal landscape since the earlier
   decisions'.[39]

The most recent case involving the Practice Direction demonstrates that, despite being given
50 years ago, it is still controversial in its ability to let the Supreme Court depart from its own
decisions.

ANALYSING THE LAW – OVERRULING THROUGH *OBITER*

In *Youngsam*[40] the High Court was faced with a novel and thorny question – could the
Supreme Court overrule its own previous decisions by comments made *obiter* **and**
without express reference to the Practice Direction? The instinctive answer may be that
this ought not to be possible because *obiter* is not part of the binding ratio of the case.

The question arose because of the Supreme Court's ruling in *Whiston*[41] where
members of the Court had made statements about how the case would have been
resolved in other circumstances. On one reading, the *obiter* would have supported
the departure from a previous decision of the House of Lords in *West*.[42] The High
Court in *Youngsam* undertook a detailed analysis of the Practice Direction and noted
a number of things.

First, that the text itself does not say that departure can only happen when the Practice
Direction is 'invoked' expressly. Second, it does not require that departure is based on
unanimous agreement of the Justices. Third, it does not require that the *ratio* in the
case in which the Practice Direction is operative to be the same as the *ratio* in the case
seeking to depart – i.e. the power to overrule can be exercised through *obiter*.

The position was helpfully summarised as follows:

> Where a majority of the Justices have in the clearest possible terms decided that one
> or more of its previous decisions are not to be followed then it is not for this court to
> seek to emasculate the later decision by reanalysing the earlier case law and reaching
> a contrary view.[43]

....

39 Ibid.
40 R (*Youngsam*) v The Parole Board [2017] EWHC 729 (Admin), [2017] 1 WLR 2848.
41 R (*Whiston*) v Secretary of State for Justice [2014] UKSC 39, [2015] AC 176.
42 R (*West*) v Parole Board [2005] UKHL 1, [2005] 1 WLR 350.
43 R (*Youngsam*) v The Parole Board [2017] EWHC 729 (Admin) [2017] 1 WLR 2848 [39].

THE SENIOR COURTS

The Senior Courts are all bound by the judgments of the Supreme Court and their effect amongst themselves varies.

COURT OF APPEAL (CIVIL DIVISION)

The Court of Appeal's decisions bind all inferior courts and the Court is bound by its own decisions unless some exception applies to this 'self-binding' rule. The case of *Young v Bristol Aeroplane Co Ltd*[44] lays out the exceptions but they are fairly narrowly understood. The exceptions are:

1   Where previous Court of Appeal decisions conflict with each other, when they usually follow the latest, but need not do so.[45]
2   Where a previous Court of Appeal decision – that has not been formally overruled – conflicts with a later decision of the House of Lords or Supreme Court, when it must follow the superior court's decision even if it believes it to be wrong!
3   Where a previous CA decision appears to have been made *per incuriam*.[46] In 1985, in *Williams v Fawcett*[47] the Court attempted to get the traditionally accepted *per incuriam* rule extended (as it was at that stage quite narrow) so as to give themselves a better chance to correct the error, which Sir John Donaldson in that case considered 'a manifest slip or error'.

This list is the most commonly used of the 'exceptions' to the self-binding rule but there are others, including the fact that the Court of Appeal may be free of the rules of precedent if the earlier judgment is incompatible with EU law. What is clear is that there is no *generalised* power for the Court of Appeal to depart from its own previous judgment. The House of Lords were quick to quash Lord Denning's attempt to establish such a power during his time as Master of the Rolls by re-affirming 'expressly, unequivocally and unanimously that the rule laid down in the [*Bristol Aeroplane Case*] as to *stare decisis* is still binding on the Court of Appeal'.[48]

COURT OF APPEAL (CRIMINAL DIVISION)

In theory the two Divisions operate the same system but in fact the self-binding rule works in a slightly different way in the Criminal Division. This has come about through two causes: (1) case law and (2) impact of the liberty of the subject being at stake in criminal appeals, thought to be more important than rigid consistency. This leads to a slightly different view being taken of precedent because of the danger of a wrongful

---

44 [1944] KB 718, [1944] 2 All ER 293 (CA) *per* Lord Greene MR.
45 *Great Peace Shipping v Tsavliris Salvage* [2002] EWCA Civ 1407, [2002] 4 All ER 689.
46 As discussed previously.
47 [1986] QB 604 (CA) Donaldson MR.
48 *Davis v Johnson* [1979] AC 264 (HL).

conviction going unaddressed. See per Lord Goddard CJ in R v Taylor.[49] Lord Woolf also
contributed to this debate in R v Simpson[50] when he suggested that the Criminal Division
had a residual discretion to treat one of its previous decisions as not binding when there
were grounds to consider the decision was wrong, pointing out that a wrong decision
in such a case could do much more harm than a wrong decision in the Civil Division.
Considering the decisions that have turned out to be wrong in recent years, this seems to
be a very sensible approach; see e.g. R v Derek William Bentley (Deceased)[51] per Lord Bingham of
Cornhill.

HIGH COURT (APPELLATE AND FIRST INSTANCE JURISDICTION)

The lowest court which creates a precedent potentially binding is the High Court and its
Divisional Courts. Precedents are only a small proportion of all the cases decided in any year,
and those which are potentially precedents are usually found to come from the High Court,
Court of Appeal and Supreme Court.

The High Court is bound by courts superior to it in the hierarchy, i.e. the Supreme Court,
the House of Lords and the Court of Appeal, but is not bound by its own previous decisions.
However, the Divisional Courts of the QBD, including the powerful Administrative Court, are
also bound by superior courts and also by their own decisions, unless a Young v Bristol Aeroplane
Co exception applies to them, although when the Administrative Court is considering criminal
cases there may be more flexibility by analogy with the Court of Appeal, Criminal Division,
and the reasons for more flexibility there, the reasons for such different treatment in relation
to being bound by their own decisions being that they are appellate courts, unlike the QBD
itself and the Divisions of the QBD which constitute the Commercial Court, the Technology &
Construction Court and the Admiralty Court.[52] These Divisional Courts of the QBD must be
distinguished from the Divisions of the High Court, viz QBD itself, Chancery Division
and Family Division, and the Divisions of the QBD, all of which conduct all or mostly first
instance business.

The more routine work of the Family Division, such as under the Marriage Acts, Matrimonial
Causes Act 1973 and associated legislation, Civil Partnership Act 2004, Gender Recognition
Act 2004, Children Act 1989, and similar statutes, is now allocated to the Family Court, in
which High Court judges also sit as Judges of the Family Court, the purpose being to bring
all levels of Family Justice into one court where possible in order to reduce the necessity
for transfers between levels or locations of court, although sometimes geographic or other
reasons still require a transfer to another location of the Family Court, or indeed to the High
Court at the Royal Courts of Justice, owing for example to the sensitivity of a case requiring

---

49 [1950] 2 KB 368 (CA).
50 [2003] EWCA Crim 1499, [2004] QB 118, per Woolf CJ.
51 [1998] 1 Cr App 21 (CA).
52 See Chapter 8 for detail of the functions of the slightly complex court structure in the High Court.

superior security which a local Family Court might not be able to provide due to local resourcing limitations.

THE CROWN COURT

This court, being a national criminal court, is bound by decisions of superior courts. However, as it is a national court sitting regionally there are other judges of this court who are making decisions in parallel, and those parallel decisions are as in the case of the High Court of persuasive but not binding authority as between the various courts sitting as Crown Courts around the country.

THE INFERIOR COURTS

These courts – including the County Court and Magistrates Court – are bound by all superior court decisions but their own decisions bind no one, not even other courts at the same level in the hierarchy.

THE FAMILY COURT

One court which is a well-known exception to the doctrine of precedent in certain circumstances is the Family Court. This is now a national court which sits in various locations including in both London and in the regions, similarly to the Crown Court, and was set up in 2014 to unite the former triple tier of Family Justice (in the Magistrates, the County Court and the Family Division of the High Court) into one specialist court, under the jurisdiction of the President of the Family Division of the High Court. The contemporary local Family Court will probably also be located in the Court Centre where it was located before 2014, especially if that is a Civil Court Centre, or Combined Court Centre, with the Crown Court often in the same building as well, although this is not always the case. The only difference is that the relatively new Family Court has had the former local magistrates who dealt with Family business relocated into the lowest level of the Family Court, just as the judges of the former County Courts dispensing Family Justice have been relocated into the next level of the Family Court (whether they formerly sat in a Divorce County Court or one which dealt with child law cases). High Court judges (or those with Deputy High Court status, i.e. the 's 9' judges, authorised under s 9 of the Courts and Legal Services Act) are also available to sit in the Family Court, so that the Family Court is now a 'one stop shop' in regard to applications that need to be made at any level, and the judiciary are all termed 'Family Court Judges (even the magistrates). Allocation of cases all now started in the Family Court, under whatever statute concerning Family Justice, are then allocated to the appropriate level by a gatekeeping system within the court.

Thus Family Justice has a different understanding of precedent since much of the legislation under which it operates is discretionary in nature; thus each decision must be made on its individual facts and precedent either does not apply at all or it applies in a different way as guidance rather than actual precedent, since the facts will always be different in some way from any previous case that in another field of law might be either binding or technically persuasive.

In particular, statutes affecting children are heavily discretionary in nature, e.g. the Children Act 1989 s 1 where s 1(1) and s 1(3) concern the principle that the child's welfare is paramount, and in particular the s 1(3) checklist is mandatory for the court to work through before the judge must consider in his discretion what will be for the child's welfare.

THE EUROPEAN COURTS

Having considered the precedential hierarchy in the English legal system it is important to point to the influence of the European courts – particularly the Court of Justice of the European Union and the European Court of Human Rights – on the domestic principles of precedent.

Each exerts a significant influence over the rulings of English courts and have had a disruptive effect on the orthodox rules of precedent. As the UK has now left the EU, the influence of the CJEU will continue to evolve and change over time both within and beyond the transition period to the UK's full disentanglement from the EU.

As you read the next two sections consider how the legal system has evolved to incorporate judgments of courts that sit slightly outside of the formal court hierarchy. Consider the challenges, to consistency, certainty and legitimacy, caused by the accommodation of judgments of these courts into domestic law and practice. Also consider the potential advantages of accommodating different systems in this way and what it says about the potential flexibility and adaptability of the English legal system.

COURT OF JUSTICE OF THE EUROPEAN UNION (CJEU)

As between the Court of Justice of the European Union and the European Court of Human Rights, arguably the former has had the most dramatic impact on the system of precedent in the English legal system.

Its own prior decisions do not bind the CJEU but it is rare for the court to depart from its own case law.

Until the UK leaves the transition period at the end of December 2020, following its formal exit from the EU in January 2020, the judgments of the Court of Justice of the European Union are binding on all courts in England and Wales. This binding effect is only active to the extent that the issue falls within the scope of European Union law. For example, if an Act of Parliament is incompatible with the CJEU's interpretation of EU law then the Act must be disapplied by courts but only so far as it applies to EU law situations. This means that a particular Act will be disapplied by the courts in those situations that activate EU law but still applied fully in purely domestic situations.

The presence of binding CJEU judgments is problematic to the English system of precedent because it upsets the hierarchical court structure. It means that a court lower down the hierarchy can be faced with uncomfortable choices. For example, the High Court may request an interpretation of EU law from the CJEU and that interpretation may conflict with prior judgments of the Supreme Court. In those circumstances the High Court is in somewhat of a difficult position. On the one hand, the rules of precedent in the English legal system state that the High Court is bound by decisions of the Supreme Court. On the other hand, the CJEU has the jurisdiction to rule on the authoritative interpretation of EU law. This conflict of precedents was resolved by the CJEU stating (in Case C-173/09 Georgi Ivnov Elchinov [2010] ECR I-8889) that in such circumstances the national courts must disregard the rulings of the higher court. The decision of the Supreme Court in such a circumstance would not be overruled but the High Court would be able to 'disapply' it in the same way that EU law empowers courts to 'disapply' Acts of Parliament that are incompatible with EU law.

The situation above will remain true during the transition period as the UK fully disestablishes its links with EU law. Most courts in England and Wales will continue to be bound in perpetuity by decisions of the CJEU given before the end of the transition period. The Supreme Court will be able to depart from CJEU judgments on the same terms as it can currently depart from its own judgments (i.e. through the use of the principles established by the 1966 Practice Direction).

Judgments given after the end of the transition period will not be binding at all but English courts, according to s 6(1) of the European Union (Withdrawal Act) 2018, may 'have regard' to them. In this way they will form non-binding, or persuasive, precedent.

DECISIONS OF THE EUROPEAN COURT OF HUMAN RIGHTS

Now that you know how the framework of binding precedent in courts fits together in the English Legal System it is time to look briefly at the Human Rights Act 1998, as this has some potential to alter the way that *stare decisis* works. The reason for this is because the European Convention on Human Rights is actually incorporated into English law in the HRA 1998. It is s 2(1) of the Act which deals with interpretation of Convention (and now HRA) rights. This subsection requires that 'a court or tribunal **must** take into account' the following: (a) judgments, decisions, declarations, or advisory opinions of the European Court of Human Rights (ECtHR), (b) opinions of the Commission adopted under Art 31 of the Convention, (c) decisions of the Commission in connection with Article 26 and 27(2) of the Convention, and (d) decisions of the Committee of Ministers under Article 46 of the Convention, whenever made or given, so far as, in the opinion or tribunal, it is relevant to the proceedings in which that question has arisen.

This inevitably creates problems. (1) What does 'take into account' mean? It seems to mean neither follow nor ignore. (2) What does **must** in s 2(1) mean? Does it mean that the ECtHR decisions are binding on our courts? English judges seem unable to agree as to the precise impact of the requirements of s 2(1) on the doctrine of precedent. And does that word 'must' mean that the hierarchy of the English doctrine of precedent is disturbed if an inferior court thinks that the decision of a superior court which it should follow is incompatible with the a ECtHR decision on the Convention? This problem arose in *Ghaidan v Mendoza*[53] where the Court of Appeal followed an ECtHR decision, *Petrovic v Austria*[54] (under which Mr Mendoza was held to have been discriminated against under Arts 8 and 14 if he were not given the succession right under his former partner's statutory tenancy of their long standing home) instead of following the House of Lords decision in *Fitzpatrick v Sterling*[55] (under which he was not entitled to more than an assured tenancy as he was not a spouse but only a same-sex partner). It seems the House of Lords in 2004 then approved the Court of Appeal decision which had effected this reversal of the English precedent rule.[56]

NON-BINDING PRECEDENT

The term used to describe this section is a little challenging as by its very nature precedent is binding. What we mean by 'no-binding' precedent is sources that may be persuasive to courts considering legal issues. Amongst the most common are:

- The *ratio* of a court lower in the hierarchy. There are plenty of excellent judges in the inferior courts and in the Senior Courts at the lower end of the hierarchy. Indeed, many of these may end up, in time, being promoted to the Court of Appeal or Supreme Court and so it may be useful for the higher courts to listen to the solutions proposed by lower courts.
- Dissenting judgments (a judgment of a judge in a bench of more than one judge who does not agree with the majority).
- A minority judgment (where a judge has agreed with the disposal of the case but for different reasons to the majority).
- The *ratio* of a decision of a foreign court or of the Privy Council (commonly decisions of other common law countries with advanced legal systems, e.g. Australia, Canada, New Zealand, whose judges sometimes sit in the Privy Council).
- The views of academic and distinguished practitioner writers and a report from a law reform body (e.g. the Law Commission or JUSTICE, the All Party Law Reform group). The latter two used never to be taken into account (particularly the writing of jurists, who were at one time not considered persuasive unless already dead) but have been much more used in recent years.[57]

---

53 [2004] UKHL 30, [2004] 2 AC 557.
54 [2001] 33 ECHR 14.
55 [2001] 1 AC 27 (HL).
56 [2004] UKHL 30, [2004] 2 AC 557.
57 See The Hon Mr Justice Beatson, Inner Temple Reader's Lecture Series, 'Legal Academics: Forgotten Players or Interlopers', 12 November 2012, in the series 'Academics and Practitioners: Friends or Foes', www.judiciary.uk/wp-content/uploads/JCO/Documents/Speeches/justice-beatson-inner-temple-lecture-12112012.pdf, in which he explains that while the work of jurists has always been a source of law, in civil law systems they have, when still living, in the past been regarded as not such an appropriate source in English law until relatively recently, prior to which the rule was 'better read when dead'!

CONCLUSION

MAKING CONNECTIONS – FROM PRECEDENT TO THE ADMINISTRATION
OF JUSTICE
++

A basic understanding of the framework of the courts and of how the doctrine of
precedent works in civil and criminal jurisdictions is essential to an understanding
of this key feature of the English Legal System and of the administration of justice
in English law. In order to do this effectively, and to avoid unnecessary repetition,
some cross referencing will be required to other chapters, such as those on legal
professionals; the judiciary; and civil, criminal and administrative justice.

However the best way to become familiar with the doctrine is to read the cases and in
particular the judgments in the leading authorities which support the framework of the
practice of following judicial precedent in English law as some of the cases referred to
have involved judgments of leading members of the judiciary who have had such cases
before them at key points of consideration of the working of this central doctrine of
the common law. It is advisable to check regularly the website of the Supreme Court[58]
as this provides unparalleled access to the judgments of the court and the videos of
the hearings so that you can witness how the most senior members of the judiciary
deal with authorities.

Beyond the text and graphics of this chapter, it is important to note some of the broader
themes that arise out of the essential information set out. First, the framework of the
application of the doctrine of precedent is not exclusively either civil or criminal, and there
are variations in how the doctrine applies in the different courts in the civil and criminal
systems, in particular the flexibility encouraged by some leading judges in criminal cases
where the liberty of the subject is at stake. This also seems to be some explanation for the
flexibility that has occurred in relation to the hierarchy of courts where human rights are
involved. Secondly, despite the framework of the specialist Divisions of the High Court, at
Court of Appeal level and above in the Supreme Court, our top judiciary are generalists rather
than narrow specialists, steeped in the general principles of English law and of the application
of it in our unique ways of statutory interpretation and application of judicial precedent, as
they were in their rudimentary first inception 1,000 years ago as members of the medieval
King's Council. This is regularly made clear when it is evident from reports of decided cases,
that whatever their previous background in practice and on the Bench, the Lords Justices of
the Court of Appeal and the judiciary of the Supreme Court are expected to sit on both civil
and criminal appeals in accordance with the demands of the service. Students of the English
Legal System should emulate their generalist approach by not confining their study to either
individual fields of law or distinct topics in the framework of English law and institutions
within their separate units but always making connections where the opportunity arises.

58 www.supremecourt.uk.

THE WEBSITE

The website that accompanies this textbook contains many useful resources that you can use to consolidate and further your knowledge of the law, to hone your skills of critical analysis and to test your knowledge. This includes a set of multiple choice questions (MCQs) that can be used to test your knowledge and understanding of the material.

PODCASTS

- The podcasts provide a summary of the area under study, bringing together the key themes and threads of analysis into a 'mini-lecture'.
- There will also be an explanation and analysis of topical and up-to-date issues related to precedent.

10

CHAPTER 10
CIVIL JUSTICE

INTRODUCTION

Early in your legal studies, you will start to read about a number of cases decided by judges in the civil court system. It is the civil courts that deal with disputes in areas of law dealing with the rights and obligations which individuals, and businesses, owe to each other in areas such as contract, tort, family and company law. Thus, civil cases happen as between private parties disputing their legal rights and obligations. This is in sharp contrast to criminal cases where the state is prosecuting an individual for a criminal offence. It is in the operation of these two justice systems that we see the administration of justice most clearly. Where an individual or business believes that one or more of its legal rights has been affected, there is usually a desire to enforce those rights in the civil courts. Once a successful court suit has concluded the court staff, including judges, generally do not take any action without prompting by one of the parties so many people still see more court action as the way forward but in recent times there has been much more emphasis on out of court settlement, which can still be enforced through the courts if necessary as a legally binding agreement.

The purpose of this chapter is to provide an understanding of the steps that a party has to take to ensure that it wins its claim at court – if going to court is what has to happen, as many cases, though not all, now do settle out of court. This process has developed over many years. The courts have to deal with a wide range of claims, broadly applying the same steps and requirements about the format of evidence whatever the value, including in low value claims, perhaps by a builder for some works to a house where the work was unsatisfactory, or possibly not even completed so that the householder had to employ someone else to finish the job properly and this is the routine stuff of small cases in the County Court, the lower of the two courts in which civil cases start. These cases lack *some* of the notoriety of their criminal counterparts – with some notable exceptions – but make up a significant part of legal practice both for solicitors and barristers. From the very highest valued contract or personal injury claim to the smallest of small claims, the civil justice system provides a pathway to justice. Indeed, civil cases make up a significant portion of the workload of cases dealt with by courts in England and Wales with around half a million claims per quarter and around 15,000 of those making it to trial. As a result the civil justice system more than pulls its weight in terms of the administration of justice and by examining its features it will be possible to learn much about the legal system 'in action' and the challenges of delivering 'justice' in the current environment.

AS YOU READ

It is well worth referring back to the chapter on the court structure[1] while reading this one, so you are clear about how cases progress through the system. For most lawyers involved in

---

1 Chapter 8.

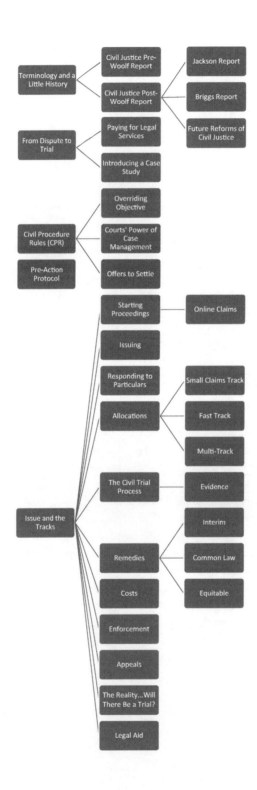

Figure 10.1

the civil justice system, much of their time will be spent dealing with cases in the High Court or the County Court, the two civil trial courts also known as the **courts of first instance**. It is in one of these courts that a claim will start. If a case involves either an important legal principle or a great deal of money, one of the parties might be unhappy with the judgment given by the High Court or County Court judge, so decide to appeal. Sometimes those appeals will be heard by judges in the Court of Appeal and, possibly, the Supreme Court (formerly the House of Lords). These are the **appellate courts** for civil justice.

As you read **consider critically** the structures and processes being described and reflect on how they impact on the ability of individuals to access justice. As you contemplate the Civil Procedure Rules **evaluate** whether they strike the right balance between certainty and flexibility. Finally, **compare** this area of the legal system, driven as it is by process, with some of the more principle-based chapters that came before it.

The purpose of this chapter is not to hope to give you a full understanding of the complex and technical rules of civil justice but rather to highlight to you the key features and to start to get you to think about how those processes shape justice.

TERMINOLOGY AND A LITTLE HISTORY

Before we move on to consider the detailed rules that apply it is important to come to terms with some of the basic terminology of the civil justice system, primarily how the main protagonists are termed. Civil justice is fundamentally a debate between individuals.[2] Those individuals and businesses are referred to as 'parties' to a dispute, perhaps an unfortunate term as even the winning party rarely has a great time – because of the costs of resolving the dispute in court, the work involved in complying with the court rules, the expense of legal advice and representation, often the delay in getting a hearing, the unpredictability of the outcome, the time taken away from other day to day activity (whether in a business or in a party's personal life) and the fact that, even if the case is won, it is very unlikely that all the costs of the litigation, both financial and non-financial, will be recovered when – and if – the judge makes a costs order against the other party!

The person bringing the civil law claim is deemed the 'claimant'[3] and the person defending the claim is called the 'defendant'. For most civil law claims the claimant has the burden of proving that alleged events took place and must discharge that burden to the civil law standard – on the so-called balance of probabilities. This means that the claimant must adduce evidence that proves his claim on the basis that the things alleged are more likely than not to be true.[4] To take an allegation of breach of contract as a starting point, the party who brought the allegation of breach of contract has the burden of proof, to prove the existence of the

---

2   Whether those are 'natural' individuals or 'legal' individuals (such as businesses).
3   Until 1998 the equivalent term used was the 'plaintiff'.
4   This is in sharp contrast to the criminal standard which requires proof 'beyond all reasonable doubt'.

contract, its terms, how the other party is in breach and the loss that has been suffered. That party needs to prove each of those to the civil standard.

Having dealt with basic terminology we move to consider the history of the civil justice system, in particular its recent history. We do this not because of a great desire to chart out this history of the legal system, as interesting as that is, but rather to give the context necessary for understanding the modern civil justice rules. The history of civil justice has been far from straightforward with multiple rounds of reforms (successful and unsuccessful) over the past 20 years amid a growth in cost, delay and complexity of process. Much has been done to streamline the process of civil justice but there is still some way to go. This pressure to reform and innovate to meet the challenges of demands on the court service has been matched with a government policy of reducing the cost of justice. Money has been removed directly from the court estate and also in support for those seeking justice through legal aid. This has led to a rise in 'litigants in person' that the legal system is having to deal with. For the purposes of this chapter we will look at the history of civil justice both pre- and post-1998 when a seismic shift in the rules was achieved, precipitated by the Woolf Report.[5]

CIVIL JUSTICE PRE-LORD WOOLF

Coming to the nub of the issue, by the mid-1990s the civil justice system was creaking from the weight of its own processes and the volume of cases it was supposed to be processing but in fact failing to do so. The rules were complex and found spread over multiple sources with different rules applying in the different courts. This, along with the parties having to manage and navigate the court processes with only very light judicial case management, meant that faith and trust in the ability of the law to deliver justice was in question. It was expensive to bring an action (with the cost often outweighing the damages sought) and the length and outcome of proceedings was too uncertain. Even if a judgment was reached, *enforcing* that judgment could be very difficult and often led to 'hollow' victories.

Against this backdrop, the Lord Chancellor commissioned the then Master of the Rolls Lord Woolf to prepare a report on access to justice and to recommend reform to the civil justice system. Lord Woolf duly prepared his interim and final reports. In his interim report, Lord Woolf highlighted the following as core to an effective civil justice system. He found that civil justice should:

(a) be *just* in the results it delivers;
(b) be *fair* in the way it treats litigants;
(c) offer appropriate procedures at a reasonable *cost*;
(d) deal with cases with reasonable *speed*;
(e) be *understandable* to those who use it;
(f) be *responsive* to the needs of those who use it;
(g) provide as much *certainty* as the nature of particular cases allows; and
(h) be *effective*, adequately resourced and organised.[6]

----

5   Lord Woolf, *Access to Justice* Reports (Interim Report 1996 and Final Report 1997). Access can be gained here – http:// webarchive.nationalarchives.gov.uk/20060213205513/www.dca.gov.uk/civil/final/contents.htm.

6   Lord Woolf, *Access to Justice* Reports (Interim Report 1996 and Final Report 1997). Access can be gained here – http:// webarchive.nationalarchives.gov.uk/20060213205513/www.dca.gov.uk/civil/final/contents.htm at para 1.

Figure 10.2 Woolf Report: Features of an Effective Civil Justice System

In order to achieve this he proposed a new landscape of civil justice based around the features shown in Figure 10.2.

These features eventually led to an overhaul of civil justice through the adoption of the Civil Procedure Rules (discussed in greater detail later) that revolutionised the way in which civil claims are issued, resolved and managed.

CIVIL JUSTICE POST-LORD WOOLF

As we shall see later in this chapter, the Civil Procedure Rules (with some modifications) that were the result of the Woolf Report are still in place today. They fundamentally changed the civil process within the English Legal System. However, things have not stopped there and over the 20 years following on from the Woolf Report and its reforms there have been further attempts at dealing with the issues generated by such high levels of demand for civil justice.

THE JACKSON REPORT

Almost ten years on from the Woolf Report in 2009, the Master of the Rolls ordered a review of the *costs* of civil litigation amid fears that such costs were spiralling out of control. Lord Justice Jackson was commissioned and produced a 557-page report in 2010 with 109 recommendations. Amongst the many recommendations that were taken up the following have the potential, in particular, to cut the cost of litigating:

- Those who were successful could no longer recover certain items in costs.[7]
- A cap was placed on certain types of fees in personal injury cases.[8]
- An extended category of fees was made available.[9]

This was coupled with a greater push, as was evident in the Woolf Report, for settlement and alternatives to litigation.

THE BRIGGS REPORT

2015 saw another Master of the Rolls (this time joined by the Lord Chief Justice) commission another review into civil justice, this time by Lord Justice Briggs, and in particular the structure of the civil courts. He reported in 2016 and identified five weaknesses in the system:[10]

- Problems with access to justice caused by excessive costs and cost risks in claims involving moderate sums
- What Briggs LJ termed the 'tyranny of paper' and the 'obsolete and inadequate IT facilities in most of the civil court system'[11]
- Unacceptable delays in the Court of Appeal
- Underinvestment in provision of civil justice outside of London
- Problems in the processes for enforcing judgments and orders

As the report was only made in 2016 there has not yet been a great deal of time for its recommendations to be adopted and put into practice. However, aspects are starting to be taken-up, most notably the piloting and introduction in 2018 of the 'Online Money Service' for making certain low value claims (up to £10,000) in the County Court.[12] This system saves the need for paper forms and replaces a very outdated online system that was in use from 2002. The pilot will run through November 2021.

---

7 'After the event insurance' and 'conditional fee arrangement' success fees. These are discussed later in the chapter when considering award of cost.
8 Success fees limited to 25% of damages in personal injury cases.
9 Contingency fees (discussed later) were made available for a wider range of claims.
10 Lord Justice Briggs, *Civil Courts Structure Review* (Final Report 2016). Access can be gained here – www.judiciary.uk/wp-content/uploads/2016/07/civil-courts-structure-review-final-report-jul-16-final-1.pdf.
11 Ibid. 115.
12 www.gov.uk/make-money-claim.

TAKING THINGS FURTHER – KEEPING UP WITH DEVELOPMENTS

Many of the recommendations of Briggs and Jackson are still being considered, piloted and implemented. It is important that you keep on top of these developments in order to keep your knowledge and understanding of the legal system current. Subscribing to blogs and updating websites can be a good way of keeping abreast of these developments. The companion website for this textbook will also contain regular updates on matters impacting on the legal system.

One of the themes that emerges from all of the preceding reports is the centrality of effective 'alternative' dispute resolution – i.e. settling claims in ways that do not involve going to court. This is one reason why this textbook has a whole chapter on 'ADR', Alternative Dispute Resolution,[13] which has thus become a new litigation trend in recent years, and to some extent an integral part of litigation rather than the 'bolt on' it once was, although the government prefers it to be called simply 'Dispute Resolution' (DR) as they want out of court settlement to become a norm within our culture, rather than an option, so as to reduce the burden of the courts' workload and the costs to the Ministry of Justice in running the courts.[14]

The remainder of this chapter will consider a civil action from claim to resolution and takes an approach that splits the civil process broadly into three phases:

- Before trial – including pre-action protocols, issuing, disclosure and track allocation
- At trial – including the typical process, remedies and costs
- After trial – enforcement

---

13 See Chapter 14.
14 See the Introduction by David Gauke, the then Lord Chancellor and Secretary of State for Justice, to the 2019 Review of the hated 'LASPO' Act (the Legal Aid, Sentencing and Punishment of Offenders Act 2012) which made stringent cuts in the provision of legal aid particularly in family law, which the government justified on the basis that of all disputes those in the family were better kept out of court. This is certainly a view shared by specialist family lawyers although not when recourse to court is actually appropriate, as it sometimes is, i.e. when settlement appears unachievable, at which point family lawyers and their professional association 'Resolution' emphasise robust court action must be utilised.

Adhering firmly to the established government policy for promoting out of court settlement in general however, Gauke's introduction says 'This review has highlighted that for too long legal support has been focussed solely on funding court disputes, with less emphasis on how problems can be resolved earlier to avoid them escalating into more problematic issues that require a court visit. Our ambition is to catch problems before this point, intervening at an early stage through services that prioritise the individual and are delivered at the right time, and in the right way for them.' While adding 'The ability of individuals to resolve their legal issues is vital for a just society, and everyone must have the ability to avail themselves of the justice system when they require it' he loses no time in adding that the government must 'explore with our partners and stakeholders innovative ways of supporting people to access the justice system and supporting placing early intervention firmly at the heart of legal support'. www.gov.uk.

FROM DISPUTE TO TRIAL

Disputes arise continually. The vast majority are resolved informally, perhaps using businesses or organisations set up to help resolve claims or through discussion by those involved. Let us look at some typical cases so as to pick one that might actually fail to resolve out of court and so go into the court process.

Many people involved in road traffic accidents contact their insurance company which helps to arrange for repairs to a damaged car and, perhaps, supplies a hire car whilst the damaged car is repaired. Most of those people do not understand the legal basis of any claim that they may have, and do not need that understanding. It is unusual that such a case goes to court, unless it might be to a criminal court – the Magistrates[15] – if one or both parties in the accident were in breach of a provision of the Road Traffic Acts or for a breach of Construction and Use Regulations, e.g. not having adequately maintained one of the cars involved, so that lights, brakes or tyres or some other part of the vehicle was found to be defective and possibly contributed to the accident, or – worst of all – one party was not insured. Mostly the ordinary road traffic accident does not result in a civil suit as there will usually be a settlement between insurers although as explained there may be associated criminal proceedings for one of, or both, the drivers. Equally, problems with contracts can often be resolved between the parties.

However, not every dispute can be resolved informally like this. For those cases, the person who believes that s/he has suffered a wrong will have to use the civil courts. In those situations, the first step for the potential claimant is to identify the legal basis of the claim. In some cases, it is simple, so for example, where a customer of a business fails to pay for the goods he receives, the business may argue that the customer breached the contract between them and the customer. The next step is then to identify the terms of the contract. Some terms will be agreed, such as the amount of goods and the price. Other terms might be imposed by laws passed by Parliament, such as the Consumer Rights Act 2015, which requires the goods to be fit for purpose and of a satisfactory quality. This would therefore be a contract claim, which you might follow with some ease as contract is often studied early in an undergraduate law course.

Another example might be a claim by a lady injured whilst driving a van. The injury occurs when another car hits the van from behind whilst the van is stationary in traffic. The lady may describe the other driver as 'negligent' without understanding the legal term she is using. If there is a dispute that cannot be resolved by negotiation someone, usually a lawyer paid for by the lady's insurers, will have to consider precisely what 'negligence' means in that context and to decide whether to issue a claim in court, which in this case would be a tort claim.

Whilst those two cases are, in legal terms, relatively simple the civil courts also have to deal with multi-million-pound disputes perhaps involving complex issues in company law or an alleged breach of trust, which are more difficult legal subjects.

---

15 See Chapter 8, The Court Structure, and Chapter 11, Criminal Justice.

PAYING FOR LEGAL SERVICES

A potential client, seeing his solicitor for the first time has a number of worries, about how soon he will recover from his injury (if at all) in the case of an accident or how he will receive goods that were not delivered or were dangerously defective. For almost all clients, one of the first questions they ask their solicitors is what a claim is going to cost them. It is a sensible and reasonable question.

Traditionally, legal costs were a simple matter, for the solicitor at least. The client would instruct the solicitor who would raise a bill at the end of the work that the client had to pay. Sometimes the client might be provided with a quotation, or estimate, indicating the fee that would have to be paid. More commonly, particularly for civil disputes, the client would be provided with some information about the hourly rate that the solicitor would charge, but usually with no indication of the number of hours of work involved. Perhaps understandably, clients and others argued that such an approach was an encouragement for solicitors to be inefficient.

The Access to Justice Act 1999 made some significant changes to the legal market in England and Wales. Amongst other things, it introduced conditional fee agreements ('CFAs'), popularly known as 'no win, no fee agreements'. As they currently operate, generally a client is not liable to pay the client's own solicitor for the work done if the claim is lost.[16] Importantly, the losing client remains liable for their opponent's costs but may be able to purchase an insurance policy to cover those fees, if they can afford the premium.[17] If the claim is successful, the client must pay their solicitor's legal costs which are usually recovered from the losing party. The client may also have to pay the solicitor a further sum, known as a success fee (which can be up to 100% of the regular fee).[18]

Solicitors can also act on the basis of 'damages-based agreements' (DBAs) that are sometimes known as contingency fees.[19] Under such an agreement the solicitor takes a share of any damages awarded rather than being paid a set hourly fee.

Otherwise, if there is no CFA and no fixed costs agreement (which some solicitors operate for common suits likely not to be complex or problematical) a client will be paying on an hourly rate which the solicitor is obliged to detail in writing to the client at the start of the case, together with other 'client care' information set out by the Law Society in its Code of Conduct, including who will have overall charge of the client's matter and who is to do the day to day work (this may usually mean two to three people in all), what position that lawyer holds in the firm, to whom to make complaints etc. and this has to be a best estimate if the

---

16 These encourage solicitors only to take on those cases where there is a good prospect of success.
17 The cost of this 'after the event' insurance policy is not recoverable if the claimant is successful. This was a revolution of the Jackson Reforms.
18 Again, not recoverable from the other side even if successful.
19 These used to be fairly restricted (e.g. to employment matters) but the Jackson Reforms liberalised them and made them available for more mainstream litigation.

hourly rate of one or more of the lawyers involved and the overall likely costs cannot be precisely detailed). This information also has to be updated regularly.

ANALYSING THE LAW – THE REALITY OF THE COSTS OF LEGAL ADVICE

In English law, the normal rule is that the loser of a case pays the other side's legal costs, the costs that the other side has paid its solicitors, barristers and other advisers in pursuing its claim. Do not forget that the loser has also to pay its own legal costs in many cases, sometimes doubling its legal bill. Costs are considered in detail later but can be considerable, in some cases running into hundreds of thousands of pounds, and sometimes over a dispute in which the value is very much less. There has been much publicity recently, for example, over the amount that some people spend over 'boundary disputes' – i.e. about a few feet of garden where it is claimed that, for some reason or another, a neighbour has sited a fence or wall incorrectly but the actual monetary value of that little strip of garden is many times less than the legal costs of even one side of the argument, and a small fraction of the legal costs bill for both sides. As a result, a mediation service has been set up involving specialist surveyors from the Royal Institution of Chartered Surveyors (RICS), who are trained mediators, to resolve such disputes, which generally results in the parties saving a substantial amount of money especially if the parties are able to obtain a fixed fee quotation from the surveyor-mediator and thus to avoid the expense of litigation.

Legal aid may be available in certain, limited circumstances. This allows for government funded support for legal actions. This applies beyond just civil cases and finds its latest incarnation in the Legal Aid, Sentencing and Punishment of Offenders Act 2012.

TAKING THINGS FURTHER – LEGAL AID AND ITS REFORM

Legal aid has proved a difficult topic for political actors with significant 'savings' being made by cutting spending on government-assisted legal action. These reforms have been deeply controversial amongst the legal profession as the amount invested in this area has fallen drastically with fewer areas being subject to the regime. As legal aid applies to civil and criminal cases, the website that accompanies this text contains additional information about the legal aid scheme as it used to apply and also the most recent developments in the reform of legal aid.

INTRODUCING THE CASE STUDY – A BREACH OF CONTRACT

One of the best ways of discussing the detail of civil process beyond this point is through the use of a typical scenario and we will follow it through the civil court process.

Jonny Jones is a marketing professional. He has for some years worked remotely from home, doing general marketing and public relations work for clients, such as new product launches, corporate identity design and crisis management, and has been so successful that he has decided to take on more staff, including some full time, and to find premises for a proper office.

He found a small run-down building on a former trading estate which has been largely taken over by a garden centre, although there are still some small industrial units occupied by small businesses which have bought their sites, and he has purchased his own, on the last available space.

He has hired a local specialist builder, Canny Conversions Ltd, to do the work of upgrading the existing building, which needs a new roof and a complete interior refit, and this construction company has, in turn, hired the landscaping service of the garden centre, Green Gardens Ltd, to relay the entrance to the premises with decorative tiling, to create decorative flowerbeds and to replant them with shrubs and seasonal perennials so that the premises always look attractive. A price was agreed of £50,000+ VAT for the work. Jonny is to provide his own freestanding office furniture, but Canny Conversions has to renew the basic services and to redecorate inside and out, and is also responsible for the payment on the sub-contract to Green Gardens.

All went well till a period of heavy rain and flooding in the spring which delayed completion by four weeks from the agreed handover date so that Jonny's new staff, who had had to work remotely, from home or at hot desks in the local Chamber of Commerce and town library, could not get into the building until the end of July when most of them were going on holiday.

Meanwhile in the summer heatwave many of the shrubs and plants were so badly affected that many died, and the office manager, Katy, tripped and fell on one of the tiles on the pathway into the main entrance door which had suddenly become raised, and is threatening to sue Johnny and/or Canny Conversions for her injuries which include a broken leg and two Colles fractures of the wrists when she put her hands out to stop herself falling onto the hard surface of the pathway, also her pain and distress, loss of earnings and general ill effects of her fall.

Jonny is furious, has refused to pay the final instalment of £30,000 to Canny Conversions Ltd, claims he has lost business and reputation, and says he will sue if the matter is not immediately resolved to his satisfaction. He is very sorry about Katy's fall but says she should have looked where she was going.

Canny Conversions says the money is due under the contract, that the dead vegetation is not their fault as Jonny's staff were clearly told to keep the new planting watered and the slightly raised tile is nowhere near as bad as the cracks, holes and raised paving stones in the high street. They try mediation but it does not work and Canny Conversions issues proceedings; Katy says she is going to sue as well.

There are, however, many steps from a dispute arising before a case goes to trial before a judge, including substantial pre-trial responsibilities which were written into the CPR 1998. We will return to Jonny and Katy's legal issues throughout the remainder of the chapter.

CIVIL PROCEDURE RULES (CPR)

The Woolf Report (discussed earlier) led to the introduction of the Civil Procedure Rules as we know them today. These Rules, known as the 'CPR', have been continuously amended and can be found in full on the internet, www.justice.gov.uk/courts/procedure-rules or in the 'White Book', the practitioners' book published annually by the law publishers Sweet & Maxwell, to which you can also obtain access online through the legal database Westlaw. The current issue is the White Book 2019 and each edition also has a 'service' of periodic supplements on recent changes in practice and amendments to the Rules and associated Practice Directions. Should Jonny and Katy wish to pursue claims then they will be subject to the rules and processes of the CPR.

However, introducing the reader at this stage to the CPR does not intend or encourage them to remember or learn the *detail* of the CPR[20] but only to introduce them to the processes, rules and procedures of the administration of civil justice. The purpose of the CPR, like any set of court rules, is to try to ensure that evidence is put before the court in a sensible, coherent form and to reduce the opportunities to cheat or abuse the court.

The CPR is divided into different Parts, each dealing with different aspects of the court procedure. There are currently 89 Parts of the CPR. Many of those Parts have a subsection, known as a Practice Direction, giving further details on the Court's approach to that Part. The CPR are reviewed and updated regularly with the 111th update being the latest in 2019 and the latest update to recent amendment pages on 7 October 2019. It is worth considering some Parts in a little more detail, particularly those that apply across the proceedings.

OVERRIDING OBJECTIVE (PART 1)

Part 1 of the CPR is the Overriding Objective, a new policy statement which was not articulated in the Rules of the Supreme Court[21] or the County Court Rules which preceded the

---

20 Which could well be the subject of a textbook all of its own!

21 This was *not* the Supreme Court brought into existence by the Constitutional Reform Act 2005 but rather the 'old' name for the Senior Courts, notably for our purposes the High Court and the Court of Appeal.

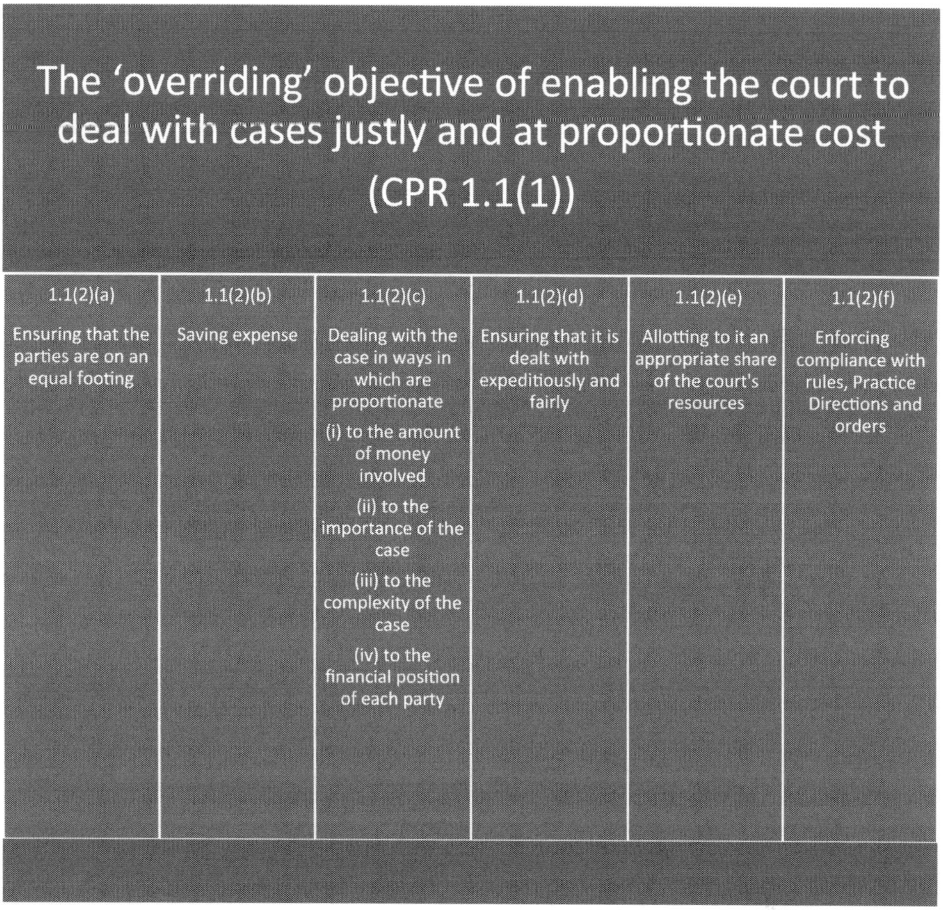

The 'overriding' objective of enabling the court to deal with cases justly and at proportionate cost (CPR 1.1(1))					
1.1(2)(a)	1.1(2)(b)	1.1(2)(c)	1.1(2)(d)	1.1(2)(e)	1.1(2)(f)
Ensuring that the parties are on an equal footing	Saving expense	Dealing with the case in ways in which are proportionate (i) to the amount of money involved (ii) to the importance of the case (iii) to the complexity of the case (iv) to the financial position of each party	Ensuring that it is dealt with expeditiously and fairly	Allotting to it an appropriate share of the court's resources	Enforcing compliance with rules, Practice Directions and orders

Figure 10.3 The Overriding Objective

CPR. This rule requires courts to deal with cases 'justly and at proportionate cost'. Amongst other things, the Overriding Objective seeks to ensure that the parties are on an equal footing and to assist the judge to deal with the case in ways which are proportionate. Proportionality requires the court to consider the amount of money in dispute, the importance of the case and its complexity as well as the parties' finances.

Importantly, the parties are required to help the court achieve the overriding objective (Figure 10.3), a slightly challenging concept for some clients who might be willing to spend considerable sums of money on legal costs to defeat their opponent. Jonny and Canny Conversions Ltd in our case study will have to remember this, and, if they do not settle and the case comes to court, that judge will have to see that Jonny is not disadvantaged, since he still seems to be a sole trader while the other businesses involved are incorporated as limited companies, and are apparently longer established which may mean that they have deeper pockets than he does.

PRE-ACTION STEPS

It is a commonly held belief that over 90% of legal cases do not go to a trial before a judge. That is probably an underestimate. As noted, there are many reasons why legal disputes never go to trial. It is widely appreciated that disputes can be resolved more easily if attempts are made soon after the dispute arises. Certainly, once parties have spent considerable amounts of money on lawyers, it becomes harder to resolve disputes as the stakes get higher.

The CPR were written to try to encourage parties to resolve claims without court proceedings. The CPR only applies to cases that have been commenced at court. At first sight, it seems illogical that the court can affect behaviour before it becomes involved. The CPR, however, achieves this in two ways. Firstly, it uses the Practice Directions on pre-action conduct and protocols. Those set out certain steps the parties are expected to carry out before commencing proceedings, such as writing detailed letters setting out the legal basis of a claim and sending with them copies of any supporting evidence, such as a copy of a contract.

In fact, the Practice Directions set out situations where rather more information must be provided in certain types of cases, and this in their specialist is the protocols. There are protocols for, amongst other things, personal injury claims – what if Katy, the office manager sues her employer, Jonny, on the basis of an unsafe system of work in having a trip hazard on the pathway into the main entrance? Or sues him as occupier of the premises under the Occupiers Liability Acts which require occupiers of buildings to which the public have access to accept liability for accidents which occur on their premises, which risk can be insured against and is usually included in any buildings insurance cover. In these circumstances in whatever capacity Jonny is likely to have public liability cover in his insurance policies so it will be worth Katy suing as Jonny's insurance company will have money to compensate her. In these circumstances, Jonny's insurer is likely to take over the management of the case on behalf of Jonny, and they will expect Katy to have provided the information to comply with the protocol when she takes out proceedings.

There are also protocols for e.g. housing disrepair, defamation and debt claims. All these protocols are designed to encourage the parties to take steps that ought to be taken in that type of claim. So, for example, the personal injury protocol requires the claimant to write a detailed letter of claim. The letter must set out the legal basis of the claim, summarise the relevant facts and detail the losses suffered by the claimant, supplying supporting documents where possible, so Katy will have to detail her loss of earnings if any, special expense in relation to treating her injury and provide further detail of her likely recovery time. Here there seems no criminal element to her accident although e.g. a claimant injured in a road traffic accident might obtain a copy of any report prepared by the police and send it with the letter, but Katy may have a report from A&E and/or her GP or even a specialist she sees at the local hospital.

The protocol requires the defendant to reply, within set time limits, allowing a period for the defendant to investigate the claim, and to put forward its version of events, if different. It should also supply documents where it has any applicable to the dispute. In this case Jonny's insurer will write these documents for him, as it is usually a condition of the insurance cover that any claim against an insured is handled by the insurance company, so as soon as Jonny receives Katy's letter he must pass it to the insurer and leave them to manage the claim.

If a 'tripping' claim such as Katy will make is by someone who has e.g. slipped in a shopping centre, causing injury, the occupier of the centre might supply a copy of the relevant part of its accident book and, perhaps, entries in its cleaning rota to show that it makes reasonable efforts to clean up spillages, but as Jonny was delayed moving in he may not have this sort of documentation in place, and the raised tile may be an initial construction defect, so in his case he may only produce, for example, the specification for the new decorative tiling outside his premises.

Importantly, the Practice Direction and all the protocols emphasise the need for the parties to use litigation as a *last resort*, using some form of alternative dispute resolution (ADR) where possible. The variety of ADR methods is discussed in detail in Chapter 14. The Practice Direction suggests negotiation, mediation and early neutral evaluation as forms of ADR that might be tried. There is also a new Practice Direction and Pre-Action Conduct Protocol 2015 which sets out what needs to be done in 13 classes of case including Personal Injury (for Katy) and Construction and Engineering for the remaining parties to the contract for the renovation work involving Canny Construction and Green Gardens, including Jonny, the client and likely claimant for the defects in his building and its outside space.

APPLYING THE LAW – LOOKING BEYOND THE LAW

When studying law, it is easy to become focussed on legal rights. It is important to understand that people and businesses have a wider perspective. For example, many shops will provide refunds to customers even if there is no legal requirement so to do, but as a gesture of goodwill and/or to avoid adverse publicity. In other situations, the parties to a dispute might reach a compromise by negotiation, perhaps having discussed the problem by telephone or in an exchange of emails. Sometimes, if the dispute is between two parties with an existing business relationship, they will wish to avoid 'souring' that relationship through court action. Other people will not take any action to enforce their legal rights because they do not understand the law or the court system and cannot afford a lawyer to help them. This means that whilst the English Legal System provides a court system for the resolution of disputes, many will not proceed for good or bad reasons.

This dispute resolution option may, however, apply particularly strongly to Canny Conversions Ltd and Green Gardens Ltd, as if Jonny has a sound local reputation and is a neighbour on their trading estate, and not only not in a business that competes with either of them, but in one whose services they may need at some stage, they may be keen to resolve the dispute, not least as the very first rule in the CPR records the overriding objective of resolving cases justly and proportionately so that this may be relevant when it comes to the judge's decision on costs. Moreover, everyone is in business in this scenario and would probably rather get on with doing business than being involved in a long argument about a few thousand pounds. This was certainly the background to the very first instances recorded of the use of DR in mercantile communities such as the ancient world's merchants, who were merchants above all and, preferring settlement to wasting time on fighting disputes formally in court, are, for example, credited with knowing and using arbitration. Legal costs which enable a party to keep trading are also usually tax deductible in contemporary developed jurisdictions, so there are usually legal costs provided for in any small company's annual budget.

However, the Practice Direction and protocols are to be used *before* court proceedings commence and are not part of the *court process.* There seems no obvious reason why the parties would not necessarily follow them assuming a claimant hires a lawyer to file the court paperwork and to handle pre-court stages required by the protocol, but in a sense they *are* part of the CPR as the CPR gives the court the power to penalise parties for their behaviour before proceedings were commenced. So, if a claimant who suffered a personal injury did not follow the protocol and send a letter of claim, the court might prevent that party, e.g. Katy, from pursuing the claim further until she has followed the steps the protocol required, and the same for a party who did not consider an offer to mediate or follow some other form of dispute resolution, although the recent case of *Gore v Naheed and Ahmed*[22] suggests that if a party wins refusing such an offer may be justified although this has been criticised as a departure from previous case law.

One of the main ways in which the courts seek to ensure that parties comply with the CPR is by imposing costs penalties. Normally, if the claimant is successful in its claim, the defendant would have to pay the bulk of its legal costs. If it ignored a step in the Practice Direction, the court might order the claimant to carry out that step but order that it cannot recover the costs of the step from the other side, even if it wins the claim. Parties have even been penalised from the early 2000s as already mentioned for not considering any DR resolution process because of thinking they had strong cases so need not. The point is that court is *not* supposed to be used if some other resolution is available! – though it may make a difference what actual strength of case is demonstrable and whether there is a need for a decision that the claimant is right about a point of law.

Figure 10.4 shows the overall court process for a standard case.

---

22 [2017] EWCA Civ 369, [2017] 3 Costs LR 509.

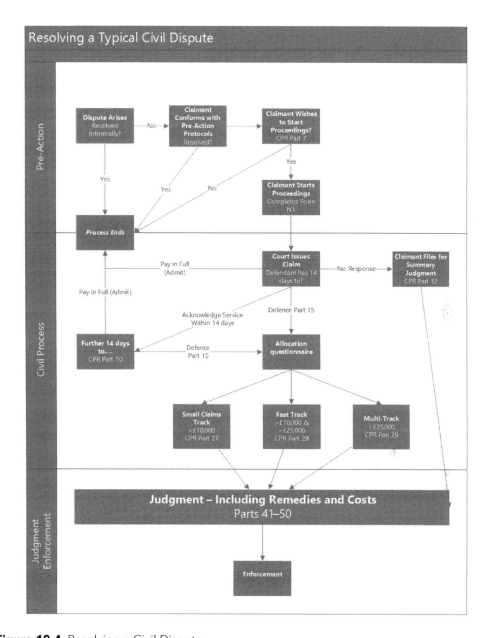

Figure 10.4 Resolving a Civil Dispute

ISSUE AND THE TRACKS

A dispute cannot be resolved in all circumstances. Sometimes the parties' valuations are too far apart, or one (or both) of the parties might simply be unreasonable. In other cases, whilst the claimant or the claimant's solicitor writes a letter of claim, the intended defendant simply ignores it. (Many solicitors find it curious that clients always seem to receive their letters whilst the other side, if not represented by a solicitor, often complains that post goes astray!) Once an impasse has been reached, or the letter of claim ignored, the claimant has a decision to make – whether or not to issue proceedings at court to start the claim. This is a critical decision for a claimant, for if later deciding to end the claim, the claimant would be the one who would have to pay the bulk of the legal costs that the defendant had incurred to that time. The claimant would, of course, also have to pay the claimant's lawyer's costs, whether the claimant is an individual or a company.

STARTING PROCEEDINGS (PART 7)

Assuming the claimant wishes to bring a claim, that party would draft a claim form. There will be two cases here: (1) *Canny Construction Ltd v Jonny Jones* (the builders suing for the contract money unpaid) and no doubt Jonny defending and filing his own 'counterclaim' along with his defence; (2) *Katy v Jonny* (claiming compensation for her personal injury). For certain claims there is a new online process but this, at the time of writing, was undergoing a pilot. This is a standard court document (Form N1)[23] requiring certain essential details, such as the names and addresses of the parties, brief details of the claim and its value.[24] In some cases the particulars[25] of claim would be set out on page 2 of the claim form. In other cases, the details would be in a separate document, called the Particulars of Claim. These documents, with copies for the court and each defendant, are sent (usually although not always electronically) to court with the appropriate court fee. The fee is paid to the court to commence proceedings. These fees vary according to the expected value of the claim and can escalate quite quickly – for claims worth over £200,000, the court fee is £10,000!

APPLYING THE LAW – A SUMMARY OF STARTING OF PROCEEDINGS

The particulars of claim are referred to as statements of case, as they state the parties' legal cases. Statements of case used to be referred to as 'pleadings', a term used by some older textbooks (and lawyers!). This old term is still useful for students to know when reading older cases which still have force and appear in subject specialism texts – so when you see this term, statements of case are what they are now.

All statements of case, as well as witness statements and experts' reports, must contain a statement of truth. This is a standard form of words, required by Part 22 of the CPR, confirming that the facts contained in that specific document are true. If a person signs a statement of truth without an honest belief that the facts are true, then that person is committing contempt of court (and that is the same if signing on behalf of a limited

---

23 Form N1, the universal claim form, can be found on the internet. See www.gov.uk/government/publications/form-n1-claim-form-cpr-part-7.
24 Covered by CPR Part 16 (Statement of Case).
25 Details.

company). Contempt is a criminal offence, so a person found guilty could face an unlimited fine, a prison sentence of up to two years or both. In *R. (on the application of Accident Exchange Ltd) v Broom*,[26] seven defendants were found to be in contempt of court having signed documents in a previous case where they knew the facts set out in the documents to be false. Each defendant was sentenced to prison for around a year. This means that Johnny, Katy and the Directors or other representatives of Canny Construction Ltd and Green Gardens Ltd must be careful in completing the forms

COURTS' POWER OF CASE MANAGEMENT (CPR PARTS 1 AND 3)

Another cross-cutting theme that emerges from the Woolf Reforms and the overriding objective of Part 1 is the changing role of the court in managing the court processes. Courts must adopt an 'active' approach to case management to ensure that justice is delivered quickly and in a cost effective manner. The courts' responsibility in this respect is to, amongst other things, encourage cooperation between the parties, encourage the use of ADR and give directions that ensure that the trial of a case proceeds quickly and efficiently. From 2015 this may include the court using Early Neutral Evaluation to assess the merits of a particular claim. The parties are *expected* to take such actions that support the court's role in this endeavour. The powers of the court to achieve this aim can be found in Part 3 of the CPR and are fairly wide-ranging.

For Katy and Jonny this may mean that they must explore ADR and may be subject to other obligations flowing from the directions of the court.

ISSUING

Once the court has received the papers and fee, it issues the claim. Issuing is the formal step when the court proceedings begin. It may involve little more than the papers being stamped but is important as many deadlines start or end on the date the claim is issued. For example, under section 11 of the Limitation Act, all personal injury claims have to be *issued* within three years of the injury occurring (there are very limited exceptions to this rule). If the claim is issued after that time, the defendant has an absolute defence to the claim. This means that the claimant would not receive compensation from the defendant, however strong the claim may be.

RESPONDING TO PARTICULARS (PART 9)

Once the claim is issued it is then for the defendant to respond to the claim. There are strict time limits that apply to the response.

....

26 [2017] EWHC 1530 (Admin).

The options open to a defendant are to file or serve:

- An *admission* (CPR 14)
- A *defence* (with or without counterclaim) where he wishes to contest the claim (CPR 15)
- An *acknowledgment of service*

If the defendant disputes the claim, then that party will file a defence, within 28 days of the claim being received from the court. If the defendant misses the deadline, then the claimant sends a form to the court to enter default judgment.[27] To give a sense of scale, of the 303,830 judgments given between April and June 2019 around 271,664 were default judgments.[28] Around 15,200 cases went to trial in the same period. This shows that a great number of claims do not receive a response and an even smaller fraction of those claims make it through to the court (many that do not end in default judgment are therefore either settled or withdrawn).

And so it will be for Canny Conversion and Katy to start the proceedings and wait to see whether the claim is *admitted* (and they can move to claiming the value) or *defended*.

OFFERS TO SETTLE (PART 36 OFFERS)

At any point during the proceedings one party may make a formal[29] offer to settle and these offers are known as 'Part 36 Offers' because they are governed by Part 36 of the CPR. Such offers are made 'without prejudice' (i.e. with no acceptance of liability).

These offers are an important strategic tool for parties because a refusal of a Part 36 Offer can result in negative consequences in terms of the award made on success. This is all part of the culture and incentives of the court in trying to get parties to settle their disputes without going through to a trial. A party has 21 days in which to consider and accept or reject such an offer.

If Jonny's insurers are acting on his behalf then they may well weigh-up the prospects of success and the likely cost of the litigation (including the prospect of paying for Katy's costs as well as their own) and make an Offer to Settle under Part 36. Equally, Canny Conversions may wish not to go through with a claim after initially serving a defence and could make a Part 36 Offer in order to bring the process to a close.

ALLOCATIONS

If the case is defended and no Offer to Settle is made or accepted then the case will be allocated for trial. When the court receives the defence, it sends the parties a form (known as an allocation questionnaire – Form N150) asking them to supply information about the claim and the steps they consider necessary for the claim to go to trial. The court will consider this

----

27 CPR Part 12.

28 www.gov.uk/government/statistics/civil-justice-statistics-quarterly-april-to-june-201.9.

29 Or any number of *informal offers*.

information but by issuing the claim, the parties at that stage lose control of the claim as the court begins its case management (now, as mentioned previously, a proactive feature of civil justice included by Lord Woolf in his suggestions in the *Access to Justice* reports for modernising civil justice and adopted in all cases since the CPR 1998 were brought into force in 1999). This means it considers the steps required taking account of the value of the claim, its legal and evidential complexity and similar matters which were another feature of Lord Woolf's reforms, in allocating cases to 'tracks', so that they could be managed more efficiently.

The court then sends out a document setting out the steps that the parties must take with a deadline for each step. As is discussed later, the steps normally involve the exchange of evidence. Thus, the order might require the parties to send each other copies of all relevant documents, by a specific date. This document is usually referred to as 'Directions', as it directs the parties as to what to do and when.

The starting point when considering the steps required is the value of the claim. It is on this basis that the court decides which of the three available tracks the case is allocated to and which thereafter the claim will follow. There are small claims, fast and multi-tracks.

SMALL CLAIMS TRACK (PART 27)

The small claims track applies to claims for less than £10,000 save for some personal injury and housing claims where the limit is £1,000. The small claims track is designed to be less formal than the other tracks. In part this is because the winning party does not ordinarily recover its legal costs from the losing party, save for the fee it paid to the court to start the claim. As a result, it is relatively rare for parties to use (or instruct) lawyers to represent them in such a claim. It is worth considering why the small claims track seems designed to remove lawyers from the court process.

Part 27 of the CPR deals with small claims track cases. Its Practice Direction provides further details, including some standard Directions for use in most circumstances, set out in Appendix B. The standard Directions provide that:

1 The parties must deliver to every other party and to the court office copies of all documents on which they intend to rely at the hearing no later than 14 days before the hearing. (These should include the letter making the claim and the reply.)
2 The original documents must be taken to the hearing.
3 The date of the trial is then fixed, and the court gives an estimate of how long the trial will take, perhaps two hours.
4 The Directions encourage the parties to contact each other with a view to trying to settle the case or narrow the issues. However, the court must be informed immediately if the case is settled by agreement before the trial date.
5 The Directions prevent the parties from relying on any report from an expert unless express permission has been granted by the court beforehand. Anyone wishing to rely on an expert must write to the court immediately on receipt of this Directions Order to seek permission, giving an explanation why the assistance of an expert is necessary.

The judge who hears the trial is often more likely to intervene than judges in fast and multi-track trials, perhaps by asking more questions of witnesses to ensure that evidence is brought out and allegations made by witnesses are challenged.

Unless the claims against Jonny are partially settled, it is unlikely that any of them are going to be on the Small Claims Track as £30,000 is being claimed by Canny Construction, and Katy's claim is unlikely to be worth less than £10,000.

FAST TRACK (PART 28)
The fast track is for those cases that are worth more than £10,000 (i.e. the small claims limit) but less than £25,000 (i.e. the multi-track lower limit). Part 26 of the CPR, which explains which track applies to cases, states that the fast track applies:

- Only if the trial is likely to last for no longer than one day and
- Oral expert evidence at trial will be limited to (1) one expert per party in relation to any expert field; and (2) expert evidence in two expert fields.

Part 28 of the CPR deals specifically with the fast track. On allocating a case to the fast track, the court is expected to set Directions to take the case to a trial, no more than 30 weeks later. Ensuring that a case is ready for trial in just over half a year does not seem that challenging, until you appreciate that some lawyers are responsible for more than 100 client files.

The court Directions set out the further steps required, again using some information provided by the parties. The timeline runs from the date that the court allocates the track and normally requires parties to disclose documents within four weeks.

Ten weeks after allocation, the parties must exchange witness statements, and four weeks later they must exchange experts' reports (if any have been obtained and not been agreed). Twenty-two weeks after the case was allocated, the parties must return completed pre-trial check lists (also known as listing questionnaires) to the court. These are standard forms and ask a series of questions to establish whether the case is now ready for trial.

Canny Construction's claim is unlikely to be on this track as the claim is for £30,000 and Jonny seems to have his own claim to include with his defence to Canny Construction's for the £30,000: in the language of the law this means that he has a counterclaim in addition to his defence to their claim for the £30,000 which may even be more than £30,000, so this is probably a complex case which needs to be on the higher track, the multi-track, for which see the following section.

MULTI-TRACK (PART 29)
The multi-track is used for the most valuable claims of over £25,000. Some lower value claims can be dealt with on the multi-track, but only in limited circumstances, such as: the case involves complex factual, legal or evidential issues; has a large number of parties; or involves a great deal of oral evidence. Importantly, such claims are still being dealt with

in the County Court. The High Court only covers claims worth £100,000 or more (and it is unlikely that the case of *Canny Construction Ltd v Johnny* (or his company if he has meanwhile incorporated) will be in the over £100,000 category.

As with the other tracks, once the case has been allocated to the multi-track, the court will want to set some Directions, setting out the steps that the parties need to take to progress the case to trial. The big difference is that, generally, the parties can have a greater say in the timetable and the steps needed. Indeed, in multi-track cases, the parties would be expected to work together to agree on some Directions. There are some standard Directions and even a menu of model paragraphs that the court makes available online for the parties to use.

THE CIVIL TRIAL PROCESS

Despite the pre-action steps and the push for parties to use ADR to resolve disputes, some cases still go to trial. Having dealt with disclosure as well as preparing and exchanging witness and expert evidence, it may seem like there is little left to do to prepare for trial. Cases that do not involve minors will be likely to be heard in public.[30] This will almost certainly be the case for Jonny and Katy. The trial will take place before a judge, sitting alone, who will have probably previously worked as a solicitor or barrister, although since the Judicial Appointments Commission was established in 2006, the pool has widened somewhat (see Chapter 7).

Having what seems like a strong legal claim is not enough for success at court. A party may consider, for example, that it has a strong claim that the other party is in breach of contract. However, it will need to prove that claim. There are, broadly, three evidential aspects that the parties have to deal with after the case has been issued through to trial. They are disclosure, witness evidence and expert evidence.

Disclosure relates to documents, with the requirements set out in Part 31 of the CPR. Each party has to gather the documents over which it has control that are relevant to the claim, then prepare a list of them. This list is sent to the other side, which can request copies of any documents that it wishes to see. Importantly, parties are required to disclose not only the documents on which they rely (to prove their own case) but also documents that harm their case and those that assist the other side.

Before the CPR, this process used to be called 'discovery', where the parties 'discovered' what documents the other side had that might be relevant. In theory, if the parties have complied with the pre-action steps just discussed, there should be little more to 'discover' at this stage.

Discovery used to be one of the most expensive steps of the litigation process, as lawyers considered many documents, perhaps thousands, to see whether they were relevant to the dispute.

30 CPR Part 9.

For fear of missing the one document that might be the 'smoking gun', the lawyers would then ask to see all of the documents disclosed by the other side. A similar trick was used to hide documents that a party did not want the other side to find. You were obliged to disclose every qualifying item, but it was not necessary to make it easy for an opponent to find! (The rules said nothing about making anything easy.) Smart litigants would then bury a document of this sort in a large category of uninteresting looking documents in the hope that the unlucky legal clerk going through all this relatively boring documentation would not persevere and would give up after no more than a cursory glance at a few documents near the start of that particular list which would be labelled something like 'Miscellaneous documents Number 1–10,001!' And if that did not do the trick the party was having an unlucky day! The Jackson reforms have changed the rules of disclosure to make them much more limited for all cases other than those involving personal injury.

For Katy, then, the usual disclosure rules will apply but the more limited version will apply for Canny Conversions.

Once the parties have all the relevant documents, they can then finalise their witness evidence. It can be unwise to do this earlier, in case a document is disclosed that can undermine a carefully crafted legal argument. The witness evidence must be set out in detailed form, as required by Part 32 of the CPR, i.e. in a statement, which becomes that witnesses' evidence at the hearing.

Historically, the first time that a party would know what a witness for the other side was going to say was when they gave evidence (known as evidence-in-chief) at the trial. Such an approach was referred to as 'trial by ambush'. The lawyer representing the other side then put questions to that witness, known as cross-examination to try to undermine the evidence given, a challenging task for the lawyer who had no advance knowledge of what was going to be said. The approach rarely suited clients although the lawyers, who were paid whether or not their clients won the trial, had little incentive to change the system.

The CPR now requires that parties should prepare detailed statements, in paper form, setting out the evidence that each person will give if the case goes to trial.[31] Importantly, those statements are exchanged with the other side weeks or months before the trial. The cards on the table approach to litigation encouraged by the CPR, including the pre-action steps, means that the witnesses and the gist of the evidence they will give ought not to be a great surprise to the party receiving them.

If the case still progresses to trial, there is a further change – the witness will not give evidence-in-chief, as the court will normally rely entirely on the contents of the statement, so the witness will go straight into being cross examined. And the lawyer for the other side will have had a chance to consider that statement, with time to devise lots of challenging questions to put to the witness!

The final piece of the evidential puzzle is that of expert evidence. Before the CPR, expert evidence was a growing area. In personal injury claims, both sides would have medical

---

31 CPR Part 32.

experts dealing with the range of injuries suffered and there might also be employment experts, giving evidence on the type of work that the injured person could do, and nursing experts, explaining how the type and extent of the ongoing nursing care that a permanently injured person would require, amongst others.

In terms of ordering, the party bringing the claim will start. Traditionally, the party's lawyer would give an opening speech, explaining the basis of the claim and how the evidence would prove it. The witnesses would be cross examined by counsel for the claimant and then the defence repeats the process. The parties' counsel then 'sum up' their cases, giving a final speech, defence first, claimant last of all, then the judge gives the decision with an explanatory judgment on the reasons.

REMEDIES

At the end of the case the judge will, on the basis of the evidence, find for the claimant or defendant. If the defendant wins then the claimant's case is dismissed and the court will make an order as to costs. If there was a (successful) counterclaim then the court may issue one of the following remedies. Equally, if the claimant wins then the court will award a remedy and costs.

There are three main forms of remedies that the court may award:

- Interim relief
- Damages
- Equitable remedy

INTERIM RELIEF

These are included in this section for completeness but, as there name suggests, will have been granted at an earlier stage in the proceedings. They are governed by CPR Parts 23 and 25 and include, amongst others, all interim injunctions, freezing injunctions and search orders.

There is nothing on the facts that suggest that this sort of interim relief is likely to be engaged in Katy or Jonny's case.

DAMAGES

The most typical remedy in a civil case will be damages. These are a common law remedy that are available as of *right* – i.e. if the case has been proved and loss has been suffered then damages will be awarded. The CPR Part 41 governs the award of such damages. They can be *compensatory, aggravated, nominal, contemptuous* or *exemplary*.

For Canny Conversion the claim would be one in contract and so the court would be looking to make an award that would put them in the same position as if the contract had been fulfilled. Those compensatory damages in the region of £30,000 are likely.

The case for Katy is more complex and would be based on the principles of tort. Damages in tort are designed to put the claimant back in the position *as if the tort had not happened*. This means that she would be able to claim for economic loss arising out of her injury. The judge would refer to existing judicial practice in calculating that loss.

ANALYSING THE LAW – ARE DAMAGES AWARDED OR WON?

Civil cases are often presented in quite a strange way in the public press. Cases are often described, in quite sensational terms, as resulting in 'bumper' or 'large' or 'record-breaking' damages with a large number of £000,000 involved. Damages are often described as being 'won' rather than 'awarded'. Having considered the complex and time-consuming nature of civil process it is important to reflect critically on these reports and their impact on the public perception of civil justice. Also reflect on the *nature* of damages in English law, which are firmly based on concepts of *loss* rather than on principles of *gain*.

EQUITABLE REMEDY

It may be remembered from Chapter 2 – Sources of Law – that many of the principles of equity find expression in *remedies* that are *discretionary* in nature. These include:

- *Specific performance* – rather than award damages the court may insist upon performance of a contractual obligation. In our example it may be that, should Jonny win a counterclaim, he would ask the court to force Canny Conversions to fulfil the terms of the contract. The court *could* issue an order of specific performance but these are rare and normally reserved for cases where damages would prove inadequate.
- *Injunctions* – these take the shape of *prohibitory* (to refrain from doing something) or *mandatory* (to make someone do something) orders.
- *Rescission* – the setting aside of a contract.

COSTS (CPR PARTS 43–47)

Costs is a complex subject with burgeoning litigation happening on this point alone (i.e. arguments over the award and calculation of costs). The courts' treatment of costs is contained within Parts 43–47. In short terms costs are paid by the losing side who bears not only their own costs but also those of the other side.[32]

---

32 Subject to some reform that came about from the Jackson Report and the advent of Qualified One-way Costs Shifting (QOCS) in certain personal injury cases.

This can be modified and adverse costs findings made if the behaviour of the winning party has been unreasonable. The Court of Appeal has recently ruled in *Dammermann*[33] that it will not provide general guidance as to what constitutes unreasonable behaviour but cited Lord Bingham's judgment in *Ridehalgh*[34] who said – 'The acid test is whether the conduct permits of a reasonable explanation.' This has included, amongst other things, an unreasonable refusal to undertake mediation and failure to follow practice directions.[35] The Jackson reforms also changed the rules regarding the recovery of 'success fees' and the 'after the event insurance' that often go along with personal injury claims.

TAKING THINGS FURTHER – THE LIFE OF A COSTS LAWYER

Even to those who work full time in the law, legal costs are rarely a thrilling topic. However, solicitors' firms and barristers have to make a profit or they cease to trade. An understanding of how lawyers charge their clients will improve your understanding of the area and your employability since this is an area of high volume work in which paralegals are often essential to a firm's ability to deal with that volume. See Chapter 15 for an understanding of the opportunities for law graduates to work in the law without qualifying as a solicitor or barrister.

ENFORCEMENT (CPR PARTS 70–74)

Unfortunately, obtaining a judgment for a sum of money does not force the losing party to pay anything. When the losing party is backed by an insurance company, payment is made relatively soon after judgment is given. In other cases, the losing party may not pay, because either they have no funds or they do not wish to do so. At that point, the winning party has a range of options. All methods of enforcement, forcing the debtor to pay, require steps to be taken by the winning party, as they are not automatically carried out by the court.

BUT, WILL THERE BE A TRIAL AT ALL?

What has gone before in this section highlights the main features and processes of civil justice from start to finish. The CPR is a vast improvement on the situation that subsisted prior to 1999 but the process is still complex and generates additional cost.

---

33 *Dammermann v Lanyon Bowdler LLP* [2017] EWCA Civ 269.
34 *Ridehalgh v Horsfield* [1994] Ch 205 (CA).
35 *Parr v Keystone Healthcare Ltd* [2019] EWCA Civ 1246.

In fact, it is very unlikely that the dispute between Jonny and Canny Construction will go to trial, so while lawyers might be instructed initially it is very likely that the case will go to Dispute Resolution, most likely mediation: there are many professional mediators, some lawyers some not, who work in this area of small business disputes. This is because Jonny owes the money claimed under the contract, so it is a debt and the liability for the actual money duly demanded is not worth pursuing in litigation as nothing can alter the fact that the sum is due, though Jonny may well be entitled to some compensation for faulty work, and/or having it put right.

It should also be noted that he has not dealt with Green Gardens directly as they are sub-contractors to Canny Construction; thus there is a whole contract in which it is Canny Construction which is primarily entitled to a satisfactory quality of work from Green Gardens who are to blame if Green Gardens' work is not up to scratch, but Jonny's claim in this respect is against Canny Construction not Green Gardens, so that Canny Construction will be seeking indemnity from Green Gardens.

It is therefore very likely that these issues will be settled between Jonny and Canny Construction, and between Canny Construction and Green Gardens on the basis that Green Gardens relays the tile properly (having checked there is not some underlying cause of the defect such as tree roots or other problem under the surface) and replaces the dead shrubs and plants (if their watering was in fact Green Gardens' responsibility, and not Jonny's staff's) and Jonny then settles the outstanding payment once the problems are put right.

Katy's claim is another matter, and that may go to trial unless Jonny's public liability insurers achieve an out of court settlement with Katy, as it is common in personal injury cases for the claimant to want full compensation and an apology for the accident having been caused to her at all, and unsurprisingly not to wish to pursue litigation if the compensation is adequate, and also not necessarily to have the money for litigation, for which the 'conditional fee agreement' mentioned previously may be used in personal injury cases. It is also common for a defendant's public liability insurers to attend mediation with the injured person's lawyer(s) in order to achieve a settlement since they prefer not to waste time and money on litigation unless essential. Moreover, there is a tariff for specific injuries, and depending on severity a medium range price is likely to be offered for both the broken leg and the wrist fractures which are common items of tripping accident damage, and for a claimant's lawyer to accept such an offer. As far as we know there are no special circumstances e.g. Katy is an office manager not a concert pianist by profession where broken wrists might be very serious, so this should not be a complex personal injury case.

In this way, it is important to understand the civil process but also to realise that much negotiation happens, as intended in the multiple reviews of civil justice, outside the courtroom door rather than inside it.

THE WEBSITE

The website that accompanies this textbook contains many useful resources that you can use to consolidate and further your knowledge of the law, to hone your skills of critical analysis and to test your knowledge. The companion website contains genuine assessment opportunities for you to monitor your progress through the text. This consists of short multiple choice questions, extended essays and problem questions.

PODCASTS

- The podcasts provide a summary of the area under study, bringing together the key themes and threads of analysis into a 'mini-lecture'.

CHAPTER 11
CRIMINAL JUSTICE

INTRODUCTION

Many students new to law immediately connect any mention of 'criminal justice' with major criminal trials in the Crown Court, even if their mental picture does not then also jump immediately to trial at the Old Bailey in London, the most famous of these Courts. It is true that any high profile trial originating in London (for which 'the Bailey' is the main Crown Court), or even in another part of England and Wales, might be allocated to the Old Bailey. In a case originating from outside London this might be, for example, because public feeling locally to the crime's commission could make it difficult for the accused to have a fair trial, or indeed difficult to empanel a jury from the local register of those eligible for jury service, or because a senior judge ticketed to try the crime in question would not be available locally for some time.

However, there is a lot more to the system of criminal justice than the sort of trial for which members of the public, as well as law students, queue for a seat in the Old Bailey public gallery. The Criminal Justice system involves a whole host of other 'actors' including the police, the CPS and an army of other legal professionals involved in the administration of criminal justice. Equally, a great deal of the Criminal Justice system takes place outside the courts, in the community and in the more than 1,000 police stations of England and Wales.

AS YOU READ

Think **critically** about the different stages in the criminal justice system, from initial investigation through charge and prosecution to full trial and conviction. By taking a holistic view of this part of the legal system, it is possible to gain a greater understanding of the principles that underpin criminal justice. The police have a great number of powers and you should **assess** whether these aid in the administration of justice.

This criminal justice system contains a great deal of procedural law and it is important that you have an **understanding** of the basic processes that govern the gathering and presentation of evidence. Also you should **think critically** about the *people* involved in the criminal justice system and the roles that they play here and elsewhere in the legal system. As you read the sections on governing the trial process try to think of the benefits and drawbacks of the trial process.

Finally, be sure to **consider** the similarities and differences between criminal justice, civil justice (already considered in Chapter 10) and administrative justice (to be considered in Chapter 13). Where there are, in particular, differences consider whether they are there for *principled* or merely *historic* reasons.

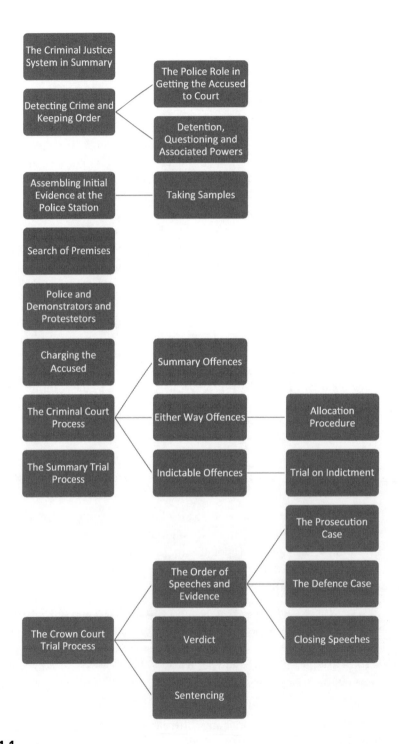

Figure 11.1

THE CRIMINAL JUSTICE SYSTEM IN SUMMARY

From the outset it is important to dispel certain of the myths and assumptions that have grown up around the criminal justice system, which is often portrayed in dramatic, glamourous and exaggerated form in popular culture. First, 98% of criminal cases are dealt with in the Magistrates Court and never reach a Crown Court, let alone the Old Bailey. Secondly, some never even reach a court as they are never 'tried' at all, e.g. the more minor Road Traffic offences, where the accused pleads Guilty by post, so the magistrates only decide the penalty; those charged with these offences usually need not even attend, having sent in their driving licences to be endorsed with whatever penalty the court awards. Thirdly, there is much to process behind the scenes before an accused can even be brought before any court, and this underlying work is done either by the police or by the Crown Prosecution Service (CPS) or both, one of whom will initially need to define the charge on which the accused would be taken to court. Fourthly, as seen in Chapter 8 on the court structure in England and Wales, all criminal cases *begin* in the Magistrates Court, whatever happens after that stage.

Fifthly, while the police can prosecute minor crime before the Magistrates where the accused is going to plead Guilty, the CPS will have to be involved once an accused decides to defend a charge, which means that, depending on its seriousness, the case might still be tried in the Magistrates Court or it may or must go to the Crown Court.

Which court a specific defendant is tried within will depend on whether it is a 'summary offence' (tried on a summons before the Magistrates) or an 'indictable offence' (tried on indictment[1] in the Crown Court) or an 'either way offence' (i.e. one which can be tried in either court depending on which form of trial the accused chooses). However, where an indictable offence is to be tried in the Crown Court, a summary offence (which would normally go for trial to the Magistrates) can be added to the indictment and the two offences tried together there: this is not as complicated as it sounds, since clearly one charging document, one court and one trial are obviously both a more efficient pathway and also cost effective; see further later in the chapter.

This apparently complex system, in which the police deal with charging the simpler and undefended cases and the CPS deals with charging more complex and defended cases, is in place because the CPS is the government body set up in 1986 to take most prosecutions out of the hands of the police, who (prior to that date) used both to investigate and initially to prosecute crimes which they detected. The Head of the CPS is the Director of Public Prosecutions (DPP) a government appointment with nothing to do with the police, and s/he is responsible to the chief government law officer, the Attorney General (AG), who is also the government's chief legal advisor, also sometimes acting as counsel for the government in very

---

1 An indictment is only a more complex form of charge sheet for the Crown Court than that used in the Magistrates Court for summary offences. There is a certain amount of technicality involved in drafting an indictment so this is normally done by the CPS, or prosecuting counsel from the Criminal Bar instructed by the CPS, a necessary precaution so as to avoid defence counsel taking some point about invalidity of the indictment.

important cases, in which the AG may personally take over or bring the prosecution. In some cases a prosecution cannot be brought without the AG's consent or that of the DPP.[2]

There are still other bodies which can investigate offences against the law and initiate prosecutions, for example local government departments dealing with weights and measures and other local regulatory matters such as breaches of environmental provisions, or the Health and Safety Executive which can prosecute for breaches of Health and Safety regulations; the police can also still initiate prosecutions for some low level offences such as under the Road Traffic Acts. However, generally speaking, the CPS is now involved in all *defended* cases because of the principle that there should be a central, specialist and independent prosecuting authority to ensure appropriate enforcement of the criminal law, which the police clearly are not if they are also the investigating authority.

Consequently, there are two separate stages of prosecuting someone for an offence – first, detection and investigation, and secondly, formulation of the charge on which an accused will be tried. The keen student of criminal justice must understand this process before taking a decision on which trial court to attend: before embarking on a first court visit, the prior practical decision at that stage will be as between the probably very *local* Magistrates or the nearest Crown Court (since unlike the Magistrates the Crown Court does not sit in every town of any size). Thus, this decision must be taken before deciding whether it is really worth travelling to the Old Bailey public gallery queue in London when a similar trial may be observed in a Crown Court nearer home or place of study. Once before a court it is, in most cases, for the prosecution to prove its case. This placing of the responsibility for demonstrating that an offence has been committed is deemed the *burden of proof*. This burden must be discharged to a certain *standard* and this, for criminal trials, is evidence that demonstrates guilt beyond reasonable doubt.

So let us begin at the beginning, with the detection and investigation of offences by the police or other bodies following which, unless the police are dealing with the simpler prosecuting work before the Magistrates, the criminal activity established must be drawn to the attention of the CPS so that its specialist personnel may decide whether there is evidence sufficient to secure a conviction and to follow that up with a prosecution.

DETECTING CRIME AND KEEPING ORDER: POLICE ORGANISATION AND INVESTIGATION POWERS AND SAFEGUARDS FOR THE CITIZEN

Surprisingly in modern times, there is still no national police force as such in England and Wales. Instead, a number of different regional forces remain locally based, mostly defined by counties, though in Greater London the local force is called the Metropolitan Police and

---

2   See www.cps.gov.uk/legal-guidance/consents-prosecute.

in the (territorially separate) City of London (the small 'Square Mile' which comprises the historic 'City' at the head of which is the Lord Mayor of London) their entirely separate force is called the City of London Police, though there are still some locations where neither of these London forces has jurisdiction, e.g. the Inns of Court, where there is also no right of public access as these are historically private properties belonging since the 14th century to the senior lawyer members of these lawyers' societies who hold their property on trust and control access to it by non-members.

These distinctions between the London and regional policing authorities are important since some police powers are only exercisable by senior officers of certain ranks whereas these two historic London forces have different titles for the ranks of their police from those of the regional forces in the remaining policing locations around the country. The heads of the two London forces are called 'Commissioners' whereas in the regional forces their most senior officers are 'Chief Constables'.

The word 'constable' is very old, and was historically in use from the Middle Ages to describe a local law enforcement officer in England and Wales (examples are found in Shakespeare's plays) and thus the term 'constable' may mean both the lowest rank in modern police forces and also any policeman of whatever rank as the word is still found having that meaning in some statutes. A police force may also thus collectively be referred to as a local 'constabulary'. 'The police' and/or 'a constable' in the widest sense have certain common law and statutory powers, including specifically to protect children, e.g. under the Children Act 1989 s 46, a child found in inappropriate circumstances[3] may be taken into 'police protection'[4] pending handing over to the local authority Children's Services for more permanent placement, since clearly the police do not have facilities for looking after children.

It should be noted that not all uniformed and 'plain clothes' staff supporting a force will actually be police officers but might instead be, for example, 'Police Community Support Officers' ('PCSOs', who are civilians wearing a different but similar uniform to police officers' and whose purpose is a 'visible' patrolling role) or 'Special Constables' who have police support roles, first developed in times of shortage of staff in wartime but now a feature of contemporary policing. Nevertheless these PCSOs do have certain defined powers, such as to issue fixed penalty tickets for littering, dog fouling, cycling on footpaths and other minor anti-social activity, and to ask for identification, seize goods and detain members of the public when an offence has been committed. However although their respective Chief Constables or

---

3   Such as where the context is such that an Emergency Protection Order under s 44 of the Act might immediately be obtained from a court by a local authority or the NSPCC e.g. where police find children in some unsuitable situation from which it is obvious they should be instantly removed. One such instance in a reported case was where a father had murdered the children's mother in front of the children, clearly a case for immediate protective action which the police are enabled to provide under the Act, their only obligation, upon immediate removal of the children, being to inform the local authority of their action as soon as possible.

4   The police do not need any order of the court to exercise this power and the child(ren) may remain in police protection for 72 hours, although in theory the local authority's resources will usually have to be mobilised at once under s 20 of the Act to provide voluntary accommodation while an EPO application is made, since the police can hardly keep children in the police station where the only resource would be the cells, even for less than 72 hours.

Commissioners may grant these subsidiary officers further discretionary powers. This does not usually include investigating offences, because extension of their routine powers is generally criticised on the basis that these personnel lack sufficient training to perform more than the basic purpose for which they were originally appointed, since they are not regular police officers and are paid at a lower rate. For one thing, in the highly technical context of modern criminal justice such lack of specific experience and specialist training at the investigation stage could actually prevent otherwise entirely deserved convictions; see further later in the chapter.

Quite apart from the professionalism now required in gathering evidence there may be some merit in this criticism on more general grounds, since the sort of extended policing provided by the PCSOs is intended to help a police force to preserve more ordinary law and order in the territory for which the particular force is responsible, rather than to address more serious crime or terrorism which may be occurring on a national or international level. All the same, these extra 'eyes and ears' can sometimes assist a force to notice indications of more serious matters, which should then be the province of the regular force.

However in the more 'everyday' context the exercise of vigilance even by regular officers has sometimes led to criticism of police 'over enthusiasm' in certain cases, for example in control of public disorder ranging from demonstrations to riots, such as in the case of the death of the innocent bystander Ian Tomlinson following a demonstration in 2009, when it seems a police constable violently pushed him during detention of a group of demonstrators in a 'kettling'[5] operation: a particularly unfortunate incident since Mr Tomlinson was in fact inadvertently caught up in the crowd while on his way home from his job as a newsvendor.

In view of the continued national fragmentation of forces, it is surprising that nothing has been done to create a more nationally integrated force at the regular police officer level; e.g. the Crime and Courts Act 2013 created a National Crime Agency (NCA), the rationale for which was addressing both organised crime and the UK's international response to certain types of crime, since it is clear that this internationalisation in the criminal fraternity does not exist simply within the James Bond film franchise. As a result the personnel who operate in this serious organised crime field combine the powers of police constables, immigration officers and customs officers. However, the various regional police forces still do not have a national computer which would obviously assist them in the large scale work of serious organised crime.

Nevertheless, the importance of the role of the police in preserving law and order as well as supporting the rule of law is recognised today in their progressive professionalisation, in the course of which the police have recently become a graduate profession with a defined career structure designed to serve the need for appropriate detection of crime and gathering of evidence for its prosecution. This means that even the lower ranks of the regular police forces, who are routinely involved in initial questioning of suspects, now need to understand the

5   A police technique for preventing or controlling actual or potential riots by cordoning off large groups and not allow-
     ing them to leave a location, sometimes for some hours, until eventually released in small numbers.

complexities of how to collect evidence in such a way that it will be admissible in a potential prosecution rather than excluded for unfairness or other flaw not compliant with the concept of human rights, which now play such an important role in the implementation of the rule of law. This is because in a liberal democracy it is recognised that, in an era of serious organised crime, there must be a balance between effective policing and individuals' rights and freedoms which may inevitably be infringed in the process of detection of offences. This professionalisation of the police has more recently been supported by the appointment of regional Police and Crime Commissioners[6] who are supposed to monitor police resources in their areas so as to ensure that the force for which they are responsible is efficient: thus their work includes setting police budgets and if necessary hiring or dismissing Chief Constables. There has however been much criticism of their role and its performance.[7]

Complaints about the police are still handled by the police themselves although in theory this is by an Independent Police Complaints Commission (IPCC) established by the Police Reform Act 2002 but funded by the Home Office. However, as it is substantially staffed by former police officers its actual independence, or any definable difference from the former system of investigation by senior officers, has inevitably been questioned.

THE POLICE ROLE IN GETTING THE ACCUSED TO COURT

This section of the chapter explores the mechanics of investigation of crime, i.e. police powers to stop and question people; to search persons and vehicles; to enter and search premises, to arrest, detain and question suspects; to take samples, photographs and impressions; and to hold identity parades.

Since the Police and Criminal Evidence Act (PACE) 1984 this has become yet another complex area of police contribution to criminal justice, so it is easy to see why the profession has had to be professionalised. Since 1984 the restrictions on what police can do when at first investigating crime and gathering evidence are contained in PACE 1984 and the Codes A to H made under it:[8] these relate to 'Stop and Search' (including the obligation to record encounters with the public) 'Search of Premises and Seizure of Property' and 'Powers of

---

6   Under the Police Reform and Social Responsibility Act 2011. This only applies to regional forces outside London, since in Greater London the PCC function is undertaken by the Mayor of London (i.e. not the Lord Mayor of the City of London or the individual Borough Mayors).

7   See Simon Cooper's paper at the annual conference of the Society of Legal Scholars, 4–7 September 2018, 'Police and Crime Commissioners: A Corrosive Exercise of Power Which Destabilises Police Accountability', a theme also taken up by The Times newspaper.

8   The codes are not actually part of the PACE statute but have indicative rather than statutory force, meaning that they should be observed by police officers but if there is a breach that does not necessarily mean that evidence gathered in contravention of any provision is necessarily inadmissible in later criminal proceedings. Inevitably this means there is a respectable case for arguing that they should be part of the statute but the contrary argument is of course that the police face enough difficulties in gathering evidence for the prosecution of crime and that PACE 1984 itself was intended to strike a balance between crime prevention and its prosecution so as to protect the public and the recognition and preservation of traditional liberties and guarantees of human rights. Also the flexibility inherent in the 'Code' model is worth preserving and fits with the discussion of secondary legislation in Chapter 5.

Table 11.1 The PACE Codes

Code	Last updated	Power covered
A	2015	The exercise of police powers to 'stop and search' people and vehicles
B	2013	The exercise of police powers to search premises and seize property
C	2019	Requirements for the detention, treatment and questioning of people in police custody not suspected of involvement with terrorism
D	2017	Identification
E	2018	Audio recordings at police stations
F	2018	Visual recordings at police stations
G	2012	The police powers of arrest
H	2019	The detention, treatment and questioning of persons in police custody who are suspected of involvement with terrorism

Arrest'. This power, contained in PACE s 24 as amended,[9] even enables arrest to ascertain a person's identity, when a potential suspect or a witness might disappear, hindering the investigation or prosecution of the crime: s 24(5). It is worth noting that the PACE Codes are regularly updated to reflect modern policing practice which goes some way to explain why the codes themselves are not statutory as the present approach allows them to develop more easily over time.

The full codes of PACE are shown in Table 11.1.

Thus the role of the police in relation to offences that may later be prosecuted often begins in the street or elsewhere in public, or even at a person's house or other premises, long before any court is reached. PACE has been statutorily updated several times since 1984, about which you will learn when you begin to study criminal law when at the same time you learn about the individual crimes and their levels of seriousness which dictate both the ways in which each crime may be tried and the appropriate level of sentence to address that relative seriousness.

You will also learn what will be the result for the police or the prosecution in court of any disregard of these now complex rules: initially the prosecution can still use evidence obtained

9   By the Serious Organised Crime and Police Act 2005.

unlawfully, improperly or even unfairly[10] but this can have adverse consequences.[11] In the Crown Court where there will be a jury the judge will decide whether such evidence is admissible and if not will prevent the jury hearing it at all; however in the Magistrates Court (where there is no jury as the magistrates are the judges of both fact and law) it is up to the Bench of Magistrates with assistance from their Legal Advisor, or the salaried or part time fee paid District Judge (Magistrates Courts)[12] sitting alone, to decide whether such evidence is admissible or not, and to disregard it in making their decision if it is inadmissible.

For the police to use any of these PACE controlled 'Stop and Search' or 'Search and Seize' powers the officers concerned must mostly have a reasonable suspicion that they are going to find prohibited articles for which the search is being conducted, e.g. blades or other offensive weapons, which are made or might be adapted or be intended for use in connection with crimes listed in section 1 of PACE, which include burglary, theft or criminal damage, in connection with terrorism or perhaps with drugs (especially dealing) all of which are subject to specialist legislation.[13] They can also search, for example, for fireworks carried in contravention of fireworks regulations.

In addition there are other restrictions: the search must take place in a location to which the public have access, the person searched must only be required to take off outer clothing[14] and stopped for search must be told what is being searched for;[15] but if the item(s) searched for are found those can be seized as evidence.[16] However the Equality Act 2010 also has an impact here, as Code A now includes a provision (called a 'reminder') that there shall be no stereotypical discrimination against any of the protected characteristics addressed in that Act. Thus the police are unlikely to be able to justify picking on any class of person known to be statistically more likely to be involved in crime. This means the police cannot stop and search people simply because they are, for example, young or black.

Even following PACE and its updates the rules are now so complex that it may be useful to follow a simple case study to see how they work – this will also help to prepare those who are undertaking legal study as the case method approach is common:

....

10 *Kuruma v R* [1955] AC 197 (PC).

11 A warning to the jury by the judge to disregard such tainted material if such evidence is wrongly admitted following a breach of PACE or the Codes; a 'stay of the proceedings' for abuse of process i.e. proceedings ended; police disciplinary proceedings; civil or criminal proceedings against the officer concerned.

12 Formerly called stipendiary magistrates.

13 PACE, s 24 provides that a police officer can arrest anyone committing or about to commit an offence when an officer reasonably suspects this is the case or that an offence has already been committed by such a person; thus the officer need not be sure, so that the test is partly objective and partly subjective: *O'Hara v Chief Constable of the Ulster Constabulary* [1997] AC 286 (HL).

14 PACE 1984 s 2.

15 Code A.

16 Ibid. s 1(6).

APPLYING THE LAW – THE CASE OF JAMES AND NAEEM AND THE FOOTBALL MATCH AT WEMBLEY

James, who is white, and Naeem, who is Asian, are two 16-year-old school friends from the Midlands who are on a weekend trip to watch a football match at Wembley. After the match they go to meet friends of Naeem's who live in Wembley and go with them to a rather rough pub where they have a few drinks, stay longer than they meant to and then get involved in a fight outside the pub in which their clothes suffer a bit; thus tired, looking a little disreputable but happy, they completely forget that they have to catch the last bus back to James's uncle's flat. It is thus rather late when, on the way back to the flat around midnight, they get off an unfamiliar bus at the wrong stop, realise they are lost, and at 1 a.m. are still wandering the streets looking for the address where they are staying.

Just as they think they have found the right road they are approached by two uniformed police officers who get out of a police car, ask the lads where they are going and what is in Naeem's pockets (one of which is bulging with a bulky item – actually a can of soft drink he had bought at the pub for the journey home). Not being very comfortable with police intervention (which they always avoid where they live in the Midlands) they ignore the officers and walk on, speeding up their pace. The police follow and one taps Naeem on the shoulder, who breaks into a run, and the other seizes James by one arm, who tells him, in an obvious Birmingham accent, to 'bl**dy drop it copper'. Both boys are then dragged back to the police car and pushed into it, one of the officers saying 'well now, you two had better come with us. Let's go down to the station where we can talk.'

Can the police do this? Is it an arrest? Would it make any difference if there had been a spate of night time burglaries in the area where the two were wandering? Attempting this sort of problem question will allow you fully to understand the legal method involved in discerning police powers.

THE POLICE STATION, DETENTION, QUESTIONING AND ASSOCIATED POWERS

Regardless of whether the police could stop and question the lads in the street in the preceding example, obviously taking anyone to a police station deprives them of liberty when that is a fundamental human right, especially when taken in a police car into which the person(s) concerned were clearly unwilling to go, and Article 5 of the European Convention on Human Rights (ECHR) guarantees that liberty. Thus a police officer acting in this way must *objectively and reasonably* believe that this action is necessary[17] so that an officer

---

17 *Hayes v Chief Constable of Merseyside* [2011] EWCA Civ 911, [2012] 1 WLR 517; *Richardson v Chief Constable of Essex* [2011] EWHC 773 (QB), [2011] 2 Cr App R 1 where the Court held that 'necessary' is an ordinary English word so no need to go into what it means.

always needs to consider whether asking a suspect to come to the police station voluntarily might be a practical alternative to arresting such a person, as if arrested such a suspect will have no choice.

Indeed, in *Lord Hanningfield of Chelmsford v Chief Constable of Essex*[18] the High Court made exactly this point about considering alternatives, although the police's explanation in that case was that if they did not arrest Lord Hanningfield (which took place at his home on suspicion of fraud) he would have had the opportunity to hide or destroy evidence or alert criminal associates.

However in that case the High Court did not accept the police explanation as there was nothing to indicate that Lord Hanningfield was *not* going to cooperate with the investigation or that he would take any of the steps the police claimed to suspect. Moreover, the judge, Eady J, said that there must be evidence that voluntary attendance had been genuinely considered so that PACE s 24 (which governs arrests in some detail) is not used to bypass the citizen's statutory safeguards. As a result Code G now provides that an officer 'must consider whether a suspect's voluntary attendance is a practicable alternative for carrying out the interview'. If however an arrest is considered necessary the officer concerned must reasonably believe that the circumstances fall within the terms of section 24, i.e. reasonable suspicion of commission or intended commission of a crime or for the protection of the person arrested. Reasonable force[19] can be used if necessary: section 117, though simply informing the subject that s/he is under arrest is also sufficient.

Further, there are strict rules as to the treatment of suspects at the police station, and as to questioning both on the way to the station and once there. Code C provides that suspects *must not be questioned* except at a police station or other authorised place of detention, since this would deprive them of rights under PACE and Codes C, E and F[20] to which they are entitled e.g. legal advice.

When suspects arrive at the police station the next step depends on whether they have gone voluntarily or have been arrested. If attending voluntarily, under PACE s 29 they can leave at any time, unless then arrested to prevent such a departure. If already under arrest, they must be brought before the Custody Officer as soon as possible. This is an officer of at least the rank of sergeant who is not involved in the investigation concerning the suspect, and who is thus independent.

The Custody Officer must open a record which details the offence for which the accused is arrested, the grounds for detention and whether legal advice has been requested; the record must also include various regular checks on the suspects' appropriate treatment, e.g. suspects have a right to regular meals at recognised meal times (two light ones and one main meal to be offered every 24 hours, plus drinks at meals and on reasonable request) and sleep (8 hours

18 [2013] EWHC 243 (QB), [2013] 1 WLR 3632.
19 This is partly objective and partly subjective, but the objective element is stronger depending on what an ordinary person would think reasonable: *O'Hara v Royal Ulster Constabulary* [1997] AC 286 (HL).
20 Code C (Detention, Treatment and Questioning of Persons by Police Officers); Code E (Audio Recording of Interviews With Suspects); Code F (Visual Recording With Sound of Interviews With Suspects).

uninterrupted, usually at night); and, by PACE ss 56 and 58, and the Annex B to Code C, there is a right to inform someone of their whereabouts as soon as possible. The notification of whereabouts and legal advice rights are only to be delayed on the authority of a senior officer (a superintendent in the case of legal advice and an inspector in the case of notification to a third party of the suspect's whereabouts on detention). Detained persons may also make one telephone call, and if they request legal advice no interview should take place until that legal advice is received. Detainees should be checked every hour, be placed in a space which is habitable (i.e. not damp, ill lit or not lit at all, also properly ventilated); they must also have clean bedding and toilet facilities and clinical attention if appearing to need it, for all of which the Custody Officer is responsible.

The Custody Officer's job is therefore a very responsible one, pro-active rather than reactive. Thus that officer must actually alert any detainee brought to his or her attention on arrival at the station to the right to legal advice and also to the services of the designated Duty Solicitor, and must monitor and review the length of any custody which is limited to 72 hours.

Moreover where a detainee is mentally disordered or 'a juvenile' (under 17) the Custody Officer must ask an 'appropriate adult' to come to the police station to give the person concerned detailed advice and assistance. This third party is normally a parent, guardian or social worker, and in any case not anyone employed by the police. Moreover, s 11 of the Children Act 2004 requires chief police officers (and some other bodies) to ensure that in the discharge of their functions they have regard to the need to safeguard and promote the welfare of all persons under the age of 18, which obviously supports the Equality Act 2010 prohibition of discrimination against a person on account of the protected characteristic of age, for example in selecting young and/or black or Asian members of the public in 'stop and search' or 'stop and account'[21] situations. However, a 2010 report identified that a black person is still six times more likely to be stopped and searched and an Asian person twice as likely than a white person.[22]

APPLYING THE LAW – JAMES AND NAEEM IN THE POLICE STATION

In the case of these two lads, as soon as James and Naeem are produced to him, the Custody Officer immediately realises that – as they are plainly 'juveniles' – they must be allowed to have an appropriate adult with them, in the circumstances obviously

21 There is an important distinction between 'stop and search' (of which a record must be kept by police) and occasions when a suspect may simply be stopped and asked where s/he is going, in respect of which Code A provides that no record must be kept. It should, however, be noted that while the police are always free to ask members of the public questions in the course of prevention or detection of crime there is no requirement under common law to answer such questions. However if they are answered rudely this may be obstruction of the police in the execution of their duty: *Ricketts v Cox* [1982] 74 Cr App R 283 (CA).
22 EHRC, 2010, Stop and think: A critical review of stop and search powers in England and Wales.

James's uncle, since he is clearly *in loco parentis* to the two of them during their visit to London. This gentleman arrives promptly at the station despite the late hour, tells them that they should simply have responded to the officers on the spot rather than running away, advises Naeem that when asked (as he almost certainly would have been) he should have instantly shown the police the can of soft drink from his trouser pocket, and also complains to the police about the waste of everyone's time owing to overzealous treatment of two youths who had apparently merely lost their way following a late journey home to their accommodation – also pointing out the boys' youth which should have been obvious to the two patrol officers to whom it must have been clear that two such young lads fell within s 11 of the Children Act 2004.

Thus in this case the police are no further forward in their investigation into the spate of night time burglaries in the area where James and Naeem were lost; also owing to the boys' age they were unable to be questioned without an appropriate adult present, and since Naeem's pocket only contained an unopened can of soft drink, the officers have not recovered any stolen property that could be seized as evidence; since the boys were apparently not even connected with the burglaries the police have not even identified any premises that it might be worth searching for property lost in the burglaries. In other words these two officers had an unlucky night!

WHAT IF THE FACTS HAD BEEN DIFFERENT?

For example, if these lads had in fact been 18, established teenage burglars, Naeem's pocket had contained a pouch of skeleton keys and James's uncle had been a modern 'Fagin' masterminding the burglaries with a successful team of unemployed youths such as themselves, and thus likely to have had stolen property at his home address?

In those circumstances James and Naeem might have been questioned at the police station (albeit with all the protection for their civil and human rights that the system provides) – see following – the police could have exercised their powers to take samples (which might have connected their two detainees to one or more of the burglaries e.g. if traces of their DNA had been found there) and if James's uncle was an established gang master likely to have some convictions under his belt, and therefore 'known to the police', they might have successfully searched his house for stolen goods.

Taking these possibilities in turn, the deployment of any of these powers at police disposal might prove to be a gateway to the criminal court process for those accurately suspected of definable offences against the law. Nevertheless, despite modern aids to investigation of crime (such as scientific tests and databases to store and retrieve computerised information) it is clear that the basic tool of the modernised police force arguably remains skilled interrogation.

ASSEMBLING INITIAL EVIDENCE AT THE POLICE STATION

As set out previously detainees at the police station, whether on arrest or merely voluntarily there 'helping the police with their inquiries', have certain basic rights to humane treatment, indeed to better treatment than the destitute homeless who regularly sleep rough in the street: police detainees not only have a cell to sleep in which might be their first roof for a long time, but must also have proper bedding, undisturbed sleep and meals at appropriate hours.

Rights while at the police station extend further: whether under arrest or voluntarily there during a police investigation, it might seem that no one is obliged actually to answer any questions at all, since questioning is usually the purpose of such police station attendance. This choice simply not to respond at all is known as 'the right to silence', one of the key freedoms under English criminal law, which except in specific circumstances requires that guilt is 'proved beyond reasonable doubt', rather than that an accused should prove innocence. This might seem really odd when a case has reached a formal investigation stage, since the purpose of police investigation is to detect crime and process its investigation.

However there is of course a downside to this for the suspect, since although the right to silence and the principle of innocence till proved guilty are absolute, 'inferences' (i.e. common sense conclusions) can be drawn if reasonable explanations that might have been given at the investigation stage are not offered when they might have been, but instead saved till a later stage – when there would have been time and opportunity for a guilty person to think them up. There are therefore more rules which have to be complied with during this key investigation stage.

First, any questioning at any stage is an 'interview' and Code C states that this must be at the police station, so not in the street or on the journey to the station, perhaps by a roundabout diversion – sometimes called sarcastically by defence counsel 'the scenic route'! – since an obvious defence is apt to claim that this was to allow more time to obtain inadvertent admissions not in the controlled location of the police station. Secondly, on arrival at the police station, that important official, the Custody Officer, must assess any person suspected of involvement in an offence as to fitness for interview, or decide that s/he is 'at risk', which may mean consulting a healthcare professional who might in turn decide that the detainee is not fit to be interviewed at all, or only in the presence of such a professional (the obvious reason being that anyone assessed as not fit may give evidence that is challenged in court as unreliable if there is a subsequent prosecution). Thirdly, before an interview can commence the interviewee must be formally 'cautioned'. This too comes from Code C, and the formal wording is as follows:

> You do not have to say anything. But it may harm your defence if you do not mention when questioned something which you later rely on in court. Anything which you do say may be relied on in evidence.

Fourthly, Code C requires that interviews must be recorded. If the suspected offence is a summary one there is a choice of method, which can be a written record, a sound recording or a video recording. If it is for an indictable offence, then Codes E and F require an audio or visual recording with sound, and the recording medium used must be unwrapped and resealed in the interviewee's presence. Moreover the record must audibly include the interviewing officers' identities and those of any others present (e.g. the health professional mentioned previously, the station duty solicitor or any lawyer that the detainee or voluntary attendee has chosen to call upon) and contain a repeat of the caution and reminder of the right to free legal advice. In addition to the regular meals already mentioned, interviews also require regular breaks e.g. every two hours, a properly lit and ventilated interview room, no requirement of the interviewee to stand, and should be ended as soon as in the opinion of the officer in charge enough information has been gathered for a viable prosecution.

Of course sometimes the interview will gain no information at all if the interviewee declines to answer any questions, possibly on the advice of the solicitor present. One result that might be hoped for is a confession or admission of some sort, for which there are more rules under sections 76 and 82. Under s 82(3) a confession is any statement wholly or partly adverse to the interviewee; it does not merely mean an admission of the offence, e.g. where s/he admits being present or in the neighbourhood of the offence but denies committing any offence. Such admissions are only admissible in evidence if not obtained by 'oppression' (s 76(2)(a) e.g. interrogation involving repeated shouting or bullying over a long period until the interviewee gives up and agrees to the interviewers' suggestions)[23] or by inducements (s 76(2)(b), defined as 'anything said or done which is likely, in the circumstances, to render any confession unreliable' e.g. offering quick and easy bail from the police station in return for admissions of guilt which the interviewee has pressing reasons to accept).[24] In these circumstances, the prosecution at a trial would have to prove that the resulting admissions were not tainted in this way, a submission which for obvious reasons trial courts tend to have reservations in accepting as they did in these cases.

TAKING SAMPLES

If questioning has not produced the evidence required to justify prosecution the police do have power to collect other potentially useful information in some cases whether or not the detainee agrees to it; for example they can take a photograph: s 64A and Code D,[25] but can only use or disclose it for a purpose in connection of investigation, detection or prevention of offences or for prosecutions or sentences. Such photographs may be retained after the purpose in question but only used again for like purposes. Obviously, such a photograph may be very useful for a variety of permitted purposes.

....

23 R v Miller [1993] 97 Cr App R 99 (CA) (13 hours questioning on suspicion of murder, 300 denials by the accused before eventually confessing).

24 R v Barry [1992] 95 Crim App R 384 (CA) (sole carer father of nine-year-old son induced to confess in return for bail to enable him to return as soon as possible to the boy).

25 Which details the information which must be given to the detainee before such samples are collected.

More useful are likely to be fingerprints, although these may be taken without the subject's consent only where the detainee has been arrested or charged with a 'recordable' offence (i.e. recordable in police records – though this would include a 'caution'[26] or warning as well as a conviction: s 61). More useful still might be an imprint of footwear, which can be taken under the same conditions as fingerprints: s 61A, or a 'non-intimate sample' (hair or a scraping from under a nail) which is also subject to the same conditions and has periodically respectively caught a burglar (so might have been helpful if James and Naeem had in fact been out burgling on the night on which they were lost) or identified a rapist or perpetrator of other serious assault or even murder.

Such samples can obviously also be useful in cases involving other incidents of theft where the accused's DNA extracted from the hair is found at the scene, or in cases of violence, criminal damage or other crimes where the offender has been left not so much red handed with the 'smoking gun' of popular fiction but with the evidence of contamination with explosives, firearms or other substances connecting the hands from which all traces of contamination have not been successfully removed.

'Intimate samples'[27] if not agreed to by the detainee may only be taken with the permission of an inspector or officer of superior rank, who has to have the same 'reasonable belief' of the subject's involvement in a recordable offence as in most cases where this objective belief is required, and if the subject refuses consent a judge or jury may later draw inferences.

The police can now retain these samples whether or not the subject is charged or convicted, except for footwear impressions which have to be destroyed after six months from their being 'necessary' for detection, investigation, prosecution etc.: s 63S, though the DNA sample itself has to be destroyed as soon as the DNA profile has been extracted.

Thus, the contemporary police have a good deal of scientific assistance at their disposal.

SEARCH OF PREMISES

For search of premises a warrant issued by a Justice of the Peace (Magistrate) is usually required (which will be issued if there are reasonable grounds to believe that an indictable offence[28] has been committed and that there is material on the premises that is likely to be of substantial importance to investigation of the offence, although pursuant to PACE s 17 it is

26 A caution is a formal process where the offender admits guilt but the police or CPS prosecutors decide to engage in this process (which will still remain on the police national computer) rather than to prosecute. This usually applies to minor offences, as it cannot be used for an indictable offence or certain either way offences: Criminal Justice and Courts Act 2015 s 117.
27 Blood, semen, urine, dental impressions.
28 This means an offence that is triable on indictment in the Crown Court rather than a less serious (summary) offence triable by the magistrates: see Chapter 8 on The Court Structure.

sometimes justified for police to search without a warrant, e.g. when they have a warrant of arrest to arrest a person for an indictable offence or for a number of summary offences (e.g. driving under the influence of drink or drugs) in any of which cases they must reasonably believe that the person to be arrested is in the premises.

There are other exceptions to the need for a warrant, such as where the search is necessary to save life or limb or prevent serious damage to property; and there is also a power under s 18 if the premises are owned or controlled by a person under arrest for an indictable offence, although in that case the police must reasonably believe that there is evidence on the premises relating to the indictable offence – or another indictable offence which is connected or similar – and, in that case, the officer(s) concerned have the authority of an inspector or more senior police officer.

Otherwise it is true that a citizen's 'house is his castle' and it cannot be entered by force unless the aforementioned conditions apply (and even if they do any force used must be proportionate). However if any relevant material is found on premises to which the police have correctly obtained access they can seize it as evidence (just as they could have seized the contents of Naeem's pockets had they managed to search him in the street, and those contents had revealed not a can of soft drink but, e.g. drugs or some other illegal item or substance, such as a housebreaking tool or one to cause criminal damage, or stolen goods or drugs, particularly if in sufficient quantity to suggest that he was a dealer).

POLICE AND DEMONSTRATORS OR PROTESTORS, OR OTHER LAW BREAKERS

By no means all police contact with members of the public ends up with no charge being brought, as in the fruitless incident with James and Naeem, and the police regularly take to the police station for questioning, detention and charge a wide variety of offenders who must then be produced to the Magistrates Court and subsequently processed by the CPS. Sometimes the police do get the wrong persons, as in the case of James and Naeem, but on the other hand the two boys might have been the burglars they were looking for at the time and in the location when and where the police were expecting to find those responsible for the criminal activity being investigated.

Equally, much of the traffic through the police station and across the Custody Officer's desk are offending drivers (whether drunk, dangerous or causing death), burglars, robbers, those guilty of assaults of varying seriousness, or of affray or other breaches of the peace, including terrorists, or demonstrators and protesters.

This last category is a common one for ordinary members of the public to be likely to become involved in, often accidentally, since the right to demonstrate peacefully is an important freedom of the citizen but, while police still have to control such large scale incidents, it is easy for anyone not part of the demonstration to become mixed up in the crowd, as in the case of Ian Tomlinson in the 2009 G20 demonstration already mentioned in which Mr Tomlinson was accidentally enclosed behind the 'kettling' cordon and mistaken for a demonstrator by a police officer when he tried to escape the containment of the crowd.

Following the Tomlinson incident, another 'kettling' incident has been to the European Court of Human Rights (ECtHR)[29] in which the Court considered whether this practice of kettling breached Article 5 of the Convention on Human Rights and decided that while it restricted movement to some extent within the cordon it was not a deprivation of liberty, since it was necessary for crowd control, although had it been maintained for longer than necessary then this would have been a breach. Accordingly, any innocent members of the public who get into this situation can unfortunately therefore commit an offence if they fight their way out!

CHARGING THE ACCUSED

With the exception of those charges brought directly by the CPS or other prosecuting agencies with the power to do so under certain statutes the usual channel into the trial process will be from the Police Station to the Magistrates Court, whether or not the case is then tried there.

Once it is clear that there is sufficient evidence to charge an offender, which pursuant to PACE s 37 will be the decision of the Custody Officer, s 37A requires that officer to have regard to guidance issued by the Director of Public Prosecutions in deciding whether to charge the accused, and with what offence, or whether to pass this matter to Crown Prosecutors, who are employed by the CPS and available within police stations to provide charging advice; this service includes a duty prosecutor out of hours. There is thus a strong link between the police station and the CPS for the purpose of settling the correct charge with a view to bringing prosecutions which do not waste everyone's time by collapsing at the trial stage (of which there have been some recent well-publicised examples, much criticised in the media).

In theory, this system should work to ensure that only sound cases are pursued (and the citizen thus not harassed by speculative charges) since the rules also distinguish between the minor 'summary' offences which can be tried by the Magistrates Court (which may include 'either way' offences where the accused will plead Guilty and sentencing by the Magistrates is likely to be suitable) and the more serious 'indictable' offences which will start in the Magistrates but be tried in the Crown Court. The Custody Officer may make charging decisions only in the case of the summary or either way offences in the first category and not in relation to indictable offences where the charging decision must be made by the CPS.

---

29 *Austin v UK* [2012] 55 EHRR 14.

Moreover, if the initial investigation stage has been properly conducted, evidence should have been appropriately gathered: however there are other options open since apart from a charge a case could be disposed of in an appropriate context by a warning or caution, or the accused could be released on police bail to enable the CPS to make a charging decision at a later date: s 37B.

Taking a decision of this sort can be quite complex so that such a delay might be justified. There is a Code for Crown Prosecutors which sets out specific tests to be applied: Prosecution of Offenders Act 1985, s 10. Clearly the first test is whether the evidence is sufficient, but the second requires the Prosecutor dealing with the case to consider whether prosecution is in the public interest, in which context the age, health etc. of the perpetrator, the seriousness of the crime and the likelihood of repetition if the offence is not prosecuted together with the impact on the victim are all relevant, and as to which the Prosecutor must form an overall view.[30]

It is obvious that there is some scope for inconsistency here, and in 2015 the Police and CPS' inspectorates considered the problem through the data that could be gathered across police forces and concluded that such likely inconsistency was indeed evident, particularly in domestic abuse cases. Unfortunately the 2015 report is no longer available since more recent inspectorate activity has concentrated more generally on widespread rape and harassment and on the continuing concern about inevitable inconsistency with the obvious potential for inconsistency within the continuing fragmentation afforded by maintaining 43 police forces in place of a united national force. There is also an EU Directive (2012/29) on minimum standards on the rights, support and protection of victims of crime which is obviously applicable to decisions not to prosecute or to stop a prosecution already started, and which (having been adopted) has led to a review system whereby the CPS looks at the case afresh and at the public interest in a prosecution, though of course this might not change the original decision.

Nevertheless, in general terms this conduit between police and Magistrates Court works as a channel to get the majority of those accused of crime out of the police station and into the trial process, and if it is not working and needs improvement this is the ongoing responsibility of the DPP for whom the AG is responsible in Parliament to which any reform will need to go in the form of amending legislation or new regulations which may need to be laid before Parliament.

Moreover once an accused has been charged no further questioning is allowed other than in exceptional circumstances: Code C 16.5, and by PACE s 38 the Custody Officer must order the detainee's release unless further detention is necessary e.g. where the charge is murder or some other reason to believe that s/he will fail to appear in court to answer to bail. So we may now move on to look at how a case progresses through the criminal justice system – even possibly to the Old Bailey, or beyond.

....

30 See www.cps.gov.uk/cps/news/publication-revised-code-crown-prosecutors.

THE CRIMINAL COURT PROCESS

Where an accused is not charged at the police station (because it is not a charge within the police powers but for the CPS to handle, or for other reasons) the CPS process is to issue a written charge together with a requisition for the accused to appear before a Magistrates Court to answer the charge. These documents are then served on the accused. The former process, still seen in some old black and white films, of laying an information before a Justice of the Peace (Magistrate) is now only available for private prosecutions i.e. that the CPS is not prosecuting or has discontinued, which members of the public discontented with the outcome of a public prosecution sometimes avail themselves of.

SUMMARY OFFENCES BEFORE THE MAGISTRATES

In view of all the attention to detail and professionalism required of the police in the investigation stage it might be thought that this would automatically get the accused into court for a trial without further delay. In practice this only tends to happen in the Magistrates Court on summary only offences where the accused can decide whether to plead Guilty or Not Guilty and if the former for the court to proceed to sentence, though there might be an adjournment for a pre-sentence report to be prepared.

THE SUMMARY TRIAL PROCESS

This will either be by three lay magistrates with the assistance of their Legal Advisor or of a single professional magistrate, a District Judge (Magistrates Courts) although certain types of uncontested summary offences which are non-imprisonable and where the accused is an adult can be heard by a single justice.[31] In such circumstances the case could also be determined only on the papers and also in the absence of the accused and counsel for prosecution and defence.

However normally the accused should be present and plead to the charge. The magistrate(s) will be both judge and jury so as to decide both facts and law, though with regard to the law the bench has the advice of the Legal Advisor whose advice must be given in the presence of the prosecution and defence so that they may make submissions on any points which arise.

The Magistrates will be trying either summary or either way offences and the trial will proceed in the same way as in the Crown Court, save that there is no jury and a majority verdict of two magistrates is sufficient. However the Magistrates also have the option of not sentencing themselves but remitting the accused to the Crown Court for sentence in the case of serious or sexual offences.[32]

....

31 Criminal Justice and Courts Act 2015 ss 46–50.
32 Powers of Criminal Courts (Sentencing) Act 2000.

EITHER WAY OFFENCES BEFORE THE MAGISTRATES AND/OR THE CROWN COURT

Either way offences in the Magistrates Court are more complicated and here there is inevitably more pre-trial work to be done, not least because if an offence is either way it is necessary to decide where it will be tried for which there is an 'allocation procedure'.[33] If the decision is to send the case to the Crown Court it will be sent there forthwith pursuant to the Crime and Disorder Act 1998 s 51.[34] Both the court and the accused have an interest in having a say as to the location of the trial. This is effected by a process called 'Plea Before Venue' in which the accused is asked if s/he would plead Guilty or Not Guilty when the case comes to be tried.[35] If the plea is Guilty the Magistrates must then decide whether their powers are sufficient to sentence the accused for the offence in question (Magistrates having only the power to award a maximum six-month custodial sentence or 12-month if two or more either way offences are involved) or whether the case should be sent to the Crown Court for sentence, where that Court's powers are usually up to the maximum or statutory limit for the offence(s) in question. Clearly the accused will also be bearing this discrepancy in sentencing powers in mind when deciding whether to go for a quick decision before the Magistrates with a lesser maximum sentence available or whether to go for a Crown Court trial before a jury where s/he might have been advised that s/he would be more likely to get off altogether, and in fact statistically acquittal is more likely in the Crown Court where the jury decides on guilt or innocence.

If the accused either says that s/he will plead Not Guilty or does not say what the plea will be, then the Magistrates must follow the Allocation Procedure in ss 19–23 of the Magistrates Courts Act 1980 as amended by the Criminal Justice Act 2003 (CJA 2003). In accordance with the Criminal Procedure Rules 2015 Part 10 (CrimPR 2015, Part 10)[36] this means that before the Allocation Procedure can commence the Prosecution must serve on the accused details of the prosecution case – otherwise, since they must prove their case not the accused disprove it, it would not be fair for the accused to have to say which way s/he would plead until the strength of the prosecution's case could be assessed by the defence team.

Thus it is seen that criminal justice in English law is as adversarial as the civil process and is regulated by rules of court very similar in format to the CPR 1998 as amended, which have reformed civil justice. Like the CPR they have numbered Parts (11 corresponding to the stages of a criminal case, preliminary hearings to appeals), are supplemented by Criminal Practice Directions (CPDs) and have an 'overriding objective' which is to:

- Acquit innocent defendants
- Deal with the parties fairly

---

33 In old reports this is called 'mode of trial' procedure.

34 The 'committal proceedings' found in old reports are now replaced by the contemporary allocation procedure.

35 Magistrates Courts Act 1980 s 17A.

36 To distinguish the Criminal Procedure Rules from the comparable civil set, the CPR 1998, the Criminal Procedure Rules are usually abbreviated CrimPR 2015. See the rules in full at www.judiciary.gov.uk/wp-content/uploads/2015/09/crim-pd-2015.pdf.

- Recognise the defendant's rights (especially the ECHR Article 6 right to a fair trial)
- Respect the interests of witnesses, victims and jurors
- Deal with cases efficiently and expeditiously
- Deal with cases in ways which take into account the gravity of offences, complexity of issues, severity of consequences and needs of other cases

The wording clearly echoes the objectives and resource issues which are articulated in the CPR 1998, and the parties are also expected to conduct the case in accordance with the overriding objective which seeks to balance the interests of both prosecution and defence just as in the CPR 1998 as amended and (in the Family Court) the FPR 2010 as amended those rules of court attempt to balance the interests of all parties as a whole (including those of HMCTS who must administer the courts so as to deliver justice and to achieve these respective overriding objectives).

ALLOCATION PROCEDURE

First, the Magistrates must decide if the case is suitable for trial by them. If they decide it is not, e.g. inherently too serious, then the accused will be sent for trial at the Crown Court and has no say in the matter (see Figure 11.2).

There are several factors the Magistrates must take into account before making their decision apart from the seriousness of the offence: nature of the case, their sentencing powers and any other relevant circumstances: they need to be told about the accused's previous convictions as this would affect sentencing.

The parties, i.e. prosecution and defence, may make representations on suitability for one trial venue or the other.

If the Magistrates decide the case could be tried by them, then the accused must decide if he will elect trial by jury in the Crown Court, or if he prefers to be tried by the Magistrates, and that is the accused's decision entirely, no doubt with the assistance of the defence team. Before deciding, the accused can ask the Magistrates for an indication of whether they would be likely to give a custodial or non-custodial sentence on a plea of Guilty, and though they do not have to answer this question they may do so.

What would influence an accused for the Crown Court?

- A judge will usually keep prejudicial evidence from the jury, unlike in a Magistrates Court who may not be able to forget it, maybe why statistically acquittal more likely.
- A Crown Court judge likely to be better able to deal with the law than magistrates and their legal advisor.

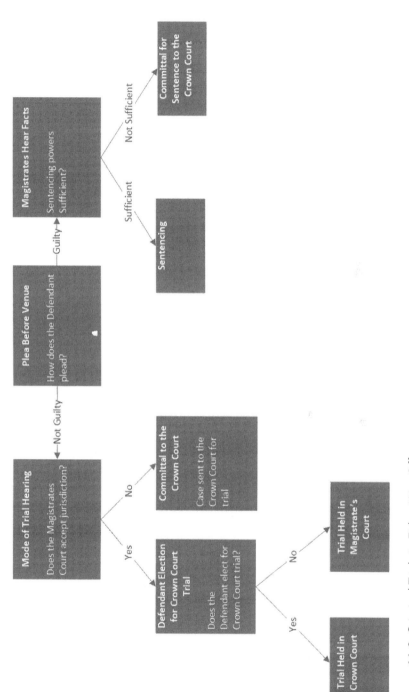

Figure 11.2 Criminal Trials in Either Way Offences

What would influence an accused against the Crown Court and for Magistrates Court trial?

- The Crown Court's greater sentencing powers
- The Crown Court is more expensive and convicted accused may have to pay part of the prosecution costs
- It may take longer to get a court hearing, which may matter to an accused unless on bail with no restrictions

There are Allocation Guidelines issued by the Sentencing Council.[37] In general either way offences are to be tried summarily unless the Magistrates' sentencing powers are inadequate.

INDICTABLE OFFENCES

Since these must go straight to the Crown Court pursuant to the Crime and Disorder Act 1998 s 51, it might be thought that that would mean these cases reached trial without more ado. However these cases have a Plea and Trial Preparation Hearing (PTPH) which must be set by the Magistrates when sending the case to the Crown Court and this must be within 28 days of despatch by the Magistrates to the Crown Court. The reason for this is that the accused must be 'arraigned' in the Crown Court, i.e. the charge must be read out to the accused who must then plead to the charge, Guilty or Not Guilty, since the plea is taken there and not at the Magistrates. Obviously if the accused then pleads Guilty there will be no need for a trial and as in the same circumstances in the Magistrates Court, the court (i.e. the Judge in the Crown Court) will proceed immediately to sentence, unless an adjournment is needed for a pre-sentence report to be prepared. However this is often not needed if a report can be prepared on the spot by a probation officer as seems increasingly the case although for many high profile cases it seems there is usually an adjournment, sometimes of some weeks, which may be for public relations purposes given that the information required seems now to be readily available in many cases in view of the fact that much is already computerised.

Where the accused pleads Not Guilty, obviously there will be more pre-trial preparatory work to do so that information will need to be gathered from the parties in order that the PTPH judge can set a timetable for the trial, and as for a more complex civil trial since this will concern

- The issues in the case
- Witnesses to be called
- Expert evidence to be relied upon

But also since this is a criminal trial

- Whether there is any 'bad character' evidence, the subject of complex rules pursuant to the Criminal Justice Act 2003, or other applications

---

37 https://www.sentencingcouncil.org.uk/wp-content/uploads/Allocation-definitive-guideline-Web.pdf.

The judge should then be able to set a date for the trial but sometimes a case might be so complex that a further PTPH will be required, called a Further Case Management Hearing (FCMH) e.g. if the case is particularly serious, includes a vulnerable witness, the accused is a child or unrepresented, or there is some other complexity such as a lengthy trial, but the Crim PR PD3A indicates that there should not be a further hearing other than in exceptional circumstances, another indication of how the Crim PR have followed the civil and Family Courts' rules in encouraging expedition and efficiency.

AS YOU READ

So far this chapter has been concerned with the way in which cases eventually heard in court are *prepared* through detection and investigation of offences and in giving detailed information on the process by which this is done so that breaches of the law *are* eventually brought to court, with a view to their reaching that stage only in circumstances where prosecution is justified and is likely to succeed. Given the frequency of collapsed prosecutions now regularly reported in the media, it might justifiably be wondered whether this aim is in fact being achieved. It is important that, as you read, **you do more than just memorise** this information so that when you go to observe some criminal trials you can form your own judgment about the extent to which the prosecution *has* – or has *not* – brought the appropriate cases to court.

While reading about the criminal justice system, you should be planning to make some criminal court visits and beginning to **think critically about how prosecutions work in English law where the defence, with some exceptions, does not have to prove innocence, but it is the prosecution which must establish its case, in default of which the accused cannot be convicted.** Of course you will understand cases that you observe more easily when you have studied some substantive criminal law and are familiar with the elements of some of the more important individual crimes, which are too detailed for you to learn at this stage when you are more concerned with **the fairness of process and the balance between prosecution and defence**. The process will be even clearer when you have also studied **the Law of Evidence** which, being also complex, is usually a second or third year undergraduate option.

Meanwhile **at last** we may have reached **a trial on indictment at your local Crown Court or even the Old Bailey**, after which it may be that you will have noticed some more differences with your previous perceptions of how criminal justice works in English law. We will return later to the accused whom we left to be tried by the magistrates.

TRIAL ON INDICTMENT IN THE CROWN COURT

After the pre-trial hearings are we ready to begin the actual trial? Not necessarily! There may be a stage called 'Plea Bargaining' to deal with and there may be issues about 'Disclosure' and these may happen right up to or even on the day of the trial, including at the door of the court, and either could hold up the trial or even prevent its taking place at all.

The object of plea bargaining is to encourage pleas of Guilty in return for a sentence benefit for the accused so that e.g. the accused might plead Guilty to a lesser charge on the same facts in return for a lesser sentence. It might be thought that this is unethical since if the police and CPS have done their job properly the accused should be coming to court on the right charge already. However a Guilty plea to a lesser charge in these circumstances can also benefit the victim as well as the administration of criminal justice, in addition to the accused: the victim because s/he will not have to give evidence of what may have been traumatic circumstances, the administration of criminal justice as a Guilty plea will free up court time and resources in a system which is overloaded, and the accused who may then have a lesser sentence since there is a discount for a Guilty plea (up to a third, and the more discount the earlier in the process the plea of Guilty occurs).

A common example is assault, street brawls often late in the evening and when the parties have been out 'celebrating'. This often seems to occur in the case of successful participants in high profile sports matches, such as the recent example involving a member of the England cricket team outside a night club in Bristol where the rumpus in the street after was so serious that the prime charge was affray. More commonly the choice of charges will be between the different levels of assault under the Offences Against the Person Act 1861, the difference being in the intent (to cause grievous bodily harm under s 18 or only to wound under s 20).

Disclosure issues which might arise at the last minute might be because of some argument about what is known as 'unused material'. The prosecution will already have given the accused all material on which it intends to rely at the trial under the initial disclosure rules, which required disclosure of anything that might reasonably undermine the prosecution case or assist the defence, and in response the accused is to provide a 'defence statement' which sets out the main points of the defence e.g. whether there is an alibi claimed, and of witnesses who are to be called: Criminal Procedure and Investigations Act 1996, s 6. However the prosecution also has a duty to keep disclosure under review[38] particularly in the light of the defence statement including material they do not intend to use but which may be necessary to disclose to ensure a fair trial, i.e. the unused material, and if the accused who has given a defence statement suspects that there is material that the prosecution has which should have been disclosed disclosure of that material can be applied for under s 8 of the Act.

The purpose of this focus on disclosure is, as in post CPR 1998 civil cases, to put an end to the former practice of 'trial by ambush', in criminal as well as civil cases, i.e. raising unsuspected last minute issues, and thus emphasising that a trial is not a game in which points are available to be scored but a serious search for the truth which should be conducted with all relevant material before the court. The value of these modern rules is obvious following revelations of past miscarriages of justice where all material in the possession of the police or prosecution had not been produced at the time.

----

38 s 7A.

THE CROWN COURT TRIAL PROCESS

Finally, we have arrived at the trial as such. This is an adversarial process, as in civil cases but the one major difference between a civil trial in the County or High Court and the criminal process in the Crown Court is the role of the jury in the Crown Court. The first stage of a Crown Court trial is to empanel and swear in a jury (see Chapter 12). The accused is then 'given in charge to the jury' which means they are then told that it is for them, having heard all the evidence, to determine whether the accused is Guilty or Not Guilty. The only role of the judge in relation to this crucial issue in the trial is to direct the jury as to whether there is sufficient evidence in law for them to find the accused Guilty, and if not that they must acquit him. (There is a procedure to hold a criminal trial without a jury, for example on application of the prosecution where there is evidence of jury tampering, but this is rare).[39]

The trial then commences, usually in public and with the accused present, though there is power to hear the case in private[40] or in the accused's absence, e.g. if an accused has absconded this will not prevent the trial being held.

THE ORDER OF SPEECHES AND EVIDENCE

A Crown Court case is perfectly choreographed with a specific running order that ensures that cases have a consistency of approach as between them and that both sides get the opportunity to put their case.

THE PROSECUTION CASE

The case for the prosecution is first, beginning with an opening speech by prosecution counsel who outlines the evidence in simple form so the jury understands what the case is about. Prosecuting counsel will then call the witnesses against the accused who will then be 'examined in chief', (which means asking them to give their evidence, in practice asking them if they stand by the evidence that they have already given when making the signed statement called their 'proof of evidence'). These witnesses are then cross-examined by defence counsel. If there are several co-defendants tried together defence counsel for each is entitled to cross examine separately. Prosecution counsel may then 're-examine' to clarify the evidence that has been given before passing on to the next witness. At this stage of giving evidence in chief the prosecution may not generally ask 'leading questions' (i.e. those to which the question suggests the answer) and in most cases witnesses must give evidence personally though if any evidence is not disputed the statement may be read out instead of the witness attending personally.

At this stage the prosecution has provided its case and so there is an opportunity to assess whether it is *possible* to demonstrate that the relevant standard of proof – beyond reasonable doubt – can be established even if all prosecution evidence is accepted. This is a question of

39 Criminal Justice Act 2003, s 44.
40 For example where the offence is under the Official Secrets Acts and to admit the public might be prejudicial to national safety.

law – i.e. whether it is *possible* for the prosecution case to be proved to the requisite standard – and so it is for the judge alone to make this determination on application by the defence.[41] Although the judge finding 'no case to answer' is rare, it is an important feature of criminal justice as it reinforces the fact that it is for the *prosecution* to discharge the burden of proof to the requisite standard. If this is, in law, impossible then the trial should be halted through a direction from the judge to acquit.[42]

THE DEFENCE CASE

Following the prosecution case the defence counsel goes through the same process, unless following the conclusion of the prosecution evidence the defence team considers that the prosecution has not established a sufficient case on which to convict the accused of the offence(s) charged, in which case they will make a submission of no case to answer. This, of course, is because of the principle that, with certain specific exceptions, it is for the prosecution to establish its case, not for the defence to establish the innocence of the accused. Thus if the submission is successful the judge will direct the jury that they must acquit the accused. The case must be proved by the criminal standard of 'beyond reasonable doubt' and the prosecution bears the burden of proof throughout including disproving any defences, with rare exceptions e.g. the defence must prove the common law defence of insanity and some statutes require the defence to assume the burden of proof, e.g. the Homicide Act 1957 s 2 in relation to diminished responsibility.[43]

There are also certain other specific rules which might change the process described previously, e.g. where the accused is acting in person (without legal representation) s/he will not be permitted to cross-examine a 'victim' or 'vulnerable person',[44] i.e. a sexual offence complainant or a child witness, whereupon such questions may only be put through the judge.

The case for the defence then follows in the same way with an opening speech by defence counsel and all witnesses, including the accused, examined in chief by defence counsel. If the accused is acting without legal representation s/he can still make an opening speech outlining the case for the jury and the evidence to be called providing s/he is going to give evidence and call other witnesses. However if the accused is the only witness or is not going to give evidence there is no entitlement to an opening speech. If there are several co-defendants their evidence is given in the order in which they appear on the indictment and they are cross-examined in the same order, with each witness also being cross-examined by counsel for the other co-defendants. Nevertheless, this is normally the limit of the prosecution's opportunity to challenge defence evidence as prosecution counsel cannot normally introduce any further evidence unless in rebuttal of any evidence given by the defence, e.g. if the accused gives evidence of good character the prosecution can then introduce evidence to the contrary.

---

41 The jury are not informed of this application for fear that it will prejudice the defendant should the trial proceed.
42 It was put in *R v Galbraith* [1981] 1 WLR 1039 (CA) that it was a judge's *duty* to stop a case in these circumstances.
43 See *M'Naghten's case* (1843) 10 Cl and Finn 200; *Woolmington v DPP* [1935] AC 462 (HL); *Mancini v DPP* [1942] AC 1 (HL).
44 Youth Justice and Criminal Evidence Act 1999.

CLOSING SPEECHES

There are then final speeches from each side. The prosecution goes first here, and the defence last,[45] usually a significant advantage as 'having the last word' means the defence's case is last in the jury's memory before they hear from the judge in his summing up.

SUMMING UP

Next the judge will 'sum up', explaining to the jury the elements of the offence(s), the burden and standard of proof and some more technical points such as 'inferences' that may be drawn from certain matters such as silence at certain points when an explanation could have been given, and also the impact of an accused's good or bad character, all often of sufficient complexity for a non-lawyer to understand, but crucial for the jury of ordinary lay people who are going to make a decision on guilt or innocence of the crime(s) charged. As a result this is one of the judge's most demanding tasks for which regular training is provided by the Judicial College but all written guidance from the College has now been brought together in the 'Crown Compendium'.

VERDICT

Following the summing up the jury will 'retire' to consider its verdict. They are first encouraged to try to reach a unanimous verdict and only if this is not possible (after a period of at least two hours) will the judge direct them that the court will accept a majority[46] verdict. The jury can ask, normally through their foreperson,[47] for clarification as to the law or the evidence. The jurors would traditionally be sequestered to a hotel if deliberations lasted more than a day but the Criminal Justice and Public Order Act 1994 altered the position and the jury may now, unless the judge directs otherwise, return home between days of deliberation.

If no majority can be reached, and it seems that this will not change then proceedings will end with a *Watson*[48] direction and it will be for the CPS to consider whether there is merit in a retrial.

Verdicts will be either 'Guilty' or 'Not Guilty'.[49] If Guilty, the judge will either proceed immediately to sentence or alternatively fix another date for sentence, e.g. if a pre-sentence report is required which cannot be provided immediately.

SENTENCING

Sentencing takes place against the backdrop of s 142 of the Criminal Justice Act 2003 which lays out the factors to which the court must 'have regard'. These include – the punishment of

---

45 Criminal Procedure (Right of Reply) Act 1964 s 1.

46 Most typically 10–2.

47 The jury will elect a foreperson from within their number and this person is responsible for structuring the discussions and will typically be the person who communicates with the judge and who speaks in court to confirm the verdict.

48 R v *Watson* [1988] QB 690 (CA).

49 In Scotland there is a second route to acquittal with a verdict of 'not proven'.

offenders; the reduction in crime; the reform and rehabilitation of offenders; the protection of the public; and the making of reparation of offenders to persons affected by their offences.

The courts can, depending on the offence, issue a range of sentences, including discharge,[50] a fine, community sentence[51] or custodial (prison) sentence.[52] Therefore a sentence can range from no particular punishment (an unconditional discharge) to a 'whole life term' which will involve a sentence with no end. There are a range of factors that will help a judge in determining the appropriate sentence; chief amongst these are the sentencing guidelines produced by the Sentencing Council[53] and any guidance issued by the Court of Appeal.

TAKING THINGS FURTHER

The website that accompanies this text contains some practical examples of how sentencing is applied in the courts. It considers very serious and less serious criminal offences and uses hypothetical situations to demonstrate how judges go about balancing the various factors that must be taken into account when calculating a sentence.

THE WEBSITE

The website that accompanies this textbook contains many useful resources that you can use to consolidate and further your knowledge of the law, to hone your skills of critical analysis and to test your knowledge. This includes a set of multiple choice questions (MCQs) that can be used to test your knowledge and understanding of the material.

PODCASTS

- The podcasts provide a summary of the area under study, bringing together the key themes and threads of analysis into a 'mini-lecture'.
- There will also be an explanation and analysis of topical and up-to-date issues related to the criminal justice system.

---

50 Complete or conditional.
51 There is a wide range of community sentences from curfew and tagging to unpaid work in the community to drug and alcohol courses.
52 Suspended, of determinate period or of an indeterminate period.
53 Governed by the Coroners and Justice Act 2009.

12

CHAPTER 12
THE JURY

INTRODUCTION

Trial by jury is an iconic and long-standing feature of the English Legal System. It is also amongst the most easily recognisable and identifiable parts of the justice system. The ability to serve on a jury is one of the few opportunities that citizens have to be intimately and directly involved in the *administration* of justice in the legal system. Equally, being tried by a jury of one's peers is an important safeguard in preventing the abuse of state power. In this way, trial by jury takes on a constitutional significance for both jurors and parties and is elevated above many other aspects of the legal system. Despite this recognition and importance, or perhaps because of it, there is also an air of mystery to the role of juror and a fair amount of wrongful perception about how widespread jury trials are and how they operate. Although seen by some as an antiquated and creaking part of the system, the concept of trial by jury is faced with some very modern problems including the rise of social media and increased press coverage of the behaviour of parties and jurors.

The purpose of this chapter is to unpick the law and policy surrounding jury trials and to assess the contribution that they make to the English Legal System. This analysis will involve looking at the development, use and function of jury trials as well as tackling some of the problems caused by trial by jury. The chapter will also briefly consider potential reforms of the system of jury trials.

AS YOU READ

By the end of this chapter you should be able to *describe the origin and function of the jury* in criminal and civil trials. In addition, you will be able to *explain the qualification requirements* for being called for jury service and the grounds on which a person may be *disqualified, excused or deferred* from jury service.

Turning to higher-order skills, as you read *consider critically the merits (and problems) of maintaining the system of jury trials* and try to *evaluate recent changes and proposals for reform* of the jury system. By doing this, you should begin to form a view of what future, if any, jury trials have in the English Legal System.

In order to try to unify the diverse strands of analysis in this chapter, consider the development of technology as both a challenge to jury service and a way of achieving greater efficiency in the selection for and implementation of jury trials.

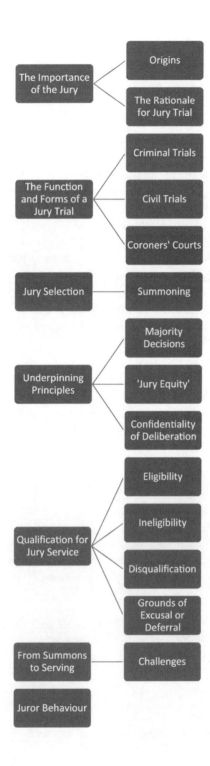

Figure 12.1

THE IMPORTANCE OF THE JURY

ORIGINS

Within the English Legal System, the origin of juries can be traced back at least to the 11th century. However, it is important to note that the juries of Saxon and Norman times are almost unrecognisable compared to the juries in use today.[1] Originally, jurors of the early and late middle ages had an investigatory role outside of a formal trial and jurors were drawn from a narrow class of persons. This extended beyond criminal matters and jurors were also involved in resolving private land disputes. The common understanding of juries today relates to criminal trials, but they were (and still are) also used in civil matters. The key unifying factor was the independent investigatory nature of the role of a juror, coupled with the highly restricted eligibility criteria to act as one. It is hardly surprising that the use of juries has changed and evolved through the ages.

The 13th century started to see a change in the function of jurors from evidence gatherers and witnesses of good standing towards the role that they occupy today as triers of fact and as those that determine guilt or innocence, since it is the jury not the judge who decides, on the evidence before the court, whether the case against the accused has been proved, on the criminal standard of 'beyond reasonable doubt'.

This 13th century, early medieval, time in the development of the English Legal System was one of some upheaval with the right to jury trial being enshrined in Magna Carta[2] after the turmoil between the barons, the Church and the King and trial by ordeal[3] losing the support of the Church. Nonetheless, juries still retained evidence gathering functions for a further 400 years. During this time, and as procedural/evidential rules developed in the common law courts, the assumption that jurors ought to have some connection with the facts of the case (an almost witness-like role) diminished and was replaced with the contrary assumption that jurors ought to have no connection with the parties or facts of the case before the trial. As we shall see later in this chapter, it is now of vital importance that a juror has no prior knowledge of the parties and that research by jurors into the circumstances of the case may lead to a conviction being unsafe. This is a clear example of how a legal system can develop as it matures and in such a process even accepted understandings can be overturned.

Thus, like many features of the English Legal System, the role of the jury has developed over time with the very function changing significantly. And yet, at the core, the principle of involving citizens in the administration of justice has remained.

----

1   It is of interest to note that one thing that has stood the test of time is the number of jurors typically used (12). This quirk (found in jury systems around the world) is discussed in Gary Slapper, How the Law Works (2nd edn, Routledge 2011) Ch 8.
2   Article 39 of Magna Carta 1215 states: 'No free man is to be arrested, or imprisoned, or disseised, or outlawed, or exiled, or in any other way ruined, nor will we go against him or send against him, except by the lawful judgment of his peers or by the law of the land.'
3   Ended by Pope Innocent III in 1215, and recognised in England by Henry III in 1219, although the practice continued in Europe for many years after that, and indeed was still prevalent in England in the Civil War and also even later in the American Colonies.

THE RATIONALE FOR JURY TRIAL

There is a great deal of legal and political rhetoric surrounding jury trial. Its place in Magna Carta has ascribed to it a constitutional value that is difficult to displace. Despite its inherent weaknesses and costs to maintain, support for jury trial is still high amongst the legal professions, the judiciary, politicians and citizens.

The emotive nature of trial by one's peers can make it difficult to pinpoint the underlying rationale for retaining the jury system. The most vocal and persuasive reason given for maintaining trial by jury relates to ensuring freedom and liberty for citizens. Perhaps most famously, Lord Devlin held that the principle of trial by jury is 'more than an instrument of justice and more than one wheel of the constitution; it is the lamp that shows that freedom lives.'[4] This had added weight when it is remembered that traditionally many crimes that would have required jury trials had the death penalty as the ultimate punishment. In those cases the need to protect the citizen from potential abuse by the state was particularly important.[5] By removing judges as the sole arbiter of fact and guilt, the potential for an accusation of state bias is reduced.

ANALYSING THE LAW – SEPARATION OF POWERS

The principle of separation of powers, and particularly the independence of the judiciary, is considered elsewhere in this text and is a theme that will be explored if you study constitutional law in any level of detail. Given that there is a well-established appeals system that is distinct from any executive interference it is unclear whether the additional safeguard of trial by jury is still necessary. Jury trials are used in a minority of cases (both civil and criminal).

Abuses of the legal process by the state are pernicious and deleterious to public confidence in the justice system. Nonetheless, are arguments in favour of jury trial that rely on the risk of 'state' or 'establishment' bias compelling? Are there examples of times where jury trials have equally led to unsatisfactory results or miscarriages of justice?

Although discussed in greater detail later, it is worth noting that the principle of 'jury equity' could also be cited as a reason for supporting jury trials. In criminal trials, juries are entitled to acquit on the basis of conscience and against the compelling evidence that the legal 'ingredients' of an offence have been satisfied.

---

4   Lord Delvin, *Trial by Jury* (Stevens & Son 1956) 164.
5   In the words of Lord Justice Cassels '[Juries] stand between the Crown and the subject, and they are still one of the main defences of personal liberty.' *R v McKenna (William James)* [1960] 1 QB 411 (CA) 329 where a judge threatened to keep a jury overnight if they could not reach a speedy verdict.

The issues discussed so far focus on the reasons why one of the *parties* may support the use of juries. Lord Denning noted that jury service gives 'ordinary folk their finest lesson in citizenship'.[6] The public duty aspect and sense of civic responsibility is an additional reason for jury trial. This may be a slightly romanticised view (particularly given the attempts that citizens go to in order to *avoid* jury service) of modern citizenship but it is a timely reminder that the justice system is as much about *cultural* and *societal* identity as it is about strict legal rules. This cultural heritage is fuelled by powerful jury scenes that are portrayed in the media and in popular culture within the UK and beyond.[7]

None of the preceding is to say that juries are not without their detractors. In a direct response to Lord Delvin's *statement*, Professor Darbyshire wrote a scathing but well-reasoned attack on jury trials, arguing that they led to 'erratic and secret decisions [that] run counter to the rule of law'.[8]

TAKING THINGS FURTHER AND ANALYSING THE LAW – JURIES AROUND THE WORLD

It is easy to become absorbed in the particular legal culture under study and to forget that there are alternative approaches taken elsewhere in the world. Given the prominence accorded to jury trial in the news and in popular fiction (particularly those emanating from high profile common law jurisdictions like the USA, which dominate the film-making industry), a student new to the study of law may be forgiven for thinking that all legal orders adopt the jury system in an extensive manner. This is far from the truth, and certain jurisdictions adopt a more restrictive system of trial by jury than that in operation in England and Wales or do not operate jury trials at all.

Different legal cultures attach different levels of importance to the various advantages and disadvantages of trial by jury. The proponents of jury trial often point to the ability of juries to acquit in the face of the law as a distinct advantage. This ability to judge according to a juror's conscience can, however, spark unease and, it is argued, led to the removal of trial by jury in India from the 1960s. The website that accompanies this textbook has more detail on the situation in India and on the case of *Nanavati* that allegedly[9] led to the breakdown of jury trials there. On the other hand, the lack of a

---

6 See more in Alfred Denning, *What Next in the Law* (Butterworths 1982) 33.

7 Some of the most memorable court scenes in major films and literature involve speeches to the jury. One of the most famous of such speeches to the jury is that of Atticus Finch, defence counsel in Harper Lee's Pulitzer Prize–winning novel, *To Kill A Mocking Bird*, filmed with Gregory Peck in the role in 1962, as he defends a black man accused of raping a white girl, at the height of Southern United States race discrimination unrest, which still has considerable impact in both film and literature, despite the passage of time.

8 Penny Darbyshire, 'What can we learn from published jury research' (2001) Criminal Law Review 970. Later research (by Cheryl Thomas *Are Juries Fair?* February 2010, Ministry of Justice Research Series 1/10) seems to suggest that some of the criticisms of jury trials were based on assumption rather than fact, as the report (described in the media as 'ground breaking' – inevitably as little or no research has been done) found that they were fair and 'effective' but also that 31% of jurors did not understand the instructions they were given.

9 There were also concerns over the way in which perverse verdicts were being returned when an offence was committed by foreigners against native Indians.

jury for the high-profile murder trial of athlete Oscar Pistorius has also led to calls for a reconsideration of the system in South Africa.

Although jury trial is a fundamental right under the British constitution,[10] it is not regarded as a facet of the basic human right to a fair trial under the European Convention on Human Rights.[11] This means that within Europe there is no common approach to jury trials. Some countries use them fairly widely (e.g. England and Wales), others save them for extremely serious criminal offences (e.g. France), some use them only in very particular circumstances (e.g. Sweden)[12] and others do not use jury trials at all (e.g. the Netherlands).[13]

Equally, when studying legal systems it is important to note that even core features can (and will) evolve over time. Japan has, within the last two decades, introduced a limited form of jury trial. Similar moves have been made in Mexico – a state which has the *potential* for jury trials mentioned in its Constitution but which has not applied extensive trial by jury since the 1930s.

Not only does understanding the way 'others' choose to do things an important way of better understanding the English Legal System, it can also be a way of enriching assessment answers. The same is true when considering the reasons why a legal system chooses to change a core feature. By including, in a meaningful way, commentary on other legal systems, you can demonstrate to an examiner a wider understanding of how the law operates within the legal system and how (and why) things might be done differently elsewhere. This involves more than just commenting that things are done differently and an effort should be made to explain *why* things may be done differently and to assess whether the alternative is more or less effective than the approach taken by the English Legal System.

Having explored briefly the origins and potential rationale(s) for the system of trial by jury, the chapter will now turn to the different purposes to which jury trials may be put in the English Legal System.

THE FUNCTION AND FORMS OF JURY TRIAL

Given the important constitutional value placed on jury trial, it is of interest to note that the *use* of jury trial is now fairly limited in the English Legal System. The trend, over the past 300 years, has been for a reduction in the types of cases that are given a jury trial. Jury trials are now predominantly reserved for serious criminal matters but still have a place in both the system of coroners' courts and in certain (albeit very limited) civil matters.

10 As evidenced by its inclusion in Magna Carta 1215.

11 The right is to an independent tribunal – this requirement can be met by a trial by judge alone (a bench trial) as found in *Twomey* [2013] ECHR 577 which is discussed later.

12 Jury trials are only for highly particular situations, such as in defamation trials.

13 Jury trials were used for a few years during the 19th century whilst the Netherlands was under French occupation.

FUNCTION OF A JURY

In addition to the symbolic and historical importance attached to jury trial the jury performs a set of practical functions.

Chief, and common, amongst the functions of a jury trial is that of determining the true facts of the case, where these are in dispute. The judge will determine matters of law and procedure and will direct the jury as to the relevant legal tests and will explain core concepts such as the burden and standard of proof. This separation of functions between the judge (determines the law) and jury (determines the facts) is of particular importance for criminal trials. A judge can direct the jury to acquit the defendant where the legal test cannot be satisfied even if the jury were to accept as true all of the facts presented by the prosecution.

In certain criminal trials, the jury also gives a verdict as to guilt. It is probably here that a jury's work is best known by the public and by law students. However, the dramatisation and widespread reporting of high-profile criminal trials leads to a distorted perception as to the use of jury trial even for criminal matters. Over 95% of criminal cases are heard, without juries, in the Magistrates' Court. It is only more serious crimes that are tried in front of a jury in the Crown Court.[14] As almost two-thirds of defendants plead Guilty when they reach the Crown Court, the number of trials that are decided with a jury is very small.

Although the jury in a criminal trial will normally determine both factual matters and produce the verdict, this is not always the case. If a defendant is unfit to be tried then the jury may still go on to determine the facts – i.e. whether the accused 'did the act or made the omission charged against him as the offence'[15] but does not determine guilt.[16] In this way, juries are sometimes involved simply to find the facts. A relatively recent example will serve to illustrate this principle. In 2015, the CPS announced that Lord Janner – a prominent politician and barrister – would not be charged for historic allegations of sexual offences against children. The CPS decided that, although there was sufficient evidence to pursue a prosecution, it was not in the public interest to do so as Lord Janner was suffering from the advanced stages of dementia. This decision was subject to a review and a 'trial of the facts' was ordered for April 2016 with the intention of determining whether Janner had committed the alleged acts.[17]

CRIMINAL TRIALS

In the criminal justice system juries are only used in trials that take place in the Crown Court. As is discussed in Chapter 11, there are two types of criminal trial – a trial on indictment and a summary trial.

---

14 www.judiciary.gov.uk/about-the-judiciary/the-justice-system/jurisdictions/criminal-jurisdiction.
15 Criminal Procedure (Insanity) Act 1964 s 4A(2).
16 R v Antoine [2001] 1 AC 340 (HL). Interestingly, the test for fitness to plead, which still depends on the ruling in the 1836 case of R v Prichard (1836) 7 C&P 303, includes whether the accused understands that s/he may challenge jurors.
17 His death in December 2015 effectively put an end to any proceedings.

Indictable offences are amongst the most serious known to the English Legal System and will take place in the Crown Court with a judge and jury.[18] Summary offences are tried in a Magistrates' Court, involve less serious offences,[19] and do not involve a jury.

There is also a category of offences known as 'either way' offences.[20] These, as the name suggests, can be settled by a trial on indictment or summarily. The initial decision as to venue is made by the Magistrates' Court in a 'mode of trial' or 'allocation' hearing.[21] If that court feels that, amongst other things, they have insufficient sentencing powers then they can commit the trial to the Crown Court. If the Magistrates' Court decides to hear the case themselves then the defendant charged with an 'either way' offence can choose instead to have the case heard by a jury in the Crown Court. It is often written that the defendant has a 'choice' in either way cases but this is not quite true.[22] A defendant can elect for a Crown Court trial if the lower court feels it can effectively exercise its jurisdiction but a defendant **cannot** elect for a trial in the Magistrates' Court if the case is committed to the Crown Court. In reality, very few defendants elect for a jury trial at such allocation hearings.

As the vast majority of criminal trials start and end in the Magistrates' Court the proportion of proceedings *eligible* for trial by jury is small. Over time, offences have been reclassified so that more are classed as summary or triable 'either way' further reducing the remit of trial by jury. For example, the Criminal Law Act 1977 made the majority of driving offences summary offences. Equally, by increasing the sentencing powers of magistrates,[23] fewer cases are committed in circumstances where the lower court is of the view that it has insufficient powers as to sentence. It is also easy to overlook the fact that even if a defendant is due to be tried in the Crown Court, it does not necessarily follow that a jury trial will happen. If a defendant pleads Guilty as is often the case,[24] then a jury will not be used.

The combination of preceding factors means that the proportion of trials that end up involving a jury is very small. Despite the incremental reduction in jury trials and their *statistical* insignificance, there is still a hesitation in removing jury trial altogether, particularly for more serious offences. Successive Governments have publicly declared their respect for and commitment to reducing the remit of jury trials.

---

18 Most common indictable offences are such as murder and robbery (triable only on indictment).

19 Most common summary offences are the less serious driving offences, e.g. careless driving and a raft of construction and use offences under the Road Traffic Acts.

20 A common either way offence example is most Theft Act 1968 varieties of stealing, including burglary, which in one sense is serious particularly because if such forced entry is committed in residential premises at night there is clear danger to the residents, so might be tried in the Crown Court if associated circumstances e.g. amount and, methodology, are also serious or might for various reasons be categorised as less serious, so the procedure as between Crown Court trial and summary hearing in the Magistrates' Court is decided on the basis of the associated circumstances.

21 For the allocation hearing, see Chapter 11, Criminal Justice.

22 For advice to the Accused on choice at the allocation hearing, see Chapter 11 on Criminal Justice.

23 For sentencing in either way cases, see Chapter 11, Criminal Justice.

24 Due to the potential benefits of a more lenient sentence for an early Guilty plea.

BENCH TRIALS IN CRIMINAL MATTERS

Through the combination of magistrates and jurors, the vast majority of criminal trials are determined by lay persons rather than by a member of the judiciary. This reinforces the fundamental principle identified earlier in this chapter, namely that criminal liability should be established whilst minimising the possibility for abuse by the state. This may help to explain why any suggestion of removing jury trials, even in very particular circumstances, tends to be treated with suspicion and attracts considerable controversy.[25] The (Labour) Government sought to introduce, via ss 43 and 44 of the Criminal Justice Act 2003, restrictions on jury trials in two circumstances – where the case concerned serious/complex frauds and where there was evidence of jury tampering, respectively. This would have led to a new practice of 'bench trials' (i.e. a trial with a judge but no jury) for these categories of criminal activity. The life of these sections is discussed later.

SERIOUS OR COMPLEX FRAUD CASES

There has been concern in the past about jurors' ability to deal with and fully to understand complex fraud issues.[26] As the suffrage for jury service has expanded and financial transactions have become more complex, the criticism of using a standard jury for this type of case has increased. This is not a new criticism and is something that even staunch supporters of the use of jury trials have commented upon.

Lord Denning, for example, supported the use of a 'special panel' of jurors in such cases or, in the alternative, proposed the use of a trial with a judge and expert assessors.[27] Denning makes the powerful point that the use of ordinary jury members in cases involving complex financial information may frustrate the oath taken in which the juror commits to understanding and using the evidence in order to come to a verdict.[28] Equally, the Roskill Report in 1986 recommended that jury trials be dispensed with in fraud cases but this recommendation was not taken forward by the then Conservative Government of the time.

The Labour Government of 2001 sought to implement the possibility for a bench trial where the case concerned complex frauds. The proposal was even put on statutory footing in the form of s 43 of the Criminal Justice Act 2003. However, the provision required an affirmative vote in both Houses of Parliament before it would come into force. The Labour Government tried on two occasions to bring into force this provision but was frustrated by the House of Lords on both occasions. Eventually the Coalition Government of 2010 brought forward legislation to repeal s 43 of the Criminal Justice Act 2003 before it was ever enacted.[29]

---

25 See later, e.g. where the Labour Government tried to do this in the Criminal Justice Act 2003 ss 43 and 44.

26 See e.g. Law Now in Canada, Charles Davison, 'Jury Trials; Cost, Controversy and Secret Powers', lawnow.org/jury-tri-als-cost-controversy-and-secret-powers/3 January 2019.

27 Alfred Denning, *What Next in the Law* (Butterworths 1982) 71.

28 Ibid. 72.

29 Protection of Freedoms Act 2012 s 113.

ANALYSING THE LAW – METHODS TO MITIGATE COMPLEX FRAUDS
_____

In the Maxwell fraud trials during 1995 and 1996, Lord Phillips of Worth Matravers, then Phillips J, tried the Maxwell fraud case in the Chancery Lane Old Bailey Annexe. Phillips used another technique (besides the obvious assistance of the IT supported Annexe court) to enable jurors to follow the complex issues: he sat every morning and gave the jurors the afternoon off to read and catch up with the developing material. The trial, reported in the *Law Gazette* of 6 June 1995, was said to cost £10 million and it involved fraud of around £100 million. It is obvious that the methodology used made it quite clear that juries *can* follow complex fraud trials if allowances are made.

SERIOUS RISK OF JURY TAMPERING

As well as trying to abolish jury trials in cases of serious fraud, the Labour Government also made provision, by s 44 Criminal Justice Act 2003, for the use of bench trials where there was a *serious* risk of jury tampering. In contrast to the section on fraud trials, this measure *was* brought into force in 2007.

The initiative for invoking s 44 lies with the prosecution[30] and the judge has no discretion in whether or not to order a trial without a jury if two conditions are satisfied.[31] The conditions are as follows:

- First, 'that there is **evidence of a real and present danger that jury tampering** would take place.'[32]
- Second, 'that, notwithstanding any steps (including the provision of police protection) which might **reasonably be taken to prevent jury tampering**, the likelihood that it would take place **would be so substantial** as to make it **necessary in the interests of justice** for the trial to be conducted without a jury.'[33]

As is obvious from the preceding extract, a risk of jury tampering is not enough for a judge to order a trial without jury. There must also be a consideration of proportionality, that is to say are there any measures that could be taken to *reduce* the risk of jury tampering and it is only where the risk would remain substantial that it would be in the 'interests of justice' to deny a jury trial. This is a reflection, built into the statute itself, of the importance attached to jury trials. It is clear that such a bench trial should only happen as a last resort. The justification for the provision, and its fairly high threshold conditions, was given in the JSM[34] case. Lord Judge, the Lord Chief Justice, noted that 'any defendant who is responsible for abusing the principle … has no justified complaint that he has been deprived of a right … which he

....

30 Criminal Justice Act 2003 s 44(2).

31 Ibid. s 44(3).

32 Ibid. s 44(4), emphasis added.

33 Ibid. s 44(5), emphasis added.

34 J, S, M v R [2010] EWCA Crim 1755, [2011] 1 Cr App R 5.

himself has spurned.'[35] While Lord Judge recognises the public policy concerns underpinning s 44 (i.e. that those who denigrate or abuse their rights can have them removed), there is also the protection of innocent citizens who may be subjected to intimidation should they act as jurors.

EXPLAINING THE LAW – JURY TAMPERING

The provisions on jury tampering were first applied and tested in the trial of John Twomey. The *Twomey*[36] case involved a high-profile armed robbery from Heathrow Airport in 2004. Trials were held in 2005, 2007 and 2009. John Twomey was unable to give evidence in the first, the jury failed to reach a verdict in the second and the third collapsed amidst allegations of jury tampering. It is estimated that the aborted trials cost in the region £25 million and that it would cost at least £6 million for protective measures to be put in place to prevent further tampering in a fourth trial and even then there would be a risk of tampering with the jurors through intimidation of their families. It was against this background that the s 44 of the Criminal Justice Act was invoked.

The subsequent conviction was challenged on appeal before the Court of Appeal[37] and the European Court of Human Rights.[38]

Before the Court of Appeal it was argued that the powers under the Criminal Justice Act 2003 interfered with Twomey's right to a fair trial under Article 6 of the European Convention on Human Rights. If we cast our minds back to the early sections of this chapter then it is worth noting that not all signatories to the ECHR operate jury trials and so it could not be successfully argued that access to trial by jury was a condition of having a fair trial. This logic was followed by the Court of Appeal and the European Court in dismissing the appeals.

The importance of the balancing exercise involved in the application of s 44 was reinforced R v J, S, M[39] where there was a successful appeal against a decision to order a bench trial in a case involving a conspiracy to pervert the course of justice. The appeal was based on the incorrect application by the trial judge of the *necessity* criterion in s 44(5). The Court of Appeal held that a judge had to be sure that other methods of mitigating the risk of jury tampering were not effective before ordering a bench trial. In the case it was held that measures to mitigate the risk of jury tampering could be sustained for the

---

35 Ibid. per Lord Judge.
36 R v Twomey, Blake, Hibberd and Cameron [2011] EWCA Crim 8, [2011] 1 WLR 1681.
37 Ibid. 8. Appeal against conviction lost before Lord Judge, CJ, Rafferty J and Roderick Evans J, sitting at the Old Bailey for security reasons.
38 [2013] 57 EHRR SE15 appeals on basis of an unfair trial without a jury unanimously rejected.
39 [2010] EWCA Crim 1755, [2011] 1 Cr App R 5.

relatively short period (two weeks) that it was expected that the trial would take place. In this way, the Court of Appeal reasserted that the provision of juryless trials was a measure of 'last resort'.[40]

TAKING THINGS FURTHER – BRITISH OVERSEAS TERRITORIES

The interaction between the English Legal System and the British Overseas Territories in relation to trial without jury can be explored on the website that accompanies this textbook. The online materials consider the recent *Misick*[41] case, decided by the Privy Council in 2015. This case concerned the high-profile trial of former members of the Government of the Turks and Caicos Islands for alleged corruption and money laundering. Treatment of the British Overseas Territories is often overlooked in a module on the English Legal System, but it can help to demonstrate that you have a sophisticated understanding of the context of interacting legal systems.

CIVIL

Jury trials used to be common for civil matters (i.e. those disputes between private parties). Land disputes and cases involving defamation[42] were commonly heard before a jury. The function of a jury was similar to that in criminal trials.

The Common Law Procedure Act 1854 marked the start of a sharp decline in the use of jury trials for purely civil matters. Section 1 of the Act allowed the parties to consent, in writing, to forgo a jury trial and to have all issues of fact and the calculation of damages to be determined solely by a judge. Thus, even in the mid-19th century, more control was given to the parties in deciding whether to have their private dispute settled with or without a jury. This was taken further over the coming century by the Administration of Justice (Miscellaneous Provisions) Act 1933[43] which abolished the right to a jury trial in most civil cases. By the 1980s, the right to jury trial in civil cases was retained in relation to a minority of actions; these included:[44]

- Defamation
- Malicious prosecution
- False imprisonment
- Fraud

---

40 Ibid.
41 *Misick and Others v The Queen* [2015] UKPC 31, [2015] 1 WLR 3215.
42 Untrue statements of fact, either in written (libel) or spoken (slander) form, that damage the reputation of a real or legal person.
43 s 6 (now repealed).
44 For cases in the High Court this requirement can be found in the Senior Courts Act 1981 s 69(1). A similar provision is in place for actions brought in the County Court can be found in the County Court Act 1981 s 66(3).

A judge could only refuse to order a jury trial in the preceding cases if the trial would involve 'prolonged examination of documents or accounts or any scientific or local investigation which cannot conveniently be made with a jury'.[45]

Outside these areas there was no right to a jury trial but a court could, in its discretion, allow one for other types of cases. In *Ward v James (No2)*[46] – a road traffic case – Lord Denning noted that there had been a steady decline in jury trials in personal injury cases, partly as a result of parties not *asking* the court to exercise its discretion.[47] Denning also noted that, in such cases where a request for jury trial is made, there is a suspicion that it is done because the party concerned has a 'weak case, or desires to appeal to sympathy'.[48] Moreover, Denning noted that juries were not accustomed or well-equipped to deal with the question of damages in certain categories of very serious personal injuries and was strongly of the view that uniformity and consistency of award were needed.[49] Therefore, the difficulties in assessing *damages* led Denning to comment that so 'important is it [calculation of damages] that the judge ought not, in a personal injury case, to order trial by jury save in exceptional circumstances'.[50]

Where they are used, civil juries decide by a simple majority.

Retaining civil jury trials, particularly, for defamation cases became increasingly problematic as the consistency of outcomes was questionable and juror involvement in the setting of damages was highly controversial. Although the criticisms have been long-standing, it was only in 2013 that real change was brought about with the passage of the Defamation Act 2013. This new Act removes the presumption of jury trial in defamation cases.[51] As such, slander and libel cases will now be heard in the same way as other civil cases, unless a judge specifically orders a jury trial.

ANALYSING THE LAW – DEFAMATION AND JURIES

The recent Defamation Act 2013 was considered in the *Yeo*[52] case involving MP Tim Yeo and a defamation suit against the *Sunday Times*. *The Times* made an application for the trial to be heard by a jury and that application was refused in 2014. Citing an earlier statement by Lord Denning, Mr Justice Warby noted that the right to a jury trial is 'of the highest importance, especially when the defendant has ventured to criticise

45 Ibid.
46 [1966] 1 QB (CA) 273.
47 Ibid. 296 (Lord Denning).
48 Ibid.
49 Ibid. 300. Denning also made the comparison to sentencing, which is not left to the jury in criminal matters.
50 Ibid. 303.
51 Defamation Act 2013 s 11.
52 *Yeo MP v Times Newspaper Ltd* [2014] EWHC 2853 (QB), [2015] 1 WLR 971.

the government of the day, or those who hold authority or power in the state'.[53] In rejecting the application, however, the judge went on to say 'Parliament no longer regards jury trial as a right of "the highest importance" in defamation cases. It is no longer a right at all.'[54]

In refusing a jury trial, the High Court not only recognises the change in the law but also dispenses with prior interpretation of the right to a jury trial in cases involving defamation. The interpretation of law that existed prior to Defamation Act 2013 had weighed *in favour* of permitting a jury trial, particularly in cases involving the reputation of politicians.[55] The High Court in *Yeo* took the opportunity to revisit this reasoning and found that having a *reasoned judgment* – i.e. one delivered by a judge and that is absent in cases involving a jury – was more beneficial than involving the public in cases involving public figures.[56] The court also noted that, despite Mr Yeo's prominence in the public eye, he was not a member of the Government. There is merit in these arguments but the High Court also went on to rely on a more dubious proportionality argument, noting the increased delay and cost involved in a jury trial needed to be taken into account when considering granting a jury trial (s 11 of the Defamation Act 2013).

The judgment in *Yeo* marks a significant change in the direction of the law. Not only does it apply rigorously the new presumption against jury trials for defamation cases, it also confirms the high hurdles necessary in order to convince a court that such a mode of trial is necessary. In this way, the classic 'special' treatment given to defamation cases is being brought more in line with other areas of law such as negligence.

CORONERS' COURTS

For the sake of completeness, it is necessary to mention that a jury is sometimes used in inquests conducted by coroners.[57] An inquest is necessary in limited circumstances surrounding certain deaths. The vast majority of such inquests are held by the coroner acting alone as finder of fact and law. However, in very limited circumstances an inquest may involve a jury. These circumstances include:

---

53 Ibid. [20].
54 Ibid. [47].
55 See *Rothermere v Times Newspapers Ltd* [1973] 1 WLR 448 (CA). It should be noted that although Tim Yeo was in an influential position, he was not a member of the Government.
56 'There are real risks of a jury verdict being unclear or misunderstood or both.' *Yeo MP v Times Newspaper Ltd* [2014] EWHC 2853 (QB), [2015] 1 WLR 971.
57 The coroner being a local judicial official who enquires into certain deaths and also has functions under the Treasure Act 1996 in respect of items of buried treasure (gold, silver and potentially some other artefacts). It is a very old office dating from at least the 11th century and is normally held by lawyers or certain members of the medical professions and others such as the police.

- Deaths that result from accidents in the workplace
- Deaths in prison
- Deaths that were the result of injuries caused by police officers[58]

The role of jury in such inquests is to establish certain of the key facts, such as the identity of the person who has died and the circumstances surrounding their death.[59] Juries used in inquests are permitted to give a range of verdicts but these do not in any way settle criminal or civil liability.[60] There is no definitive list of verdicts but commonly used verdicts include:

- Natural causes
- Accident/misadventure
- Neglect
- Suicide
- Unlawful killing
- Dependency on drugs
- Suicide
- Industrial disease
- Open verdict (used where there is not enough evidence to establish a definitive verdict)

JURY SELECTION

Having discussed the nature, origins and form of jury trials in the English Legal System in the previous section, this part of the chapter will turn to the more practical principles and processes that underpin the *selection* of potential jurors. Although the rules surrounding the eligibility, excusal and summoning of jurors could appear to be mechanical and overly formalistic, it is nonetheless a crucially important part of the legal system. How juries are selected determines the composition of the final jury and, if conducted improperly or erroneously, could potentially influence the outcome of a given case. Also, improperly constituted juries could damage the public perception of this historic institution.

This section will look at the eligibility criteria for selection, the process of summoning a jury, the jury in waiting, challenges and swearing-in. The focus will be on the method of selection in criminal trials.

---

58 The precise form of wording can be found in the Coroners and Justice Act 2009 s 7(2).

59 Coroners Act 1988 s 11(5).

60 Inquest conclusions must not even appear to determine such matters – Coroners and Justice Act 2009 s 10(2) in force since 2013. The Act largely repeals the 1988 Act.

SUMMONING

The summoning of potential jurors is undertaken by the Central Summoning Bureau (CSB) but formal responsibility for the summons lies with the Lord Chancellor.[61] The CSB uses a method of random selection based on the *eligible* entries contained on the electoral register.

It is an important point to note that there are no restrictions as to where a person may be required to report in order to discharge their duty as a juror[62] but the Lord Chancellor is required to be mindful of the 'convenience of the persons summoned and to their respective places of residence, and in particular to the desirability of selecting jurors within reasonable daily travelling distance of the place where they are to attend'.[63]

The Juries Act 1974 also allows the court to make additional 'exceptional' summons if a jury is likely to be incomplete. This power permits the court to make summons, without the normal formal written notice, to those in the court or in the vicinity[64] of the court at the time.[65] Jury service is compulsory and a failure to serve when summoned is an offence and can be punished by a fine.[66]

UNDERPINNING PRINCIPLES

In executing their duty to try a defendant and to give a verdict based on the evidence, there are some general principles that underpin how a jury trial operates. The most important of these principles are the requirement for **majority decisions**, the concept of '**jury equity**' and the **duty of confidentiality**.

MAJORITY DECISIONS

In criminal trials, the normal number of jurors is 12. This number can, as a result of jurors being dismissed by the judge during the course of a trial, be as low as nine. The Criminal Justice Act 1967 abolished the long-standing tradition of unanimous judgments where all jurors had to agree to a verdict. This was a principle of long-standing with Lord Denning discussing a rather extreme example from the 14th century where a judge initially threatened a juror with imprisonment unless he agreed with the other 11 jurors.[67] It was not uncommon for jurors to be kept without basic necessities ('without meat, drink, fire or candle')[68] to ensure that a majority be reached. The current position, contained in s

---

61 Juries Act 1974 s 2(1).
62 Ibid. s 2(3).
63 Ibid. s 2(2).
64 This could include those passing in the street on which the court building is located.
65 Juries Act 1974 s 6(1).
66 Juries Act 1974 s 20.
67 Alfred Denning, *What Next in the Law?* (Butterworths 1982) 36.
68 Ibid. 37 citing Blackstone's Commentaries III, 375.

17 Juries Act 1974, is that majority verdicts are acceptable.[69] The change to majority decisions has led to the more efficient administration of justice but also sought to mitigate the risk of jury tampering (dealt with elsewhere in this chapter) and of juror bias. The underlying rationale of a jury *deliberating* is now secured in criminal proceedings by the requirement that majority, as opposed to unanimous, verdicts can only be accepted by the Crown Court where there have been at least two hours of deliberation.[70] In the case of a Guilty verdict, the numbers in agreement and in dissent must be read out in open court.[71] The removal of the requirement of unanimous verdicts was a significant change in policy and further demonstrates the significant evolution of the legal system over time.

'JURY EQUITY'

As has been mentioned previously, jury trials are still justified as a means of involving citizens in the administration of justice. The principle of 'jury equity' seeks to balance the administration of justice with individual conscience. The principle allows a jury to acquit a defendant despite the fact that the necessary *legal* ingredients of an offence is made out or despite the fact that a defence that is pleaded is not technically available to the defendant. In this way, and for more serious criminal offences, the cold law is injected with some sense of community morality, albeit the morality of a small proportion of society. The principle finds favour as early as the 17th century in *Bushel's Case*[72] where it was held that jurors, as sole finders of fact, could not be *punished* on the basis that they exercised judgment in coming to a conclusion (i.e. verdict) on those facts. It later developed into a more sophisticated ability for the jury to come to so-called perverse verdicts to acquit.

The principle of jury equity affords the rigidity of the law a certain degree of flexibility but only where that flexibility favours the defendant. This means that a judge can order an acquittal where a *legal* test necessary for conviction cannot be made out on the facts but cannot order a conviction. This has been recently reaffirmed in *Brandford*[73] with the Court of Appeal making it clear that any attempt to withdraw a defence from the jury should be handled carefully so as not to violate the principle that a judge cannot direct a jury to convict.

EXPLAINING AND ANALYSING THE LAW – JURY CONSCIENCE

Discovering the *actual* motives of a jury in acquitting (or convicting) a defendant is almost impossible due to the requirement of confidentiality in deliberations. However, it may be that the use of 'jury equity' is more likely to occur in two categories of case – where the case has a *political* dimension or where the jury is *empathetic* to the position of the defendant.

---

69 A minimum of ten with juries of 11 or 12 members. In cases of ten jurors, nine must agree.
70 Juries Act 1974 s 17(4).
71 Juries Act 1974 s 17(3).
72 *Bushel's Case* (1670) 124 ER 1006.
73 *R v Brandford* [2016] EWCA Crim 1794, [2017] 4 WLR 17 [49] citing *R v Wang (Cheong)* [2005] UKHL 9, [2005] 1 WLR 661.

On the political side the case of *R v Ponting*[74] is often cited as the leading example of a political acquittal in the face of overwhelming evidence of guilt. The sinking of the Argentinian warship – the *Belgrano* – was a particularly controversial development in the Falklands Crisis of the 1980s. Clive Ponting, a senior civil servant at the Ministry of Defence, sent governmental documents concerning the sinking of the *Belgrano* to a Labour MP. He was subsequently charged with an offence under the Official Secrets Act 1911. During the trial the judge made it clear to the jury that the elements of the offence had been made out (and were not in dispute) and that Ponting's attempt to rely upon a defence under the OSA was doomed to fail. Nonetheless the jury refused to convict and acquitted Ponting of the charge.

Jury equity also allows the law to be applied compassionately. For example, the case of Dr Biezanek[75] demonstrates how a jury can inject empathy into the rigid application of the law. Dr Biezanek was charged with various drugs offences – primarily possession with intent to supply and supply of cannabis (a controlled drug). At no point did Dr Biezanek deny the facts and so a conviction may be assumed to have been inevitable. However, the jury acquitted her of all charges. She had been supplying the drugs to her daughter to help manage a serious illness. Although we cannot know the basis of the acquittal it is widely believed (and reported by the press at the time) that in this case, as in others involving the provision of drugs for medical purposes, that the jury were sympathetic to the actions of a parent attempting to alleviate the suffering of a child.

When looked at from an *individual* level the principle of jury equity, as applied in the preceding cases seems, at the least, understandable and, at the most, laudable. It softens the hard edges of the law. However, it can cause confusion in the public's understanding of the purpose of a jury trial and also in the reporting of the outcomes of particular cases.

CONFIDENTIALITY OF DELIBERATION

In order to protect the discussions of jurors it is important that their deliberations are confidential. Equally, jurors ought to decide cases based on the evidence presented and not on matters (or prejudices) extraneous to the case.

The matter was traditionally governed by s 8 of the Contempt of Court Act 1981 which stated that it was 'a contempt of court to obtain, disclose or solicit any particulars of statements made, opinions expressed, arguments advanced or votes cast by members of a jury in the course of their deliberations in any legal proceedings'. This served to protect juror

---

74 R v Ponting [2015] Crim LR 318 (CA).

75 Reported in the public press – www.independent.co.uk/news/uk/drug-case-doctor-is-cleared-solicitor-calls-for-legal-reform-to-enable-gps-to-supply-cannabis-1511893.html.

deliberations but it also acted as a barrier to investigating jury deliberations and could make appealing against convictions on the basis of improper conduct by jurors very difficult.[76] There were a number of cases where it became increasingly difficult to justify the harsh line that s 8 drew in balancing juror and defendant rights, despite the efforts of the judiciary to distinguish between matters that fell within deliberations (which were covered by s 8) and those that were extraneous to it (which were not covered by s 8). The situation led some to question whether s 8 was compatible with Article 6 of the European Convention on Human Rights, which seeks to ensure that all accused are given a fair trial.

TAKING THINGS FURTHER – CASES ON CONFIDENTIALITY OF DELIBERATIONS

The website that accompanies this text takes some further examples of issues caused by the tensions inherent in determining the proper limits surrounding the confidentiality of juror deliberation.

Advances in technology and the advent of social media have led to increased access to information and this presents two particular challenges for jury trials. First, the internet can be a tempting place for jurors to perform additional 'research' into either the law or the lives of those who are subject to judicial proceedings. This challenge, which comes *at the time of* the trial, can lead jurors to try the case other than on the evidence admitted and presented to court. Second, social media in particular presents *post trial* risks in that jurors may be tempted to share information about the deliberations that they, and their fellow jurors, engaged in on online platforms.

Within the context of a rise of jurors investigating and researching the cases on which they sat the Law Commission published a report in 2013.[77] The recommendations of this report were adopted and enacted via the Criminal Justice and Courts Act 2015 which created a range of new criminal offences within the Juries Act 1974. These include:

- Jury research during the trial period[78]
- Sharing research with another juror[79]
- Jurors engaging in other prohibited conduct[80]
- Disclosing jury's deliberations[81] (other than in limited circumstances)[82]

---

76 *R v Mizra; R v Connor and Rollock* [2004] UKHL 2, [2004] 1 AC 1118.

77 Law Commission, *Contempt of Court: Juror Misconduct* (Law Comm No 340, 2013).

78 Juries Act 1974 s 20A.

79 Juries Act 1974 s 20B.

80 Juries Act 1974 s 20C – prohibited conduct means 'conduct from which it may reasonably be concluded that the person intends to try the issue otherwise than on the basis of the evidence presented in the proceedings on the issue.'

81 Juries Act 1974 s 20D.

82 Governed by ss 20E–G which essentially allows for disclosure to certain named bodies for the furtherance of justice.

In this way the legal position has sought to evolve to be responsive to changes in technology but this has not prevented some jurors from still acting in ways incompatible with their important role (as discussed later in this chapter).

This is again evidence of the legal system operating in a way that is dynamic with solutions to new problems finding their way into the law through a mix of technological advancement and real-life cases. In this instance the law is seeking to ensure the integrity of the system and to secure rights to a fair trial for those accused of serious crime, while punishing (or deterring) behaviours incompatible with these aims.

QUALIFICATION FOR JURY SERVICE

ELIGIBILITY

The eligibility criteria for serving on a jury have been simplified over time and are relatively straightforward to understand.[83] A person is qualified to serve, according to s 1 of the Juries Act 1974, provided that they:

- Are registered as an elector for local or parliamentary elections
- Are aged between 18 and 75[84]
- Have been ordinarily resident in the UK, Channel Islands or Isle of Man for five years or more since the age of 13
- Are not ineligible or disqualified

Partly in order to widen the potential pool of jurors, there is a statutory basis – in s 68 of the Criminal Justice and Courts Act 2015 – for increasing the upper age limit for those serving on a jury to 76.[85] At the time of writing, the provision has yet to be brought into force.

INELIGIBILITY

Despite the wide scope of s 1 of the Juries Act 1974, there has traditionally been reluctance for the legal system to allow those in certain professions to sit on a jury. Thus, barristers, solicitors, judges, magistrates, police officers and members of the clergy were, until 2004, ineligible to serve on a jury (along with peers, criminals and lunatics). The Criminal Justice Act 2003 s 321 swept away this whole category of ineligible persons and now only those who are 'mentally disordered' are ineligible for service.[86]

The reform of the law to increase the numbers eligible for jury service has not been without controversy. More particularly, the extension of eligibility to police officers, lawyers and others involved in the administration of justice has been subject to close judicial consideration and reconsideration in a number of subsequent cases. It is important to understand that the

83 Prior to 1972 a juror also had to be a homeowner, with the consequence that around 95% of women were ineligible to serve on a jury.
84 The upper age limit was changed from 70 to 75 by s 68 Criminal Justice and Courts Act 2015.
85 The provisions of the new CJCA 2015 would further amend the Juries Act 1974.
86 This change was the result of a recommendation out of Auld LJ in the *Review of Criminal Courts* (2001) Stationary Office.

inclusion of the preceding, previously ineligible categories was without statutory caveat or condition and so it would appear that Parliament had intended to include these jurors without reservation. As we shall see the courts have developed a more nuanced approach that looks very closely at the personal circumstances of certain jurors in assessing whether there is a risk of bias.

APPLYING AND ANALYSING THE LAW – ELIGIBILITY TO SIT

The issue of the interpretation of s 321 of the Criminal Justice Act 2003 came to the fore in the conjoined cases heard on appeal under the name of the lead appellant *Abdroikov*.[87] The case concerned three defendants who had been convicted by separate juries, each of which had included a person involved in the administration of justice. The jurors had been: a solicitor directly employed by the Crown Prosecution Service, a serving police officer with no prior involvement in or connection with the case being tried and, finally, a police officer who had served for a short period with another officer who was the victim in the case but there was no suggestion that they knew each other.

When the case reached the House of Lords on appeal against conviction, a split decision was reached. The majority allowed the appeal in the first and final case outlined previously. For the police officer who had served alongside the victim the majority found that, because the evidence was in dispute there was a real risk of the appearance of bias.[88] In the case of the CPS employee it was held that being a salaried employee of the prosecutor would call into question the appearance of an impartial jury.

The outcome in *Abdroikov* demonstrates that even unambiguous changes to the law, brought about by statute, do not automatically equate to certainty in the law. The development of the law has been controversial amongst academics and members of the judiciary. In *Abdroikov* itself Lord Rodger's dissent was critical of the majority view going so far as saying that the decisions would 'drive a coach and horses through Parliament's legislation'.[89] His view was that Parliament had acted unequivocally in extending the eligibility criteria and that the courts should follow this intention. Academic criticism has also focussed on the lack of certainty that *Abdroikov* has created following Parliament's attempt to extend the eligibility criteria.[90]

---

87 R v *Abdroikov* [2007] UKHL 37, [2007] 1 WLR 3538.
88 Applying the standard *Porter v Magill* [2001] UKHL 67, [2002] 2 AC 357 test for bias, namely 'the question is whether the fair-minded and informed observer, having considered the facts, would conclude that there was a real possibility that the tribunal was biased'.
89 Lord Rodger's dissenting judgment starts at paragraph 28 and continues to paragraph 43 of the *Abdroikof* judgment.
90 Nicola Lacey, Celia Wells and Oliver Quick, *Reconstructing Criminal Law* (4th edn CUP 2003); Terence Morris and Louis Blom-Cooper, *Fine Lines and Distinctions: Murder, Manslaughter and the Unlawful Taking of Human Life* (Waterside Press 2011).

DISQUALIFICATION

In addition to those who are ineligible to serve on a jury, there are also those who are disqualified from sitting on one. If such a person knows that s/he is disqualified but still sits on a jury then that person will have committed a criminal offence, punishable by a fine.[91] Table 12.1[92] contains details of those who are disqualified for life and those who are disqualified for ten years following certain events.

GROUNDS FOR EXCUSAL OR DEFERRAL

If an eligible person is called for jury service then that person is under a strict obligation to obey the summons. In the past there were broad and generous grounds for being excused from jury service, as of right. Members of Parliament, those aged over 65 and doctors were amongst those who would be granted automatic excusal if they so requested.[93] This system was changed by the Criminal Justice Act 2003 and now (limited provision for the armed forces aside)[94] the right to excusal is limited to those who have previously served in juries within the past two years.[95] The Central Summoning Bureau is also able to defer or offer discretionary excusal if a person can show that they have 'good reason'.[96]

The Lord Chancellor has issued statutory guidance, under s 9AA of the Juries Act 1974, on the application of principle of excusal and deferral.[97] The opening paragraph makes it clear that applications for excusal or deferral must be considered 'carefully, sympathetically and with regard to the individual circumstances of the applicant' but, perhaps more strikingly, the CSB should 'not hesitate to refuse a request if no "good reason" is given'.[98] This statement, so early in the guidance notes, reinforces the message that excusal should be exceptional. The guidance notes go on to say that deferral should be considered before excusal is granted, thereby ensuring that all selected persons have the opportunity to be summoned. This not only ensures that citizens are involved (irrespective of their initial wishes) but also means that they can be excused service for good reason.

The guidelines go on to give some indication of the sorts of application that would justify different responses. The following list outlines these situations and the responses:

- Insufficient understanding of English – *excusal* [para 6]
- Caring responsibilities – *deferral* in first instance [para 7]
- Beliefs (religious or secular) that are incompatible with jury service – *excusal* [para 8]

91 Juries Act 1974 s 20(5)(d).
92 Drawn from the Juries Act 1974 Schedule 1.
93 Juries Act 1974 s 9(1) (now repealed).
94 According to the government website, www.gov.uk, members of the armed forces (all three services) are ineligible for service if on full pay. However it appears that there is also an excusal provision which would cover other circumstances e.g. reserve if jury service would interfere with duties.
95 Juries Act 1974 s 8(1).
96 Juries Act 1974 ss 9A and 9AA.
97 HMCS, *Guidance for Summoning Officers When Considering Deferral and Excusal Applications* (2009).
98 Ibid. [1].

Table 12.1 Those Disqualified from Jury Service

Disqualified for life	Disqualified for ten years
A person who is on bail in criminal proceedings	Convicted of an offence under section 20A, 20B, 20C or 20D of the Juries Act 1974
Sentenced to imprisonment for life	Convicted of an offence under paragraph 5A, 5B, 5C or 5D of Schedule 6 to the Coroners and Justice Act 2009 (equivalent offences relating to jurors at inquests)
Sentenced to detention during her Majesty's pleasure or during the pleasure of the Secretary of State	Convicted of an offence under paragraph 2, 3, 4 or 5 of Schedule 2A to the Armed Forces Act 2006 (equivalent offences relating to members of the Court Martial)
Sentenced to imprisonment or detention for public protection	Served any part of a sentence of imprisonment or a sentence of detention
Sentenced to an extended sentence under section 226A, 226B, 227 or 228 of the Criminal Justice Act 2003 (including such a sentence imposed as a result of section 219A, 220, 221A or 222 of the Armed Forces Act 2006) or s 210A of the Criminal Procedure (Scotland) Act 1995	Had passed on him a suspended sentence of imprisonment or had made in respect of him a suspended order for detention
Sentenced to a term of imprisonment of five years or more or a term of detention of five years or more	Had made in respect of him a community order under section 177 of the Criminal Justice Act 2003, a community rehabilitation order, a community punishment order, a community punishment and rehabilitation order, a drug treatment and testing order or a drug abstinence
A person for the time being liable to be detained under the Mental Health Act 1983	
A person for the time being resident in a hospital on account of mental disorder as defined by the Mental Health Act 1983	
A person for the time being under guardianship under section 7 of the Mental Health Act 1983 or subject to a community treatment order under section 17A of that Act	
A person who lacks capacity, within the meaning of the Mental Capacity Act 2005, to serve as a juror	

- Participation in religious festivals – *deferral* [para 8]
- Geographical difficulties in getting to the court building – *an alternative court to be considered* [para 9]
- Holiday – *deferral* [para 10]
- Business reasons – will be 'looked at closely' but *excusal* only granted for 'unusual hardship' (e.g. small businesses) [para 11]
- Shift workers – *excusal* or *deferral* depending on context [para 12]
- Students and hardship for vacation workers – application to be treated *'sympathetically'* [para 13]
- Teachers and students during term time/during exam periods – *deferral* in first instance [para 14]
- Conflicting with other public duties – *deferral* [para 15]
- Members of Parliament and conflict parliamentary duties – *deferral* [para 16]
- Speaker of the House of Commons – *deferral* to a time when Parliament is not sitting [para 17]
- Those involved in the administration of justice and the judiciary can apply on the basis that they might be known to the parties – *deferral* or relocation to another court in the first instance [para 18]
- Additional consideration should be made to granting *excusal* when the application is from an employee of the prosecuting authorities, serving police officers in locality or serving prison officers [para 18]
- Members of the Armed Forces where the Commanding Officer certifies that the absence would affect operational efficiency – *excusal* or *deferral* to be considered [para 19]
- Work commitments – *deferral* in the first instance [para 20]
- Physical disability making attendance difficult – treated *sympathetically for excusal* [para 21]

The very detailed guidance, just touched upon, makes it very clear that every effort will be made to accommodate jury service through deferral before an excusal is to be considered. The normal position is that a person should apply in advance of appearing at court but it is possible for a person to request excusal or deferral at the court in person.[99]

FROM SUMMONS TO SERVING

Once at the court building, the potential jurors are split into groups of between 15 and 50. There is no set number to this part of the process but larger groups are often used where a case is likely to take more than two weeks, as this gives plenty of scope for non-selection on the basis of other commitments. If a trial is likely to take many weeks or months, then the judge will question the availability of the jury for this period of time.[100] An official of the court will then randomly select, via names written on paper, 12 persons to sit in that particular case and the remaining people are returned to the pool for selection in

---

99 The Consolidated Criminal Practice Direction – Criminal Procedure Rules IV.42.1.
100 Criminal Practice Direction IV.42.2.

another case.[101] The prosecution and, in more limited circumstances, defence then have the opportunity to challenge the selection of the jury as a whole or of individual jurors. Challenges are discussed in more detail later. The jurors are then sworn in (by oath or affirmation) to 'try the defendant and give a true verdict according to the evidence'.[102]

CHALLENGES

During the process of jury selection, and before the jurors are sworn in, both the defence and prosecution have the opportunity to challenge membership of a particular jury under the conditions that follow.

CHALLENGING THE ARRAY

Under a challenge to the array, it is possible for the membership of the *whole panel of jurors* in a particular case to be put in question. The Juries Act 1974 permits such a challenge on the basis that the person responsible for summoning the jurors is biased or has acted in an improper way in the execution of this duty.[103] Given that the selection is now largely produced centrally by random selection from a database, the scope for bias or improper conduct is greatly reduced. The effect of this is that challenges on this ground are very rare.[104]

CHALLENGE FOR CAUSE

The Juries Act 1974 gives both the prosecution and the defence the opportunity to challenge individual jurors for cause. The Act indicates that alleging that a juror is disqualified is a potential ground for review but otherwise is silent on the potential other 'causes' that may apply, stating only that 'nothing in this Act affects the law relating to challenge of jurors'.[105]

In addition to disqualification, the other major ground for establishing 'cause' to challenge is that the juror is biased. The test for bias is that which is well-established in public law by Lord Hope's statement in *Porter v Magill*: 'The question is whether the fair-minded and informed observer, having considered the facts, would conclude that there was a real possibility that the tribunal was biased.'[106] As the *deliberations* of the jury are not admissible evidence in an appeal, determining whether there is a real possibility that a juror (or entire jury) is biased can be difficult. As a challenge for cause must happen before a juror is sworn in, it is unlikely that a challenge for cause on the basis of bias will be successful unless such bias is manifest and obvious from the outset.

---

101 Twelve is the normal size of the jury, but a trial may continue with a lesser number provided that number does not fall below nine.

102 The Consolidated Criminal Practice Direction – Criminal Procedure Rules IV.42.4.

103 Juries Act 1974 s 12(6).

104 For example, the most recent but ultimately unsuccessful attempt at such a challenge came from the British Virgin Islands in *Director of Public Prosecutions of the Virgin Islands v William Penn* [2008] UKPC 29. There has not been a reported challenge to the array from within the English Legal System for more than 20 years.

105 Juries Act 1974 s 12(4).

106 *Porter v Magill* [2001] UKHL 67, [2002] 2 AC 357 [103] (Lord Hope).

ANALYSING THE LAW – DEALING WITH BIAS

Based solely on the preceding reasoning, it is possible to criticise the English Legal System's approach to challenge for cause as being too restrictive. By considering challenges for cause *in isolation* it would appear that there is the opportunity for biased, or even disqualified, jurors to sit and taint the whole process of jury trial.

However, when a broader view is given to the criminal justice system it soon becomes apparent that there are *other* safeguards to prevent this injustice from happening. This is because challenge for cause is only *one step* in the trial process. It is more common, but that does not mean that it happens frequently, that potential for bias becomes apparent during the course of a trial. For example, in *Pintori*[107] it was emphasised that a juror working with officers called as witnesses in a case may have the appearance of bias and should not have sat on the jury.[108] This meant that the conviction was unsafe and the appeal was allowed.

It is possible to draw out from the preceding an important lesson of more general application when studying the English Legal System. It is often easy to take a single element of the system, such as 'the jury', or even an aspect of that element 'challenges to the jury' and to subject it to intense scrutiny. Indeed, any form of legal study will encourage this sort of critical analysis. However, it is always important to remember the 'bigger picture' (i.e. where this 'piece' fits in the broader machinery of the legal system. One of the hallmarks of success is to take an issue or area of law and balance the detailed analysis against a more general framework. Achieving that balance well provides for more convincing and sophisticated assessment answers.

There is a further important qualification on a challenge for cause. This is that neither party is entitled to ask questions of the jurors before making the challenge. This means that unless a juror is known to the defence or prosecution, it will be extremely difficult to know whether there is or is not cause. In this regard the prosecution sometimes has a distinct advantage over the defendant due to the (controversial) practice of jury vetting.

STAND BY (AND JURY VETTING)

Stand by is available to the prosecution only. Technically this is a completely open challenge but is, in reality, reserved to cases where 'jury vetting' has occurred. As such, it is subject to tight controls (discussed later) from the Attorney General.

As a point of principle, and to qualify the discussion that follows, it is important that some form of 'vetting' of potential jurors is possible. For example, it is now routine for there to

---

107 [2007] EWCA Crim 1700, [2007] Crim LR 997.
108 Ibid. [24].

be a Disclosure and Barring Service (DBS) check of all jurors to ensure that they are not disqualified by virtue of their own past criminality.[109] This saves relying on the potential jurors' own assessment as to eligibility to serve and prevents trials from taking place that include disqualified jurors. This is perfectly acceptable and is part of administering justice in an efficient manner. It is investigations conducted by the state into jurors that go *beyond* a DBS check that are anathema to the principles of jury trial.

In the 1970s it became clear that certain additional checks had, in certain cases, been taking place into the backgrounds of particular jurors to ensure that they did not hold views that would make them unsuitable for jury service. This came to light following the so-called ABC trial concerning the Official Secrets Act 1911. These additional, and covert, checks were controversial because one of the core principles of trial by jury is that state interference was reduced by selecting from a large and open pool of jurors and that the grounds for ineligibility had been set down by statute.[110]

Again we see the legal system attempting to balance competing interests as an argument could be made that additional checks are conducive to the administration of justice in certain cases, for example ones concerning national security or terrorist activities. To allow for proper accountability for the use of additional checks, the process of jury vetting is now subject to guidance and personal approval from the Attorney General following a request of the Director of Public Prosecutions.[111] The cases in which the Attorney General would authorise a challenge as a result of vetting are restricted to those cases of great public importance (i.e. not routine cases). The justification for cases of national security is that the evidence may be given in camera[112] and that certain jurors may put at risk the sensitive nature of the material. The second justification is that, in such cases, there is a real risk to the administration of justice if a juror were themselves to hold extreme views that created such bias that they could jeopardise the case.

JUROR BEHAVIOUR

Before departing from the jury it is important to consider juror behaviour in a slightly broader sense. Lord Denning – speaking extrajudicially – once harked back to the 19th century as 'the golden age of trial by jury'[113] and lamented the wider selection in place during his time on the bench, going so far as to suggest that jury service should require an interview

---

109 A process that has received judicial endorsement – *Mason* [1981] QB 881 (CA).
110 Lord Denning was particularly scathing of any attempt to 'vet' jurors beyond the basic statutory grounds of disqualification in *R v Sheffield Crown Court Ex parte Brownlow* [1980] QB 530 (CA) holding that, in his view it was 'unconstitutional for the police authorities to engage in "jury vetting"' at 542.
111 Issued first in 1989 as 'Attorney General's Guidelines on Exercise by the Crown of Its Right of Stand-by' (1989) 88 Criminal Appeal Reports 123 and updated in 2012 – https://www.gov.uk/guidance/jury-vetting-right-of-stand-by-guidelines--2.
112 In private and not as part of an open, public process.
113 Alfred Denning, *What Next in the Law* (Butterworths 1982) 46. It is worth noting that all jurors at that time were male, middle class and householders.

and references.[114] This is very far away from a random, peer-based system intended to generate the absolute minimum of 'state interference' necessary for the proper administration of justice.[115]

Jurors doing strange or inappropriate things as part of the trial process is rare but not unknown. Most trials are conducted entirely appropriately and with a jury acting with the propriety and earnestness we would expect.[116] However, there are occasions where the behaviour of jurors lays bare the broader criticism of involving ordinary citizens in the most serious criminal trials.[117] The brief examples that follow are intended to highlight some of the challenges faced by the justice system but should not be 'over read' as requiring, of themselves, a fundamental rethink of the role of juries.

The case of Young[118] provides a startlingly bleak examination of the challenges posed by jury trials. Stephen Young had been convicted on two counts of murder. He appealed against his conviction when it came to light that four jurors, in the hotel accommodation provided between two days of their deliberations, had constructed and consulted a Ouija board in order to commune with the spirit world and speak with one of the deceased victims. He alleged that this demonstrated that his conviction had not been based on the evidence presented and was successful in his appeal. The case also demonstrates the difficulties caused by the old s 8 of the Contempt of Court Act 1981 inasmuch as the court could only investigate the claim because it had not happened in the jury room as part of the deliberations but in the hotel between sessions. Had the jurors undertaken this course of action *during* deliberations in the jury room then s 8 would have prevented an investigation of the conduct of the jury by the Court of Appeal.

ANALYSING THE LAW – JUROR BEHAVIOUR AND THE INTERNET

There is no doubt that advancements in technology (as discussed previously) bring with them new forms of idiocy and challenge. What might once have been private folly[119] can now be laid bare for all to see. This takes two distinct forms – the use of social media and the use of the internet to search for material relating to the case.[120]

---

114 Ibid. 76 where he said – 'Nowadays virtually every member of the population is qualified to sit as a juror. No matter how illiterate or uneducated or unsuitable he may be. And where the changes, by sheer weight of numbers, are loaded heavily against the jurors being the sensible and responsible members of the community.'

115 And could be said to be inconsistent with his strong (judicial) criticism of state interference in the selection of jurors in *Ex parte Brownlow* discussed earlier in relation to jury vetting.

116 And, as discussed in Chapter 7, the judiciary is not immune from lapses in judgment.

117 Including the juror who was jailed for feigning illness on the fifth day of a trial when, in truth, they had gone to watch a theatre production – www.bbc.co.uk/news/uk-england-manchester-16288257.

118 *R v Young* [1995] QB 324 (CA).

119 But not more acceptable for it.

120 Littered throughout the case reports, there are plenty of examples of such conduct – *R v Thompson* [2010] EWCA Crim 1623, [2011] 1 WLR 200;

To take an example of the first, in the case of *Fraill*[121] the juror communicated with an acquitted defendant over text message, despite the fact that they were still hearing the trial of a co-defendant. Whilst some instances of juror impropriety are a result of naïve ignorance, this juror was well aware of the risks to the trial that they were posing as the following was admitted in evidence in her contempt hearing – 'pleeeeeese dont say anyhting cause jamie they could call mmiss trial and i will get 4cked to0.'[122] Social media also proved to be the undoing of Kasim Davey who expressed inappropriate views about his role as a juror in a child sex offence case and was sentenced to two months in prison.[123]

For an example of the second, the new range of offences relating to jury research (discussed previously) have started to bite in more recent times. The first case to consider these new offences involved the conviction for contempt of Theodora Dallas for sharing information with other jurors about the defendant's prior involvement in a rape case when hearing a case about grievous bodily harm. The case eventually made its way to the European Court of Human Rights where the UK was found not to have violated Dr Dallas's rights by prosecuting her for contempt.[124] A more recent example came in the form of *Stoddart*[125] where a juror was convicted of contempt for researching the previous criminal history of a defendant in a burglary trial.

THE WEBSITE

The website that accompanies this textbook contains many useful resources that you can use to consolidate and further your knowledge of the law, to hone your skills of critical analysis and to test your knowledge. This includes a set of multiple choice questions (MCQs) that can be used to test your knowledge and understanding of the material.

PODCASTS

- The podcasts provide a summary of the area under study, bringing together the key themes and threads of analysis into a 'mini-lecture'.
- There will also be an explanation and analysis of topical and up-to-date issues related to juries.

121 *Attorney General v Fraill* [2011] EWHC 1629 (Admin), [2011] 2 Cr App R 21.
122 Ibid. [16].
123 *Attorney General v Davey* [2013] EWHC 2317 (Admin), [2014] 1 Cr App R 1 where Davey had said: 'Woooow I wasn't expecting to be in a jury Deciding a paedophile's fate, I've always wanted to Fuck up a paedophile & now I'm within the law!' at [6].
124 *Dallas v United Kingdom* (2016) 63 EHRR 13.
125 *Solicitor General v Stoddart* [2017] EWHC 1361 (QB).

CHAPTER 13
ADMINISTRATIVE JUSTICE AND THE TRIBUNAL SYSTEM

INTRODUCTION

Administrative Justice unfortunately seldom has the same appeal to the average student of the English Legal System as Criminal Justice. Even Civil Justice casts more rays of glamour (where defamation may be found in the Queen's Bench and celebrity divorce in the Family Court). However, Administrative Justice is of fundamental importance to the proper functioning of the legal system and provides access to less expensive forms of specialist justice (in the form of tribunals) and allows individuals to challenge the unlawful actions of the government and its agencies. Administrative Justice reinforces the separation of powers by allowing the judiciary to perform an important check on executive action.

Many of the most significant judgments to be handed down in English courts over the last 100 years have been on the basis of the processes and principles of administrative law. Although generally it is the criminal cases that are raised in the public consciousness through the press, the ruling by the Supreme Court in September 2019 that the Prime Minister had acted unlawfully in advising the Queen to prorogue Parliament gained widespread coverage.[1]

AS YOU READ

Much of this chapter is concerned with the different ways in which cases heard by our judges are distributed between the Administrative Court and the Tribunals Service, and in giving more detailed information on the process by which this is done and how the system works in general. Particular attention is given in relation to the Tribunals Service which is relatively new, but as already mentioned, is likely to have a closer relationship to the life of the student than the Administrative Court, in which it is unlikely that many will be quickly going for judicial review or requiring *habeas corpus*. It is important that, as you read, **you do more than just memorise** this information.

As you read, **consider critically** the purpose of the structures that you read about and **compare** how they contrast with other court-based actions. Also **evaluate** the distribution of power that results from Administrative Justice.

---

1   R (on the application of Miller) v The Prime Minister; Cherry and Others (Respondents) v Advocate General for Scotland [2019] UKSC 41, [2019] 3 WLR 589.

It is also important that you view administrative law in action and you can achieve this by visiting the tribunals and **comparing** the descriptions here with the real-life workings. A visit to the Employment Tribunal is a good place to start as the subject matter of the cases is often relatable and easy to follow.

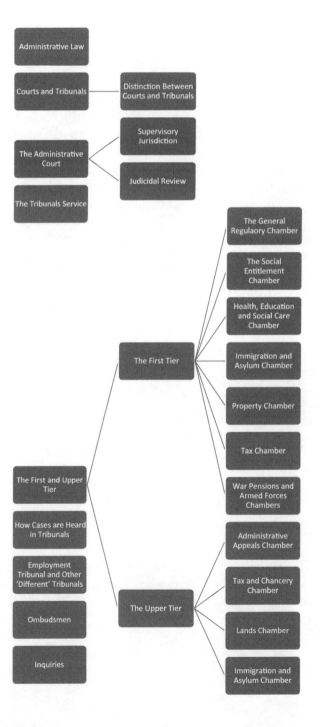

Figure 13.1

ADMINISTRATIVE LAW AND JUSTICE

Administrative law is the field of law that a trainee or newly qualified solicitor might be likely to come into contact with even more so than with either of the mainstream areas of civil or criminal justice, since 'Administrative Justice' refers to areas of law which are more common in the lives of the individual citizen than either civil or criminal justice. This is because this term 'Administrative Justice' has several meanings. It can mean:

1   The mechanisms for reviewing the decisions of those who exercise public powers, in order to ensure that they are lawful. The most obvious of these mechanisms are judicial review and the prerogative writs (now called 'orders') such as *habeas corpus* (an ancient remedy requiring production and/or release from any form of potentially unjustified detention). These actions were historically assigned to the Administrative Court and are thus a contemporary function of the Divisional Court of the Queen's Bench Division.[2]
2   The work of the 70 plus administrative tribunals on which the Leggatt Review reported in 2001, and which have since been reformed and their work enlarged by the Tribunals, Courts and Enforcement Act 2007. In this sense the term covers a huge field of law administered in tribunals by a much greater number of judges than populate the mainstream courts.
3   The other mechanisms for administrative accountability including the work of ombudsmen and inquiries.

These overlapping forms for raising and resolving disputes between individuals and states all have – at their heart – the same core purpose of attempting to hold an increasingly large range of public bodies to account for their exercise of public powers (see Figure 13.2). When taken together they provide an effective and robust system of accountability that is stronger and more effective than would be possible in a system based entirely on court action.

Judicial review is the most formal and legalistic of the methods of accountability and can incur great cost (emotional and financial) and take a long time to resolve. The tribunals were intended to provide (less) formal methods for resolving disputes within specialised tribunals that can deal with often technical decisions within cognate subject areas. The tribunals are expected to deal with cases at pace and at such volume that would prove difficult for the generalist courts. It is important to recognise that the Courts Service and Tribunals are part of a unified system of Her Majesty's Courts and Tribunals Service (HMCTS) but within which courts and tribunals still keep their distinct functions: whereby judges in the courts always *determine* cases and their role is exclusively *judicial*, but technically it seems the tribunal judiciary's functions are partly judicial and partly administrative, which is why the separate tribunal system was set up in the first place because their partly administrative functions were considered unsuitable for the court process.

---

2   See Chapter 8 on court structure.

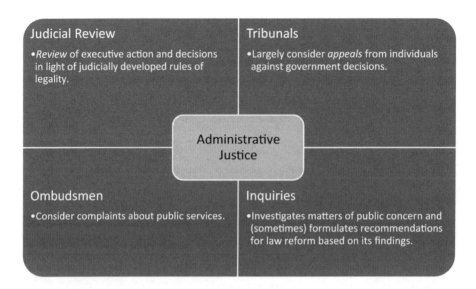

Figure 13.2 The Elements of Administrative Justice

In the course of this 2007 reorganisation, the numbers and remits of the various pre 2007 tribunals have been expanded to around 100 tribunals dealing with ever more numerous jurisdictions, resolving disputes between government ministries and the citizen and between other non-government organisations and the individual. Accordingly, while the distinguished 19th-century jurist A V Dicey considered[3] that there was no such thing as a separate corpus of Administrative Justice outside the common law (which was arguably incorrect even at that time, since there were still the first category of cases heard by the QBD Divisional Court), this could not logically be said now, in view of the wide and more recently expanded tribunals' jurisdiction.

Ombudsmen are used widely and where the questions are not necessarily *legal* or in need of 'determination' by a court and are often linked to levels and quality of 'service' provided by important public bodies, such as the Parliamentary and Health Service Ombudsmen, or private service Ombudsman like the Pensions Ombudsman or the Legal Services Ombudsman. The use of an Ombudsman is important where actions falling below a certain quality standard may not necessarily be *unlawful* but, nonetheless, should be capable of readdress – this is often termed 'maladministration'. The present Ombudsman service in the UK had its origins in an influential 1961 report of the All Party law reform society JUSTICE, The Citizen and His Council, which when followed by three further reports not only resulted in the establishment of UK Ombudsman services, but facilitated the developing Dispute Resolution services which generated the spread of mediation in the 1990s; the importance of such key Ombudsman influence was recognised by the judicial mediation movement in Europe (founded as the European Association of Judges for Mediation (GEMME) in 2003), of which the Ombudsman of the three Scandinavian countries were early members.

----

3   In *Introduction to the Study of the Law of the Constitution* (1885) (10th edn. Macmillan 1959).

Finally, inquiries can be used to ensure that 'public scandals' or 'public tragedies' can be properly investigated and *recommendations* made to prevent recurrence.

MAKING CONNECTIONS – PUBLIC LAW
+ +

This chapter only sketches out the main institutions, functions and principles of Administrative Justice and does not seek to subject them to a comprehensive or exhaustive treatment. This is because this area of law properly falls under the label of 'public law' being concerned as it is with the control of exercise of state power. If you go on to study 'public law' in greater detail then you will need to consider these institutions and structures more fully. Our purpose here is simply to draw attention to the features of Administrative Justice as they appear most relevant to the English Legal System.

The remainder of this chapter will explain the structures of each of these methods of achieving 'Administrative Justice' and some consideration will be given to their effectiveness.

COURTS AND TRIBUNALS

The post-2007 reforms and the unified HMCTS have in no way sought to blur the distinction between the courts and the tribunals, but merely to bring both forms of formal dispute resolution under the umbrella of one government department, that of the Ministry of Justice. While in general terms the civil and criminal courts continue to deal with court based civil and criminal justice, the tribunals deal with decisions in the fields of central and local government administration and regulation, which have always been regarded as less suited to the court process: such as decisions in relation to social security and welfare benefits, housing and town & country planning, education, employment and numerous other everyday concerns likely to touch a citizen's life, even down to the detail of the regulation of buses, coaches and heavy goods vehicles and of estate agents and consumer credit, all of which have their post-2007 slot in the Tribunals Service.

There are thus, as identified previously, two distinct types of Administrative Justice for us to examine that are based on the exercise of a judicial function: (1) the classic public law element which is an extension of the courts' jurisdiction and is dealt with in the Administrative Court, which includes judicial review of actions of public bodies and officials, including inferior courts (such as appeals on cases stated in Magistrates Courts and use of the prerogative writs) and of the decisions of local councils and members of the executive, and even including those of individual government ministers[4] although the prerogative writs

---

4   For example, *R v Secretary of State for the Home Office ex p Fire Brigades Union* [1995] 2 AC 513, [1995] 2 WLR 464 (HL) where the Home Secretary changed the payment rates for criminal injuries by introducing a new tariff when he should have replaced the former non-statutory scheme by legislation as intended by Parliament in the Criminal Justice Act 1988 and not to do so was an abuse of power.

cannot be used against the Crown, and (2) the numerous specialised government agencies and other organisations which deal through the Tribunals Service with all these everyday sectors of the framework of modern life which the citizen usually calls our personal 'admin'.

Category (1) has already been encountered in the chapters on civil and criminal justice and the court structure, which is why the reader is signposted back to those chapters.

Category (2), dealt with in the tribunals, which have existed for around 200 years, is therefore probably more deserving of the name 'Administrative Justice' than (1), which is still mostly dealt with in the High Court within the court system, since the tribunals were originally set up to deal specifically with administrative matters in relation to the public, thus providing greater accessibility for the public than to the courts which were not originally created or later adapted to deal with the public other than through their lawyers.[5] Unfortunately, the general public often thinks that hearings in the 'Tribunals Service' are as much 'courts' as those in the 'Courts Service', especially since the two have been unified within the MOJ as 'HMCTS'.

The first tribunals were, however, set up for dealing with such technical matters as tax (late 18th and early 19th century) and later in the 19th century to deal with issues in connection with the large numbers of Irish labourers employed to dig the canals and build the railways. Nowadays the successors to these original tribunals still have a place in the post-2007 tribunals system, which now provides a modern tax jurisdiction, serviced by Tax Judges, in the Tax Chamber, whereas the successors to the 19th-century tribunal regulating the canal and railway workers are to be found in the Transport lists, serviced by Transport Judges, in the General Regulatory Chamber of the First Tier of the Tribunals Service and the Administrative Appeals Chamber of the Upper Tier: these two Chambers deal with appeals from the national network of Traffic Commissioners who regulate the road haulage and bus and coach industries and also allied jurisdictions such as appeals in relation to driving instructors' qualifications, which go to the First Tier General Regulatory Chamber.

Disputes in employment of all sorts have now achieved their own tribunal, the Employment Tribunal which has its own Employment Appeal Tribunal, and these two tribunals sit under what is called a 'separate pillar', distinct from the main framework of the rest of the Tribunals Service. The Employment Tribunal is mentioned here for the sake of completeness but is not (formally) part of the system of Administrative Justice, concerned as it is with the private disputes of labour contracts. Employment Tribunals share many of the features or perceived benefits of the other tribunals – such as ease of access, ability to deal effectively with high volumes of cases while maintaining specialism and all in a (relatively) inexpensive and less formal way than is possible from within the court environment.

---

5   Which is one reason why the present influx of litigants in person (LIPs) causes so many problems for both LIPs and
     court judiciary, see e.g. per Black LJ in Lindner v Rawlins [2015] EWCA Civ 61 where the respondent husband, a busi-
     nessman who was not a lawyer, got the law wrong, leaving the Court to research the law he should have relied on, and
     which counsel representing him would have known and already submitted to the court.

DISTINCTION BETWEEN COURTS AND TRIBUNALS

Despite the formal unification of courts and tribunals within HMCTS, courts and tribunals do thus remain distinct, and although originally tribunals were intended to be sufficiently informal[6] (providing accessibility to the public without lawyers) this has not really been maintained since many tribunals have become formalistic and technical e.g. the Employment Tribunal, which hears cases about employees' pay and conditions of work and unfair and discriminatory dismissal. Moreover, all tribunals now have some rules, formal or informal, plus some recognised 'practices' which bring their processes ever closer to those of the courts. Nevertheless, the present Senior President of Tribunals, Sir Ernest Ryder, who has a background as a judge in the North West of England, is extremely proactive in bringing the latest skills to the tribunals under his supervision, including recognising that tribunals have the historic purpose of dealing directly with people who will not necessarily have lawyers, and in promoting dispute resolution methodology to the Tribunal Service jurisdiction e.g. by encouraging the use of mediation or other DR methods before resorting to hearings.[7]

The word 'tribunal' is also sometimes used in a general dictionary definition sense in relation not to a tribunal in the Tribunals Service sense but to a *court*, and the reader must look out for this meaning in other contexts e.g. when in a glossary or dictionary a tribunal is defined as 'a body appointed to adjudicate in some matter or to inquire into some disputed question': this would clearly cover courts as well as tribunals, also for example professional conduct committees and indeed arguably many other self-regulatory committees, whether having a judicial or administrative function. This is compounded by the fact that some tribunals (such as the one dealing with immigration and asylum) sit in places that look very much like courts, while others are much less formal. Thus 'tribunal' has both a general and a legal definition, in the latter case defining its position in relation to the framework of the English Legal System.

Some cases may be found in the reports where the distinction between courts and tribunals has been debated, and it seems that does not depend on the name given to the body in question, e.g. *AG v BBC*[8] where the House of Lords decided that a 'local valuation court' was not a court, even though it had the word 'court' in its title, and in *General Medical Council v BBC*,[9] the Court of Appeal held that the Professional Conduct Committee of the GMC was not a court (the point of these decisions being that generally for a person to be found 'in contempt of court' within the meaning of the Contempt of Court Act 1981, s/he must have been in a *court*). Rather confusingly the Employment Appeal Tribunal (EAT) is a *court* for the purpose of the Contempt of Court Act. This is a good example of the well-known maxim that Parliament is 'supreme' and can enact anything it decides to – in detailing the composition and functions of the modern Employment Tribunals in the Employment Tribunals Act 1996 as amended it, *inter alia*, decided the EAT was a *court*. This can make the study of this area quite difficult but one of the features of the English Legal System is its constant evolution and readiness to accept bodies for what they *are* rather than just what they are labelled to be.

---

6 Particularly in relation to processes and rules of evidence.
7 His address to the joint Academics' Conference of the Civil Mediation and Family Mediation Councils, October 2017.
8 [1980] 3 All ER 161, HL.
9 [1998] 3 All ER 426, CA.

THE ADMINISTRATIVE COURT

It will be remembered from perusal of the chapters on the court structure[10] and criminal justice[11] that the Divisional Court of the Queen's Bench Division has one important distinctive function as a court for hearing of judicial review, certain statutory appeals and cases of *habeas corpus* and other historic remedies, and as such is the most important of the Divisional Courts of the QBD. It is based in London, besides in other major provincial cities, i.e. Birmingham, Cardiff, Leeds and Manchester. The court has a website which explains its functions, which include declaring 'vexatious litigants', i.e. those who needlessly and irritatingly pursue groundless litigation which is inappropriate in some way, and stopping them from taking any legal proceedings without permission: www.gov.uk/courts-tribunals/administrative-court.

The Divisional Court of the Queen's Bench Division is thus distinct from the other three QBD Divisional Courts already mentioned in the chapter on court structure (Chapter 8), as it is the court for the purpose of hearing applications for judicial review, statutory appeals and *habeas corpus* and similar suits protective of the liberty of the subject. When it exercises these functions it is known by the separate name of the 'Administrative Court' and you will sometimes see reports of cases heard in it in *The Times* Law Reports, or of course in other reports series.

SUPERVISORY JURISDICTION OVER OTHER COURTS, TRIBUNALS AND AUTHORITIES

The Senior Courts Act 1981 s 28A gives the court jurisdiction in 'case stated' on points of law from the Magistrates Court, and both Magistrates and County Court are subject to the supervisory prerogative[12] jurisdiction of the High Court. These cases and use of the orders of *mandamus* (now called a 'mandatory order'), *certiorari* (now called a 'quashing order') and prohibition (now called a 'prohibiting order') are normally heard in the Administrative Court. Also, for example, pursuant to the Senior Courts Act 1981 s 29(3), the High Court can quash any decision of the County Court if it has exceeded its jurisdiction and the same is true of Magistrates' decisions. These functions may be carried out by a single judge or by a divisional court of two or three judges, and if such a court is constituted the chair of the three justices is likely to be a Lord Justice of Appeal who normally sits in the Court of Appeal.

The writ of *habeas corpus* (which still goes by this old Latin name which means 'you have the body' of the individual sought for production from detention) can be obtained from a single judge, sometimes even over the telephone.

The court also has some supervisory jurisdiction over coroners under the Coroners Act 1988.

---

10 Chapter 8.
11 Chapter 11.
12 So called as they used to be the way that sovereigns controlled the actions of their officials which is why they cannot be used against the Crown but can be against individual ministers who are servants of the Crown.

JUDICIAL REVIEW

This used to be a prime function of the Administrative Court when judicial review became a growth industry from the late 1980s e.g. in human rights, immigration and asylum, which produced a large number of such reviews, particularly in the field of immigration and asylum. These have more recently reduced significantly since immigration appeals were transferred to the Upper Tribunal Chamber for Immigration and Asylum in November 2013.

Grounds for judicial review enable a person with a sufficient interest in the matter to be brought to the court to ask a judge to review the lawfulness of:

1 Any enactment short of an Act of Parliament[13]
2 A decision, action or failure to act by someone with responsibility to exercise a public function

MAKING CONNECTIONS – SEPARATION OF POWERS
+++

Judicial review is not about assessing the *merits* of the original decision but its *lawfulness*. It is also not an *appeal* against the decision but, as the name suggests, a *review*. It will be remembered that a core theme of this text is about the distribution of powers within the English Legal System, something that was explored in Chapter 3 in terms of the institutions. Judicial review distributes powers towards the judiciary (and legislature)[14] at the expense of the executive. This helps to explain why the government is keen to curb the powers of the court in relation to judicial review, often under the guise of cost savings or the burden of judicial review to public services.[15]

By not entering into discussions about the *merits* of decisions and restricting the analysis to lawfulness, we can see that the court is attempting to abide by the principles of separation of powers by not *becoming* the decision-maker but rather adjudicating on the lawful basis of the decision. This is an important 'check' on the powers of the executive and not only bolsters the courts' position within the legal system but ensures that Parliament's will in passing legislation enabling the use of public powers is not misused.

13 In the English Legal System it is impossible for the court to review the lawfulness of an Act of Parliament, which is to be contrasted with other jurisdictions (such as the United States of America) where courts may be able to call into question the legality of primary legislation.
14 The court is often keen to stress that it is undertaking its judicial review function in a way that is compatible with and protective and respectful of parliamentary sovereignty – see R (on the application of Miller) v The Prime Minister; Cherry and Others v Advocate General for Scotland [2019] UKSC 41, [2019] 3 WLR 589 [41] and R (on the application of UNISON) v Lord Chancellor [2017] UKSC 51, [2017] 3 WLR 409 at [68].
15 https://consult.justice.gov.uk/digital-communications/judicial-review.

The fault or flaw complained of may be either procedural or substantive. 'Procedural' in this instance means not following an appropriate procedure set down for the purpose or context, or failure to observe natural justice, e.g. not allowing one side to make representations. 'Substantive' means doing something unauthorised, but also includes making an unreasonable decision, such as in *Associate Provincial Picture House v Wednesbury Corporation*,[16] the case which gave its name to the principle of 'Wednesbury unreasonableness' because of the fact that in that case Lord Greene established the potential for challenging a discretionary decision because it was plainly unreasonable.

This was later confirmed by Lord Diplock in *Council of Civil Service Union v Minister for the Civil Service*[17] where he took Lord Greene's concept further, articulating the grounds more clearly – to include illegality, irrationality and procedural *impropriety*, rather than simply not following an appropriate procedure – and also including *proportionality* between the decision challenged and the purpose for which it is made.

This means that in judicial review cases the doctrine of proportionality requires a reasonable relationship between the decision and its objectives, so the decision should be no harsher on the individual's rights than strictly necessary to achieve the objective which generated it. This is not a new idea now, though it might have been in 1984, and has echoes in the proportionate approach of the European Convention on Human Rights (ECHR), which has become reflected in some aspects of national law in England and Wales[18] and indeed in European law generally. However it was a controversial idea at the time although supported by Lord Slynn in *R v Secretary of State for the Environment, Transport and the Regions ex p Holding and Barnes plc*,[19] although Lord Reed in the Supreme Court in *R (on the application of Lumsdon) v Legal Aid Board*[20] was still insisting that the principle of proportionality in EU law which has crept into some English law is not the same as that applied in the ECtHR under the ECHR.

Nevertheless, proportionality is clearly a concept which has a place in judicial review, indeed sometimes entirely appropriately used against the applicant by the judiciary, for example in *Frank Cowl & Others v Plymouth City Council*[21] in which an application was brought against the Council for JR of their decision to close a residential home for the elderly whereas they had already said they would consider the matter within a statutory complaints scheme. Lord Woolf criticised this overuse of JR in court as opposed to the obvious advantage of out of court dispute resolution.

------

16 [1947] 1 KB 223 (HL).

17 [1985] AC 374 (HL).

18 For example under the Children Act 1989, in which the imposition of a care or supervision order requires the court to choose the least intrusive into family life if at all possible, i.e. the much lighter supervision order under s 35 (where the child remains at home under the supervision of the designated supervisor) rather than the more restrictive care order under s 33, where parental responsibility (and the right to override parents' decisions if necessary) will be acquired by the local authority,

19 [2001] UKHL 23, [2003] 2 AC 295.

20 [2015] UKSC 41, [2016] AC 697.

21 [2001] EWCA Civ 1935, [2002] 1 WLR 803.

It seems that overactive use of JR may have had some contribution to make to the decision to expand the Tribunals Service jurisdictions, see next section. However the judiciary have been keen to preserve their control over both courts and tribunals, and attempts in drafting to exclude JR have not succeeded as they tend to have been interpreted to exclude other appeals (where, for example, a provision states that a decision shall be 'final and conclusive') as the courts have interpreted such phrases narrowly, as meaning that other appeals are excluded but not JR. An early case in this category was R v Medical Appeal Tribunal ex p Gilmore[22] where Lord Denning said 'The word "final" … does not mean without recourse to certiorari' (now a quashing order) and in S E Asian Fire Bricks Sdn Bvd v Non-Metallic Mineral Products Manufacturing Employees Union[23] where the drafting did manage to exclude certiorari for error of law on the face of the record; the Privy Council noted that that did not exclude JR if there had been action which was ultra vires or in breach of natural justice.

THE TRIBUNALS SERVICE – REFORMED FRAMEWORK OF THE TRIBUNALS

The expansion of tribunals in fact began before the Leggatt Report and the Tribunals, Courts and Enforcement Act 2007, and was much earlier generated by the 1945 Labour government whose reforming zeal itself generated the Welfare State; and in the course of passing a number of Acts which would inevitably create conflicts between government and individuals which immediately necessitated a forum for dealing with those the need for a tribunal system must slowly have become apparent. The courts were clearly unsuitable for this task, and thus it was not long before the tribunals were obliged to shoulder the burden. Conceptually, the Franks Committee[24] thought that their role was adjudicative rather than administrative, but it seems now to be generally agreed that their role is more administrative than adjudicative though inevitably they also make determinations in a quasi-judicial role. To this end the current chairs of their chambers and of the committees into which they are formed to make these determinations are classed, and addressed as, judiciary, although the specialist 'wing' members who sit alongside the judicial chairpersons are usually not 'judges; but 'tribunal members'. One purpose of the creation of tribunals was to relieve the pressure on overloaded courts. The original supervisory body was the Council on Tribunals, but this was replaced by the Administrative Justice and Tribunals Council, which was then itself abolished under the Public Bodies Act 2011,[25] was briefly replaced by an Administrative Justice Advisory Group in 2012, and then in 2013 by an Administrative Justice Forum, an independent body sponsored by the MOJ whose job it was to 'gauge how the administrative justice and tribunals system is working … to identify any areas of concern or good practice and to provide early, informal

---

22 [1957] 1 QB 574 (CA).

23 [1981] AC 363 (PC).

24 Appointed on 1 November 1955, their report on Administrative Tribunals and Enquiries was published in 1957, Cmnd 218.

25 This Act is discussed in greater detail in Chapter 4 on Primary Legislation.

testing of policy initiatives'. This organisation was itself replaced in 2017 by a new supervisory body hosted by the law reform society JUSTICE.

Development over the decade and a half since the Labour Government decided to work on the tribunal system has been extensive. In 2001, the then Lord Chancellor, Lord Irvine, appointed Sir Andrew Leggatt, a retired judge,[26] to review the administrative tribunals which were then dealing with nearly a million cases a year although only three had very substantial work (social security and child support – which did the bulk of the work – employment and immigration and asylum, while of the rest many had little work and some were virtually defunct). He recommended creating a unified tribunal system, thus making them independent of their sponsoring government departments, providing a coherent and unified appeal system, and overhauling the position of the lay members so that no members actually sat on any tribunal unless they had a function to fulfil. These recommendations were adopted in 2003; the new Tribunals Service was inaugurated in 2005 and began to operate in 2006–2007 when the Tribunals, Courts and Enforcement Act 2007 was passed. In 2011 the new Tribunals Service amalgamated with the courts (up to and including the Court of Appeal) to form HMCTS, becoming an agency sponsored by the MOJ. Gradually the former separate tribunals were inducted into the new systems, except for the Employment Tribunal and its appeal body, the EAT, which was planned to remain as a 'separate pillar' alongside the framework of the First and Upper Tiers of the unified Tribunals. Both tiers were divided into Chambers which usually housed more than one tribunal of similar or at least non-conflicting fields of operation, and the Tribunals Service was headed by a Senior President of Tribunals (currently Sir Ernest Ryder, Ryder LJ from the Court of Appeal).

Appeals go from the First Tier to the relevant Chamber of the Upper Tribunal, and with permission an appeal may go from there to the Court of Appeal, on point of law only. The Senior President of Tribunals is responsible for training, guidance and welfare, and for representing the views of the tribunal judiciary to the government and to Parliament. The Lord Chief Justice has also delegated some of his powers under the Constitutional Reform Act 2005 to the Senior President, mainly concerning discipline of the tribunal judiciary.

Figure 13.3 shows the structure of the First and Upper Tribunals and their relationship through appeals.

THE FIRST AND UPPER TIERS

Figure 13.3 captures the complexity of the system of tribunals and their interrelationship. The following section will seek to explain, in outline, the work of each of the chambers.

FIRST TIER

The First Tier has seven Chambers.

26 Not to be confused with George Leggatt, his son, who has recently been appointed to the Supreme Court.

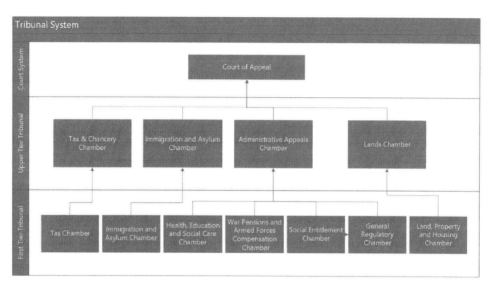

Figure 13.3 The Tribunal System

THE GENERAL REGULATORY CHAMBER (GRC)

This has nearly 20 subject lists which are now brought together to continue the regulatory work that used to be done in separate tribunals before the GRC was established in 2006. Details of their work can be found on the HMCTS website which now provides one destination to go to for information. These separate areas of GRC responsibility include (in alphabetical order) charities, claims management services, community rights to bid, copyright licensing, electronic communications and postal services, environment, estate agents, examination boards, food, gambling, immigration services, information rights, letting and managing agents, microchipping dogs, pensions regulation, professional regulation and transport. Two of the commonest here are regulation of estate agents under the Estate Agents Act, and of HGVs and buses and coaches by the Traffic Commissioners.

THE SOCIAL ENTITLEMENT CHAMBER (SEC)

This deals with Asylum Support (but not with asylum claims or with other immigration matters) as it has in effect a welfare benefits focus. It also deals with Criminal Injuries Compensation and Social Security and Child Support. This Chamber is very busy and has a heavy workload for obvious reasons. (The bulk of the work here is welfare benefits under numerous such Acts as child support under the Child Support Acts 1991–1995 and the Child Maintenance and Other Payments Act 2008.)

HEALTH, EDUCATION AND SOCIAL CARE CHAMBER

This one deals with Care Standards (that is, appeals against decisions from organisations concerned with children and vulnerable adults, and those regulating social, personal and healthcare); Special Educational Needs and Disability; Mental Health Review; and Primary Health Lists (that is appeals and applications from decisions made by Primary Care Trusts as part of the local management of such lists concerning medical practitioners).

IMMIGRATION AND ASYLUM CHAMBER

This is the Chamber that deals with appeals from immigration and asylum applications and decisions made by the Home Office (in connection with which the SEC deals only with provision for applicants' and appellants' support). The Appeals concern decisions which refuse asylum in the UK, refuse entry or leave to remain, or to deport someone who is already in the UK.

PROPERTY CHAMBER

This is a busy Chamber dealing with residential property disputes, such as under the Leasehold Reform, Housing and Urban Development Act 1993; Commonhold and Leasehold Reform Act 2002 (CLARA 2002); land registration under the Land Registration Act 2002; and agricultural land and drainage matters.

TAX CHAMBER

Two main areas of work are done by this Chamber: any Tax appeals from decisions of HM Revenue and Customs (HMRC); and MPs' expenses where the decisions are made by a Compliance Officer appointed by the Independent Parliamentary Standards Authority (IPSA). The Compliance Office is responsible for determining and paying MPs' expenses and appeals are made under the Parliamentary Standards Act 2009.

WAR PENSIONS AND ARMED FORCES COMPENSATION CHAMBER

This Chamber hears appeals against refusal of war pensions refused by the Secretary of State for Defence.

THE UPPER TIER

The Upper Tier has four Chambers: Administrative Appeals, Tax and Chancery, Lands, and Immigration and Asylum.

ADMINISTRATIVE APPEALS CHAMBER

This is a busy Chamber which hears appeals from the First Tier Chambers unless there is a more specialist Chamber in the Upper Tier to hear their appeals, e.g. Transport appeals will go automatically to the Administrative Appeals Chamber as this is a regulatory jurisdiction which fits perfectly with the Administrative Appeals diet, but appeals from First Tier Tax Chamber will of course go to the Upper Tier Tax and Chancery Chamber; likewise appeals from the First Tier Property Chamber will fit with the Upper Tier Lands Chamber; and First Tier Immigration and Asylum appeals go to the Upper Tier Immigration and Asylum Chamber.

TAX AND CHANCERY CHAMBER

This and the First Tier have brought together four previous tribunals to hear the full range of direct and indirect Tax cases, replacing other variously named tribunals.

LANDS CHAMBER

This Chamber hears appeals from the First Tier Property Chamber but also continues the work of the pre-Tribunals, Courts and Enforcement Act 2007 Lands Tribunal, which joined the Tribunals Service in 2009. The Chamber is often still called the Lands Tribunal!

IMMIGRATION AND ASYLUM CHAMBER

This Chamber hears appeals from the First Tier Chamber of the same name; both Chambers at First Tier and Upper tier level were established in 2010, and as the Upper Tier is a superior court of record it seems that this Chamber can hear appeals from both the First Tier and its own Asylum Chamber decisions.

> MAKING CONNECTIONS – TO CIVIL AND CRIMINAL JUSTICE
> +++
> Now that you know how the framework of courts and tribunals fit together in delivering Administrative Justice, it is time to look at the content of the Tribunals Service jurisdictions so that you can appreciate how this system works in relation to the everyday life of the citizen, and how it may even already impact on that of the reader while still an undergraduate. This is likely to make a visit to some tribunals more personally interesting.
>
> We have, in the course of tracing the civil and criminal outlines, already looked briefly at both civil and criminal justice including their appeals systems. We are now going to look at the detail of the tribunals' fields of law which form their separate jurisdictions.

HOW CASES ARE HEARD IN TRIBUNALS

This adversarial system used in the courts is completely different from the Tribunal Law Systems' approach which is not only more informal than a court hearing but also inquisitorial, and has more similarity to the inquisitorial system in civil law systems, though much adversarial style has made its way into tribunal hearings as the law they administer has become more technical. A key example of this is the Employment Tribunal (which exists in its 'separate pillar' outside the main Tribunal Service framework, delivering its decisions much as it did when all tribunals were completely independent and where it is frequently the case that a full professional team may be employed, including instructing solicitor, counsel as advocate and expert witnesses. The same is true in the Property Tribunals where, for example, expert valuation in property cases may be needed because under e.g. the LRHUDA 1996 and the Leasehold Enfranchisement Act 1967 technical calculations and professional judgment are required to determine what figure should be paid to the lessor by the lessee. However, the tribunals system as a whole is still built on the original tribunal ethos, i.e. that lawyers are not needed although this may not be the situation for optimum results in some specialist cases. In theory it should also cost less than in the court system.

The judges of the **Tribunals Service** are of three types: (1) the lawyers, (2) the specialist wing members and (3) the lay members, who are no longer used in some jurisdictions owing to the need for economy. All are appointed by the Lord Chancellor and take a judicial oath though appointment is through the Judicial Appointments Commission (JAC) as with judges for the courts, and some will already have been inducted into other jurisdictions in the courts e.g. existing magistrates who sit as lay members. Some of the wing members are also appointed by the Lord Chancellor as judges in the same way as the lawyers, in the same way as when in pre-2007 days, they were called Lawyer and Valuer Chairs respectively, rather than judges.

EMPLOYMENT TRIBUNALS AND OTHER 'DIFFERENT' TRIBUNALS

Before departing from discussion of the system of tribunals in the context of administrative law it is important to note the existence and role of the Employment Tribunal. Employment Tribunals (ETs) and the Employment Appeal Tribunal (EAT) are governed by the Employment Tribunals Act 1996. The ET and EAT consider statutory claims arising from employment law – such as unfair dismissal, redundancy, unlawful deduction of wages and a whole raft of discrimination based claims.[27] The regular courts retain jurisdiction to deal with certain matters arising out of employment disputes, largely those concerned with common law claims – such as wrongful dismissal. The vast bulk of the work of the Employment Tribunal is focussed on the private law disputes between workers/employees and employers.

There is a Judicial Mediation Scheme which has been in operation since 2006 and ACAS, the Advisory, Conciliation and Arbitration Service also offers an arbitration service as an alternative to using the tribunals.

Along with the Employment Tribunals in their separate pillar, there are some other tribunals which do not belong to the Tribunal Service framework, e.g. the Special Immigration Appeals Commission (SIAC) established under the Special Immigration Appeals Act 1997. This is the special 'secret' jurisdiction that deals with some cases with such high national security risks that the person before the Commission may not even know what risk he is alleged to present and the issue is usually whether s/he should be allowed into the UK or if s/he should be deported for security reasons. Curiously it is sometimes possible for the public to attend such hearings although even the parties and their lawyers are also warned that they may have to leave the hearing at some point because of the secrecy, in national security interests, of the evidence to be heard.

---

27 Employment Rights Act 1996; Equality Act 2010.

A CRITICAL APPROACH TO THE COURT AND TRIBUNAL STRUCTURE

It may be that the Tribunals Service has not yet reached its optimum performance. It has been said to be 'quicker', though this may only be in comparison with the courts which are notoriously slow. They are also said to be cheaper as it is not necessary to be represented by lawyers though experience and some research has shown that parties fare better if they are represented. However, it is not necessary to be represented by the most expensive lawyers: paralegals and non-lawyers and other professionals are usually accepted as representatives in tribunals e.g. a valuer or surveyor may be used in property cases, and such a person may not be a regulated professional as in fact a 'surveyor' does not necessarily have to belong to the Royal Institution of Chartered Surveyors (RICS) (unlike an architect who must be formally qualified as it is an offence to pretend to be an architect if not so qualified), although a judge can always refuse permission if a non-lawyer is disruptive and wasting the hearing's time. Similarly, other volunteers such as students from Law Clinics may be used, although there is sometimes concern about 'McKenzie Friends'[28] who often give free advice, but sometimes charge, and have sometimes been found to give wrong information to their clients!

OMBUDSMEN

Turning away from essentially adjudicative forms of administrative law, the Ombudsmen schemes in operation provide a useful alternative when individuals wish to complain about the *quality* of service received from public bodies as opposed to making allegations of unlawful behaviour. Ombudsmen are deemed 'representatives of the people' and are given specific remits to consider complaints brought to their attention. It is important to note that here we are concerned with Ombudsmen schemes as they apply to *public* bodies and not the Ombudsmen who act as consumer and service watchdogs for a whole host of *private* services.

The primary Ombudsman in England and Wales is the Parliamentary and Health Service Ombudsman who considers complaints about public authorities, the National Health Service and UK Government Departments. There are several reasons that undermine the effectiveness of the Ombudsman. First, in respect of issues about the NHS, the Ombudsmen can receive direct complaints but concerns about Government departments must come from an MP. This hinders the effectiveness of Administrative Justice and essentially places additional hurdles in the way of bringing justice to wronged individuals. Secondly complaints must

---

28 *McKenzie v McKenzie* [1970] 3 WLR 472 (CA), gave the McKenzie name to anyone who accompanies a litigant in person to court to help organise papers, documents and books, but does not have the right to speak for that LIP because such an unqualified non-lawyer friend will have no right of audience, which is reserved to counsel, solicitors (who have limited rights of audience) and in some cases legal executives.

be about 'maladministration' – a rather hazy concept – that can be best described as 'bad governance'.[29] By having such uncertain terms as part of the core activity of the Ombudsman it may dissuade people from calling upon the service. Finally, whilst the Parliamentary and Health Service Ombudsman has a wide ranging remit, the Ombudsmen cannot accept complaints about government policy.

In this way the Ombudsman scheme provides a small piece in the overall puzzle that is Administrative Justice in the English Legal System. It provides both direct and indirect means of addressing the public use of power but in a way that is not related to the lawfulness of that use.

INQUIRIES

Inquiries were briefly mentioned in relation to the institutions of the legal system in Chapter 3. They play an important role in terms of Administrative Justice as they allow for failings of public bodies or the law to be brought to light and for suggestions for changes to the legal position to be made in response. Lord Butler commented that such inquiries also acted as the 'lightning rod' for the public's anger and the call for an inquiry can be a way that governments diffuse public disquiet or as a political weapon used by politicians to criticise the incumbent government.

The Inquiries Act 2005 lays down a specific statutory basis for Ministers to establish an inquiry. The purpose of such inquiries is to find facts and, in some cases, make recommendation. Inquiries, according to s 1, can be held when it appears to a Minister that:

a) particular events have caused, or are capable of causing, public concern, or
b) there is public concern that particular events may have occurred.[30]

Such inquiries are often held in haste following a public scandal. There is often a 'muddying' of the role of inquiries with the judicial role performed in courts. This misconception should be dispelled from the outset. They do not have the power to 'punish' any wrongdoing and, generally, any obvious criminal charges should be dealt with through the courts before an inquiry is launched.[31] Inquiries are intended to be fact finding and may (but do not have to) make recommendations as to law or political reform. The Francis Inquiry published an incredible 290 recommendations following its investigation into the failing at Mid Staffordshire NHS Foundation Trust.

29 For the difficulties in defining the term, see R (Liverpool City Council) v Local Commissioner for Local Government [2001] 1 All ER 462 (CA).
30 Inquiries Act 2005 s 1(1)(a)–(b).
31 This happened in the Bichard Inquiry (into the murder of two young girls that eventually led to reform of the system of criminal record checks) but did not happen in relation to the Leveson Inquiry (into Press Standards) and this caused significant disruption to the workings of the inquiry.

EXPLAINING THE LAW

For example, following the disastrous fire at the Grenfell Tower that killed 72 people a public inquiry was launched by the (then) Prime Minister Theresa May and chaired by Sir Martin Moore-Bick (a retired judge of the Court of Appeal).[32] The remit of the inquiry is to examine the circumstances of the fire and to make recommendations. At the end of 2018 there were eight ongoing inquiries that had not yet reported their findings, and by October 2019 the Grenfell Inquiry was amongst those that had not reported.

As was mentioned in Chapter 3, inquiries can be led by judges provided certain formalities are followed including consultation with senior members of the judiciary.[33] Judges have been used in a number of high profile inquiries.[34] The advantages of utilising the skills of a judge (or a retired judge) to lead such an inquiry are clear:

- They may well have expertise in the subject matter considered.
- They will carry authority with those involved, including senior politicians.
- They will have credibility with the public.
- They will be used to dealing with complex (and, at times, distressing) evidence.
- They may have the ability to understand the practical consequences of any recommendations.

One of the issues of using judges is that it further 'muddies', in the public's mind, the role and purpose of inquiries and how they are intended to be distinct from court proceedings. This is not helped by the fact that the involvement of judges often ends up with a more formalised approach to the giving of evidence and the involvement of additional QCs to ask questions of the witnesses.

ANALYSING THE LAW – MAKING LAW IN HASTE

There is no question that public inquiries are an important aspect of Administrative Justice and the legal system. They allow a very public light to be shone on the innermost workings of the English Legal System and can identify gaps in the legislative landscape. However, such a public and sometimes emotional way of generating law reform can be problematic. The Bichard Inquiry is a good example of this. It was set up following the murder of two young girls by a man known to them and who had had police involvement in the past, before he gained a job at the girls' school.

---

32 www.grenfelltowerinquiry.org.uk.

33 Inquiries Act 2005 s 10.

34 Including – the Leveson Inquiry into press standards, Lord Saville's Inquiry into Bloody Sunday, the Hutton Inquiry into the death of Dr David Kelly.

The inquiry (rightly) identified failings in the system of criminal checks for those working in certain roles that brought them into close proximity with children. Out of the recommendations was rapidly born the Criminal Records Bureau (CRB) and a system of 'enhanced' and 'basic' criminal checks. The legislation had been ill thought through and was passed too quickly. These CRB checks grew in volume and became a significant administrative burden that was out of proportion with the *actual* protections that they gave against former criminals (and those accused of certain crimes) gaining access to vulnerable people. The CRB system was very wide and left it to individual police forces to decide the extent to which historic (and, in some cases, very historic) criminal offences could be revealed.

Eventually, the CRB system was replaced with the Disclosure and Barring Service (DBS) – which set time limits on the sharing of certain minor offences and established specific rules for young offenders – following a successful challenge to the scheme on the basis that it breached human rights.[35] Even the new DBS scheme was not improved enough to avoid a declaration from the Supreme Court upholding the issuing of a declaration of incompatibility by the Court of Appeal in January 2019.[36]

THE WEBSITE

The website that accompanies this textbook contains many useful resources that you can use to consolidate and further your knowledge of the law, to hone your skills of critical analysis and to test your knowledge. This includes a set of multiple choice questions (MCQs) that can be used to test your knowledge and understanding of the material.

PODCASTS

- The podcasts provide a summary of the area under study, bringing together the key themes and threads of analysis into a 'mini-lecture'.
- There will also be an explanation and analysis of topical and up-to-date issues related to Administrative Justice.

35 R (T) v Chief Constable of Greater Manchester Police [2014] UKSC 35, [2015] AC 49.
36 R (P, G and W) v Secretary of State for the Home Department and Another [2019] UKSC 3, [2019] 2 WLR 509.

14

CHAPTER 14
ALTERNATIVE DISPUTE RESOLUTION (ADR)

INTRODUCTION

Having spent the last seven chapters discussing the various facets and intricacies of the formal judicial system one could be forgiven for believing that every dispute involving legal rights or obligations will inevitably end up being resolved through formal court proceedings. That, indeed, used to be the default position, which has, however, been steadily eroded since the late 1980s when the focus first shifted from that of providing legal aid to those who could otherwise not afford access to justice, and instead became refocussed towards alternative means of dispute resolution, giving rise to the term 'ADR'. This shift might be said to be a culmination of the reports and reforms which began with the Benson Commission in the 1970s, and ultimately resulted in the passage of the Courts and Legal Services Act (CLSA) 1990 which changed the way that the courts, legal services and legal profession had worked in the second half of the 20th century.

Any protracted study of the English Legal System is likely to skew perception about the extent of use of litigation. In reality very many legal issues had by 1990 for some time only ended up in litigation when other, less formal, methods of resolving disputes had proved unsuccessful. The very organisation of the legal system had certainly by 1990 for some time been predicated on the notion that early settlement and resolution of disputes is preferable, both for the parties concerned and for society more generally, to formal court proceedings. Despite the foundation in 1990, with the support of the Confederation of British Industry (CBI) of the not-for-profit Centre for Effective Dispute Resolution (CEDR) it has been a hurdle to the acceptance of ADR as an integral part of the litigation system, rather than a 'bolt on', that its implementation has been seen as an economy rather than as a range of tools in their own right for resolving the disputes which are at the core of all litigated disputes.

Both the Woolf Reforms[1] and the Jackson Reports[2] on the costs of civil litigation (discussed in Chapter 10) have attempted to promote and encourage the use of alternative forms of resolving disputes but it may be that the historic 'economy' taint has still inhibited both the development and public acceptance of 'Non-Court' Dispute Resolution (as the process has been imaginatively renamed in the Family Court which also enjoys the only statutory and court rule based automatic referral to ADR in England and Wales).[3]

---

1 The final report was published in 1996 and with recommendations implemented in the Civil Procedure Rules in 1998.
2 Preliminary report in 2009 and final report in 2010.
3 Although such automatic referral has been very successful in reducing the volume of court traffic in Europe (e.g. Italy) and North America (in Canada as well as in some states of the USA).

This chapter will explore the meaning of these 'alternative' forms of dispute resolution and how they now operate not as adjuncts or satellites to litigation but as an *integral part* of civil justice in the legal system. The chapter will explain the rationale for alternative dispute resolution (ADR) and explore its operation through the processes of arbitration and mediation.

AS YOU READ

As you read this chapter it is important that you gain an **understanding** of the rationale and principles of Alternative Dispute Resolution. This will allow you to be able to **describe** and **assess critically** the different types of ADR that operate within the English Legal System.

Consider critically the benefits to the parties and the English Legal System of facilitating effective ADR. As you read try to **compare and contrast** the mechanisms here with the more formal concepts of litigation that are discussed elsewhere in this textbook.

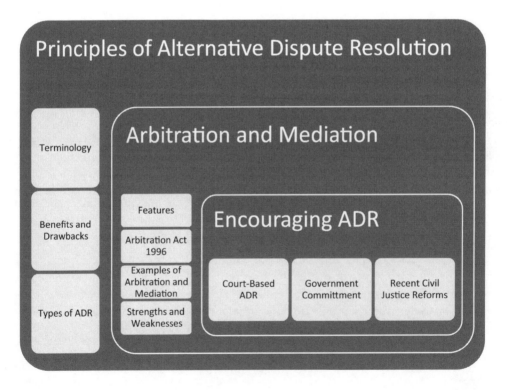

Figure 14.1

PRINCIPLES OF ALTERNATIVE DISPUTE RESOLUTION

The problem encountered in Chapter 6 on statutory interpretation, in terms of the flexibility of words, is also present in trying to determine what is (and what is not) covered by the phrase Alternative Dispute Resolution (ADR). It is a notoriously flexible term that has different meanings to different people (see Figure 14.2). In the broadest sense, the term could be applied to any form of procedure (formal or informal) that seeks to provide an alternative to resolving disputes through litigation. This would include arbitration, negotiation, mediation, conciliation and a range of other methods discussed later. A narrower construction of ADR is that it applies to forms of dispute resolution that do not involve the **outcome** of the process being determined by a **third party** (i.e. methods that are not adjudicative in nature). This meaning is not apt since it excludes mediation where the mediator facilitates the parties' own decision in a form of assisted negotiation, so makes no determination, and this would not do since the only form of statutory dispute resolution in English law at present is the MIAM (Mediation Information and Assessment Meeting) in force in the Family Division through the FPR 2010, s 3 and the Children and Families Act 2014, s 10.

This chapter takes a very broad view of the term, similar to that taken by Parliament in its Standard Note on ADR:

> Alternative dispute resolution (ADR) is the collective term for settling civil disputes with the help of an independent third party and without the need for a formal court hearing.[4]

This would therefore include both mediation and arbitration. This broad understanding of ADR is chosen because the current chapter comes at the end of a series of chapters that are mainly linked to litigation and a broad understanding of ADR will act as a counterpoint to that discussion. There are those in the academic world who would argue that this is too broad a conception and that the focus of ADR should be on the *parties* resolving the dispute *themselves* with or without the aid of a third party, rather than including more adjudicative methods of dispute resolution which involve the issue being *determined* by a third party.[5]

The chapter could have taken the even broader view of ADR adopted in the Practice Direction (Pre-Action Protocol) as the 'collective description of methods of resolving disputes otherwise than through the normal trial process'.[6] However, this view would include an almost unmanageable number of extremely informal dispute resolution methods that are

---

4   Diana Douse, 'Mediation and Other Alternatives to Court' (House of Commons Library, 2013), www.parliament.uk/briefing-papers/SN04176/mediation-and-other-alternatives-to-court.
5   For the difficulties in language surrounding ADR, see Sir Laurence Street 'The language of ADR' (1992) 58(2) Arbitration 17.
6   PDPAC 3.1(3).

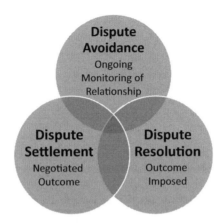

Figure 14.2 The Different Understandings of ADR

only tangentially linked to the more formal legal system. It would also include methods of resolution already discussed elsewhere in the textbook – particularly Chapter 13 on the Administrative Justice System – such as ombudsmen and tribunals. Again, we are wrestling with the fluidity of language and its impact on our understanding of the legal system. Many of the principles discussed later apply in relation to mediation and arbitration.

ANALYSING THE LAW – JUST 'DISPUTE RESOLUTION'?

There is an inherent danger in using the term 'ADR' that relates to the word 'alternative'. In this context the word should not be misunderstood. It does not mean unusual or unorthodox. It does not mean a different choice to the normal or regular way of resolving disputes. It is not an inferior term to 'litigation'. It is simply being used to describe methods other than litigation. This is an important issue as it goes to both the credibility and attractiveness of ADR as a way of resolving disputes.

Methods of ADR were traditionally viewed as stemming from the failings of the court system (a point explored in Table 14.1) and so as some kind of second choice. In many ways the opposite situation is true. Litigation is the alternative that arises when formal or informal forms of dispute resolution fail and the parties are left turning to the law and formal court structure to resolve disputes that they could not themselves resolve. As is explored throughout this chapter, far from being 'alternative' in the pejorative sense, ADR is a mainstream device for resolving disputes. The legal system itself – through the rules of civil procedure in particular – now more formally recognises and supports ADR even within the system of litigation. This process began with the new CPR 1998, which introduced a concept of 'hands on case management' in which the judiciary were charged with the task of 'actively managing' cases listed before them for interlocutory appointments, which were for the first time intended to be the subject of a proactive stocktaking of the optimum handling of a claim, whether by traditional litigation or by ADR or a combination of the two.

Unfortunately when the CPR 1998 were drafted (over 20 years ago) the culture was not yet ripe for imposing automatic referral and neither the original Rules nor any subsequent amendment has yet introduced such a system either except in the Family Court as mentioned previously, but judges were given power to adjourn at any time for ADR to be considered and attempted and some have used such powers more energetically, persuasively and determinedly than others, however stopping short only of direct compulsion – although case law (as discussed later) has developed a well-defined cost penalty system suitable for complete failure by a party even to consider ADR when it might be appropriate.

Table 14.1 lays out some of the problems that parties face when using traditional court-based litigation, and these may go some way to explaining the enthusiastic adoption of ADR in some quarters.

Table 14.1 Problems with Litigation

Delays
■ From lodging initial applications to final judgment, the court system is by no means quick. Although things have improved following on from the Woolf and Jackson Reports and ongoing routine CPR amendments court is still not an attractive option if parties wish to settle disputes quickly.
■ The delay is often caused by the specific and technical procedures used by English courts.
Costs
■ It is a banal truism (though one worth repeating) to point to the high cost of litigation. There is also increased risk in litigation as the losing party will normally need to pay not only his own costs but the costs of the other side.
Public hearings and reporting
■ Court hearings are (generally) open and so parties can have their commercial transactions exposed to competitors. Parties may also be reluctant to have the fact that they are in dispute made public.
Lack of technical expertise
■ Although there are Divisions within the High Court, there is a risk that generalist judges are not well-equipped to deal with certain technical subjects and the calling of expert witnesses and the writing of expert reports will only add to the costs of the proceedings.

(Continued)

Table 14.1 (*Continued*)

Adversarial
■ The adversarial nature of the English Legal System has many benefits but it can be unsuitable for certain types of dispute, including those involving families although Family Justice has enthusiastically absorbed arbitration because of its faster and cheaper delivery of an award which there is confidence the court will enforce if made by a trained professional Family Arbitrator.

Lack of party control (process and outcome)
■ Parties must follow the procedural rules laid down by the English Legal System and may not opt for procedures of their own creation when a case is heard in court under court rules. Another reason why parties seeking a Family Justice determination will often opt with confidence for Family Arbitration by a member of the Institute of Family Law Arbitrators, which can enable a dispute to be determined within a more flexible and less costly system – into which they can have much more case management input into setting up the arbitration than within the confines of court rules on evidence and procedure.
■ ADR also enables the parties to pick their own arbitrator, whereas they cannot pick their own judge since the Court will list cases in accordance with its own gatekeeping system., when and before whom they decide.
■ As an adjudicated outcome, a court decision is one that is imposed on the parties with only the potential for appeal if the result is unwelcome. While this notionally means that there will be a 'winner' in the case, it could well be that neither party is happy with the outcome.

TYPES OF ADR

Figure 14.3 gives an indication of the major forms of alternative dispute resolution and gives a brief description of how they normally operate. The figure is not intended to be exhaustive but rather to give a flavour of the variety of methods that are available to parties to resolve their disputes. The contents of the figure are based on the guidance notes accompanying the Government's Dispute Resolution Commitment.[7] The nature and implications of this Commitment are discussed later in the chapter.

MUTUALLY EXCLUSIVE OR HYBRID FORMS OF ADR?

It is also very tempting to separate out the different types of ADR completely and to laud the advantages and decry the disadvantages of each. This typology risks ignoring the fact that, quite often, the different forms of dispute resolution interact with each other and can form part of a *system* of methods of resolving disputes that escalates,

---

7   Ministry of Justice 'The Dispute Resolution Commitment: Guidance for Government Departments and Agencies' (May 2011), www.justice.gov.uk/courts/mediation/dispute-resolution-commitment.

Negotiation	• Parties come together to resolve their disputes (normally either personally, with no independent person present, or through solicitors). • Normally used where continuation of relationship is essential and where time is of the essence.
Mediation	• A more formal and structured form of negotiation involving a third party. Normally called 'facilitative'; mediation where the parties are helped to reach their own agreement. • The mediator normally meets with parties individually and acts as 'go between'. • The process reduces antagonism caused by face to face meetings especially if 'shuttle' meetings of the mediator and parties in different rooms means the parties either need not meet at all or only in infrequent plenaries – this is called 'caucusing'. • The outcome of the mediation itself is not binding but can be written up into a contract usually by the parties' lawyers working from Heads of Agreement.
Conciliation	• Very similar in form and substance to mediation. • The key difference is that the conciliator takes a more **active** part in the discussions similar to 'adjudicative' mediation or a hybrid mediation style which blends both styles. • Conciliator will comment on the relative merits of the arguments and suggest solutions. A mediator can also do this if asked to do so; this would then be 'evaluative' mediation, or 'hybrid' mediation.
Neutral Evaluation	• Where a dispute revolves around a point of law, neutral evaluation can be used to help resolve differences in views about the legal position. • Parties submit outlines of their claims to a third party with legal expertise (such as a retired judge). • The expert gives a (non-binding) opinion on the legal issues of the case that the parties can then use as the basis for further negotiation.
Adjudication	• Widely used in the construction industry particularly under specific statutes addressing interim decisions on contractual payments so as to preserve cash flow on large civil engineering projects, e.g. pursuant to the Housing Grants, Construction and Regeneration Act 1996. • An adjudicator will make an interim decision until full determination is made (thus giving some form of legal certainty).
Arbitration	• Largely governed by the Arbitration Act 1996 and contract law but a special type of arbitration is used in Family Justice under the IFLA Scheme where an IFLA Arbitrator makes a decision where the Award is recognised by the Family Court. • Case is submitted to an independent arbitrator who decides the outcome of the case. • Wide party discretion in the process and execution of the arbitral tribunal.

Figure 14.3 Forms of Dispute Resolution

normally, towards arbitration or litigation. However, that escalation can be cyclical with several attempts at different forms of ADR. To put this differently, the methods of ADR are not intended to be mutually exclusive, except (in England and Wales) mediation and arbitration, since these two methods are a contradiction in terms if undertaken by the same person. This is because in arbitration an arbitrator is always a neutral arbiter making a decision known as an 'Award' and thus must know nothing confidential that is not known to the other party, whereas in mediation a mediator must not disclose to the other party anything disclosed by one party in confidence without the discloser's permission since s/he is a third party neutral facilitator. So a mediator can never become an arbitrator but an arbitrator can become a mediator.

In some other jurisdictions however e.g. Canada, there is an accepted process called 'Med-Arb' where if a mediation does not settle all outstanding issues the mediator may act as an arbitrator to make an Award on the outstanding issue(s). It is still possible, however, for a mediator to settle as many issues as possible in mediation and to refer the outstanding issues to another arbitrator who comes fresh to the case and this is sometimes done.

EXPLAINING THE LAW AND TAKING THINGS FURTHER – HYBRID DISPUTE RESOLUTION

The most common type of hybrid process outside England and Wales is Med-Arb. This method combines mediation and arbitration into a single dispute resolution process. This type of process is common in construction agreements, particularly in the USA and also in Canada which has refined the hybrid system.

Under Med-Arb the parties, when they have exhausted their informal efforts to resolve their disputes, first enter into mediation. If the mediation process is successful, then the agreement can be transposed into a contract that would then bind the parties. If the mediation fails outright to resolve the dispute, the process progresses to a full arbitration with either a new arbitrator appointed (essential in England and Wales) or in other jurisdictions the mediator 'stepping into the shoes' of an arbitrator. During the mediation (or after it) parties are free to enter into further rounds of negotiation before progressing to arbitration if there is no prospect of settlement. The whole idea of Med-Arb allows parties to have certainty of process without progressing straight to adversarial proceedings. However, having knowledge that, should the cooperative fail, there is the prospect of an adjudicated solution can be very attractive and can focus negotiations at earlier stages.

English law considers Med-Arb methodology using the same mediator and arbitrator practised elsewhere quite unsuitable as the mediator's neutrality is compromised since s/he may know too much of a confidential nature to be able to undertake an arbitration in the same case in which that mediator has already acted. The Americans and Canadians respond that this is not true because the mediator turned arbitrator is no more compromised than a judge faced with a 'voir dire' in a criminal trial in English criminal law, where s/he must make a determination on the evidence when deciding the facts in that 'trial within a trial' that sometimes occurs in a criminal trial.

The most common hybrid processes in England and Wales are therefore not Med-Arb but: Negotiation flowing into Mediation or Arbitration, or directly to litigation, depending on the subject matter or use may be made of Early Neutral Evaluation, ENE (especially in commercial cases) then Arbitration or Litigation if not settled; ENE is now in increasing use as a tool for gauging later likely litigation success.

If arbitration and mediation are to be tried together in England and Wales, arbitration will thus be first; then the arbitrator is not compromised. Figure 14.4 indicates the shape of a cyclical 'hybrid' process.

RATIONALE FOR ALTERNATIVE DISPUTE RESOLUTION

The desire to resolve disputes through methods other than litigation can arise for a number of reasons and some of these reasons are explored during the following section of the chapter. In analysing these multiple rationales, you should bear in mind that certain forms of dispute

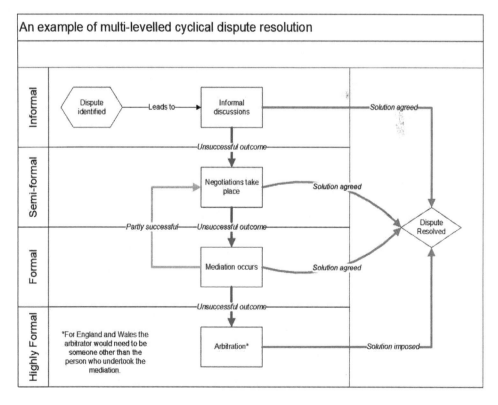

Figure 14.4 Hybrid Forms of Dispute Resolution

resolution achieve these different purposes to varying degrees. It should also be remembered that stakeholders within the process may have different reasons for wishing to encourage the use of ADR that cannot be so easily classified and categorised. For example, some disputants are suspicious of forms of dispute resolution that do not lead to binding results as they can just prolong what they see to be the inevitability of court action. This never need be the case with e.g. mediation as binding Heads of Agreement can be signed to be incorporated into a draft consent order for the court or even simply a contract. Similarly, with negotiation or conciliation, and district judges do this every day when they broker agreements and reduce them to binding force in an order of the court, particularly in the Small Claims Court. In family law there is a similar process called Collaborative Law, where all parties and their advisers agree to stay out of court and if discussions break down without settlement everyone involved in the dispute instructs new lawyers for litigation or any other form of ADR. If on the other hand agreement is reached, again Heads of Agreement and a Consent Order/ Contract can be binding. Equally, some disputants may have preference for a form of ADR (whether it is appropriate to a particular dispute) because of familiarity and successes with that form in the past.

PARTY CONTROL OF THE PROCESS

One of the primary reasons for supporting ADR within a legal system relates to its ability to respect party choice and party control over the process. The concept of party choice being a central plank of the English Legal System's incorporation of ADR is recognised both in the case law[8] and in statutory form.[9] Although party choice is often treated as a single principle, it can actually be split into two (or possibly more) sub-principles: party choice over *outcome* and party choice over *process*.

The former is most easily demonstrated when talking about mediation (discussed later) and conciliation where the independent third party is not determining a given dispute but facilitating the parties in coming to an *agreed* solution. This is particularly useful in family disputes, where the parties are thought more likely to abide by, and feel satisfied with, outcomes which they are involved in creating. Party choice as to *process* is more evident in arbitration (discussed later) where the outcome is imposed by the arbitrator (and so is adjudicative) but the whole process, including issues of evidence and even choice of arbitrator, can be controlled by the parties. For one thing the parties to an arbitration will sign an agreement to arbitrate and to be bound by the Arbitrator's Award and (assuming there is no issue about jurisdiction) the court will enforce this in the absence of error of law or procedural irregularity. This is a major advantage to parties privy to international commercial relations who wish to settle any dispute according to the law of England but without having to use the court system.

---

8   Lloyd v Wright [1983] QB 1065 (CA) 1072 where it was held that 'the court does not claim a monopoly in deciding disputes between parties. It does not, of its own initiative, seek to interfere when citizens have recourse to other tribunals'.
9   Arbitration Act 1996 s 1(b) reads as follows: 'the parties should be free to agree how their disputes are resolved, subject only to such safeguards necessary in the public interest'.

COSTS

Like party choice, the issue of cost is multifaceted. While discourse normally focusses on the benefits to the individual in terms of cost,[10] it must also be remembered that the legal system itself saves money and time when disputes are resolved other than at court through litigation. This can occur due to 'settlement at the courtroom door' where those in dispute only avoid litigation late on in proceedings and thereby waste court time in the case management process. The Woolf Report[11] and the Jackson Report[12] on the costs of civil litigation both advocate the use of ADR as a method of avoiding spiralling costs. As was discussed in Chapter 10, the Access to Justice Act 1999[13] and changes to the Civil Procedure Rules (also discussed later) encourage and support the use of ADR.

Generally, the costs of using certain forms of ADR are lower for disputants than the costs of litigation. Some jurisdictions take this idea much further, particularly where there are perceived problems in relation to access to justice. As just one example, the Legal Services Authority Act 1987 of India regularises the concept of Lok Adalat (the People's Court) where retired judges, amongst others, sit in public in order to resolve disputes through compromise, sitting on up to 150 cases in one day.[14] As such it is a quick and efficient form of dispute resolution that attracts no fees whatsoever. Although this could be accused of being second class justice, it does allow those who would otherwise struggle to afford court fees to have access to justice. However, within the English Legal System, this idea that ADR leads to reduced costs should not be taken too far. Although it is true that the services of a skilled mediator are likely to be less expensive than the sum cost of pursuing a case through litigation, it should be remembered that not all mediations are successful. Where a particular mediation fails outright, the parties are likely to revert back to pursuing the action through the courts. The total cost would be greater than if litigation on its own had been pursued.

APPROPRIATE FORUM FOR DISCUSSION

Much of the growth of the use of ADR is linked to an acceptance that different disputes raise different issues and so may require different solutions. In this regard, two distinct but interrelated factors (in addition to costs) should be taken into account when considering the processes of dispute resolution (including whether to progress to litigation): *the relationship of the parties and the importance of the issue.*

Determining the relationship of the parties is an important step in selecting the *appropriate* form of dispute resolution. If the relationship is familial in nature, then the importance of both maintaining a continuing relationship and of the parties feeling ownership over the final

---

10 In one case, for example, the costs of litigation far outstripped the amount recovered: *Seventh Earl of Malmesbury v Strutt* [2008] EWHC 424 (QB), [2008] 5 Costs LR 736 [6] – this was described as 'a horrendous figure' by Jack J.

11 Lord Woolf Final Report 'Access to Justice' (HMSO July 1996).

12 Lord Justice Jackson Final Report 'Review of Civil Litigation Costs' (HMSO Jan 2010).

13 Access to Justice Act 1999 s 4(4)(c) for example requires those administering legal aid to take decisions to 'achieve the swift and fair resolution of disputes without unnecessary or unduly protracted proceedings in court'.

14 For a brief description of the operation of Lok Adalat, see Soumita Majmundar 'Lok Adalats (People's Courts) in State of Gujarat' (1991) 9(2) Commonwealth Judicial Journal 18.

outcome is paramount. This is why family law disputes are often dealt with via mediation which is seen as less confrontational than a court hearing and has the advantage of being an agreed, as opposed to imposed, solution. Similarly, if the relationship is one of equal commercial actors in an industry that requires a high level of technical knowledge, or where transactions take place over multiple countries, and especially where the particular industry involves a small circle of principal companies and individuals who must all associate with one another e.g. at annual industry conferences, or where their product is so specialised that they must all contract with one another, then having the dispute settled by an expert under pre-agreed procedures may be the most appropriate solution. Therefore, many disputes concerning international commercial contracts are settled via arbitration. If there is significant imbalance in the power relationship between the parties then, depending on the skill and gravitas of the mediator, mediation may not adequately protect the weaker party and so conciliation may be a better option. This is why ACAS is often involved in conciliation in employment situations. Finally, if the relationship is one of consumer and provider of services that are of low value, a progressive 'complaints' system that incorporates multiple methods of dispute resolution may prove sensible as court action is likely to be prohibitive in terms of costs. This is the system that is operated in relation to disputes between members of the Association of British Travel Agents (ABTA) and consumers who have booked holidays through ABTA members.

Similarly, determining the importance of the issue is a key step in assessing which is the most appropriate form of dispute resolution for a particular dispute. For example, if the outcome is likely to govern future relationships then an adjudicated solution (or a neutral evaluation) that can be relied upon in the future will be the most desirable outcome, as opposed to a negotiation that could be re-opened the next time the dispute is made. Equally, if the legal position is extremely unclear there may be a *strategic* advantage in avoiding litigation that may settle the point against a party. Similarly, if determination of *legal rights* is unimportant then a negotiated settlement may be better as it allows for strategic bargaining to occur with low cost risks.

TAKING THINGS FURTHER – THE WEBSITE

The companion site to this textbook contains an exercise that can help you to test your understanding of the different needs of, and relationship between, parties when considering ADR. You will be presented with a number of scenarios and must recommend, with reasoning, the most appropriate form of dispute resolution. This type of applied reasoning is essential for legal practice where clients will want to be told not necessarily of all of the options but rather of the ones that are most likely to produce the desired result.

The following sections of the chapter will focus on two methods of dispute resolution: arbitration and mediation. These are chosen as they are the most prevalent forms of dispute resolution and represent the dispute resolution (arbitration) and dispute settlement (mediation) forms of ADR. As a result, the discussion contained in the following sections will reveal some of the principles of the broad categories of dispute resolution as well as their strengths and weaknesses.

ARBITRATION

The nature of arbitration is adjudicative. The parties submit their case to an independent third party (or panel of such people) sitting as an arbitral tribunal which determines the outcome and whose findings, called 'Awards', are normally legally binding and can be enforced as if they were ordered by a court. Arbitrators act in a judicial manner and follow the rules of natural justice[15] but do not have to follow the strict procedural rules of litigation in the civil courts. The arbitrator normally has specialist expertise in the subject matter of the dispute that is far beyond that which could be expected from a judge sitting in a generalist court. Quality of arbitrator can be assured through using one listed by professional bodies, such as the Chartered Institute of Arbitrators (CIArb).[16] Arbitration is attractive to those dealing with sensitive commercial information as confidentiality can be assured.

Being adjudicative and adversarial in nature, arbitration is the method of ADR that bears the greatest resemblance to litigation. However, there is a danger of confusing the two. Lord Scarman gave a concise and accurate statement of the similarities and differences in *Bremer Vulcan*.[17]

> **Litigation ... is a compulsory process** available as of right to anyone who issues a writ: it is not to be compared with the process of arbitration, which arises from **consent** and is **conducted according to terms agreed, expressly or impliedly by the parties**. Arbitration is, of course, subject to a measure of statutory control: but this control in no way detracts from the **essentially contractual nature of arbitration**.... But arbitration, while consensual, **is also an adversarial process**. There is a dispute, the parties having failed to settle their difference by negotiation. Though they choose a tribunal, agree its procedure and agree to accept its award as final, the process is adversarial. **Embedded in the adversarial process is a right that each party shall have a fair hearing, that each should have a fair opportunity of presenting and developing his case**. In this respect, there is a comparability between litigation and arbitration. In each **delay can mean justice denied** (See Figure 14.5).[18]

---

15 A point recently reinforced by the Privy Council in *Cukurova v Sonera* [2014] UKPC 15, [2015] 2 All ER 1061 [31].
16 www.ciarb.org.
17 *Bremer Vulkan v South India Shipping Corporation* [1981] AC 909 (HL).
18 Ibid. 999 (Lord Scarman).

Figure 14.5 The Relationship Between Arbitration and Litigation

ARBITRATION ACT 1996

Much of the law surrounding the conduct and principles of arbitration within the English Legal System can be found within the Arbitration Act 1996. The Act arose in the wake of the UNCITRAL Model Arbitration Law of 1985 which the UN provided in order to promote greater consistency in the arbitration laws of the various member countries. In response to the Model Law, Lord Justice Mustill, who chaired the UK Departmental Advisory Committee on Arbitration Law, suggested that the English Legal System should not fully adopt the Model Law.[19] It was felt that to adopt the Model Law would be to harm the existing, highly developed principles of arbitration law that had arisen via common law and statute. Instead, Lord Mustill's Committee reported in 1989 that an attempt should be made to lay down 'in statutory form … the more important principles of the English Law of arbitration, statutory and (to the extent practicable) common law'.[20] Out of this, and some seven years later, came the Arbitration Act 1996.

RATIONALE OF THE ARBITRATION ACT 1996

The purpose of the Arbitration Act 1996 was twofold. Firstly, and as noted previously, it was about consolidating the existing statutory framework and the existing case law. As you will recall from Chapter 4 on primary law-making, this type of Act is a partly consolidating Act. Secondly, the aim was further to increase the attractiveness of England as the seat and, more particularly, London as the location for international commercial arbitration. This was a process which had already begun at the time owing to the reputation of our superior judiciary and of our international commercial arbitrators, many of whom were retired judges of the Commercial Court, other High Court judges and Court of Appeal and House of Lords judiciary. In many ways the first aim arises out of the second, with a codified set of principles reducing uncertainty for those who wish to use English commercial law to

---

19 Departmental Advisory Committee on Arbitration Law, 'A Report on the UNCITRAL Model Law on International Commercial Arbitration' (HMSO 1989).

20 Ibid. [108].

settle their disputes. This reveals one of the most important motivations for using arbitration as opposed to litigation, namely that parties sometimes wish to utilise the *legal principles* of a system without having to pursue those principles through the formal system of courts. If you cast your mind back to Chapter 1 of this textbook, you will recall that a distinction was drawn between the 'law' and the 'system' of laws that govern a nation. Arbitration allows parties to use, for example, the legal principles of English commercial law to settle their disputes without having to be at the mercy of English judges sitting in English courts applying English court procedures. Arbitration can, therefore, be law without a legal system, but reinforced by the international reach of the CIArb and its regulatory framework.

It is important to note from the outset that the Arbitration Act 1996 applies only to written agreements to arbitrate.[21] These written agreements will usually be found in contracts and so formal arbitration happens most commonly where the parties have a contractual relationship. The underlying contract, which will normally give rise to the dispute, need not be written itself providing that the agreement to arbitrate is in written form. The agreement to arbitrate is classed as a distinct agreement even if it forms part of the contract.[22] This doctrine of separability is particularly important as it means that if the validity of the contract itself is called into question during the arbitration proceedings then the legitimacy of the arbitration cannot itself be questioned for that reason.

Much of the Act applies only where the seat of arbitration is England and Wales.[23] The seat of arbitration relates to the law that governs the actual arbitration procedure and the way in which, and where, an award can be enforced. Some sections of the Act apply where the seat is elsewhere but the law of England and Wales has been selected to settle the dispute.[24] Finally, some provisions apply regardless of the law chosen to settle the dispute or the seat of arbitration.[25] It should, therefore, be recognised that the Arbitration Act 1996 can apply, to varying degrees, in a wide range of circumstances where arbitration has been selected as the method to settle the dispute.

As will be discussed in greater detail later, the Arbitration Act 1996 can be viewed through a number of lenses: the powers it gives to arbitral tribunals, the powers it gives (or reserves) to courts and the matters it leaves to parties' choice. Figure 14.6 attempts to illustrate these different aspects of the Arbitration Act through categorising some (but not all) of its provisions.

----

21 Arbitration Act 1996 s 5 – 'The provisions of this Part apply only where the arbitration agreement is in writing, and any other agreement between the parties as to any matter is effective for the purposes of this Part only if in writing.'

22 Arbitration Act 1996 s 7.

23 Arbitration Act 1996 s 2(1).

24 For example, Arbitration Act s 7 on separability of the agreement to arbitrate and s 8 on the death of a party. These requirements are laid down in the Arbitration Act 1996 s 2(3). Some clauses of an agreement to arbitrate are therefore non-negotiable and must be included.

25 Most notably the Arbitration Act ss 9–11 on the ability of the court to stay proceedings and s 66 on enforcement of awards. These requirements are laid down in the Arbitration Act 1996 s 2(2).

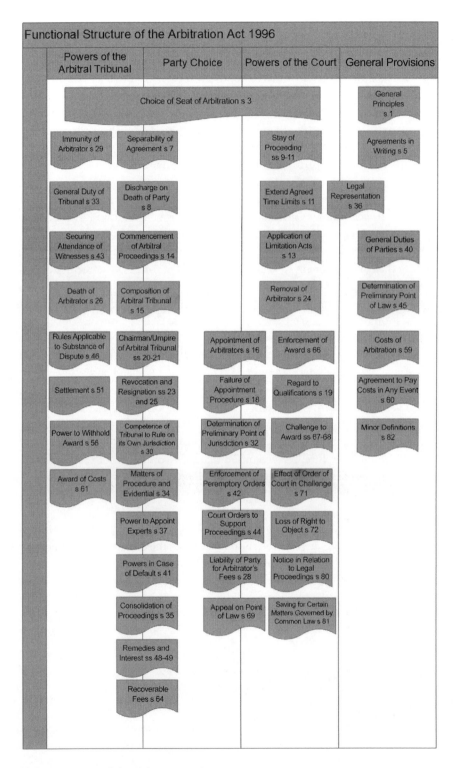

Figure 14.6 Structure of the Arbitration Act

A note of caution should be applied to Figure 14.6. It is unlikely, in a study of the English Legal System, that you will need to know all of the listed provisions in any level of detail. Instead, the diagram should be used only as a way of understanding that the Act is sculpted around these broad themes, with particular emphasis on party choice. Where a provision straddles a line in the diagram it represents a situation where parties *can* decide what happens in that situation but there is a default position if the parties do not deal with the issue in their agreement to arbitrate.

GENERAL PROVISIONS OF THE ARBITRATION ACT 1996

The wording of the Arbitration Act 1996 is unusual for an Act of Parliament in that it opens with very 'principle-based' sections. This is likely to indicate the importance of the second purpose of the Act, as described previously – to improve the attractiveness of London as a centre of worldwide arbitration. It is a 'sales pitch', intending to explain what place arbitration holds in the English Legal System and is particularly useful in international arbitration where a party from a civil law jurisdiction would be expecting these points to be spelled out, as everything is in the format of such a jurisdiction's Constitution and codes so that their mind-set looks for such articulation. The more important sections of the Arbitration Act 1999 are laid out later, starting with those that reinforce the idea of party choice before moving on to discuss the powers that are granted to the arbitrators under the Act and ending with a discussion of the role of the courts under the Act. It is clearly a positive feature of the Act that while some sections of the Act must be followed, and cannot be changed by the parties, any not so designated are optional.

EXPLAINING THE LAW – ARBITRATION ACT 1996

Section 1 of the Act transcends these themes and lays down the following principles:

S 1: (a) the object of arbitration is to obtain the fair resolution of disputes by an impartial tribunal without unnecessary delay or expense;

 (b) the parties should be free to agree how their disputes are resolved, subject only to such safeguards as are necessary in the public interest;

 (c) in matters governed by this Part the court should not intervene except as provided by this Part.

Section 1 gives out a number of important messages about the nature of arbitration in the English Legal System. Firstly, it explicitly recognises one of the perceived advantages of arbitration in cutting cost and delay (s 1(a)). Secondly, it emphasises party choice in the process (s 1(b)). Thirdly, it expressly and unequivocally limits the jurisdiction of the ordinary courts in becoming involved where an arbitration agreement exists. This is a clear indication of support for ADR as a matter of public policy. Rather than reading as the opening section to an important and very technical Act of Parliament, it reads as an open advertisement on the benefits of using England as the seat for arbitration. It strongly reinforces the three key benefits of arbitration as a method of ADR: avoidance of cost and delay, the importance of party choice and the limited involvement of the formal institutions of the legal system.

The desire for arbitration to be an expeditious method for parties to resolve their disputes is reinforced by the case law. In *Bremer Vulcan*[26] the House of Lords held that excessive and unreasonable delay to answer a claim of arbitration may lead to a repudiatory breach of the arbitration agreement, entitling the other party to treat the requirement to refer disputes for arbitration as void. This is because excessive delays prejudice a right to a fair hearing. As Lord Denning reminisced in the Court of Appeal:

> When I was young, a sandwich-man wearing a top-hat used to parade outside these courts with his boards back and front, proclaiming 'Arbitrate, don't litigate.' It was very good advice so long as arbitrations were conducted speedily: as many still are in the City of London. But it is not so good when arbitrations drag on forever.[27]

PARTY CHOICE

The Arbitration Act 1996 gives the parties involved a large amount of autonomy over not only the choice of arbitration as a method of dispute resolution but also over how the Arbitration Tribunal conducts itself. Schedule I of the Act lists the mandatory provisions that apply notwithstanding any agreement between the parties. These are minimum standards that provide some level of consistency and certainty to the disputants. Aside from this, the parties can determine whether other sections of the Act apply. In most instances, each issue is left to the arbitration agreement, but the Act gives default positions, should the parties not cater for the particular issue in their agreement. The following is subject to an overriding duty on the arbitrator to 'act fairly and impartially as between the parties, giving each party a reasonable opportunity of putting his case and dealing with that of his opponent, and adopt procedures suitable to the circumstances of the particular case, avoiding unnecessary delay or expense, so as to provide a fair means for the resolution of the matters falling to be determined'.[28] The parties have the power to determine, amongst other things, the following aspects of the arbitration:

1 The seat of arbitration (s 3)
2 The date on which arbitral proceedings are commenced (s 14)
3 The number, identity and process of appointment for the arbitrator (s 15 and s 16)
4 The function of any Chairperson (s 20)
5 The revocation of the authority of a particular arbitrator (s 23)[29]
6 The procedures of the tribunal and any rules of evidence that will apply (s 34)

In the absence of agreement on any of the preceding points, the Arbitration Act 1996 details within the relevant section how the matter is to be resolved.

....

26 *Bremer Vulkan v South India Shipping Corporation* [1981] AC 909 (HL).
27 *Bremer Vulkan v South India Shipping* [1980] 2 WLR 905 (CA) 933 (Lord Denning MR).
28 Arbitration Act 1996 s 33.
29 This power must be exercised by both parties acting jointly (s 23(1)) and in writing (s 23(4)), unless they have a different procedure detailed in their arbitration agreement.

EXPLAINING THE LAW – PARTY CHOICE

Given the prominence of party choice in the Arbitration Act 1996, it is not surprising to find the courts placing similar emphasis on its importance. Thus, in the *Channel Tunnel*[30] case, Lord Mustill was keen to emphasise that when parties have chosen a form of dispute resolution, such as arbitration, to settle their contractual disputes then '[h]aving made this choice I believe that it is in accordance … with the interests of the orderly regulation of international commerce, that having promised to take their complaints to the experts and if necessary to the arbitrators, that is where the appellants should go. The fact that the appellants now find their chosen method too slow to suit their purpose, is to my way of thinking quite beside the point.'[31]

POWERS OF COURT

Although s 1 of the Act makes it clear that courts should not lightly intervene in the arbitral process, that same section does make clear that the court itself is given powers under the Act. A court, for example, has the power to stay proceedings under s 9(1) of the Act where one of the parties tries to bring a legal action before the arbitration is allowed to run its course. This power ensures that the courts are not used to bypass the agreement of the parties to settle their dispute by arbitration and helps to achieve the rationale of s 1(c) Arbitration Act 1996, namely of non-interference by the court in private agreements. S 9(4) creates a presumption that the court will grant such a stay unless it is satisfied that the agreement to arbitrate is 'null and void, inoperative, or incapable of being performed'. The court also has a power to extend any time limits within the arbitration.[32] In order to invoke this power the court must be satisfied that either it would be unjust, due to the behaviour of one of the parties, to hold the other party to the time limit or where the delay was due to circumstances outside of the 'reasonable contemplation' of the parties.

The previous subsection of this chapter dealt with the appointment of a suitable arbitrator or arbitrators and noted that this was left to party choice. The courts are only permitted to intervene, by virtue of ss 16 and 18, where this process fails or where there is nothing in the arbitration agreement pertaining to appointment.

The courts maintain jurisdiction to remove an arbitrator in the following circumstances:

- Where there are doubts as to impartiality[33]
- Where the arbitrator does not contain qualifications stipulated by the arbitration agreement[34]
- Where there are doubts as to mental or physical capacity to conduct the proceedings[35]

---

30 *Channel Tunnel Group v Balfour Beatty Construction* [1993] AC 334 (HL).
31 Ibid. 353 (Lord Mustill).
32 Arbitration Act 1996 s 12.
33 Arbitration Act 1996 s 24(1)(a).
34 Arbitration Act 1996 s 24(1)(b).
35 Arbitration Act 1996 s 24(1)(c).

- Where the arbitrator has failed to conduct the hearing properly *and* where 'substantial injustice has been or will be caused' to the person applying for the court's intervention[36]
- Courts can also order enforcement of the award, which will be treated in the same manner as enforcement of a court order.[37]

The preceding powers of the court in the case of arbitration are largely about ensuring that there are procedural safeguards in place so that parties feel confident in electing arbitration as their method of ADR and to govern situations where party choice fails.

In addition to the aforementioned powers, the courts have a role in ensuring that arbitral awards are fairly arrived at and managing the process of challenge to an award. It is here that we see an inherent tension between the stated aims of arbitration. By this we mean that the legal system has to try to balance the wants of the parties in avoiding litigation and in ensuring that awards made are fair and do not distort the established law. Thus, even after the completion of an arbitral hearing, the parties may still end up in court. Due to the wish of the English Legal System to make the UK an attractive choice for international commercial arbitration the circumstances for challenging an award of an arbitral tribunal through the court system are extremely limited. The following circumstances give rise to potential for challenge:

- If the substantive jurisdiction of the tribunal is in issue (s 67)
- If there were serious irregularities that risk causing injustice to the applicant (s 68)[38]
- If there is an alleged error of law (s 69)

The possibility for appeal on a point of law has proved to be controversial as it risks undermining the speed and efficiency of the arbitration process and introducing many of the pitfalls of litigation. To prevent recourse to the 'error of law' becoming too frequent the Act lay down a strict test for the courts to apply. In exercising this jurisdiction and granting leave for an appeal, the courts must follow strict guidelines of s 69(3), which have their origin in the common law test of *The Nema*:[39]

(a) that the determination of the question will substantially affect the rights of one or more of the parties,
(b) that the question is one which the tribunal was asked to determine,
(c) that, on the basis of the findings of fact in the award –

   (i) the decision of the tribunal on the question is obviously wrong, or
   (ii) the question is one of general public importance and the decision of the tribunal is at least open to serious doubt, and

(d) that, despite the agreement of the parties to resolve the matter by arbitration, it is just and proper in all the circumstances for the court to determine the question.

....

36 Arbitration Act 1996 s 24(1)(d).
37 Arbitration Act 1996 s 66.
38 This can include failure of the tribunal to comply with its duties, where the tribunal acts outside of its agreed powers or where the tribunal has failed to act according to the procedures agreed by the parties.
39 *Pioneer Shipping v BTP Tioxide (The Nema)* [1982] AC 724 (HL) 742 (Lord Diplock).

Parties can even attempt, through agreement, to circumvent the potential of challenge to an arbitral award. This attempt to oust the jurisdiction of the court is controversial as it runs the risk of violating fundamental rights, such as the right to a fair trial/hearing. This very issue was raised in the *Sumukan*[40] case.

MAKING CONNECTIONS AND ANALYSING THE LAW – OUSTING THE JURISDICTION OF THE COURT
++

The English Legal System protects certain fundamental rights. One of those rights is the right to a fair trial under Article 6 of the European Convention on Human Rights. In the *Sumukan* case a contract contained, by reference to a statutory scheme, an arbitration agreement that itself excluded the possibility of appeal on a point of law. In essence, the arbitration agreement wished to exclude the court's jurisdiction under s 69 of the Arbitration Act 1996.

Although s 69 of the Act states that an appeal on a point of law is possible '[u]nless otherwise agreed by the parties', in *Sumukan* the question was whether the exclusion of s 69 jurisdiction needed to be expressly stated, rather than incorporated by reference. The line of argument was that to exclude the jurisdiction of the court was a serious issue that should only be used where parties expressly agreed to it. To decide otherwise, the claimants argued, would violate the right to a fair trial. The court disagreed, holding that excluding appeal by reference was not a violation of the ECHR.

The reasoning of the High Court here is interesting as it based on the purpose of arbitration as preserving 'privacy and confidentiality'[41] and 'to reflect and preserve the twin objectives of finality and party autonomy'.[42] In doing so, the court has placed great emphasis on contract, as opposed to public law, principles. Indeed, in supporting the finding, Mr Justice Colman made express reference to the general law of contract on exclusion agreements.[43] He went further in saying that, in comparison to a contract law issue on excluding *liability*, the exclusion of a right to appeal did not go to substantive rights but went '**only** to the ancillary dispute resolution machinery'.[44]

What is clear from the *Sumukan* case is that in the balance between procedural rights and contractual freedom, the court will place special emphasis on the latter due to the policy objectives – party freedom and independence from the courts – where arbitration is involved.

---

40 *Sumukan v Commonwealth Secretariat* [2006] EWHC 1148 (Comm), [2006] 1 All ER (Comm) 621.
41 Ibid. [16].
42 Ibid.
43 Ibid. [19] (Colman J) citing Lord Justice Bingham in *Circle Freight International Ltd v Medeast Gulf Exports Ltd* [1988] 2 Lloyd's Rep 427 (CA), 433 (Bingham LJ).
44 Ibid. [20] (Colman J).

POWERS AND DUTIES OF ARBITRATORS AND THE ARBITRAL TRIBUNAL

Although not appearing until the mid-portion of the Arbitration Act 1996, it is important to note that each individual Arbitration Tribunal is under an overarching duty to:

> act fairly and impartially as between the parties, giving each party a reasonable opportunity of putting his case and dealing with that of his opponent, and adopt procedures suitable to the circumstances of the particular case, avoiding unnecessary delay or expense, so as to provide a fair means for the resolution of the matters falling to be determined.[45]

The preceding general duty reiterates the points made at the start of this section of the chapter, namely that the Arbitration Act 1996 has a dual purpose of achieving a fair and just outcome according to the wishes of the parties and of allowing for an expedient and cost-effective resolution of the dispute. The arbitral tribunal is under a duty to decide the dispute according to the law chosen by the parties and/or any other considerations that the parties may agree.[46]

As well as the general duty to act fairly, the arbitral tribunal has general powers in relation to the organisation of arbitration proceedings. Amongst these general powers is the ability to require and administer oaths and affirmations.[47] The arbitrator(s) has important powers in relation to the jurisdiction of the Arbitration Tribunal. This power extends to determining the validity of the arbitration agreement itself and to the subject matter of the dispute to be determined.[48]

In addition, and if the parties do not agree otherwise, the tribunal can determine evidential and procedural issues from basic decisions such as the location of the arbitration proceedings to more complex rules on disclosure of documents and whether the proceedings will be through written statements only or whether oral arguments would be heard.[49] These powers include the determination of admissibility of evidence and any weight that will attach to particular types or pieces of evidence.

The arbitrator has a very strong immunity for acts done in discharge of his or her duty. This extends beyond acts undertaken negligently and s 29 makes arbitrators only liable for acts or omissions made in bad faith. Should a party cause 'inordinate and inexcusable delay' then the tribunal has the power to make an award dismissing the case.[50] In relation to remedies, the tribunal, agreement notwithstanding, has powers to issue a range of remedies that are broadly similar to those available to an ordinary court. The arbitral tribunal can order a payment of money (akin to damages) and order things similar to injunctions and specific performance.[51] The arbitral tribunal can also order an award of costs.[52]

45 Arbitration Act 1996 s 33.
46 Arbitration Act 1996 s 46.
47 Arbitration Act 1996 s 38.
48 Arbitration Act 1996 s 30.
49 Arbitration Act 1996 s 34.
50 Arbitration Act 1996 s 41(3).
51 Arbitration Act 1996 s 48(4)–(5).
52 Arbitration Act 1996 s 61.

Figure 14.7 Common Forms of Arbitration

COMMON EXAMPLES OF ARBITRATION

The principles of arbitration, as they now find expression in the Arbitration Act 1996, that apply within the English Legal System have developed largely in the context of English commercial law. The importance of freedom of contract/party choice, confidentiality and speed of process has therefore dominated the understanding of formal arbitration as a dispute resolution mechanism. As a result, much of what is talked about in relation to the Arbitration Act 1996 is directly relevant for and related to commercial arbitration. Nonetheless, and more recently, the Arbitration Act 1996 has increasingly been used by a wider range of disputants to settle their disagreements. The forms of arbitration discussed in this section are summarised in Figure 14.7. Most recently arbitration has been extended outside the civil and commercial context to family law, both in determining financial and property cases and issues in the private law relating to children. This initiative was undertaken by a pan professional group of stakeholders centred on the Chartered Institute of Arbitrators, which undertook the training of specialist arbitrators for the scheme, which was guided by the Family Law Bar Association and Resolution (the Solicitors Family Law Association which uses this style as a business name). The entire scheme was inspired and brought to life by an academic and practitioners' research committee known as the Centre for Child and Family Law reform, usually chaired by a specialist Family judge, and sponsored by City University of London. The Scheme was launched, originally only for Financial and Property cases, in 2012; is administered by Resolution; and its regulatory board initially chaired by the former Labour Lord Chancellor, Lord Falconer of Thoroton. The current Chairman is Lord Neuberger of Abbotsbury, recently retired President of the Supreme Court and the scheme was extended to include private child law cases in 2016. Training of new arbitrators continues annually and the scheme is already gathering sufficient momentum to provide significant assistance to the Family Court in addressing its volume of work and in particular reducing delay in awaiting hearings for disposal of their cases since a study by one arbitrator[53] has shown that an arbitration can be completed within three or four months, half the time that might otherwise be spent in awaiting a hearing date at the Family Court.

COMMERCIAL ARBITRATION

Even within the ill-defined arena of 'commercial law' certain transactions and relationships lend themselves more to arbitration than others. For example, arbitration agreements (and adjudication) are common in construction contracts. This is due primarily to the need for disputes to be dealt with swiftly and with relevant expertise over costs when construction projects overrun on time or budget or require significant amendments. This was evident

---

53 Dennis Sheridan and Suzanne Kingston, *Family Arbitration: Practice and Precedents* (2nd edn, Law Society 2017).

with the *Channel Tunnel* case just discussed. The case involved the valuation of changes to the original agreed work. As well as being a construction case, *Channel Tunnel* also demonstrates the other major area where arbitration is used and that relates to relationships that take place, or operate, in the international arena – in the case of the Channel Tunnel project, primarily between companies and governments in the UK and France.

The term 'international commercial arbitration' is often used when describing the use of the Arbitration Act 1996. The term has connotations that suggest resolution at the international level but as there is no supranational system of arbitration this has to have a national context. We are talking about *international disputes* that take place in a *national jurisdiction* according to *domestic* rules of the chosen jurisdiction.

The lack of a supranational forum or of a fully harmonised set of international rules for settling arbitrations results in competition between jurisdictions to become the seat of individual arbitrations. It is from this competition that the 'sales pitch' of s 1 of the Arbitration Act 1996 arises. Consequently, commercial contracts involving cross-border activity often contain arbitration clauses. This adds a great deal of certainty to proceedings and prevents 'forum shopping' – a practice by which a party in dispute will pick the most advantageous jurisdiction within which to launch an action. Where a contract is to be executed by parties in different countries or where goods are to be shipped across many territorial waters it can lead to a great deal of uncertainty. Arbitration can help to strip away that uncertainty and allows parties to dictate, before a dispute even arises, where and by which law their disagreement is to be resolved.

FAITH-BASED ARBITRATION

Traditional textbook discourse on the English Legal System tends to focus on commercial arbitration and will analyse the merits and disadvantages of arbitration as a whole in relation to the commercial world. That presents a very narrow view of the role of arbitration (and ADR more generally) in society. This chapter takes a broader view and will consider the use of faith-based arbitration as a mechanism of resolving disputes. This is seen as a growing area of ADR within the English Legal System. For example, in 2007, the Muslim Arbitration Tribunal (MAT) was established. It allows Muslims to have certain types of dispute determined in accordance with Schools of Islamic Sacred Law. The tribunal sits with at least two members: one a scholar of Islamic Law and the other a qualified solicitor or barrister. The integration of faith into the ADR system is a highly charged political issue and also tells us a great deal about the flexibility of the legal system and of acceptance of faith considerations within that system. The degree of sensitivity over the issue of faith-based dispute resolution was drawn into sharp focus by the comments of the Archbishop of Canterbury in 2008, when he appeared to advocate the adoption of religious law within the English Legal System.[54] His comments found some support from Lord Phillips, speaking extrajudicially.[55]

---

54 For academic comment, see Julian Rivers, 'The secularisation of the British Constitution' (2012) 14(3) Ecclesiastical Law Journal 371, 391, https://www.cambridge.org/core/journals/ecclesiastical-law-journal/article/secularisa-tion-of-the-british-constitution/40886A0AB7A0E649D2AC109EFCA01A75.

55 http://news.bbc.co.uk/1/hi/uk/7488790.stm.

EXPLAINING THE LAW – FAITH-BASED ARBITRATION

The recent judgment in *AI v MT*[56] is revealing as to the approach of the courts to faith-based arbitration. The case concerned an orthodox Jewish couple whose marriage ran into difficulties and as a result the British born mother refused to return to Canada with her children. Initially, the father sought an order from the English courts requiring the return of the children. The parties then agreed that their dispute be resolved using a specific Jewish religious arbitration tribunal whose decision they would respect – that of the Beth Din in New York.

In the case at hand, the English courts were asked to dismiss the father's initial claim, given the agreement of the parties to proceed to a binding religious tribunal through the New York Beth Din. The court refused to make the order on this basis but, after examining the principles that would be used in the religious tribunal, Mr Justice Baker indicated that the award of the New York Beth Din would be 'likely to carry considerable weight with the court … [but] … would not be binding and would not preclude either party from pursuing applications to this court in respect of any of the matters in issue'.[57] On this basis a consent order was granted and the father's initial claim dismissed. When the matter returned to court after the completion of the Beth Din hearing, Mr Justice Baker endorsed the findings of the Beth Din and transferred them into an order. Sadly this humane decision of a leading Family judge, now Lord Justice Baker of the Court of Appeal, was immediately misunderstood by the global press, including The Times in London: one leading broadsheet published a picture of the Dome of the Rock in Jerusalem above a headline indicating that Sharia law would henceforth be applied in England and Wales (not even apparently appreciating that the case was about a Jewish rather than a Muslim family.)

In this case the English Legal System managed to accommodate the wishes of the parties, based on their deeply held religious views, while not threatening the consistency of the legal system. As a result, the faith-based tribunal was respected within a secular court system. This was possible because the principles by which the New York Beth Din came to its conclusions were equivalent to those that would have been followed by an English court. However, and unlike a commercial arbitration, the Beth Din award could not be binding and enforced in the English Legal System without final approval from a court. As the interests of the children were paramount to the determination of the Beth Din, the court felt able (cautiously) to respect the choice of the party. However, Mr Justice Baker made it clear that if he was 'independently of the view that it was not in the child's best interests I would unhesitatingly say so and refuse to order it, notwithstanding the very great respect this Court has for the deliberations of the Beth Din.'[58]

----

56 *AI v MT (Alternative Dispute Resolution)* [2013] EWHC 100 (Fam), [2013] 2 FLR 371.
57 Ibid. [15] (Baker J).
58 Ibid. [18] (Baker J).

Although mediation is a more prevalent form of dispute resolution in this area, it is clear from this case that many of the perceived benefits of commercial arbitration can extend into the realm of family law. It is worth noting that Mr Justice Baker made particular reference to the benefits of speed, cost and the ability of the parties to choose the specific arbitrator who will settle their dispute.[59] The 2011 judgment of the Supreme Court in Jivraj,[60] an early decision following its inauguration in 2009, marks an important step in the recognition of faith-based arbitration as an integral part of the English Legal System. In the case, Lord Mance's comments are particularly enlightening in that he held that arbitrator's contracts are of a *sui generis* nature which means that arbitrators are not employees and are not subject to discrimination rules.[61] This, contrary to the judgment of the Court of Appeal in this case,[62] means that it is lawful for those of faith to have a contractual requirement that an arbitrator be drawn from a particular faith without breaching the rules surrounding discrimination on the basis of religious beliefs.

Turning back to *AI v MT* Baker J went even further so as to suggest that party autonomy, even in sensitive family law disputes, underpins both the Children Act 1989[63] and Article 8 of the ECHR.[64] However, and as demonstrated by the case, due to public policy issues surrounding the welfare and protection of children the benefits of arbitration must be hemmed in with additional safeguards. Thus, parties are unable to oust the jurisdiction of the court through agreement in certain matrimonial and family matters.[65] The *quid pro quo* being that the court will give significant weight to the award given by a tribunal that follows principles common to English law. The judgment in *AI v MT* is of particular importance in debunking the assumption that recent trends in the growth of ADR have been traced to the 'waning role of some of society's traditional [dispute resolving] institutions – the family, the church and the community'.[66] The case demonstrates that religion, dispute resolution and the legal system can not only co-exist but can have a meaningful and beneficial relationship.

While *AI v MT* represents a seemingly satisfactory accommodation of belief and party autonomy within the Legal System, the principle is not without controversy. Concerns have been expressed about the practice of certain faith-based Arbitration Tribunals where (1) the principles adopted to resolve disputes are not in accordance with English law and (2) where certain tribunals are falsely claiming jurisdiction to adjudicate on matters (including certain family and criminal matters) that they should not be deciding.

----

59 Ibid. [32] (Baker J).
60 Jivraj v Hashwani [2011] UKSC 40, [2011] 1 WLR 1872.
61 Ibid. [77]–[78] (Lord Mance).
62 Jivraj v Hashwani [2010] EWCA Civ 712, [2011] 1 All ER 50.
63 Which vests, via s 2, responsibility for the welfare of children primarily with the parents.
64 Which secures the right to a family life.
65 A principle laid down as long ago as the 1920s in Hyman v Hyman [1929] AC 601 (HL) 613 – a case concerning an agreement of a wife not to petition the court for maintenance on the ending of her marriage.
66 Frank Sander, 'Alternative dispute resolution in the United States: an overview' in Julio Betancourt and Jason Crook (eds), *ADR, Arbitration, and Mediation* (AuthorHouse 2014) 2.

MAKING CONNECTIONS AND ANALYSING THE LAW – LEGISLATIVE
REACTION TO FAITH-BASED ARBITRATION
+ +

Chapter 4 examined the process by which legislation is passed. The chapter discussed
the prospect of non-government bills being introduced into Parliament, particularly on
sensitive matters. In order to address the concerns over false claims of jurisdiction and
threats to equality Baroness Cox introduced a Private Members Bill – the Arbitration
and Mediation Services (Equality) Bill – in the 2012–2013 session.

The Bill sought to criminalise false claims of jurisdiction and to ensure equality
(particularly in relation to sex) in execution of arbitration proceedings and other
proceedings available under English law based on faith. Baroness Cox made an
impassioned speech on the introduction of the Bill to the House of Lords, indicating
existing problems in relation to certain Sharia 'courts' and community pressure on
Muslim women not to resort to the more formal legal proceedings.[67] These issues
range from problems over substantive differences in treatment of men and women to
those relating to evidence and procedure.[68]

While the concerns were aimed at parts of the Muslim Arbitration Tribunal, the vast
majority of problems seem to arise in less formal fora where women (who might as
well e.g. have sought divorce and financial provision under English law) are led to
believe that the Sharia 'court' has binding powers. During the Second Reading of the
Bill, Baroness Donaghy noted that the problems caused by certain forms of faith-
based dispute resolution risk bringing the whole system of ADR into disrepute.[69]
As was mentioned in the Second Reading Stage of the Bill in the House of Lords,
certain faith-based dispute settlement processes are questionable because women
often suffer 'a language barrier, huge cultural or family pressure, ignorance of the
law, a misplaced faith in the system or a threat of complete isolation' that means
that the process is 'as consensual as rape'.[70] While the Bill ultimately did not make it
through the process to become an Act of Parliament, it is indicative of the strength
of feeling and concerns around faith-based arbitration. The Bill was re-introduced in
subsequent sessions, most recently in 2016–2017 but again failed to progress and
become law.

Indeed, the immediate misunderstanding and later equally misunderstood backlash
in the media against the eminently sensible judgment in *AI v MT* demonstrates that
separating out the 'appropriate' ADR from the 'inappropriate' ADR is by no means
easy.

---

67 HL Deb 19 October 2012, col 1683.
68 Ibid. col 1693.
69 Ibid. col 1687.
70 Ibid. col 1687.

FAMILY LAW ARBITRATIONS

Family law issues have since the early 1980s been more traditionally resolved by conciliation or mediation, partly due to the need for party engagement in forming the solution and in an effort to reduce the antagonism that goes along with adjudicative, adversarial processes. Nonetheless, in February 2012, the Institute of Family Law Arbitrators (IFLA)[71] was able to establish a scheme of family law arbitration. This was not based on any statutory framework. The IFLA creation, however, demonstrates the growing popularity of arbitration in a growing number of fields. Although certain issues (such as divorce) cannot be definitively determined by such arbitration, other issues such as financial arrangements and inheritances could be resolved using this new scheme, and the accompanying private child law issues were added in 2016, so as to enable an 'all issues' determination by an arbitrator qualified under both sets of rules.[72]

TAKING THINGS FURTHER – WEBSITE

The website that accompanies this text contains a more detailed consideration of the IFLA scheme with some commentary on its potential operation. This is provided to further your understanding not of particular areas of family law (which you may study in a distinct modules on a law degree) but to give a deeper insight into a form of arbitration that is not 'commercial' in nature. The scheme has seen well over 200 arbitrations and the 'all issues' children inclusive arbitrations have been popular though the real benefit is in the cohabitation disputes (as the court fee for a Chancery application to dispute ownership of a cohabitant couple's home of average value is otherwise £10,000).

ROLE OF ABTA

Before departing from specific examples of arbitration in action, a final example of the process will be considered. This time it comes from the distinct arena of consumer relations. The Association of British Travel Agents (ABTA)[73] is, as the name suggests, a trade association for tour operators and travel agents. As part of its remit it operates an escalating complaints procedure for consumers.[74] This starts with a consumer complaining to a company that is an ABTA member. If the complaint cannot be settled using the internal complaints procedure of the company then the matter can be referred to ABTA who will advise on options for the consumer. If no solution is forthcoming then, at the apex of the scheme, is a system of arbitration. To put this differently, if a complaint cannot be settled using ABTA's complaints procedure there is the option to have the matter referred to binding and independent arbitration. Again, the important point is not the precise process of the ABTA scheme but

71 http://ifla.org.uk.

72 The IFLA Rules (two separate sets for the Financial Scheme and the Children Scheme) can be obtained from the IFLA website, www.ifla.org, or the website www.familyarbitrator.com, or Frances Burton, *Core Statutes on Family Law 2020–2021* (Palgrave Macmillan, published August 2020).

73 http://abta.com.

74 http://abta.com/go-travel/travel-clinic/complaints.

Advantages	Disadvantages
•Technical expertise of arbitrator •Parties able to choose precisely who will decide dispute •Confidentiality can be ensured •Parties can be involved in deciding the procedures to be used •Provided they comply with principles of English law, parties can have disputes settled according to own beliefs and standards •Hearings can be organised at parties' convenience	•Lack of legal precedent •Dispute may turn on points of law that a technical expert in subject matter cannot adequately decide though usually arbitrators are keen specialists likely to be able to reason through potential judicial approaches •No agreed outcome (an imposed solution) though room for the skilled arbitrator to bring the parties closer together •Can be overly formal and so runs same risks of delay •Can be as expensive (due to fees) as litigation though there are fixed fees available •Very limited rights of appeal/challenge

Figure 14.8 Advantages and Disadvantages of Arbitration

rather what it tells us about the nature and extent of arbitration in the English Legal System. The ABTA scheme is designed to offer consumer protection to those booking services with ABTA members and a certain and defined dispute resolution scheme for the companies who are members. The collapse of Thomas Cook in September 2019 has brought greater public attention to the work of ABTA.[75]

ADVANTAGES AND DISADVANTAGES OF ARBITRATION

The brief set of examples of arbitration discussed in this section has revealed, or at least alluded to, both the advantages and disadvantages of arbitration when compared to litigation and other forms of ADR. These advantages and disadvantages are detailed in Figure 14.8.

Due to the adversarial nature of arbitration, you will notice that some of the drawbacks of arbitration are the same as the drawbacks of litigation. It is similarly adjudicative and adversarial in nature. Indeed, many would argue that some of the problems of the court system, such as delay, are now equally ingrained in the system of arbitration, though this is likely to apply only to the largest arbitrations where the scale is in itself the problem.

While Figure 14.8 is useful to get a snapshot of the merits of arbitration, one must not lose sight of the fact that many arbitral tribunals proceed in a less than perfect way and we should not view them in an overly idealised manner. Some of the cases discussed previously demonstrate this. *AI v MT* demonstrated that speedy resolution of disputes is not always possible within arbitration although there are likely to be fewer delays than within the court system since the case focusses only on the interests of the parties to which

---

75 And ATOL.

the plentiful supply of arbitrators is likely to be able to conform. The concerns over the treatment of women within some faith-based Arbitration Tribunals question the fairness of certain tribunals. While party choice is said to be a core of arbitration the case of *Sumukan* demonstrates that some parties are not fully aware of the consequences of the arbitration agreements that they enter into.[76]

MEDIATION

PRINCIPLES OF MEDIATION

Mediation differs from arbitration in that it is not *adjudicative* in nature, which is to say that the outcome is not determined by an independent third party. Rather, the role of the mediator is to facilitate the parties in coming to a mutually agreed outcome. The theory behind mediation is that parties are placed in a 'win-win' situation where each side is involved in creating the 'solution'. This is to be contrasted with litigation (or, indeed, arbitration) where a solution is imposed on the parties, leading to a 'win-lose' situation.

Having the parties actively engaged in the process of creating the solution is of particular importance to disputes that will have a continuing impact on the relationship of the parties. For this reason mediation is frequently the 'best solution' where the parties are likely to have or have had an ongoing relationship and where differences may be exacerbated by litigation. Thus, it is often the case that mediation is used in family disputes (such as divorce) or those involving an employment relationship.

The other significant difference between arbitration and mediation is that while arbitration is regulated, both by statute and the courts and by the professional organisations, such as the globally active CIArb, mediation is generally not regulated. However there are operative codes for mediation, such as that of the EU, and international organisations which offer 'certification' and in the UK, the Civil Mediation Council, which requires members to do annual CPD (continuing professional development), be qualified through a recognised providers' course of at least 40 hours, or five days plus assessment and observations of live mediations, as well as doing a minimum amount of mediation practice each year and having professional negligence insurance. The CMC also provides a complaints procedure. Only the FMC (Family Mediation Council) actually purports to 'qualify' Family Mediators, who are the only mediators who can conduct MIAMs (Mediation Information and Assessment Meetings) compliant with the Family Procedure Rules (FPR) 2010 as amended, r3 and PD3A and the now statutory requirements for observation of these FPR provisions included by the Children and Families Act 2014 s 10. Only those trainers approved by the FMC may train Family Mediators. However many mediators undertake other family work whether as members of the CMC or without such membership since there is no regulation in this respect in fact.

---

76 Although this is affecting the court system as well with the significant rise in Litigants in Person who may have little understanding of the process or potential outcomes.

Many retired judges, obviously well qualified to do so from experience of the former 'day job' do this work and are IFLA qualified arbitrators as well.

MAKING CONNECTIONS – OTHER JURISDICTIONS
+ +

Chapter 1 discussed how cultural identity can help to shape the way in which the legal system operates. This is evident in the emphasis (or lack of it) that is placed on the use of mediation in legal systems around the world. One of the core principles or aims of mediation is to avoid conflict and to promote consensus as a method of dispute resolution.

This helps to explain why certain legal cultures emphasise the importance of mediation over litigation or arbitration. For example, in China, with its strong basis in Confucian (and Communist) moral philosophy, there has traditionally been a focus on mediation as it allows parties to 'save face' due to its 'win-win' nature.[77]

As well as being its major strength, having to reach a consensual decision is also the greatest weakness of mediation. This is because there will, inevitably, be times when the parties are unable to come to an agreement. To this end the statement of Lord Justice Thorpe in *Marsy*[78] that: 'there is no case, however conflicted, which is not potentially open to successful mediation, even if mediation has not been attempted or has failed during the trial process'[79] is perhaps a little optimistic. Where parties fail to come to agreement in their mediation, the option for litigation is still available and the parties will have spent time and money on the services of a mediator. As such, while successful mediation is normally less costly than litigation, a failed mediation will only add to the cost and delay of the process although it may have narrowed the issues and solved some since it is rare for a trained mediator to achieve nothing at all unless one or both parties attended only for 'show' so as to say they 'tried it'.

Mediation also offers a wider range of remedies that cannot be ordered by a court. As the Court of Appeal in *Halsey* stated 'for example, an apology; an explanation; the continuation of an existing professional or business relationship perhaps on new terms; and an agreement by one party to do something without any existing legal obligation to do so.'[80] The very nature of these remedies is different to those available to a court. This is an important point because it demonstrates that not only is the *process* of dispute resolution different for certain methods of ADR but so are the *outcomes*. This further reinforces the idea that selection of the correct forum for deciding disputes is crucial to obtaining the 'appropriate' solution.

---

77 Gabrielle Kaufmann-Kohler and Fan Kun, 'Integrating Mediation into Arbitration: Why it Works in China' (2008) 25(4) Journal of International Arbitration 479, 479.

78 *Al Khatib v Masry* [2004] EWCA Civ 1353, [2005] 1 FLR 381.

79 Ibid. [17] (Thorpe LJ).

80 *Halsey v Milton Keynes General NHS Trust* [2004] EWCA Civ 576, [2004] 1 WLR 3002 [15].

The use of mediation is not a panacea for all disputes. Manifestly, there will be cases that are unsuitable for mediation. These include where the case raises a point of law that is of general interest to a particular sector or market and that is likely to arise again in the future. In that instance, the benefits of having a binding precedent may outweigh the additional costs involved in litigation. Similarly, where a party is likely to need interim relief or where there are allegations of malpractice by one of the parties litigation may be the better option.

EXAMPLES OF MEDIATION IN THE ENGLISH LEGAL SYSTEM

MEDIATION IN FAMILY CASES

Given the consensual nature of mediation, it is not surprising to find that mediation is prevalent in relation to family matters and particularly used in settling issues around divorce. The Family Act 1996 sought to promote the use of mediation in family disputes and even went as far as to aim for compulsion to mediate in divorce cases but this was later repealed after strong opposition. It then became compulsory under the FPR 2010 for divorcing couples relying on public funding to attend a mediation information and assessment meeting (MIAM) before starting proceedings. This meeting, which is not itself mediation, sought to explain and, in appropriate cases, recommend mediation to all divorcing couples but proved difficult to enforce as the lower judiciary, who first saw these cases in court, were often apt to decline to demand evidence of the MIAM observance and the Senior District Judge took the view that he could not enforce this upon the judiciary's independence. The Children and Families Act 2014 which gained Royal Assent in March 2014 however then addressed this issue statutorily by requiring all applicants (with the exception of those in cases alleging domestic abuse) to attend an MIAM meeting. This obviously goes a long way towards encouraging mediation, especially now that the form the mediator must sign is incorporated into the form of application to commence proceedings, so the MIAM cannot now be dodged except in exceptional circumstances, e.g. the other party will not come, but still does not require that mediation itself takes place.

COURT-BASED SCHEMES

Many of the courts of the English Legal System have been involved in developing the use of ADR, including mediation. Some of these are outlined here, just to give a flavour of how the courts are involved in the process of mediation. There is a great deal of experimentation within the English Legal System and, in particular, the courts in relation to ADR. What is described here represents the most well-known of those experiments.

COURT OF APPEAL MEDIATION SCHEME (CAMS)

The Court of Appeal has jurisdiction to recommend mediation when it is dealing with permission to appeal on certain areas of law. The scheme has been in operation since 2000 and applies to all non-family cases that come to the Civil Division of the court, unless they are claims of a very high value (over £250,000). From 2012, the CAMS entered a pilot system where *all* eligible cases involving sums less than £100,000 are automatically referred for mediation through the Centre for Effective Dispute Resolution (CEDR, already mentioned previously).[81] CEDR, the original not for profit ADR centre to be set up in the UK, is now probably the leading dispute resolution consultancy centre in the world, and its members (retired English judges as well as leading barrister and solicitor commercial DR specialists) are independent of the courts and, unlike the court based mediation schemes set up by the Ministry of Justice, this means the CAMS scheme is not manned by court staff or Ministry of Justice appointed mediators. This independence is crucial because if the mediation process fails then the disputants will return to the Court of Appeal which should have no knowledge of the discussions that took place during the mediation. The cost of the service is £950+VAT per party for claims up to £1 million and £1,900+VAT for claims above £1 million and covers preparation and a fixed number of hours of mediation. Another advantage of this scheme is that CEDR is probably also the largest and most diverse global source of expertise in conflict resolution so that the service has access to both the best theoretical expertise and practical experience available anywhere. Thus if mediation cannot fix a dispute at this level it probably is an exceptionally difficult one to settle though that may not mean that some other choice of third party neutral could not facilitate a settlement, as the *Masry* case has already shown.

The Commercial Court (part of the new Business Courts group) also promotes ADR (see the Commercial Court Guide, new edition September 2017, pp 62–64) though not through a specific reference to CEDR neutrals but via its specifically proactive case management systems through which it will if necessary nominate a neutral or panel of neutrals suitable for any particular case.

CENTRAL LONDON COUNTY COURT

One of the most established experiments in court-based mediation comes from the Central London County Court which first established a mediation scheme in the 1990s which was then evaluated by Professor Hazel Genn.[82] The original pilot scheme had a much lower cost (£25) than the Court of Appeal scheme detailed earlier and allowed for time-limited mediation services (usually three hours after court hours) to be offered in cases other than those allocated to the small claims track. The scheme has since been extended to small claims and the fee is now £100.

SMALL CLAIMS TRACK MEDIATION

The small claims track mediation scheme has gained widespread approval within the various court areas of England and Wales. The major benefit of the scheme is that, in comparison to the other schemes detailed previously, it is free for parties to use. The system is funded by HMCTS. The mediation is usually operated using the telephone and a face to face meeting is not necessary.

---

81 www.judiciary.gov.uk/announcements/news-release-mediation-pilot-court-of-appeal.
82 Hazel C Genn, *Central London County Court Mediation Pilot Scheme: Evaluation Report*, Lord Chancellor's Department, 1998.

By considering (albeit briefly) the different schemes of mediation on offer from within the formal structures of the English Legal System it should become clear that there is evidence of growing reliance on ADR as an integral part of the process of litigation. Mediation is an important element of the whole picture of dispute resolution both within and outside the formal structure of litigation (see Figure 14.9 for the advantages and disadvantages of mediation). The courts have been central in ensuring the growth of mediation and further developments (such as the introduction of a small claims track to the Patent Court) suggest that this will continue in the future. Meanwhile the Government 'PR machine' has been keen to promote the use of the term 'dispute resolution' rather than 'ADR', in order to erase (if it can) the unfortunate dependence on the word 'alternative' to suggest that ADR is a mere option as an alternative to litigation which the public can ignore at will. It was for this reason that Sir James Munby, the immediate Past President of the Family Division, chose the alternative of 'non-court dispute resolution' or 'N-CDR' for the version he promoted in the newly established Family Court, since the holistic approach to litigation and ADR is of course to recognise that both litigation and ADR are 'dispute resolution' methodologies, and thus that 'ADR', or 'DR', is an integral part rather than some sort of 'bolt-on' of the litigation system which has been known to English courts for centuries. Along with the term 'automatic referral' (as opposed to the essentially contradictory 'compulsory mediation') terminology is probably going to be key in establishing the new era of reduced court hearings and increased DR which is the Government aim.

ADVANTAGES AND DISADVANTAGES OF MEDIATION

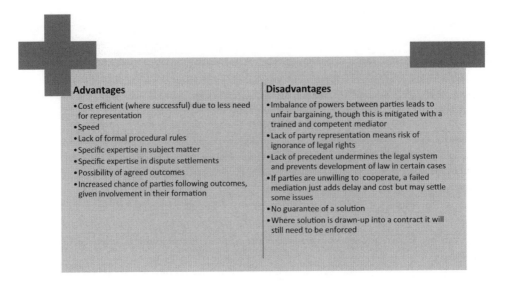

Advantages
- Cost efficient (where successful) due to less need for representation
- Speed
- Lack of formal procedural rules
- Specific expertise in subject matter
- Specific expertise in dispute settlements
- Possibility of agreed outcomes
- Increased chance of parties following outcomes, given involvement in their formation

Disadvantages
- Imbalance of powers between parties leads to unfair bargaining, though this is mitigated with a trained and competent mediator
- Lack of party representation means risk of ignorance of legal rights
- Lack of precedent undermines the legal system and prevents development of law in certain cases
- If parties are unwilling to cooperate, a failed mediation just adds delay and cost but may settle some issues
- No guarantee of a solution
- Where solution is drawn-up into a contract it will still need to be enforced

Figure 14.9 Advantages and Disadvantages of Mediation

ENCOURAGING THE USE OF ADR

When we talk of alternatives to litigation it is an easy assumption to make that this also means that the formal court structure will not be involved in the resolution of ADR-based disputes. As has been demonstrated previously, in relation to mediation, this is simply not true and the courts have an important dual role of encouraging the use and managing certain aspects of ADR as well as in reducing mediated settlement terms to consent orders to end disputes on terms agreed in Heads of Agreement with the help of the mediator who acted as third party neutral to facilitate the agreement. Indeed, many of the innovations of the English Legal System's treatment of ADR can trace their roots to actions of the courts. Alternative forms of dispute resolution also have support from the Government in the form of a commitment to settle their own disputes using ADR, where appropriate. The implications and content of that commitment are discussed later in further detail.

MAKING CONNECTIONS – WOOLF REFORMS
+ +

As was discussed in Chapter 10, the civil justice system has been (re)designed in such a way as to encourage parties to consider ADR. The reforms of Lord Woolf marked a turning point for the use of ADR in the civil courts. New powers and procedures were introduced to help facilitate the use of ADR. When this is coupled with changes to the way in which public funding of legal disputes is administered there is a strong impetus and incentive for parties to use ADR.

Some of the powers and duties of the court to encourage the use of ADR can be found in the Civil Procedure Rules (CPR) which were enacted following on from the Woolf Report. Part 1 of the CPR is concerned with the overriding imperative of empowering the courts to manage cases 'justly and at proportionate cost.' As part of the changes brought about by the Woolf Reforms, courts are under a duty actively to manage cases.[83] In particular, under CPR 1.4(2)(e) the court must '[encourage] the parties to use an alternative dispute resolution procedure if the court considers that appropriate and [facilitate] the use of such procedure'. In order to fulfil the duty of facilitating ADR, courts are empowered to 'stay' proceedings so that the parties can explore the possibility of using an alternative method of resolving their dispute.[84] This can either be where the parties request a stay[85] or where the court of its own motion thinks it would be appropriate to order a stay.[86]

---

83 CPR 1.4.
84 CPR 26.4.
85 CPR 26.4(2).
86 CPR 26.4(2A).

The case of Cowl[87] demonstrates the strength of feeling that the courts should use their case management powers in a way that strongly encourages ADR. In that case, Lord Woolf held that '[t]he courts should not permit, except for good reason, proceedings for judicial review to proceed if a significant part of the issues between the parties could be resolved outside the litigation process.'[88] Although his comments can be applied very broadly, he was of the view that where public funds were concerned an attempt to use mediation as a cost saving measure was of paramount importance: 'Today sufficient should be known about alternative dispute resolution to make the failure to adopt it, in particular when public money is involved, indefensible.'[89]

COMPULSION

One of the major questions arising, particularly in relation to mediation, is the *extent* to which the courts should 'encourage' the use of alternative methods of dispute resolution when the parties are reluctant to do so. Here we have something of a continuum from the courts having no role at all in the promotion of ADR to the very different position of courts forcing parties into attempting a form of dispute resolution when they are reluctant to do so (Figure 14.10).

In relation to mediation, the English courts have settled on something of a halfway house, falling short of compulsion but by no means allowing parties freely to disregard the prospect of mediating their dispute, and without penalties. An analysis of the case law will demonstrate the approach the English Legal System has taken to forcing disputants to use ADR.

The case of Dunnett[90] continued the progress, started by Cowl, towards cost sanctions for refusals to mediate. The court in Dunnett specifically sought to raise the profile of mediation and the consequences for parties for failing to engage with ADR: '[i]t is to be hoped that any publicity given to this part of the judgment of the court will draw the attention of lawyers to their duties to further the overriding objective in the way that is set out in CPR Part 1 and to the possibility that, if they turn down out of hand the chance of alternative dispute resolution when suggested by the court, as happened on this occasion, they may have to face uncomfortable costs consequence.'[91]

The consequences alluded to in Dunnett of parties refusing to consider ADR (in this case, mediation) were fully considered in the Halsey case where useful clarification of the preceding cases was given.

....

87 Cowl v Plymouth City Council [2001] EWCA Civ 1935, [2002] 1 WLR 803.
88 Ibid. [14] (Lord Woolf CJ).
89 Ibid. [25] (Lord Woolf CJ).
90 Dunnett v Railtrack Plc [2002] EWCA Civ 303, [2002] 1 WLR 2434.
91 Ibid. [15].

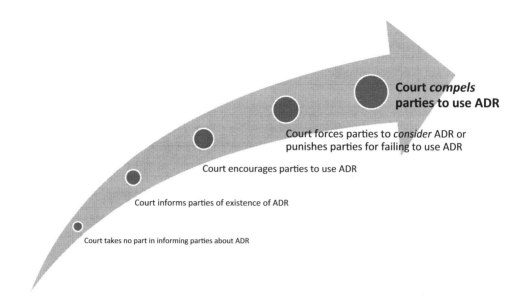

Figure 14.10 The Continuum of Compulsion

FACTS AND OUTCOME

To put it simply, in *Halsey v Milton Keynes NHS Trust*[92] the Court of Appeal held that a party should not be compelled to use a form of ADR against his will but *unreasonable refusal* to mediate could lead to an adverse costs order.

Halsey was a joined case where the appellants sought a cost sanction against the defendants for refusing to participate in mediation. Mrs Halsey had made a claim against Milton Keynes NHS Trust under the Fatal Accidents Act 1976 on the basis that the death of her husband was caused by alleged medical negligence. Mrs Halsey was happy to mediate (and accept a very small sum of money) but the Trust persistently refused her offer on many occasions. The Court held that the Trust had not acted unreasonably in refusing the offers to mediate and refused to make an adverse costs order. In coming to its conclusion the court made general points about the role of ADR and gave more detailed guidance on the circumstances under which a court would make an adverse costs order.

ENCOURAGING ADR

On encouraging the use of ADR, the court held that: 'It is one thing to encourage the parties to agree to mediation, even to encourage them in the strongest terms. It is another to order them to do so. It seems to us that to oblige truly unwilling parties to refer their disputes to mediation would be to impose an unacceptable obstruction on their right of access to the court.'[93]

The court went on to say that an order compelling parties to mediate would potentially breach the parties' right to access to the court and thus be a violation of Article 6 of the European Convention on Human Rights.

BURDEN OF PROOF

When discerning who should prove or disprove the reasonableness of the refusal to follow through with ADR, the Court of Appeal noted that as this was a departure from the general rule that costs should follow the event 'the burden is on the unsuccessful party to show why there should be a departure from the general rule'.[94] In other words it is for the party who offered to mediate, and not the party refusing, to prove that the refusal is unreasonable. The desirability of the burden of proof being decided in this way will be discussed further later in the chapter.

FACTOR

The Court of Appeal in *Halsey* put forward a number of (non-exhaustive) factors that will help future courts to determine whether a party has acted reasonably in refusing an offer to decide the matter by ADR:

1 The nature of the dispute
2 The merits of the case
3 The extent to which other settlement methods have been attempted
4 Whether the costs of the ADR would be disproportionately high
5 Whether any delay in setting up and attending the ADR session would have been prejudicial
6 Whether the ADR attempt had a reasonable prospect of success[95]

As mentioned previously, this is not compulsion but encouragement of the strongest possible form. The threat of a costs sanction could, if applied liberally, be akin to a requirement to mediate when one party so requests. The principles laid down in *Halsey* have been applied in a number of subsequent cases.[96] More recently, the Court of Appeal has commented upon the

---

93 Ibid. [9].
94 Ibid. [13].
95 Ibid. [16].
96 *Reed Executive Plc v Reed Business Information Ltd (No 2)* [2004] EWCA Civ 887, [2004] 1 WLR 3026; *Burchell v Bullard* [2005] EWCA Civ 358, [2005] BLR 330.

application of *Halsey* in cases where one party wishes 'to have his day in court'. The court in *Rolf*[97] noted that this was one of the reasons that the court in *Halsey* fell short of compelling parties to enter into a process of ADR. However, the court went on to state that wanting one's day in court does not seem to be 'an adequate response to a proper judicial concern that parties should respond reasonably to offers to mediate or settle and that their conduct in this respect can be taken into account in awarding costs'.[98] In concluding, Lord Justice Rix noted that the rationale of a *Halsey* sanction on costs is not to give the impression that mediation will always be successful but that it can be a useful exercise in potentially saving the parties time, money and frustration: 'It is possible of course that settlement discussions, or even mediation, would not have produced a solution; or would have produced one satisfactory enough to the parties to have enabled them to reach agreement but which [the Defendant] might now, with his hindsight of the judge's judgment, have been able to say did him less than justice.'[99]

Returning to the *Halsey* case, the safeguards (or, as some would have them, obstacles) laid down in that case may water down what would otherwise be a very strong incentive to consider mediation. Two aspects of *Halsey* have troubled the minds of academics and judges since the decision was handed down. These relate to the assertion that the burden for proving that refusal to mediate was unreasonable falls not on the person refusing the mediation but on the person seeking an adverse costs order and that compulsory orders for mediation would breach the European Convention of Human Rights. By placing the obligation to prove unreasonableness not on the person who has refused, the court in *Halsey* introduced evidential difficulties for those willing to mediate.[100] It would have been much more conducive to the encouragement of ADR if the party unwilling to enter into dispute resolution (particularly when recommended by the courts) had the burden of demonstrating that their behaviour was reasonable.

The proposition regarding Article 6 of the ECHR put forward in *Halsey* has been largely discredited by academics[101] and subsequent developments outside the English courts. Although initially finding passing domestic support in *Hickman v Blake*,[102] the judgment of the Court of Justice of the European Union in *Alassini*[103] would seem to settle the issue that, on the face of it, an order to mediate would not necessarily impinge upon a party's right to access to justice.[104] The finding that Article 6 is not, as a matter of course, violated if a party is ordered to mediate is further strengthened when looking at legislation emanating from European Union provisions[105] and the fact that other jurisdictions have automatic referral to

---

97 *Rolf v de Guerin* [2011] EWCA Civ 78, [2011] CP Rep 24.

98 Ibid. [41].

99 Ibid. [48] (Rix LJ).

100 For a response to the criticism, see Lord Dyson, 'A Word on *Halsey v Milton Keynes*' (2011) 77(3) *Arbitration* 337.

101 Brenda Tronson, 'Mediation Orders: Do the Arguments Against them Make Sense?' (2006) 25 CJQ 412.

102 [2006] EWHC 12 (QB), [2006] 3 Costs LR 452 [21].

103 Joined Cases C-317–320 *Alassini v Telecom Italia* [2010] ECR I-2213.

104 Having said this, it should be noted that the facts of *Alassini* are slightly different given that the scheme of mediation would not have cost the parties anything and had an extremely limited timeframe of operation.

105 Directive 2008/52/EC on certain aspects of mediation in civil and commercial matters [2008] OJ L136/3. Article 3(a), for example, talks of mitigation that is 'ordered by a court or prescribed by the law of a Member State'.

mediation, although they take care not to refer to this as 'compulsory mediation'.[106] Despite this, the reluctance in *Halsey* to compel parties to enter into ADR appears to have stultified discussions about moving from encouragement to compulsion, even to the extent that a pilot of automatic (and compelled) reference to mediate in the Court of Appeal had to be changed to include an opt out.

Furthermore, on one construction of the Civil Procedure Rules, it is possible to argue that the courts are already able to order parties to use ADR to resolve their dispute. It should not be forgotten that just because a court *could* order mediation, it would not be the case that the court *would* order mediation. As part of the general duties of the court towards good case management, it could be argued that the court should have the *discretion* to order mediation in cases where the facts suggest that it would have some prospect of success. Indeed, it can be argued that, despite the reticence shown in *Halsey*, the court already has the power to order ADR through a combination of CPR 1.4(2)(e) (on the duty to encourage ADR) and CPR 3.1(2)(m) (on the power of the court to 'take any other step or make any other order for the purpose of managing the case and furthering the overriding objective'). This would safeguard parties from having to mediate in every case, particularly where there is no prospect for success.

The *Halsey* position has been extended to cover not only outright refusals to mediate but also where a party ignores an offer to mediate[107] or where a party acts unreasonably *during* mediation. The case of *Strutt*[108] is the leading case on the latter development.

EXPLAINING THE LAW AND ANALYSING THE LAW – UNREASONABLE BEHAVIOUR IN MEDIATION

In the case of *Strutt*, James Carleton Harris (7th Earl of Malmesbury) pursued a negligence claim against surveyors for failing adequately to negotiate a commercial lease of the claimant's land to be used as a car park for Bournemouth International Airport. It was common for such leases to include 'turnover' clauses that were heavily in favour of the landowner. Such a clause was not negotiated at the time of the original lease.

The parties entered into mediation, with the claimants wishing to settle originally at a figure of around £100 million. By the time of the trial this had reduced to some £5 million. They eventually won the case and were awarded just short of £1 million.

---

106 For example, Italy and Canada, as set out at the 2017 Academics' Conference of the CMC and FMC in London on 13 October 2017, where it was revealed that Italy had done 80,000 automatic referral mediations in the previous year, and that in Ontario, Canada, the level of hearings had been reduced by successful automatic referral to 2% of previous volume.
107 *PGF II v OMFS* [2013] EWCA Civ 1288, [2014] 1 WLR 1386.
108 *Seventh Earl of Malmesbury v Strutt* [2008] EWHC 424 (QB), [2008] 5 Costs LR 736.

As such, their position during mediation had been greatly exaggerated and so the behaviour during the mediation was unreasonable. The court therefore severely restricted (but did not completely remove) their ability to recover costs 'by reason of their attitude in mediation'.[109]

In coming to a judgment Mr Justice Jack held that unreasonable behaviour during a mediation was similar, in effect, to unreasonable refusal to mediate. The court held that 'a party who agrees to mediation but then causes the mediation to fail by his reason of unreasonable position in the mediation is in reality in the same position as a party who unreasonably refuses to mediate. In my view it is something which the court can and should take account of in the costs order in accordance with the principles considered in *Halsey*.'[110]

On first blush, the outcome in *Strutt* seems sensible but it is not without dangers. By continuing formally to integrate forms of ADR into the legal system, the courts risk ending up acting in a supervisory role and the result is likely to delay the process as the 'conduct' of the parties is examined. As the court is not party to the actual mediation, this may prove difficult and an overly interventionist court would detract from some of the perceived benefits of the process of mediation. It also goes expressly against part of the rationale in *Halsey* (at paragraph 14) when discussing the issue of failed mediations more generally: 'if the integrity and confidentiality of the process is to be respected, the court should not know, and therefore should not investigate, why the process did not result in agreement.'

If one looks at the case from the perspective not of the substantive issues but from the point of costs alone then the decision may seem more reasonable. Costs had risen to some £5.3 million and were 'wholly disproportionate to the sum actually recovered by the claimants',[111] which was in the order of £1 million. As such, the issue of who should bear the costs of the litigation were as materially important as the question of liability.

ENCOURAGEMENT FROM WITHIN THE FORMAL LEGAL SYSTEM

The previous section of this chapter dealt with some of the court-based mediation schemes that exist within the English Legal System. However, there are other schemes that are in operation outside mediation but that happen within the courts. In addition, the Government has committed itself to pursuing ADR within the disputes that arise in the operation of Departmental Business.

---

109 Ibid. [88].
110 Ibid. [72] (Jack J).
111 Ibid. [6].

SMALL CLAIMS TRACK

Perhaps the most notable innovation of ADR within the civil justice system was the development of the small claims track of the County Court.

MAKING CONNECTIONS – THE COURT STRUCTURE
+ +
More detailed examination of the 'track system' of the County Court can be found in the chapter (Chapter 8) concerned with the court structure of the English Legal System.

The majority of cases dealt with by the small track are of low value. Recent changes mean that non-personal injury cases of up to £10,000 are likely to be allocated to the small claims track. Consultation is underway, at the time of writing, to increase further the value of claims that will be automatically allocated to the small claims track.

Where the small claims track is used, the procedures of the court are simplified and costs are rarely awarded meaning that most people allocated to this track will appear without legal representation. The intention behind this simplification of the small claims track was to remove the formality and overly legalistic processes of the County Court where cases were relatively straightforward and of low value. This, it should be noted, is a similar aim to that of certain forms of ADR. By adopting a more flexible approach to these claims, the Woolf Reforms hoped to encourage a greater range of claimant to gain access to the justice system in a way that did not have prohibitive costs.

THE COMMERCIAL COURT

In 1993, following a Practice Statement,[112] the Commercial Court began issuing ADR orders in appropriate cases. If the court issues an ADR order then the parties must inform the court of the method of ADR attempted and, where unsuccessful, why the ADR failed. This helps to focus the mind of those involved but falls short of compulsion. Such strong support of ADR coming from the Commercial Court is unsurprising given that it is familiar with the process of arbitration as many cases that come before it will contain arbitration agreements. As was noted in *Halsey* the Commercial Court scheme 'is the strongest form of encouragement…. It is to be noted, however, that this form of order stops short of actually compelling the parties to undertake an ADR.'[113]

GOVERNMENT ENCOURAGEMENT

As well as the court system embracing the principles of ADR, central Government has also had an important role in facilitating the spread and 'normalisation' of ADR. In 2001, in the wake of the Woolf Reforms and the Access to Justice Act 1999, the Lord Chancellor Lord Irvine made a 'Pledge' committing Government departments to use ADR to settle their own disputes

---

112 [1994] 1 WLR 14 (QB).
113 *Halsey v Milton Keynes General NHS Trust* [2004] EWCA Civ 576, [2004] 1 WLR 3002 [30].

wherever appropriate. The importance of this step should not be underplayed given that this will cover many high-value contracts awarded through procurement.

In 2011, the Ministry of Justice reconfirmed the commitment of central Government to the process of ADR.[114] The new Dispute Resolution Commitment was launched and sought to build on the work of the ADR Pledge. The Commitment aims 'at encouraging the increased use of flexible, creative and constructive approach to dispute resolution'.[115] It is interesting to note that the original Pledge was launched shortly after the Woolf Reforms came into force and the new Commitment came shortly after the Jackson Report on the costs of civil litigation. The restatement and further development of the Pledge is hardly surprising given that the Ministry of Justice estimate that the Pledge saved almost £400 million of litigation costs in the ten years of operation.[116] Given the high success rate of Governmental settlements, this would seem a sensible approach both as a matter of public policy and as a matter of cost saving. The Government Pledge/Commitment neatly demonstrates the benefits of ADR both to the legal/political system and to the individual parties involved.

Alongside the Commitment, the Ministry of Justice has published detailed guidance on how the Commitment will work in practice.[117] The guidance makes it clear that procurement contracts for goods and services will include clauses that require ADR (as appropriate) to be used before litigation is considered. Government contracts will therefore have 'a full framework for the escalation of disputes beginning with a reference to the project board, followed by negotiation between named representatives of the parties and thereafter, if necessary, recourse to a non-binding ADR procedure (primarily mediation) and, in the event of failure to agree a settlement, ultimate resort to litigation in the courts or, if preferred, arbitration'.[118]

Nevertheless, despite this 'Pledge' the Government has not in fact always honoured its promise, for example in the long running 'O'Brien' litigation where the Recorder O'Brien and other part time fee paid judiciary have been obliged to sue the Government to obtain the pensions to which they were entitled under the Part Time Workers (Prevention of Less Favourable Treatment) Regulations (PTWR) 2000 and the Working Time Regulations (WTR) 1998. While the formal claims in the Employment Tribunal to pensions due under these Regulations were made some seven or more years ago, upon Recorder O'Brien's initial success in the EU and thus ultimately in the English courts, this complex, wearisome and costly litigation with a large number of former part time judges is still going on. This appears to be because their requests for a mediated settlement had all apparently been refused. Considering the cost and delay for all concerned which has been occasioned in this seven years, it seems odd that the very Government department which owes these pensions should have chosen to ignore the Government's own ADR Pledge and that the costs involved in the conduct of the Government

114 www.gov.uk/government/news/djanogly-more-efficient-dispute-resolution-needed.
115 Ibid.
116 Ibid.
117 Ibid.
118 Ibid.

case in establishing the very lowest level of liability on its part might have been better spent in putting the very pensions which have had to be claimed into payment. The analysis that follows may explain why this has happened as it has, since it seems that there has always been a query as to whether the pledge was enforceable.

ANALYSING THE LAW – THE GOVERNMENT PLEDGE IN ACTION

Despite the Government pledge to use ADR in the settlement of disputes that may arise in departments, a question remained as to whether this Pledge was enforceable in court. The issue of the enforceability of the pledge arose in *Royal Bank of Canada v Ministry of Defence*.[119] The case concerned the construction of a lease, with the Secretary of State as the defendant. The Ministry of Defence, despite the Pledge, turned down offers by the claimant to mediate the dispute. When it came to the issue of costs, the court was swayed to issue a *Halsey*-type costs sanction because of the refusal.

Mr Justice Lewison gave an extremely strong judgment stating that 'the formal pledge given on behalf of all government departments is something which I must take into account and to which I ought to attach great weight.'[120] By talking about the weight of the Pledge in determining costs, Mr Justice Lewison is implying that the Pledge itself is not legally binding but forms a persuasive factor that courts should bear in mind. In concluding, he found that the Pledge was 'the most important'[121] feature in determining costs.

What is particularly interesting from the extracts of the case just given is that the court did not focus (at all) on the *reasonableness* of the refusal of the MoD to countenance mediation. To this end, *Halsey* was not mentioned at all in the costs judgment. Thus it is unclear whether the same types of factor are relevant when considering Government refusal to attempt ADR. The preceding clearly indicates that the Lord Chancellor's Department has not advised the Government to consider ADR whenever it is offered. This would appear to place Government Departments in a more restricted position, even where they are acting in a private capacity. One suggestion could be that the public declaration/pledge will reverse the burden of proof issue of *Halsey* with the Government Department having to justify a choice not to enter into ADR.

SUMMARY OF USE OF ADR *WITHIN* THE FORMAL LEGAL SYSTEM

Figure 14.11 attempts to summarise some of the different forms of ADR that are used at various points in the formal institutions of the legal system. This will help to consolidate

---

119 *Royal Bank of Canada v Ministry of Defence* [2003] EWHC 1841 (Ch).

120 Ibid. [10] (Lewison J).

121 Ibid. [12] (Lewison J).

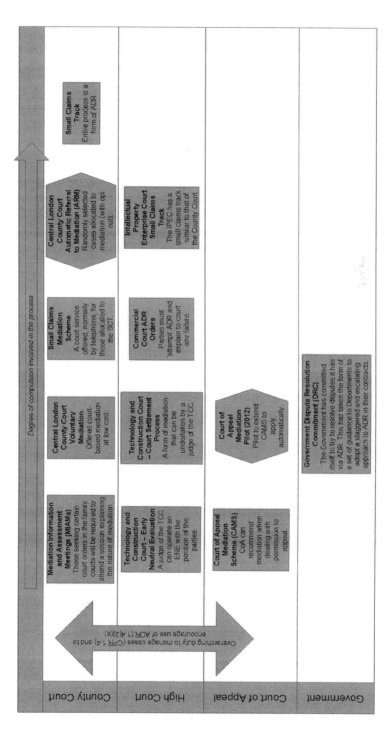

Figure 14.11 Summary of the Use of ADR in the Legal System

knowledge of the points discussed previously and also to set them into the broader institutional context. Given the strong emphasis on early settlement in the CPR it is not surprising that many of the schemes developed so far occur in the lower levels of the court structure.

CONCLUSION

There are two dangers involved in adopting, as this chapter has done, a very liberal understanding of ADR. Firstly, we create the impression that there is 'litigation' on the one hand and 'everything else' on the other. The implication of that would be that litigation is the gold standard and everything else is second class justice. This is simply untrue since the time has now come to make it clear that DR is part of litigation, not a bolt on even if the Government and HMCTS have not yet quite managed to align the court systems and underlying rules with the practical reality which also fortunately appears to coincide with how they see the access to justice provision for which in a liberal democracy they are responsible. Moreover, the methods described previously should already now be viewed as part of a suite of options that can be used by disputants in addition to or in place of litigation, rather than waiting for the arrival of the future which is clearly envisioned in the Civil Justice Council's latest official interim report on the future of ADR, or DR as they would rather both view and label it.[122]

The second risk is that by discussing the forms of ADR (be it arbitration, adjudication, mediation, conciliation, early neutral evaluation or med-arb) within a single chapter it could create the impression that each is designed to deal with the same issues. This is equally untrue. Fundamentally, methods of alternative dispute resolution should be used when they are appropriate for the dispute – both objectively in terms of the type of dispute and subjectively for the needs of the particular parties in dispute.

With such strong and growing support from the judiciary and Government the prospects for ADR seem very strong within the English Legal System. When this is coupled with the changes to legal aid, particularly in family disputes, the incentive for increased use of ADR seems particularly strong. While this may be beneficial in terms of Government spending and for 'balancing the books' of civil justice, one should not ignore the law of unintended circumstances. A Marxist analysis of the current drive to cut costs of the legal system could suggest that, where there is significant imbalance of power between the parties, alternative dispute resolution turns into inferior dispute resolution with litigation remaining the domain of the wealthy and powerful.

---

122 CJC ADR Working Group, *ADR and Civil Justice*, October 2017.

THE WEBSITE

The website that accompanies this textbook contains many useful resources that you can use to consolidate and further your knowledge of the law, to hone your skills of critical analysis and to test your knowledge.

PODCASTS

- The podcasts provide a summary of the area under study, bringing together the key themes and threads of analysis into a 'mini-lecture'.
- There will also be an explanation and analysis of topical and up-to-date issues related to ADR including a discussion of the new family law arbitration scheme set up by the Institute of Family Law Arbitrators.

15

CHAPTER 15
LEGAL PROFESSIONALS

INTRODUCTION

The reader may be surprised by the title of this chapter since it might well be thought by the average non-lawyer studying law for the first time that there is basically only one legal profession in England and Wales, that of a 'lawyer' (as in most jurisdictions in the world) or at most two, those of the 'solicitor' (practising in the city or the high street in towns around the country and belonging to the Law Society) and the 'barrister' (appearing in courts in wig and gown, belonging to one of the ancient Inns of Court in London and represented by the Bar Council).

For at least the past three or four decades this has no longer been the case, as the practice of English law has moved with the times, and the Law Society and the Bar Council are no longer the only professional bodies associated with their respective parts of the profession: since the publication of the Report of the Clementi Review[1] commissioned in July 2003 there has been a perception that the representation and regulation of both the Law Society and the Bar should be separate because these functions were otherwise in conflict: thus the functions were split and the Law Society's representation role on behalf of the profession is now complemented by the Solicitors Regulation Authority (SRA), the solicitors' new professional regulator, and the Bar Council similarly by the Bar Standards Board (BSB) as the barristers' new professional regulator. However, this was only the start of the expansion and elaboration of the various groups of law professionals now required to service our system of justice.

This chapter will explore the different roles of the fully qualified, as well as the variously partly or wholly unqualified sectors of the workforce, which together process English law through the justice system. This variegated workforce, which deals with the cases which end up in law reports and textbooks, but which set out as just someone's dispute, are now operated in as many as eight distinct legal professional specialisms, each ssupervised by their specific regulators (or by none). This army of practitioners is already numerous without even considering the peripheral professions, such as psychologists, psychiatrists, accountants, surveyors, secretaries and administrators who support the administration of justice, and the wide range of other specialist experts who support the specific legal professionals in the administration of justice. Nor are all those who might consider themselves to be legal practitioners, including those who might have either started out as law graduates or taken some law modules in a mixed degree with other disciplines, since in the case of the newest group of employees of legal professionals, the 'paralegals', there will be a significant group who perhaps will not have studied any law at all prior to taking up legal employment where they will aim to learn 'on the job'.

---

1 Sir David Clementi, *Regulation in the Legal Services Market*, Department for Constitutional Affairs, 2004.

Besides the 'paralegals' there are also some other puzzling terms which need explanation, such as 'attorneys' (who are not simply foreign lawyers, particularly in America where the word is much used to describe legal professionals, since they also exist in England and Wales) and 'counsel' (which is not simply another word for lawyers in some other countries, particularly other common law jurisdictions, or for an English or Welsh 'barrister', but is

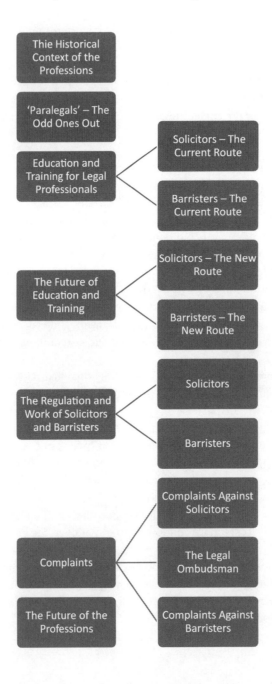

Figure 15.1

commonly used by companies to describe their 'in-house' lawyers who may be barristers or solicitors, or possibly neither). Counsel is also normally used to describe a barrister who is instructed in a particular case.

AS YOU READ

Think about the wider picture of contemporary British life and the roles and functions of the working population, and to what extent the law touches their lives and occupations if they are not themselves lawyers. From the examples given, consider whether any of these roles might suit you as an eventual law graduate.

Assess the extent to which the knowledge you will then have of the law and its practice would assist you in an occupation you would like to have, either in practising the law as such or in carrying out another occupation such as in a business, whether that might be in a large corporate entity, a medium sized or even small business or in a completely different occupation which will inevitably be touched by the law in one way or another.

Consider the different roles of the practising barrister or solicitor; the chartered legal executive; the partly qualified 'paralegal', largely learning on the job but also sometimes taking training courses to formalise their work based learning; the **'in-house' lawyer** working in the law department of a company or of local or central government; **the specialist lawyers** – dealing with **trade marks and patents**, or **wills, inheritances and property** transactions; and then of the many other occupations in which lawyers may now be found, such as in the **'Alternative Business Structures'** into which lawyers – including barristers – are now permitted to enter … suddenly lawyers and quasi-lawyers may seem to be everywhere and their many varieties will need to be distinguished from one another, particularly when, in an age of consumerism and requirement for redress for unsatisfactory services or supply, it is necessary for a member of the public to know to whom to complain.

THE HISTORICAL CONTEXT OF THE PROFESSIONS

The beginning of the generous expansion of what used to be two complementary halves of a single profession – with work traditionally divided between solicitors and barristers supported by their clerks – originally lay in the Royal Commission on Legal Services chaired by Lord Benson, which reported in 1979. Having looked at the extent to which the public was satisfied with the work of lawyers, the report unanimously rejected any idea of fusion of the solicitors' and barristers' separate sectors, which had been criticised as bad value for their clients, owing to duplication of work and cost but which in fact and upon closer examination, did not genuinely duplicate each other.

On the contrary there was a logic in the division, since in the commercially expansive 19th century the two sectors had chosen their own preferred work areas, when barristers gave up all conveyancing work and direct access to clients in return for a monopoly of rights of audience in the higher courts, and solicitors decided largely to remain in the office and to do the documentary work. Now that is all changed: many barristers now work as in-house lawyers, e.g. as particular specialists where a great command of detail is required, such as tax, intellectual property and other sectors previously relying on the Bar for its elite referral expertise when any solicitor needed a specialist, and many solicitors go to court, since they have rights of audience in the lower courts and can obtain 'Higher Rights' permitting them to appear in the superior courts, when they are then called 'Solicitor Advocates'[2] (and when appearing in the Royal Courts of Justice are permitted to lunch in Hall at the Inns of Court).

Thus, the Benson review was not so much one of research for more effective ways of working for clients as an attempt to address ongoing criticisms of lawyers, and in particular their price structures. Lawyers have always had a bad press, since Shakespeare's time and probably before, but only in the image conscious later 20th century was much attempt made to address this.

The immediate results of the Benson Report, regardless of the rejection of fusion, were therefore some expansionist statutes, such as the Administration of Justice Act 1985, Part II, which created a new sector of the profession – Licensed Conveyancers – which enabled non-solicitors to do this work which had previously been a solicitors' monopoly, and thus to introduce competition so as to reduce costs in that field. The Courts and Legal Services Act (CLSA) 1990, s 37, which required such conveyancers to be suitably qualified and insured against loss to the client, continued this development.

Thus was inserted the thin end of the wedge into a handy gap in the accumulated corpus of traditional practices, not least as the CLSA 1990 s 27 also enabled professional bodies to grant rights of audience in the higher courts to their suitably qualified members: accordingly, from 1993 the Law Society was able to grant Higher Rights certificates to solicitors to appear in the higher courts, either for All Proceedings or for Civil Proceedings in those courts (including for judicial review) or similarly for Criminal Proceedings. As a result, such solicitors could then, like barristers, also apply for the rank of QC (Queen's Counsel), and ultimately, as qualifications for advancement were routinely uprated, for high judicial office as well, which had previously been reserved for barristers.[3]

2　These are a branch of the profession that have attracted some criticism, most notably from a former Justice Secretary – Michael Gove, 'What is Really Criminal about our Justice System?' (Longford Lecture 16 November 2018) – who suggested that 'there is also no doubt that, individual for individual, barristers provide a better service'. In levelling this criticism he cited the Jeffrey Report *Independent Criminal Advocacy in England and Wales* (May 2014) which seemed to be concerned with the level of experience of *some* solicitor advocates. His comments also prompted a spirited defence in Jeremy Robson, 'Gove's nonsense: barristers v solicitor advocates' (2016) 160 Solicitors Journal 19.

3　A distinguished solicitor led the way into the higher judiciary and up the ladder of the judicial hierarchy in establishing this norm: first as Mr Justice Collins (2000–2007), then in the Court of Appeal and Supreme Court. Formerly Lawrence Collins, he was a partner in the well-known city firm of Herbert Smith, now Herbert Smith Freehills.

Eventually the Legal Services Act 2007, hot on the heels of Clementi's changes to lawyers' professional regulation, introduced the concept of the new entity of the Alternative Business Structure (ABS), which for the first time permitted a professional service provider to provide all of the services for a particular range or type of transaction(s) in partnership with other specialists in those associated fields but from different professions – so that not only solicitors but also barristers can now be in partnership with other professionals, including non-lawyers such as accountants, a concept previously completely alien to the Bar, members of which previously could not even be in partnership with one another, since they had always worked either as sole traders in the loose affiliation of Chambers or (for 'in-house' lawyers) as employed barristers in the role of employees of a commercial entity of some sort which required a law department.

These ABS structures have proved popular with the big accountancy firms,[4] those who provide other services 'branching out' into the law and national personal injury firms[5] all of which have been licensed by the SRA. To date at least one University Law Clinic has successfully set up as an ABS.[6] At the time of writing there were just over 1,000 licensed ABSes.

In addition to creating this new business model, the LSA 2007 also created a new body to oversee the now wide regulation of legal services: this was the Legal Services Board (LSB) and (since the complaints about lawyers' performance and their alleged poor value which had been tendered to the Benson Commission decades before had always continued to be sustained by some sectors of the public) the Act created an Office for Legal Complaints (OLC) to deal with all consumer complaints in relation to legal services.

In step with these changes those lawyers working under the supervision of solicitors, but who were neither solicitors nor barristers themselves, succeeded in upgrading their own organisation, the Institute of Legal Executives (dating in that format from 1963 but originating in the Solicitors' Managing Clerks Association of 1892). This was achieved in 2012 by their obtaining a Royal Charter, thus becoming the Chartered Institute of Legal Executives and finally establishing themselves alongside both solicitors and barristers as the third major group of law professionals and, in accordance with the Clementi principles, maintaining as its Professional Conduct Committee a separate regulator, CILEx Regulation, formerly ILEx Professional Standards Ltd (IPS). This organisation of legal executives is now known as CILEx and its members are identified by grade up to Chartered Legal Executive (Fellow)[7] and recognised as potentially qualifying to apply for judicial office,[8] along with solicitors and barristers.

---

4   Price Waterhouse Coopers, KPMG, Enrst &Young.
5   Such as National Accident Law.
6   SHU Limited of Sheffield Hallam University – www.sra.org.uk/solicitors/firm-based-authorisation/abs-regis-ter/650129.
7   Lower levels of recognition include Student, Affiliate, Associate and Graduate Member.
8   There are a number of members of the judiciary who come from a CILEx background, including the first woman mem-ber of CILEx to become a judge – Elizabeth Johnson as a fee-paid judge of the First-Tier Tribunal (Social Entitlement Chamber).

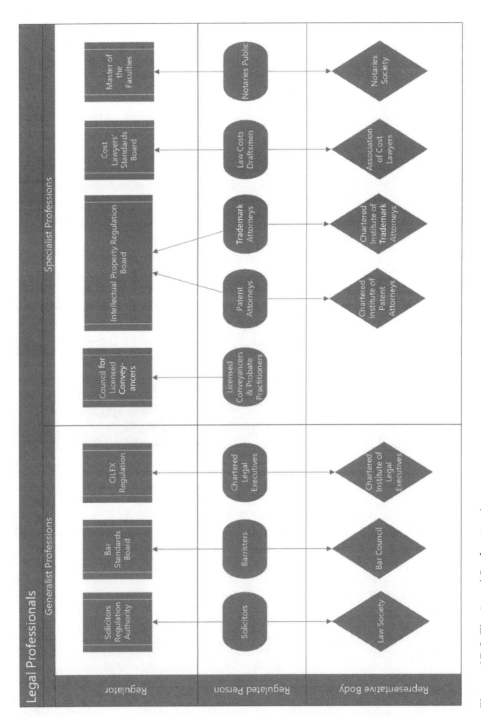

Figure 15.2 The Legal Professionals

Thus, along with the smaller specialist lawyers' groups which also have their own regulation, have we achieved *eight* regulated legal services professions, and without counting the new and fast growing group of 'paralegals' who, unless they also belong to one of the other groups, are as yet unregulated, but may perform, under the supervision of a qualified solicitor (or other qualified legal professional) such tasks as their responsible supervisor permits. Many of such 'paralegals' might have been known at an earlier time as 'legal secretaries'.

Figure 15.2 provides a diagram that lays out:

1   The three main groups of generalist[9] legal professionals
2   The five groups of specialist legal professionals

It is worth noting that in Figure 15.2 there are two groups of individuals whose name includes the word '**attorneys**' – historically in English law and language, an attorney was anyone, including a lawyer, who had a legal right to act for another and who was an early equivalent of a solicitor who prepared clients' cases for an advocate to present in court. The word is still used in both these contexts in the USA. In England and Wales the term is not much used in the first sense, of having formal standing to act for someone save in the form of the patent, trade mark and IP specialist lawyers listed previously, and in the case of the office of 'Attorney General' (the senior of the Government's two law officers – the other is the Solicitor General – who advise the Cabinet and government departments on legal issues and sometimes appear in court for them). The role of acting on behalf of another person has also preserved the use of the word 'attorney' in the term 'power of attorney', meaning the legal document by which formal authority to sign documents on behalf of another is given to that person's representative, for example to conclude a transaction such as a property purchase on behalf of that other.

'PARALEGALS' – THE ODD ONES OUT

Thus remaining outside the formal professional groups (see Figure 15.2) are the 'paralegals' who are not qualified as barristers, solicitors or chartered legal executives, but may be, and often are, law or non-law graduates or indeed qualified as a member of some other profession, but whose distinguishing characteristic is to have obtained work in a law firm or other legal context so as to learn 'on the job', often to have obtained expertise in particular areas of work which can be performed to a high specialist standard but then their 'billable hours' charged to clients at a lower rate than the services of the qualified solicitors who supervise them.

The existence of this formally unqualified but 'time served' workforce may be because, having attempted to qualify as a barrister or solicitor, such persons were unable to obtain a

---

9   Which is not to say that these groups will not 'specialise' in particular areas but rather that they have a general license to practice.

pupillage to complete Bar training, or a tenancy to practise at the self-employed Bar, or, if on the solicitors' pathway, to obtain a training contract, or an associate solicitor position in a firm of solicitors, or other employment as a solicitor. Some law graduates also choose the paralegal route with a view to completing qualification as a solicitor later (see further the section on Education and Training) or simply with a view to gaining experience before deciding on a permanent career path. School leavers can also choose this route, in particular following the introduction of law apprenticeships pursuant to the government's apprenticeship levy, collected as a tax by HMRC from 6 April 2017, through which law firms with a wage or salary bill of £3 million or over are obliged to pay this apprenticeship levy exacted by the government. Firms can then best amortise this expense by sending staff on day release to complete such courses.

Figure 15.3 illustrates the legal apprenticeships available at the time of writing.

Moreover in whatever way such 'paralegals' have come to work in a firm of solicitors, the SRA Code of Conduct, which regulates solicitors' professional work, is satisfied if the firm's paralegals are supervised by a qualified solicitor, thus explaining the vast expansion of this business model for delivering a firm's time intensive but less lucrative workload.

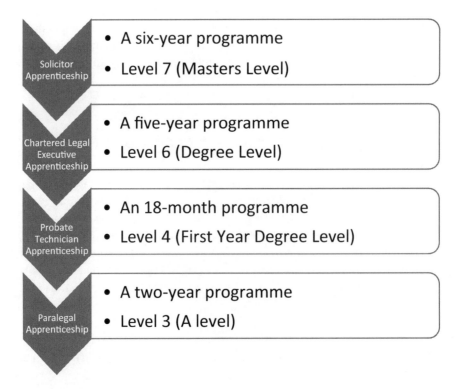

Figure 15.3 Legal Apprenticeships

Naturally this system saves considerable expense over employment of qualified solicitors actually to do the work that such paralegals can be trained to perform, and also often saves costs to the client since a paralegal's hours can clearly be charged to the client at a lesser rate than that even for an inexperienced but qualified associate solicitor. In some contexts this may be crucial, for example in the case of work that must be done on behalf of lessors but paid for by lessees under the leasehold legislation enforcing the terms of the leases in question, such as the Leasehold Reform, Housing and Urban Development Act 1993. This work is subject to review by the First Tier Tribunal Property Chamber of HM Tribunals, which may strike down excessive costs since the lessor is of course spending the lessee's money in such cases. Thus the lessor's solicitors can be expected to use paralegals on paralegal rates for much of such routine work, instead of charging the rate for a solicitor in each case, who could merely be supervising a large number of paralegals actually carrying out such work under a number of individual leases.

Paralegals often take courses, such as at A level, BTEC or similar training, often online, within the continuing professional development suites of modules offered by law training companies (there is also one course offered by CILEx for applicants who do not qualify for their regular training framework). This is in addition to the new apprenticeship route indicated previously. However while these are designed to instruct paralegals formally in their work so as to increase a firm's efficiency, they do not in fact formally qualify such paralegals for any purpose as a professional lawyer, other than either supplying background knowledge or confirmation of skills which are learned 'on the job', even if a paralegal may belong to a paralegals' organisation such as the Institute of Paralegals. Nevertheless, the system is obviously mutually beneficial to both law firms and the staff involved, and can also provide cost effective staff in similar contexts wherever 'in-house' legal services are provided, such as in local government and commercial enterprises generally.

EDUCATION AND TRAINING FOR LEGAL PROFESSIONALS

Qualification of both barristers and solicitors is currently under review and modernisation, in which neither the SRA nor the BSB has yet fully detailed what is proposed. Some background may therefore be helpful in understanding the likely options, which appear to be adopting an element of 'back to the future' in their planning, particularly in the case of the SRA.

Training of legal professionals used to be fairly straightforward – qualification was for many years obtained either by an undergraduate degree, in law or a non-law subject, which was taken first and then supplemented by the centrally set and marked written Final Examination of the Law Society for solicitors, or the Bar Final Examination for intending barristers; either of these was able originally to be studied for separately from a degree so that the candidate proceeded directly to the relevant Examinations, a degree not being essential until 1982. Thus, a non-graduate would take a Part I covering the subjects otherwise already studied and passed by a graduate, who would be exempt from Part I if the degree transcript revealed that a sufficient standard had already been obtained in the subjects for which exemption could be sought. Part II then covered further heads central to general practice either as a barrister or solicitor, including the more important specialist subjects ranging from company law to family law. Only black letter law, and no vocational knowledge, skills or aptitude was required for these examinations which did not differ greatly from those under university syllabuses although they were supposed to be somewhat more vocationally orientated.

Examination preparation (including for the Part I Examinations for those without a degree, or for which a candidate had not obtained a sufficient standard for exemption) was historically undertaken by private endeavour, with the aid of specialist instruction if required: this was done either in class at specialist law tutors, by distance learning (in those days a hard copy or postal course) or on the candidate's own. Part II usually required a little more study, either through a postal course or in a specialist class, a system still in use for most State Bar Examinations in the USA, where self-study is usual because the candidate will already have completed a law degree which will in any case have involved a graduate course undertaken following a foundation first degree as in all states within the USA, law is only available as a graduate course.

Up to the 1960s the Law Society ran such classes for solicitors in its own School of Law, and the Inns of Court School of Law in Gray's Inn ran those for the Bar. Inevitably private enterprise meant that commercial tutors eventually offered targeted tuition courses, the best known up to the 1980s for both Law Society and Bar students being that of long established law tutors, Gibson & Weldon, originally in Chancery Lane, which amalgamated with the Law Society's School of Law in 1964, whereupon a new name, 'the College of Law', was assumed and the entire framework of preparation for the (centrally set and marked) solicitors' qualifying examinations were devolved to the College and a number of universities. The name has been kept, although for a short time it was re-badged as 'the College of Law of England and Wales' until more recently it obtained university status and is now known as 'the University of Law'.

At this time formal pupillage was not required of barristers though solicitors were obliged to enter practical training within formal 'articles of clerkship' with a qualified solicitor.

There matters rested until 1979 when the Inns of Court School of Law (ICSL) designed and implemented a genuine Bar Vocational Course (BVC) for barristers intending to practise in England and Wales, a course which included both knowledge of law and practice and vocational skills such as advocacy and other interpersonal competences closely allied to a barristers' work. It was also decided to make both Bar and Law Society qualification a graduate course, either through candidates obtaining a Qualifying Law Degree (QLD) encompassing what were seen as the agreed 'foundations of legal knowledge' required by either Bar or Law Society, or a non-law degree plus fast track conversion course for non-law graduates, called at first a Common Professional Examination (CPE) or later a Graduate Diploma in Law (GDL).

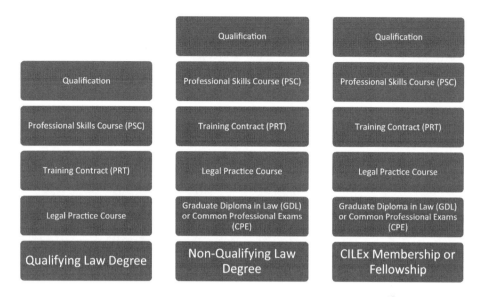

Figure 15.4 The Routes to Qualification as a Solicitor

The former Bar Examinations were initially retained for barristers not intending to practise in England and Wales and for overseas students, but then phased out in the 1990s, and the ICSL's original monopoly devolved to a handful of universities and similar institutions. In the meantime, the Law Society had followed the style of the BVC with a Legal Practice Course (LPC) implemented in 1993, which required both much the same black letter knowledge of the law and range of vocational skills as the BVC.

There matters again rested, with a stage of training (a QLD or non-law degree + GDL, supervised by a joint committee of Bar and Law Society called the Joint Academic Stage Board, the JASB) until the end of the first decade of the 21st century, when once again the BVC and LPC duo were subjected to further modernisation, in the process of which the BVC also became the Bar Practical Training Course (BPTC).

SOLICITORS – THE CURRENT ROUTE TO QUALIFICATION

There are a number of routes to qualification as a solicitor, but the main ones are:[10]

1 Law graduate route
2 Non-law graduate route
3 CILEx route

These routes are summarised in Figure 15.4.

As you can see from Figure 15.4, the starting point for the different pathways towards qualification may be different but they soon converge.

10 There is also the Qualified Lawyers Transfer Scheme for those who have qualified in another jurisdiction.

THE INITIAL STEP

Students who complete a 'Qualifying Law Degree' – one that satisfies the requirements of the Academic Handbook – are currently exempted from taking the Common Professional Exams. Such degrees must contain substantial study of the Foundations of Legal Knowledge subjects (broadly speaking – public law, contract, tort, land, equity, crime and European Union law with some form of study of the legal system of England and Wales).

Those without a 'Qualifying Law Degree' currently either take the Common Professional Exams or undertake a period of study on a programme that covers the Foundations of Legal Knowledge – most commonly by completing a Graduate Diploma in Law.

For the CILEx route an individual must satisfy the requirements necessary for *Membership* or *Fellowship* before progressing to a GDL.

THE LEGAL PRACTICE COURSE (LPC)

The LPC is split into two stages. At Stage 1 students currently study property law and practice, litigation (both civil and criminal), business law and practice, ethics, tax, probate and the administration of estates and trusts. At Stage 2 students study a range of electives drawn from corporate client and private client areas – such as family, dispute resolution, employment, advanced criminal practice and commercial property practice. Alongside this there is also training provided into some key legal skills including client interviewing, advocacy, drafting, legal writing and research.

PERIOD OF RECOGNISED TRAINING (THE TRAINING CONTRACT)

The Period of Recognised Training (more commonly known as the Training Contract) can be undertaken either after or alongside study on the LPC. It lasts for two years and must be supervised by a solicitor. In large firms trainees normally rotate around different departments so that they experience a number of different practice areas. In smaller firms the trainee does not normally take 'seats' but must be exposed to at least three practice areas.

PROFESSIONAL SKILLS COURTS (PSC)

The PSC is a short course for those undertaking their Period of Recognised Training to ensure that they receive formal instruction in a common core. The core is comprised of Financial and Business Skills, Advocacy and Communication Skills and Client Care and Professional Standards. In total there are 48 hours of training in this core which is then supplemented with 24 hours of training in elective subjects. The intention is that the PSC builds on the skills first encountered on the LPC.

QUALIFICATION

The final stage is to apply for admission to the roll of solicitors to the SRA (this used to be part of the role of the Master of the Rolls) and provided the person is of 'good character'[11] this will then be the final step in becoming a fully qualified solicitor.

---

11 www.sra.org.uk/solicitors/handbook/introAuthPrac/suitabilitytest.

Figure 15.5 The Routes to Qualification as a Barrister

BARRISTERS – THE CURRENT ROUTE TO QUALIFICATION

The route to becoming a barrister is similar in structure to that of becoming a solicitor in the sense that there is an academic and vocational stage (see Figure 15.5).

THE INITIAL STEP

The initial step is the same for barristers as it is for those who wish to become solicitors – i.e. completion of a QLD or a Non-QLD + GLD/CPE.

BAR PROFESSIONAL TRAINING COURSE (BPTC)

Before joining the BPTC a student must join one of the 'Inns of Court' – the honourable societies of which every barrister must become a member. The Inns of Court are Lincoln's Inn,[12] Inner Temple,[13] Middle Temple[14] and Gay's Inn.[15]

Students then progress to the BPTC. This is a formal course of study that normally lasts for a year. During the BPTC students will be given instruction in skills and knowledge and will need to study advocacy; ethics; opinion writing; resolution of disputes out of court; civil litigation, evidence and remedies; criminal litigation, evidence and remedies; conference skills; and drafting. Students may then be called 'to the bar' by their Inn, provided that they have also completed their 12 'Qualifying Sessions'.[16]

---

12 www.lincolnsinn.org.uk.
13 www.innertemple.org.uk.
14 www.middletemple.org.uk.
15 www.graysinn.org.uk.
16 A mixture of lectures, moots, debates, training and dining.

PUPILLAGE

Students must then obtain a pupillage of 12 months, or two of six months each,[17] with a pupil supervisor who has at least seven years' experience since Call and is registered as a pupil supervisor with the Bar Council. There is no right of audience during the first six months but in the second a pupil may conduct his or her own cases under the supervision of the pupil supervisor, whose professional indemnity insurance covers the pupil's work as well as the supervisor's own. Pupillages have been paid since 2000 and the pupil is now to be guaranteed a living wage,[18] assuming that the newly called barrister has managed to obtain a pupillage since there are now only around 400 pupillages available annually, approximately a third of the number of those taking the BPTC who are likely to want to try for one. Just over half of those on the BPTC are now women, and women also score as highly, if not slightly higher, in obtaining pupillage as men; however the comparative figures fall sharply when it comes to retention after the initial few years in practice, as the latest retention figures on the Bar Council website unfortunately indicate.[19]

QUALIFICATION

Upon completing pupillage a barrister will need to find 'Tenancy' with a Chambers or otherwise 'squat' in their existing Chambers without Tenancy. A barrister must then complete the 'New Practitioners' Programme' whicis a form of continuing professional development that takes place during the first three years post qualifications.

Thus there are still some challenges in qualifying for the Bar which is expensive to achieve, even if a scholarship is obtained and even if a further scholarship is obtained from Chambers where the student will be a pupil, some of which can be drawn down for the BPTC year before the promised 'living wage' is available for the pupillage year.

THE FUTURE OF EDUCATION AND TRAINING

Although we have now considered the current routes to qualification, there is much that is still up in the air. In 2011 it was decided to have a Legal Education and Training Review (LETR) in order, in summary, to study in further detail whether existing training was appropriate and/or whether other associated aims, such as achieving wider access to the profession especially at less cost to students, and/or greater satisfaction of clients could be better served. It was the first major review of the Ormrod Report 1971. The Review reported in 2013 recommending the development of 5- to 7-year apprenticeships and further attention to the quality of diversity in pathways into the regulated professions. In the meantime, the JASB was discontinued and Bar and Law Society training went their separate ways.

....

17 If not offered 'tenancy' at the end of a pupillage a pupil barrister can continue to take an additional 'sixth' known as a
    'Third Six Pupillage'.
18 *The Lawyer*, 30 May 2018.
19 *Women at the Bar*, BSB Report, 16 July 2016, www.barstandardsboard.org.uk.

At this point it seems that both the SRA and the BSB decided to treat the entire era of the expensive LPC and BVC/BPTC as a mistake and to find ways of reverting to the old, cost saving system of centrally set qualifying examinations which students could prepare for how they pleased, plus (in the Bar's case) specialist Advocacy Teaching. There is some doubt as to whether the cost savings, particularly for the SRA, will be achieved when the cost of preparation for the new scheme is factored in.

SOLICITORS – THE NEW ROUTE TO QUALIFICATION

The SRA, which of course regulates and controls admission to the solicitors profession, has since decided in effect to go back to the late 20th-century system of requiring no further tuition to be provided for its Final Examination than what might reasonably be expected to be covered on an undergraduate law degree, as it envisages definitely abandoning the expensive LPC in favour of a centralised Solicitors Qualifying Examination (SQE – in two parts as before) but for which *no discrete course of study* will be *required* (at least by the Law Society) although the framework for the examination has already been revealed and it seems likely that commercial training providers are likely to provide 'crash' courses, either online or in person, perhaps both full time short daytime courses and regular evening courses so that those with employment, either law related or not, could attend after work – as indeed many 19th-century academic and professional courses used to provide 'night school' opportunities in city colleges such as the Metropolitan Evening Classes for Young Working Men in the City of London, which was the origin of the later City of London Polytechnic. The new scheme, at the time of writing still subject to approval by the Legal Studies Board, will take effect from 2021 with those entering onto the old route able to qualify on that route with a long transition period through to 2031.

Whether this SQE, which is, according to the SRA, built on the goal of saving students the escalating cost of the LPC, is a sound development remains to be seen. While it does cover some subject areas taught in what used to be regarded as the core legal knowledge comprising the QLD, but in a vocational rather than academic manner, it also lays great emphasis on associated skills (such as dispute resolution) without, however, requiring as much elementary work as was considered important in the now abandoned LPC framework. Nevertheless, what it lacks is any form of specialist law and practice, such as those common modules which used to be featured as 'electives' e.g. family law, employment, immigration, tax, commercial law, etc. of which any new practitioner will probably need to have some grasp.

Some universities have already started making changes to their degree programmes to address the likely lack of student capacity or willingness to undertake much further study or expense in addressing the new arrangements. This new system is still expected to be implemented despite a chequered history of opposition to the training model by the four learned societies most interested, i.e. the SLS (Society of Legal Scholars, the main legal scholarly society, which represents many university law lecturers and academic researchers), the SLSA (Socio Legal Studies Association), the ALT (Association of Law Teachers) and CHULS (Committee of Heads of UK Law Schools).

TAKING THINGS FURTHER

At the time of writing there is still significant uncertainty about the final form of the proposed reform to the route to qualification as a solicitor. The website that accompanies this textbook will contain updates as progress is made towards reform of the pathways to qualification as a solicitor, including a full explanation of the new requirements found within the SQE Part 1 and Part 2.

BARRISTER – THE NEW ROUTE TO QUALIFICATION

The Bar regulator, i.e. the BSB, is meanwhile planning further modernisation, possibly by also reverting to the former Part I and Part II of the pre-BVC/BPTC system, but it seems not on such radical lines as the SRA, although the BSB also seeks to reduce costs to students and to improve the resulting training. The Council of the Inns of Court (COIC) which has created a joint Advocacy College, has instead envisaged a new BPTC Part I, covering what has for decades been the seven foundations of legal knowledge, for which students may prepare in any way they wish – such as on their undergraduate degrees, by self-study or through a customised course, perhaps online – and if they pass that, and an application process, a Part II will then teach Advocacy and associated skills, within the knowledge fields covered in Part I, to those deemed by Part I performance and the application process to have an aptitude for practice at the Bar. However, this suggested scheme, which appears to have found favour with the profession and the Inns in the consultations that have been conducted, is not necessarily what the BSB may choose when it announces its own new arrangements.

TAKING THINGS FURTHER

The current future uncertainty of training systems for barristers and solicitors can be confusing especially owing to the number and detail of changes already made in these systems since 1979. The best way to keep up to date and to engage in the debate, which is still to some extent open until final detail is announced, is to visit the SRA and BSB websites.

The SRA has one called Training for Tomorrow at **https://www.sra.org.uk/globalassets/ documents/sra/consultations/education-training-consultation.pdf.**

The BSB's, called Future Bar Training, is at **www.barstandardsboard.org.uk/qualifying-as-a-barrister/future-bar-training.**

However, for the Bar, much may be learned from the websites of the four Inns of Court, the original Bar trainers, whose 'Readers' (in the medieval era of chained books) were charged with teaching would be barristers what they needed to know about the law and its practice. The Inns continue this function today, providing Education Days and sessions in conjunction with the associated 'dining' tradition during student membership when a student must complete 12 'qualifying sessions' between joining the Inn as a student and starting the BPTC and eventual Call to the Bar. The qualifying sessions are still to some extent delivered at Dinners, where the theory is that students meet with and learn from barristers of the Inn dining with them, and also from the 'Benchers' (the senior barristers and judges who, as 'Masters of the Bench' comprise the governing body of the Inn) and that this education imparts not only some core knowledge of law and practice, but also the ethics and traditions of the profession which it is essential for Bar students to learn in order to conduct their eventual practice appropriately within the Code of Conduct and traditions of the Bar. Barristers participating in these 'qualifying sessions' do so voluntarily in the spirit of support of the profession and of the Inn, as do the Benchers, who undertake to support such Inn activity when accepting an invitation to join the 'Bench'. Such invitations are extended not only to the most senior barristers (the QCs, also known as 'Silks') but also to some senior members of the profession who have not 'taken Silk', including academics and some non-lawyers, particularly those in public life whose contribution might be regarded as inspiring to the student membership. Each Inn normally has at least one 'Royal Bencher' e.g. the Prince of Wales is a Bencher of Gray's Inn, The Dukes of Kent and York are Benchers of Lincolns Inn, The Duke of Cambridge of Middle Temple and The Princess Royal of Inner Temple.

Given the changes that have occurred over the past 40 years it appears that at least the old debate about whether there should be fusion of the two parts of the profession occupied by barristers and solicitors is largely over, since each sector appears to have settled into its own area of activity which is in fact more flexible than previously, especially now that barristers may be involved in a partnership with other professions in one of the Alternative Business Structures permitted by the LSA 2007. The result of such a development (e.g. the ABS granted to a set of barristers' Chambers in 2013) means that while the individual barristers in such a set remain regulated by the BSB, the ABS entity, the Chambers itself, is regulated by the SRA and may include non-lawyers.

This development, unheard of little over a decade ago, is now one of the surest indicators that the Bar has moved out of historic times and firmly into the 21st century, along with the more flexible approach to division of work between the two sectors of barristers and solicitors, and indeed between those two main players and the smaller sectors ranging from CILEx to the narrower specialisms such as Conveyancers to Notaries.

THE REGULATION AND WORK OF THE PROFESSIONS

Readers may ask themselves why they should gain a working knowledge of the legal professionals and their respective remits when studying the English Legal System. The reason is to be found not only in the large numbers of personnel involved in the professions supporting the administration of justice but also in the eight regulatory objectives set out in s 1(1) of the Legal Services Act 2007:

1   Protecting and promoting the public interest
2   Supporting the constitutional principle of the rule of law

3   Improving access to justice
4   Protecting and promoting the interests of consumers
5   Promoting competition in the provision of services (i.e. services which are provided by
    authorised persons, including services which do not involve activities which are reserved
    legal activities)
6   Encouraging an independent, strong, diverse and effective legal profession
7   Increasing public understanding of the citizen's legal rights and duties
8   Promoting and maintaining adherence to the professional principles

This may sound like one of those theoretical statements of which statutes sometime seem
over full, without necessarily impacting on any result in practice, but in fact this particular
statute has largely encapsulated in identifiable effects the aims set out in the sub section and
have altered the fabric of the legal system.

ANALYSING THE LAW

What has the section in fact generated?

The statute created a Legal Services Board (LSB) to oversee all the regulation
mentioned in connection with the divisions of the legal profession whose details are
set out previously, replacing former self-regulation with greater transparency and
safeguards.

It has created an Office for Legal Complaints (OLC) which deals with complaints
about services provided by all lawyers and the OLC has created a Legal Ombudsman
(discussed in a later section).

It did create the ABS system thus providing a new business model to bring services in
one field together so that legal professionals, even barristers, can be in partnership
with other disciplines, which is a major benefit in consumer terms, since law applies in
all other professionals' lives and in the lives of the ordinary citizen who may need those
services.

Regulation and the ABS model have already been addressed. For the importance of
the unified complaints system, see the section on complaints against solicitors later.

The Legal Services Act 2007 also created the concept of the 'reserved legal activity' (s 12)
which can only be carried out by 'authorised persons' (s 18) or 'exempt persons' (s 19). This
statute permits some 'non-solicitors' to carry out some legal activities subject to authorisation
and regulation (hence the importance of the various regulators). This mainly affects what
barristers and solicitors can do (since a barrister is of course a non-solicitor) and what e.g.
a notary can do since 'notarial activities' are included in the 'reserved legal activities' as
are 'reserved instrument activity' e.g. preparing a document for the purposes of the Land

Registration Act 2002 and 'probate activities'. The latter two will come under the umbrella of the licensed conveyancer as well as of the solicitor's work.

Other important reserved legal activities include the 'right to conduct litigation' (Schedule 2) which belongs to solicitors (and not therefore to barristers) and this includes issuing legal proceedings or taking any step in an action such as entering an appearance unless of course a barrister is acting in person (but not the advocacy required in such proceedings which belongs to barristers) and the exercise of 'a right of audience' (which belongs to barristers except in a court where a solicitor may appear for a client, i.e. before coroners, magistrates, County Courts and tribunals) unless, of course, the solicitor has 'higher rights' accredited by the SRA (CLSA 1990, s 31 amended by the Access to Justice Act 1990) for which see **https://www.sra.org.uk/solicitors/accreditation/higher-rights-of-audience.**

Both barristers and solicitors owe duties not only to their clients but to the courts. This means that they must not mislead or lie to the court and this overriding obligation can sometimes result in a conflict in representing a particular client and can result in a particular legal professional having to withdraw from representing a client.

Some legal services can be provided by Citizens Advice Bureaux (CAB) and law centres, also by charitable organisations and **pro bono** organisations (although these have much reduced owing to the cuts in legal aid made by the Legal Aid, Sentencing and Punishment of Offenders Act 2012).

SOLICITORS

Solicitors potentially undertake a wide range of work, but it is only those 'reserved activities' that are subject to the greatest degree of regulation and control. They can also work in a wide range of environments – from partnerships to sole practitioners to LLPs and ABSs. There are also differences in terms of location (which has an impact on work undertaken) such as between the City, the regions and high street practice.

A solicitor must maintain a practising certificate in order to undertake reserved activities.[20] Solicitors are licensed for a general practice[21] and so their work includes, but is not limited to:

- Offering legal advice to private clients – on relationships (personal and commercial), on land transactions, on the administration of their estates
- Offering legal advice to corporate clients – advice on commercial transactions, company form etc.
- Offering legal advice in public law environments – such as in relation to the work of solicitors employed by Local Authorities

20 SRA Practice Framework Rules 2011.
21 That is, there is no formal concept of 'specialisation' in terms of regulation, outside of some quite niche areas – such as advising at police stations or gaining higher rights of audience.

- Offering legal advice and supervision in pro bono[22] situations – such as at Law Clinics and Law Centres
- Preparing cases for trial – such as completing and submitting court forms and preparing bundles for use by barristers

Solicitors are divided in the SRA statistics into the total of those on the Roll (around 190,000 currently) and those with practising certificates (currently just over 140,000). Like barristers they practise either individually or in partnerships in firms of solicitors (in which they may be remunerated as a partner with a share of profits depending on their partnership agreement, or as salaried partners or associates). They also work in employed practice as General Counsel in the same variety of entities as barristers or in the new ABS entity in partnership or employment with other non-solicitor professionals. There are also two forms of partnership available, if a solicitor is in a partnership rather than employed as an associate or consultant, namely a traditional partnership under the Partnership Act 1890 or under the more recent LLP entity under the Limited Liability Partnerships Act 2000, introduced in 2001. In both cases there will be a partnership deed setting out the solicitor's rights and obligations.

BARRISTERS

Barristers are either self-employed (practising from sets of Chambers sharing administration and expenses, but not in partnership, or after three years in practice may operate from home as sole practitioners) or may be employed by a company, local or central government (which operates a Government Legal Service) or even by a law firm. When self-employed by a corporate entity as their 'in-house' lawyer, a barrister is often referred to as the company's 'General Counsel'. The largest employer of barristers is the Crown Prosecution Service. Employed barristers are all now equally regarded as 'practising' although this was not always the case, since until the reconstitution of the Bar Council now nearly 20 years ago, so as to give employed barristers a seat on it, employed barristers were not regarded as 'practising'. When in practice as self-employed, barristers are subject to the **'cab rank rule'** which means that they cannot refuse a case in their area of work and before their regular court(s) and for their regular fee. This rule exists to ensure that no unpopular case is ever left without a barrister for representation in court, e.g. in the case of a terrible crime which might disgust every normal person.[23]

Barristers[24] undertake a range of work, most visible the advocacy that defines them in the eyes of the public. Barristers have rights of audience in all courts in the English Legal System. When appearing in criminal matters (other than in the magistrates court) they will be wearing the wig and gown that has become such a part of our shared cultural heritage. Another big section of work is the giving of expert opinion on legal issues, normally at the

---

22 Unpaid work that is still regulated to the same standard as for work attracting a fee.
23 www.barstandardsboard.org.uk/media/1460590/bsb_-_cab_rank_rule-paper_28_2_13_v6_final_.pdf.
24 Here we are talking primarily about the self-employed Bar as opposed to the employed Bar where work is organised and requested by the 'employer'.

request of a solicitor. This use of 'Counsel's Opinion' can be used not only to assess complex legal issues but as part of the decision-making on whether to litigate by providing the instructing solicitor with an idea about potential success.

The vast majority of work for barristers comes from solicitors via 'instructions'. The most important relationship here is between the solicitor and the barrister with whom the client then takes a lesser role in receiving their advice and deciding whether to act on it. Barristers may now also accept Direct Access work pursuant either to the Bar's Licensed Access route whereby certain organisations e.g. firms of accountants or specific individuals may apply to the Bar Council to be licensed to instruct barristers directly owing to their expertise in such work, or pursuant to the Bar's Direct Access Rules 2004 (this is mainly in civil work and excludes crime, family and immigration work and requires the barrister to whom Direct Access is sought to have undertaken a specialist course on the conduct of such access without the usual instructions from a solicitor).

There were in 2017 (most recent figures on the Bar Council website) just over 16,000 practising barristers, of whom 1,665 were Queen's Counsel (QCs or 'Silks' – called thus as they wear a silk gown). QCs are regarded as the pre-eminent advocates of the legal system. Since 2005 QCs have been selected by an independent nine-member **Queen's Counsel Selection Panel** established by the Bar Council and the Law Society, assisted by the Ministry of Justice, and which comprises two solicitors, two barristers, a judge, three lay members and a lay chair. They select on the basis of competence criteria: integrity, understanding and use of the law, oral and written advocacy, working with others and diversity.[25]

There is also an employed version of Honorary Silk, open to solicitors as well as non-practising barristers and academics who are not members of the practising Bar, for which an annual announcement invites nominations, which must be on a specified form, and cannot be sent in personally by the nominee. This has revived the former practice of granting the honorary QC rank to employed barristers who have performed distinguished work contributing to the development of the law (such as to Baroness Hale, when as Professor Brenda Hoggett she was a Law Commissioner in the 1980s, and to her husband, Professor Julian Farrand, also a Law Commissioner and later also Pensions Ombudsman and Insurance Ombudsman). In logic, this system (which prior to 2005 also depended on the former patronage of the Lord Chancellor) probably did not survive the recasting of Silk appointments from 2005 when the Queen's Counsel Selection Panel was instituted, but the recent system has acknowledged some significant contributions outside the practising Bar, such as Professor Hazel Genn's ADR research; Professor Graham Virgo's academic work at Cambridge University, in particular in the field of teaching Equity & Trusts; and the work of Dawson & Cornwell solicitor Anne-Marie Hutchinson OBE in the development of family law, in particular through her work for the charity Reunite on international child abduction and forced marriage.

---

25 www.qcappointments.org.

COMPLAINTS

Complaints systems are a feature of modern life. Every well-run business of whatever size now tends to have an internal complaints system which is the consumer's first port of call. This has been much influenced by the Consumer Rights legislation which has impacted on English law owing to influence from the EU, just as the EU influence has already for many years impacted on our employment law. Complaints against legal professionals are particularly important given the central role solicitors and barristers play in the administration of justice. They are often the public's only conscious interaction with the legal system and a breach of trust or falling public confidence in the professions may lead to a fall in confidence in the law and the legal system.

COMPLAINTS AGAINST SOLICITORS

The first level of complaint is in house at a solicitors' firm and this is regulated by the Solicitors Code of Conduct 2011 which requires observation of the ten core principles which were written into the new version of the code published in that year and which addressed principles and behaviours which were to be pervasive within a solicitor's performance rather than, in the style of the previous edition of the code, requiring certain positive actions and prohibiting certain negative ones. This change is because it is now considered that no completely comprehensive code can be provided to address every context individually; thus an approach to a solicitor's work is now the preferred system.

The core principles are that a solicitor must:

1 Uphold the rule of law and the proper administration of justice
2 Act with integrity
3 Act in the best interest of each client
4 Not allow independence to be compromised
5 Provide a proper standard of service to each client
6 Behave in a way that maintains the trust that the public places in a solicitor and in the provision of legal services
7 Comply with legal and regulatory obligations and deal with regulators and ombudsmen in an open and timely manner
8 Run the firm's business /carry out the solicitor's role in the business effectively and in accordance with proper governance and sound financial and risk management principles
9 Encourage equality of opportunity and respect for diversity
10 Protect client money and assets

Solicitors, whether individual practitioners or working in a firm, should have a formal complaints procedure and this should be brought to clients' attention at the outset of any matter. It must be easy to understand and enable clients to complain by any reasonable means. It must be responsive to individual clients e.g. those who are vulnerable in some way. Complaints must be dealt with promptly and fairly, enabling them to be investigated sufficiently. There must be appropriate remedies and no charge must be made for handling a complaint. This is normally addressed by the issue of a client care letter when instructions are first taken, indicating who will handle the client's matter and to whom in the firm any complaint should be made.

The SRA, being the regulator, deals with compliance with the code in this respect, and, if the complaint is not resolved in house, can take regulatory action e.g. issuing a reprimand or closing the practice in extreme circumstances.

Reference can also be made to the Solicitors' Disciplinary Tribunal,[26] a statutory tribunal which decides cases of professional misconduct and has powers arising under the Solicitors Act 1974, which include striking off the Roll, suspension, reprimand and (under SA 1974 s 43) prohibiting any solicitors' employee from working in a law practice without the consent of the Law Society. The SDT can also issue fines and order the costs to be paid to the investigating authority (normally the SRA on behalf of the Law Society). Direct applications can be made to the SDT but all evidence and investigation will have to have been submitted at that time (i.e. the SDT does not have power to investigate or gather evidence about any matter). The SRA also holds the Compensation Fund used to compensate for the activities or omissions of dishonest solicitors and every solicitor makes an annual contribution to this fund.

There is a right to appeal from the SDT to the High Court. If the various methods of redress are deemed insufficient then the complainant can still sue the solicitor for professional negligence which will engage the solicitor's professional negligence insurance and the insurers will take over the solicitor's defence and pay any damages awarded by the court. See for example *Griffiths v Dawson* [1993] 2 FLR 315, where the damage to the client was loss of a pension claim owing to early automatic application for a decree absolute of divorce, precluding such a claim being made, a very expensive mistake indeed.

THE LEGAL OMBUDSMAN

This may have been a positive innovation which works rather better than previous methodologies. The service, set up in 2010, is independent and impartial and can deal with complaints about any regulated lawyer. It publishes an annual review, providing a single, free gateway for consumers' complaints which it then analyses so as to provide feedback to the profession in order to enable improvement in accordance with the regulatory objectives of the LSA 2007 as set out in s 1(1). The Ombudsman can direct that a faulty service can be put right, e.g. by apologising, doing remedial work, reducing or refunding unlimited fees or paying compensation up to £50,000. Outcome statistics are available.

Figure 15.6 shows the complaints process up to the Legal Ombudsman and, if the consumer is still dissatisfied, to the ultimate remedy of a civil suit for professional negligence.

---

26 www.solicitorstribunal.org.uk.

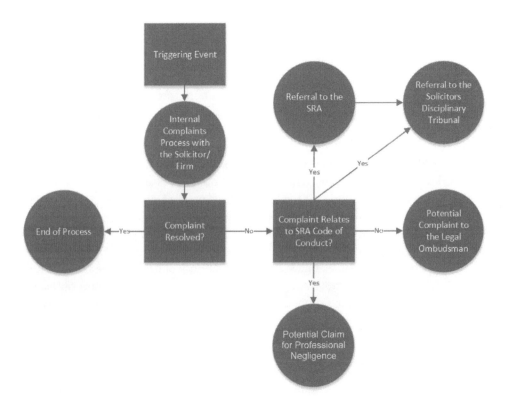

Figure 15.6 Procedure for Complaints Against Solicitors

COMPLAINTS AGAINST BARRISTERS

This is regulated by the Code of Conduct of the Bar of England and Wales which similarly to the SRA's for solicitors puts up some general flags against unacceptable behaviour but does not go into as much detail as to what positive behaviour is expected. Basically, it expressly forbids a barrister to

(a) Engage in conduct whether in pursuit of his profession or otherwise which is:

  (i)   dishonest or otherwise discreditable to a barrister;
  (ii) prejudicial to the administration of justice;
  (ii) likely to diminish public confidence in the legal profession or the administration of justice or otherwise bring the legal profession into disrepute;

(b) Engage directly or indirectly in any occupation if his association with that occupation may adversely affect the reputation of the Bar or in the case of a practising barrister prejudice his ability to attend properly to his practice.[27]

---

27 www.barstandardsboard.org.uk/for-barristers/bsb-handbook-and-code-guidance/the-bsb-handbook.html.

However as the Bar is largely a referral profession the first step in a complaint will usually be to the instructing solicitor, before raising the issue with the barrister and then, if the complaint is still unresolved, with the BSB, which can address either professional misconduct, e.g. dishonesty or incompetence, or alternatively inadequate professional service, which means service falling significantly below the norm expected of a barrister. The BSB can disbar the barrister (similar to striking off a solicitor from the Roll), suspend them for a period, impose a fine or require repayment of fees, or simply requiring the barrister to apologise to the client.

Equally, a complaint can be taken to the Legal Ombudsman.

Similarly to the situation in relation to solicitors, barristers can now in the last resort be sued for professional negligence and like solicitors will have professional negligence insurance in place to handle the case and to pay any damages awarded. It was not always the case that barristers could be sued, originally because the barrister did not enter into any contract with either the solicitor or the lay client as the fee paid was an honorarium to which there was no contractual entitlement (hence the little pouch sewn into the pleats at the back of the barrister's gown for the honorarium discreetly to be paid!) This concept of a barrister's fee being only some sort of glorified 'tip' dated originally right back to Roman times. Immunity from suit lasted into the 20th century when the CLSA 1990 s 62 confirmed the immunity and extended it to solicitor advocates, but in 2003, in the case of *Arthur J S Hall v Simons* [2003] 3 All ER 673, HL, it was decided that the immunity was an anomaly, since no other profession had any such privilege, so a barrister is now as liable to be sued in negligence as any other professional.

THE FUTURE OF THE LEGAL PROFESSION

As we are now at the start of the third decade of the 21st century it would be easy to think — if one watches the barristers decant from the Crown Court robed with wig box under arm — that the system that governs the profession remains the same as it did 200 years ago. However, looking beyond some of the imagery, symbolism and pageantry of the law we do see evolution. This evolution comes in terms of the regulation and conduct of the professions and technology would seem to be putting pressure on the professions to go further in reforming the ways of working of barristers and solicitors.

TAKING THINGS FURTHER

The website that accompanies this textbook contains a podcast about the concept of 'Legal Tech' and its implications for the work of solicitors. It is a concept that concerns both the regulation of new technologies (such as cryptocurrencies) and also the way in which legal practice engages with the technological revolutions of the 21st century. It considers the impact of artificial intelligence and machine learning on the development of law and legal practice. An awareness of the future shape of the professions as they embrace these changes will help to gain a better understanding of the 'modern' legal professions.

Fusion of the professions – a discussion of significant pedigree – now seems a dead topic with all the change that has occurred to widen access, increase diversity and expand cost effective services. The Bar Council insists that 'The existence and structure of the Bar has … very substantial public advantages. Barristers develop expertise in advocacy and in specialist areas of the law which enables them to provide expert advice and services to solicitors and other professional clients.'[28] Besides coming from the Bar Council itself, which should know the strengths of its own profession as well as anyone, this is manifestly only another way of putting the point that the Bar has the facilities to provide an elite referral service to solicitors which saves both the smallest firms without extensive in-house expertise in recondite areas of law, and even medium and large size firms which cannot cover every specialism, from having to allocate precious research time to specialist subject areas of which a specific barrister or set of Chambers may be experiencing day-to-day up-to-date familiarity in the course of advocacy in the higher courts.

Cautiously, one may opine that for the first time in nearly 70 years the use to which a lawyer's education, training and skills can be put is relatively extensive. While England and Wales are nearing full employment, it is clear that there is now substantial choice available (albeit competitively won) to the law graduate which was not the case 20 or more years ago when employed barristers were not regarded as practising, nor did they have representation as such on the Bar Council. The qualified barrister now has a choice of practising in Chambers or as an employed barrister, and although the number of pupillages has fallen to around 400 a year (which is much reduced from earlier figures, possibly since pupils now have to be paid and since 2018 have had a 50% rise in their minimum pay[29]) the growth of the use of paralegals has meant that there is an alternative to going directly to the Bar and there may be further advantages of starting work in the solicitors' side of the profession. Another alternative is to be a legal executive, now fully recognised as a third branch of the profession alongside solicitors and barristers. From this position it is possible to qualify as a practitioner through CILEx[30] and ultimately even as a solicitor if the firm in which a paralegal has worked satisfactorily as a legal executive is willing to provide a training contract. Thus, this also is somewhat 'back to the future' since this is exactly how a clerk in a solicitors' firm would have qualified in the first half of the 20th and in the 19th century, so we are returning to this old work-experience-related qualification route. From the solicitors' office it is then possible to transfer to the Bar which is a pathway regulated by the Bar Standards Board[31] and as the Bar remains a referral profession except for the few who have trained to receive direct access from clients, inevitably a former solicitor is welcome along with his or her contacts.

Alternatively, a CILEx qualification is valuable in its own right, and the lawyer can give up the progression to the other two sides of the profession at any time if s/he has a change of mind

---

28 The Bar Council response to the 2004 Consultation Paper 'Review of the Regulatory Framework for Legal Services in England and Wales'.
29 See *Law Gazette*, 7 December 2018.
30 See www.CILEx.org.uk, CILEx runs its own law school and examinations so that a paralegal may qualify first as a legal executive and then later as a solicitor.
31 www.barstandardsboard.org.uk, there is a special information section for transferring solicitors.

and direction, while the alternatives for a law graduate include working as an academic in a university. Alternatively again, the spread of dispute resolution means that there are opportunities to work as a mediator for which training is much shorter and less expensive.[32]

MAKING CONNECTIONS
+ + + + + + + + + + + + + + + + +

Whether the ordinary member of the public takes any notice of the extensive changes in regulation of the various branches of the legal profession, let alone the changes in appointment of QCs, or of the re-introduction of employed/academic Honorary Silk, the general tidying up of the detail in all these contexts is probably a positive feature, in particular as it has also coincided with the new Equality Act 2010 which has consolidated the various anti-discriminatory statutes as a result of which the Codes of Conduct of both the Bar and the Law Society have been updated as well. This is important in the context of improving access to the legal professions and in particular the Bar, which has always been seen as a particularly stiff hurdle to surmount from atypical backgrounds, owing to the cost, the low number of pupillages in relation to the numbers taking the BPTC and the fact that once qualified a barrister is self-employed and has no 'soft cushion' of a salary (as does a newly qualified solicitor) so that inevitably establishment at the Bar is easier for a person of private means. Thus, the strict adherence to diversity and equality in the professions is important in securing protection at least against discrimination against minorities, including women and minority ethnic backgrounds. There remain, however, Associations at the Bar, or of all three main professions and judges, which continue to support women lawyers either at the Bar or across the various sections of the profession which now have a significant women's membership (e.g. the Association of Women Barristers, www. womenbarristers.co.uk, whose President is Lady Justice Hallett, herself the first woman to be Chairman of the Bar; the Association of Asian Women Lawyers, www.aawl.org.uk, which has a wide membership of barristers (including QCs), solicitors, CILEx members and judges; the UK Association of Women Judges founded by Baroness Hale, www. ukawj.org; and one or more which support black lawyers, such as the Society of Black Lawyers).

However other societies which used to support other minority groups seem to have ceased active work in recent times, perhaps since both the Bar and the Law Society have recently queried whether such associations are any longer required in the 21st century. In particular **the Law Society has disbanded the Association of Women Solicitors**, which (dating from the post 1919 period following the Sex Discrimination (Removal) Act 1919) for many years was the role model for the AWB – the Law Society now prefers to address its diversity and equality issues through its **Equality Committees**, and the Bar (which now has a unified **Equality Policy Committee**) was recently reported to be of the view that no AWB was any longer necessary since

---

32 See the Civil Mediation Council (CMC), www.civilmediation.org; Family Mediation Council, www.familymediation-council.org.uk; and the leading training organisations such as Cedr, www.cedr.com.

women have been achieving equality at the point of admission so that the only issue was retention which was a practical problem of work life balance rather than an equality issue in qualification or establishment at the Bar. While it is true that every set of **Chambers must now have formal equality policies** in order to comply with the code, there remain many individual issues concerning women who if they have a family will inevitably need to take maternity leave and to be assured of return to Chambers, issues which tend to be much more easily managed in the employed context of a solicitors' practice or in an in-house employment.

CONCLUSION

The preceding account of the contemporary professionals can only be a snapshot within the limited chapter length. For a genuine understanding of the profession and how it works today some limited fieldwork will be necessary. This is one of the benefits of joining an Inn if you intend to go to the Bar as this can be combined with applying for the valuable scholarships which are awarded to likely potential candidates for a career at the Bar at that stage. In the meantime the best thing you could do to familiarise yourself with the profession is to apply for a mini-pupillage at the Bar (two or three days or possibly a week shadowing a barrister in Chambers practising in a field of law which interests you) or a summer placement at a firm of solicitors, again in an area of practice in which you might wish to specialise. Summer placements are usually advertised in *The Lawyer*'s student edition published around Christmas each year, the *Lawyer2B*, which usually includes a table of the top firms' summer placement details, including cut off dates for application (usually no later than the end of January in the year in which you hope to have such a place).

TAKING THINGS FURTHER

In order to promote your critical awareness, it is important that you can do more than simply setting down a descriptive account of how the legal profession, in all its contemporary sectors, actually works. You must be able also to identify the relevant advantages and disadvantages of the changes in structure of the profession and the methods by which they are regulated, as well as being able to take a critical view of whether the current systems are likely to work or indeed actually working, which may be difficult unless there has been some empirical evaluation. It is not enough to present answers to such questions as a list of advantages and disadvantages followed by a brief effort to evaluate the strength of the arguments in favour of or against the changes made in the conclusion. As commented elsewhere in this book, this is an overly simplistic way of approaching legal essays and often leads to bland, generic answers.[33] Better answers

---

33 This applies to all forms of legal essays and not just those relating simply to a module on the English Legal System.

attempt to consider the rationale for the changes and to relate them to contemporary life in a practical manner.

To be able to do this you need to keep in touch with changes in policy and its implementation, which inevitably requires some regular reading about current affairs and also about current affairs in the profession. A good source of the former is the broadsheet newspapers, *The Times, Telegraph, Guardian* and *Independent*, including *The I*, the *Independent* digest which is supported by its website, www.inews.co.uk (website edition is free). The latter can be read in the Law Society's publication, Law Society Gazette, the weekly newspaper for solicitor since 1903, www.lawgazette.co.uk, and/or in the Bar Council's monthly publication since 1985, *Counsel* magazine, https://counselmagazine. co.uk, published by Lexis Nexis. All of these publications should be available in any law library. Alternatively, you can use *The Lawyer* website which is read by the entire profession, https://thelawyer.com.

If reading a newspaper is not viable for some reason, then you could listen to Radio 4's *Today* programme.

There are also many blogs which address the Bar, e.g. www.thesecretbarrister.com, and see the book of the same name also reviewed by *The Guardian*, on 28 April 2018, in which it is said that the author 'writes engagingly' on various current topics interesting the Bar.

THE WEBSITE

The website that accompanies this textbook contains many useful resources that you can use to consolidate and further your knowledge of the law, to hone your skills of critical analysis and to test your knowledge.

PODCASTS

- The podcasts provide a summary of the area under study, bringing together the key themes and threads of analysis into a 'mini-lecture'.

CHAPTER 16
THE EUROPEAN UNION AND THE LEGAL SYSTEM OF ENGLAND AND WALES

INTRODUCTION

When studying the English Legal System it is very easy to turn our analytical lens inwards, looking only at the rules, systems and procedures that have their origins from within the legal system in question. However, it is important to realise that much of what forms the core of the legal system is influenced, or even formed, by external factors and forces. It is both dangerous and unwise to study a legal system in a vacuum without an appreciation of that wider context. One of the clearest examples of this type of external influence comes from the UK's membership of the European Union that, at the time of writing, was being rescinded (the process has become widely known as 'Brexit'). An understanding of the European Union is therefore crucial to understanding the English Legal System. As Lord Denning put it 'the [EU] Treaty is like an incoming tide. It flows into the estuaries and up the rivers. It cannot be held back, Parliament has decreed that the Treaty is henceforward to be part of our law. It is equal in force to any statute.'[1] European Union law will continue to be relevant, but perhaps not in the powerfully poetic language of Denning, to the English Legal System long after the Brexit date. This is both in terms of the substantive law that will be subsumed into the domestic legal order and also in the imprint that membership will leave on the institutions, principles and personnel of the legal system.

This chapter will start by sketching out the institutional structure of the EU and its independent law-making capacity. It will then move on to examine the far-reaching influence that European Union law has exerted over the English Legal System in a number of important areas, some of which have already been discussed in earlier chapters of this work. Finally, the chapter will then look to the future and consider what the UK's exit from the European Union will mean for the status and lasting influence of EU law over the legal system of England and Wales even after the UK revokes its membership.

AS YOU READ

As noted in the Introduction, this chapter seeks to achieve a number of purposes: looking backwards to the effect of EU membership on the legal system, looking forwards to a post-Brexit future, comparing the EU's legal system with that of England and Wales and placing the domestic legal system into its broader international context. As you read, keep these purposes in mind and reflect upon how the issues under discussion interact with the discussion in earlier chapters.

---

1 *HP Bulmer Ltd and Another v J Bollinger SA and Others* [1974] Ch 401, [1974] 3 WLR 202 (CA) 418.

By the end of this chapter, the reader should have an **emerging understanding** of the legal framework that governs European Union law. You should be able to **consider critically** the impact of EU law on the legal system of England and Wales in the past and **evaluate** its potential continuing impact once the UK ends its membership through an appreciation of categories of retained EU law.

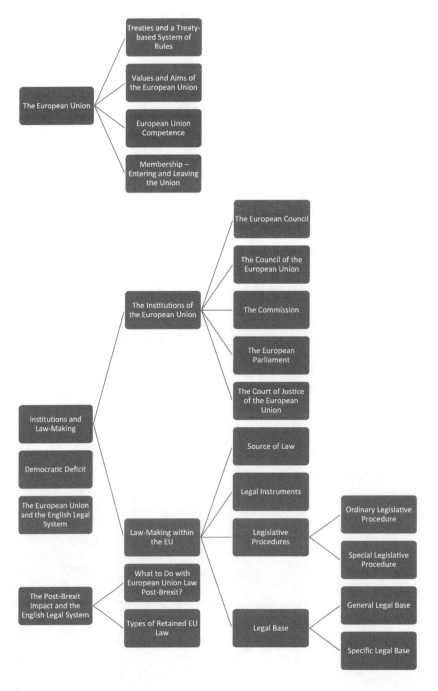

Figure 16.1

THE EUROPEAN UNION

The European Union is an international organisation of, at the time of writing, 27 Member States. Over its more than half a century of operation, the European Union and its influence over its member countries has changed beyond all recognition through a process of wider and deeper integration of the law and legal systems of the Member States.

The UK joined the EU in 1973 but it is important to note that a referendum on the UK's continued membership of the EU was held in 2016 and, by a margin of 51.89% to 48.11%,[2] it was decided that the UK would leave the European Union (a process that has come to be known as 'Brexit').[3] The process of leaving has proved to be fraught with legal and political challenges and, following a number of extensions to the two-year process for leaving, the UK finally left the EU on 31 January 2020, entering a transition period due to end on 31 December 2020.

This section will explore some of the key features of the EU's legal order and consider the operation of the major institutions and mechanisms of law-making.

TAKING THINGS FURTHER – THE EU AND THE ACCOMPANYING WEBSITE

At the time of writing the process of the UK leaving the European Union was entering into its final stages, and there are still significant developments unfolding in the Brexit saga. The website that accompanies this text will contain regular updates – both text- and video-based – on the process of Brexit as it develops.

TREATIES AND A TREATY-BASED SYSTEM OF RULES

The defining characteristic of the EU is that it is a system of legal rules based on the Treaties agreed between the Member States. The two treaties[4] that govern the EU are:

- The Treaty on European Union (TEU)
- The Treaty on the Functioning of the European Union (TFEU)

This treaty-based system, where the powers of the institutions are defined and constrained by the formal agreement, is common in international law but stands in stark contrast to the way in which power and sovereignty exist in the legal system of England and Wales. The consequence of this arrangement is that the focus of law-making in the EU is on the *aims* defined within the Treaties and law can only be enacted within the areas of *competence* laid out in those Treaties.

....

2   On a turnout of 72.21% of the eligible electorate.
3   A contraction of 'Britain's Exit'.
4   Originally there was one Treaty but a second was added in 1992 and both have been amended over the lifetime of the EU.

VALUES AND AIMS OF THE EUROPEAN UNION

The European Union's purpose has developed over time, since the original European Coal and Steel Community in 1951, which preceded the development of the Union as we know it today. What started as an endeavour to use trade[5] to promote peace and unity following the horrors of the Second World War has now developed into a sophisticated organisation that governs an increasingly wide range of policy areas. The aims and purpose of the EU can be found in the opening Articles of the Treaty on European Union, which reinforces the concept that the EU is intended to be a process of 'ever closer union'[6] between its member countries. This is fleshed out in Article 2 TEU, which confirms the *shared values* upon which the Union is based:

> Respect for human dignity, freedom, democracy, equality, the rule of law and respect for human rights, including the rights of persons belonging to minorities. These values are common to the Member States in a society in which pluralism, non-discrimination, tolerance, justice, solidarity and equality between women and men prevail.

The primary aims of the EU can be found in Article 3 TEU:

1   The Union's aim is to **promote peace**, its values and the **well-being of its peoples**.
2   The Union shall offer its citizens an area of freedom, security and justice without internal frontiers, **in which the free movement of persons is ensured in conjunction with appropriate measures with respect to external border controls**, asylum, immigration and the prevention and combating of crime.
3   The Union shall **establish an internal market**. It shall work for the sustainable development of Europe based on **balanced economic growth and price stability**, a highly competitive social market economy, aiming at **full employment and social progress**, and a high level of protection and **improvement of the quality of the environment**. It shall promote scientific and technological advance.
    It shall combat **social exclusion and discrimination**, and shall promote social justice and protection, **equality between women and men**, solidarity between generations and protection of the **rights of the child**.
    It shall promote economic, social and territorial cohesion, and solidarity among Member States.
    It shall **respect its rich cultural and linguistic diversity**, and shall ensure that Europe's cultural heritage is safeguarded and enhanced.
4   The Union shall establish an ***economic and monetary union whose currency is the euro***.
5   In its relations with the wider world, the Union shall uphold and promote its values and interests and contribute to the protection of its citizens. It shall contribute ***to peace, security, the sustainable development of the Earth***, solidarity and mutual respect among peoples, free and fair trade, ***eradication of poverty and the protection of***

---

5   By creating an integrated market in the materials of war – coal and steel.
6   Article 1 TEU.

human rights, in particular the rights of the child, as well as to the strict observance and the development of international law, including respect for the principles of the United Nations Charter.

6   The Union shall pursue its objectives by appropriate means commensurate with the competences which are conferred upon it in the Treaties.'[7]

From the preceding we can see that the EU has a multitude of goals, some of which are economic and some of which embrace social or political aims. In this way the EU is pooling or sharing the sovereignty of its members in order to tackle both global and local issues and is no longer, if it ever really was, just about trade.

EUROPEAN UNION COMPETENCE

Central to an understanding of the difference between a sovereign state and an international organisation such as the EU is the principle of 'conferred competence'.[8] A sovereign state (such as the United Kingdom) has ultimate, original legislative power. This means that the UK Parliament can make or unmake any law it wishes.[9]

MAKING CONNECTIONS – THE NATURE OF SOVEREIGNTY
+ +
What is being described here is the doctrine of parliamentary sovereignty. If you study public law in the future then you will return to this doctrine as it is an extremely important principle of the British constitution. Chapter 4 of this textbook also briefly considered the notion of a supreme legislative authority when considering the law-making process of the English Legal System.

The EU is very different and can only do things it has been given the express power to do. This is the doctrine of 'conferred competence'. For this reason, and as you will notice, the current chapter of the textbook is also different to the ones that have gone before with a much closer focus on precise Articles of the Treaty and less on principle-led discussion. The doctrine of conferred competence operates through three types of Union competence: *exclusive*, *shared* and *supporting/coordinating* competences (Figure 16.2).

If the EU attempts to act in an area where it has no competence to do so, the measure could be challenged before the Court of Justice of the European Union.[10] It is therefore of paramount importance that you can tell the difference between the different types of competence listed.

---

7 Author emphasis in bold italics.

8 A principle noted in Articles 1, 3(6), 4 and 5 TEU. For discussion of conferred competence see Franz Mayer, 'Competences – Rreloaded? The vertical division of powers in the EU and the new European constitution' (2005) 3 IJCL 493.

9 This is not saying that the UK Parliament *would* pass any law, only that it has the power to do so.

10 This is referred to as an 'action for annulment' in Article 263 TFEU.

Figure 16.2 Types of EU Competence

EXPLAINING THE LAW – CATEGORIES OF COMPETENCE

Article 2(1) TFEU – 'When the Treaties confer on the Union **exclusive competence** in a specific area, only the Union may legislate and adopt legally binding acts, the Member States being able to do so themselves only if so empowered by the Union or for the implementation of Union acts.'

Article 2(2) TFEU – 'When the Treaties confer on the Union a **competence shared** with the Member States in a specific area, the Union and the Member States may legislate and adopt legally binding acts in that area. The Member States shall exercise their competence to the extent that the Union has not exercised its competence. The Member States shall again exercise their competence to the extent that the Union has decided to cease exercising its competence.'

Article 2(5) TFEU – 'In certain areas and under the conditions laid down in the Treaties, the Union shall have competence to carry out actions **to support, coordinate or supplement** the actions of the Member States, without thereby superseding their competence in these areas.'

The Treaty also details the areas that are covered by *exclusive, shared* and *supporting* competences. These are detailed in Figure 16.3.

MEMBERSHIP – ENTERING AND LEAVING THE EUROPEAN UNION

The European Union is not open to all nation states. There is a legal process for acceding to and for leaving the European Union and the benefits of membership only accrue to those who meet the criteria for joining.

To join the European Union a potential Member State must meet the so-called Copenhagen criteria that lay down geographical, legislative and economic conditions for entry.[11] The process of joining the EU is governed by Article 49 TEU. Once negotiations are opened the candidate country must satisfy that the detail of 35 policy areas,[12] or chapters, have been

---

11 Such as the country being located in Europe and demonstrating respect for democracy, human rights, the rule of law and having a functioning market economy.

12 These include passing laws in relation to, amongst other things – the free movement of goods, the freedom of movement of workers, company law, competition law, intellectual property law, agriculture, fisheries, energy, taxation, economic and monetary policy, social policy and employment, environment, external relations and institutions.

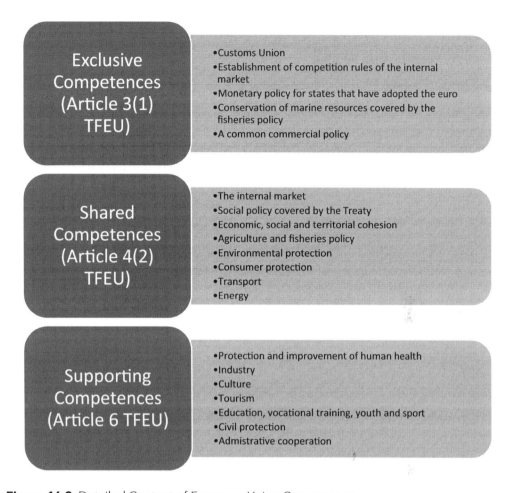

Figure 16.3 Detailed Content of European Union Competence

achieved before a final decision can be taken as to whether to allow accession of the country to the Union as a full Member State.[13]

Until the reforms brought about by the Lisbon Treaty in 2009, there was no Article within the Treaty that provided a mechanism by which a Member State could *leave* the European Union. This was remedied by the inclusion of Article 50 TEU in 2009, which reads as follows:

1   Any Member State **may** decide to withdraw from the Union **in accordance with its own constitutional requirements**.
2   A Member State which decides to withdraw **shall notify the European Council of its intention**. In the light of the guidelines provided by the European Council, **the Union shall negotiate and conclude an agreement** with that State, **setting out the arrangements for its withdrawal**, taking **account of the framework for its future relationship with the Union**. It shall be concluded on behalf of the Union by the

13 A decision that requires unanimous agreement amongst the current members.

Council, **acting by a qualified majority**, after obtaining the consent of the European Parliament.

3   The Treaties shall **cease to apply to the State in question from the date of entry into force of the withdrawal agreement** or, failing that, **two years after the notification** referred to in paragraph 2, unless the European Council, in agreement with the Member State concerned, **unanimously decides to extend this period**.[14]

It is according to this process that the UK has implemented its decision to leave the EU. The process for the English Legal System has been (putting it mildly) fairly difficult, triggering two General Elections and the fall of Theresa May's and David Cameron's Governments as well as numerous court cases.[15] Nevertheless, at the time of writing, the process of leaving had completed on 31 January 2020.

TAKING THINGS FURTHER – KEEPING UP WITH BREXIT

Given the fluid nature of the Brexit process, the website that accompanies this text includes an updated and detailed consideration of the stages of Article 50 TEU as it applies to the UK's exit from the European Union.

INSTITUTIONS AND LAW-MAKING

This section will consider the major institutions of the EU and the law-making processes. It is important to understand these concepts as EU law has traditionally been an independent source of law within the English Legal System. Even following on from Brexit, EU law passed prior to 'exit day' will remain a source of English law, as discussed in a later section – The Post-Brexit Impact of European Union Law – and so understanding the processes by which it is made is important to understanding law-making in England and Wales now and into the future.

THE INSTITUTIONS OF THE EUROPEAN UNION

The EU comprises a number of institutions, each of which has a distinct role in the Union's legal system. These roles are determined by and detailed in the Treaty. Some of the institutions also have powers and obligations in relation to the process of making and enforcing the law. The official institutions of the EU can be found in Article 13(1) TEU that states that the 'Union's institutions shall be:

---

14 Emphasis added.

15 R (on the application of Miller and another) v Secretary of State for Exiting the European Union [2017] UKSC 5, [2018] AC 61. This case considered whether the Government could issue the notification triggering Article 50 TEU without recourse to Parliament.

- the European Parliament,
- the European Council,
- the Council,
- the European Commission (hereinafter referred to as 'the Commission'),
- the Court of Justice of the European Union,
- the European Central Bank,
- the Court of Auditors.'

What follows is a brief explanation of the composition of the major institutions[16] along with an explanation of their role in the EU's legal structure and the process of law-making. As mentioned previously, the EU is an international organisation that is organised and limited by its Treaties. It is therefore sensible to begin with the Articles that govern the roles of the institutions.

THE EUROPEAN COUNCIL

Article 15(1) TEU: 'The European Council shall **provide the Union with the necessary impetus for its development** and shall define the general political directions and priorities thereof. It shall not exercise legislative functions' (emphasis added).

It should be clear from the preceding that the European Council (not to be confused with the Council of Europe or 'the Council')[17] is a *political* institution. It provides high-level direction to the EU and sets the agenda for law-making over a long period of time. The European Council used to meet informally and was outside the institutional structure of the EU as the Member States used to meet at impromptu summits to discuss matters and this became regularised over time. The European Council was, eventually, brought fully within the EU legal structure as an institution by the Treaty of Lisbon and it now meets 'twice every six months.'[18]

COMPOSITION

The European Council consists of the Heads of State or Government of the Member States and its President and the President of the European Commission.[19] The preceding demonstrates that the European Council is extremely 'high level', in terms of policymaking. The UK was represented by the Prime Minister and the other Member States by the equivalent Head of State.

The President of the European Council is a relatively new post, created by the Treaty of Lisbon. The thinking was to provide some consistency to the operation of the European

---

16 The European Central Bank and the Court of Auditors have only a marginal role in the law-making process and are not discussed further in this chapter.

17 The Council of Europe is *not* an EU institution. It is responsible for the European Convention on Human Rights – an international law system of rules governing human rights and fundamental freedoms.

18 Article 15(3) TEU.

19 Article 15(2) TEU.

Council and to give the EU real 'weight' on the world stage. The post of President of the European Council proved to be highly controversial, as the President is not elected by the European people. The choice of Herman Van Rompuy as the first President also proved controversial due to a perceived lack of charisma and absence of democratic legitimacy or accountability. Nigel Farage, leader of the Brexit Party,[20] likened Van Rompuy, the former Belgian Prime Minister, to a 'damp rag' and labelled him the 'quiet assassin' of national sovereignty.[21]

THE COUNCIL OF THE EUROPEAN UNION

Article 16(1) TEU: '**The Council shall, jointly with the European Parliament, exercise legislative and budgetary functions**. It shall carry out policymaking and coordinating functions as laid down in the Treaties' (emphasis added).

The Council of Ministers (hereinafter 'the Council') has many roles and responsibilities. It takes the 'high level' policy decisions of the European Council and turns them into the outline for a legislative programme (but does not propose the legislation itself, which is a job for the Commission). It represents the interests of the Member States.

For the purposes of this textbook, the most important role of the Council is that it is the final decision-maker on the majority[22] of secondary legislation passed by the EU. In other words, nearly no piece of secondary law can come into force unless it has been approved by the Council, either acting unanimously or by a qualified majority. You should think to yourself why the Member States reserved ultimate decision-making competence to themselves and were not content for this decision to be taken by a body, such as the Commission, that does not represent Member State interest.

COMPOSITION(S)

The Council is comprised of a representative of each Member State who will be of ministerial level.[23] The precise composition of the Council will depend upon the subject matter being discussed. If, for example, Finance legislation is being discussed, the Finance Ministers from each Member State will be in attendance (the Chancellor of the Exchequer for the UK). There are many configurations of Council and, as such, it is not composed of a static membership but the membership will vary according to policy area. Figure 16.4 demonstrates the different configurations of the Council.

---

20 But who, at the time, was leader of the United Kingdom Independence Party.

21 Bruno Waterfield, 'Nigel Farage Fined After Herman Van Rompuy Slur' The Telegraph (London, 2 March 2010), www. telegraph.co.uk/news/worldnews/europe/eu/7352572/Nigel-Farage-fined-after-Herman-Van-Rompuy-slur.html.

22 There are a few exceptions that you need not concern yourself with, including an extremely complex and technical process of the Commission making law on its own, known as 'Comitology'.

23 Article 16(2) TEU.

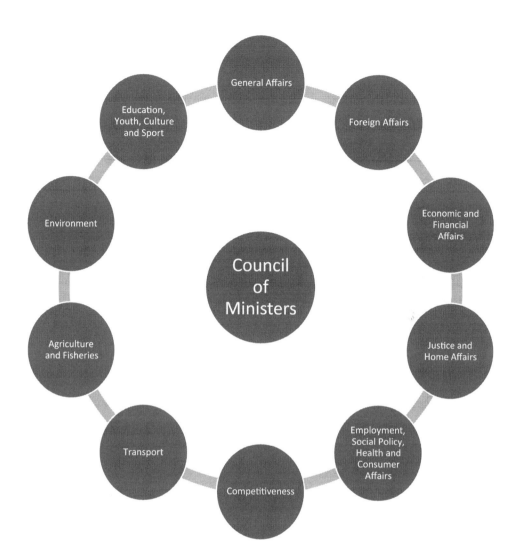

Figure 16.4 Configuration of Council Meetings

TAKING THINGS FURTHER – THE POLITICAL DIMENSION OF VOTING IN COUNCIL

The internet contains useful modelling apps whereby you can see the various voting combinations in qualified majority voting and how they would impact on the success of legislation. The apps are very easy to use and can help you visualise the dominance of the Member States holding the most influence within the EU. For example, you will see that the chances of a measure passing without the support of the 'big 5' Member States (Germany, France, UK [as at the time of writing], Italy and Spain) are severely reduced. The general position is that 55% of Member States, representing 65% of the EU population, must approve a measure before it becomes law.[24]

---

24 Article 16(4) TEU.

THE COMMISSION

Article 17(1) TEU: 'The Commission shall promote the **general interest of the Union** and take appropriate initiatives to that end. It shall **ensure the application of the Treaties**, and measures adopted by the institutions pursuant to them. It shall **oversee the application of Union law** under the control of the Court of Justice of the European Union' (emphasis added).

It can be seen that the Commission has a relatively wide-reaching mandate. In essence, it has three major roles[25] under the Treaty:

1   To represent the Union
2   To ensure the application of the Treaties (by monitoring Member States' compliance with EU law)
3   Law-making

This final role is extremely important. The Commission has (with a few exceptions) the sole right to initiate legislation under Article 17(2) TEU. It is important to think about what the sole power to initiate legislation means for the direction of the European Union. It is in this regard that the Commission is most frequently criticised as the sole right to initial legislation is a significant power and is vested in, as we shall see, an unelected institution.

COMPOSITION

The Commission is headed by a President, who is proposed by the European Council and then approved by the European Parliament. The current President-elect of the Commission is Ursula von der Leyen and her Commission took up office in December 2019 for a period of five years until 2024. The President is supported by Vice-Presidents (one of whom is the High Representative for Foreign Affairs and Security Policy). Each Member State then proposes a Commissioner. Given the planned departure of the UK, the British Government did not put forward the name of a Commissioner in 2019. This placed the UK in breach of European Union law and, at the time of writing, the Commission was due to launch infringement proceedings[26] against the UK for this failing. The von der Leyen Commission was due to take office in early November 2019 but there were problems with the confirmation of the French, Romanian and Hungarian nominees that delayed matters until December 2019.

Each Commissioner is responsible for an area of European Union policy and is then supported by several departments that are referred to as Directorates General (Figure 16.5 explains the structure of the Commission). The College of 27 Commissioners must then, collectively, be approved by the European Parliament. The Commission is further supported in its work by a (relatively) large number of civil servants from the European Civil Service.

....

25 It also has many other important roles (such taking decisions against companies in breach of competition law).
26 Under Article 258 TFEU.

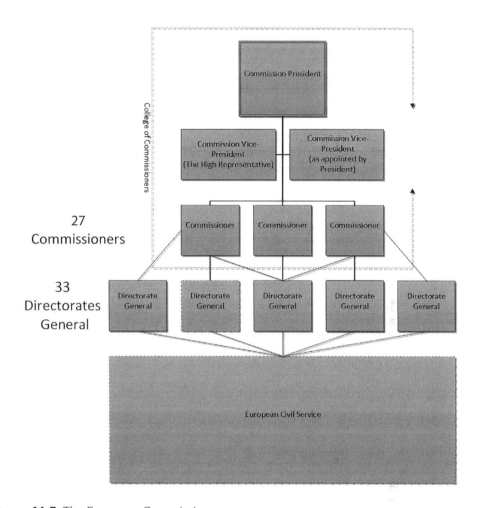

Figure 16.5 The European Commission

THE EUROPEAN PARLIAMENT

Article 14(1) TEU: 'The European Parliament shall, jointly with the Council, exercise legislative and budgetary functions'.

As is clear from the preceding description, the Parliament has an important role in law-making. Post-Lisbon, it co-decides (with the Council) the majority of law proposed by the Commission, under the 'ordinary' legislative procedure. It also has a role in holding the Commission to account and has the power to force the entire College of Commissioners to resign. The Parliament threatened to use this power in 1999 essentially forcing the Santer Commission to resign, amid reports of mass fraud and mismanagement.[27] In addition, the Parliament has control over the budget of the EU. Indeed, and in an unusual situation within

---

27 For further discussion, see Paul Craig, 'The fall and renewal of the commission: accountability, contract and administrative organisation' (2000) 6(2) ELJ 98.

the EU structure, the Parliament has the ultimate say on whether or not to approve the EU budget. It has exercised the power to reject the EU budget on two occasions (in 1984 and 1988).

The Parliament began as a simple 'Assembly' with little power and has gained significant new competences as the EU has evolved. For example, the Parliament only used to have the right to be 'consulted' over proposed legislation and now it normally shares final decision-making powers with the Council.

COMPOSITION

The Parliament is made up of 751 (to be reduced to 705 following the UK's departure)[28] Members of the European Parliament (MEP) and has been directly elected since 1979. The distribution of seats to Member States is the result of tense negotiations and there are deep disagreements whenever the issue is discussed. Although based largely on population size (with bigger states getting more seats) the system is one of 'degressive proportionality', which means that the smaller states get more seats than a strictly proportional system based on population would suggest. The UK was allocated 73 seats in the European Parliament (the third highest) coming after France (74) and Germany (96).[29] The smallest states are Malta, Luxembourg, Cyprus and Estonia, each of whom get six seats.

The UK elected its MEPs using a system of proportional representation that is, therefore, different to the 'First Past the Post' system used in the UK General Elections, as described in Chapter 3. This means that smaller parties have greater representation within the European Parliament than they do in Westminster. For example, the Brexit Party secured 23 of the UK's 74 seats in the European Parliament elections of 2019 despite having no representation in the UK Parliament. Turnout at European elections is generally poor within the UK and has hovered at around 35% in the nine elections that have occurred since the UK's membership in 1973 with 2019 providing the second largest turnout at a paltry 37.18%.

THE COURT OF JUSTICE OF THE EUROPEAN UNION

Article 19(1) TEU: 'The Court of Justice of the European Union shall include the Court of Justice, the General Court and specialised courts. It **shall ensure that in the interpretation and application of the Treaties the law is observed**' (emphasis added).

It should be clear from the outset that the EU court actually consists of two courts: the Court of Justice (this chapter will refer to it as the 'ECJ' or 'the Court') and the General Court. The Court has 27 judges with one from each Member State and is assisted by Advocates General who give non-binding legal Opinions on how particular cases should be resolved. The Court sits in different configurations and can sit in 'full court' with all 27 judges, in a smaller 'Grand Chamber' of 15 judges or in even smaller panels of three or five judges.

28 The intention was that the UK would have left by the start of the 2019 Parliament but, due to extensions to the Brexit process, the UK did participate in the European Elections.

29 The full split of seats can be found here: www.europarl.europa.eu/aboutparliament/en/0005bfbc6b/Number-of-Members-per-Member-State.html.

As well as the general duty of ensuring that the 'law' is observed, the Court has specific jurisdiction over the following issues:

1   It hears 'preliminary references' under Article 267 TFEU. The procedure allows for[30] national courts and tribunals to ask questions to the ECJ about the interpretation of EU law that is relevant to cases that are being heard in a national court. It is an extremely important procedure as it allows for interaction and dialogue between the European and national legal orders.
2   Rules on the *validity* of EU law through a form of judicial review called 'action for annulment' under Article 263 TFEU.
3   It hears cases, brought by the Commission or other Member States, of alleged infringement of EU law by a Member State and has the power to impose lump sum and periodic payment fines on Member States under Article 258–260 TFEU.
4   It can award damages to individuals for violations of EU law committed by an EU institution under the principle of non-contractual liability found within Article 340 TFEU.

In exercising the preceding jurisdiction, the Court has significantly extended the reach of EU law. It has influenced both the direction and depth of the penetration of the EU legal order into the English Legal System to the extent that the Court has been labelled by some as exercising 'judicial activism'.[31]

LAW-MAKING WITHIN THE EU

Turning our attention to law-making, this section will consider the sources of law, law-making process and concept of 'legal base' in the European Union.

SOURCES OF LAW

The European Union has a multitude of legal sources. Some of these are also, as will be remembered, sources of law for the English Legal System.

The main sources of EU law are:

- The Treaties (the Treaty on European Union [TEU] and the Treaty on the Functioning of the European Union [TFEU])
- Acts of the Union (Regulations, Directives, Decisions, Recommendations and Opinions)
- The case law of the European Courts
- The European Charter of Fundamental Rights
- The 'common constitutional traditions of the Member States'[32]
- Other international treaties (most notably, the European Convention on Human Rights)

---

30 And in some cases requires.
31 Gareth Davies, 'Activism relocated. The self-restraint of the European Court of Justice in its national context' in Susanne Schmidt and Daniel Keleman (eds), *The Power of the European Court of Justice* (Routledge 2013).
32 This is a phrase that the Court favours in its case law. See, for example Case C-28/08 P *Commission v Bavarian Lager* [2010] ECR I-6055, para 100.

LEGAL INSTRUMENTS

The European Union is empowered to further its objectives using a number of legal instruments found within Article 288 TFEU.

EXPLAINING THE LAW – SECONDARY LEGISLATION IN THE EUROPEAN UNION

Article 288 TFEU:

'To exercise the Union's competences, the institutions shall adopt regulations, directives, decisions, recommendations and opinions.

A regulation shall have general application. It shall be binding in its entirety and directly applicable in all Member States.'

Regulations apply to the whole of the EU (i.e. they have 'general application') and do not require national law to implement them (i.e. they are directly applicable). A particular regulation will be published in the Official Journal and will specify the date on which it will come into force. They are generally used where a high level of consistency is needed as they fully harmonise and override inconsistent national law.

Article 288 TFEU: '**A directive** shall be binding, as to the result to be achieved, upon each Member State to which it is addressed, but shall leave to the national authorities the choice of form and methods.'

Directives are addressed to the Member States and set out general aims and goals. Member States then have a period of time, usually about 18 months, to 'implement' the directive in question. They can use existing national law or pass new laws in order to achieve the aims of the directive. In the English Legal System, directives are most often implemented using statutory instruments and powers under section 2(2) of the European Communities Act 1972. When the Member State has implemented a directive they must report that implementation to the Commission.

Article 288 TFEU: '**A decision** shall be binding in its entirety. A decision which specifies those to whom it is addressed shall be binding only on them.'

Decisions can be addressed to the world or to specific legal or natural persons (Member States, individuals or companies). Decisions are commonly adopted by the Commission acting alone, under its executive powers, to enforce the competition law of the EU.

LEGISLATIVE PROCEDURES

Before the reforms of the Treaty of Lisbon 2009 simplified the process there were a myriad of legislative procedures for adopting law and they involved different powers and processes for the institutions to adopt. Following on from Lisbon there are now two primary methods for passing legislative instruments within the EU. These are:

- The 'ordinary' legislative procedure under Article 294 TFEU
- The 'special' legislative procedure under Article 289(2) TFEU

You do not need to know any level of detail about these processes in order to understand English law but it is useful to observe how different legal systems distribute powers amongst its institutions.

ORDINARY LEGISLATIVE PROCEDURE

This is now the 'normal' way of making law in the EU. The process is represented by Figure 16.6.

SPECIAL LEGISLATIVE PROCEDURE

The special legislative procedure is more likely to be used in sensitive areas (Figure 16.7).

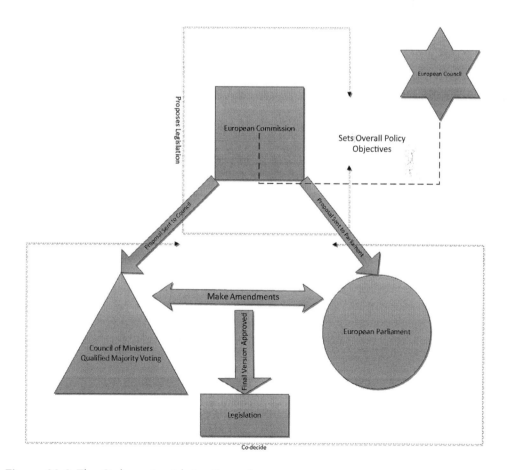

Figure 16.6 The Ordinary Legislative Procedure

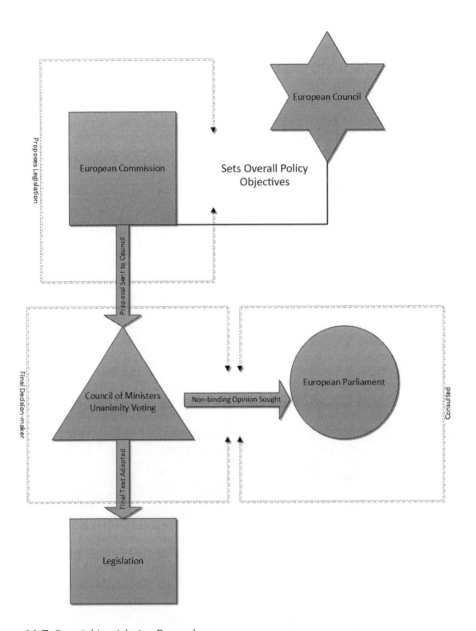

Figure 16.7 Special Legislative Procedure

LEGAL BASE

Given the issue of conferred competence, and the possibility of annulling unlawful legal instruments, the Commission must be very careful in identifying the precise Article of the Treaty that confers powers on the Union to pass law when they are proposing legislation. The Article of the Treaty that empowers the Union to act is called the 'legal base'. Selection of the incorrect legal base can lead to the legal instrument being annulled under Article 263 TFEU.

The legal base will tell you:

1   The policy area
2   The types of act that the EU can pass (if no specific measure is mentioned, the EU can adopt regulations, directives or decisions)
3   The powers of the institutions in relation to this area
4   The process of law-making

Figure 16.8 demonstrates the operation of an exemplar legal base.

SPECIFIC LEGAL BASES
These can be extremely narrow and prescriptive. For example, Article 153 TFEU is the legal base for actions that can be taken by the EU in relation to social security. Article 153 TFEU:

> In the field of social security the EU 'may adopt...by means of directives, minimum requirements for gradual implementation. The Council shall act unanimously, in accordance with a special legislative procedure, after consulting the European Parliament and the said Committees.

Therefore Article 153 TFEU defines the policy area (social security), the types of act that the EU can pass (directives), the powers of the institutions (unanimity in Council, consultation of the Parliament) and the process of law-making (special legislative process). It is unnecessary to learn specific legal bases of EU law in a study of the English Legal System. The preceding are just examples of the principle of conferred competence in action. They demonstrate the need for EU law to have a solid legal base in order to avoid challenge. By contrast there is no

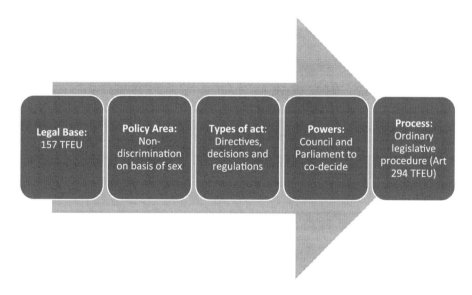

Figure 16.8 Legal Bases

such need to identify a 'legal base' for the passage of Acts of Parliament in the English Legal System but the equivalent would be the 'Parent Act' for the passage of secondary legislation.

GENERAL LEGAL BASES

In addition to the specific legal bases there are also general legal bases. These are broadly defined legal bases that give the EU potentially wide-ranging powers and are not really linked to a particular policy area. The clearest example is Article 114 TFEU:

> The **European Parliament and the Council** shall, acting in accordance with the **ordinary legislative procedure** and after **consulting** the Economic and Social Committee, adopt the measures for the approximation of the provisions laid down by law, regulation or administrative action in Member States **which have as their object the establishment and functioning of the internal market**.

You can see that this is a very broad Article, giving the EU wide powers to legislate. The use of Article 114 TFEU (and its outer limits) has been the subject of many ECJ judgments. It was in issue in the landmark *Germany v European Parliament and Council*[33] case. This case concerned a directive that banned the advertising of tobacco in various forms. The measure was adopted under Article 114 TFEU. Germany[34] challenged the measure, claiming that it had been adopted using the incorrect legal base. Had a different legal base been used, Germany argued that the EU would not have been permitted to adopt the measure that it did.

This case demonstrates the need for careful thought on the part of the Commission about the concept of conferred competence when adopting legislation. It also demonstrates the difference between the English Legal System and the EU legal system. Using the correct legal base is important precisely because the EU is a body of *conferred* competence. This means that technical arguments over competence can be as important as the substance of a case. This was also evident in *Kadi*.[35] The case involved human rights, terrorists, secret phone calls and the freezing of bank assets. However, despite the excitement and intrigue raised by the facts of the case, a very substantial part of the judgment was dedicated to whether the Union had adopted measures on the correct legal base![36]

DEMOCRATIC DEFICIT

One of the most frequent (and vocal) criticisms of the EU relates to its lack of democratic legitimacy. There is a strong argument that the presence of a democratic deficit was a major factor in public opinion moving towards Leave in the 2016 election. Whilst there are many

---

33 Case C-376/98 *Germany v European Parliament and Council* [2000] ECR I-8419.

34 This demonstrates the implications of Qualified Majority Voting, where Member States can be outvoted.

35 Cases C-402/05 P and C-415/05 P *Kadi and Al Barakaat* [2008] ECR I-6351.

36 Ibid. paras 121–205.

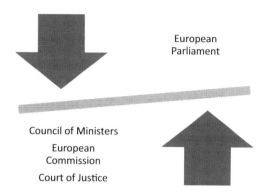

Figure 16.9 The Balance Between the Powers of the EU Institutions

superficial (and inaccurate) statements on the topic,[37] there are some very real concerns about democratic legitimacy and these are most often expressed in terms of a perceived 'democratic deficit'.

There is no generally accepted definition of 'democratic deficit'[38] but this chapter takes it to mean the gap between the strength of the voice of the people of Europe in the institutions of the EU and powers exercised on their behalf. The democratic deficit can be demonstrated on the vertical (as between the people and the institutions) and the horizontal level (as between the different institutions).

On the horizontal level academics have questioned whether the allocation of powers between the institutions is democratically legitimate. In particular, the role (or lack of it) of the European Parliament is highlighted.[39] It is the only directly elected institution of the EU and yet it can only 'co-decide' and not propose legislation or authorise legislation independently from the other institutions. This argument, however, does not recognise that the Parliament has gained significant law-making powers over the lifetime of the EU and now co-decides on the majority of EU law.[40] It also fails to address the significant powers that the European Parliament has in holding the Commission, as a whole, to account and the powers to reject the EU budget in its entirety (Figure 16.9).

On the vertical level, there is a sense of 'disconnection' between the people of Europe and the EU itself. This is compounded by the progressive transfer of powers to the EU and the failure of democratic exercises, such as the national referenda in France, the Netherlands and

---

37 See, for just one example, Macer Hall, 'EU Plot to Scrap Britain' *The Daily Express* (London, 4 May 2012), www.express. co.uk/news/uk/318045/EU-plot-to-scrap-Britain.

38 For some attempts, see Andreas Follesda and Simon Hix, 'Why there is a democratic deficit in the EU: a response to Majone and Marovcsik' (2006) 44(3) JCMS 533; Giandomenico Majone, 'Europe's "democratic deficit": the question of standards' (1998) 4(1) ELJ 5.

39 Andrew Moravcsik, 'In defence of the "democratic deficit": reassessing legitimacy in the European Union' (2002) 40(4) JCMS 603.

40 Andreas Maurer, 'The legislative powers and impact of the European Parliament' (2003) 41(2) JCMS 227, 230–234.

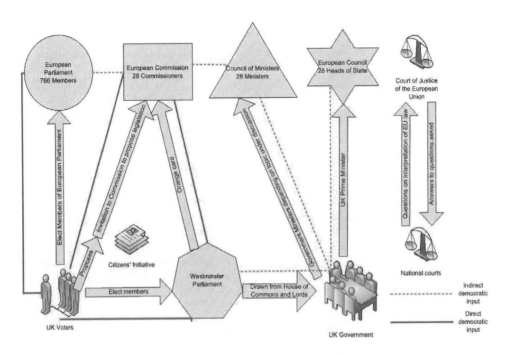

Figure 16.10 Direct and Indirect Democracy in the European Union

Ireland in relation to the Constitutional and Lisbon Treaties. In addition, the use of degressive proportionality to apportion seats in the European Parliament has attracted criticism from the very influential German Constitutional Court due to the overrepresentation of smaller states at the expense of bigger states (including Germany).[41] Figure 16.10 exemplifies the limited nature of direct democracy within the EU, with a focus on the institutions.

Figure 16.10 is complex but that is because the question of democracy is not straightforward. What the figure reveals is that in judging the democratic deficit of the EU both the presence of direct and indirect democratic input should be examined.

On the notion of direct democracy, there are two important points to discuss in relation to Figure 16.10. Firstly, European citizens directly elect Members of the European Parliament, which has an important law-making function in that it is the joint decision-maker for the EU.[42] Secondly, and as a result of the Treaty of Lisbon, citizens can petition the Commission and invite the institution to bring forward legislative proposals in a particular area.[43] This new procedure, called the Citizens' Initiative, requires a minimum of one million signatures from at least seven Member States with a minimum number of signatories (based on total population) in each country, gained within a year.[44] As such, the effectiveness of the

41 BVerfG, 2 BvE 2/08 judgment of June 30, 2009 (the Lisbon Judgment), para 284.
42 Refer back to the 'Institutions' section of this chapter for a brief discussion of whether the direct elections achieve true representation in the European Parliament.
43 Article 11(4) TEU and Article 24(1).
44 These requirements are laid down in Council Regulation (EU) 211/2011 on the citizens' initiative' [2011] OJ L65/1.

procedure can be questioned as the requirements involve coordination that would be beyond the reach of most European citizens.[45]

From the perspective of indirect democracy, the EU does demonstrate checks and balances between the various institutions, as indicated in Figure 16.10. Although the European Parliament is the only directly elected body, this does not mean that the other institutions completely lack democratic credentials:

- The Council is composed of Ministers drawn largely from the national parliaments. This had a level of indirect democratic credibility in the UK as these will be drawn from the Government who sit in the UK Parliament and who remained accountable to that Parliament and the people.
- The European Commission is not elected, nor are its President and Vice-President(s). As previously mentioned, the European Parliament (which is elected) has an important role in approving the Commission as a whole and in holding them to account. Equally, the appointment of Commissioners could be said to gain some democratic legitimacy from their selection by the Council which itself has indirect democratic accountability.
- The President of the European Council and the High Representative also hold unelected positions but derive some legitimacy from their selection by the indirectly accountable Council.

Finally, Figure 16.10 demonstrates another form of indirect democratic accountability through the 'orange card' system operated by the national parliaments, another innovation that was introduced by the Treaty of Lisbon. If a national parliament believes that a proposed piece of EU legislation would be better achieved at the national level then it can send an opinion to the Commission and if one-third of national parliaments send such an opinion then the Commission is required to review, amend or discard the proposed legislation. Similar to the Citizenship Initiative discussed previously, the threshold and time limit restrictions may harm the effectiveness of this indirect form of democratic accountability.

ANALYSING THE LAW – DEMOCRACY AND STANDARDS

One of the difficulties in assessing the standard of 'democracy' we expect from the EU is finding a suitable comparator. Is it some ideological notion of a perfect democracy? Is it the same as we expect of a sovereign state (such as the UK)? Is it the same as an international organisation (such as the UN)?

Think of some of the earlier chapters of this textbook and what they revealed about the nature of democracy within the English Legal System. In particular, consider some

---

45 Michael Dougan, 'What are we to make of the Citizens' Initiative?' (2011) 48(6) CMLRev 1807.

of the issues with democratic accountability, which are highlighted in relation to law-making in the English Legal System:

1 The role of the Monarch in the English Legal System (Chapter 3)
2 The highly controversial role of the unelected House of Lords in the law-making process (Chapter 4)
3 The extensive use of secondary legislation that is subject only to minimal scrutiny by Parliament (Chapter 5)

THE EUROPEAN UNION AND THE ENGLISH LEGAL SYSTEM

Much of the discussion of this chapter so far has focussed on the features, principles and processes of the European Union as an *independent* legal system. There is utility in understanding the EU in these terms – so that you can compare and contrast with similar features of the English Legal System and, should you be engaged in a fuller legal education, it will prepare you to undertake further study of European Union law. It is also important to understand how these features, principles and processes interact with the English Legal System.

Various chapters have sought to bring to your attention the times and ways in which EU law has had an impact in the English Legal System. The fact that this has spread over so many chapters is indicative of the reach of European law into English and Welsh law but can make the impact feel fragmented. This short section will try to draw together (using the textbook chapters as a framework) the various influences of EU law on the English Legal System into a single place. This will help bring home to the reader the importance of the UK's more than forty-five-year membership of the EU for the development of the legal system.

MAKING CONNECTIONS – THE EU AND THE ENGLISH LEGAL SYSTEM
+ +
Starting right at the beginning, Chapter 1 dealt with questions of law and legal systems. The European Union provides an effective foil against which the English Legal System can be examined and is an example of how legal systems co-exist, interact and (sometimes) collide.

Chapter 2 considered the question of 'sources' of law in England and Wales. Here EU law has a dramatic impact insofar as it is of itself an 'independent and overriding source of domestic law.'[46] This means that EU law has shifted traditional

---

46 R (on the application of Miller and another) v Secretary of State for Exiting the European Union [2017] UKSC 5, [2018] AC 61 [65].

understandings of the hierarchy of law in the English Legal System in a way that will remain long after the UK leaves the Union. Although often portrayed in a 'one-way' fashion, English law has also exerted an influence on the development of general principles of law in the EU.

Chapters 4 and 5 looked at law-making in the legal system of England and Wales. Here, the EU also exerts an influence. Much as the preceding, it alters our understanding of the force and application of Acts of Parliament (primary law) and provides a source of power for ministers to pass secondary legislation intended to implement EU law. Also, the process of leaving the European Union has led to a whole new swathe of powers for UK Ministers to pass secondary law to 'fill the gap' in our statute book and to repeal and reshape law that previously originated in the EU.

In Chapter 6 we examined statutory interpretation. The EU has given[47] to the English and Welsh Legal System an enhanced method of interpretation in the form of *purposive* or *teleological* interpretation. This has empowered the English courts to go beyond more textual reasoning and to explore the purpose of particular pieces of legislation. While this largely applies when interpreting national law in light of European law, it has started to be adopted more widely by English judges.

Chapters 7, 8 and 9 considered the role of judges and courts in the English Legal System. Here, again, we see the profound impact of membership of the EU on the underlying legal system. During the period of membership, all UK courts were also regarded as European courts with the consequence that they gained new powers (previously unknown to the English Legal System) to disapply Acts of Parliament.[48] Even the doctrine of precedent – the cornerstone of the common law – was disrupted by membership with 'lower' courts being freed from the strictures of the judgments of even the Supreme Court where these conflicted with EU law.[49] As well as new powers, the EU brought new responsibilities including the ability to refer questions of interpretation outside of the formal court structures and directly to the Court of Justice of the European Union under Article 267 TFEU.

Chapters 10 through 13, which considered the various 'justice' systems in operation, were amongst those least affected by membership of the European Union. Although there are enhanced opportunities for the enforcement of judgments given in other jurisdictions, the European Union has not sought to harmonise to any great degree the procedural rules of its Member States' justice systems.[50]

---

47 In conjunction with the European Convention on Human Rights.

48 *R v Secretary of State for Transport, ex parte Factortame (No 2)* [1991] 1 AC 603 (HL).

49 Case C-173/09 *Georgi Ivnov Elchinov* [2010] ECR I-8889.

50 Indeed, there is a principle in European law of preserving the autonomy of national procedural rules: Case 33/76 *Rewe-Zentralfinanz eG and Rewe-Zentral AG v Landwirtschaftskammer für das Saarland* [1976] ECR 1989, para 5 – 'it is for the domestic legal system of each member state to designate the courts having jurisdiction and to determine the procedural conditions governing actions at law intended to ensure the protection of the rights which citizens have from … [EU] law.'

Even if we turn to alternative methods of resolving disputes, as found within Chapter 14, such as mediation or arbitration, then the EU has had an influence on how the English Legal System approaches such matters with Directives on the harmonisation and encouragement of certain forms of ADR.

Finally, our legal professions – discussed in Chapter 15 – need to understand and be able to apply EU law in order to be licensed to practise law in England and Wales. This is largely because of all of the other aspects of EU law discussed in this box – i.e. because of the profound impact that EU law has on the *legal system* of England and Wales. This textbook has not touched upon *substantive* legal areas (e.g. contract law or company law or environmental law) and here also the EU's law-making shapes the law and policy in the English Legal System.

THE POST-BREXIT IMPACT OF EUROPEAN LAW ON THE LEGAL SYSTEM OF ENGLAND AND WALES

This final section of this chapter looks to the future and to how law originating from the European Union will be treated by the English Legal System after 'exit day' (the day on which the UK is to leave the European Union). In this way, European law may continue to exert an influence over substantive policy and the legal system for many years to come. What follows is a short summary of the position of European Union law, now that the UK left on 31 January 2020. What is **not** intended is a consideration of the likely direction of the trade negotiations on the future relationship between the EU and the UK as this is a process that either will be likely to take many years or be abandoned in favour of no such relationship. Instead, this section will explore the status and ongoing impact of EU law on the English Legal System.

WHAT TO DO WITH EUROPEAN UNION LAW POST-BREXIT?

If the UK was simply to repeal the European Communities Act 1972 – which gives effect to EU law in the UK – then there would be a significant hole in the statute book and many areas of law would become simply unworkable. Many employment, environmental, trade and other rules have their origins in European law and not all of that EU law needed to be 'implemented' in order for it to be effective in the English Legal System. These EU laws have been supplemented with thousands of judgments of the CJEU over many decades. It would not have been possible, even had all of the parliamentary time over the last three years been dedicated to the task, for the Government to assess the ongoing necessity of *every* piece of EU law before 'exit day' and decide whether to 'save' it on a case-by-case basis. Therefore, the Government passed an Act of Parliament – the European Union (Withdrawal) Act 2018 – that sought to maintain the continuity of rights and obligations without creating a legislative 'black hole'.[51]

---

51 The situation has been complicated by the Government of Boris Johnson, which sought to implement his Withdrawal Agreement with a transition period until the end of 2020 (a situation not envisaged by the Act already discussed).

At the risk of oversimplification, the broad impact of the EU (Withdrawal) Act 2018 is to repeal the European Communities Act 1972 – the conduit through which EU law currently takes effect – but to incorporate a large amount of EU law into the English Legal System by converting it to a special form of English law that will be termed 'retained EU law'. This would apply to EU law as it stood before 'exit day' and not to EU law passed subsequent to 'exit day'. Subsequent to the passing of this Act, the Government has proposed a further Bill that had made it through to Second Reading before the 2019 General Election – the European Union (Withdrawal Agreement) Bill 2019–2020. The main effect of this Bill is to 'save' the European Communities Act 1972 for the period of the proposed transition arrangements that form part of Boris Johnson's 'deal' to leave the EU until the end of 2020. In short, this would mean that EU law would have full effect until then and that 'retained EU law' would only come into effect at the end of the transition, rather than on 'exit day'.

Whether a particular Treaty Article, directive, regulation or court judgment of European law is 'retained' is a matter of statutory interpretation. The form of 'retained law' and its ongoing impact is determined by application of the Act.

TAKING THINGS FURTHER – THE WEBSITE

On the companion website you will find exercises that will help you to test your understanding of this complex and novel area of law. The skill of being able to determine whether a provision is 'retained EU law' will be increasingly important in the years following Brexit. This is because it will impact on the rights and obligations of individuals and so be of direct relevance and concern to the legal profession. The exercises on the website should be attempted following on from this chapter as you will be able to trace the *type* of retained law and the implications for interpretation and application.

TYPES OF RETAINED EU LAW

Retained law is defined in section 6(7): '"retained EU law" means anything which, on or after exit day, continues to be, or forms part of, domestic law by virtue of section 2, 3 or 4 or subsection (3) or (6) above.' This demonstrates that only certain categories or types of law will be retained once the UK leaves the Union and you should always check whether a particular law is exempted by virtue of s 20 or Schedule 6.[52]

Before considering the specific types of retained EU law we should contemplate how such retained law will interact with other forms of domestic law. Section 5(2) confirms that the supremacy of retained EU law will continue to apply to any domestic law that was passed before 'exit day'. Any domestic law that is passed *after* 'exit day' will take priority over retained EU law according to section 5(1).

---

52 Such exemptions include those EU law measures which the UK was exempt from during membership (such as those relating to the eurozone), EU directives (as opposed to the national law implementing them), the European Charter of Fundamental Rights (s 5(4)) and the Treaties (as opposed to the directly effective rights contained within them).

EU-DERIVED DOMESTIC LAW

Section 2 of the European Union (Withdrawal) Act 2018 seeks to save certain measures of national law at 'exit day'. There are two ways in which EU law could have become national law – through the laying of *secondary* legislation or by the passage of *primary* legislation.

Most notably this would include UK secondary legislation that was made under section 2(2) of the European Communities Act 1972. These will be easy to identify as they will reference the ECA 72 and will have been passed specifically to implement EU law into English law. For example, the Working Time Regulations[53] was the UK's implementation of the EU's Working Time Directive[54] that sought to regulate aspects of Employment Law. At 'exit day', or at the end of the period of transition, those Regulations will be classed as 'retained EU law' under s 2 of the European Union (Withdrawal) Act 2018. Although these are already a form of English law (as secondary law), their status as 'retained' law has consequences for their interpretation and force in the future that will mark them as different to 'regular' secondary law.

Primary law (i.e. an Act of Parliament) that was passed to implement EU law (most likely a directive) will also be retained as EU-derived national law under s 2 of the European Union (Withdrawal) Act 2018. This can be harder to recognise as the link to EU law is often less obvious. There also may be controversial distinctions that will need to be drawn in the future. *Aspects* of the Equality Act 2010 were arguably implemented in order to bring UK law in line with EU law – for example, the concept of discrimination by association was included following on from the CJEU's decision in *Coleman*.[55] In such cases, it is doubtful that the *whole* of the Equality Act 2010 was intended to implement EU law. It is to be expected that this category of EU-derived domestic legislation will prove to be problematic and occupy the time of the English and Welsh courts in the years following on from 'exit day'.

DIRECT EU LEGISLATION

This third category of retained law is intended to incorporate and save all *relevant* regulations, decisions and tertiary law of the European Union. This category is covered by section 3 of the European Union (Withdrawal) Act 2018. As discussed elsewhere in this chapter, not all EU law required *implementation* through a UK Act of Parliament or by means of secondary law. It is this directly applicable EU law that will be saved by section 3. This will mean that legal professionals will need to make reference to EU regulations and decisions into the future.

ALL OTHER RELEVANT RIGHTS, POWERS, LIABILITIES, OBLIGATIONS, RESTRICTIONS, REMEDIES AND PROCEDURES

Section 4 of the European Union (Withdrawal) Act 2018 is a catch-all provision that seeks to save those directly effective rights and obligations that are part of EU law not covered in the preceding sections of the Act.

53 The Working Time Regulations 1998, SI 1998/1833.
54 Council Directive 93/104/EC concerning certain aspects of the organisation of working time [1993] OJ L307/18.
55 Case C-303/06 *Coleman v Attridge Law* [2008] ECR I-5603.

RETAINED EU CASE LAW

An important question that the Act seeks to resolve relates to the status of judgments of the CJEU after the UK leaves the EU. This is of importance because this jurisprudence has proved to be a significant source of rights and of interpretation of EU law principles. Section 6 of the Act governs the status of retained EU case law. It treats judgments handed down *before* 'exit day' differently to those judgments handed down *after* 'exit day'.

UK courts must follow CJEU case law rendered before 'exit day' when interpreting other forms of (unmodified) retained EU law.[56] This means that most courts in England and Wales would be *bound* by interpretations given of retained EU law by the CJEU. Of note is that the Supreme Court would *not*, according to section 6(4)(a), be bound by such judgments. Where the Supreme Court wishes to depart from CJEU judgments after 'exit day' then they can only do so in the same way that they would depart from their own rulings (i.e. by application of the 1966 Practice Direction[57] discussed in Chapter 9). This creates an interesting situation where retained EU case law could be displaced by future Supreme Court rulings but that such retained EU case law will have the status of a Supreme Court judgment until that point.

UK courts are *not* bound by CJEU case law handed down on or after 'exit day' but may 'have regard' to it.[58] This means that EU case law handed down after 'exit day' will continue to be a source of *persuasive* precedent in the future.

TAKING THINGS FURTHER – CHANGING RETAINED EU LAW

The European Union (Withdrawal) Act 2018 gives significant (and controversial) powers to Government Ministers to pass new secondary legislation to *deal with deficiencies arising from withdrawal*[59] and to *implement the withdrawal agreement*.[60] These provisions are controversial because they include so-called Henry VIII powers for Ministers to use secondary legislation to amend Acts of Parliament with only minimal parliamentary scrutiny. The concern is compounded by the likelihood that the powers will be heavily used in the run up to, and immediately after, the UK's exit from the EU. So far more than 500 SI have been laid as a result of Brexit and there is a risk that there will be insufficient parliamentary time to consider these SIs effectively.

The Government's legislation website can be used to explore recent SIs and to undertake a more detailed examination of those that have been passed in order to make use of the powers provided by the European Union (Withdrawal) Act 2018.[61]

----

56 European Union (Withdrawal) Act 2018 s 6(3)(a).
57 Practice Direction *Judicial Precedent* [1966] 1 WLR 1234.
58 European Union (Withdrawal) Act 2018 s 6(1).
59 European Union (Withdrawal) Act 2018 s 8.
60 European Union (Withdrawal) Act 2018 s 9.
61 www.legislation.gov.uk/all?text=%22European%20Union%20%28Withdrawal%29%20Act%22.

THE WEBSITE

The website that accompanies this textbook contains many useful resources that you can use to consolidate and further your knowledge of the law, to hone your skills of critical analysis and to test your knowledge. This includes a set of multiple choice questions (MCQs) that can be used to test your knowledge and understanding of the material.

The website will be a particularly important resource for this chapter of the textbook. This is because, as has been mentioned on several occasions throughout this chapter, the question of Brexit has not been fully resolved at the time of writing. The website will contain text and video updates of how the process continues to unfold post-publication.

PODCASTS

- The podcasts provide a summary of the area under study, bringing together the key themes and threads of analysis into a 'mini-lecture'.
- There will also be an explanation and analysis of topical and up-to-date issues related to European Union law and its impact on the English Legal System.

INDEX